Latin-American Political Thought and Ideology

Latin-American Political Thought and Ideology

by Miguel Jorrín
and John D. Martz

The University of North Carolina Press
Chapel Hill

*To Tessie
and Mary Jeanne*

Contents

Preface

In any such volume involving a partnership of co-authors, the reader should have an explicit understanding of the nature of the collaboration and the division of responsibilities. In the present case, the arrangement is of an unusual nature, and it is appropriate to review the intellectual history of the work. Professor Miguel Jorrín of the Department of Government at the University of New Mexico was long a pioneer in the study of Latin-American political thought and ideology, one of the few scholars to be deeply concerned with the subject. Over a period of years he undertook the writing of a work that would review and analyze the contributions of Latin American *pensadores*. His untimely death in 1965 found the projected manuscript approximately half-written, and it was at this point that the junior author, on the kind invitation of Professor Jorrín's widow, became involved in the work.

My own personal and professional acquaintance with Professor Jorrín had been all too brief, although my contacts with him during visits to the University of New Mexico were most cordial. Given the opportunity to examine the manuscript and accompanying notes, I concluded that my undertaking the completion of the work would not be inappropriate. At The University of North Carolina at Chapel Hill, the late Professor William Whatley Pierson had for many years encouraged the study of Latin-American political thought, and I had fallen heir to the teaching of the course that he had introduced two generations earlier. My own emphasis has been upon the ideological movements of twentieth-century Latin America, and this proved fortuitous upon reviewing the manuscript.

The material that I received included the draft of the first six chapters—in effect, the material that appears in Part One under the rubric of "The Conflict between Liberty and Authority, 1800–1900." Although not in final form, neither was it merely a preliminary draft. There was need for some minor editing, which I have done; in some instances brief passages have been added to provide somewhat greater historical background for the setting within which the Latin-American thinkers articulated their ideas. The material and analysis for Part One remains that of the senior author, with my own role a minimal one.

By contrast, Part Two, "The Conflict between State and Society, 1900–1970" is, for better or worse, my own work. Professor Jorrín left no rough draft, no outline, and virtually no notes to suggest his intentions regarding the organization and presentation of what is essentially the twentieth-century material. There were a few short pieces he had written for other purposes: for example, public lectures on "The Concept of the State in Latin America" and "The Crisis of the Liberal State in Latin America." He had also prepared the section on "Development of Latin-American Political Thought," which was incorporated in the study conducted some years ago by the University of New Mexico for a congressional report on Latin America. These were useful in reflecting some of his ideas on the broad distinctions between nineteenth- and twentieth-century thought in Latin America, and contributed to the Introductions to both Parts One and Two. Otherwise, however, there was no indication as to his plans for the remainder of the volume. I have attempted to maintain the analytical approach and organizational patterns that he employed in Part One, but in all other particulars, these latter chapters reflect my own study, research, and experience. Unless otherwise indicated, all translations in the text are by the authors.

In summary, then, Part One represents the work of the senior author, slightly edited and with minor historical additions to provide a fuller transition from one body of thought to another. Part Two is my effort, as is the Introduction to the volume. For myself, I can say in all honesty that the final result would have been more satisfactory had the original author been able to complete the entire work. As this proved impossible, I have attempted to complete the study in the fashion that was judged most fitting and appropriate. The opportunity to do so has been a privilege, for which I am deeply indebted to Mrs. Teresa Woodell. It is not customary for a preface to be in the nature of such a personalized statement, but under the circumstances it was deemed both necessary and proper.

I wish to express my indebtedness to the University Research Council of The University of North Carolina at Chapel Hill for aid in publication of this book.

John D. Martz

January 1970
Chapel Hill, North Carolina

Latin-American Political Thought and Ideology

Introduction

Latin-American Political Thought
and the Role of the Intellectual

The role and contribution of the intellectual elite in Latin America has traditionally been one of great significance.[1] The membership of this group has historically been in the forefront of major political and social movements, and there has been somewhat less of the distaste for politics and public responsibility than has often been found elsewhere. Germán Arciniegas, a towering intellectual figure, has remarked that it is "in the oldest Latin-American tradition for intellectuals to intervene in politics. . . . What is singular in Latin America is not the phenomenon of the participation of intellectuals in public life, but the extent of their participation." In short, leading intellectuals have been widely respected and nationally prominent, enjoying a degree of prestige that is not commonly found in other geographic and cultural regions. The much-lauded *pensador*—sometimes likened to the eighteenth-century

1. This essay, as well as the introductory statements preceding Parts One and Two, includes passages excerpted from John D. Martz, "Characteristics of Latin American Political Thought," *Journal of Inter-American Studies*, VIII, No. 1 (January 1966), 54–74. Appreciation is expressed to the editor for permission to incorporate portions of that article.

3

philosophe—has been intimately involved in major political movements from colonial times forward. Indeed, the long-accepted function of the Latin American intellectual has been well characterized by Mannheim in a passage not written specifically with this area in mind: "Intellectual activity is not carried on exclusively by a socially rigidly defined class, such as a priesthood, but rather by a social stratum which is to a large degree unattached to any social class and which is recruited from an increasingly inclusive area of social life. This sociological fact determined essentially the uniqueness of the modern mind, which is characteristically not based upon the authority of a priesthood, which is not closed and finished, but which is rather dynamic, elastic, in a constant state of flux, and perpetually confronted by new problems. . . ."[2]

If such a statement has frequently been regarded as holding broad validity for Latin America, in recent years there have been voices of dissent that contend that, at least in the contemporary period and perhaps even earlier, the role of the intellectual has in point of fact been minimal. One close observer has written that to the "charges against cultural elites of barren sycophancy, imitativeness, and disconnection from local realities have been added the more contemporary accusations of disloyalty and deliberate subversion."[3] In concluding this commentary, he has further stated that if "the task of national development truly hinges on massive cultural reconstruction—educational, ideological, moral and scientific—and the present assessment of the status of cultural leadership [i.e., negative] is approximately correct, the prospect is disheartening indeed."[4] And finally, while the cultural elite remains politically radical and socially conservative, its individual member "gains no true leverage on the shape of his own life, that of his class, or of his society."[5] Given such an evaluation of the contemporary role of the Latin American intellectual, further exposition becomes necessary.

The Latin-American Intellectual and His Socio-Political Role / At the very outset, there must be a clearly delineated idea of what and who is meant by the "intellectual," the *pensador*, or the member of the "cultural elite." There is little general consensus on the question. Perhaps the broadest definition, and one which is not infrequent

2. Karl Mannheim, *Ideology and Utopia* (New York: Harcourt, Brace and Co., 1946), p. 139.
3. Frank Bonilla, "Cultural Elites," in *Elites in Latin America*, ed. Seymour Martin Lipset and Aldo Solari (New York: Oxford University Press, 1967), p. 234.
4. *Ibid.*, p. 250.
5. *Ibid.*, p. 251.

in the literature, can best be exemplified by Bonilla, who argues that "higher education is equated with intellectual status,"[6] although he subsequently qualifies this statement in some respects. Given the status of education in Latin America, even such an inclusive category leaves only a small minority who could be regarded as intellectuals. Thus, for example, one learns from Brazilian data that in 1950 only 0.5 per cent of the population over twenty years of age held professional degrees or were professionally active; the ratio of 1 per 200 adults is contrasted to a figure of 1 per 20 in the United States.[7] Taking Latin America as a whole, moreover, it has been shown elsewhere that about a decade ago, there were some 350,000 university students in all of Latin America, and of these only a small percentage ever completed their studies, received degrees, and began to pursue professional careers.[8]

There is little disposition here to dispute the contention that the bulk of university graduates in Latin America have not necessarily exerted great influence on society, culture, and politics in their respective countries. At the same time, however, such an encompassing definition of intellectuals is not believed to hold a large degree of analytical or heuristic significance. In the present context, at least, the completion of university training will not be regarded as necessarily qualifying one for membership in the intellectual elite. While such an elite obviously includes many who have completed their university studies, it by no means embraces *all* of them. What might best be termed a "cultural elite" also includes among its numbers a substantial group of artistic and creative individuals, many of whom have at least a peripheral concern and commitment to social and political matters.

The sociopolitical role of artistically inclined members of the cultural elite is highly variable. It is true that the painter, musician, architect, sculptor, and poet may not necessarily participate directly in the political sphere. In some cases he will, however, fulfill essentially a dual role in which his activities may be represented as either artistic or political; frequently the dividing line may be either obscure or nonexistent. The latter case is strikingly illustrated by the famed revolutionary muralists of Mexico, particularly Diego Rivera, David Alfaro Siquieros, and José Clemente Orozco. The last of these has himself traced the political stages through which the Mexican mural movement passed following that

6. *Ibid.*, pp. 242–43.
7. John Friedmann, "Intellectuals in Developing Societies," *Kyklos,* XIII (1960) 520.
8. K. H. Silvert, "The University Student," in *Continuity and Change in Latin America,* ed. John J. Johnson (Stanford: Stanford University Press, 1964), p. 213.

country's great Revolution and, incidentally, revealed many of the problems inherent in the relationship between art and politics.[9]

There are those who point to the difficulty confronted by the Latin-American artist who seeks to pursue a dedication to aesthetic creativity while standing outside the interplay of political and socioeconomic events. One leading authority on the arts in Latin America has stated, for instance, that the general theme of change "keeps recurring like a Wagnerian leitmotiv throughout the contemporary arts in Latin America; with each decade it becomes more insistent—and more effective, as the pressures of the modern world work in favor of the new forces."[10] The same author further cites one observer who, writing from Latin America, maintained, "Intellectuals down here are all disciples of change. Most of them aren't sure of what they want to change to, but they are looking for something different. And I'm talking about change in their art *and* their social and political conditions."[11] A clear articulation of the position that artistic interests are inseparable from the sociopolitical environment emerges from the following:

> Today, Latin America finds itself at a critical juncture, with many of its traditional values demolished or strongly threatened by social, political, and economic pressures. There is clamor for change everywhere, clearly reflected in the new realistic literature and in the restless activity of the masses. . . . Nearly all agree that there are wrongs to redress in Latin America, but there is sharp disagreement on the means to remedy these wrongs. . . . A climate of reform prevails, impelled by a sense of urgency. Whatever the outcome, the rich cultural heritage of Latin America, and the historic role of its intellectuals as men of action, give promise that the humanities will be among the main sources of renewed vitality and social progress.[12]

Undoubtedly the sociopolitical role of Latin-American intellectuals with artistic commitments is variable across time as well as in individual

9. For further discussion of the artist and his relationship to national life, see Jean Franco, *The Modern Culture of Latin America: Society and the Artist* (New York: Frederick A. Praeger, 1967), especially Chapters 5, 7, and 8 ("Art and the Political Struggle," "The Writer as Conscience of his Country," and "The Writer and the National Situation,") pp. 133–74, 205–80. Also see Gilbert Chase, "The Artist," in Johnson, *Continuity and Change*, pp. 101–36.

10. Chase, "Artist," in Johnson, *Continuity and Change*, pp. 113–14.

11. David D. Zingg, "The Wind of Change: South America's Lively New Generation of Artists," *Show: The Magazine of the Arts*, II (November 1962), 58.

12. Pedro Henríquez Ureña, *A Concise History of Latin-American Culture*, tr. (and with a supplementary chapter) by Gilbert Chase (New York: Frederick A. Praeger, 1966), pp. 161–62.

countries. There is fairly general agreement that the direct political role of the writer has been more fully and consistently observable than that of painters, musicians, and the like. As will be seen later, some of the more significant expositions of political thought in Latin America have come from the pens of novelists and essayists. Moreover, some of the most telling analyses of political and related problems have appeared in the form of novels and, in a few isolated cases, poetry. In the contemporary era, the involvement of the writer with politics has often been strong, even granting that the actual degree of influence is scarcely susceptible to precise measurement. It might well be valid to extend to all of Latin America the analysis of Mead in 1956 relating to Mexican writers, which classified competing factions into a Marxist-nationalist group and a more cosmopolitan "universalist" element.[13] Men of letters, in short, have often been politically as well as intellectually involved in contemporary national problems. Whatever the source of ideological inspiration, they have frequently served as powerful agents of political change; the specific nature and content of proposed changes and reforms has naturally varied greatly. Dealing specifically with Latin-American writers, Ellison sees them as performing "time-honored tasks as political and social thinkers," while being accorded both prestige and responsibility by their societies.[14] Perhaps the concluding word might come from the author of a recent study of art and culture in Latin America:

> To declare oneself an artist in Latin America has frequently involved conflict with society. . . . Although to the despairing observer Latin America seems to have made little progress in the direction of the social justice for which its intellectuals have always fought, the artistic scene has not remained static. . . . While so much of Western art is concerned with individual experience or relations between the sexes, most of the major works of Latin-American literature and even some of its painting are much more concerned with social phenomena and social ideals. . . . Here lies the true originality of Latin-American art: it has kept alive the vision of a more just and humane form of society and it continues to emphasize those emotions and relationships which are wider than the purely personal.[15]

That members of the contemporary cultural elite, whether artistically and aesthetically inclined or not, hold a great potential as agents of change seems unquestionable. The certainty that they will in fact perform

13. Robert G. Mead, Jr., *Temas hispanoamericanos,* as cited in Johnson, *Continuity and Change,* p. 92.
14. Fred P. Ellison, "The Writer," in *ibid.,* p. 100.
15. Franco, *Modern Culture,* pp. 280–82.

this function remains an unanswered question. It should be kept in mind, clearly, that whatever its precise definition by any scholar, the Latin-American cultural elite is fundamentally heterogeneous in composition, and generalization must therefore be of a guardedly selective nature. The *pensador* who discusses and attempts to influence political affairs may have any given social, educational, and occupational background, Moreover, especially in the twentieth century, some of the most influential political thinkers do not meet the generally accepted qualifications expected of the intellectual. Many of the recent and contemporary political leaders whose views, as discussed subsequently, have been politically important cannot in a narrow sense by regarded as intellectuals. To be sure, there are men such as the Chilean, Eduardo Frei, who established himself as a Christian Democratic theorist and philosopher of note many years before achieving political eminence. By contrast, such individuals as Rómulo Betancourt of Venezuela or Juan Perón of Argentina would not customarily be regarded as intellectuals or political theorists.

Finally, it must also be borne in mind that while many of the great figures of Latin-American political thought have been activists in the sense of immediate and lasting political involvement—including the achievement of the presidential chair in their republics—others have helped to shape the course of events while secluded from regularized political strife. As but one example of many, consider Peruvian José Carlos Mariátegui, who, although a leading writer on political issues of the day, rarely engaged in formal competition for office and died prematurely in his mid-30s; yet Peruvian political and social thought has never been the same since. An even better illustration would be represented by Brazilian Gilberto Freyre, whose influence on contemporary Brazilian thinking about social and political questions has been exercised through academic and scholarly investigation. This would suggest that there are many sources of relevant social and political thought in contemporary Latin America, as there have been for more than a century and a half. This condition is not likely to change, and the potential for significant influence from members of the cultural elite will remain as an important variable in any analysis of Latin American political thought and ideology. It now becomes necessary to state precisely what is meant by the use of these latter terms.

The Nature and Content of Latin-American Political Thought and Ideology / A descriptive explanation of the boundaries of this study, despite the dangers of merely stressing the obvious, is nonetheless appropriate. The basic purpose is that of examining political ideas, philosophies, doctrines, and ideological movements that have accompanied and to differing degrees have affected the evolution of the Latin-American republics. Political thinking and writing in any given country is regarded as crucial to its intellectual and cultural history. With this assumption explicit, we have endeavored to consider the general philosophical trends that have predominated in the several historical epochs. To understand the sociopolitical culture of Latin America, it is indispensable to know what the leading thinkers believe to be their reality, problems, and alternative approaches to the resolution of difficulties, whatever the normative and evaluative judgments of any specific formulation.

As indicated by the title of this volume, emphasis has been consciously placed upon what is regarded as political thought and related ideological movements rather than "political theory" or "political philosophy" more narrowly construed. "Political" itself is used with the broadest of connotations, embracing many works that have substantial socioeconomic or humanistic and literary content. The writings of Latin Americans are broad in textual scope, often ambitiously sweeping in their subject matter. Their implicit intellectual bias against specialization and narrow, restrictive analysis is such that a flexible definition of "political" writings will include materials with social, cultural, economic, and humanistic as well as issue-oriented concerns. Thus our emphasis throughout will be directed toward intellectual trends and expositions that have relevance to political questions. We must therefore refer to a wide variety of literary contributions and political documents, running a kaleidoscopic gamut of novels, essays, criticisms, constitutions, manifestoes, party proclamations, and even poetry.

The word "thought" is used deliberately, for only a limited portion of writing could be genuinely denoted as political "theory" in the classical sense. Aside from the tendency of most writers to be more eclectic and derivative than original, the writings that concern us here—in many cases bearing major impact on the course of events in a particular country—only infrequently proffer new or different contributions to the body of political thought. There have been in Latin America intellectual followers of such original political minds as those of Rousseau, Comte, Spencer, Hegel, and Marx. However, it is questionable whether any Latin American has formulated the kind of unique or innovational thought that might on its own intellectual merits attain comparable universality. "Political thought" therefore requires us to focus upon works that may well be predominantly legal, juridical, historical, sociological, economic, or philosophical.

It can be argued that the literature of Latin-American *philosophy* can be more precisely identified than that of political thought. It is not, perhaps, coincidental that North American scholars have devoted relatively greater attention to the former body of thought.[16] Much of it has, indeed, verged on the sociological and anthropological in dealing with diverse aspects of "culture," variously defined.[17] Yet frequently the more important *pensadores* have written essentially philosophical works that have been politically important. Our usage of the term political thought must therefore permit a substantial infusion of philosophical inquiry. The more significant intellectual trends also flow from ventures into the fields of fiction and poetry, as already suggested. In addition to the fact that literary surveys and anthologies[18] often contain significant political passages, there are numerous cases in which literary essays, novels, and poetry must be considered in terms of political content. The ideology of the Mexican Revolution, for example, is seen in a clearer light after a reading of Mariano Azuela's *The Underdogs;* the autobiographical writings of José Vasconcelos are important in the same country; Rubén Darío's *Ode to Roosevelt* is representative of the litera-

16. It is not possible, for example, to find a discussion of political thought that parallels Arthur Berndtson's "Teaching Latin-American Philosophy," *The Americas,* IX (January 1953). Furthermore, translations of Latin-American writings have, to the present, been more concerned with largely philosophical matters. See Aníbal Sánchez Reulet, *Contemporary Latin-American Philosophy: A Selection* (Albuquerque: University of New Mexico Press, 1954); Luis Recasens Siches, *Latin-American Legal Philosophy* (Cambridge: Harvard University Press, 1948); Samuel Ramos, *Profile of Man and Culture in Mexico,* tr. Peter G. Earle (Austin: University of Texas Press, 1962); and Octavio Paz, *The Labyrinth of Solitude: Life and Thought in Mexico* (New York: Grove Press, 1961), as examples.

17. A few of these, which sometimes are themselves philosophically oriented, include: John P. Gillin, "Modern Latin-American Culture," in *Readings in Latin-American Social Organization and Institutions,* ed. Olen E. Leonard and Charles P. Loomis (East Lansing: Michigan State College Press, 1953); John Gillin, "Changing Depths in Latin America," *Journal of Inter-American Studies,* II, No. 1 (January 1960); William J. Kilgore, "One America—Two Cultures," *Journal of Inter-American Studies,* VII, no. 2 (April 1965); and René de Visme Williamson, *Culture and Policy: The United States and the Hispanic World* (Knoxville: University of Tennessee Press, 1949).

18. To name but a few, one can cite Germán Arciniegas, ed., *The Green Continent: A Comprehensive View of Latin America by Its Leading Writers,* trans. Harriet de Onís et al. (New York: Alfred A. Knopf, 1944); Isaac Goldberg, *Brazilian Literature* (New York: E. P. Dutton, 1922); Isaac Goldberg, *Studies in Spanish American Literature* (New York: E. P. Dutton, 1920); Pedro Henríquez Ureña, *Literary Currents in Hispanic America* (Cambridge: Harvard University Press, 1945); Arturo Torres-Ríoseco, *The Epic of Latin American Literature* (New York: Oxford University Press, 1942); and Arturo Torres-Ríoseco, *New World Literature: Tradition and Revolt in Latin America* (Berkeley: University of California Press, 1949).

ture of Yankeephobia, if but a pale image of his finest poetry; and Da Cunha's *Rebellion in the Backlands* is a classic that the student of Brazilian political thought ignores at his peril.

Our title suggests a distinction between political thought and ideology, although there is no intention of establishing a dichotomy between the two. One scholar has recently proposed the following differentiation:

> Let us say that political theory, at least where Latin America is concerned, is a body of prescriptive beliefs about how the body politic and its government *ought* to function, what should be the optimal preferred set of relationships between man and the State, and what values and goals ought to be organically central to the system. Theory also may consist of descriptive and analytical statements and hypotheses about the way the political system *does* operate in organic but non-prescriptive terms. . . . Political ideology, in comparison, refers to "the body of beliefs which are habitually evident in the actions of a political society." The characteristic that distinguishes ideology from theory is that the former is a set of beliefs which are popularly held, shared, and acted upon. Theory may never be believed by anyone except its protagonist. However, theory may ultimately come to be ideologically embraced by a populace.[19]

While it is true that much political writing is clearly prescriptive in nature rather than representing the beliefs of a society, such a distinction with regard to ideology is not fully satisfactory. What are later described in this study as ideologies do not necessarily enjoy broad and habitual support. Moreover, there are rather grave analytical problems in determining the point at which a set of political ideas would achieve substantial enough popular support to pass from political thought or theory into the realm of ideology. Without setting up two mutually exclusive categories, then, let it be said that political ideology is regarded as a set of reasonably integrated beliefs to which a set of policy positions are attached, the articulation and support for which can be identified with an organized group of political actors. Thus, the writings of Chile's Eduardo Frei and his colleagues become an ideology of Christian Democracy which relates philosophical and theoretical exposition of specific policies and programs for action, advocated by an effective and vocal political party. The same can be said of the *apristas* and Haya de la Torre in Peru. In its purest sense, political ideology is an all-encompassing set of beliefs from which are derived programs that become

19. Kenneth C. Johnson, "Latin American Political Thought: Some Literary Foundations," in *Political Forces in Latin America: Dimensions of the Quest for Stability*, ed. Ben Burnett and Kenneth C. Johnson (Belmont: Wadsworth Publishing Company, 1968), p. 479.

sufficiently accepted and supported to enter the arena of political competition. It will not be argued that a body of thought can be identified as ideological only when accepted by the society in general. But such doctrines take the form of a political creed that, despite possible internal or logical inconsistencies, represents an overarching set of ideas that become translated into the action program of a specific political force.

The pair of essays introducing the two major divisions of this volume attempt to set forth the broad characteristics differentiating between the attitudinal approach of *pensadores* in the nineteenth and twentieth centuries respectively. During the former period, this is described as a fairly antithetical clash between the concepts of individual liberty and governmental authority. Moreover, the heritage extending from the late colonial period until the beginning of the 1900s was typified by political writing that with scattered exceptions emphasized the role and impact of Spain and of things Spanish. Although the emphasis varied somewhat, consistent attention was devoted to the relevance of the colonial experience and the continuing domination of Spanish modes of life, social attitudes, and institutional traditions. Not until the introduction of positivism in the latter half of the century did the negativist emphasis on the Spanish legacy begin to recede. Moreover, various elements of European intellectual influence encouraged a philosophically formalistic preference for abstract formulations. While certain prominent thinkers concentrated on the realities of socioeconomic and political conditions, these were more the exception than the rule. Furthermore, with the exception of the politico-military leaders of the revolutionary wars, the majority of the *pensadores*, while writing of political affairs, tended not to engage actively over an extended period of time in public life. For those who did play a part in public affairs, the most usual career pattern carried them into the field of education and a reform of that system.

The present century reflects a perceptible change. Advocates of political thought have tended increasingly to be party leaders and national political figures, with pragmatic considerations given far greater attention than previously. Among other things, this has meant that an understanding of twentieth-century political thought has come to require a heavy component of ideological movements such as Social Democracy, communism, and Christian Democracy, as well as the varied forms of nationalistic populism. The great historical movements of the Mexican and Cuban Revolutions as well must properly be viewed through an examination of historical and ideological factors. Such noted political figures as Cárdenas, Vargas, Perón, Betancourt, Frei, and many others must be studied as exponents of doctrinal and political movements. Consequently, the elaboration of the contemporary conflict between society and the state is told in large part through a critical account of political events in selected republics. If the political thought of the 1800s was often mirrored by a succession of fairly abstract philosophical schools, that of the twentieth century derives from pragmatic and issue-oriented as well as ideological political forces.

Characteristics of Latin-American Political Thought / Over the years there has been a certain ambivalence on the part of many who have studied Latin-American intellectual thought, as well as some disagreement over the more general characteristics. Harold E. Davis has put it well when observing that the frequent reaction has been either one of "presenting the thought as a pale, attenuated, corrupted version of European social philosophy, having little connection with realities of the Latin American scene or, going to the other extreme, naively picturing a thought which has no roots in the past, either European or American."[20] Certainly any effort to characterize the literature must consider the relative degree of originality. Given the impact of European and occasionally North American contributions, originality is often minimal. In view of the historical and geographical circumstances, this is less than startling. A student of Latin-American philosophy has spoken of Latin-American thought as being manifested by the proclivity of many *pensadores* to prefer "not . . . the creative development of the content of philosophy but rather . . . support which philosophical positions could provide proponents of the status quo or reformers with a basis for justification of social, political, educational, economic or religious programs."[21]

L. L. Bernard has written that problems in the social sciences have often been handled with imagination and ingenuity, and yet "the fact that this civilization was less well developed than those of Europe and North America has made the Latin Americans in large measure dependent upon their distant neighbors for much of the method and content of that part of their social sciences which is not of indigenous origin."[22] Although the search for a distinctly American philosophy has been a continuing phenomenon, little of real significance has failed to owe a

20. Harold Eugene Davis, *Latin-American Social Thought: The History of Its Development Since Independence, with Selected Readings* (Washington: University Press of Washington, D.C., 1963), p. 1.

21. William J. Kilgore, "Latin-American Philosophy and the Place of Alejandro Korn," *Journal of Inter-American Studies,* II, No. 1 (January 1960), p. 7.

22. L. L. Bernard, "The Social Sciences as Disciplines: Latin America," *Encyclopedia of the Social Sciences,* I (New York: Macmillan Co., 1950), p. 320.

debt to some source outside Latin America itself. Thus, Latin-American social thought "can be seen as an unfulfilled search for a distinctive and compelling synthesis of ideas that might give sense, coherence, and dramatic expression to regional life for more than a select minority."[23] The major collective exception would lie with twentieth-century advocates of *indigenismo;* yet this has been limited, due in no small part to the irrelevance of Indian problems in many countries.[24] The Latin-American experience has either directly or indirectly been related to the philosophy and spirit of Catholicism. Harvey L. Johnson has commented pertinently that Spanish American culture was neither wholly European nor Indian. While largely Catholic, it has been different in many ways from that of Spain. Indeed, the culture "tends to be humanistic. Ideologically, Spanish America has been influenced by the Enlightenment, by the American and French revolutions, by Existentialism, etc." A page later he also underlines the fact that Spanish American culture can best be understood and evaluated in terms of its own history and present circumstances.[25] This seems an obvious point, yet it bears repetition here.

There is much of a derivative nature in the political ideas that this volume presents. One cannot fully understand Latin-American political thought and ideology without at the same time have some acquaintance with the foreign writings upon which it has so often been based. Thus attention must be directed at times to the specific European origins, as for example the Comtean basis of positivism. Running through a large portion of Latin-American thought, additionally, has been a prominent strain of optimism (although there have been individual instances of pronouncedly bleak pessimism). Beginning with the *criollo* rebellion against authority and continuing to the present day, one sees the continuing belief that progress and development will in one fashion or another be achieved. Today this has emerged in the recent writings treating of national development and socioeconomic reform.

Among the important characteristics is the individual societal position of the *pensador* and ideologue, which has already been debated briefly. The role and influence of many thinkers has given an historical impetus to national affairs. Such a man will occasionally be projected directly into political issues of the day, as with the Generation of 1837 in Argen-

23. Bonilla, "Cultural Elites," in Lipset and Solari, *Elites,* pp. 240–41.
24. Bonilla would add that "the exaltation of indigenous cultures in order to affirm unique regional values and achievement has never placed a high value on the social or human worth of contemporary Indian populations." *Ibid.*
25. Harvey L. Johnson, "Some Aspects of Spanish American Culture," *The Americas,* XVII, No. 4 (April 1961), p. 355.

tina or the *científicos* in Mexico. In some cases an individual has assumed the kind of position exemplified by Peru's Manuel González Prada, becoming the conscience of his country; similar roles have been played by Martí in Cuba, Rodó in Uruguay, and Darío in Nicaragua. The content of the literature is notable for its intellectual range. Although this may today be in the process of change, it has been historically true that Latin Americans have been widely concerned with many different facets of human knowledge and inquiry. Generalists rather than specialists, they have dealt with broad issues of life, society, culture, and civilization. As already noted, it is frequently impossible to distinguish purely "political," "economic," or other writings by a given individual. More likely than not, his concerns over a period of time will impinge concurrently upon history, philosophy, education, science, and humanism. There is a concomitant tendency of many writers to avoid close identification with or advocacy of ideas representing a particular political and philosophical school. Positivism stands as the major exception in the nineteenth century, yet even there, given the widely differing interpretations and sometimes contradictory teachings of different European positivists, most of the prominent *pensadores* have been fairly eclectic. In the twentieth century, the influence of Marxism has been great, yet the variants have been many.

Latin-American political thought has been consistent in its concern with the place of individual countries and of the entire region in the stream of history. National development, broadly defined, has usually been central to the thought of the *pensadores*. The past has been examined in spiritual and cultural as well as political and economic terms, often leading to prescriptions whereby the development and self-fulfillment of the individual within society would be possible. The element of humanism has emerged through the intellectual search for individual as well as national progress. There has been a feeling that, at least potentially, Latin-American civilization has a role to play that might contribute to the march of mankind in general. Occasionally one finds an aura of superiority; once directed toward the life and ideas of the Old World, especially the Iberian Peninsula, this later came to be argued in contrast with the United States.

A final trait inherent in much Latin American thought has been the commitment to revolution and to drastic socioeconomic and political change. While outsiders have too often applied the word "revolution" to palace *golpes de estado,* which alter little except the names of office holders and wielders of power, such profound movements as the Mexican and Cuban Revolutions have dramatically illustrated the depth and breadth of profound transformations in social policy and the very structure of politics. Sensationalized books by foreign observers in recent years, arguing that violent revolution and turmoil is around the immediate corner, neglect the traditional Latin-American acceptance of the fact that a society that is or must become dynamic will inevitably experience prompt or impending revolutionary change. While it is possible to identify a stream of conservative thought running through the literature, best exemplified by defenders of traditional authoritarian regimes, revolutionary ideas have been present in Latin-American intellectual life since the latter part of the colonial period. As one commentator has written,

> Certain persistent elements are to be seen, including the right of revolution, concepts of human rights, concepts of American international law, anti-colonialism and anti-imperialism, insistence on a secular society and a secular state, freedom of oppressed social classes, notably the emancipated Negro slaves and the retarded indigenous peoples, and the responsibility of the state for improving the general welfare. Nationalism has tended to make this thought assert its independence of European intellectual patterns, as of European social movements. Its most characteristic note, as Felix Schwartzmann of Chile has shown in a broad study of American literature, has been a generally optimistic concept of man, as contrasted with what Latin Americans have conceived to be a more pessimistic European view of human nature.[26]

Among the major characteristics of political thought and ideology in Latin America, then, we can identify the derivative nature of many writings, the breadth and scope of the literature, the influential and occasionally pre-eminent role of the *pensador,* the concern with historical and environmental forces, a broadly revolutionary commitment, and an optimistic faith in both the inevitability of hemispheric progress and the uniqueness of Latin America in the sweep of world civilizations. We would conclude, finally, that the effort to identify an indigenous, singularly American approach to the problems of humanity continues. Today this often takes the form of a somewhat amorphous "third position" resting somewhere between the understanding applied to capitalism and to communism, seeking to combine the best features of both while shedding harmful or destructive elements. *Peronismo* and Christian Democracy are among those disparate movements that have explicitly claimed to represent a centrist or "third" position. Some might argue that the intellectual quest is overly ambitious, that it seeks a utopia

26. Harold Eugene Davis, "Revolutions and Revolutionary Thought in Latin America," *Afro-Asian and World Affairs* [New Delhi], (1967), p. 121.

that intellectuals elsewhere have concluded to be beyond the capacity of humanity. Yet it is through the deep-seated humanitarianism, the blending of the cultural and the spiritual with the material and the tangible, that speculative inquiry by Latin-American thinkers has attempted to realize its fullest development.

SELECTED BIBLIOGRAPHY

BOOKS

Arciniegas, Germán, ed. *The Green Continent: A Comprehensive View of Latin America by Its Leading Writers.* Translated by Harriet de Onís et al. New York: Alfred A. Knopf, 1944.

—————. *Latin America: A Cultural History.* New York: Alfred A. Knopf, 1967.

Clissold, Stephen. *Latin America: A Cultural Outline.* New York: Harper & Row, Publishers, 1966.

Cosío Villegas, Daniel. *American Extremes.* Translated by América Paredes. Austin: University of Texas Press, 1964.

Crawford, William Rex. *A Century of Latin American Thought.* Cambridge: Harvard University Press, 1961.

Cruz Costa, João. *A History of Ideas in Brazil: The Development of Philosophy in Brazil and the Evolution of National History,* Translated by Suzette Macedo. Berkeley and Los Angeles: University of California Press, 1964.

Davis, Harold Eugene. *Social Science Trends in Latin America.* Washington: American University Press, 1950.

—————. *Latin-American Social Thought: The History of Its Development Since Independence, with Selected Readings.* Washington: University Press of Washington, D.C., 1963.

Del Río, Angel, ed. *Responsible Freedom in the Americas.* New York: Columbia University Press, 1955.

—————. *The Clash and Attraction of Two Cultures: The Hispanic and Anglo-Saxon Worlds in America,* Translated and edited by James F. Shearer. Baton Rouge: Louisiana State University Press, 1965.

Echanove Trujillo, Carlos A. *La sociología en hispanoamérica.* La Habana: Imp. Universitaria, 1953.

Franco, Jean. *The Modern Culture of Latin America: Society and the Artist.* New York: Frederick A. Praeger, 1967.

Gaos, José. *Sobre Ortega y Gasset y otros trabajos de historia de las ideas en España y la América Española.* México: Imp. Universitaria, 1957.

Goldberg, Isaac. *Brazilian Literature.* New York: E. P. Dutton, 1922.

—————. *Studies in Spanish American Literature.* New York: E. P. Dutton, 1920.

Heath, Dwight B., and Richard N. Adams, eds. *Contemporary Cultures and Societies of Latin America.* New York: Random House, 1965.

Henríquez Ureña, Pedro. *A Concise History of Latin American Culture.* Translated and with a supplementary chapter by Gilbert Chase. New York: Frederick A. Praeger, 1966.

————. *Literary Currents in Hispanic America.* Cambridge: Harvard University Press, 1945.

Jacobini, H. B. *A Study of the Philosophy of International Law as Seen in the Works of Latin American Writers.* The Hague: Martinus Nijhoff, 1954.

Kempff Mercado, Manfredo. *Historia de la filosofía en Latino-América.* Santiago: Editorial Zig-Zag, 1958.

Larroyo, Francisco. *Filosofía americana.* México: Universidad Autónoma Nacional, 1958.

Masur, Gerhard. *Nationalism in Latin America: Diversity and Unity.* New York: Macmillan Co., 1966.

Medina Echeverría, José. *Panorama de la sociología contemporánea.* México: Casa de España en América, 1940.

Onís, Harriet, ed. *The Golden Land: An Anthology of Latin American Folklore in Literature.* Rev. ed. New York: Alfred A. Knopf, 1961.

Paz, Octavio. *The Labyrinth of Solitude: Life and Thought in Mexico.* Translated by Lysander Kemp. New York: Grove Press, 1961.

Picón-Salas, Mariano. *A Cultural History of Spanish America from Conquest to Independence,* Translated by Irving A. Leonard. Berkeley and Los Angeles: University of California Press, 1962.

Pike, Fredrick B., ed. *Freedom and Reform in Latin America.* Notre Dame: University of Notre Dame Press, 1959.

Ramos, Samuel. *Profile of Man and Culture in Mexico.* Translated by Peter G. Earle. Austin: University of Texas Press, 1962.

Recasens Siches, Luis. *Latin-American Legal Philosophy.* Cambridge: Harvard University Press, 1948.

Sánchez Reulet, Aníbal. *Contemporary Latin-American Philosophy: A Selection.* Albuquerque: University of New Mexico Press, 1954.

Terry, Edward D., ed. *Artists and Writers in the Evolution of Latin America.* University: University of Alabama Press, 1969.

Torres-Ríoseco, Arturo. *Aspects of Spanish-American Literature.* Berkeley and Los Angeles: University of California Press, 1963.

————. *New World Literature: Tradition and Revolt in Latin America.* Berkeley: University of California Press, 1949.

Villegas, Abelardo, ed. *Antología del pensamiento social y político de América Latina.* Washington: Unión Panamericana, 1964.

Whitaker, Arthur P., and David C. Jordan. *Nationalism in Contemporary Latin America.* New York: Free Press, 1966.

Wilgus, A. Curtis, ed. *The Caribbean: Its Culture.* Gainesville: University of Florida Press, 1955.

Williamson, René de Visme. *Culture and Policy: The United States and the Hispanic World.* Knoxville: University of Tennessee Press, 1949.

Zea, Leopoldo. *The Latin-American Mind.* Translated by James H. Abbott and Lowell Dunham. Norman: University of Oklahoma Press, 1963.

ARTICLES

Bernard, L. L. "The Social Sciences as Disciplines: Latin America," *Encyclopedia of the Social Sciences,* I (New York: Macmillan Co., 1950).

Berndtson, Arthur. "Teaching Latin-American Philosophy," *The Americas*, IX (January 1953).

Bonilla, Frank. "Cultural Elites," in *Elites in Latin America*, edited by Seymour Martin Lipset and Aldo Solari. New York: Oxford University Press, 1967.

Chase, Gilbert, "The Artist," in *Continuity and Change in Latin America*. Edited by John J. Johnson. Stanford: Stanford University Press, 1964.

Davis, Harold Eugene. "Revolutions and Revolutionary Thought in Latin America," *Afro-Asia and World Affairs* [New Delhi], (1967).

————. "History of Ideas in Latin America," *Latin American Research Review*, II, No. 4 (Fall 1968).

————. "Trends in Social Thought in Twentieth Century Latin America," *Journal of Inter-American Studies*, I, No. 1 (January 1959).

Ellison, Fred P. "The Writer," in *Continuity and Change in Latin America*. Edited by John J. Johnson. Stanford: Stanford University Press, 1964.

Frondizi, Risieri. "Tendencies in Contemporary Latin American Philosophy," *Inter-American Intellectual Interchange*. Austin: Institute of Latin American Studies, 1943.

Gillin, John P. "Changing Depths in Latin America," *Journal of Inter-American Studies*, II, No. 1 (January 1960).

————. "Modern Latin-American Culture," in *Readings in Latin-American Social Organization and Institutions*. Edited by Olen E. Leonard and Charles P. Loomis. East Lansing: Michigan State College Press, 1953.

Johnson, Harvey L. "Some Aspects of Spanish American Culture," *The Americas*, XVII, No. 4 (April 1961).

Kilgore, William J. "Latin-American Philosophy and the Place of Alejandro Korn," *Journal of Inter-American Studies*, II, No. 1 (January 1960).

————. "One America—Two Cultures," *Journal of Inter-American Studies*, VII, No. 2 (April 1965).

Martz, John D. "Characteristics of Latin American Political Thought," *Journal of Inter-American Studies*, VIII, No. 1 (January 1966).

Zea, Leopoldo. "Philosophy and Thought in Latin America," *Latin American Research Review*, III, No. 2 (Spring 1968).

PART ONE

*The Conflict between Liberty
and Authority*

1800–1900

Introduction

Beginning with the Spanish and Portuguese Empires in their final death throes, the nineteenth century came to reflect a broad conflict between liberty and authority. From the writings of the precursors of independence to the revolutionary wars, and moving through successive periods of romantic liberalism, positivism, and idealism, liberty was conceived as meaning protection for the individual against possible abuses of power by the rulers. For the majority of Latin-American thinkers, this appeared to be the main dilemma of political thought. Freedom from colonial abuses was crucial to the ideas of the revolutionary period, and in the immediate postindependence era this was extended to cover social and intellectual as well as more obvious political emancipation. In time, the *pensadores* came to recognize that the majority of the people did not enjoy genuine individual liberty, whether political or socioeconomic. This prepared the ground for the acceptance of European positivism and, later, of idealism. The underlying assumption continued to be the conviction that, given a proper intellectual and philosophical framework, individual freedoms might be enhanced. Once the protection of the individual was definitively attained, accompanying national problems, be they social, economic, educational, or other, would be eventually and inevitably solved. Or such, at least, was the reasoning of most thinkers.

Initially, the ideas that inspired the emancipation of the American

23

colonies were those of the Enlightenment, more of the French and Spanish Enlightenment of the eighteenth century than of seventeenth-century British rationalism. Latin America was also negatively influenced by the political thought of the Hispanic counterreformation. The seventeenth century had inaugurated in the Western world the urban life of science and the common man. That period was characterized by a scientific and philosophical revolution in western Europe, with the exception of the Iberian Peninsula. As Picón-Salas has written,[1] outside of imperial China, no country has shown a more extraordinary "defensive energy" than Spain in the seventeenth century. Unwilling or reluctant to accept meaningful change, this attitude contrasted with British and Dutch economic achievements and their basic political liberalism, while in France the absolutism of the state was being challenged by Huguenot writers and leaders.

The struggle for religious liberty which emanated from the Reformation concentrated on the question of the real function of the state. Democratic apprenticeship in such countries as England, France, and the Netherlands was a natural consequence of the religious wars. Western Europe was influenced more by the Reformation as a whole than by the leading reformers such as Calvin and Luther. At the end of the religious struggle there was need for an intellectual truce. The policy of Henry IV in France and John Locke's philosophy of toleration are but two examples of this trend. By contrast, given the policy of counter-reformation established in Spain and Portugal, nascent democratic forces registered little impact there. The absence of seventeenth-century liberal thought in Latin America tended to shackle the newly independent countries in developing a more fruitful evolution toward genuine democracy.

The Enlightenment, drawing to a close in Europe just as it began to reach the Spanish and Portuguese colonies in significant degree, offered above all else a conviction of the general progress of civilization, a belief that intellectual and social advance was inevitable. Humanity was marching toward perfectibility, with pure reason destined to be the ultimate master. And although the Enlightenment by the time of the French Revolution was in a state of deterioration, it was nonetheless providing for many Latin-American intellectuals the beliefs that themselves were basic to Western civilization. Until fairly late in the 1700s, as Lanning has observed, intellectual predilections in Latin America

1. Mariano Picón-Salas, *A Cultural History of Spanish America from Conquest to Independence*, tr. Irving A. Leonard (Berkeley and Los Angeles: University of California Press, 1963), p. 18.

favored an almost reverent repetition of Condillac and similar writers.[2] The Lockean argument that the spiritual and physical man constituted one harmonious whole in nature was widespread. Furthermore, the increasing trade and exchange of books and other materials brought a growing familiarity with Rousseau, Paine, and others.

In addition to the European Enlightenment, the example of the emancipation of the British colonies in North America influenced Latin America. It is important to note, however, that the political ideas of the Revolutionary War of North America were closer to Locke and Montesquieu than to Rousseau, while in Latin America the latter was more widely read and repeated. North American liberalism was therefore somewhat more individualistic and tolerant in intellectual matters, while the Latin-American version was emotional and self-assertive. Rousseau's liberalism extended from the intellectual sphere to that of the passions. Latin-American political leaders in this early period tended to associate their own will with Rousseau's "general will" and were ruthlessly intolerant of opposition. This rather romantic interpretation of liberalism was ultranationalistic, and the worship of liberty was mixed with the splendor of war and the cult of the successful hero. The admiration of the strong man soon found its way into constitutional practices with the executive dominance in the structure of new governments.

Early European liberalism represented a middle-class revolt against aristocratic and ecclesiastical privilege. It aimed at political reform and was willing to compromise and to tolerate dissenters. The Latin-American independence movement, however, was not a revolt of the middle class since none truly existed. Independence instead was merely a victory of the colonial oligarchs over the authority of the mother countries. The new republics were governed at the beginning by the landed gentry and the military caste. Rousseau's theory that society naturally endows the state with its all-powerful general will—from which it is treason to dissent—drew widespread acceptance by many of the new rulers.

From Rousseau and from lesser thinkers, the political thought that inspired the leaders of Latin-American independence was, therefore, utopian and romantic. The utopian element was reflected in the belief that social and economic progress was to come about as the result of the free play of natural laws unhampered by unnecessary state control. Romanticism was marked by the emotionally assertive nature of thought. Among important political thinkers of the late colonial and revolutionary

2. John Tate Lanning, "The Reception of the Enlightenment in Latin America," in *Latin America and the Enlightenment,* ed. Arthur P. Whitaker (New York: D. Appleton-Century Co., 1942).

period were Manuel Belgrano, an Argentine greatly inspired by the egalitarianism of the French Revolution, and his countryman, Mariano Moreno, whose affinity for Rousseau led him to translate and publish the *Contrat Social* in Buenos Aires. From Venezuela came the greatest revolutionary precursor, Francisco Miranda, who had actually been a general in the revolutionary armies in Paris; the famed liberator himself, Simón Bolívar, whose formative years were influenced by a disciple of Voltaire and Rousseau; and the eminent Andrés Bello, a scholar whose more moderate philosophy later helped to shape the Chilean educational system. Colombia produced Antonio Nariño, a precursor who was imprisoned for publishing in Spanish and distributing the French Declaration of the Rights of Man. Others included Mexican priests Miguel Hidalgo and José Morelos, who were followers of the encyclopaedists and led popular mass uprisings in their country. The importation of Freemasonry from Europe also was important, especially in the thought of another Mexican, José Joaquín Fernández de Lizardi.

When independence from Spanish authority was achieved in the 1820s, the early romantic brand of liberalism had to struggle with those ideas that had developed in Europe during the period of the Restoration. Spanish conservatism during the wars of independence was unreflective, limiting itself to the defense of the *status quo*. The conservatism of the Restoration differed somewhat, for it attacked reason and proclaimed the supremacy of historical forces over the free actions of individuals. In the early days of the new republics, Latin-American conservatives were able to profit from the freedoms postulated by the liberators. As the state was not supposed to intervene in religion, economy, or culture, the conservatives used the Roman Catholic church, their own economic power, and social prestige either to acquire or to preserve political power. While freedom from Spain had been gained, the struggle for domestic and individual freedom began with the initiation of the independence period.

The leaders of this early era were well aware of prevailing conditions. Simón Bolívar envisaged by the end of his career a sort of paternalistic state under the rule of a strong executive. Andrés Bello warned the Chileans not to confuse independence with democracy and favored a slow evolution toward a representative government. In Mexico, Fernández de Lizardi took an anticonservative position, challenging the power of the Church and recommending the expropriation of all lands of the *haciendas* in excess of four square leagues. For some years, then, Latin-American political thought was concerned primarily with the preservation of the achieved freedom and the organization of the new countries.

They accepted as the only possible political condition the concept of the liberal state based on the free play of natural law, expecting that progress would come gradually but surely. The National Reorganization movement in Argentina, the more radical *reforma* of Mexico, and the utopian socialism of several Chilean thinkers pointed to the need for economic, educational, and social changes. Nevertheless, this early concern with reform was conceived of as being contained within the ongoing political structure of the liberal state.

A notable feature that became prominent from the 1830s forward was the embittered denunciation of the colonial heritage; the Latin Americans discoursed extensively on the continuation of colonial forms despite the departure of European rule. While there was some attention to socioeconomic matters, the major emphasis had been placed on the expulsion of agents of the crown and the institution of local rule in place of that controlled by *peninsulares,* those who had actually been born in Spain. It was supposed by many thinkers that military victory would more or less automatically bring about a drastic new order. As the early years of independence gave the lie to this expectation, complaints multiplied over the fact that the exchange of Spanish or, for that matter, Portuguese for national rulers had brought little true political emancipation. The disillusionment over the continuation of Iberian habits, customs, and traditions became widespread. Only slowly did a growing number of *pensadores* come to recognize that the negativism of attacks on past evils of royal control was largely an exercise in futility. And at this same time, political struggles were being conducted between conservative and liberal factions who vied for control of government and policy making. By and large, these were to continue until the 1860s, after which, in at least some of the countries, new political hues and colorations began to tint the landscape.

Conservative forces found support from the military, clergy, and landed aristocracy, while the liberals drew backing largely from intellectuals and a nascent middle class. The battle was joined most importantly in Argentina and Mexico, later appearing elsewhere. In Argentina, where the main need was reorganization, liberal statesman Bernardino Rivadavia abolished ecclesiastical privilege, facilitated the acquisition of land by peasants, fostered immigration, and even tried to help the liberals in Spain in 1823. Although these reforms were interrupted by the long dictatorship of Rosas, they were resumed as Juan Bautista Alberdi authored a liberal Argentine Constitution in 1853 under which the economic development of his country progressed along laissez-faire lines. Argentina's liberal political thinkers were romantics of the traditional school, and there was a tendency to close their eyes to the country's social realities, although this was not true of such writings as Sarmiento's sociological and demographic works.

In Mexico the liberal movement, known as the *reforma,* was drastic and revolutionary. Armed and ideological conflicts between liberals and conservatives continued unabated from 1824 to 1867, with political power oscillating between the two. The liberals demanded an end to Church and military privilege while advocating civil liberties and land reform. Their creed was expressed in the important constitution of 1857 and accompanying reforms of the Juárez government. Among the liberal philosophers of this period were Valentín Gómez Farías, the first to advocate the complete separation of Church and State; José María Luis Mora, a pronounced liberal who articulated the need for revolutionary changes in the rigid structure of society but insisted that they be achieved by consent; Benito Juárez himself, the most distinguished statesman of the *reforma;* the brothers Miguel and Sebastián Lerdo de Tejada, formulators of several of the important laws of the *reforma;* and Ignacio Ramírez, a bitterly anticlerical and materialistically inclined lawyer and writer. The extremism of Mexican liberal thinkers is accounted for by the extraordinarily privileged position of the Church and the uncompromising attitude of the oligarchy. The political thought of the 1824–67 period constituted the prelude to the important revolutionary changes that took place in Mexico after 1910.

In Chile, Francisco Bilbao, whose well-known study *La sociabilidad chilena* was publicly burned by the conservative authorities, responded to the confrontation with a long period of conservatism by seeking a synthesis in the historical process. For Bilbao, the solution lay in his conception of the new utopian liberalism, with some ingredients as well of the Christian socialism of Lamennais. His countryman, José Victorino Lastarria, later an exponent of positivism, wrote in the vein of romantic liberalism in calling for the eradication of past Spanish influence. With the struggle for independence having left untouched the social and economic bases produced by three centuries of colonialism, he argued that his countrymen needed to discard remaining customs and practices, thereby renouncing the past and committing themselves to the sovereignty of law. In Cuba, meanwhile, Fathers Caballero and Varela, as well as José Antonio Saco, were fairly realistic liberals who demanded a degree of self-government under Spain. Saco, perhaps the ablest Cuban political thinker before Martí, opposed premature insurrection while demanding first the emancipation of slaves and the encouragement of sufficient European immigration. José de la Luz y Caballero was another

Cuban to wrestle with the implications of political independence as influenced by the problems already being encountered by the new republics of the hemisphere. Seeing the continuation of a struggle between principles of enlightened self-government and the well-entrenched landed aristocracy, he was to spend his final years in training a new generation of Cubans, many of whom were to participate in the ferment that culminated in armed rebellion against Spain.

The years of romantic liberalism in the hemisphere, which in some countries extended from the winning of independence to the introduction of positivism in the 1860s, were characterized broadly by the search for a new basis to a truly American order of things. At the same time, the preoccupation with the past remained strong, consistently leading to a reiteration of the conviction that political independence had accomplished relatively little. With true freedom a mere façade, postindependence developments had been discouraging, especially to dedicated intellectuals. Dictatorships such as those of Iturbide, Francia, and O'Higgins had been created allegedly to permit extensive popular freedom and economic well-being; instead, conditions had worsened, while privilege and elitist rule remained prevalent. Thus renewed efforts were necessary if the spirit of feudalism were to be overcome. Given the need for a new approach, the intellectual soil was fertile for the introduction of positivism. Receptive to new ideas, the *pensadores* gradually turned toward positivism in freeing themselves from the almost psychopathic preoccupation with Spain. While various European intellectual currents became significant, the Iberian emphasis began to recede. It was this abatement of the preoccupation with Spain and its heritage that permitted a clear distinction between the prepositivist years and those that followed.

By midcentury, the *pensadores* began turning toward positivism, and it became the dominant political philosophy of the 1870–1900 era. The main inspiration came from Auguste Comte, the French originator of positivism, although many Latin Americans blended in the philosophies of John Stuart Mill, Herbert Spencer, and occasionally Charles Darwin. Since positivism aimed at the improvement of human society by scientific means and at peaceful social transformation through scientific progress, it seemed to fit in well with the needs and conditions of Latin America. It shone out as a redeeming doctrine that was seen as "suitable for imposing a new intellectual order which would replace the one destroyed, thus ending a long era of violence and political and social anarchy."[3]

3. Leopoldo Zea, *The Latin-American Mind,* tr. James H. Abbott and Lowell Dunham (Norman: University of Oklahoma Press, 1963), p. 27.

It was believed that such problems as the failure of constitutional democratic forms, the absence of economic prosperity, the increasing social tensions arising among classes and in some cases among races, and the unending frustrations of Church-State relations might all be solved through a reliance upon positivism. Members of the ruling classes also interpreted positivism as a justification of efforts to disrupt the activities of radical and impatient reform elements. Progress would mean for the rulers economic development in which order would be paramount. For those who hoped to continue in the exercise of relative political, social and economic hegemony, positivism permitted a rationalization of the status quo.

Among intellectual circles, there were expectations that positivism would first remove all vestiges of the colonial heritage, then guide the region toward true progress. After the 1860s, when the political turmoil of the early national period had somewhat abated and respect for law and order began to characterize political action, the positivists' influence became strong in Latin-American education and politics. Public education, especially, was made more practical and scientific, and the old humanistic approach was altered. This positivist educational reform began in Mexico under the Díaz regime and was extended to a number of other countries, last of all to Cuba in the early twentieth century. Gabino Barreda and Enrique José Varona were the leading educational philosophers in Mexico and Cuba respectively. The adaptations and adjustments of positivism were diverse, depending as they did upon the situations in specific countries. Politically, most positivists were initially progressive liberals, emphasizing evolutionary change. This image gradually became clouded with the passage of time, however.

In Mexico, positivism began with the educational reforms of Gabino Barreda, and was later continued under the guidance of Justo Sierra, the teacher and scholar who stood for years in the forefront of Mexican positivism. Arguing that the country's future strength must be based on an educational foundation, he believed that the pursuit of positivist goals would in time develop the true national conscience necessary for the achievement of an organized social order conducive to progress and growth. With the lengthy rule of Porfirio Díaz, which was inaugurated in the 1870s, Mexican positivists assumed increasingly important governmental positions. By the end of the century, these so-called *cientificos* provided the major impetus to governmental administration, enshrining positivism as the official philosophy from 1890 to 1910. In time, however, the ethical elements of Comtean thought were forgotten in favor of the "scientific" approach as a justification of the rule of the educated elite through a military ruler. The *científicos*, obsessed with the progress of the white European nations, ignored the miserable living conditions of the *mestizo* and Indian masses. Only if President Díaz became the arbiter of social peace and order could the populace, it was held, come to appreciate and understand freedom and liberty. The positivist gospel was reiterated as emphasizing honest and effective, scientifically rational administration. In the end, Mexican positivism became a conservative movement that contributed to internal crisis and made the revolution of 1910 inevitable.

Far to the south, the Chileans and Argentines were concerned with a different set of questions. In both countries the intellectual influence of positivism was represented by rival schools, and incessant polemics were exchanged between the orthodox and heterodox positivists. While the first Chilean school was led by the Lagarrigue brothers, the opposing group accepted only portions of Comtean thought, preferring the selective enunciation of José Victorino Lastarria in his final years. These latter thinkers, plagued by the logical problems of reconciling order with progress, never escaped an underlying suspicion that positivism might well lead to the sanctification of absolutist government; the commitment to positivism, indeed to Mill as well as to Spencer and Comte, was less than wholehearted. The Argentines divided similarly, differing widely in their interpretations. Traditional Comtean positivism was advocated by those affiliated with the Normal School at Paraná. Established by Sarmiento in 1870, it sought a totally new and different order, arguing that the tendencies personified earlier by Rosas had to be totally eradicated. There were others, however, who preferred the stimulation of an "individualistic" brand of positivism. Men like J. Alfredo Ferreira spent years arguing in favor of original, creative approaches, underlining experimental and innovational interpretations while discarding many aspects of positivism as irrelevant.

Perhaps nowhere in the hemisphere was the assimilation of positivism more extraordinary than in Brazil, where it was adopted with very little alteration from the Comtean original. Benjamín Constant Botelho de Magalhães was responsible for the founding of the Positivist Society in 1871, and within a decade a positivist church was disseminating the ideas of Comte's religion of humanity, which the Spanish Americans had generally rejected. Brazilian positivists joined others who urged the overthrow of the Empire, calling for a "positivist republic" that, rather than democratic or representative, was to provide a means of stable, effective, rational management of national affairs. For a few months after the forced abdication of Dom Pedro II in 1889 the positivists exercised some governmental responsibility, but the military soon asserted its primacy, and positivism receded rapidly.

A less influential but perceptible European philosophy that also began to reach Latin America after the 1860s was German idealism. The philosophical "historicism" of Hegel and Schelling had inspired the German historical school of jurisprudence that became highly regarded in a number of Latin American universities. European neo-Kantianism and neo-Hegelianism began to register in Latin America; these philosophies, together with those of Boutroux, Bergson, Croce, and James arrived some years later. An important philosophical revival, developed in Spain by Julián Sanz del Río, voiced the obscure thought of the German Krause. The Spanish interpretation, as represented by Sanz del Río's great disciple Francisco Giner de los Ríos, influenced a growing number of *pensadores* toward the end of the century, among them the Cuban, Martí. As Latin-American idealism began to emerge, it became an outspoken critic of the liberal state as it was then seen. Uruguay's José Enrique Rodó opposed the culture that had resulted from liberalism, revolting against the growing materialism of the times. The Peruvian Manuel González Prada, bitterly disgusted with conditions in his country, went even further to become a protesting libertarian anarchist. Further attacks on liberalism were mounted by anarchists and by utopian socialists, while the arrival of Marxian socialism just before the close of the century led to the introduction of clubs, pamphleteering, and in a few cases the founding of the earliest socialist political parties.

With few exceptions, these philosophical schools and expressions of political thought stressed the conflict between individual liberty and authority. The transferral of socioeconomic and political power from the Spanish to the aristocratic elite following the expulsion of Spain left the individual in a position of continued subordination. The advent of romantic liberalism and, in several countries, the temporary ascendancy of liberal political movements articulately defended the principle of freedom and human dignity without extending the practice and observance to the masses. Positivism provided a philosophical rationale for the somewhat authoritarian, order-oriented governments such as that erected by Díaz and the *científicos* in Mexico. Idealism seemed to illuminate philosophical insights but answered few of the hard pragmatic political issues that had survived from the colonial era. By the turn of the century, the growing impact of industrial development, the wave of European immigrants in the River Plate region, and the growth of both an urban proletariat and an expanding middle sector all combined to provide a societal setting that differed fundamentally from that of the

1800s. Attitudes toward the role and responsibility of the state began to change, and thus the central focus shifted from the polarized struggle between individual liberty and authority to the more complex competition between state and society. As a consequence, the basic context of political and theoretical issues was transformed, and the flavor of the literature changed from the philosophically oriented writing of the nineteenth century *pensadores* to an examination of practical political and socioeconomic conditions in which the content became more explicitly ideological.

I

The Eighteenth-Century Background

Since the earliest days of intellectual speculation and theorizing in Latin America, European influences have been significant. While by no means all of the formulations of the *pensadores* have been derivative, it is generally true that original insights have been less frequent than imaginative adaptations of philosophical currents that were elaborated in foreign lands. This was clearly the case in the later years of the colonial era, as the accumulation of resentment against the mother countries and a rising surge of independence sentiment moved the sympathies of the educated elite away from generations of allegiance to the Iberian princes. Many of the ideas to reach the New World belonged properly to seventeenth-century thinkers, although the more influential ideas came largely from those of the eighteenth century. The writers of the 1600s had initiated in large part the revolt against the dogmatism of traditional scholastic thought, inaugurating in its stead a new rationalism. As Lanning has written, "the Americans, taking their cue from Descartes, Gassendi, Leibnitz and Newton, viewed the philosophical principle of authority with the same horror, if not with the same frenetic unrestraint, as the [eighteenth century] *philosophes* viewed the whole structure of the supernatural."[1]

While the eighteenth century became commonly regarded as the age

1. John Tate Lanning, "The Reception of the Enlightenment in Latin America," in *Latin America and the Enlightenment*, ed. Arthur P. Whitaker (New York: D. Appleton-Century Co., 1942), p. 77.

34

of reason, it might be called more properly the age of a *new* reason, for its conception of rationality differed from that of earlier years. The thinkers of the seventeenth century, whether empiricists or believers in innate ideas, had always relied on a method that began with a first original certainty from which reason could derive its truth. The eighteenth century, however, under the influence of Newton, depended upon analysis more than deduction; it rested upon the basic proposition of the existence of a universal order, subject to investigation and based on data collected through observation. The eighteenth-century mind was also characterized by a different conception of logic. By a long process that can be traced back through various centuries, the old scholastic method of definitions was gradually abandoned. The approach to definition by means of similarities and differences gave way to the genetic or causal definition. Thinkers aspired to know not what a thing was, but *why* it was, and *what* produced the object of knowledge. This development of causal logic and its application to political theory constituted an important characteristic of eighteenth-century thought.[2]

The empiricism of the seventeenth-century thinkers, especially the British, was also of great importance in the following century. If there were no innate ideas to guide a thinker, knowledge therefore became an acquistion rather than a heritage. Reason was necessarily more moderate, representing not the sum of all innate ideas but instead an intellectual force leading man toward the discovery of truth. The writers of the early European Enlightenment generally did not advocate a drastic or revolutionary change in the structure of the state. They wanted a tolerant ruler who respected civil liberties, emancipation from the dominance of the Church, and certain necessary economic and legal reforms under a normative order based on reason in accord with nature. Their goal was education of the ruler that he might be persuaded to implement such reforms. They desired, in short, an enlightened despotism. Political goals consistent with this attitude dominated educated circles in Latin America until late in the 1700s, when the success of the North American Revolution, the writings of Rousseau, and the French Revolution led them to consider their political problems from a different perspective.

Voltaire, the best representative of the early Enlightenment in France, was the champion of civil liberty and religious toleration. Before Rousseau in France, only Diderot, Condorcet, and a few others could be included among those with something of a democratic philosophy. Economic conditions were the concern of many French *philosophes*, for

2. For a detailed treatment, see Ernst Cassirer, *The Philosophy of the Enlightenment* (Boston: Beacon Press, 1955).

such thinkers hoped that a freer economy might bring about a concomitant improvement of the political picture. The condition of the poor, it was argued, should be attended to by the enlightened ruler, but revolutionary social or political means were not to be used. It can generally be said, then, that the ideas of the European Enlightenment were by no means fully homogeneous. As a consequence, the interpretations that emerged from the Spanish and Portuguese colonies were also varied. Before directing our attention to the Latin-American setting, however, further discussion of the European Enlightenment is appropriate.

Political Thought of the European Enlightenment

Perhaps the single most important conviction held by European intellectuals during the seventeenth and eighteenth centuries was their faith that right reasoning could bring the discovery of true knowledge, ultimately leading man to happiness. In pure political theory, this was consistent with an emphasis on natural law, stressing the advocacy and prescription of what is, and even more importantly, of what *ought* to be. Existing human conditions were obviously less congenial than they should be; the Enlightenment was therefore critical of reality while attempting to focus on proposed changes and reforms. A broadly humanitarian spirit protested against observable inhumanity of the age, arguing that all men were somehow linked by nature into a universal brotherhood. Partially in reaction to the absolutist strains of Thomas Hobbes's sovereign state, rationalism responded with a call for world citizenship. Voltaire and others attacked what they regarded as patriotic prejudice— an early form of inward, insular nationalism—for its deterring effect on the progress of civilization.

With the old framework of Renaissance religious life and thought being shattered, the Enlightenment came to consider for itself the nature of man, while inquiring also into the circumstances that produced the state. For many this led to a search for an original kind of social contract, those resulting in such expositions as those of Hobbes and later of John Locke in his *Two Treatises on Government*. Politically, England settled into a somewhat complacent solidity following Cromwell in the mid-seventeenth century and later the Glorious Revolution of 1688. Turbulence was more evident in France, as the slow deterioration of royal absolutism indirectly helped to promote what became a voluminous outpouring from the pens of French political theorists. Voltaire helped to introduce Locke to the French, and then Rousseau's contributions added complexities that in time helped to speed the decline of the Enlightenment itself.

There was an important common denominator of the political thought of the reformist Enlightenment and the forerunners of Latin American independence: a new conception of the state. As the rationalism of the Enlightenment inquired into the basic causes of conditions and institutions, the state had to be defined in terms of its origin, and political conditions in particular demanded explanation. When the conditions were found to be unsatisfactory, they had to be removed. This intellectual framework suggested a desire for reform and change. While thinkers often disagreed as to the means, there was a consensus that the political structure should somehow be transformed. This became a common proclivity of Latin-American thinkers toward the latter half of the eighteenth century. Implicit in such considerations of change was a strong spirit of negation. The seventeenth-century scientific and rationalistic impulse had in its time negated scholastic dogmatism. In philosophy, art, and literature as well, the growth of such a new movement was initiated by a condemnation of existing forms of expression and creativity. Just as the French condemned their old order in 1789, so had the North American colonies in 1776 rejected British political control. In Latin America, eighteenth-century thinkers gradually repudiated the absolutism of the Hispanic central government while attacking the system of rigid statism that characterized the colonial administration. In time, the opponents of the Hispanic order therefore advocated a new liberal ideal in which political society would enact a set of laws preventing abuses of power by the rulers while guaranteeing basic liberties to the individual.

It is necessary to keep in mind the difference between the eighteenth-century conception of the liberal state from the political ideas of the following century, which included the desire for unqualified independence. With the exception of Rousseau, the advocates of this early liberalism were essentially utopian, arguing that social and political perfection was to come about only as a result of the free play of man's behavior, unhampered by unnecessary state control. After negating absolutism and curbing the abuses of governmental power through new constitutional forms, political and economic *laissez faire* would bring mankind both progress and happiness. Utopian liberalism was individualistic in intellectual as well as in economic matters but was not emotionally self-assertive. It was a philosophy of a nascent middle class in its struggle against the state-supported Church, the powers of the king and the landed gentry. This was well represented in the thinking of Locke who, in order to restrict the power of the king, formulated the theory of government by consent, defending religious tolerance and advancing the theory that property should be only the result of man's labor. Utopian liberalism during the French Revolution was typified by the Girondists, while practical success was achieved in North America, unhampered by feudalism or a state church.

The utopian liberals, by the use of new logic, identified the causes of their problems and formulated a new system in order to correct unsatisfactory conditions. When this phenomenon was repeated, the forerunners of independence followed the somewhat different inclinations of Rousseau. With Rousseau, as Bertrand Russell has said, there began a new political thought that became the antithesis of early tolerant liberalism and created the cult of the hero, as later developed by Carlyle and Nietzsche.[3] This hero-cult helped to create the "providential ruler," who even today is influential in Latin America.[4] The interpretations of Rousseau have always been and will continue to be sharply divided, with political leaders all too often inclined to confuse their own wishes with the general will. The enlightened *criollos* of the eighteenth century were familiar with Rousseau but at first devoted more attention to his general philosophy of the cult of nature and the goodness of man. The influence of his *Contrat social*, with its theory of the sovereignty of the people and its conception of the rights of man, came later. His ideas of the primacy of will over reason fitted perfectly into the need for political action and insurrection against Spain. Thus the calm rationalism of the reformists and the hopes for improvement under an enlightened despot gave way in time to the preromantic liberalism of the drive for independence.

Utopian liberalism was closely related with the economic thought of the last decades of the 1700s. The economic criticism of Spanish writers, especially Campomanes and Jovellanos, found an echo among educated Latin Americans. The conditions denounced in Spain existed also in the colonies. The major grievances were the feudalism of the landed gentry, the wasted lands controlled by the Crown, the system of entailed estates, monopoly and a primitive system of agriculture. The needed changes were advocated under the influence of Adam Smith. His *Wealth of Nations* (1776) was translated into Spanish in 1792 and circulated widely. In Chile, Manuel de Salas and, in Argentina, Manuel Belgrano described the difficulty of economic conditions and demanded urgent

3. Bertrand Russell, *A History of Western Philosophy* (New York: Simon and Schuster, 1945), p. 600.
4. Miguel Jorrín, *Government of Latin America* (New York: D. Van Nostrand, 1953), discusses this point in various contexts.

reforms. Economic *laissez faire* marched hand in hand with political *laissez faire*. The economists felt that the natural law of supply and demand, with a free trade policy, would cure all economic evils, just as the free application of natural law would create the ideal political community.

During the Enlightenment, the old concept of natural law was given a new emphasis, just as reason had a new meaning. Natural law was no longer the *jus naturale* of the scholastics, conceived as the participation of the rational being in the eternal law. The thinkers of the Enlightenment were not concerned with the divine legal order as much as with the natural rights of man. In other words, natural law became not a static system of norms but the privilege that man enjoys as an individual rather than as a part of a political order. These natural rights belonged inherently to man, existing before the establishment of the state. They were inalienable and never to be surrendered to the political community.

Although such a brief summary cannot do justice to the long and varied elaborations of the thought of the Enlightenment, it should again be stressed that inherent was a faith in the over-all general progress of mankind. There was a belief in the continual intellectual and humanitarian progress of life and society. Perhaps the last great exposition of this view came as late as 1793 from the Frenchman, Condorcet, although he was at the very time in hiding from the authorities then directing the excesses of the French Revolution. Condorcet regarded humanity as being on a steady march toward perfectibility, claiming that in due course all men everywhere would be free, with pure reason alone as their ultimate master. There were many in Latin-American educated circles who were familiar with Condorcet's beliefs. It is true that the Enlightenment was approaching a state of disintegration even as he wrote. Faith in eternal principles was being shaken, as natural law gradually slipped from its pinnacle. For Latin-American *pensadores,* at least, the significance of the Enlightenment was a moral belief that was declaring in new language what were actually among the oldest values and beliefs in the history of Western civilization. It was these, along with the later practical lessons of revolution, which found a receptive audience in the Iberian colonies toward the close of the 1700s.

Major Sources of Enlightenment Influence

While the general ideas of the Enlightenment were broadly reflected in the colonies, more specific sources of influence can be identified.

A common generalization holds that the ideas of the Enlightenment that spread to Latin America came largely from the French, sometimes through the interpretive writings of the French-oriented Spanish "*afrancesados*." While this is basically true, it tends to obscure the fact that other sources were also significant. British scientific and political ideas of the seventeenth century, for example, reached many scholors in the New World.[5] There were also significant contributions from Italy, Germany, and the United States. In the first case, Italian intellectual ties with Spain were strong, and the Spanish king, Charles III, had himself been exposed to Italian teachers and cultural life during his youth in Naples.[6] Germany and Spain also enjoyed fairly close intellectual matters; thus in 1760 the Academy of Natural Science at Azcoitia—later renamed the Sociedad Económica—began to send scholars to Germany and later participated in German-directed scientific expeditions to the New World.

From the United States there were exchanges of publications between Latin-American educational centers and Harvard, the New York Historical Society, and the American Antiquarian Society. The American Philosophical Society maintained a subscription to the progressive *El Mercurio Peruano*, which itself reprinted timely expressions of North American ideas. Yet the paramount source of political doctrine, in the last analysis, was France. There, from approximately 1680 forward, such authors as Fénelon, Jurieu, and Saint Simon had led the criticism of monarchical absolutism. The work of philosophers helped to free history and science from the bonds of dogma, placing them on a more independent footing.[7] In time it became necessary to distinguish between the reformist programs of the French *philosophes* and the preromantic influence of Rousseau which developed after the North American Revolu-

5. The philosophic "sensationalism" of Locke and Hobbes, the rationalism of Hume, and the writings of Bacon were known. The Spanish Jesuit Antonio Eximeno, for one, was influenced by Locke, while the works of Diego de Avendaño concerning the theory of the state also mirrored Locke's influence. In his *Thesaurus Indicus* of 1668, Avendaño manifested his concern with the plight of the indigenous masses, and described European ideas of the divine right of kings as unprincipled absolutism, demanding instead a popular will and social contract as preferred bases of political association. For additional discussion, see Mariano Picón-Salas, *A Cultural History of Spanish America from Conquest to Independence,* tr. Irving A. Leonard (Berkeley and Los Angeles: University of California Press, 1962), esp. pp. 115–16.

6. Italian ministers such as Gimaldi collaborated in Charles' administrative reforms, and Alejandro Malaspina formulated a forward-looking plan for colonial reform.

7. Characteristic contributions came from the skepticism of Fentenelle and the materialism of Bayle.

tion. In short, the single most important focal point for the eighteenth-century attack on conventional institutions and traditions was France, where such forces were strong even before the climactic events of the Revolution. The intellectual figure of pre-eminence was, of course, Jean Jacques Rousseau.

Although almost totally ignorant of conditions in the New World, he nonetheless wrote glowing descriptions of the so-called noble savage. Coupling these passages with a consideration of original man in the state of nature, he wrote extensively about the high quality of preconquest indigenous life and the subsequent degradation brought about by the unmitigated evils of the *conquistadores* and their descendents. In his classics *Contrat social* and *Emile* the extraordinary Genevese stressed the innate worth of man and the relevance of government based upon the consent of the governed. His description of the plight of the aboriginal peoples and their debasement by European exploiters enflamed imaginations across Europe, while an increased acquaintance with his works by young *criollos* in the colonies led to enthusiasm for the totality of his writing. The impact of Rousseau was joined with that of Voltaire and Raynal in criticizing the role of the Jesuits, and anticlerical diatribes were circulated both before and after the expulsion of that order, in 1759 from Brazil and in 1767 from the Hispanic regions.

The reformism of the *philosophes* reached Latin America not only directly from France but through Spain itself, especially during the reign of Charles II. Enlightened despotism in Spain under that king was characterized by the belief that the authoritarian government of a good ruler could be conducive to the welfare of the people. The Spanish Crown contributed to the development and spread of the Enlightenment throughout the Empire. This was not entirely altruistic, for the shock experienced by defeat in the Seven Years' War brought a recognition of the need to improve colonial trade and commerce in preparation for the anticipated forthcoming war with England. There was an urgent need to increase the military and to strengthen fortifications in the colonies, especially in Cuba, Puerto Rico, and Mexico. Spanish statesmen, thinkers, and administrators, conscious of their country's relative decline, were themselves increasingly receptive to new ideas, even in the realm of political and religious reform. Greater emphasis, however, was placed on the promotion of scientific knowledge for practical purposes. It was not until the aftermath of the French Revolution that a reaction brought about the abandonment of the reform program for the colonies. Once this fact was fully recognized in Latin America, there was little real alternative to independence.

In addition of official royal policy, Spain also produced thinkers in the 1700s who were concerned with social and economic problems. Father Benito J. Feijóo (1676–1764), in his *Teatro crítico universal* and *Cartas eruditas y curiosas* was influenced by the French Enlightenment and was widely read in Latin America. Inquiring as to what he regarded as Spain's departure from the paths of European cultural development, he called for precise analysis of facts in preference to hollow verbalism and the free use of critical reason in place of blind reverence for official authority. Demanding an end to the labyrinthian verbosity of Spanish intellectual thought derived from the sources of scholasticism, he insisted upon the value of experimentation and the observation of nature. The natural sciences, in his view, required a renewed study and understanding in Spain, while in lieu of superstition he called for "religious feeling shorn of a numbus of miracles, needless terror, and silly fables."

The Count of Cabarrús (1752–1810) was concerned with the goodness of man and the impact of society upon him, indicating a familiarity with the teachings of Rousseau. Another writer influenced by Rousseau was the Count of Campomanes (1732–1803), and together with Melchor Gaspar de Jovellanos (1744–1813) he expressed concern over economic problems of the day. Jovellanos' thought was well represented by his *True Excercise of the Arts and Crafts* (1785) and *Concerning the Agrarian Law* (1795), in which he drew parallels between the causes of poverty and backwardness in Spain and in the colonies. The gravity of technical and productive stagnation, combined with the ignorance of the neglected peasant, made inevitable for Jovellanos the depressing reality that lay before him. At the court itself, Charles III's most trusted minister, the Count of Aranda (1719–98) was something of a follower of Rousseau. His *Memorial* of 1783 analyzed perceptively the repercussions that North American independence would have on Latin America. Predicting the rapid and powerful development of the United States, he recommended to the government hat a Spanish commonwealth be created to prevent the disintegration of the colonial empire.

Another important cultural development of the Spanish Enlightenment was the creation of the Sociedades Económicas de Amigos del País, the first of which was founded in Biscay in 1746. Sponsored by the government, these societies established centers for teaching applied science, especially chemistry, agriculture, and industrial textiles. Parallel organizations were later initiated in the colonies as well. Reforms also reached other centers of higher learning. Thus, in 1769 the University of Salamanca began to modernize its curricula, moving away from scholasticism rapidly. In many other institutions, students were required to read such philosophers as Bacon, Descartes, Gassendi, Newton, and Condillac.

The colonies were also influenced to a degree by the writings of Jesuit scholars. The Company of Jesus was the most important institution of higher learning in eighteenth-century colonial Latin America, enjoying both economic power and social prestige. Together with substantial agricultural and mining property, the Jesuits owned considerable urban land and took advantage of the economic opportunities afforded their schools and missions. The Venezuelan historian, Mariano Picón-Salas, for one, has argued that following the formal expulsion of the Order in 1767, the Jesuits turned against the Spanish king. It is his contention that their subsequent criticism of the Spanish government and praise for the colonies helped to prepare the national consciousness over independence. For Picón-Salas, the Jesuits revealed a religious enlightenment in contrast to a lay and revolutionary one. By way of illustration, the Jesuit, Francisco Xavier Clavijero (1731–87), in his *Storia antica de México* showed a nostalgia for his American native land, writing with admiration of Mexican aboriginal culture. He criticized the Spanish policy of colonization and stressed the fact that the Indians' native language was richer than many European ones.

Another exiled Jesuit, Andrés Cavo (1739–1802), pointed in his *Tres sigles de México* to an interesting animosity against the Spaniards in Mexico, attributing it to the Spanish policy of discrimination against Indians and *mestizos,* whose values and social organization he admired. Yet another representative Jesuit was Francisco Xavier Alegre (1729–88), whose *Instituciones teológicas* dealt with political philosophy and attempted to find the basis for a more efficient Christian society. Maintaining that Christianity and representative government were not inimical to one another, he contended that the origin and source of political power was only the consent of the community embodied in a social contract. Alegre also criticized the cruelty and incomprehension of Spanish policy in the Americas, singling out the trade monopoly, Negro slavery, and exploitation of the Indian for special condemnation. These men, along with other exiled Jesuit scholars, undoubtedly helped to call European attention to the importance of the Latin-American lands. They also contributed to a feeling of nationalism in the colonies, one that centered on the suggestion that Spanish administrative practices were both corrupt and inept. Yet although the Jesuits clearly exerted influence on the spread of independence sentiment, in terms of political theory they represented less an outgrowth of the Enlightenment than an extension of the traditional writings of earlier Jesuits.[8] For Jesuit thought had been formulated earlier than and largely apart from Enlightenment teachings, and that legacy was perhaps the major intellectual base for later Jesuit criticism of Spain.

Reception and Dissemination of the Enlightenment

The ideas of the European Enlightenment found fertile soil in Latin America. The New World was in a sense an experimental ground for these philosophical formulations. Despite the ban imposed by Spanish authorities, fairly large numbers of books were shipped in from abroad, and intellectuals in the colonies were informed, if belatedly, of changing European currents. Especially by the 1700s, as the sea passage became swifter than before, personal contacts and the broadening influences of travel and foreign study became significant factors. Many of the wealthy *criollos* succeeded in returning from Europe with new books and publications of various sorts. Secrecy was required to circulate the books, but neither the censors nor the officials of the Inquisition were rigid in the enforcement of the laws. As one noted student has written, "The bibliographical avenue of the Enlightenment was never so thoroughly barricaded as the statute indicated."[9] The Inquisition was never especially effective in the colonies, and as education gradually became more secularized than in earlier years, intellectual curiosity and investigation grew rapidly.

The Hispanic Reception / The ideas and writings of North American and French revolutionaires were commonly read in educated circles. The works of Locke, Voltaire, Montesquieu, and Rousseau were all to be found in the private libraries of the intellectuals, and in the final years of the century there were those who reprinted Spanish translations of revolutionary proclamations and declarations, as for example the

8. There was a clear parallel to the earlier thought of Francisco Suárez and Juan de Mariana. In his *De legibus,* Suárez (1548–1617) had maintained that all men were born free, and he suggested a theory of social contract. To him, natural law meant that man was not obligated to accept axiomatically any specific form of government. Juan de Mariana (1536–1623) in *De rege et regis institutione* argued against absolutism, saying that the King of Spain had no authority to issue arbitrary decrees. He expressed regret that the rights of the people under ancient Spanish law had fallen into disuse. Furthermore, he advocated the medieval right of tyrannicide when the king violates the basic laws of the country.

9. Lanning, "Reception of the Enlightenment," in Whitaker, *Enlightenment,* p. 7.

Colombian, Antonio Nariño, and his circulation of the French Declaration of the Rights of Man. Another who did much to further knowledge was José Antonio Rojas, a Chilean who traveled as far as Russia, collecting a library of banned works that he smuggled back into his native land. Among the Spanish officials were a number who acquired prohibited works for themselves, and these were subsequently passed from hand to hand. The censor of the Inquisition in Callao, Diego Cisneros, was among those who gathered works of the *philosophes* and distributed them to friends. In Chuquisaca, Canon Terrazas kept the books of Mariano Moreno in the metropolitan palace. Viceroys Manuel de Amat in Lima and Juan José Vertiz in Buenos Aires even recommended that "students should be free to select the system of ideas which made the greatest appeal to them."[10] While these cases were exceptions to the general rule, perhaps, they illustrated the mood of tolerance that was demonstrated by many of the royal authorities in the colonies, both secular and clerical.

The works that fell into the hands of the inquiring and curious Latin-American audience were widely varied. Perhaps none were as familiar as the major works of Jean Jacques Rousseau. Montesquieu's *Spirit of the Laws* was well known, as was Smith's *Wealth of Nations*. The demand of the latter for the removal of official trade and commercial restraints in the interests of classical economic *laissez faire* was especially appealing to the Latin Americans, of course. There was also exposure to somewhat less eminent authors who dealt in various ways with colonial problems. Among the most widely read books of the times was the popular *Philosophical and Political History of the Indies* by Abbé Guillaume Raynal. More than fifty editions of this work were issued in a thirty-year period, with its Rousseau-like conception of the noble savage so dear to the *philosophes*. Themes treating the American indigenous peoples and their oppression by the Spanish were frequently repeated. The sixteenth-century classic by Father Bartolomé de Las Casas, *Historia de las Indias*, was revived and widely distributed. Indeed, somewhat unfair criticism of Spanish mistreatment of the Indians proved highly popular, giving further support for the growing resistance of the *criollos* to the existing colonial system.

Among the important roles in the dissemination of the Enlightenment in Latin America was that played by the Sociedades Económicas de Amigos del País. Some of these organizations were called Patrióticas, while others took the title Sociedades de Amantes del País, and that in Quito was known as the Escuela de Concordancia. These institutions,

10. *Ibid.,* p. 82.

as the names suggest, were economic societies that generally stressed the need to change from a feudal and purely agricultural society to a manufacturing or industrial one. These were not royal societies, but associations of "friends of the country" for whom the idea of the Spanish kingdom was giving way to loyalty to the native environment. The aims of the institutions were eminently practical. A reading of their regulations and bylaws reveals their genuine concern with immediate and measurable progress. Without exception they called for agricultural development, the improvement of crafts and artisanship, the introduction of machinery for industrial purposes, respect for the laboring groups and the education of the youth.

It was also noteworthy that these economic societies came into being as the result of the private initiative of wealthy *criollos* or educated *peninsulares* whose presence in the New World had led to the growth of interest in its future welfare. It is true that the Spanish government approved of these organizations, especially during the reign of Charles III, but the initiative for reform rested with those actually residing in the colonies. Interest in education and the transmission of knowledge dominated the thought of the membership. In the field of education, their main objective was to encourage and implement the teaching of subjects that had been neglected in the schools and universities. One of the founders of the economic society of Santiago, Cuba, in 1783, Pedro Valiente, clearly expressed this sentiment when he said that "the Economic Society is a school to learn what is not taught in the universities."[11] One of the early acts of the society formed in 1793 in Havana was to endow a chair of political economy in the university.

The influence of the Sociedades Económicas de Amigos del País in preparing the political thought of the independence was obvious and was connected with another powerful force—that of Freemasonry. The historical antecedent of the Spanish economic societies was the Royal Society of England. There was in turn a close relationship between the Royal Society and the Honorable Society and Fraternity of Freemasons which, under the influence of deism, was fighting for scientific progress and religious toleration. The Royal Society itself defended the experimental method, the use of reason and a belief in human progress based on man's own efforts. Some historians have maintained that the first economic societies in Biscay were actually established by Freemasons and that at first they functioned as secret masonic lodges. The point is debatable, but the fact remains that there was always a close connection

11. Fernando Ortíz Fernández, *La hija cubana del iluminismo* (La Habana: n.p., 1943), p. 32.

between Freemasonry and many thinkers of the eighteenth century. It is by no means irrelevant that Charles III's administrative and ministerial confidant, the Count of Aranda, was a personal friend of Voltaire and served as first grand master of the lodge Gran Oriente Español, founded in 1780. The Count of Campomanes was also a Freemason and a leading sponsor of the economic societies in Spain. A correspondent with the American Philosophical Society and friend of Benjamin Franklin, the grand master of the Philadelphia Lodge, he provided further testimony to the importance of the role of Freemasonry in the spread of reformist ideas in the New World.

By the latter years of the eighteenth century, ideas of the Enlightenment spread with increasing rapidity because of the appearance of a number of important journals and newspapers. Since early in the 1600s, leaflets and bulletins had been published in the capitals of the viceroyalties, with the first official publication, the *Gaceta de México,* appearing in 1667, although only at irregular intervals. After periods of publication in the first six months of 1722 and then from 1728 to 1739, it was succeeded by *Mercurio de México* from 1740 to 1742. A more enduring revival dated from 1784 under the editorship of Manuel Antonio Valdés. By the middle of the eighteenth century there were similar gazettes in Guatemala City and in Lima. Established newspapers also appeared in Havana (1764), Bogotá (1785), Buenos Aires (1801), Veracruz (1805), Santiago de Cuba (1805), and elsewhere.[12] The first actual daily was Lima's *Diario Erudito, Económico y Comercial,* which began publication in 1790. By the end of the century, there were four Mexican journals devoted to literature and natural sciences, while similar important publications were *El Mercurio Peruano* of Lima, *El Mercurio Volante* of Mexico, *El Papel Periódico* of Havana, *Las Primicias de la Cultura* of Quito, and Bogotá's *Semanario de la Nueva Granada.*

Not all of the newspapers in the New World supported the rising chorus of criticism, to be sure, and there were royalist organs that strongly defended Spanish authority. However, the imposition of censorship was sufficiently erratic to permit the appearance of editorials, essays, and even news items that furthered the dissemination of dissenting views. And by the beginning of the revolutionary period itself, the decree by the Spanish Cortes favoring freedom of the press resulted in even more frank discussions of contemporary problems. Among new publications that took advantage of this newly acquired freedom were Lima's *El*

12. Pedro Henríquez Ureña, *A Concise History of Latin-American Culture,* tr. (and with a supplementary chapter) Gilbert Chase (New York: Frederick A. Praeger, 1966), pp. 34–35.

Cometa (1811–14), El Peruano (1811–12), and El Argos Constitucional (1813), along with the series of newspapers published in Mexico by José Joaquín Fernández de Lizardi.[13] By this time the supporters of freedom and independence also published periodicals abroad, including Francisco de Miranda's El Colombiano (1810) and the Guatemalan Antonio José de Irisarri's El Censor Americano (1810), both in London.[14]

Some years earlier, El Espíritu de los Mejores Diarios in Madrid began printing digests of important world news. Published in the form of a booklet, this could easily be folded and carried in the pocket, therefore being passed readily from person to person in the colonies. An organ of political liberalism, El Espíritu published statements such as the following: "Man is born free and remains restrained only as long as his weakness does not permit him to be independent, but as soon as he is able to use his reason, he is free to select the country and government that will best fit his ideas."[15] The Latin-American newspaperman of the eighteenth century demonstrated considerable scientific curiosity, and was omnivorous in seeking news and information about facts and conditions in the other colonies. Newspaper writers exchanged ideas and published information of a scientific, economic, and social nature; they kept in close contact with and sought collaboration from the editors and publishers of other newspapers.[16]

Added to this was the increased literary output of both Spanish and Latin American writers, in which the appearance of irony as a means of social criticism became common. Father Feijóo, although a fervent Catholic, became known as a Spanish Voltaire from his biting commentaries on the superstitious exaggerations of ignorant clergymen. His use of polemical irony was followed in Latin America as well. Picón-Salas aptly observed, "Every period of social change and of a break in tradition is preceded by waves of sardonic humor and satire."[17] Among characteristic practitioners of irony as a vehicle of social protest were the quiteño Francisco Javier Eugenio Espejo and Concolorcorvo (the pen name of Calixto Bustamante). The latter remarked that, as a mestizo, his highest aspiration in colonial officialdom would be that of dogcatcher of the Cuzco cathedral, while native-born Spaniards continued to be regarded

13. For more on Fernández de Lizardi, see Chapter 2, section B.
14. Henríquez Ureña, Latin-American Culture, pp. 51–52.
15. Germán Arciniegas, Este pueblo de América (México: Fondo de cultura económica, 1945), p. 109.
16. For an extended discussion, see José Torre Revello, El libro, la imprenta y el periodismo en América (Buenos Aires: Casa Jacobo Peuser, 1940).
17. Picón-Salas, Cultural History of Spanish America, p. 152.

as brilliantly unique children of the sun. Other writers of the period satirized the colonial social structure, arguing that racial prejudice and an exaggerated sense of honor were used by the privileged class to protect itself from the drudgery of work.

The Brazilian Experience / At one time the common conception held that the Enlightenment in Brazil did not begin until 1808 when, fleeing Lisbon in advance of Napoleonic troops, the royal family transferred its court to Rio de Janeiro. This interpretation has long since been proven fallacious, however. A small handful of Jesuit colleges in the late 1500s and after provided an outlet for the version of European scholasticism then current in Portugal. This broad humanism was received uncritically and admiringly in Brazil for some years, and there was virtually no effort to consider local conditions in the light of such abstractions. By the eighteenth century, humanistic scholasticism went into gradual decline at the same time that the influence of the Jesuits tended to cut off the colonists from the scientific revival and renewal of intellectual curiosity in Europe. The political decline of the Iberian Peninsula in the 1700s was especially marked in Portugal where the glories of the Empire were receding further into the past. Indeed, retrogressive forces in Portugal unfolded more rapidly than in Spain; the country slipped back to a minor rank among European powers although, as the contemporary Brazilian Gilberto Freyre has noted, it figuratively stood on tiptoe in order to retain some semblance of its earlier prominence.

During much of the colonial period in Brazil, the Jesuits played the major civilizing and unifying role, and this continued until their expulsion in 1759. The official Portuguese interest was largely economic, and a series of temporary waves of prosperity were alternately based on sugar and on diamonds. In the eighteenth century cotton developed for a time as a major source of revenue, and by the close of the 1700s Brazil was actually outstripping the mother country in its economic growth. Intellectual life developed more slowly than in the Hispanic colonies although, to repeat, there was more energy and activity than many scholars once believed. The domination of plantation life—the society centered on the *fazenda*—was not conducive to a stimulation of intellectual investigation, and there was relatively little excitement during much of the period. For more than three centuries there were no universities whatever, although this was offset in part by a number of theological centers and colleges. The Jesuit school in Bahia ranked on a par with Portugal's University of Evora until the expulsion of the order, but for Brazilians who desired professional training in medicine or law, it was necessary to matriculate in Europe, usually attending Portugal's University of Coimbra.

The impetus of intellectual development and the dissemination of Enlightenment thought consequently arrived somewhat later than in the Hispanic area. Much of the belated impetus came from the emergence of enlightened despotism in Portugal during the reign of João I, with the program of reform outlined by the Marquis de Pombal. Private initiative for intellectual development culminated in the creation of institutions of advanced studies there, such as the Academia dos Generosos and the Academia Real de História. These were devoted almost exclusively to literature and history. Attention to scientific studies soon followed through the organization of the Academia Real das Sciencias. The Portuguese eighteenth-century interest in learning, while less advanced and reformist than that which grew up in Spain, nonetheless began to influence Brazil many years before independence. A variety of private or semipublic academies grew up in the colonies, beginning with the Academia dos Esquecidos in 1724. In 1759 the Academia dos Renascidos was created, although later ordered closed by the authorities under the charge of harboring a conspiracy. The Sociedade Científica do Rio de Janeiro was established in 1772, contributing substantially to the initiation of native studies while gathering a valuable library and scientific collection. Later, it too was to be disbanded and its members arrested under suspicion of spreading "Jacobinism."

Newspapers were unknown to Brazil throughout the colonial period, and the lack of universities was a major deterrent to intellectual development. At the same time, however, it is a great exaggeration to disregard those signs of intellectual curiosity that did exist. Pedro Henríquez Ureña goes so far as to say that, in colonial Brazil, "books compensated for the lack of universities. One cannot detect a substantial difference in cultural levels between the overseas subjects of the Portuguese Crown and those of the Spanish Crown—except in the two great centers of learning, Lina and Mexico City."[18] Alexander Marchant has also concluded that Brazil did indeed experience the impact of the Enlightenment, less important in quantity and quality than that of Lima and Mexico City but the equal of that in the other Spanish colonies.[19] He has written that the Brazilian poet Claudio Manoel da Costa (1728–89) in his *Cartas chilenas* satirized the colonial administration in the manner

18. Henríquez Ureña, *Latin-American Culture*, p. 33.
19. Alexander Marchant, "Aspects of the Enlightenment in Brazil," in Whitaker, *Enlightenment*, p. 115.

of Montesquieu's *Lettres persanes,* as well as undertaking a translation of Adam Smith. The legendary 1789 revolt in Minas Gerais, the "Infidencia Mineira," was enthusiastically narrated by the writings of several Brazilian poets, including Tomás Antônio Gonzaga (1744–1810) and Alvarenga Peixoto (1744–93). Private libraries also included the works of Condillac, Montesquieu, Voltaire, and the forerunner of socialism in France, the Abbé Mably.

By the close of the 1700s, as Cruz Costa has written, "Brazil had reached a stage of development which has outspaced the inefficient tutelage of the Portuguese, unable to serve the growth of the colony." He further remarks that when "the monopoly of external trade was abolished, the colonial experience was shaken. Revitalizing forces were unleashed, which progressively confirmed the change from a colony into an autonomous national community."[20] In short, if the colonial preparation for independence in Brazil was less extensive and active than that of Hispanic America, it was far from nonexistent; by the end of the eighteenth century, the small but articulate circle of Brazil's educated elite had been exposed to the major philosophical treatises of the Enlightenment. The spirit of tolerance in social matters, more noticeable than that in the Spanish colonies, included attitudes toward race, caste, and inheritance. To this innate tendency was added the sheer fact of Portuguese colonial rule, far less effective and restrictive than that of Spain. With the arrival of the royal family in 1808, measurable stimulus to intellectual development appeared. The routine of court life spurred the rapid development of an urban social elite that waxed enthusiastic over the possibilities of both spiritual and material progress. There was a new animation from the broad spirit of scientific renewal, which received further acceleration from the expanded importation of European writings and the appearance of newspapers and irregular pamphlets following the introduction of the printing press. Backwardness was no longer the hallmark of the society, as a group of French artists was brought in to initiate an Academy of the Arts; a Royal College was also established which drew on the contribution of exiled scholars from the University of Coimbra, who had fled the invading French forces.

With this impetus from the presence of Portugal's King Joâo VI, the pace of colonial intellectual life increased, and the new European spirit launched a frontal attack upon the fortifications of elitist tradi-

20. Joâo Cruz Costa, *A History of Ideas in Brazil: The Development of Philosophy in Brazil and the Evolution of National History,* tr. Suzette Macedo (Berkeley and Los Angeles: University of California Press, 1964), p. 35. Also see Caio Prado Júnior, *História econômica do Brasil* (São Paulo: Edit. Brasiliense, 1945), p. 134.

tionalism. Faculties of mathematics and philosophy were established, and a veritable transformation was well under way before the proclamation of independence of João's son Dom Pedro I in 1822. The disintegration of the colony of Brazil reached its culmination in the events of the early nineteenth century, after a process of many years. The French legacy in particular was strong, and this fact was underlined when the newly established Empire in 1823 proceeded to draw up the constitutional form of government over which Don Pedro was to rule.[21] Both the original working draft and to a somewhat lesser extent the finished product reflected the heritage of the French revolutionary writers. This tendency, bound up with the Europeanized views of the dominant class, permitted the consolidation of a constitutional monarchy through which Brazil was to avoid much of the turmoil and travail that followed the winning of independence in the Hispanic colonies.

Summary / In viewing this background to the emergence of independence through the revolutionary wars in Latin America, one must recall that Europe from the mid-1700s had been increasingly the scene of great intellectual ferment. Moreover, this was more extensive than simply the writings of a few giants such as Voltaire, Rousseau, and Montesquieu. Conventional ideas were everywhere under attack, and the traditional values regarding mercantilism and trade, monarchical authority, and the role of religion were all being questioned. Overtones of explicit partriotism were accompanying the rise of the European nation-state and the international overtones of clerical influence were being held up for scrutiny and criticism. While the process of challenging old and traditional ideas in Europe had by no means run its full course by the year 1800, old notions of authority were being questioned with growing force. Furthermore, as Whitaker has remarked, the New World itself contributed to European intellectual development, for there was a two-way exchange of ideas and influences flowing across the Atlantic. While much of the spirit and body of Enlightment thinking moved from Europe to the colonies, a deep impression was registered on many Europeans as a result of the events and circumstances in Latin America.[22]

A final point revolved about the fact that as late as 1800, there were few in the colonies who foresaw significant political changes in the immediate future. The adoption of the Enlightenment generally called for a reform and amelioration of conditions; few recognized that in

21. Cruz Costa, *History of Ideas in Brazil*, pp. 42–43.
22. Arthur P. Whitaker, "The Dual Rôle of Latin America in the Enlightenment," in Whitaker, *Enlightenment*, pp. 11–12.

actuality the colonial empires were poised on the brink of destruction. As political events—most notably the Napoleonic invasion of Spain and Portugal—brought about the cataclysmic revolutionary movement against the mother countries, moreover, there were few who realized that the Enlightenment and eighteenth-century liberalism were, in Latin America, fundamentally destructive rather than creative. Society was seen in fairly realistic and hence critical terms, placing in question the traditional social and political roles of the Church, monarchy, and peninsular elite while suggesting opposition to the *status quo*. Few new substitutes were offered, until a generation of independence-minded *pensadores* began to enunciate the more positive values of emancipation from Spain and Portugal. As events were to prove, even the exponents of natural rights and popular sovereignty were characterized by a preponderant strain of destructive negativism, and it was not until the post-independence rise of romantic liberalism and the concomitant advocacy of utilitarianism that intellectuals in the New World came to devote more systematic thought to the creation of a new order in the hemisphere.

SELECTED BIBLIOGRAPHY

Arciniegas, Germán. *Este pueblo de América.* México: Fondo de cultura económica, 1945.

Cassirer, Ernst. *The Philosophy of the Enlightenment.* Boston: Beacon Press, 1955.

Cruz Costa, Joâo. *A History of Ideas in Brazil: The Development of Philosophy in Brazil and the Evolution of National History.* Translated by Suzette Macedo. Berkeley and Los Angeles: University of California Press, 1964.

Diffie, Bailey W. *Latin American Civilization: Colonial Period.* Harrisburg: Stackpole, 1945.

Griffin, Charles C., ed. *Concerning Latin American Culture.* New York: Columbia University Press, 1940.

Haring, Clarence H. *The Spanish Empire in America.* New York: Oxford University Press, 1947.

Henríquez Ureña, Pedro. *A Concise History of Latin American Culture.* Translated and with a supplementary chapter by Gilbert Chase. New York: Frederick A. Praeger, 1966.

Jane, Cecil. *Liberty and Despotism in Spanish America.* New York: Oxford University Press, 1929.

Lanning, John Tate. *Academic Culture in the Spanish Colonies.* New York: Oxford University Press, 1940.

———. *The Eighteenth-Century Enlightenment in the University of San Carlos de Guatemala.* Ithaca: Cornell University Press, 1956.

Moses, Bernard. *The Intellectual Background of the Revolution in South America, 1810–1824.* New York: Hispanic Society of America, 1926.

Ortíz Fernández, Fernando. *La hija cubana del iluminismo.* La Habana: n.p., 1943.

Picón-Salas, Mariano. *A Cultural History of Spanish America from Conquest to Independence.* Translated by Irving A. Leonard. Berkeley and Los Angeles: University of California Press, 1962.

Russell, Bertrand. *A History of Western Philosophy.* New York: Simon and Schuster, 1955.

Torre Revello, José. *El libro, la imprenta y el periodismo en América.* Buenos Aires: Casa Jacobo Peuser, 1940.

Torres-Ríoseco, Arturo. *New World Literature: Tradition and Revolt in Latin America.* Berkeley and Los Angeles: University of California Press, 1949.

Whitaker, Arthur P., ed. *Latin America and the Enlightenment.* New York: D. Appleton-Century Co., 1942.

Zavala, Silvio. *Filosofía política de la conquista de América.* México: Fondo de cultura económica, 1947.

Zea, Leopoldo. *The Latin-American Mind.* Translated by James H. Abbott and Lowell Durham. Norman: University of Oklahoma Press, 1963.

2

Natural Rights
and Popular Sovereignty

The influence of the reformists in the Enlightenment ended during the decade of 1790 to 1800, when the ideas and examples of the French Revolution and the abandonment of the program of reform by Spain led the *criollos* increasingly to see independence from the mother country as a possible solution to their problems. The notion of independence was far from new, with brief flashes of the suggestion dating back as far as the years of the Conquest itself.[1] And before the shift in Spanish policy, the Count of Aranda had advised Charles III in 1783 to create three monarchies headed by Spanish princes—one in North America and two in South America. By the start of the nineteenth century, a sympathetic knowledge of both the North American and the French Revolutions had contributed a note of practical reality to the discontented musings of Latin American *pensadores* and would-be political leaders. As Henríquez Ureña wrote, the educated colonists had been reading the works of French and English thinkers whose writings contained such doctrines as the social contract, popular sovereignty, and the separation of governmental powers. "With the revolutionary turn of events in France and North America, these doctrines acquired a dangerous vital-

1. Pedro Henríquez Ureña, *A Concise History of Latin-American Culture*, tr. (and with a supplementary chapter) by Gilbert Chase (New York: Fredrick A. Praeger, 1966), p. 43.

55

ity—dangerous for traditional authority. The Spanish Americans not only ignored the injunctions against reading works containing these doctrines, but persisted in reading the documents of both great revolutions and the writings of the thinkers who had participated in them or had supported them, such as Thomas Jefferson. The Declaration of the Rights of Man promulgated by the Constituent Assembly in Paris, translated into Spanish by Antonio Nariño . . . and printed clandestinely in Bogotá in 1794, circulated throughout a large part of Spanish America."[2]

The climactic event leading to the wars of revolution was the invasion of the Iberian Peninsula by Napoleon in 1808, which led to the abdication of the Spanish king and the flight of the Portuguese royal family to Rio de Janeiro early in the year. While the latter permitted the continuation of colonial authority in Brazil, patterns of legitimacy and allegiance were weakened significantly. At first the *ayuntamiento* or municipal council assumed authority in the name of the deposed monarch, while the *cabildo abierto* or open town meeting provided necessary governmental direction. The increased participation by the *criollos* in these bodies underlined the doctrine of popular sovereignty, and within a few years the first outbreaks in the fight for independence took place. In Spain, a legislative body loyal to the royal family was convoked, and the famed Cortes met in Cádiz with representatives of Spanish America for the drafting of the liberal constitution of 1812, Spain's first. This failed to satisfy the rising sentiment for independence, however, and insurrection, which had already reached major proportions in Mexico, soon spread. Notwithstanding the withdrawal of Napoleon and the restoration of the monarchy in Spain, the struggle continued until the ultimate victory of the Latin Americans in the 1820s.

The Precursors of Independence

In considering the political ideas of this period, it is useful to distinguish between two groups of men: first, the forerunners of the revolutionary wars and, second, the actual political and military leaders of the movements. There is scarcely a single Latin American country today which does not claim, legitimately, one or more forerunners of the movement for independence. These men lived in effect before their time, realizing the inevitability of a final break with the mother country. While giving voice to both intellectual and political demands, these precursors generally advocated ideas of liberty and freedom, equality, class opportunity, and the dignity of man. Weight was given to the doctrine

2. *Ibid.*, p. 44.

of popular sovereignty, which opposed the traditional concentration of all authority in the figure of the monarch. Not only was full liberty and equality to permit the removal of class and race distinctions, but economic freedom was also proclaimed. There was a deep-rooted belief, naturally shared by merchants and businessmen, that the colonial mercantilism of Spain should be abolished if commerce were to be increased.

Among the leading precursors, only a few can be mentioned, and it will be helpful to stress the impetus for independence which came to Venezuela and Argentina, two of the first important centers of rebellion, along with Mexico. In the first instance, the dominant intellectual figure was perhaps the greatest and most important of all precursors, Francisco de Miranda (1750–1816).[3] Born in Caracas of Spanish parents, Miranda was to experience one of the most remarkable, indeed bizarre careers imaginable. Alternately regarded both during his lifetime and since as hero and coward, patriot and ambitious self-seeker, scholar and opportunistic libertine, he began a military career by buying, at the age of twenty-two, a commission in the Spanish army, not an uncommon practice of the time. Serving with the Spanish and French forces against the British during the Revolutionary War in the United States, he then joined the French and, in 1792, commanded the forces that captured the city of Antwerp.[4] After his departure from France following brief imprisonment by jealous opponents in Paris, he went to London, which served as his base of operations for much of the time until 1810. During the interim, however, he traveled widely in Europe, ranging as far as Turkey and Russia, where he became an admired confidant of royalty.

During his extensive studies and reading throughout these years, Miranda became firmly committed to the vision of independence for Spanish America, and especially for his native Venezuela. Whether he was motivated more by patriotic or selfish ambitions remains a subject of debate among historians. Whatever his ultimate reasons—and they were in all probability mixed—Miranda worked for the realization of colonial liberation, an idea that he had proffered as early as 1782. Convinced that European support was a necessary ingredient, he sought to rally support in England. His campaign was formally launched in 1806, when he landed at the head of a small band near Coro, in Venezuela. Promised British naval support was withdrawn for use elsewhere, however, and

3. A classic study is the two-volume work of William Spence Robertson, *The Life of Miranda* (Chapel Hill: University of North Carolina Press, 1929). Among more recent studies, also consult J. F. Thorning, *Miranda: World Citizen* (Gainesville: University of Florida Press, 1952).

4. Briefly a member of the pantheon of revolutionary heroes, Miranda's name was subsequently inscribed on the Arc de Triomphe in Paris.

the expected enthusiastic reception by Venezuelans did not occur. Miranda therefore returned to London, where he undertook once again a personal campaign to gain acceptance and, importantly, material assistance from the British. In 1810 the *cabildo* of Caracas proclaimed Venezuela's independence, and Miranda joined with Bolívar, Andrés Bello, and Luis López Méndez in a collaborative effort to gain a formal commitment from London. While the mission of this delegation was unsuccessful, it brought Miranda into direct contact with the Venezuelans, as well as introducing him to Simón Bolívar. Soon, at the age of sixty, he returned home to lead the military forces against Spanish troops.

Named the commander-in-chief of the revolutionary armies, he rapidly gained popular acceptance, and when independence was formally proclaimed in Caracas on July 5, 1811, Miranda assumed the powers of dictator. From that moment forward, his fortunes went into rapid decline. He was a hesitant and vacillating leader, and the unity of the movement fragmented on the rocks of personal jealousy and enmity. The following July he capitulated to the Spanish and was arrested as the result of a conspiracy in which Bolívar, who had angrily turned against him, played a major role. His captors denied his wish to go to the United States; instead he was returned to Spain in chains, where he died a martyr's death in prison in 1816. Historical controversy still surrounds the events of his capture, and Bolívar's role is somewhat ambiguous, notwithstanding the latter's repeated attacks on Miranda's "treachery and treason." An eminent North American scholar has well suggested the violently contradictory views of Miranda's activities.

> On one side, the view may be taken that Miranda merely sold his services to the best bidder. His career may be interpreted to mean that he was a shifty adventurer, who betrayed the liberty of his fatherland for gold. . . . On the other side, the view may be taken that Miranda was an exalted patriot. Under the influence of this conception, some writers have overemphasized Miranda's services to the cause of South-American independence. . . . The writer takes an intermediate view: there were many occasions when Miranda must have been impelled by mixed motives: resentment toward Spain mingled with love for Venezuela. With Miranda the revolutionizing of Spanish America became a profession,—he was a patriot-filibuster.[5]

A true man of the Enlightenment, Miranda never permitted his peripatetic revolutionary life to monopolize his attention. An avid reader

5. William Spence Robertson, *Rise of the Spanish-American Republics As Told in the Lives of Their Liberators* (New York: Collier Books, 1961), p. 80. The original of this important work was published in 1918 by D. Appleton and Company.

and man of considerable learning, he was described by John Adams as "a man of universal knowledge." Yale President Ezra Stiles termed him "a learned man and a flaming sun of liberty."[6] Even Napoleon expressed the opinion, "He is a Don Quixote, except that this one isn't crazy."[7] Not in the formal sense what might be termed a political philosopher, Miranda nonetheless had definite views on contemporary political questions, and the influence of Rousseau was evident in his defense of popular sovereignty and his conception of the rights of man. For independent Hispanic America he advocated a kind of constitutional monarchy, to be headed by a descendant of the Incas. The idea of an hereditary Inca was later modified to the proposal of two such rulers for a ten-year period, one of them responsible for administration from the capital the other traveling continually throughout the realm.

Supporting the hereditary monarchical leader there was to be a two-house legislature. The upper body was to be composed of *caciques* or chieftain-like rulers with life tenure, while the lower would be elected every five years. The monarch would name a judicial body whose members would enjoy life tenure, while a fourth power—that of censors— would maintain vigilant supervision over legislative actions. Miranda was implicitly reflecting the attitudes of Montesquieu, with whom he was familiar, in the reliance on a division of national power among diverse branches, which he contended should enjoy an equality of authority. In all of his conspiratorial planning and thinking, Miranda maintained his commitment to the eventual unification of Hispanic America. Perhaps not uncharacteristically, he was unwilling to think in terms of many independent entities but rather proceeded to the more grandiose dream of hemispheric unity. Further insight into his preference for divided authority among federal branches can also be gained from the Venezuelan constitution proclaimed in 1811, in whose drafting and formulation he was influential.[8]

Especially representative of the enlightened *criollo* in the final years of colonialism was the wealthy Colombian lawyer, Antonio Nariño (1765–1823). A great admirer of Voltaire, Rousseau, and Montesquieu, he was a prosperous land-owner whose 6,000 volume private library in Bogotá was among the largest collections in the hemisphere. Nariño also owned a small hand printing press, on which he reproduced per-

6. Henríquez Ureña, *Latin-American Culture,* p. 52.
7. Jean Descola, *The Conquistadores,* tr. Malcolm Barnes (New York: Viking Press, 1957), p. 37.
8. For a fuller discussion of his ideas and activities, see Víctor Andrés Belaúnde, *Bolívar and the Political Thought of the Spanish American Revolution* (Baltimore: Johns Hopkins University Press, 1938).

tinent excerpts to be distributed to friends. When he received a bound volume including the French *Declaration of the Rights of Man and of the Citizen*, he enthusiastically translated it into Spanish. He then printed the seventeen articles of that document, although by his own later testimony only a small number of copies were distributed. When the authorities learned the source of the Spanish version, he was promptly jailed and his property confiscated. Later escaping and taking refuge in France, Nariño unsuccessfully endeavored to secure the help of the revolutionary government in Paris on behalf of Colombian independence. Although he later stated, "The seventeen articles of the Rights of Man cost me more than that number of years of imprisonment and persecution,"[9] Nariño's message had wide repercussions. He eventually returned to participate in the independence movement, and was named to the Colombian vice-presidency by Bolívar in 1822, but he was prevented by political opponents from taking office and died a year later.

Thousands of miles from the locale of Miranda and Nariño, the independence movement in Argentina took shape largely apart from the influence of events in Venezuela and Colombia. Among the most noted figures in the Plate region were Manuel Belgrano and Mariano Moreno. Belgrano (1770–1820) was notable for his reflections on economic liberalism as interpreted during his times. Inspired by the French Revolution, he championed the principles of liberty and equality, defended free trade for the colonies, and proposed the introduction of machinery as a means of overcoming obsolete production methods. Thus he wrote that "the nearer a state is to complete liberty in its internal and external trade, the nearer it is to a steady prosperity. If it is fettered, its steps toward prosperity are slow and far apart."[10] For Belgrano, the keynote to economic freedom was an infusion of democratic governmental processes and procedures.

Historical evidence is inconclusive, but it is generally believed that Belgrano was among those who inspired and perhaps contributed to the *Representación de hacendados y labradores de Buenos Aires* (1793), one of the first official economic protests filed with the Spanish authorities in Buenos Aires. Belgrano's varied activities, aside from participation in the growing wave of protest, included such things as the founding of the Naval School of Buenos Aires in 1799. In time, like Nariño, he joined the revolutionary movement to become an able officer in the

9. Quoted by Mariano Picón-Salas, *A Cultural History of Spanish America from Conquest to Independence*, tr. Irving A. Leonard (Berkeley and Los Angeles: University of California Press, 1963), p. 172.
10. *Ibid.*, p. 169.

conflict. He was withdrawn from the military and sent to Spain in an early diplomatic effort to gain recognition of Argentine independence but was unsuccessful. He then turned to the direction of *El Correo del Comercio,* in which he published articles in favor of economic reforms. In his final years, Belgrano grew disillusioned over the prospects of republicanism in Argentina, harboring monarchical sentiments while favoring aristocratic rule.

Mariano Moreno (1778–1811) is a particularly characteristic figure of the period. Born in Buenos Aires of a family long resident in the New World, he received his early education there, then traveled to Chuquisaca in what was to become Bolivia to enter the University of San Francisco Javier, a center of legal and theological study. Deciding against the priesthood in favor of law, he practiced first in Chuquisaca before returning home, where he became prominent as a representative of wealthy farmers. During these early years Moreno combined the enlightened ideas of the *porteño* aristocracy with liberal economic teachings of Gaspar Melchor de Jovellanos, whose *Concerning the Agrarian Law* in 1795 was an influential economic critique of colonial trade policies. He coauthored the *Representacion de hacendados y labradores de Buenos Aires* in 1810,[11] a demand for free commerce and other economic reforms. In May of that year, amid confusion over the nature of local authority and its relationship to officials in Spain, the May Revolution was produced, with a provisional junta including Belgrano among its membership assuming control.

As the junta was organized, two major departments were created, one for financial matters and the other for military and political affairs. Moreno was designated the secretary responsible for the latter. He also organized and became the editor of the *Gaceta de Buenos Aires,* the first issue appearing on June 7, 1810. This became the official organ of the regime and provided Moreno a source of substantial influence through the wielding of his facile pen. As the leader of fairly radical young men who tended to differ with the more conservative and aristocratic views of Belgrano and his colleagues, Moreno became the guiding genius of the junta and was soon its dominant member. Basically he held a moderate position between outspoken advocates of either federal democracy or strong central government. Caught in the crossfire between

11. His important writings are available in edited form, with accompanying commentary, by Ricardo Levene, *Mariano Moreno: Escritos,* 2 Vols. (Buenos Aires: Editorial Estrada, 1943). Also see Harold F. Peterson, "Mariano Moreno: The Making of an Insurgent," *Hispanic American Historical Review,* XIV, No. 2 (May 1934), 450–76.

warring factions, in December, 1810, he was eased out of the junta. In a farewell statement he declared his abiding conviction in democratic and republican beliefs. Then, receiving full authority as diplomatic agent to win acceptance from the British, he sailed in January, 1811, from Buenos Aires, accompanied by aides and assistants. The stress of preceding months had weakened his constitution and he died at sea in March, only thirty-three years old.

Despite the brevity of his public career, Moreno looms large as a crucial leader of independence movement; the major figure in the Revolution of May, he was the first of a series of liberal leaders who are still revered in the forefront of that tradition in Argentina today. Moreno was an avowed follower of Rousseau, translating and publishing the *Contrat Social* in Buenos Aires. In the introduction he called Rousseau "immortal," a man who had "placed in a clear light the rights of the people," teaching them the true origin of their obligations" as well as the importance of seeking "in the social compact the root and only origin of obedience."[12] Calling for the exercise of the general will in creating true democracy, he saw in independence the necessary basis for individual liberty and human dignity. Rejecting Rousseau's religious ideas, he eliminated all such references from his translation of the original, stating in the preface that he believed Rousseau's treatment of the subject invalid. "Since Rousseau had the misfortune to rant and rave when he dealt with religion, I suppressed that chapter and the principal passages in which he has treated these matters."[13]

His political ideas, according to one scholar, were based fundamentally on his belief in the natural rights of man, together with abstract principles of stoic philosophy, the teaching of the Church fathers and the Roman lawyers.[14] Like most of his contemporaries, Moreno believed that a proper constitution provided the cure-all solution for all problems, including the organization of the state and the defense of popular sovereignty. He advocated the convening of an Estates General, in the French tradition, as the proper authority to draft a constitution and code of laws. In a series of editorials for the *Gaceta de Buenos Aires* from November 1 to December 6, 1810, he also called for a division of powers in the coming government. Declaring that Hispanic America had the right to constitute itself as a group of independent nations,

---

12. Quoted in Robertson, *Spanish-American Republics,* p. 157.
13. Quoted in José Luis Romero, *A History of Argentine Political Thought,* tr. Thomas F. McGann (Stanford: Stanford University Press, 1963), p. 70.
14. Enrique de Gandía, *Las ideas políticas de Mariano Moreno: Autenticidad del plan que le es atribuído* (Buenos Aires: Peuser, 1946).

he opposed as utopian those who called for a massive continental confederation. At the same time, he saw much merit in the possibility of a union between Chile and the province of the Río de la Plata. In his editorial of December 6, he wrote the following lines:

> If we consider the diverse origin of the group of states which forms the Spanish monarchy, we cannot discover a single reason why they should remain united in the absence of the king, who was the bond of their unity. . . . It is chimerical to claim that all of Spanish America should form one state. . . . The colonies should form constitutions; they should do so for themselves; nature herself has ordained this conduct because of the products and the boundaries of their respective territories. Every arrangement which diverts them from this procedure is a trick to misdirect the enthusiasm of the people until the occasion is ripe to furnish them with a new master. . . .

> I desire that the provinces would restrict themselves to the limits which they have had up to the present time; that they always observe the just maxims of mutual aid and succor; and that, postponing all thoughts of a federal system which under present conditions is not suitable and may be injurious, they consider only the formation of close alliances which would encourage the fraternity that should always reign, and which is the only thing that can save us from domestic passions,—a more terrible enemy to a state that is in process of formation than the armies of foreign nations which oppose it.[15]

In sum, Mariano Moreno believed in the people, hated demagoguery, and feared anarchy. Historically representative of the political thought of the eighteenth-century Enlightenment, when confronted with England's invasion and temporary occupation of Buenos Aires in 1806 and then the Napoleonic Wars in Spain, he joined the Argentine revolutionary movement and fought for independence.[16] With an almost naïve faith in the doctrine of public law, he pursued a liberal political position despite misgivings over the admitted ignorance of the masses. A somewhat sickly individual who enjoyed a keen intellect, his uncompromising love of justice and equality provided an inspiration that survived his premature death. An exaggerated and flowery eulogy written in 1855 gives some measure of the regard in which he has been held by his countrymen.

> As eloquent as Mirabeau, as ardent as Camille Desmoulins, as republican as Junius Brutus, he was endowed with a remarkable

---

15. Quoted in Robertson, *Spanish-American Republics,* pp. 158–59.
16. For a careful treatment, see Ricardo Levene, *El pensamiento vivo de Mariano Moreno* (Buenos Aires: Edit. Losada, 1942).

faculty for the transaction of administrative affairs. His comprehensive intelligence appreciated all the circumstances of a situation which was beset with difficulties. The light of the junta,
he dispelled doubts, and calmly promulgated the most audacious
reforms. Under the guidance of his surpassing talents and copious
knowledge, the press freely scattered ideas upon all subjects concerning which the American people were summoned to act when
extricating themselves from the rule of Spain. . . . With un-
daunted front he fought prejudices, attacked abuses, and laid
the foundations of the Argentine republic.[17]

In Mexico, the third of the major centers of agitation for independence, one of the most important of all the precursors was Father
Miguel Hidalgo y Costilla (1753–1811), the leader of a popular uprising
initiated by his historic *Grito de dolores* in 1810. Mexican thought in
the eighteenth century had shown a marked tendency toward more intellectual autonomy and philosophical criticism than in most of Hispanic
America. In the university, there were professors who openly condemned
Aristotle and defended Descartes' rationalism. Benito Díaz de Gamarra,
to name but one, was an eclectic seeking truth in all philosophical systems, attempting to apply philosophy to the actual conditions of Mexico.[18] There was also an important tradition of independent thought
among many members of the Church, and it was in this atmosphere
that Father Hidalgo studied at the university, where he received the
degree of Bachelor of Arts and Theology. He served as a parish priest
in several cities before moving to Dolores. A noted scholar and for a
time also head of the Seminary at Valladolid, Hidalgo soon became
both controversial and beloved.

He was frequently attacked by higher ecclesiastical authorities for holding heretical views. In 1800, for example, he was officially charged with
criticizing the Scriptures, speaking disrespectfully of the popes, and
doubting the virginity of the Mother of Christ. In the political realm,
he was also charged by his critics with desiring to see the establishment
of French revolutionary ideals in Spanish America and with questioning
whether a monarchy might be inferior to a republic as a governmental
form. Although frequently harassed through such attacks, Hidalgo managed to retain his clercial position. His parish of Dolores was in the
meantime exposed to his interest in agricultural development, as well
as local industry and crafts. Of his reading little is known, although
at some point he had been exposed to the ideas of the French Revolution,

17. Quoted in Robertson, *Spanish-American Republics*, pp. 163–64.
18. Samuel Ramos, *Historia de la filosofía en México* (México: Imp. Universitaria, 1943).

and especially to Rousseau. Mexico was in the meantime experiencing the agonies resultant from the situation in Spain and diverse personal and political controversies in Mexico City. In December of 1809 an unsuccessful conspiracy in Valladolid had aimed at establishing a special junta to rule on behalf of the deposed Ferdinand VII. In September, 1810, a new viceroy was named—Francisco Javier Venegas—and three days later the revolutionary conflagration was kindled by Father Hidalgo.

There had been a number of conspiratorial discussions in the earlier months of 1810, and after a time Hidalgo entered into the group. The uprising was scheduled for later in the year, but authorities learned in advance of the plot, including the name of Hidalgo as a prominent leader. Consequently the rebellion was launched hastily on September 16, beginning a civil disturbance that for the next eleven years, in the words of one historian, "crimsoned the soil of Mexico with blood."[19] Despite some interpretive ambiguity, it appears fairly certain that the goal was the independence of Mexico, despite the pretext of defending the rights of Ferdinand VII. Of particular relevance, however, was the appeal to both Indians and *mestizos,* as well as a number of revolutionary symbols including the banner of the Virgin of Guadalupe, the patron saint of Mexican Independence. What soon emerged was an uncontrolled social uprising that took on racial overtones and, in the process, alienated many *criollos* who at first were favorably disposed.

Indian workers and peons joined behind the standard of the Virgin of Guadalupe, and lower class support was pronounced. The authorities responded by adopting a variety of measures, including a rapid preparation for military action. For many of the Indians, the battle became a war of revenge against all Spaniards, although this development had not been foreseen or intended by Hidalgo. Gradually the ranks of his followers reached nearly thirty thousand, and on October 30, 1810, he won a victory at Monte de la Cruces, a locale commanding the road running from Toluca to Mexico City. Instead of marching on the capital, however, Hidalgo hesitated for two days then turned back. Fighting continued in the weeks to follow, while Hidalgo issued a variety of manifestoes and declarations. In mid-January his forces were routed in battle, however, and from that time his military fate was sealed. In March, Hidalgo was taken prisoner; following a trial, he was shot by a firing squad on July 30, 1811.

Hidalgo's political platform, pieced together from a number of assorted documents and proclamations, revealed his admiration for France and the ideas of that revolution. Opposed to the practice of slavery, he fought

19. Robertson, *Spanish-American Republics,* p. 19.

against monopolies, called for the sponsorship of industrial and agricultural projects, and advocated the distribution of land to the peasants. His leadership of the insurgency was frank and open, as he declared at his trial prior to execution. "I placed myself at the head of the revolution, raised armies, manufactured small arms and cannon, appointed chiefs and officers, directed a manifesto to the nation, and sent to the United States a diplomatic agent. . . ."[20] Later during the cross-examination he reiterated that his purpose had been the winning of independence, although not having a specific governmental plan to be implemented. Despite his limitations as a military tactician and an inability to control the behavior of his own undisciplined followers, Hidalgo had rudely awakened the dscontented in Mexico, fanning the smoldering embers of rebellion and elevating the ideal of independence.

The banner of protest soon passed to the hands of another priest, José María Morelos (1765–1815). Born to a poor family and unable to complete his studies until he was thirty years old, Morelos, of mixed blood, prepared for the priesthood at Valladolid while Hidalgo was rector. Although there is little evidence of a close relationship between the two, the experience opened to Morelos the liberal revolutionary ideas of the day. Serving as a village priest in 1810, he immediately joined Hidalgo's forces following the *Grito de dolores*. When Hidalgo captured, Morelos and a small group moved their zone of operations to the south, where several victories were won. The royalists were unable to fight a major engagement with Morelos, and by September, 1813, he controlled much of southern Mexico. Morelos called into session a congress at Chilpancingo, where he attempted to outline his program.

Repeating Hidalgo's call for independence from Spain, Morelos argued in the best liberal tradition of the day that sovereignty was vested in the people and that it was their will to establish a new and free Mexican government. Slavery, monopolies, and personal taxation were to be abolished, as well as all forms of Indian tribute payments and special privilege in general. Morelos promised to support the Catholic religion, adding that no other faith would be tolerated. Following the adoption of this program at Chilpancingo, Morelos attempted to negotiate a favorable settlement, and at one point issued an act declaring—for the first time—the independence of Mexico. The new revolutionary congress was soon disbanded by royalist forces, however, and the situation became even more confused following the shifting policies of the restored Spanish monarch, the untrustworthy Ferdinand VII. A Morelos-inspired revolutionary constitution was drafted and adopted in October, 1814, in Apat-

20. *Ibid.*, p. 105.

zingan, declaring again that popular sovereignty was supreme and that its authority was to be vested in congress. A three-man executive was also created, including Morelos. Nearly a year later, however, with fighting and bloodshed still a common occurrence, Morelos fell into Spanish hands, and in December, 1815, was executed after having been declared both heretic and insurgent. An abler military leader than Hidalgo, Morelos had followed many of his predecessor's political views, and these were to live after him as Mexicans continued their fight until full independence was ultimately achieved.

From Mexico, then, such figures as Hidalgo and Morelos joined the heroic and near-legendary ranks of the great precursors, along with Belgrano and Moreno, Miranda, Nariño, and less familiar figures. Each of these men was affected by the writings of the European Enlightenment as changed and remolded by the realities of the French Revolution and its aftermath. As has been remarked, "Ideas are begotten of circumstance on the human mind, and rarely, if ever, is their major source to be found in books. What books supply is chiefly forms and conventions of expression. They further categories and classifications and, perhaps, 'arguments,' they supply needed contrasts and parallels; they suggest ways of putting things. But the continuity of political thought arises from the continuity of circumstance."[21] The political expression of nearly all the enlightened *criollos* of the era, in looking for liberal reforms, adjusted itself to the facts of the struggle for independence. As will be seen, what helped to differentiate the ideas of the precursors from those of the revolutionary and military leaders was the new circumstance faced by the latter: namely, the need to organize the countries politically after their liberation.

As the struggle for independence began to assume significant proportions in much of the continent by the years just before the 1820s, a further influence, both philosophically and practically, was the force of moderate liberalism in Spain. This had been represented by those who took part in the Cortes of Cádiz, from 1809 to 1813. The patriotic assembly had been constituted by four classes of deputies: these included delegates from the Spanish cities, others from the provincial juntas, a third group chosen by the people by direct vote, and, lastly, a small group of representatives from the American colonies, who received one vote for every 100,000 white inhabitants. There was a strong current of the French Enlightenment among the Cádiz legislators, and several of those present were notable exponents of such ideas. Martínez Marina

21. J. W. Allen, *A History of Political Thought in the Sixteenth Century* (London: Methuen, 1957), p. 282.

(1754–1833), for one, combined his liberalism with historical Spanish traditionalism, considering the Cádiz assembly a revival of the medieval Cortes in Castile. Father Joaquín Lorenzo de Villanueva (1757–1837) demanded official recognition of the dogma of national sovereignty and recommended the exile of those who would repudiate the principle. Antonio Alcalá Galiano (1789–1865) based his liberalism on natural law, with ingredients of utilitariansim. Despite the influence of such men, the Spanish constitution of 1812 that proceeded from the Cortes had its conservative elements, including a proclamation that national sovereignty be exercised by the monarch. The government created by the Cortes was not precisely a liberal monarchy, but the brief constitutional period enjoyed by the mother country added to the influences exerted on Latin Americans who were struggling to achieve their freedom from Spain.[22]

The Revolutionary Leaders

Those who were successfully to lead in the open conflict with the Spanish were, generally, more inclined toward military than political affairs. Despite the talents and ideas of Bolívar and a few others in the governmental realm, the majority of the revolutionary leaders had a much less clear picture of post-independence institutions and procedures than they did of the actual campaign against the troops of Spain. Obviously, the writings and declarations of Simón Bolívar are of primary importance in the political thought of the period. Yet he was not the only figure of the period, having been preceded not only by the several precursors but also by revolutionary leaders elsewhere. Of these latter, mention is due both Tupac Amaru and Toussaint L'Ouverture. While neither enjoyed more than fleeting success in the quest for independence, both men typified the spirit that had begun to well up even before the rise of Bolívar.

The Leaders of Mass Rebellion / Tupac Amaru (1740–1782) was a descendant of the Inca line who achieved some intellectual repute during his lifetime. Educated in the Spanish tradition by the Jesuits, he became prominent among the Indians as well. Although honored with wealth and a Spanish title, he preferred his Indian name, taken from that of a famous ancestor. He adopted the cause of the indigenous

22. Luis Recasens Siches, *Los temas de la filosofía del derecho* (Barcelona: n.p., 1934), pp. 332–33.

masses in what later became Peru, pleaded for their welfare with Spanish authorities, and demanded the elimination of virtual slavery and the wide practice of deceit and fraud against the Indian. Repeatedly rebuffed by the agents of the crown, he began to piece together a largely unarmed native army, launching a bloody uprising in November of 1780. "The kings of Castile," he proclaimed, "have usurped crown and the sovereignty of my people for three centuries by imposing upon my vassals an unbearable burden of tributes, imposts, tithes, excises, and taxes of every kind, along with tyrannical viceroys, judges, magistrates, and other officials who have treated the natives of this kingdom like beasts."[23] When he had won control over much of southern Peru and parts of today's Bolivia, he naïvely believed that the Spanish would respond by granting the claims of his people. Instead, reinforcements were sent from Buenos Aires, and his force of an estimated 75,000 was systematically divided and defeated. Tupac Amaru's capture and execution by dismemberment led to further bloodshed, but the Spanish ultimately controlled the situation and put down the final glimmerings of native rebellion.

On the French-controlled western third of the island of Hispaniola, the Negroes found their early liberator in a former slave named Toussaint L'Ouverture (1743–1803). Haiti had been a lucrative colony for France throughout the 1700s, and the spread of revolutionary ideas after 1789 contributed to a movement of violence which by 1791 had assumed major proportions. There were rival revolutionary groups for several years, and by the end of the decade the island was caught up in virtual civil war. L'Ouverture, born a slave but later freed and becoming in time a man of substantial wealth, had joined rebel forces in 1791. By 1800 he had established himself as the dominant figure in the colony, and within two years his forces controlled the whole of Hispaniola, including the once-Spanish eastern portion. From France, an irritated Napoleon sent a large complement of troops to deal with the Haitians; L'Ouverture was eventually defeated, imprisoned, and died in 1803. While the battle had been lost, the war was soon to be won, for in 1804 Haiti became the first of the Latin-American countries to gain independence. Toussaint L'Ouverture had been a product of violence and unrest and did not prove a significant exponent of political ideas. He was, however, an excellent example of the impulses of a people emerging from slavery. It is unduly melodramatic to call him, as some have done, a Black Napoleon. Broadly committed to freedom and emancipation. L'Ouverture was the embodiment of new forces struggling to be born in defiance of French rule.

23. Quoted in Picón-Salas, *Cultural History of Spanish America*, pp. 135–36.

The Political Ideas of Simón Bolívar / Of all the revolutionary leaders on the continent, it was the liberator Simón Bolívar (1783–1830) who rightly stands as the pre-eminent figure of the age. As a military leader and activist, his accomplishments were seriously rivalled by only one man—San Martín. Bolívar's political and intellectual ideas were the most important and influential of the day and have long since been enshrined in virtual immortality by the several countries whose independence he won. A complex personality who was alternately humble and vain, selfless and ambitious, magnanimous and petty, his political thought passed through a lengthy period of evolution and change that mirrowed his own experience as well as the changing conditions in the lengthy struggle for freedom from Spain. Born to a wealthy aristocratic *criollo* family in Caracas, Bolívar received an excellent private education, counting among his tutors such distinguished men as Miguel José Sanz, Andrés Bello, and Simón Rodríguez, the last of these a brilliant eccentric who imparted to Bolívar his personal predilection for Jean Jacques Rousseau. During extended travels in Europe as a young man, Bolívar found repugnant the absolutism of Napoleon, and through the teaching of Rodríguez became as a young man an advocate of republicanism. At the outbreak of Venezuelan rebellion in April of 1810, he sailed for home and joined the first provisional government. From there, his career was to carry him to the heights of glory before his embittered death two decades later.[24]

Among his voluminous writings, proclamations, manifestoes, and personal correspondence, Bolívar's thought can be seen as passing through a series of stages, each of them represented by at least one major pronouncement. During the initial phase, he was concerned largely with military action and a break with Spain. Dedicated to the destruction of Spanish influence, he tended to favor a strong and stable unitary government as the necessary basis for a successful military campaign.

24. The commentaries and biographies of Bolívar are, of course, voluminous. For the English reader, an excellent and judiciously selective two-volume source is Vicente Lecuna and Harold A. Bierck, eds., *The Selected Writings of Bolívar,* 2 Vols. (New York: The Colonial Press, 1951). Among the many treatments of his life and thought, in addition to Robertson, *Spanish-American Republic,* and Belaúnde, *Bolívar,* might be included Gerhard Masur, *Simón Bolívar* (Albuquerque: University of New Mexico Press, 1948); Hildegard Angell, *Simón Bolívar: South American Liberator* (New York: W. W. Norton & Co., 1930); and Waldo Frank, *Birth of a World: Bolívar in Terms of His Peoples* (Boston: Houghton Mifflin Company, 1951). A highly controversial but important study is that of the Spanish intellectual Salvador de Madariaga, *Bolívar* (London: Hollis & Carter, 1952).

On November 27, 1812, his message to the Congress of New Granada[25] provided insight into his thinking at the time. In what is commonly referred to as the Cartagena Manifesto, he explained his view of the collapse of the first Venezuelan republic (headed, 1810–11, by Miranda) and then offered his own ideas on the nature of governmental forms. Miranda's leadership was criticized for unrealistic policies and a fatal predilection for moderation, for "a spirit of philanthropy" when aggressive action against Spanish troops was called for. He also censured religious fanaticism by parts of the clergy, which he said confused an uneducated and superstitious public. Upholding South American freedom as the great ideal, he asked all the peoples of New Granada to fight for the deliverance of Caracas, where the citizenry was determinedly republican.

Bolívar's thinking at this early point was further revealed a month later in his *Memorial to Citizens of New Granada by a Citizen of Caracas,* which was widely distributed in 1813. He described a federal governmental system as the most perfect and ideal form in theory but added that it was inappropriate to the infant states then struggling against Spain. "Our fellow-citizens are not yet able to exercise their rights themselves in the fullest measure, because they lack the political virtues that characterize true republicans—virtues that are not acquired under absolute governments, where the rights and duties of the citizen are not recognized."[26] Moreover, a truly federal system was regarded as too weak to direct the kind of extended and intensive warfare that the situation demanded. Calling for the centralization of government within a democratic framework, he added that in 1810 and 1811, "if Caracas had established the simple government that its political and military situation required, instead of a slow-moving and insubstantial confederation, Venezuela would still exist and enjoy its freedom today!"[27]

As both this *Memoria* and the Cartagena Manifesto underlined, Bolívar was at the time convinced of the merits of republicanism but inclined through the initial period of military action to prefer a centralized government providing necessary unity and stability. A further statement, perhaps his most famous, came in a letter dated September 6, 1815, and entitled *Reply of a South American to a Gentleman of this Island, Jamaica.* Popularly known as the Jamaica Letter, this tract was written while the liberator was in temporary exile before renewing action on

25. New Granada was later to become Gran Colombia, including today's republics of Venezuela, Colombia, Panama, and Ecuador.
26. Lecuna and Bierck, *Writings of Bolívar,* I, 21.
27. *Ibid.,* p. 22.

the mainland. Arguing in favor of independence, he maintained that Spain could no longer hope to retain its colonies, let alone reconquer what had already been lost. He began with a description of Spanish abuses in the New World, showing deep familiarity with colonial history as well as with the geography of South American. In this connection he strongly criticized the Spanish neglect of both orthodox and political education of the people. "We have been harassed by a conduct which has not only deprived us of our rights but has kept us in a sort of permanent infancy with regard to public affairs."[28] Bolívar also criticized the Spanish economic policies, especially the prohibition of planting European crops, as well as the existence of Spanish-controlled monopolies and trading privileges. Attacking the systematic exclusion of *criollos* from local government, he remarked: "We are never viceroys or governors, save in the rarest of instances; seldom archbishops or bishops; diplomats never; as military men, only subordinates; as nobles, without royal privileges."[29]

Bolívar carefully analyzed revolutionary conditions in Hispanic America, revealing detailed knowledge of the liberation movements in Mexico, Argentina, and Venezuela. There was a touch of Montesquieu in his discussion of the diversities of geography, ethnic composition, and economic systems from one region to another, and he agreed with the French *philosophe* that climate and regional conditions played a definite role in the political structure of nations. Retrospectively, his treatment of the various colonial regions and nationalities is particularly intriguing. Opposing the common intellectual tendency to consider America as a single monolithic Spanish colony about to become a single huge state, he speculated perceptively about the future countries in terms of national and individual regional traits, as well as economic and psychological factors. He visualized some fifteen states emerging and opposed the institution of monarchy in them while insisting upon a somewhat paternalistic governmental approach.

Again he expressed misgivings over the efficacy of republicanism in Latin America at that time. He echoed a common opinion of European thinkers of the Enlightenment in suggesting that a republic was feasible only in a small country. "Almost all small republics have had long lives. Among the larger republics, only Rome lasted for several centuries, for its capital was a republic. The rest of her dominions were governed by diverse laws and institutions."[30] Despite his distaste for monarchy,

28. *Ibid.,* I, 111.
29. *Ibid.,* I, 112.
30. *Ibid.,* I, 116–17.

he was so convinced of the inherent difficulties of a large republic that he predicted the larger states of Latin America might find themselves forced to create monarchies. Opposed to a federal system as inappropriate, he maintained that it was "overperfect, and . . . demands political virtues and talents far superior to our own."[31]

Following the divisions outlined by the proindependence French publicist Abbé de Pradt, Bolívar expected that Chile would become a republic, where the chances for a long and happy life were good. Peru, long dominated by the desire for gold and silver and a state of indigenous slavery, reflected strong factors clashing with liberal principles and individual freedom; Bolívar was not sanguine over its prospects. Mexico he saw as potentially a great representative republic, which would require a strong executive with extensive powers. Unless a wise man should emerge, popular revolts and internal strife would be a commonplace occurrence. Monarchy was a possibility there, but would also degenerate into violence in the absence of a wise ruler. He anticipated the establishment of a confederation by the nascent states of Central America and saw the prospects as essentially favorable. New Granada and Venezuela in combination would have difficulty in agreeing upon the terms of consolidation. He advocated the location of the capital in either Maracaibo or else a new city named Las Casas in the border region. Otherwise the countervailing forces of Bogotá and Caracas would lead to a shattering of unity. He recommended a nonhereditary, lifetime executive, with a bicameral legislature encompassing a hereditary upper chamber and a lower body based on popular representation.

The Jamaica Letter concluded that after the expulsion of Spain, the numerous individual countries should not unite as one gigantic entity but rather should establish an "American Federation." Genuine integration would only come slowly, given the class and ethnic differences that existed. Ultimately, however, this was destined to grow and prosper. In the meantime, despite divisive policies adopted by Spanish generals, the peoples of the continent would stand alongside one another in the revolutionary undertaking. "Surely unity is what we need to complete our work of regeneration. The division among us, nevertheless, is nothing extraordinary, for it is characteristic of civil wars to form two parties, *conservatives* and *reformers*. The former are commonly more numerous, because the weight of habit induces obedience to established powers; the latter are always fewer in number although more vocal and learned. Thus, the physical mass of the one is counterbalanced by the moral

31. *Ibid.*, I, 118.

force of the other; the contest is prolonged, the results are uncertain. Fortunately, in our case, the mass has followed the learned."[32]

By this point, in short, Bolívar's political and governmental ideas were increasingly suggesting that true republicanism lay well in the future and that in some cases individual circumstances might even justify a form of monarchy or lifetime ruler. In the years ahead, his disillusionment with the capacity of the masses was to grow, and the importance of domestic tranquility and order led him further along the road toward a more authoritarian form of government. This was underlined in 1819 by his *Angostura Discourse*.

On February 15, 1819, the second national congress of Venezuela met at Angostura—today's Ciudad Bolívar—following several military victories against Spain. The liberator delivered his address to the legislators as the outline of a constitutional plan. Along with the Bolivian Constitution of 1826, this provided a representative statement of his thought on the subject of constitutions and forms of government. Beginning with the customary placing of guilt on Spain for past and present evils, he quoted both Rousseau and Montesquieu in outlining his philosophy of the sovereignty of the people and his belief in the rights of man. Accepting the principle of natural law but suggesting that it should be moderated by historical experience, Bolívar returned repeatedly to Montesquieu in arguing that legislators should study history and compare political structures before adopting constitutional forms: "laws must take into account the physical conditions of the country, climate, character of the land, location, size and mode of living of the people."[33]

The *Angostura Discourse* warned about the threat to democratic rule posed by the authority of any one man, but this was contrasted with expressions of concern over the chaos resulting from absolute and unfettered liberty. Bolívar came out forthrightly in favor of unitary, centralized government as the most efficient, although noting some of its inherent weaknesses, as he had done in earlier years with respect to federalism. A single executive was to be chosen, although Bolívar was unclear on the matter of tenure. In addition to the usual judicial and bicameral legislative bodies, he also advocated a fourth or "moral" power somewhat reminiscent of Miranda's "censors." This governmental branch would oversee the education of the young while promoting patriotism and national well-being, vigilantly guarding against violations of ordinary social precepts. This proposal was suggestive of the liberator's growing conviction that an intellectual and political elite with the capacity for ruling

32. *Ibid.*, I, 121.
33. *Ibid.*, I, 179.

was a necessary constitutional component. This idea was to grow in the decade of life left to the Venezuelan.

The years following the *Angostura Discourse* were fraught with the difficult but climactic series of battles that ultimately forced the Spanish withdrawal from the continent. Not long after the final victories, Bolívar was invited to draft a constitution for Bolivia, the southern portion of the former Viceroyalty of Peru which took its name from him. His *Message to the Congress of Bolivia,* delivered on May 25, 1826, stands as the fullest statement of his political ideas during the final period of his life. The result was a highly imaginative and ingenious plan that was so complex as to have strained the capacity of the most progressive and homogeneous state, let alone one of the poorest and most fragmented of the new republics. There were several oddities in the document. Bolívar designed four branches of government, adding the electoral to the usual executive, legislative, and judicial. This fourth branch was intended to represent the needs of local and provincial governments, guard the interests of the people, and balance the central authority of the national government, thereby enhancing the representative nature of the system. In addition to the usual judicial body, he recommended a three-chamber legislature, another constitutional curiosity.

The tribunate was responsible for taxation and finances, for deciding issues of war and peace, and for dealing with matters of citizenship and nationality; its members were to enjoy forty-year (in effect, lifetime) terms. Senators, named for eight-year terms, were to be responsible for a codification of the laws and, ultimately for legal and judicial matters in co-operation with the courts. The chamber of censors, whose members were chosen for life, were responsible for the preservation and protection of the constitution and laws, resembling in broad outline the "moral" power described in the *Angostura Discourse* of 1819. Among the most interesting and controversial recommendations was that of a lifetime president (*presidente vitalicio*); the first would be chosen by congress, after which he would name his own vice-president, who would succeed to power upon the death of the president, then assuming his own life tenure. In an intricate effort to create a strong and stable executive that would nonetheless be prevented from assuming authoritarian control, Bolívar attempted to limit the powers of the president. He would appoint officials of only three ministries, while also serving as military commander-in-chief. His vice-president, however, would be responsible for administrative services, acting as a kind of manager of public affairs.

The *Message* included a strong statement calling for the absolute separation of Church and State. Man of the Enlightenment that he was,

Bolívar was a deist; although condemning the abuses of Catholicism in Latin America, he held that religion was ultimately a matter of individual preference. Beyond this, he reiterated the importance of the freedom of the individual and the dignity of man. Although accepted by the Bolivians, these recommendations lasted only two years in practice. Constitutional difficulties included the executive arrangement in which the vice-president proved in actual fact almost as powerful as the president, thereby causing a confused fragmentation of authority. Far too sophisticated for Bolivia, the document was, among other things, typical of many subsequent Latin American constitutions in its undue complexity of operation for an ill-trained and inexperienced people.

As a political thinker, Bolívar provided a mystical inspiration and zeal for independence and human progress with liberty, one that has never been extinguished. His military actions led to the freeing of a half-dozen states from the Spanish, each of which today regards him as a great national hero. His various governmental plans were in time discarded, however. The forced union of Gran Colombia broke apart into Venezuela, Colombia, and Ecuador in 1830, and when the liberator died toward the end of that year in Santa Marta, Colombia, he was a bitterly disillusioned, prematurely aged figure who complained of the futility of a career that, in the end, had merely "plowed the sea." Having encountered divided loyalties and divisive forces among his countrymen, his essentially complex intellect had changed, sometimes contradictorily, with the evolving events of the times. The Peruvian scholar Víctor Andrés Belaúnde saw in Bolívar something of a Hamlet, and in retrospect one can see traits and tendencies that have troubled pensadores and political leaders in Latin America ever since. Among these are the conflict between the absolutist tradition and the original revolutionary democratic ideal; the stress exerted on continental solidarity by cultural differences and deeply rooted nationalistic impulses; and the conflict between the demands of the uneducated masses and the paternalistic but competent administrative role of the small intellectual elite.[34] By the end, Bolívar seemed to prefer a transitional period during which the people would be educated for democracy. Accused by his enemies of seeking a crown, his dictatorial and personalistic proclivities of the final years were his ultimate response to the impossibly trying circumstances of the revolutionary era.

The Generation of Revolutionary Heroes and Thinkers / There are many remembered names in addition to that of Bolívar, among

34. Belaúnde, *Bolívar*, especially the Preface, pp. ix–xix.

them Santander, San Martín, O'Higgins, Sucre, Rivadavia, Páez, and Valle. Some of these were simple military men at heart, although frequently either choosing or being forced into more direct political activity. Strictly speaking, it is difficult if not imposible to classify them as political thinkers. Certainly the philosophical aspects of their ideas are slight. To understand the intellectual currents of the revolutionary period however—perhaps the least productive era in terms of philosophical and theoretical speculation—it behooves us to highlight the goals and ideals held by various of the leading figures. Among those who had dealt for years with Bolívar was Francisco de Paula Santander (1792–1840),[35] Colombia's "man of laws" and first president following the 1830 separation of Venezuela and Ecuador, he has often been remembered for his many differences with Bolívar, with whom he argued and debated while at the same time collaborating in the effort to oust the Spanish. Santander had emerged as a recent law graduate when the revolutionary fighting began, and for a time he served as Bolívar's military lieutenant in New Granada, as Colombia was called for a time.

Soon he turned his major attention to political and legal matters and for years served as the ruling vice-president in Bogotá while Bolívar was absent on his series of campaigns. On the whole he shared Bolívar's ideas for reform and progress but came more rapidly to grips with the limitations of existing environmental and social realities. In 1825 he was re-elected vice-president and directed his attention primarily to the undramatic but basic problems of consolidation. The worsening of his relations with Bolívar led to his temporary eclipse in 1828 while the Venezuelan assumed virtual dictatorial powers. After some three years, however, Santander returned in 1831 and became president the following year. During his term Santander put down a serious challenge from separatist forces and negotiated a settlement of major border disagreements with both Venezuela and Ecuador. Opposing the Bolivarian preference for centralized government, Santander was inclined toward a federalist solution, and his followers were to maintain a strong movement in Colombia for many years. He founded a system of public education, helped to organize the final victory over Spain, and provided in contrast to the visionary Bolívar a talent for practical administration and organization. Colombia's establishment on a constitutional basis under the guidance of liberal democratic ideas was in large part the work of Francisco de Paula Santander.

Standing in a different relationship to Bolívar was the other dominant

35. For a standard English biography, see David Bushnell, *The Santander Regime in Gran Colombia* (Newark: University of Delaware Press, 1954).

military figure, José de San Martín (1778–1850). Born in Yapuyú on the right bank of the Uruguay River, San Martín chose a military career, serving with Spanish troops against the Moors in North Africa and later against France and, in 1801, against Portugal. In 1811, he withdrew from the Spanish army and returned to Buenos Aires, arriving in March, 1812, and immediately becoming active in a secret proindependence society called the Lautaro Lodge. Almost as rapidly he began to train the revolutionary troops, and in January of 1814 he was appointed commanding general of a large detachment of troops. He began to reorganize and to prepare his forces, and by the opening of 1817 he initiated one of the best known military operations of the Americas. Brilliantly moving his forces across the supposedly impassable Andes, he descended into Chile and defeated loyalist Spanish troops, after which attention was shifted to the north and Peru.[36]

After a series of battles effectively secured Chile for the revolutionaries, the systematic San Martín began preparations once more, and in 1820 began the campaign into Peru. By the middle of 1821 he had won victory and was proclaimed the "protector" of the country by local authorities. Resentment by traditionalist *limeños* in the capital rendered his task difficult, and it was not a happy time for the Argentine. The rivalry with Bolívar was also mounting, encouraged as much by followers as by the two great generals themselves. On July 26 and 27 of 1822, the two men conferred privately at the famous and still mysterious interview at the port of Guayaquil. Whatever the precise content of the discussions, the result was San Martín's withdrawal, first from Guayaquil, then his resignation to the Peruvian congress in Lima and, shortly thereafter, his final sailing from Argentina for Europe. There he spent years of lonely solitude before dying in 1850, two decades after his Venezuelan rival.

San Martin's constitutional and political ideas were fairly direct and straightforward. An advocate of independence, he was not given to protestations of loyalty to Ferdinand VII. He also developed rapidly a conviction that the people of the La Plata provinces were ill prepared for republicanism, and the result was his slow evolution toward monarchist views. He wrote a friend in February of 1816, "I feel as though I might die every time that I hear people speak of a federation. . . . A federa-

36. Among the better sources for his biography are the following: Bartolomé Mitre, *Historia de San Martín* (Buenos Aires: n.p., 1890); Ricardo Rojas, *San Martín: Knight of the Andes,* tr. Herschel Brickell and Carlos Videla (New York: Doubleday & Company, 1945); and Anna Schoellkopf, *Don José de San Martín, 1778–1850* (New York: Liveright Publishing Corp., 1924).

tion! How could this be established? If a country like the United States with an established government, well populated, artistic, agricultural, and commercial had so many difficulties under a federal system of government during the last war with England, what would happen if the provinces of La Plata became jealous of each other? If you consider also the rivalries and the clashing interests of various regions, you will agree that the United Provinces would become a den of beasts of which the royalists would be the masters."[37]

In mid-1816 he received enthusiastically a statement by Belgrano urging the establishment of a monarchy with a member of the Inca dynasty on the throne. Later he began to consider the value of a European prince, while the establishment of his personal authority in Peru led some critics to call him "King José." While serving in Lima he sent a secret mission to Europe, with the avowed objectives of gaining recognition of Peruvian independence and of negotiating a large loan. Special instructions were also included to empower the diplomatic agents to discuss with a prince of the House of Brunswick the possibility of acceding to a Peruvian throne, and similar proposals were to be made to Russia, Austria, and other royal families. Although the mission was unsuccessful and the Argentine was soon to quit the scene after his meeting with Bolívar, his monarchist ideas became his final political legacy, as was suggested by a letter to Bernardo O'Higgins of Chile. "I am persuaded that my views will meet with your approval, for I believe that you will be convinced of the impossibility of erecting republics in these countries. In brief, I desire only the establishment of that form of government which is adapted to the existing circumstances, thus avoiding the horrors of anarchy."[38]

The recipient of this letter, Bernardo O'Higgins, was less agreeable than San Martín had hoped, having his own personal ambitions in Chile, where he had provided the major support to the troops of the Argentine. The Chilean national hero of the revolutionary epoch, O'Higgins was the natural son of an Irish adventurer who had served as viceroy in Peru. O'Higgins (1776–1842) had been educated in both South America and Europe before taking up the leadership of Chilean independence fighters in the period immediately preceding the entry of San Martín in 1817. Following the victory over royalist forces and San Martín's rejection of an offer to become governor of Chile, O'Higgins was chosen supreme director of Chile by influential Santiago citizens, thereby vesting in him virtual dictatorial powers. Remaining opposition was overcome

37. Quoted in Robertson, *Spanish-American Republics,* p. 180.
38. *Ibid.,* pp. 204–5.

by O'Higgins, and he proclaimed the declaration of Chilean independence on January 1, 1818. Chile, it was stated, would henceforth become "a free, independent, and soverign state, which will remain forever separated from the Spanish monarchy with full power to adopt a suitable system of government." And on February 12 of the year, the formal announcement of independence was repeated.

O'Higgins soon gained a more formal authorization for his authority, providing a more precise organization of power while retaining nearly unlimited personal command. Initially enjoying widespread popularity, he gradually fell from favor. Strongly anticlerical, he provoked sharp attacks from the Church. Members of the *criollo* elite resented the fact that, as the son of an Irishman, he was presumably not a true Chilean. In time, his five-year rule became increasingly stormy, as a variety of uprisings, protests, and defiant demonstrations plagued him. By 1823 the pressures had grown too great, and the supreme director was forced from power. While he had temporarily provided stability through the initiation of a centralized government, the maintenance of the regime proved impossible. With O'Higgins' fall, some half-dozen years of domestic turmoil were to follow before the conservatives under the guiding genius of Diego Portales asserted the beginning of a long period of hegemony in 1830.[39]

In Central America, the most notable figure was José Cecilio del Valle (1780–1834), who was born in Choluteca, Honduras. The Enlightenment in Central America had been centered in Guatemala City, where the University of San Carlos de Guatemala had been authorized by royal order in 1676. Father Antonio Liendo y Goicochea (1735–1814) had sponsored important academic reforms, introducing the experimental method in the sciences, condemning scholasticism, and expounding the philosophy of Descartes. Father Antonio Larrazábal (1769–1853), who represented Guatemala before the Spanish Cortes of 1812, was another noted scholar. An ardent defender of the ideas of national sovereignty and constitutional monarchy, he was an important forerunner of the movement for independence. It became the task of Valle, however, to play the leading role in the region, both politically and intellectually.

The scion of a distinguished *criollo* family, José Cecilio del Valle graduated in law from the University of San Carlos, and much of his adult life was actually spent in Guatemala. In 1820 he founded the newspaper *El Amigo de la Patria,* which became a source of moderate liberalism. Even earlier, he had served as professor of political economy at San Carlos and as deputy to the Supreme Central Junta of Spain.

39. See Chapter 3, pp. 95, 99–100 for further discussion.

When Mexico declared its independence in 1821, Central America promptly followed suit, and Valle was the principal author of its official declaration of independence. Although he was opposed to Central American annexation by Mexico, he served as a deputy to the Mexican congress during the brief period of amalgamation. When Iturbide fell from power in Mexico and Central America declared its independence as a single federal entity, Valle became one of the leading political figures. He was a member of the three-man provisional executive that ruled Central America until a constitutional government was formed, and he then served as deputy to the congress. He ran for the presidency of Central America twice but was unsuccessful, and his last years were occupied as director of the Sociedad Económica, which advanced the teaching of economics with a marked utilitarian bent.[40]

Valle was one of the leading early *pensadores* to show an affinity for the ideas of Jeremy Bentham. He believed in liberal economic ideas and wrote that government should play a carefully circumscribed role. He agreed with the English writer in a somewhat conservative brand of social reformism that depended upon legislative adjustment rather than violent action. At the same time, he differed from Bentham in accepting the concepts of natural law and natural rights. As a consequence, Valle presented a mixture of early utilitarianism with nineteenth-century romanticism, those two intellectual currents that were to become widely popular in Latin America a few years after the end of the independence wars. A close reading of Valle also shows his divergence with Bentham on a variety of points, although Valle often made explicit reference to his admiration for Bentham. Thus he could write in a letter to the Englishman:

> The past month of March was one of very great satisfaction for me. I received, forwarded by the consul of your nation, the letter and the books which you kindly sent me. Each one filled me with the sweetest sentiments. . . . your works will have the distinguished place deserved by the wise Institute of legislators of the world. Through their influence, I hope for a beneficent revolution among all the nations of the earth. You have provided the scientific basis, establishing the fecund and enlightened principle of Universal Utility. . . . You will also bring about a revolution in codes of legislation by making a science of it, and peoples will at last come to have a body of law which will not be a

40. For a full length biography, see Louis E. Bumgartner, *José del Valle of Central America* (Durham: Duke University Press, 1963); also useful is the study of Franklin D. Parker, *José Cecilio del Valle and the Establishment of the Central American Confederation* (Tegucigalpa: University of Honduras, 1954).

reproach but an honor to Reason—which will bring not misery but happiness to man.[41]

As a statesman of Central America, Valle advocated independence in the final years of colonialism and, although accepting the temporary merger with Mexico, was not displeased when it failed. His underlying conservatism was suggested by the frequent references in his writings to the fact that independence was peacefully achieved, as well as expressions of apprehension over the possible abuses of excessive and uncontrolled freedom. Sharing in the contemporary conviction that Spain was wholly responsible for the problems encountered after the expulsion of royalist forces, he firmly supported those who advocated the creation of an inter-American system, and at one point formulated a plan for an American congress whereby all the newly independent countries of the hemisphere were to form a federation for mutual defense and economic development. Valle's interest in history, economics, law, and social problems was well manifested in *Acta de la independencia* (1821), *Manifesto a la nación guatemalteca* (1825), and especially in his *Discursos* (1826), where he defended America's sovereignty and the principle of nonintervention.[42]

To the north of Central America in Mexico, the popular uprisings of Hidalgo and Morelos are recalled as helping to set the stage for the ultimate defeat of the Spanish. Rural fighting by bands of insurgents was never completely halted, despite the capture and execution of the two parish priests. The 1820 liberal revolution in Spain led to a government in Mexico City that was hostile to the Catholic clergy and other privileged groups. Mexican conservatives, seeing independence as the best means of defending their property and interests, plotted with *criollo* General Agustín de Iturbide, and under his leadership the viceroy was overthrown in 1821. Iturbide soon proclaimed himself Emperor, but this effort to create a native monarchy soon crumbled. In these years of turmoil in Mexico, society was characterized as the survival of the medieval sense of life. Order imposed from above had pervaded all social behavior, with life conditioned largely by status. The survival of

41. Originally published in Rafael Heliodoro Valle, *Valle* (México: Secretaría de Educación Pública, 1934), pp. 156–58. The quotation here is from the English translation in Harold E. Davis, ed., *Latin-American Social Thought: The History of Its Development Since Independence, with Selected Readings* (Washington: University Press of Washington, D.C., 1963), pp. 92–93.

42. The best single source of Valle's writings is in the edited work of Rafael Heliodoro Valle cited in note 41. Also see the treatment by a prominent nineteenth-century Honduran in Ramón Rosa, *Biografía de don José Cecilio del Valle* (Tegucigalpa: Talleres Tipográficos, 1934).

vestigial feudalism dominated community life. The corporative spirit, in Church, army, the university, and the landed gentry, hampered the limited national spirit that existed. Mexico was typified by a series of "states within the state," with an oligarchy of classes, especially that of the clergy supported by the military. Both army and Church enjoyed privileged status and a series of *fueros,* special rights that were generally not subject to the common law of the land.

It was in this setting that "El Pensador Mexicano," José Joaquín Fernández de Lizardi (1776–1827), emerged as a political and philosophical conscience of the land. Born in 1776, Fernández de Lizardi's early life is largely unknown, but he first became recognized around 1810 when his writings began to appear. He was largely self-taught in philosophy and law and rapidly became known through the founding of the newspaper *El Pensador Mexicano,* from which he derived his pen name. A royalist at heart, he nonetheless was sharply critical of existing social conditions and attacked injustice in sharply pointed prose. He appealed to the popular taste and became familiar to many who could not themselves read his newspaper. Basically he agreed with Hidalgo and Morelos but called largely for an amelioration of traditional abuses of authority. He offered a comprehensive national plan for free and obligatory education in 1814, following the ideas of the French *philosophes.* In subsequent years he maintained a stream of reformist proposals and demands. Through much of the decade he continued to believe that change could be achieved under Spanish authority, and the adoption of the liberal Spanish constitution of 1820 briefly encouraged his hopes.

Fernández de Lizardi continued to publish *El Pensador Mexicano* until his death in 1827, and after 1815 he also introduced other journals, notably *Alacena de Frioleras, Las conversaciones del Payo y el Sacristón,* and the *Semanario de México.* His best-known statement, however, was a critically realistic novel of Mexican society, *El periquillo sarniento,* or *The Itching Parrot* (1816).[43] This work led later commentators to regard him as the founder of Mexican national literature. During the gradual process of independence, *El Pensador Mexicano* stood as the most influential organ of the times. It was here that, following the Spanish refusal to implement the constitutional principles of 1820, Fernández de Lizardi announced in time his support of Iturbide's movement for independence, although he later opposed the founding of the shortlived Empire.

43. A useful source of Fernández de Lizardi's works is in *El pensador mexicano* (México: La Universidad Nacional Autónoma, 1940), including a critical analysis by Agustín Yáñez.

The Mexican, although by his own lights a staunch Catholic, experienced constant difficulty with Church officials. He realized that the freedom of the people could not be attained unless the Church would yield its authority to the civil government. While never questioning religious dogma, he said that if a bishop used the pulpit to attack him, it was only right that he respond from the columns of his newspaper. In one exchange, he wrote to the Bishop of Sonora that he should first cleanse his lips before pronouncing the names of Voltaire, Rousseau, and Montesquieu, all of whom he admired although with certain reservations.[44] Fighting for the separation of the Church and State, he believed with Voltaire that the traditional position of the Church represented an obstacle to civil liberty. When in 1823 he wrote on constitutional matters, he therefore proposed that ecclesiastics be banned from election to congress unless proven to be "enlightened" and that in any event they could not attend or participate in discussions of nonecclesiastical matters. He also suggested that the clergy should be required to preach from the pulpit that all men are free by nature and free to act as they wish under the laws of the country. Fernández de Lizardi was eventually excommunicated for his writings. The immediate cause was his defense of the Freemasons against the papal bulls of Clement XII and Benedict XIV.

Following the overthrow of Iturbide in 1823, Fernández de Lizardi offered his views on forthcoming constitutional discussions through a dialogue between fictitious legislators entitled "Political Constitution of an Imaginary Republic," which appeared in his *Conversaciones.* There are reminders of his early interest in a constitutional monarchy, for he was fearful of the excesses of Jacobinism, worrying about the dislocations that might emerge from the rapid transition to republican status. In the manner of Montesquieu he discussed the importance of "taking into account the character and customs of the country to which the law is given," and he also supported the principle of natural rights, which he described in terms of liberty, equality, security and property. He advocated a federal republic, which he saw as doing away with the heritage of Spanish centralism and the survival of the medieval society.

His imaginary legislature also examined social and economic problems. The forthcoming constitution should deal, therefore, with such matters as the problem of the *latifundia.* He considered it unjust for a few men to control extensive lands, saying "it is well known that there are rich men who own ten, twelve or more *haciendas,* some of which

44. Jefferson Rhea Spell, *The Life and Works of José Fernández de Lizardi* (Philadelphia: University of Pennsylvania Press, 1931), p. 98.

cannot be traversed in four days, at the same time that there are millions of individuals who do not have a palm of land of their own."[45] He recommended the expropriation of all excess land on *haciendas* larger than four square leagues. Fernández de Lizardi was also interested in the development of industry and immigration. Skilled European workers were to be attracted to Mexican shores and placed in national workshops where they might engage in activities beneficial to the nation while also serving to train native apprentices.

Ever an industrious pamphleteer and journalist, Fernández de Lizardi remained active until his death. He helped to set up reading societies, proposed a variety of educational reforms, and contributed to a movement that created a system of libraries. Never personally or politically ambitious, he was perhaps the principal intellectual leader of democratic reform in Mexico's early independence period, and his pen was always poised for the defense of justice and the rights of the underprivileged. In his works, Mexico was to find suggestions for the necessary reforms that, in many cases, were not meaningfully adopted until after the Revolution of 1910.

SELECTED BIBLIOGRAPHY

Belaúnde, Víctor Andrés. *Bolívar and the Political Thought of the Spanish American Revolution*. Baltimore: Johns Hopkins University Press, 1938.

Bumgartner, Louis E. *José del Valle of Central America*. Durham: Duke University Press, 1963.

Bushnell, David. *The Santander Regime in Gran Colombia*. Newark: University of Delaware Press, 1954.

Fernández de Lizardi, José Joaquín. *El pensador mexicano*. México: La Universidad Nacional Autónoma, 1940.

Frank, Waldo. *Birth of a World: Bolívar in Terms of His Peoples*. Boston: Houghton Mifflin Company, 1951.

Gandía, Enrique de. *Las ideas políticas de Mariano Moreno: Autenticidad del plan que le es atribuído*. Buenos Aires: Peuser, 1946.

Henríquez Ureña, Pedro. *A Concise History of Latin American Culture*. Translated and with a supplementary chapter by Gilbert Chase. New York: Frederick A. Praeger, 1966.

Humphreys, R. A., and John Lynch, eds. *The Origins of the Latin American Revolutions, 1808–1826*. New York: Alfred A. Knopf, 1965.

Jane, Cecil. *Liberty and Despotism in Spanish America*. Oxford: Clarendon Press, 1929.

Lecuna, Vicente, and Harold A. Bierck, eds. *The Selected Writings of Bolívar*. 2 Vols. New York: The Colonial Press, 1951.

45. Quoted in Davis, *Latin-American Social Thought*, p. 51.

Levene, Ricardo. *El pensamiento vivo de Mariano Moreno.* Buenos Aires: Losada, 1942.

———. *Mariano Moreno: Escritos.* 2 Vols. Buenos Aires: Editorial Estrada, 1942.

Madariaga, Salvador de. *Bolívar.* London: Hollis & Carter, 1952.

Masur, Gerhard. *Simón Bolívar.* Albuquerque: University of New Mexico Press, 1948.

Moses, Bernard. *South America on the Eve of Emancipation.* New York and London: G. P. Putnam's Sons, 1908.

———. *The Intellectual Background of the Revolution in South America, 1810–1824.* New York: Hispanic Society of America, 1926.

Parker, Franklin D. *José Cecilio del Valle and the Establishment of the Central American Confederation.* Tegucigalpa: University of Honduras, 1954.

Picón-Salas, Mariano. *A Cultural History of Spanish America from Conquest to Independence.* Translated by Irving A. Leonard. Berkeley and Los Angeles: University of California Press, 1963.

Robertson, William Spence. *Rise of the Spanish-American Republics As Told in the Lives of Their Liberators.* New York: Collier Books, 1961.

———. *The Life of Miranda.* Chapel Hill: University of North Carolina Press, 1929.

Rojas, Ricardo. *San Martín: Knight of the Andes.* Translated by Herschel Brickell and Carlos Videla. New York, Doubleday & Company, 1945.

Romero, José Luis. *A History of Argentine Political Thought.* Translated by Thomas F. McGann. Stanford: Stanford University Press, 1963.

Schoellkopf, Anna. *Don José de San Martín, 1778–1850.* New York: Liveright Publishing Corp., 1924.

Spell, Jefferson Rhea. *Rousseau in the Spanish World before 1833.* Austin: University of Texas Press, 1938.

———. *The Life and Works of José Fernández de Lizardi.* Philadelphia: University of Pennsylvania Press, 1931.

Thorning, J. F. *Miranda: World Citizen.* Gainesville: University of Florida Press, 1952.

Valle, Rafael Heliodoro. *Valle.* México: Secretaría de Educación Pública, 1934.

Wilgus, A. Curtis, ed. *South American Dictators During the First Century of Independence.* Washington: Seminar Conference on Hispanic American Affairs, 1937.

3

Romantic Liberalism and Realism

The thought of the early independence period was undoubtedly based on the liberalism of the Enlightenment, but it was necessarily conditioned to a degree by the succession of drastic political changes in Europe. France, one of the major inspirational sources, passed in rapid order through constitutional monarchy, the republic, Jacobinism, the directory, the consulate, the empire, and finally the Restoration. In European politics the post-Napoleonic years saw the emergence of the Holy Alliance, with its negation of the principle of self-determination challenging the right of independence for the new countries of Latin America. The struggle for that right had engaged traditional European conservatism as represented by Spain, a conservatism that was largely unreflective and had consciously limited itself to defense of the *status quo*. For the liberals of the independence era it was easy to challenge these ideas with the popular principles of natural rights and popular sovereignty. The answer was assumed to be a new type of government based on certain abstract conceptions that would secure man's liberty, its power to be strictly defined by constitutions that would maintain civil order and assure individual justice. This new government would have little to do with the regulation of life and social relations. Economy, culture, and religion were regarded as the exclusive domain of private individuals in their own voluntary associations, standing outside the political jurisdiction of the state.

When independence was achieved in the 1820s, a revival of European conservatism was occurring with the emerging Restoration period, expressed in France by the writings of Joseph de Maistre and in Spain by Donoso Cortés. Their philosophy asserted the supremacy of historical forces over the actions of individuals guided by reason. They mounted an attack on abstract reason as disturbing the harmony of society and creating anarchy instead. What society needed, it was argued, was authority based on a well-defined conception of social hierarchy. The traditional forces in Latin America adopted these ideas for their own protection. While shrewdly profiting from the freedoms postulated by the liberals and supporting the position that the State was not to play an intervening role, the spokesmen of conservative authority employed the Church, economic power, and their own social position to acquire and control political power in the new republics. Consequently, although freedom from Spain was achieved, the struggle for the implementation of domestic freedom only began with the closing of the books on colonial rule of the Iberian Peninsula. For the philosophically inclined *pensadores* of the early independence period, therefore, there was the task of engaging the conservative elements of society and politics.

The philosophical trends that had been developing in Europe found their reflections in Latin-American thought. As a consequence, at least two major streams of influence appeared in the newly independent countries, the first identified with utilitarianism and the contemporary realism of the ideas of British political economy, and the second responding to the romantic or utopian socialism of such French thinkers as Claude Henri Saint Simon. Of these, the former stemmed in large part from Jeremy Bentham and James Mill, whose philosophical commitment was to the sloganeering hallmark of utilitarianism—a pragmatic seeking of the greatest good of the greatest number. In practical terms utilitarianism included as a major component the ideas of free trade and *laissez faire* in economics, accompanied by a commitment in domestic affairs to minimize the role and influence of the state. The theories of Bentham were being taught by the University of Buenos Aires as early as 1821; Andrés Bello and José María Luis Mora were exemplary exponents of utilitarian concepts in Latin America.

Romantic socialism had its advocates too, among whom Francisco Bilbao in Chile and Esteban Echeverría in Argentina were especially prominent. While this intellectual current was less susceptible of precise formulation than utilitarianism, it was no less influential. Fundamentally concerned with social welfare and with individual rights, it was an early form of socialism that was adopted by a number of *pensadores* as useful in achieving economic progress without unduly restricting personal freedoms and the dignity of man. Moreover, there was a mystical quality that at least hinted optimistically at the ultimate perfectibility of man and his society. Believing that the expulsion of the Spanish had removed all major obstacles to development, many anticipated the swift attainment of economic growth, social advance, and an orderly political stabilization that would permit the citizen the widest possible exercise of individual prerogatives. It was the eventual disappointment of these thinkers, even more than that of the followers of utilitarian concepts, which brought about the intellectual preconditions for positivism in the later years of the nineteenth century.

An important ingredient in the thinking of both the utilitarians and the romantic liberals was a sympathetic curiosity toward events in the United States. The increasing success of that republican experiment, with its reliance on constitutional institutions and a written charter with specific delegations of authority and responsibility, seemed to provide an attractive if superficial parallel to Latin America. The North American westward expansion into largely unpopulated regions suggested the importance of a similar movement, and this loomed large in the pro-immigration policies and writings that were frequent in Latin America for many years. Particularly in Chile and Argentina, there was a belief in the fundamental importance of an influx of Europeans, especially of urban workers and farmers. Many agreed with the dictum that the sparsely populated interior expanses had to be developed if a modern nation were to be created. The North American experience with federalism also drew substantial approval, suggesting to many that the highly centralized colonial administrative network should be broken up into smaller entities with sufficient authority to govern their own affairs. This was an important contributory factor to the years of bitter struggle between federalists and centralists, and has been enshrined in the constitutions of four nominally federal republics—Mexico, Venezuela, Brazil, and Argentina.

A final intellectual proclivity that underlay much of the thinking during this period was the negative and destructive interpretation of Spanish colonialism. There was a natural opposition to Spain and all things Spanish, leading to a *desespañolización*, a "de-Spanishization," in which many proposals were supported simply because they were diametrically opposed to past Spanish practice. *Pensadores* therefore developed a strong emphasis on their search for an "American" approach or ideology within which more specific policy problems might be identified and dealt with. It became a commonplace in the literature of the time to argue that the removal of Spanish attitudes and institutions would bring not only political independence but an intellectual, social, and cultural emancipation. Again, it was the eventual realization that this reasoning was basically fallacious and meaningless which created the deeply rooted disappointment from which positivism was to spring. For those who came to adulthood during roughly the first quarter of the 1800s, however, the experience with independence was not sufficiently lengthy to reflect this intellectual disaffection. Consquently, the underlying tone during much of the early independent period, typified philosophically by romantic liberalism and utilitarian realism, was basically optimistic and hopeful.

Early Exponents of Utilitarian Realism

In Mexico the most representative writer was José María Luis Mora (1794–1850). Born and educated in the capital, he earned a doctorate in theology at San Ildefonso. As historian, educator, and political observer, he became Mexico's most outstanding thinker in the immediate postindependence era. A prolific writer of essays and historical studies, he emerged to be the most articulate advocate of economic and political liberalism in his country. Profoundly disturbed in his youth by the uprisings of Hidalgo and Morelos, he only later conceded that they had been necessary precursors to the final emancipation of Mexico. While still in his twenties Mora began to publish *El Semanario Político*, thereby launching his carreer as a political commentator and from 1821 became an acute critic of the governments of both the first Mexicans to realize that a genuine sense of nationalism was necessary if the old social order were to change. In 1822 he was a member of the Constituent Congress and, upon its dissolution by Iturbide, was imprisoned. Following his release Mora later served in congress again and contributed importantly to the drafting of legislation. He resumed his studies to earn a law degree in 1827 and then founded another paper, *El Observador de la República Mexicana.*[1]

With the advent of the liberal government of Valentín Gómez Farías in 1833, Mora became an adviser and close collaborator, but after a year conservative forces regained power, and Mora left for France. Living in Paris in great poverty for many years, supported by small donations from a handful of friends, he was eventually appointed minister to Great Britain in 1846 when Gómez Farías returned to power. In London when the Communist Manifesto was issued, Mora was a witness to the revolu-

---

1. Among the available publications of Mora's writings, consult Arturo Arnáiz y Freg, ed., *Ensayos, ideas y retratos* (México: Universidad Nacional, 1941); also José Maria Luis Mora, *México y sus revoluciones* (México, 1950).

tions of 1848, writing to Gómez Farías, "Things here are going badly, and socialism and communism have done more harm to republican principles than the efforts of all kings together."[2] Not long after he returned to Paris, where he died on Bastille Day of 1850. Despite the relative brevity of his political activities, however, Mora had continued to write whether in Mexico or Europe, and while his complete works have not been published, the more significant of them serve to justify his characterization as the leading spokesman of Mexican liberalism.

The fullest statement of Mora's political writings appeared in the Paris publication of his *México y sus revoluciones* in 1836.[3] Therein he discussed his concept of the state, the theory of revolutions, the responsibilities of government, and the role of the economy in the state. For Mora the approach to the origin of the state was contractualist, closely following the broad outlines of Locke and Hobbes. The Mexican held that natural liberty was granted to man by God, but in order to avoid anarchy, man agreed to assist his fellow man under certain conditions; this agreement was the first social contract. The origin of laws came as a result of the failure of some members of society to observe the contract, with the group creating regulations in order to guarantee the observance of the pact. A sort of *pacta sunt servanda* had produced the first primitive legal order. When disagreement inevitably arose as to the meaning of the laws, the judiciary would appear, and soon an executive would become necessary for the enforcement of judicial decisions. The completion of the process would mean the founding of the state, with one of its essential attributes the power of coercion. Mora was presenting nothing either novel or original, but he did subsequently add that the goal of the state ultimately was the happiness of the individual, a postion suggesting the influence of Condillac and Bentham.

José María Luis Mora was as fearful of the tyranny of the majority as he was of an absolute king or despot. Although familiar with Rousseau, he rejected the despotism of a general will, which he considered antisocial. Preferring Montesquieu, whom he frequently quoted, Mora placed his faith in a constitutional government with a balance of powers to counteract the possibility of despotic rule. And above all, he sought security for the individual against any possibility of oppression. Sounding at times highly reminiscent of Jeffersonianism in the United States, he advocated the least government as the best one. As one student has stated, "Today he might be classified as a cultural determinist, with,

---

2. Quoted in Morris L. Simon, "The Political Thought of José María Luis Mora" (Master's thesis, University of New Mexico, 1951).

3. We have used the edition indicated in note 1.

of course, the reservations granted to a nineteenth century liberal."[4] It was further true of Mora that, despite the power of coercion granted to the state, he was opposed to violent measures, whether employed in support of or opposition to a given regime. Although conceding the need for revolutionary changes in Mexico, he was unwilling to accept the application of force as a legitimate weapon.

The political consequences of the use of force, he argued, were never enduring. He envisaged changes in the hierarchical structure of Mexican society but insisted that they should be attained only on a base of popular consent. The ruling classes were warned that the best way to prevent revolution was to be more fully aware of the revolutionary times and demands with which they were living and therefore to grant what was required. It might be inserted parenthetically that this is as valid for many Latin American countries even today as it was for the Mexican oligarchy of the 1830s. Mora believed that the need for order in society was sacred and that all changes for a better Mexico should be peaceful. If forced to choose between order and freedom, Mora would clearly have opted for the former. Never forgetting that during his youth his own family had suffered seriously from the Hidalgo uprising, he decried the repercussions of violent mass movements. This led him to the conviction that the avoidance of such outbursts could only come from a responsive and basically democratic regime in which the governing class would be largely responsible, promoting individual liberties through gradualistic reforms. In this as in many of his other positions Mora, although true to the spirit of Mexican liberalism in the 1830s, was expressing what today would be regarded as conservative political views.

Discussing forms of government, Mora preferred a republic but was sufficiently perceptive to see that the only immediate change of power resulting from the establishment of independence was the shift from the representatives of the Spanish monarch to the new national congress. Unlimited power in the hands of congress was dangerous and could only be avoided through the limitations emanating from a proper and meaningful distribution among the three branches. He called for a bicameral legislature, with the upper chamber composed of property owners and professors, the lower body largely popular in its composition. Suffrage was to be qualified by the ownership of property, and in Mora's opinion, universal suffrage was premature for Mexico. In an independent judiciary he saw the best guarantee for civil liberties. Above all this, and in agreement with Fernández de Lizardi, he advocated federalism to counteract the rigid centralism of Mexico's colonial society. Consistent

4. Simon, "Political Thought of Mora," p. 10.

with the liberalism of his times, Mora maintained that decentralization was an effective means of reducing the possibility of arbitrary political power. The excesses of stratified social control were also to be curbed by the abolition of Church and military principles. It was his opinion that religious beliefs were a matter of private conscience beyond the purview of governmental concern, and he urged that the clergy be limited to its original function, the spiritual mission. If this were done, then the Church could properly serve the national interest, since religion was necessary for man.

In economic matters, Mora followed the traditional individualism of Adam Smith and his French disciple Jean Baptiste Say. He was concerned with the problem of the land, and on several occasions wrote that Mexico's most serious difficulty was that of the *latifundia*. Mora also condemned the large accumulation of property in the hands of the Roman Catholic church. While agreeing with Locke that the right of the individual to private property preceded the coming into existence of society, he argued that a corporation, such as the Church, enjoyed property only as a civil right, which was posterior to society and subject to the limitations placed upon it by society. This argument was to be revived and applied by Benito Juárez years later during the great Reform.

Although opposed to violence and respectful of private ownership, Mora defined many of the social and economic changes needed in Mexico if meaningful and lasting progress were to be achieved. In large part a spokesman of Mexican creoles, Mora was essentially sympathetic to the Indian but unprepared to grant him equal status. He saw the Indian as constituting a major social problem for the country but, although advocating an improvement in his status, he held that emphasis should be placed on Mexico's European traits. The development of national culture was among the major long-range goals for which Mexico must strive. As an immediate measure, he recommended the establishment and supervision of a national network of schools under the aegis of the central government. Spain had followed a policy of keeping its colonies ignorant, and thus newly independent Mexico was at a disadvantage in its dealings with the rest of the world. The best possible use of recently won independence would be intellectual development. If ignorance were not thereby dissipated, demagoguery might establish a new form of despotism in the name of freedom. "The word liberty has often served for the destruction of the substance of liberty."[5] The practical benefits of education could scarcely be exaggerated. An appreciation of true freedom, the establishment of intelligent governmental

5. José María Luis Mora, *Obras sueltas,* II (Paris: Rosa, 1837), p. 78.

administration, and the appropriate minimizing of interference in economic and social life would all be encouraged as a result.

Somewhat similar views were expressed by one of the great intellectual figures of Latin-America history, Andrés Bello (1781–1865). Born in Caracas, the Venezuelan studied law and medicine at the university, after which he entered public life and held several modest government positions. The early revolutionary outburst in 1810 sent him to England on a diplomatic mission with Bolívar; when the rebels were defeated, he remained there and did not return to Latin America for eighteen years. Earning his livelihood by private tutoring and occasional translating, he served for several years after 1822 as secretary at the Colombian embassy. It was an intellectually rewarding time for Bello, as he became familiar with the leading British thinkers of the day and established close relations with both Jeremy Bentham and James Mill.[6] In 1829, following strong recommendations on his behalf by Chilean Mariano Egaña, Bello accepted an important post in that country's foreign office. He was to pass the last thirty-six years of his long life in Chile, where he served in the Ministry of Foreign Relations and in the national senate. At the pinnacle of his career he was appointed rector of the University of Chile, which he founded in 1842.

The first and most important true humanist in independent Latin America, Andrés Bello's versatility was reflected by his work as a poet, educator, jurist, diplomat, philosopher, literary critic, historian, occasional journalist, and *pensador*. Our concern here is of course with his philosophical and political contributions.[7] In contrast to many of his contemporaries, Bello was familiar with the French *philosophes* but stood apart from their writings. Thus he mentioned Voltaire only as a literary figure, for example, while he referred to Rousseau merely to comment on biographical anecdotes, not ideas.[8] His philosophical theory of knowledge was similar to that of Kant, and he was critical of Descartes' mechanistic conception of reality. Of the French philosophers of the times Bello was closer to such figures as Destutt-Tracy and Victor Cousin than to the thinkers of the Enlightenment. For Bello, philosophy in all its branches was a science based on observation and reason.[9] Something of a Christian moralist, he believed in free will and the immortality of the soul.

6. Germán Arciniegas, *El pensamiento vivo de Andrés Bello* (Buenos Aires: Editorial Losada, 1946), p. 35.
7. Andrés Bello, *Obras completas* (Santiago: Imp. Pedro G. Ramírez, 1881).
8. See Rafael Caldera, *Andrés Bello* (Caracas: Parra León Hermanos, 1935).
9. *Ibid.*, p. 59.

It is useful to recall the political conditions in Chile when the Venezuelan-born Bello arrived there from England. In broad outline, the situation was not dissimilar to that of Mexico following the expulsion of Spain. Disorder was prevalent, with civil war filling the period from O'Higgins' fall in 1823 until 1830. In that year the conservative elements, popularly known as the *pelucones* (bigwigs), became dominant through the leadership of Diego Portales, a successful businessman and financier who set the tone and temper of the era although never himself serving as president. The *pelucones* were composed of the landed aristocracy and the clergy, with important support coming from organized military forces in Chile. In their effort to establish dominion over the country, they were guided by Portales' "religion of government," which promised to impose order on the country while ignoring the principles of democracy and republicanism. From 1830 until his death by assassination in 1837, Portales created political and economic institutional patterns that survived him. The liberal opposition was persecuted, the press controlled, the Church favored, and wealthy landholders encouraged. The government at the same time was vigorous in public works, encouraged foreign trade, and strengthened centralized government through Portales' constitution of 1833, which was to survive until 1891.

The opposing liberals or *pipiolos* (novices) came largely from the middle classes, advocating among other things political decentralization and the curbing of clerical influence. Major liberal demands included the abolition of the entailed estates (*mayorazgos*), the separation of Church and State, and the reinforcement of civil governmental authority. Years were to pass before the bulk of these measures were accomplished.[10] In the meantime, the intellectual climate was somewhat ambiguous; certainly it differed from the comparable period in Argentina under the despot Rosas. Although many opposed the Portales-inspired conservative regime, conditions were different from the dramatic polar extremes existing in Argentina, and as a consequence the views of Chilean thinkers tended to be less than homogeneous, with disagreements and jealousies frequently acute. The most dramatic development in intellectual life came from the rising Generation of 1842, with such fiery spokesmen as Lastarria and especially Bilbao. However, much of the setting for the emergence of these young men was provided by the work of Bello, whose influences continued for many years until his death in 1865. Indeed, the very phrase "Generation of 1842" derived from the opening of the National University of Chile under Bello's rectorship.

10. For a useful discussion of these years, see Ricardo Donoso, *Las ideas politicos en Chile* (México: Fondo de Cultura Económica, 1946).

Already esteemed as a great intellectual figure in the Venezuelan independence movement and standing largely as a transitional figure, Bello was forty-seven years old when he arrived in Santiago, already a mature thinker with the important formative years in England behind him. Among his practical accomplishments were the codification of laws and the establishment of the university. Regarding the former, Bello as early as 1832 in his *Principios de derecho de gentes* had established himself as a believer in natural law. Holding that it was obligatory and eternal, standing above and superior to positive law, Bello also regarded it as the foundation of the law of nations, obligatory upon all states above the requirements of ordinary municipal law. Then and later, Bello showed the clear influence of the classical conceptions of Roman law in his legal writings, deriving his thinking from Aquinas and the seventeenth-century Spanish Thomists while he rejected Rousseau's notions about the presocial natural rights of man. After more than twenty years' labor, his definitive *Código civil* appeared in 1855, and the massive four-volume code served Chile for generations.

The establishment of the National University was also a task that engaged Bello for years. Only after great difficulty with strong political opposition did he finally gain governmental approval in the early 1840s. Named the first rector despite the candidacy of several native-born Chileans, he thereby received national recognition of his predominant intellectual position. In his inaugural address he called for a national program of education and cultural development, beginning with primary education. Regarding this as the best means of promoting national progress, he urged upon the government an awareness of the educational potential for development. He was staunch in his demand for practical studies; typical was his insistence that a program of economics should contain matters of practical utility to Chile rather than the customary classical theoretical approach. While his speech was among his major statements on the subject, it had been preceded by earlier essays, including a representative declaration in 1836.

> The distinctive character of man is in his susceptibility of improvement. Education, which enriches his mind with ideas, adorns his heart with virtues, and is an efficient means of promoting his progress. . . . Whatever be the equality which political institutions establish, there is nevertheless in all peoples an equality . . . of condition, of needs, of mode of life. To these differences, education must adjust itself. . . .
>
> In a matter of such vital importance, government for a limited portion of the people is not to develop education, for it is not enough to turn out men skilled in the learned professions; it

is necessary to form useful citizens, it is necessary to improve society; and this cannot be done without opening the path to advancement to the most numerous part of the public.[11]

Bello also stressed the importance of developing a singular American and Chilean philosophy and science. The New World, he argued, had a duty to respond collaboratively to the European desire for universal study and knowledge. In 1848, speaking of the cultural autonomy of Latin America, he used the following terms:

> Europe has already influenced us more than it should. While we are taking advantage of European Enlightenment we should, at the same time, imitate its independence of thought. . . . Young Chileans! Learn to judge for yourselves; aspire to independence of thought. . . . Inquire into each civilization as revealed in its works; ask each historian for his sources. That is the first philosophy that we must learn from Europe. . . .
> Our civilization will also be judged by its works; and if they see us servilely copying European civilization, even that which is not applicable, what will a Michelet, a Guizot think of us? They will say: "America still has not taken an original thought in her works, nothing original, nothing indigenous; she copies the forms of our philosophy without absorbing its spirit."[12]

It was the effort to break these chains which motivated Bello throughout his career. And the generations-long educational effort was in keeping with his over-all moderation, by which he saw gradual evolution as the preferred course toward political progress and the improvement of the nation's political and legal order.

A facet of Bello's thought which set his apart from Bolívar, Fernández de Lizardi, and other contemporaries was his refusal to totally reject Spain and all things Spanish. In his *Investigación sobre la influencia de la conquista y del sistema colonial de los españoles en Chile*,[13] he argued that the problems of the newly independent republics were not necessarily attributable to the Spanish influence: "Injustice, atrocity, perfidy in war were not common to the Spaniards alone, but to all races in every country." The Spanish contribution was by no means

---

11. Bello, "Educación" [1836], *Obras*, VIII, pp. 213–20.

12. Andrés Bello, "Discurso en el aniversario de la humanidad," *Anales de la Universidad* (Santiago, 1848), as quoted in Leopoldo Zea, *The Latin-American Mind*, tr. James H. Abbott and Lowell Dunham (Norman: University of Oklahoma Press, 1963), p. 102.

13. Andrés Bello, *Investigación sobre la influencia de la conquista y del sistema colonial de los españoles en Chile* (Santiago: 1842), reprinted in José Gaos, ed., *Antología del pensamiento de lengua española en la edad contemporánea* (Mexico: Editorial Seneca, 1945).

wholly negative, for the spiritual inheritance from the mother country had been important in the growth of the revolutionary movement itself. Thus, "Whoever observes philosophically the history of our struggle with the mother country will quickly recognize that it was precisely the Iberian element that made it possible for us to defeat her. . . . Native Spanish persistence clashed with the inborn stubbornness of the sons of Spain. The patriotic instinct in the hearts of American led them to deeds similar to those of the Spaniards at Numancia and Zaragoza. . . . The captains and the veteran legions of European Iberia were defeated and humiliated by the *caudillos* and improvised armies of another young Iberia which, rejecting its name, maintained the indomitable spirit of the ancient defense of its homes."[14] While Spain had obstructed the development of the "republican spirit," it had nurtured the seeds of magnanimity and heroism that helped to motivate the independence movement. Spain had therefore instilled a feeling of dignity and courage in the *criollos* that explained their deeds in the wars of independence. His fellow countrymen were reminded that they should retain the cultural values of their Spanish forebears, such as their language, religion, and respect for human dignity.

In analyzing the independence of Latin America, Bello differentiated between the political emancipation from Spain and the organization of internal political freedom and the necessary intellectual emancipation. The battle begun by Simón Bolívar would have to be completed by the educators. "No one loved liberty more sincerely than General Bolívar but he, like everybody else, was caught up in the nature of things. Independence was necessary for liberty, and the champion of independence was and had to be a dictator. . . . Bolívar triumphed; the dictatorships triumphed over Spain; the governments and the congresses still waged war against the customs of the sons of Spain, against the habits formed under the influence of the laws of Spain. It was a war of vicissitudes in which ground was won and lost, an insensible war in which the enemy had many powerful allies among us."[15] Rejecting the contention that independence had been a consequence of the example set by France and the United States, Bello saw it rather as the natural effect of the desire of any society to administer its own interests and not to receive its laws from other countries. But he continued to emphasize that it was a misconception to confuse freedom from Spain with domestic political freedom. The Latin-American people were well prepared for the former but not for the latter. He argued that the patriots of the inde-

14. *Ibid.*
15. *Ibid.*

pendence movement had erred here; history was to demonstrate, of course, the accuracy of Bello's contention. The task of mental freedom had to be the work of the Latin Americans themselves, free from Spanish involvement, and it was this that he envisaged as the emancipatory task of the emerging generation.

Regarding the problem of political institutions, Bello reflected the influences of Bentham and the utilitarians. Although he was not receptive to utilitarian empiricism and liberalism, he followed his former British acquaintances in a deep-seated belief in reform through legislation. Retaining a sympathy toward monarchy, he apparently believed that the absence of such a tradition in Latin America would make it inappropriate for the newly independent states. He was never entirely candid on the matter, however, and there is still historical debate as to whether or not he favored a constitutional monarch for the New World. In principle he approved of a strong executive, and supported the life presidency designed by Bolívar in the constitutional plan for Bolivia. Essentially a pragmatist in his analyses of political and constitutional questions, Bello was fearful of possible exaggerations by political theoreticians. Learning through the experience of his public career the importance of realistically evaluating political conditions and changing historical forces, he maintained, not unlike the utilitarians, that the ultimate success of a government depended more on the character and honesty of the rulers than on the philosophy inspiring the formulation of constitutional principles.

A final revealing note stems from his broad political position within the Chilean context. Bello arrived in Chile just as the conservative hegemony was about to emerge under Portales' guidance, and he has been charged by some as being personally opportunistic by trimming his sails, in effect, to the near reactionary views of the dominant political elite. It is undeniable that Bello first affiliated with the liberals and then changed. More importantly, however, he held himself largely aloof from partisan affairs, although involved in public duties much of his life. He expressed the private belief that, as a foreigner, it was incumbent upon him to remain outside the interplay of domestic politics. In a broad sense, his conservative as well as pragmatic inclinations permitted an accomodation with the conservative regime. He saw positive benefits in orderly government and the collaboration of commercial and landed interests on behalf of economic development. At the same time he shared a fairly common belief in Chile that Portales was laying the foundations for a future which would be prosperous and well organized, as well as protective of personal freedoms and liberties. Perhaps the fairest assessment would place him in the position of championing moderate reform within a conservative order. Neither a radical nor a liberal by temperament, he saw the values of stability as necessary in the progressive achievement of reforms.

The Quest of Romantic Liberalism

The influence of European romantic liberalism and the utopian socialism of Saint Simon was most noticeable in Chile, Argentina, and Uruguay. In the first of these countries, while Bello did not fit this pattern, he stood as an intellectually transitional figure whose lasting impact included the creation of the National University and the encouragement of independent thought by two generations of young Chileans. A visible manifestation was the Generation of 1842; although José Victorino Lastarria was initially among this group, his gradual mental development eventually carried him far in the direction of positivism, and his most important work came years after the heyday of the Generation of 1842.[16] A more representative figure was the fiery and volatile Francisco Bilbao (1823–65). Bilbao was influenced from his earliest years by his father, a staunch admirer of the French Enlightenment. At the age of eleven, Bilbao's father was driven into Peruvian exile by the Portales regime, an experience that further affected the youth who became a prime example of romantic liberalism in Chile. After returning with his family from exile, Bilbao attended the Instituto Nacional, where he learned the revolutionary thought of the Frenchman Felicité de Lamennais. Already an ardent defender of freedom of thought and religion, he became a member of the *Sociedad Literaria* headed by Lastarria. Three years later, at the age of twenty-one, he exploded on the intellectual scene amid a wave of national notoriety.

The publication in 1844 of his *Sociabilidad chilena*,[17] which might be translated into *Chilean Social Reason*, drew a government his expulsion from the Instituto Nacional, the public burning of his book, and his forced exile to Europe. In it Bilbao set about a quest for the ideal political structure for the new American republics. His starting point was the familiar theme that held Spain responsible for the political evils currently being experienced. Spain represented the Middle Ages, which consisted in a synthesis of Catholicism and feudalism. Latin Americans should emancipate themselves from the cultural habits inherited from

16. See Chapter 4.
17. Francisco Bilbao, *Sociabilidad chilena,* Vol. X of *Obras completas* (Buenos Aires: Manuel Bilbao, 1866).

Spain, thereby creating a new synthesis that could produce the equality of liberty or liberty for all. Bilbao was not an atheist, but he placed the blame on the Roman Catholic church for the survival of medieval rural structures in Latin America. Regarding Catholicism of the Middle Ages as struggling against the republicanism of the times, he saw them as directly contradictory forces; only one could survive, for in no way did they complement one another. Catholicism, he contended, denied the fundamental principles of republican government and of popular sovereignty. On the other hand, republicanism and equality denied the kind of obedience to dogma that he felt was characteristic of the Church. Should the conflict be won by Catholicism, monarchy or theocratic rule would result. The alternative was liberal republicanism, which would free the people from Catholic domination and enhance the values of freedom.

Bilbao was among the most eloquent writers of his generation to examine the problem of the liberators in establishing a new order following the winning of independence from Spain. While he offered nothing unique, his statement was among the most effective. The combatant Chilean regarded the great revolutionary leaders as having been equipped only with a negative brand of critical destructiveness. When the Spanish were expelled, therefore, they had few genuine philosophical ideas by which to establish the foundations of a modern liberal order. The result was postindependence turbulence from which emerged strong man rule as the defender of order and stability. In Chile, for example, O'Higgins had honestly attempted the organization of politics and society in accord with national traditions but had been unequal to the task. The military fight with Spain had been so bitter and deeply felt that few had seen any ultimate objectives beyond the defeat of the colonial masters. Thus traditional beliefs had survived, and there was only an inadequate comprehension of the true implications of liberty and freedom.

During Bilbao's enforced exile in France, he grew familiar with both the exponents and writings of utopian socialism, witnessing the revolutionary upheavels of 1848. He became more imbued with the ideals of Father Lamennais, later praising in particular his *Paroles d'un Croyant* (*Words of a Believer*).[18] Upon returning to Chile in 1850, Bilbao showed the intellectual impact of his exile through the effort to interpret history by epochs, following Saint Simon's distinction between organic and critical periods of civilization. He returned to his quest for a new synthesis in the historical process while continuing to reject the traditional one.

18. Hugues Félicité Robert de Lamennais, *Paroles d'un croyant* (Paris: Garnier Frères, 1834).

The solution, he felt, was to be found in the implementation of a true liberalism although, as an essentially destructive critic, he was fairly vague in specific proposals and philosophical formulations. Contrasting at one point the rapid progress of the United States following its revolution, he referred to Latin America as the "disunited states," calling for an effective union among the Hispanic republics. He later formulated a plan for a Latin American federation, including a customs union and a hemispheric court of justice. Bilbao's last major work before his death, *Evangelio americano* (1864),[19] written after a second exile in Peru and, finally, in Argentina, restated once more his criticism of Spanish influence and urged a new revolution to eradicate that legacy. Liberty could only be achieved when the people understood that it consisted in man's action under the guidance of reason; the principle of popular sovereignty could work only when it became the sovereignty of reason.

The best exposition of the Chilean's general philosophy was his *Ley de la historia* (1858), where he rejected the notion that the historian should limit himself to a descriptive account of conditions. He also expressed his opposition to the philosopher-historian who accepts with resignation and understanding the calamities of mankind. Bilbao believed in the existence of a normative ingredient in historical knowledge; man had a duty toward his fellow man that prescribed a norm of action, which was the true law of history as commanded by the Creator. This normative command would ultimately culminate in man's freedom, which was the political expression of the idea of the people's sovereignty. Linking a concern for institutional reform and constitutional principles with the study of the philosophy of history, he presented an idealistic defense of faith in human progress through freedom, divine inspiration, and respect for one's fellow man. He reiterated his lifelong conviction in the dissemination of understanding throughout the populace. While saying relatively little beyond a common declaration favoring educational reforms, Bilbao through his flaming rhetoric and deeply personal statements helped to spark an intellectual revival that in time carried Chilean *pensadores* in the direction of positivism.

On the other side of the Andes, Argentina was producing some of the most eminent political thinkers of the period, three of whom assumed a front rank in the intellectual currents of the day. These men—Esteban Echeverría, Juan Bautista Alberdi, and Domingo Faustino Sarmiento—were intellectually and politically instrumental in carrying Argentina beyond the dictatorship of Juan Manuel de Rosas which had endured for

19. Francisco Bilbao, *Evangelio americano,* prepared and with commentary by Dardo Cuneo (Buenos Aires: Editorial Americalee, 1943).

twenty years from the early 1830s. The years before the rise of Rosas in Argentina, were, if anything, even more disturbed than the comparable period in Chile. The adoption of a centralized constitution had been bitterly opposed by the federalists from the provinces, and this inaugurated the struggle between *porteño* (the resident of the port of Buenos Aires) and *provinciano* (the rural provincial citizen) which was to characterize Argentine political life for years to come. Another centralist constitution in 1826 undertook to placate the provinces by granting them a modicum of autonomy, but the federalists were still dissatisfied and the intensity of their contest with the *porteños* mounted.

For several years the city of Buenos Aires functioned independently of the provinces. The polarization between Buenos Aires and the interior was pronounced. Federalists backed by a number of regional *caudillos* demanded local power and authority, while centralist unitarians, as they became known, advocated a national union in which the port city would direct a centralized government. In 1831 Juan Manuel de Rosas emerged at the head of the Buenos Aires government, and through agreement with federalist leaders of the interior, he gained domination over the unitarions. The virtual ruler of Argentina from 1829 to 1852, he paradoxically established a strong central government in Buenos Aires while lashing out vehemently against the efforts of the "savage, filthy Unitarians." His political acumen contributed to his effective unification of the country even while he consistently claimed to be the defender of federalist interests. Following on a national basis the traditions of small rural *caudillos*, Rosas developed a harshly tyrannical regime over which he presided as "El Restaurador"—the restorer.

Although long denounced by Argentine historians, Rosas in recent years has become a slightly less distasteful figure. Clearly he halted the process of disintegration that had started, restoring order and stability in the process. Despite his federalist declarations, in point of fact he laid the groundwork for the eventual unification of Argentina along unitarian lines. Moreover, it was under his regime that a *criollo* reaction grew against the Rivadavia program of modernizing Argentina by imitating European experience. The emphasis on Argentine nationalism that gradually evolved was to characterize the thinking of the country's intellectuals from that era forward. At the same time, it is equally true that his regime was brutal and oppressive; among other things, Rosas established the first effective secret police in Latin America, his dreaded *mazorca*. His success in winning and consolidating national authority engendered a bitter reaction on the part of educated elements, especially in Buenos Aires, and it was inevitable that highly critical opposition would result. The first organized exposition of protest came with the emergence of the so-called "Generation of 1837," which was composed of a number of young intellectuals, among whom Esteban Echeverría and Juan Bautista Alberdi were prominent.

The members of the Generation of 1837 represented the first group to mature in Argentina after the winning of independence, and they shared a belief in the principles of freedom of the May 1810 Revolution. Concentrating on the political destiny of Argentina, they comprised a brilliant elite of enlightened *porteños* who, while influenced by European romanticism, kept their eyes on political reality. Among the earliest evidences of such ideas came from a young Esteban Echeverría upon his return home in 1830 after some five years in France. He became one of the first to express the sentiment that Argentina's national destiny would have to be molded from its natural and human resources, its geographical, climatic, and topographical characteristics. This impact of romantic liberalism became more pronounced in 1837 when, in the bookstore of Marcos Sastre, young intellectuals formed a Salón Literario. This literary circle gained notoriety when it was promptly closed by President Rosas, and its membership then organized a secret society known as the Asociación de la Joven Generación Argentina. Among those active in the association were Echeverría, Miguel Cané, and Juan María Gutiérrez. The first two men collaborated in the preparation of a *Credo* setting forth their principles; these were later incorporated into Echeverría's *Dogma socialista* in 1846. Domingo Faustino Sarmiento, exiled in Chile at the time, expressed his sympathy with the association although he did not formally join.[20]

Rosas' break of relations with France and the introduction of a lengthy period of hostility between the two countries provoked pointed opposition from the members of the association, and resultant criticism led the dictator to intensify his persecution of the group. Nonetheless, the emerging thought of the Generation of 1837 continued to mirror their inheritance of the ideas of utopian liberals, and the strongly European flavor placed them closer to Rivadavia than to Rosas in this respect. Although there were, inevitably, differences among various of these embattled young Argentines, they shared an approving response to Saint Simon, Fourier, and Leroux. Drawing a distinction between political and social problems, they argued that a political solution alone would not meet national needs, for any efficient political system should represent not only free and well-organized institutions but a sound and coherent community.

20. José Luis Romero, *A History of Argentine Political Thought*, tr. Thomas F. McGann (Stanford: Stanford University Press, 1963), p. 129.

Europeanized formulations were offered as appropriate to the resolution
of national weaknesses. As others had done, they said that the remnants
of "backward" Spanish elements should be purged. They outlined modernizing characteristics that were derived from the North American experience even more than the European.

Among the first exponents of this movement in Argentina was Esteban
Echeverría (1805–51). He had been born in Buenos Aires and was educated both there and in France, pursuing a literary career that included
poetry and fiction as well as political writings. The latter dealt primarily
with political and social interrelationships. Echeverría was not a student
of economics, and his major work, *Dogma socialista*,[21] was neither concerned with economics nor socialism in the modern sense. By socialism
he meant a dedication to the study of social realities but by no means
state intervention in the economy. Major emphasis was placed on ideas
of equality, mortality, and freedom of association, although Echeverría
was an elitist in some of his views. He believed, for example, that universal
suffrage and unlimited freedom of expression were inherently dangerous,
preferring society to be ruled by an educated group of property owners.
In this his writing was suggestive of the Saint Simonian belief in the
natural inequality of man.

Echeverría was among the early members of the chorus proclaiming
that the Americas still retained many traits of colonialism, with true
emancipation unrealized. He, too, called for a complete repudiation of
the Spanish inheritance and held that Argentina's original May Revolution had been only partially successful in freeing the people from Spain.
The task of his generation, therefore, was the attainment of a society
fully emancipated from the colonial past. In 1810 the Argentine people
had become politically sovereign but lacked the training and civic voca-
tion for proper self-rule. The inevitable result, in time, was a regressive
shift in the direction of tyranny, which he saw embodied in the person
of Juan Manuel de Rosas. Two Spanish traits in particular had survived:
social customs and legislative regulation. In the first case, the long-ac-
customed obedience of the colonial era had made authoritarianism the
natural political inclination of the early independence period. Beyond
that, the inherited forms of government also blocked the progress of
true revolution.

Effective emancipation from Spanish practices depended in large part
upon education. This remedial proposal of Echeverría's was also common
to many of his contemporaries. Holding that true liberty would come

21. Esteban Echeverría, *Dogma socialista: Con noticias biográficas de José
María Gutiérrez* (Buenos Aires: La Cultura Argentina, 1915).

only from knowledge and understanding, the people had to learn to be competent for self-rule. Until this might be achieved, Argentina would continue to be stifled by pervasive colonialism rather than developing its own modern spirit. There was no true understanding of the practical organization of democracy and representative forms. Not in the ordinary sense a political partisan, Echeverría in his youth had seen some positive benefits in the rule of Rosas for, with many of his colleagues, the Argentine believed in the necessity of bringing about meaningful political unification. As the dictatorial excesses mounted, however, he soon became critical of Rosas. Indeed, both the federalists and unitarians were the subject of his scorn. The former were a divisive and fragmenting influence on the country, while the latter were either ineffectual or authoritarian. Both federalists and unitarians had contributed to the destruction of true and authentic progress, setting in motion those traditional forces that permitted a return to the despotism of the past. Such was the message of Echeverría: a social and political liberalism that called for the creation of a society in which individual freedom would be the cornerstone for progress and development.

Perhaps a more typical representative of the Argentine Generation of 1837, and one who made a lasting impression on national politics, was Juan Bautista Alberdi (1810–84). An original member of the *association* and close colleague of Echeverría, he was somewhat less strongly influenced by European utopian socialism, and his intellectual debt was perhaps as strong to England as it was to France. Thus his writings were a mixture of utilitarian realism and pragmatic political analysis as much as a reflection of the romantic liberalism that was current in Argentina. Economic ideas of *laissez faire* and a commitment to minimal governmental activity also underlined his views. Born of Basque ancestry in the provincial capital of Tucumán, he was educated in Buenos Aires, where he studied law and philosophy. He rapidly became a bitter critic of the Rosas dictatorship, and was forced into exile in 1839, going across the Plate estuary to take up residence in Montevideo. His absence from Argentina was extended, and he traveled first to France and then to Chile before returning home at the time of Rosas' defeat in 1852.

As the military campaign against Rosas approached its conclusion, Alberdi rapidly wrote his famous *Bases y puntos de partida para la organización política de la república Argentina.*[22] Rushed into print and sent to the constitutional convention that drew up the federal constitution

---

22. Jaun Bautista Alberdi, *Bases y puntos de partida para la organización política de la república argentina,* in *Obras completas* (Buenos Aires: La Tribuna Nacional, 1886).

of 1853, the *Bases* was employed as the guide for discussions and the eventful drafting of that document, one of the most long-lasting and justly famed constitutions of all Latin America.[23] Although written swiftly and hurriedly under the pressures of time, *Bases* was the result of many years' experience and study of Argentine problems. Even today this work is among the greatest single contributions to Argentine political thought, and it is the best expression of Alberdi's ideas and convictions. Roughly similar in purpose and impact to the Federalist Papers in the United States, it has been described as "one of those rare books in the history of the human spirit which capture the sense and meaning of the experience of an age."[24] It was the initial edition of this work which shows Alberdi at his best. Subsequent editions included changes introduced because of Alberdi's partisan political interests, and several of these made the author a more controversial figure in Argentine political history than would otherwise have been the case.[25]

Before discussing Alberdi's *Bases*, it is pertinent to mention his doctoral thesis, *Preliminar al estudio del derecho* (1837), which clearly showed an influence of traditional liberalism intermingled with familiarity with the writers of the historical school of jurisprudence. Here as well as in other early writings Alberdi reflected an intellectual proclivity for the more traditional and classical studies that typified Argentina at the time. By the year of his *Bases,* however, Alberdi had developed into a more mature thinker, aware of Argentina's need for a political organization that could harmonize the divergent interests of city and country-side with existing geographic and ethnic realities. His immortal phrase "gobernar es poblar"—to govern is to populate—was an echo of views already expressed by Domingo Faustino Sarmiento but was less an over-simplification than some have believed. For Alberdi envisaged a particular kind of population; he intended a colonization of large unpopulated rural areas and did not advocate the unqualified acceptance of any and all immigrants. Encouragement of European immigration was directed at the introduction of competent farmers and agriculturalists into the Argentine interior. What the countryside lacked at the time, he averred, was a knowledge of crops, soils, seeds, and the effective utilization of the land. Thus European immigration should be primarily that

23. Although temporarily replaced by a *peronista* document nearly a century later, the Constitution of 1853 was restored in Argentina following the overthrow of Juan Perón.

24. Harold E. Davis, "Juan Bautista Alberdi, Americanist," *Journal of Inter-American Studies,* IV, No. 1 (January 1962), 53.

25. See Ricardo Rojas, *Historia de la literatura argentina,* VI (Buenos Aires: Editorial Losada, 1948), 565–71.

of competent and skilled farmers. To a lesser degree he also hoped to attract urban workers with industrial skills, but this was less important. He further explained that the population, ideally, should be doubled every ten years in Argentina.[26]

At the time in which Alberdi was writing, it was commonly held that two different schools existed in the art of constitution making. The Anglo-Saxon approach consisted of incorporating in a public normative order the legal institutions and practices of a nation. The French position was more dogmatic and theoretical, with the assembled representatives of the people attempting to create the public order that they believed necessary. Alberdi adopted an eclectic position that undertook to combine both approaches, aiming at a liberal constitutional order consistent with historical realities. What he therefore undertook in his political and constitutional recommendations was the erection of a system that might grapple effectively with the traditional counterpressures between federal and unitary forms of government. Recognizing that the conflicting abstract dogmas of centralism and federalism had failed in practice, Alberdi sought harmony, conciliation, and in general a compromise with existing conditions. In this he reflected what Argentine scholar José Luis Romero has labeled as the period of *pensamiento conciliador* (conciliatory thought) in Argentina.[27] He took from the centralists their cherished institution of a strong presidency, allowed political decentralization for the provinces, and vested the central government with the power to intervene in local affairs under certain specified circumstances.

Alberdi recognized that, notwithstanding the tyrannical nature of Rosas' rule, Argentina had progressed under his guidance as a unified entity. Committed to a strong central government, he recognized at the same time that local and provincial autonomy was important if loyalties to the central government were to be strengthened. He therefore introduced the practice of national *interventores* with the authority, in extraordinary cases, to intervene in provincial and local affairs. He intended this power to be used by the central government only on rare occasions; in practice, however, this was later used as a means of reducing provincial autonomy. In the twentieth century both Hipólito Irigoyen and, later, Juan Perón were to make extensive use of the power in furthering the authority of the national government in Buenos Aires. In the long run, the Alberdi-inspired constitution, while nominally federal, proved to be

26. Even today Alberdi is frequently cited by Latin Americans in the context of discussions of family planning and population questions.

27. Romero, *Argentine Political Thought*, see Chapter V, pp. 126–64, and especially pp. 145–49.

largely centralist in practice. Yet the document was instrumental in encouraging the further development of Argentina as a unified entity, and the form of compromise embodied by the constitution was a noteworthy effort to meet the future needs of national development while recognizing existing conflicts within society.

Alberdi's political philosophy in general can be described as liberal realism. He maintained a faith in liberalism, identifying his concept of law with the general will of Rousseau. Nevertheless, he believed that French thought of the postrevolutionary period concentrated on social and economic conditions. Alberdi also reflected the writings of British political economists in his attention to economic problems. His political views included a strong element of internationalism that emerged in his advocacy of an efficient inter-American system. In 1844 he presented a *Memoria* to the University of Chile recommending the celebration of a general American congress. In this document he joined Bolívar, Moreno, Gutiérrez, Bilbao, and others in anticipating the present hemispheric system. The proposed congress was to deal with the international problems of the new republics, such as boundary disputes and wars, for which he recommended disarmament and mediation The *Memoria* included constructive suggestions, years ahead of his times, such as a customs union and an international court. He also envisaged the possibility of intervention in local situations as a means of preserving orderly relations among the republics of Latin America.

Alberdi's career, at least in a public sense, reached its climax with the publication and influence of *Bases*. Shortly thereafter he was appointed to a diplomatic post in Europe, and most of his remaining years were spent there in disillusionment with the politics of the day. He did not return home until 1880, but instead of the anticipated triumphal reception he was received with an outburst of criticism from political opponents. He shortly returned to Paris, where he died in 1884. Although he wrote little during the long years in Europe, his disillusionment was revealingly illustrated by *Luz del día* (1872), a mediocre satire on the politics of his day. Describing the behavior of the "sheep" of an imaginary republic founded by Don Quijote in Patagonia, he presented a crude caricature of the democracy he had dreamed of for his homeland and blamed its corruption on the negativism of ruling politicians. He complained about the hypocrisy of business and the venality of the press; he charged the old liberals with apathy and disinterest in national progress. It was a sad footnote to the career of one of Argentina's most eminent sons.

Contrasting with the long and final eclipse of Alberdi's political career was the public service of Domingo Faustino Sarmiento (1811–88), one of the great figures of the hemisphere whose life was capped by service as president of Argentina. His impoverished childhood in the western region of the country was a Lincolnesque struggle for education and knowledge, and he could not afford university training. Sarmiento was therefore largely self-taught, and at an early age he turned to journalism as a career. At sixteen he first suffered political persecution for the expression of critical views, and in 1831 his writing resulted in his expulsion from Argentina, which stretched out into some two decades of exile. Most of these years he spent in Chile as an active newspaperman and essayist who, contrary to the usual exile pattern, entered enthusiastically into the politics of his host country. Sarmiento was an ardent admirer of Manuel Montt, the conservative president of Chile.

Sarmiento's activities included the editorship of *El Mercurio,* the establishment of the first normal school in Chile, the authorship of two significant works on education, the preparation of Chile's first speller for classroom use, and a ceaseless encouragement of the writing of textbooks for popular use. His romantic and humanistic orientation contrasted with the coolly rational classicism and traditionalism of Andrés Bello, with whom he exchanged numerous polemical articles and pamphlets. Always a difficult and contentious personality, Sarmiento made many enemies in Chile. His differences with Bello were serious, and the frankness of his comments on national politics was unappreciated, coming as they did from the pen of an alien. He maintained a long and outspoken criticism of the Rosas government, and consequent demands by Argentina for his extradition were a source of difficulty for the Chileans. His egotistical assurance led him to be known by some as "Don Yo," because of endless references to the first person in both conversation and writing. His presence in Santiago proved increasingly embarrassing to the government, and finally in 1845 he was sent abroad to study foreign educational systems. The result was an extended exposure to Europe and to the United States, which furthered his interest and understanding of educational problems. It was this experience that made him an enthusiastic admirer of North American Horace Mann and the developing educational system in the United States.

Returning to Chile in 1849 from this kind of educational sabbatical, he soon re-entered Argentina to join the insurgents of the regional *caudillo* Justo José Urquiza in the fight against Rosas and was present for the ultimate defeat of the latter. His career unfolded rapidly from that point. By 1855 he was editing the newspaper *El Nacional* in Buenos Aires, and he soon was elected as a member of the Senate. After serving as governor of his native province of San Juan in the 1860s, Sarmiento was sent to the United States as his country's minister. The experience provided him with material for acute and perceptive comments on North American society and political life. He returned home in 1868 and was elected to the presidency for a six-year term. Sarmiento continued to be active politically following his retirement from that office, and he remained an acerbic and out-spoken figure until his death, writing in newspaper columns as well as from the floor of the Senate, to which he returned after his presidency.

The tract that best reflects Sarmiento's political thought is *Facundo,* written and published in Chile in 1845 with the subtitle of *Civilización y barbarie.*[28] One of the classics of the literature, the book was puportedly a biography of the regional *caudillo* Juan Facundo Quiroga but was aimed directly at Rosas. The subtitle is indicative of Sarmiento's major theme: civilization was the city, with its European culture and progress, as contrasted to the barbarism of Argentina's vast unpopulated plain. There, in the *pampas,* primitive little clusters of people associated in *montoneras* or bands, following the inspiration of a personalistic man of the soil and living by brute force. It was from the *pampas* that Argentine violence was derived. Sarmiento's sociological and demographic preoccupation pointed up the realistic strain of his thinking. Theoretical political solutions and ideal constitutions did not promise a rebirth of Argentine nationality. The country could never become a nation until the plains were incorporated into civilization. Time would be required, and in the meantime a political truce between warring factions was necessary in order to allow economic development, population growth and, above all, education.

While Alberdi's motto was *gobernar es poblar,* that of Sarmiento might be said to have been *gobernar es educar*—to govern is to educate. His *Educación popular* in 1849 contained the report prepared for the Chilean government after his observations of foreign educational systems. Covering the principal problems of public education in the new republics of Latin America, he contributed substantively to the understanding and subsequent educational development of both Chile and Argentina.

28. Domingo Faustino Sarmiento, *Civilización y barbarie: La vida de don Juan Facundo Quiroga* (Santiago: 1845). For an English translation, see that of Mrs. Horace Mann, entitled *Life in the Argentine Republic in the Days of the Tyrants, or Civilization and Barbarism* (New York: Hurd and Houghton, 1868). For an excellent biography in English, see Allison Williams Bunkley, *The Life of Sarmiento* (Princeton: Princeton University Press, 1952). For a selective anthology, see Stuart Edgard Grummon, ed., *A Sarmiento Anthology* (Princeton: Princeton University Press, 1948).

When he ascended to the presidency of his country, Sarmiento reorganized the educational system completely, and this was among the most important accomplishments of his administration. He once told congress in a presidential message, "If I do not advance popular education, all of my earlier words and deeds stand as vain ostentation." He succeeded in expanding school facilities and doubling enrollment during his presidency, while introducing such North American innovations as a nationwide network of normal schools and the establishment of night classes for adult education. Second only to his educational accomplishment was an active encouragement of immigration, which brought the entry of 280,000 Europeans during his six-year term, reaching an annual high of 70,000 during his final year in office. Material accomplishments also included the building of railroads to open the interior, the settlement of virgin lands, the extension of highways and postal service, and the beginning of the modernization of Buenos Aires port facilities.

Domingo Faustino Sarmiento was not a systematic thinker who scrupulously followed any definite school of thought with unwavering consistency. In an era of romanticism in Argentina, he was neither poet nor philosopher, but rather an observer and analyst of social conditions. Argentine Ricardo Rojas was to say of him, "Sarmiento was more than a writer; he was a great man who spoke. His [written] words seem to come from his mouth and not from his pen."[29] In a broad sense, it can be said that three major influences helped to shape his attitudes: the Enlightenment, nineteenth-century romantic liberalism, and the practical impact of his observations of the United States.[30] The Enlightenment taught him the importance of the concept of government by law, emphasizing the obligatory supremacy of the constitution. From its teachings he also derived the idea of progress and a broad optimism that was seen in his overwhelming confidence in the role of education. A romantic impact emerged from his self-reliance and his emphatic conviction about the ability of the individual to overcome all handicaps. This was also, of course, a direct result of his personal experience. And lastly, the North American contribution was not only strong in the educational field but impressed him as well with the relative progress in establishing a domestic political consensus permitting internal development in transportation and communications, in the economy, and in agricultural progress. Fundamentally opposed to the Argentine brand of political personalism that was sometimes called "gauchocracy," Sarmiento dreamed of elevating the people through education, a migratory influx

29. Rojas, *Literatura argentina,* V, 376.
30. This point is developed fully in Bunkley, *Sarmiento.*

a devotion to laws and, in the final analysis, a total recasting of society and civilization itself.

The Philosophical Drive for Cuban Independence

On the island of Cuba, the continuation of Spanish colonialism through the nineteenth century confronted its intellectuals with a different situation. Although there were those who restricted their writings to abstract theoretical speculation, the most prominent touched upon political questions in one fashion or another. For most of the Cuban *pensadores* of the nineteenth century, two basic problems were paramount: the question of relations with Spain and the concomitant matter of the governmental forms appropriate to the island. Cuba had enjoyed a period of enlightened despotism in the latter portion of the eighteenth century. The University of Habana, founded in 1738, had become an important center of learning. Following the expulsion of the Jesuits, the Seminario de San Carlos had adopted a more advanced curriculum than the university itself, which was yet dominated by the philosophy of scholasticism. With the faculty in the Seminario composed largely of secular clergymen and in some instances laymen, it is not surprising that scholasticism first went into decline there rather than at the university.

In Cuba, where throughout much of the century preceding its independence the emphasis was first on intellectual and only second on political independence, the teacher was more influential than the soldier. Among the first to achieve prominence was Father José Agustín Caballero (1765–1835), whose *Philosophia electiva,* written in Latin and published in 1797, was devoted basically to logic. A follower of Descartes, Caballero's epistemology showed such influences as those of Locke, Condillac, and Bacon, and his was the first philosophical tract written in Cuba. Regarding Cubans as descendants of Spain but also inhabitants of a land with its own distinctive environment, Father Caballero was at one with his contemporaries in accepting Spanish dominion while requesting a recognition of its own unique qualities. In 1810 he served in a diplomatic capacity to present before the Spanish Cortes of Cádiz a project requesting a degree of self-government for Cuba. A provisional council was requested, providing a native Cuban body to work with the Spanish governor general. As Caballero fruitlessly explained, "Those who clamor for reforms do not aspire to establish a state with its complete juridical independent organization; they only want Spain to recognize the personality of the colony. They believe that there will be a more tranquil and prosperous coexistence if the mother country decentralizes its governmental status."[31]

A disciple of Caballero, Father Félix Varela y Morales (1788–1853), became the philosophical mentor of a brilliant group of Cuban thinkers in the early nineteenth century, and during a brief period of Spanish liberalism in the 1820s he taught constitutional law at the Seminario de San Carlos. He was also a professor at the University of Habana and was responsible for the introduction of rational philosophy into Cuba, using an eclectic approach that derived from Destutt de Tracy while containing elements of Descartes and Locke as well. Differentiating philosophy from theory, Varela held that truth was found only through reason confirmed by experience, and the authority of the Christian fathers in philosophy was the same as that of the philosophers that they themselves followed. This meant that apart from matters of faith, there was an obligation to accept the teaching of the fathers. As a good Christian, he followed Saint Augustine rather than the official Thomistic philosophy of the Roman Catholic church. There was in Varela an affinity between the Augustinian concept of the primacy of the will and the Cartesian method, which he developed and expanded in his teachings.[32] It was through the teachings of Varela in particular that scholasticism was abandoned at the Seminario and replaced by a new independence of thought, at a time when the University of Habana was maintaining its Thomistic orientation until the 1840s.

Father Varela's lectures on constitutional law attracted much interest from students and from the general public. He prepared a text based on the Spanish constitution of 1812, entitled *Observaciones sobre la constitución de la monarquía española*.[33] In spite of some conservatism in that charter, Varela attempted to stress the liberal elements, which he traced to the medieval Spanish rights. In that document, he pointed out the influence of Montesquieu in the suggestion of a need to devise effective separations of power.[34] In the years following the publication of *Observaciones*, Varela became increasingly vocal in his views. At the Spanish Cortes of 1823 he presented his *Proyecto para el gobierno de las provincias de ultramar* as his recommendation of self-government for Cuba and Puerto Rico. The forthcoming restoration of Ferdinand

---

31. Medardo Vitier, *Las ideas en Cuba: Proceso del pensamiento político, filosófico y crítico en Cuba, principalmente durante el siglo XIX,* I (La Habana: Edit. Trópico, 1938), 114.

32. *Ibid.,* II, 95–97.

33. Félix Varela y Morales, *Observaciones sobre la constitución política de la monarquía española: Biblioteca de autores cubanos* (La Habana: Universidad de La Habana, 1944).

34. Adolfo Posada, *Tratado de derecho político* (Madrid: V. Suárez, 1924).

VII to the Spanish throne led to Varela's flight from Spain before his project was considered. Traveling to the United States, he lived modestly as a parish priest in New York, Philadelphia, and finally in Florida, where he died.

Varela, who in a very real sense stands apart from the other Cubans mentioned here, became well known in North American ecclesiastical circles and founded two churches in New York City. At one point he was even considered as a candidate for the bishopric of that city.[35] Cuban problems, however, were always in his mind, and he edited the newspaper *El Habanero* from exile until 1826. Later he continued his campaign for Cuban political independence in *El Mensajero Semanal,* which he edited in collaboration with José Antonio Saco y López. The correlation of his religious principles with a belief in individual freedom represented an important early example of liberalism in Cuba, and he is remembered for this in his native land even today. Even more directly influential during this period was his sometime collaborator, Saco. It was the frequent public exposition of Cuban problems by the latter which encouraged a more general public awareness of the political and economic status of the island within Spanish colonial mercantilism.

During the early and middle years of the nineteenth century, there were four different opinions in connection with colonial problems. One favored complete independence, to be won by revolutionary means; another advocated educational and economic reforms to prepare the citizenry for self-government; the third demanded political autonomy under Spanish aegis; and the fourth, while desiring either self-government *or* independence, was mainly concerned over the small white minority on the island. This last group was probably the most realistic in its understanding of the Cuban situation, and its best known figure was José Antonio Saco y López (1797–1879), who succeeded Varela in the chair of philosophy at the *seminario.* Receiving his higher education in law and philosophy, first in Santiago and later in Habana under Varela himself. He began his literary career at an early age and rapidly acquired a reputation as a brilliant prose writer on a broad range of subjects. An enlightened liberal from his youth,[36] Saco retained his chair of philosophy only until 1834, when he was deported by order of the Spanish Captain General Miguel de Tacón. The rest of his long life was spent in Europe, with the exception of two brief stays to Cuba.

Although he desired independence, Saco was opposed to the use of

35. José Ignacio Rodríguez, *Vida del presbítero don Félix Varela* (Nueva York: Imprenta de "O Novo mundo," 1878).
36. Fernando Ortíz, *José Antonio Saco y sus ideas cubanas* (La Habana: Imp. El Universo, 1929).

violent means; his opposition toward Spanish rule was no less firm than his denunciation of revolutionary activity. Described by the Cuban writer Orestes Ferrara as a statesman rather than revolutionary,[37] Saco explored Cuban political reality with a depth of knowledge and objectivity unparalleled by his contemporaries. His study of Cuban political conditions centered on four topics: Spanish despotism, slavery, annexation by the United States, and political reforms under Spain. Among his significant writings was Saco's *Paralelo entre la isla de Cuba y algunas colonias inglesas*.[38] In this monograph, published in Madrid in 1837, he attempted to shatter the Spanish claim that Cuba was the happiest and most prosperous of all European colonies. Saco analyzed the administrative institutions, economic and educational conditions, and the position of individual liberties in several British colonies as a measure for comparison with the political despotism and material backwardness in Cuba under Spanish rule. The work, persuasive in its language and argument, illustrated Saco's realistic approach and his amassing of facts to support his theses.

His strain of realism kept him constantly preoccupied with the ethnic problem of the Negro population and the institution of slavery. He saw Cuba as a colony with two slaveries, one that of the Negro, the other that of the native *criollo* deprived of all political rights. He strongly attacked the institution of slave trade and demanded the abolition of slavery. His conviction was forcefully underlined by his multi-volume historical study of slavery, which he began in the 1840s. The *Historia de la ésclavitud* did not appear until 1875, with the second and third volumes following between that date and 1892.[39] He was well into the fourth of five projected volumes when he died; the fourth provided a valuable if incomplete study of Negro slavery in the Americas, and the final one had sketched insightful sections on the history of Indian slavery in the New World. Throughout this major work, as well as in articles and essays, Saco reiterated the importance of attracting desirable European immigrants to Cuba as a means of balancing the disproportion between the white and Negro inhabitants. Without this demographic adjustment, he argued, Cuba was not ready for full independence.

Saco's position on the role of the United States vis-à-vis Cuba was also revealing. At the time, North American policy desired that the island remain in the hands of Spain, a weak power, as an alternative

37. Orestes Ferrara, *Las ideas políticas de José Antonio Saco* (La Habana: n.p., 1909).
38. See José Antonio Saco y López, *Papeles sobre Cuba,* II (Paris, 1859), 149–79.
39. José Antonio Saco y López, *Historia de la Esclavitud,* 3 Vols. (Paris: n.p., 1875–92).

preferable to the possibility of ultimate British control. At the same time, there was sentiment in the United States which favored the annexation of the island, to be followed by the later granting of some degree of self-government. There were also Cuban leaders who favored annexation, especially after the United States' war with Mexico in 1846. They even went so far as to form a Consejo Cubano in New York with the explicit purpose of encouraging the annexation movement. Saco was strongly opposed, despite a general sympathy for the United States. He feared that Cuba's identity would be lost in the culture of the larger country. "I would have Cuba be not only rich, cultured, moral and powerful, but also a Cuban Cuba, and not an Anglo-American one. . . [for] nationality is the immortality of all peoples and the basis of the purest patriotism. If Cuba had four or five million white inhabitants, with what pleasure I would see her go to our neighbor's arms! In that case, no matter how many of them would immigrate to us, they would be assimilated, and Cuba, growing and prospering to the world's amazement, would always be Cuban."[40] Saco's refusal to join the supporters of annexation was also a courageous move, for many of his close friends backed the movement, including several who were contributing financially to support his exile existence.

Saco stayed on in Spain, struggling for mental enlightenment and political liberty for Cuba. In many of his writings, he said that as the island was legally a part of the Spanish kingdom, the civil liberties existing in the mother country should also be extended to Cuba. In 1865 the Spanish government called a meeting in Madrid of delegates from Cuba and Puerto Rico to discuss the political situation of the two islands, and Saco was among the delegates to this Junta de Información. When negotiations failed, he drafted a dissenting opinion, or *voto particular,* in which he brilliantly restated his ideas. Again demanding self-government for Cuba, he realistically opposed her representation in the Spanish Cortes as a solution, holding that the small Cuban delegation would be without influence and constantly subject to being outvoted by the Spanish majority. The failure of the Junta de Información was a bitter blow to many Cubans, who had previously trusted the possibility of negotiated solutions. With this hope apparently crushed, the liberals led by Carlos Manuel de Céspedes began an uprising on October 10, 1868. The result was a ten-year struggle that ended in a truce, with Cuba still a colony. Saco had always opposed any such premature fight for liberation; seventy-one years old when it started, ill and half blind,

40. Saco, *Papeles,* III, 316.

he neither encouraged nor fought it, believing that with the violence finally unleashed, there was nothing to be done but continue until the end.

A contemporary of Saco's was José de la Luz y Caballero (1800–62), the man most responsible for educational progress during the slow movement toward ultimate independence. Lacking in the revolutionary zeal of many of his associates, Luz y Caballero filled the role of educator of a new revolutionary generation, and it was his chair of philosophy to which the famed Enrique José Varona y Pera later succeeded. Even more strongly opposed to violence than was José Antonio Saco, he foresaw the attainment of freedom through moderate and measured progress. As one of his students later wrote, Luz y Caballero "really never dreamed of disturbing the people's minds by preparing them for immediate and destructive action; he longed, on the contrary, to enlighten them with the truth and to settle them in virtue, but nevertheless in the end he did perturb them."[41] Although he was influential in training a generation of revolutionaries, Luz y Caballero never taught war or violence but concentrated instead on freeing Cubans socially and intellectually from the weaknesses imposed upon them by Spain. Without entering into a discussion of his philosophical teachings, which on the whole were fairly eclectic, it can be said that the great educator instilled in an emerging generation a positive sense of Cuban reality. "It is necessary to have reason strongly fortified in order to cast off the yoke of authority in any form in which it appears. And what more terrible form than the words of a teacher for the weak understanding of his disciples? One owes respect to teachers, but not faith. . . . My aim has been to demolish authority and at the same time to stop presumption."[42]

Along with Caballero, Varela, and Saco, José de la Luz y Caballero contributed to the emergence of a national consciousness among Cubans, both the educated elite and, increasingly, the general public. An awareness of reality grew, accompanied by a belief that drastic measures would be necessary if political freedom were to be achieved. Toward the end of the century, thinking Cubans had concluded that armed rebellion was necessary. While there was a fairly general recognition of the fact that liberation from Spanish colonialism would not bring with it an immediate enjoyment of material prosperity and individual enlightenment, the decision to win political independence as the first step became

41. Manuel Sanguily, *José de la Luz y Caballero* (La Habana: Edit. O'Reilly, 1890.

42. José de la Luz y Caballero, "Documentos para su vida," as quoted is Zea, *Latin-American Mind,* p. 114.

widely accepted. It was within this milieu that José Martí,[43] along with others of his generation, were able to launch the movement that culminated in the Spanish-American War of 1898 and the renewed struggle for emancipation, which, in a sense, was continued by Fidel Castro a half-century later.

Owing to the situation peculiar to Cuba in the nineteenth century, its *pensadores* were less concerned with philosophical abstractions than were Latin Americans elsewhere. Moreover, they were inclined in many cases to focus upon the immediate achievement of freedom from Spain, rather than the postindependence quest for philosophical rationalizations to assist in the eradication of destructive tendencies left behind by the Spanish heritage. This also meant that the Cubans, preoccupied with colonial relationships, sought far less guidance from Europe than did the intellectuals elsewhere. Outside Cuba during these years between the expulsion of Spain and the advent of positivism, an early optimism gradually gave way to frustration over the inability to move away from past traditions toward a new and orderly prosperity in which the dignity of man might be enhanced. Thus, as has been seen, there came into being a growing preoccupation with the reality of the past, and foreign, non-Spanish models were studied as possible means of achieving a renaissance of cultural and social well-being. It was toward the end of the era of romantic liberalism and realism that the impossibility of transplanting European and North American patterns on basically dissimilar environmental conditions became more widely appreciated. The optimism inherited from European philosophical currents of the early 1800s went into decline as liberty and freedom became increasingly restricted. In addition, economic prosperity seemed an elusive and unattainable chimera. The intellectual groping for a new order, diffuse and eclectic, was soon to give way to a philosophical force that was to be regarded as embodying all the necessary truths. That force, European positivism, was to sweep the hemisphere in the latter half of the century.

SELECTED BIBLIOGRAPHY

Alberdi, Juan Bautista. *Bases y puntos de partida para la organización política de la república argentina,* in *Obras completas.* Buenos Aires: La Tribuna Nacional, 1886.

Arciniegas, Germán. *El pensamiento vivo de Andrés Bello.* Buenos Aires: Editorial Losada, 1946.

Bello, Andrés. *Obras completas.* 7 Vols. Santiago: Imp. Pedro G. Ramírez, 1881.

43. See Chapter 5.

Bilbao, Francisco. *Sociabilidad chilena.* Vol. X in *Obras completas.* Buenos Aires: Manuel Bilbao, 1866.

Bunkley, Allison Williams. *The Life of Sarmiento.* Princeton: Princeton University Press, 1952.

Donoso, Ricardo. *Las ideas políticas en Chile.* México: Fondo de Cultura Económica, 1946.

Echeverría, Esteban. *Dogma socialista: Con noticias biográficas de José María Gutiérrez.* Buenos Aires: La Cultura Argentina, 1915.

Gaos, José, ed. *Antología del pensamiento de lengua española en la edad contemporánea.* México: Editorial Seneca, 1945.

Grummon, Stuart Edgard, ed. *A Sarmiento Anthology.* Princeton: Princeton University Press, 1948.

Hale, Charles A. *Mexican Liberalism in the Age of Mora, 1821–1853.* New Haven: Yale University Press, 1968.

Mora, José María Luis. *Obras sueltas.* 2 Vols. Paris: Rosa, 1837.

Ortíz, Fernando. *José Antonio Saco y sus ideas cubanas.* La Habana: Imp. El Universo, 1929.

Piñera, Humberto. *Panorama de la filosofía cubana.* Washington; Pan American Union, 1966.

Rojas, Richardo. *Historia de la literatura argentina, ensayo filosófico sobre la evolución de la cultura en el Plata.* 8 Vols. Buenos Aires: Editorial Losada, 1948.

Romero, José Luis. *A History of Argentine Political Thought.* Translated by Thomas F. McGann. Stanford: Stanford University Press, 1963.

Sarmiento, Domingo Faustino. *Civilización y barbarie: La vida de don Juan Facundo Quiroga.* Santiago, 1845.

Varela y Morales, Félix. *Observaciones sobre la constitución política de la monarquía española: Biblioteca de autores cubanos.* La Habana: Universidad de la Habana, 1944.

Vitier, Medardo. *Las ideas en Cuba: Proceso del pensamiento político, filosófico y crítico en Cuba, principalmente durante el siglo XIX.* 2 Vols. La Habana, Edit. Trópico, 1938.

Zea, Leopoldo. *The Latin-American Mind.* Translated by James H. Abbott and Lowell Dunham. Norman: University of Oklahoma Press, 1963.

4

Positivism and Its Interpreters

The period of romantic liberalism and realism represented the concerted postindependence attempt to identify and elaborate upon a philosophical schema appropriate to the emergence of a new region and its peoples. The anti-Spanish element was inevitable, yet it did not, as we have seen, prevent the early *pensadores* from following fairly derivative lines. At least one of several reasons for the diffuse and sometimes contradictory nature of writings during this period was the variety of European schools from which the Latin Americans drew inspiration. In the early attempts to formulate an American political philosophy, therefore, the eclectic approach of many *pensadores* prevented the development of a single, consistent, and clearly enunciated set of ideas. In much of Latin America, a full half-century passed following the expulsion of the Spanish before political philosophy received systematic treatment. When this came to pass, it took the form of positivism. And although there were varying interpretations, especially from the respective exponents of either Comtean or Spencerian postulations, the advent of positivism made it possible for the first time to speak of a specific and carefully enunciated political and philosophical system. Before examining some of the Latin-American voices of positivism, however, a discussion of the European origins is in order.

European Positivism and Its Appeal for Latin America

Philosophically, the seventeenth century in Europe had been over-shadowed by Newton and stood out as an age of physics and the physical sciences. This was superseded in the eighteenth century by the age of the Enlightenment. In the nineteenth, there was a tremendous desire to be scientific, and the dominant tendency stressed the importance of personal and intellectual observation. This first emerged through an emphasis on history and historical study but later shifted to analytical observation of contemporary behavior. Among those who contributed to the nineteenth-century intellectual formation of Europe were Auguste Comte, Herbert Spencer, and Karl Marx, while John Stuart Mill also loomed large. Of these, Comte was important in helping to set the tone of the age, creating a kind of closed scientific system described in theoretical terms. With Comte came the belief that there was no problem confronting society which science could not solve.

Comte and his followers held that the world was rationally ordered, with laws of social development and interaction that might be discovered by rational thought and study. Moreover, man enjoyed sufficient native intellect to accumulate and to understand the knowledge of life and society. Reason made it possible to discover both the laws of social behavior and the goals and aspirations toward which man was striving. Comte himself was fully convinced of the rational nature of man and society, believing that the millenium, an ultimate scientific utopia would shortly be achieved, either during his lifetime or shortly thereafter. Reflecting the spirit of the age, it was Comte in particular who contributed to the intensification of the reliance upon and belief in rationality and scientific investigation. Comte symbolized the European commitment to the establishment of a single, all-knowing philosophical framework within which all the problems of humanity might be understood and, once comprehended, dealt with for the collective welfare of all mankind.

The foundation of what became identified explicitly as the school of positivism emanated most importantly from the Frenchman Auguste Comte (1798–1857). Influenced in his youth by the pre-Marxian utopian socialism of such thinkers as Saint-Simon, he presented his classic work in the six-volume *Cours de philosophie positive* (1830–42). He was concerned with the creation of a new science of society and used the methodology of the physical and natural sciences. The approach was purely scientific, while the ingredients of transcendental metaphysics received minimal attention. In this work Comte first set forth his law of the three stages of philosophical thought: the theological, the metaphysical, and, at the culminating pinnacle, the positive. The first of these was characterized by a reliance upon the supernatural, with divine beings endowed with the capacity of explaining all occurrences. Second, the metaphysical was a supernatural being or God replaced by abstractions, by rational entities of various sorts. Climactically, the third or positive stage found man able to observe and understand facts in their empirical certainty.

In discussing the positive stage, Comte presented a general classification of the sciences, which developed from bottom to top in terms of the increasing complexity and difficulty of its subject matter. He placed mathematics at the bottom of this hierarchy, seeing it as more general and less complex than those above it. He then continued to move up through astronomy, physics, and a further succession of various of the sciences, until reaching the apex of the pyramid in sociology. It was sociology, wrote Comte, which, because it represented the observation of human facts and relationships, was the most advanced and most complicated of the many sciences. The peak of Comte's hierarchical classification was therefore sociology, and the Frenchman pursued his research and speculation within this general realm. It is from his speculation and theorizing on this level that Comte has become known as the father of modern sociology.

His particular concerns were those of order and progress. It was, indeed, this slogan that his followers and enthusiasts enshrined; the flag adopted later by the Brazilian republic, for example, contained these words in Portuguese in the center of the banner. Comte saw sociology as being divided into what he called social statics and social dynamics. The former referred to order, to the proper interaction between habit and tradition, between custom and practice. Social dynamics meant for him the development of society and his schema of the three stages of philosophical evolution, thereby representing the concept of progress. It was from the dependence upon this overarching system that Comte's influence in Europe was the greatest. Within this framework, his broader philosophical presuppositions were adopted by a great number of European intellectuals. Both Mill and Spencer were to rely upon it to varying degrees, and it was at first from Comte and later from his many disciples that the era of positivism and of science in human thought began to develop.

Following the publication of his *Cours de philosophie positive* by four years was his *Politique positive,* in which Comte attempted to create a new ethic through his so-called Religion of Humanity, based on the worship of the great benefactors of mankind. While criticizing the usual form and belief of Christian religion as belonging to the theological and to the metaphysical stages that preceded the positive, he advocated the adoption of a new kind of worship. This Religion of Humanity in effect embraced most of the external qualities of Roman Catholicism but without Christianity. In a philosophical sense, Comte attempted to establish himself as its high priest, presenting a kind of rationalized spiritualism that was to be guided by the tenets of positivism. During his later years Comte devoted himself increasingly to the advocacy of this pseudo religion, and in France as elsewhere his followers in many cases actually attempted to put it into practice, establishing several positivist temples dedicated to the Religion of Humanity. As will be noted later, this aspect of his teachings held little attraction in Latin America, although there were some efforts to develop it in Brazil. Generally, however, the Latin-American positivists were interested in Comte's broader theoretical statements, stressing his scientific emphasis on the achievement of order and progress in society.

Although Comte's major works appeared shortly before the midpoint of the 1800s, it was some years later when positivism became the intellectual vogue in Europe. Romantic liberalism remained strong until 1848, the year in which a series of liberal revolutions broke out in Europe, most of them ending in failure and defeat. However, by the 1850s there was a perceptible erosion of the aristocratic undertones of preceding years, and in the more advanced European nations the rise of a politically significant urban middle class was developing. The intellectual pull of positivism grew increasingly influential, even among some of the small circles of early socialism. Not long after the appearance of Comte's major works, the writings of Herbert Spencer (1820–1903) appeared on the scene, providing a contrast that was to prove attractive to Latin-American *pensadores*. Many regarded him as the leading philosopher of nineteenth-century evolutionism and the Darwinian doctrine of natural selection.

Looming large among the politically oriented works in his lengthy bibliography were *Social Statics* (1850) and *The Man Versus the State* (1884). Spencer believed that evolution would ultimately lead to the perfect society, in which a state of equilibrium between the individual and the social organism would exist and emphasized the importance of accumulated experience and its acquisition through the years. This led him to the position that the state should play a minimal role in society, a stance that clearly differed from that of the Comteans. The principle of *laissez faire* was to be applied in all areas of life and politics for, in the final analysis, evolution could do no wrong if only left alone.

In economic terms, the state should be prohibited from any and all intervention that might impinge upon private enterprise. With society reflecting an organismic growth toward the attainment of its ultimate perfection, he therefore led his followers away from the "scientific" authoritarianism that in some instances based itself on Comtean principles.

Consequently, those Latin Americans who were familiar with Spencerian thought sometimes reflected contradictory positions, especially with regard to the role of the state. Generally, however, they preferred the "scientific" direction of national authority while speaking vaguely of the concomitant evolutionary movement toward a higher condition of progress and material well-being for mankind. In the New World, political and socioeconomic problems, which to the surprise and disappointment of many *pensadores* had not vanished with the departure of the Spanish, led to the gradual adoption of positivism as a philosophical guide. The sense of failure that accompanied the early years of experience with the practice and institutions of constitutional democratic government had been interpreted by many as indicating the inapplicability of the North American model to the Latin-American political and cultural milieu.

Not only had existing political institutions proved unsatisfactory, but the removal of Spanish mercantilistic and monopolistic policies had not led to the expected economic development. In much of Latin America, it was recognized, a kind of insularity had grown up, with backward and primitive economies staggering along on their own, no better and sometimes even worse than they had been under colonial rule. A new set of social dynamics was also springing forth in some countries owing to the emancipation of Negro slaves. By mid-century, only Brazil and Spanish-controlled Cuba had failed to free their slaves, and labor problems had resulted in many places, along with sociological, occupational, and other conflicts. To such political, economic, and social difficulties were added the continuing frustrations of the unending conflict of Church and State. During the colonial period the distinctive position of the Church had made it a major instrument in material as well as spiritual affairs. Independence had failed to bring about a clear resolution of the situation. While the fight for freedom from Spain had been supported by a number of liberal ecclesiastics who desired that the Church conclude its political activities, much of the force behind this drive had been ineffectually dissipated. By mid-century, many of the Latin-American countries were still faced by the preeminent position of the Church in society and culture, even though its material wealth had diminished somewhat. The essentially reactionary political views that it continued to enunciate had driven many liberals into a blind and bitter opposition, which only added to frustrations and irritations.

Such, in brief, was the experience of Latin America in the years that followed the revolutionary wars, and it could scarcely have been better designed for receptivity to the scientific sociology of Comte and his successors. Probably nowhere in the world did the evolutionary, scientific thought of the European positivists become so popular with the governing class as in Latin America. At the same time, it inevitably acquired a peculiarly American flavor; moreover, the internal conditions of the individual countries varied in some ways, leading to a variety of different interpretations and applications. The Argentine, Chilean, Mexican, and Brazilian variants of positivism all had their distinctive features. But whatever the individual forms, Latin-American positivism became the core of intellectual and political thought in the last half of the century, reaching a pinnacle of popularity from 1880 to 1900. In Mexico it constituted the dominant philosophy of the *científicos*, who formulated official policy during much of the lengthy rule of Porfirio Díaz. In Brazil, positivism was virtually the official philosophy of the nation. Benjamín Constant founded a Positivist Society in 1871, and ten years later a positivist Temple of Humanity was founded—this the major exception to the general Latin-American rejection of Comte's Religion of Humanity.

The ruling classes found especially attractive the rationale behind the political aspects of Comtean positivism, which argued that government should be vested in those most capable of ruling. The popular franchise was not considered to be the best means for selecting rulers. This, rather, would be carried out by the positivist priesthood which, although not directly responsible to the people, was regarded as the servant of humanity and therefore concerned with the interests of the masses. Government was to be placed in the hands of socially minded bankers and businessmen chosen by the priesthood. Comte himself rather naïvely believed that bankers in particular were not a part of any vested interest, serving rather as intermediaries and therefore assuring impartiality in their rule. Those who governed in Latin America thus found appealing the contention that, by the application of the "scientific" outlook to national problems, a new and better life might be possible. Positivism became for many of them a justification in combating and opposing the radicalism of impatient reformers. This spirit was typified by the attitude of the Mexican government under Porfirio Díaz, which identified itself with positivism in undertaking scientific progress through gradual, orderly evolution rather than the revolutionary violence that obviously would have meant its loss of power, position, and wealth.

Positivism seemed to many Latin Americans to provide an explanation of things as they were, as well as a course of action for the amelioration of existing problems. The ruling class saw positivism as strengthening its authority through the idea that institutions should act as continuing guides toward gradual reforms. Nonrevolutionary in tenor, positivism seemed to be concerned with national specifics yet was couched in an impressive panoply of philosophical abstractions of a high order. It is misleading to imply, however, that Latin-American positivism was little more than an after-the-fact effort by the governing elite to justify its administration of public affairs. Intellectually, positivism appealed to many as a truly constructive rather than purely critical body of thought. After several decades of destructive criticism of Spain and colonial rule, it was time for a less negative kind of philosophical speculation; here too, positivism answered a genuine need in Latin America. Now, many intellectuals felt, they had something to contribute beyond the sheer fact of political emancipation that was now well into the past.

The philosophy of Comte, then, appeared on the Latin-American horizon with all the promise of a new and redeeming philosophy; although formulated in another world, it appeared suited to the needs of the New World. It was believed that positivism could impose a new intellectual order in place of that destroyed by past events, which had led to years of violence, instability, and virtual anarchy. The Latin Americans hopefully believed in this new ability to order the reality of life through positivism, achieving the kind of utopia that was supposedly to germinate and flourish following the removal of Spanish dominion. Now, they argued, all traces of the colonial heritage could be swept away, superseded by a philosophically oriented evolution that would lead to great spiritual and material accomplishment. Positivism, in each of the countries, would permit the eradication of national evils while enhancing the best qualities of the people.

With its mystical, magical promise of a better world, positivism meant somewhat different things in different countries. Mexico saw it as a means of ending the perpetual anarchy that had repeatedly swept the country since the winning of independence. Argentina believed that positivism would eliminate the absolutist, personalistic tendencies long exemplified by the *caudillistic* dictatorship of Juan Manuel Rosas. Uruguay felt it held moral qualities that might reduce military intervention in politics and endemic political corruption. In Chile, positivism promised to convert traditional ideas of political liberalism into reality. A few years later, Peru and Bolivia saw it as a framework for the rebuilding and reordering of national affairs and social policy in the wake of their national humiliation during the War of the Pacific with Chile. The

Cuban interpretation stressed positivism as a justification of their desire for independence from Spain. In each of these countries, positivism was regarded as particularly pertinent in the field of education, implying a removal of superstition and warped misconceptions inherited from the colonial legacy. The result would be the creation of a new Latin-American man, an individual capable of achievement in practical as well as aesthetic and intangible matters.

Latin-American adaptations of positivism, while often a reflection of Comtean dogma, in some cases owed a greater intellectual debt to the evolutionary modifications subsequently introduced by both Herbert Spencer and Charles Darwin. Especially in its Darwinian interpretation, it represented a belief in the evolutionary progress that would mean a transformation of social illness and political instability toward a healthy state of order and prosperity. As events were to prove, it indeed helped to provide greater political stability than had previously existed. In the countries with a large indigenous population, notably Mexico and the Andean states, the Comtean belief in the supremacy of the white race over all others was sometimes used as justification for a continued neglect of the Indians. Comte had maintained that the peoples of western Europe were superior in intelligence to nonwhite races, and especially in Mexico this part of his teachings was used as an excuse to ignore the problems of Indians and lowborn *mestizos*.

While positivism was seized upon by better-educated members of the elite as a means of strengthening their personal positions of material and political domination, it appealed at the same time to many intellectual reformers who saw it as a new and promising instrument for the attainment of their long-frustrated goals. Among these latter were intellectual freedom, which implied a destruction of the omnipresent spirit of Spain through an educational transformation of mind and character. Once this had been achieved, a given national citizenry would be capable of rising to the level of the great civilized nations, matching the material accomplishments of even the most advanced. A new order, neither colonial nor theological, would inevitably emerge. Based on scientific understanding of reality and an educated citizenry, it would bring industry, social welfare, and such material public works as roads, telegraphs, and communications. By the 1880s, then, much of the Latin-American intelligentsia was embued with optimism, and there was a deep-seated conviction that, through the science of positivism, liberty and unlimited progress were soon to be attained. By the end of the century, this optimism had given way to a disillusionment that brought about the defection of intellectuals, as happened with the precursors of the revolution in Mexico. For some years, however, positivism was enshrined as the panacea by which the peoples of Latin America were destined to achieve the greatness that had been denied them, first by Spanish colonial rule and then by the legacy that romantic liberalism had proved unable to dissipate.

Positivism in Mexico

Perhaps nowhere was the evolution of positivist influence more striking than in Mexico, where a succession of *pensadores* provided the intellectual framework within which the dictatorship of Porfirio Díaz found a fashionable philosophical rationale. The precursor of Mexican positivism, Ignacio Ramírez (1818–79), was illustrative of the mental framework of liberals of Mexico's reform period, although actually calling himself a positivist. Born in Guanajuato, Ramírez studied law and soon gained eminence through his unusual abilities. He first gained attention through the reading of a paper in the Academia de San Juan de Letrán under the title *No hay Dios: Los seres de la naturaleza se sostienen por si mismo.*[1] Denying the existence of God, Ramírez based his thesis on the principle that matter was indestructible and eternal, and that there was no need for a Creator. The result of this atheistic pronouncement was persecution and harassment from both conservative and liberal elements, but Ramírez resisted intimidation and continued to defend his ideas. He established a reputation as lawyer and journalist and subsequently held public office, holding the ministries of justice and of public education.

Described by his biographer, Ignacio Manuel Altamirano, as a Voltaire of his times,[2] Ramírez was a brillantly outspoken advocate of national progress. During his ministry of public instruction, he executed laws that embodied his strong anticlericalism and dealt a major blow to clerical influence in the educational system. His philosophical belief that matter is eternal was a result of his reading of Lucretius' *De rerum natura* which, in turn, emanated from Epicurus and the Greek atomists. Although an atheist, however, he was not in the orthodox sense an Epicurean, since we are told that Epicurus believed in the gods.[3] In all likelihood, Ramírez knew Epicurus only at second hand through the work of Lucretius. Scorning metaphysics and theology, he employed

1. For further discussion, see Ignacio Manuel Altamirano, *Biografía de Ignacio Ramírez* (México: Editora Nacional, 1889), p. 14.
2. *Ibid.*
3. Norman W. De Witt, *Epicurus and his Philosophy* (Minneapolis: University of Minnesota Press, 1954).

his materialism as a justification for attacking the Roman Catholic church. This materialism was wielded as an iconoclastic weapon against the political power of the clergy. As Altamirano noted, Ramírez was basically a materialist who "looked for truth in the reality of things."[4]

Ramírez' materialism helped to pave the way for true Mexican positivism, which emerged as less a new and complete philosophical view than a method and argument with which to combat the social power of religion. The struggle also extended to include all metaphysical conceptions and to everything connected with the survival of the colonial social order. It was this attitude that helps to explain the anticlericalism of the Mexican thinkers of the late reform period and the emergence of positivism in the country. The true initiator of Mexican positivism was Gabino Barreda (1820–81). Born in the town of Puebla, Barreda studied medicine in Mexico City before going abroad to continue his studies in Paris. There he became acquainted with Comte and his followers, later returning to Mexico a convinced positivist. When the French occupied Mexico City a few years later, Barreda fled to Guanajuato and did not return until after the fall of Maximilian's empire. That same year, 1867, Barreda delivered his *Oración cívica* in which he outlined the evolution of Mexican history. Following Comte, he described it in terms of the theological, metaphysical, and positivist stages. The first of these was the colonial epoch, the second the war of independence against Spain, and the third the victory of Benito Juárez and his reformers over the incursions of foreign invaders. Juárez' Liberal party, he proclaimed, would fulfill the historic responsibility of introducing positivism into Mexico, under the slogan of "Liberty, Order and Progress."

As Juárez set about his plans to reform the nation, Barreda's positivism fitted admirably into the political mood of the leadership. Barreda's demand for national reconstruction along scientific lines was attractive, and Juárez soon called upon him to mount a campaign of intellectual emancipation. So it was that Barreda in the educational field assumed a position that was to orient public instruction along positivist lines and pave the way for a generation of positivist intellectuals. The anticlerical Juárez and his counselors had already initiated strong measures against the Roman Catholic church, having previously disestablished it while nationalizing Church property. Now the need to break the traditional Church monopoly on education made possible the introduction

4. Ignacio Ramírez, *Obras* II (México: n.p., 1889), p. 529. For a more recent collection, see *Obras de Ignacio Ramírez*, 2 Vols. (México: Editora Nacional, 1952).

of sweeping reforms under the guidance of Gabino Barreda and a lesser-known positivist, Pedro Contreras. In December, 1867, a law was promulgated creating a series of primary and secondary lay schools throughout the country, while Church schools at the same time were banned. This law also created the Escuela Nacional Preparatoria in Mexico, with Barreda its director. The school's curriculum followed Comtean philosophy closely, with such "nonscientific" subjects as metaphysics and classical languages eliminated. Regardless of the professional careers for which the students were being trained, the curriculum remained the same. Barreda served more than ten years as head of the school before resigning to accept a diplomatic post in Germany.

In outlining the educational policies that he pursued, Barreda held in mind his image of the state as the "guardian of material order." That social order, originating in the mind of the educated, would appropriately be limited by the directives of the state. Only thereby might true liberty be possible for all. "I hope that in the future a complete freedom of conscience, an absolute freedom of exposition and discussion which will admit all ideas and all inspirations, will shed its light everywhere and will make every disturbance that is not spiritual and every revolution that is not intellectual unnecessary and impossible. . . . I hope that the material order, preserved at all costs by those who govern and respected by the governed, will be a sure guarantee and a safe way by which to continue ever on the happy road to progress and civilization."[5] Barreda's "material order" envisioned a government that would see that the rights of the people would be respected. Having been critical of the privileged classes in years past, he added that the state, in the interests of society, should limit the material wealth of the individual. Since he believed that wealth was a function of society, he did not advocate, as had Comte, that the state should actively intervene. Rather, he argued that the wealthy had a moral responsibility to contribute to the common good and common progress.

Barreda, whose positivism was in advance of the more traditional ideas of many around Juárez, found himself in sharp disagreement with them on several occasions. A continuing dispute centered on the definition of freedom. The liberals were suspicious of the possible authoritarian impulses behind the positivist emphasis on order; some of their leaders feared a possible dogmatism as rigid as that of the Church. Barreda argued heatedly that the positivist concept of freedom was not incom-

5. Gabino Barreda, *Opúsculos, discusiones y discursos,* as quoted in Leopoldo Zea, *The Latin-American Mind,* tr. James H. Abbott and Lowell Dunham (Norman: University of Oklahoma Press, 1963), p. 278.

patible with order. What it implied was a submission to the controlling law of order, wholeheartedly entered into by the citizen. He denied that form of freedom that meant the right to do anything, regardless of the dictates of law and social custom. The true freedom saw man as limited by the society that gave him laws, while his freedom consisted in obeying them.[6]

Barreda left no important written work; his single best-known exposition was his 1867 *Oración cívica*. His greatest contribution was undoubtedly his educational reform. José Vasconcelos, who was among the leading critics of positivism after the turn of the century, remarked nonetheless that "the positivism of Barreda had the virtue of having restored modern science in our secondary school system."[7] Barreda represented the educational ideas of positivism in Mexico, and after his death, the new generation trained in the Escuela Nacional Preparatoria applied his ideas to government and politics, opening another phase of positivist influence. The contemporary Mexican Leopoldo Zea has written that Barreda and the early orthodox positivists thought of Comte's teaching as a doctrine, while later the political positivists considered it only as a method to be applied to Mexican reality.[8] The method was used to rationalize the political position of the positivists and to support the government of Porfirio Díaz. Almost totally an orthodox Comtean positivist, Barreda even accepted the Frenchman's Religion of Humanity. Only a few of his disciples continued this aspect of Barreda's teaching, most notably Porfirio Parra and Agustín Aragón.

For a full quarter-century, Comtean positivism as shaped by the teachings and works of Gabino Barreda guided the thought of educated Mexicans. The students were in most cases the children of the rich, either *criollo* or *mestizo;* the children of the poor did not attend the preparatory school, not being expected to follow a professional career. As Schulman has noted, "They were the first generation of well-to-do Mexicans that were educated in the laic tradition. They were at the same time race-conscious, money-conscious and Comte-conscious."[9] There were also important influences from Herbert Spencer, with evolutionary theory also a factor in the thinking of many whose careers were shaped by study under Barreda. The Spencerian opposition to a coercive state was appeal-

6. *Ibid.,* p. 279.
7. José Vasconcelos, *Historia del pensamiento filosófico* (México: Ediciones de la Universidad, 1937).
8. Leopoldo Zea, *Apogeo y decadencia del positivismo en México* (México: El Colegio de México, 1944).
9. Sam Schulman, "A Study of the Political Aspects of Positivism in Mexico" (Master's thesis, University of New Mexico, 1949).

ing to those who saw an authoritarian strain underlying much of Comte's philosophy. With Spencer, there was a desire for a state that would protect the individuals who comprised society. The Spencerian image of progress suggested an ideal of freedom that was less restricted than that of Comte.

The students of Barreda differed with his teachings in maintaining that Mexican society had not yet reached the positivist stage to the extent requisite for the full enjoyment of individual freedoms. While deeply concerned over the liberty of the individual citizen, they felt that social evolution had not yet progressed sufficiently for the achievement of civic responsibility by the populace. As a consequence, stress was placed upon the importance of material advancement. Mexico, it was argued, was not yet truly modern, thus the immediate task was to create a strong state capable of promoting economic development. Only then would the social order be equipped to accept the fullest enjoyment of individual freedom. Society remained heterogeneous in Mexico, and the state had yet to establish it as fully integrated and homogeneous. Once Mexico succeeded in ordering affairs away from the traditional turbulence and near anarchy of preceding years, Spencerian laws of progress could be meaningfully applied. First, however, that order would have to be won; only then could true freedom develop.

The application of Comtean thought to political affairs became the work of a number of Barreda's disciples, who later became known as the *científicos*—the scientific ones. Political positivism came into prominence after Porfirio Díaz won the presidency in 1876, although the term *científicos* was not widely used until the 1890s. The group was not an organized political party but, rather, an elite who influenced the President and supported his inclination to rule with a rod of iron. Of Comte's idealism and utopianism, the group retained only the "scientific," while popular sovereignty allowing the masses to pass judgment on the government was "nonscientific."[10] Especially in its formative years, the *científico* group voiced its views in the columns of the newspaper *La Libertad*, which bore on its masthead the positivist slogan "order and progress." The emphasis of its writings was placed largely on order rather than progress, in keeping with its political proclivities. Stressing repeatedly the importance of education, the contributors to *La Libertad* staunchly maintained that anarchy would have to be curbed and the obligation to observe the laws ingrained in the public mind before individual liberty might be fully realized.

It was in 1892 that these positivists acquired their informal name.

10. *Ibid.,* pp. 78–80.

That year a political group known as the Liberal Union proclaimed a manifesto to the nation supporting the fourth re-election of Porfirio Díaz. Presenting a platform designed to appeal to the growing Mexican *bourgeoisie,* the manifesto spoke of "scientifically" analyzing social conditions and problems in Mexico. Opponents spoke of the signers of the manifesto scornfully as the *partido de los científicos,* and thus the name was born. The proclamation was significant in that it called for the granting of fuller freedom to Mexican society in view of the material progress that had developed. Moreover, the internal order that the Díaz government had achieved made it possible to further the granting of individual liberty. "We believe that just as peace and material progress have attained this objective [e.g., a new historical era], it now falls to the lot of political activity to consolidate order; it is its turn to demonstrate that from this day hence rebellion and civil war will be an accident, and peace based on the interest and will of a people are normal; to obtain this, it is necessary to place peace on the touchstone of freedom."[11]

Mexicans, it was declared, were now ready for a new set of freedoms. These did not, however, include the popular franchise. There were other freedoms that, at the time, were more important; primary among these was freedom of commerce and the abolition of internal customs duties. This would constitute an economic freedom to accumulate capital. The *científicos* were therefore advocating a reduction of state intervention in the economic field, but not yet in the political. Díaz' administration of the political order was henceforth to encourage the economic freedom of the bourgeoisie, while political rights remained secondary. All of this supported the importance of re-electing Porfirio Díaz. The republic was "aware that it is the effective cause of the nation's progress and tranquillity, but it knows that a man has helped, in the first place, to give a practical form to the general tendencies, and this citizen is the one the convention has chosen . . . to occupy the presidency again!"[12]

At the head of the *científicos* were Justo Sierra, Francisco Bulnes, José Yves Limantour, Agustín Aragón, and Porfirio Parra. All of these men were either products of the Escuela Nacional Preparatoria or, in practical terms, followers of Gabino Barreda. Sierra and Bulnes provided the philosophical direction, Limantour advised Díaz as his most trusted and powerful lieutenant, while Aragón and Parra helped to protect the

11. Zea, *Latin-American Mind,* p. 286. It should be remarked that this translation of Zea's *Dos etapas del pensamiento en hispanoamérica,* first published in 1949, is the single best English source on Latin-American positivism.
12. The manifesto of Unión Liberal appeared in the volume by Antonio Manero, *El antiguo régimen y la revolución* (México: n.p., 1911).

political front. To varying degrees they were eclectic positivists who derived inspiration from Spencer and John Stuart Mill as well as Comte; Limantour in particular used positivism for his own political advancement. The importance of Sierra and Bulnes was especially noteworthy as philosophical defenders of the *porfiriato*, as Díaz' regime became known. Both men achieved genuine intellectual distinction, however, and are worthy of consideration as important *pensadores* in the Mexico of the 1880s and 1890s. Sierra was perhaps the more influential of the two, serving officially and otherwise as the leading authority on education during the Díaz years.

Justo Sierra (1848–1912) was born in Campeche, Yucatán, and completed his education in the capital city, where he later taught history at the Escuela Nacional Preparatoria. For a time he served as Díaz' minister of education, and he edited several different journals. His greatest material contribution was the re-establishment of the National University as an integrated institution. Previously, the several different professional schools had existed as independent economic units. Poet, novelist, and prolific propagandist of *científico* thought, Sierra's more important writings were *Historia patria* (1898) and *Evolución política del pueblo mexicano* (1910),[13] which became a near classic. Based largely on his lectures at the Escuela Nacional Preparatoria, the work set forth his positivist reading of Mexican history. Society was described as a living organism, which evolves and is transformed with the passing of time. The colonial era had ended in creating new personalities or nations that lacked the knowledge necessary to govern themselves. The legacy of Spanish administrative despotism left in Mexico many of the same weaknesses that had existed before the coming of independence. The result was an endless succession of civil wars that prevented either material or moral growth.

Only slowly did an intellectual nucleus come to recognize the problems demanding resolution. This was especially true in the economic sphere. "The economic problem . . . stood out clearly before their eyes, and they understood that it was necessary to undertake its solution, relying upon these principles: that Mexico, because of the lack of means for developing her natural resources, is one of the poorest countries of the globe, and that the spirit of adventure is a form of energy which needs to be channeled by force into labor. If the problem is so understood, its resolution demands the adoption of a policy completely opposite to

13. Justo Sierra, *Evolución política del pueblo mexicano* (México: La Casa de España en México, 1940).

that of conquering Spain, raising all barriers both internal and external."[14] The proper approach to this, as to other problems, was positivist. Moving beyond the anti-Spanish attitude that is evident above, Sierra nonetheless insisted upon the total elimination of the influence of Spanish culture in Mexico, condemning clericalism while defending the financial oligarchy that supported President Díaz. He also turned his attention to racial explanations, although somewhat ambivalent in his attitude toward the Indian. His discussions of educational policy resembled those of Barreda, although reflecting a strain of evolutionary thought that was scarcely noticeable in his predecessor. A political conservative, Sierra advocated "practical liberty" based on domestic order, but without the abstract notion of freedom that many positivists expressed.

Sierra's contemporary, Francisco Bulnes (1849–1924), was an iconoclastic controversialist who did not fall neatly into prevailing positivist patterns. He was regarded in his day, nevertheless, as among the leading *cientificos,* and in the political sphere he maintained that a science of government existed which must be understood by those who ruled. Bulnes began with the not unusual conviction that the nation had inherited destructive tendencies from the Spanish. Believing that miscegenation was leading to the substitution of the *mestizo* for the Indian and the *criollo,* he demanded a society based on the economic interests of all. National unity required the harmonious relationship of all social classes, whereby the qualities of truth and justice might be enhanced. Blind patriotism was inadequate; what Mexico needed was a scientifically rational economic policy that would raise the material well-being of all. The majority of Mexicans were little more than barbarians, yet contained within themselves the traits that, with proper direction, might be elevated to a civilized level.[15]

Politically the most immediately influential of the positivists was José Yves Limantour (1854–1935). Born in Mexico City, he became one of Barreda's most ardent admirers while studying at the Escuela Nacional Preparatoria and later took a law degree from the National School of Jurisprudence. After a brief trip to Europe, he returned to Mexico and began a career as writer, financier, and politician. Between 1878 and 1884 he served on the editorial board of the *cientifico* newspaper *La Libertad.* Elected national deputy in 1880, he was appointed to a commission with the responsibility of studying the instability of the national

14. *Ibid.,* p. 188.
15. Francisco Bulnes, *Las grandes mentiras de nuestra historia* (México and Paris: La vida de C. Bouret, 1904), and *Los grandes problemas de México,* rev. ed. (México: Editora Normal, 1952).

currency. His great financial ability attracted the attention of the president, and he became in time the virtual economic master of Mexico, serving as minister of finance for eighteen years. He agreed with his fellow positivists in the application of scientific principles to administrative problems and looked down upon *mestizos* and Indians as inferior. His admiration of North American and European economic achievement led him to plan a reconstruction of its economy. Foreign capital was regarded as necessary for the financing of development, and Limantour's advice led Díaz to negotiate a series of agreements with outside investors. By 1910, it was estimated that fully half the worth of the economy was in North American hands.

Through Limantour's influence, Mexico adopted a variety of important economic measures, including the consolidation of the foreign debt, the establishment of the gold standard, and the building of railroads and assorted public works. The regime also concentrated on the strengthening of agriculture in the production of export crops; this resulted in the encouragement of large *haciendas* that extended the state of servitude under which the Mexican *campesino* lived. The brilliant success of Limantour's financial and economic policies brought Mexico a long distance from its pre-Díaz backwardness, while the dictator's ruthless crushing of opposition provided the order within which material progress might evolve. With the passing of time, however, the tightly knit establishment of the day grew increasingly stagnant; the upper classes and foreign business interests were the only ones to benefit from economic growth. As the *pax porfiriana* aged, it also grew increasingly bureaucratized and unimaginative, both unable and unwilling to recognize the growing discontent that was to burst forth in the great revolutionary movement that toppled the *porfiriato* in 1911.[16]

The influence of positivism in Mexico was as great as anywhere else in Latin America, coinciding as it did with an important era in the unfolding of Mexican history and the search for genuine nationhood. The excesses of the Diáz regime, especially in its latter years, have tended to obscure the favorable aspects. In combination with the political and military talents of the president, positivism succeeded in eradicating the endemic turbulence of the preceding half-century. Through the educational policies of such men as Barreda and Sierra, it brought about the professional training of a generation of competent public administrators who were at least the equal and in most cases clearly superior to their counterparts elsewhere in the hemisphere. And although the fruits of positivist economic policies did little for the mass of the citizenry,

16. See Chapter 7, pp. 209–27.

they helped to attract capital sufficient for the initiation of industrial development, which was to prove an asset to the revolutionary leaders who were to follow. Philosophically, the Mexican positivists typified the tendency of the movement to regard itself as the holder of the ultimate truths whereby an unprecedentedly prosperous and modern society would be created. As was the case elsewhere, however, the positivists found themselves more concerned with the "order" than the "freedom" of Comtean writings. In Mexico this meant, over a period of time, a perceptible shift from the libertarian outlook of Juárez and the reform to the enforced subservience of the masses under Díaz.

The Diffusion of Positivism

Brazil and the Coming of Republicanism / Elsewhere in the hemisphere, the configurations of positivism varied substantially from one country to the next. The Brazilian experience was especially striking, for it embraced certain elements of positivism which were not widely accepted elsewhere, notably the Comtean exposition of the Religion of Humanity. As in Mexico, positivism for a time enjoyed the status of an official state doctrine, although proving short lived. The historical bases for positivism in Brazil differed sharply from those in the Hispanic nations, however, and these are crucial to an understanding of the effort to adapt positivism to its own peculiar circumstances. The latter part of the colonial period saw a relative degree of intellectual stagnation, although the arrival of the Portuguese royal family in Rio de Janeiro in the early 1800s brought about notable change. Intellectual activity grew slowly through the coming of independence, the establishment of an empire, and the elevation of a new emperor, Dom Pedro II, in 1838. Coming to the throne while a child, Dom Pedro's own intellectual breadth was not fully apparent until the 1850s, at which time cultural and intellectual ferment in Brazil became more evident.

Education, although not as advanced as in Chile and Argentina, began to progress. The emperor's own interest was important, as reflected in his statement that he might have become a schoolteacher had he not succeeded to the throne. Dom Pedro II was also enthusiastic in supporting such activities as the Brazilian Historical and Geographical Institute, which became one of the most advanced such groups in Latin America. Less a scholar than a highly curious intellectual dilettante, he nevertheless helped to provide the impetus to educational and mental development. Thus, the advent of positivism fell upon a land in which serious philosophical speculation had been slight, and the small number of educated

Brazilians responded eagerly to the promise of an all-embracing doctrine. Among the first manifestations of positivism was the presentation at the military school in Rio de Janeiro which outlined certain positivist ideas. Indeed, the central technical and the military schools were among the first educational institutions to show a growing adherence to positivism.

The first true Brazilian positivist publication, according to the scholar Fernando de Azevedo, was the *Elementos de matemática* by Muniz de Aragão in 1858, although more than a decade passed before the Comtean influence became widespread. Tobias Barreto showed positivistic inclinations in his *A religão perante a psicologia* (1868), although turning to German idealism later in life. In *As tres filosofias* (1874), Luis Pereira Barreto introduced Comte to the Brazilian public in detail. Texeira Mendes was one of the most influential exponents of orthodox positivism in his *Primeiros ensaios positivistas* (1877) and, together with Miguel Lemus, was a follower of the Religion of Humanity that still has some churches in Brazil today. As the literature of positivism gradually accumulated, it came to reflect the same divisions that developed in Europe and especially in France following the death of Comte in 1857.[17]

One group of disciples followed Comte's philosophy without qualification and may be called orthodox. Under the leadership of Pierre Lafitte, this group accepted Comte's theory of the religious and political organization of society as well as the cult of humanity with its worship, feast days, and sacraments. A second group, under the guidance of Maximilien Paul Emile Littré, rejected Comte's political and religious ideas, retaining only the scientific and sociological part of his teachings. This same division took place among Brazilian positivists. The group to which Miguel Lemus and Texeira Mendes belonged followed Lafitte's interpretations, while the faculty of the military school, directed by Benjamín Constant Botelho de Magalhães, preferred the more selective approach to Comte's ideas as represented by Littré. It was from the instruction at the military school that Brazilian positivism was largely derived and developed, much as was the case of Barreda's Escuela Nacional Preparatoria in Mexico.

The tendency in early positivist writings was toward a high level of abstraction in which complex philosophical inquiry was largely unrelated in any substantive way to national problems. The first concrete area

17. For a detailed analysis of Brazilian positivism, see Chapter 5, "The Advent of Positivism," pp. 82–176, in João Cruz Costa, *A History of Ideas in Brazil: The Development of Philosophy in Brazil and the Evolution of National History*, tr. Suzette Macedo (Berkeley and Los Angeles: University of California Press, 1964).

to which Brazilian positivism turned its attention was religion. The orthodox positivists naturally argued for the replacement of Catholicism by the Religion of Humanity. The prevailing view held that the Church influence was decadent and feudal; nothing less than its complete eradication from Brazil would suffice. The Church provided a ready target for this early positivist effort to relate Comtean beliefs to practical matters, for it had become embroiled in a series of disputes that had weakened its authority and prestige. The issue of freemasonry had become a burning political issue, with lay orders known as *irmandades* or "brotherhoods" expanding in size and including Freemasons among their ranks. Initially, anticlericalism was not an important factor; it was illustrative that when, in 1865, the Pope announced an encyclical ban on Freemasonry, the Catholic emperor refused to permit its publication in Brazil. Furthermore, when two Brazilian bishops forbade church members to maintain their Freemasonry, Dom Pedro II ordered their imprisonment for going against his wishes.

The Brazilian positivists therefore found a somewhat mixed if increasingly agitated situation in the dispute over the Church. They offered positivism as a doctrine capable of replacing the kind of intellectual and educational role customarily exercised by the Church. Thus Brazil soon became the first and, as it developed, the only Latin American country to accept the Religion of Humanity and to establish Temples of Humanity. The growth of these institutions and an expanding membership gave significant impetus to the positivist movement, and by 1880 it emerged as one of the country's major forces. In 1880 the positivists held a national conference in Rio de Janeiro which was followed by a "civic procession," at which the official Flag of Humanity was displayed for the first time. The following year the Positivist Society in the capital celebrated a Festival of Humanity, with public sermons and speeches commemorating the opening of a new Temple of Humanity. Before the close of 1881 an official Positivist Church of Brazil had been organized, with branches sprouting in various cities.

Through the decade of the 1880s the positivists were increasingly active on the political front. They took a highly conspicuous position on the growing debate over slavery, which had been growing in intensity for years. Such legislation as the Rio Branco Law of 1871 was gradually moving the country in the direction of abolition,[18] but progress was not rapid enough to satisfy the advocates of absolute and immediate

18. Among other things, the Rio Branco Law said that all children born to slave mothers would be free. This was characteristic of the slow-moving legislative approach to the eradication of slavery in Brazil.

emancipation of all slaves, and the positivists were among the most vocal. In discussing the nature of society and culture in Brazil, they considered at length the proper place of the Negro in society. While their position was less than forthright egalitarianism, they nonetheless concluded that slavery should be outlawed at once. Added to the positivist agitation over this issue was its role in the growing controversy over the respective virtues of monarchical or republican forms of government. Dom Pedro II was an honored and revered personage who represented a father figure for much of the country, and even the outspoken critics of imperial rule avoided attacks on his person. At the same time, the cry for an end to monarchy mounted, and the positivists were among the vanguard of those demanding institutional change.

As early as 1870 the positivists had begun to publish in their newspaper a justification of republican governmental forms. The columns of the first issue of *A República,* in fact, included a "Republican Manifesto" calling for an end to the empire. Advocating a positivist republic, they proposed a highly centralized and implicitly authoritarian regime. They were not concerned over a representative democratic system but with the replacement of the hereditary imperial dynasty of civilian leaders. The positivists were not, unlike some Brazilians, advocating the removal of Dom Pedro II in order to create a more representative or popular regime. What they demanded was a well-ordered centralized government that, over a period of time, could help to bring about rational socioeconomic and cultural progress. As the positivist campaign attacked the emperor with increasing fervor, nonpositivist forces also added their criticisms of the regime. Young military officers, many of them trained at the military school, also rebelled against the prospect of serving under an empress, since Dom Pedro's only heir was a daughter, Isabel. The fact that she had married a foreigner—a nephew of France's Louis Napoleon—helped things not at all.

The positivist teachings of the military school were important, and the focal person was Benjamín Constant Botelho de Magalhães, who for years was its director. A heterodox positivist with a variety of ideas somewhat unsystematically gleaned from various European philosophers, Constant shared the mounting concern over the general disorder of society, the lack of education and the relative paucity of intellectual enlightenment. For him, the overthrow of the empire seemed the important first step toward a drastic transformation of the *status quo.* Constant and influential military leaders therefore co-operated in the movement against the aging emperor, and in November, 1889, he was deposed and shipped into exile. The ambitious leader of the revolutionaries, General Manoel Deodoro de Fonseca, assumed collective leadership of the new regime with Floriano Peixoto and Benjamín Constant, organizing a provisional government that rapidly approved several broadly liberal measures, including the official separation of Church and State. A constituent assembly was convoked and the charter of the first Brazilian republic went into effect in February of 1891. The assembly proclaimed Constant the founder of the republic as a tribute to his services, and the new republican flag included the motto "Ordem e Progreso"—Order and Progress—at its center.

It was during this period of early republicanism that the philosophy of positivism played an important and direct role in the political life of the country. Although the famed jurist Rui Barbosa[19] denied that positivism was such a strong influence at the founding of the republic,[20] its real importance was clear. Fernando de Azevedo has explained that, although the republic did not owe its existence to positivism, this doctrine exercised a moderating and conservative influence that helped to establish and preserve sound republican institutions. "The demagogic republicanism in which the new regime was struggling met, in fact, in the armed classes, in the Church and in positivism, some of the principal points of resistance to its expansive force."[21] As minister of education in the early republican era, Constant created a new program of instruction that reflected his positivist ideas. He introduced in the normal and secondary schools a curriculum based on a series of abstract sciences that followed Comte's classification, doing away with the traditions of classical education that had previously predominated. The program was less productive than were the reforms of Barreda in Mexico, at least in part because Brazil did not face the Mexican problem of freeing education from a strong Church monopoly. Moreover, Constant's educational reforms met with strong opposition, and modifications were soon forced upon him.

The Brazilian break from the empire was clean and bloodless; it was more a barracks revolt than a popular uprising, and there was more than a little public consternation at the departure of Dom Pedro II. The subsequent rule of Deodoro and then of Peixoto was marked by a few years of confusion, and regularized civilian control was not established until the turn of the century. The positivist influence on govern-

19. For a discussion of Barbosa's thought, see Chapter 5, pp. 167–69.
20. Rui Barbosa, *Discursos e conferencias* (Porto: Emprêsa litteraria e typographica, 1907.
21. Fernando de Azevedo, *Brazilian Culture: An Introduction to the Study of Culture in Brazil,* tr. William Rex Crawford (New York: Macmillan Co., 1950), pp. 159–61.

ment was short-lived and then went into decline. The crusading zeal of Constant and others did not long survive the introduction of republican government, and by the turn of the century the philosophical zenith of positivism was past. Its influence during the accumulation of pressures against the empire had been important, however, as had its impact on the officer corps. Moreover, positivism was the first recognizable philosophical school to emerge forcefully in Brazil, and as such, it provided impetus to the self-awareness of the country's intelligentsia. Also, it was a formative contribution to the thinking of one of the country's most revered literary figures, Euclydes da Cunha.

Educated in Rio de Janeiro, Euclydes da Cunha (1866–1909) came early under the influence of Benjamín Constant. Later he received more specialized training at the Escola Militar de Praia Vermelha, which included a large measure of positivist thought. In 1896 he concluded a brief military career to become a civil engineer, and this took him to the state of São Paulo during the Canudos revolt. Da Cunha was sent by the newspaper *Estado de São Paulo* to report on a military expedition to subdue a revolt by the rural populace. The result of this experience was the publication in 1902 of his *Os sertões*,[22] a masterpiece of representative Brazilian thought and literature. The boldness and vigor of da Cunha's writing was also illustrated by such later works as *Contrastes e confrontos* (1907) and *A Margem da história* (1909). In each of these works, the Brazilian responded to the heroic peoples of the backlands, and these *sertanejos* he described as the "bedrock of the Brazilian race."

Os sertões was a narrative of a land and a people seemingly without a history, and yet representative of an important segment of Brazilian life and culture. In presenting life in the interior, da Cunha showed his skill as a geographer, historian, and social observer. While the lot of the *sertanejos* was primitive and brutal, it was not without its redeeming features. The *sertanejos* themselves were depicted as a new ethnic group, formed of a mixture of European, Negro, and Indian traits under the distinctive conditioning circumstances of the tropical environment. The harsh climatic and geographic extremes had given birth to a new race, one which for da Cunha typified the inherent courage and vitality of Brazil. The leader of the backlands rebels was portrayed as a messianic figure for a new race in need of spiritual leadership. Although the author provided a scrupulously objective and realistic analysis of social conditions, he went beyond this in the quest for the true Brazilian. Da Cunha

22. For the English version, see Euclydes da Cunha, *Rebellion in the Backlands*, tr. Samuel Putnam (Chicago: University of Chicago Press, 1943).

exemplified a strong spirit of nationalistic pride, and the peoples of the cities and littoral population centers were held responsible for the backwardness of the interior. Echoing a mystical belief that contributed more than fifty years later to the construction of the new national capital of Brasília in the midst of a wilderness, he argued that Brazil's future as a great nation would be the result of the integration of the rural masses into the national mainstream.

Da Cunha's timeless description of the rebellion at Canudos reflected the approach to social problems of a man trained in positivism, yet it sharply contrasted with the attitude of many Mexican *científicos* toward the Indians in that country. His narrative has survived the onslaught of time to stand as one of the true classics of Brazilian and Latin American literature. It also promoted an intensified study of the peoples of the interior which in time produced more than a generation of interpreters of Brazilian cultural and ethnic factors. In a work that was at once a literary gem and a scientific description of life as observed in the *sertão,* da Cunha infused his writing with an intangible spirit that has survived in Brazil. He helped to tear down the narrow provincialism of urban intellectuals, holding up the promise of a new national life drawing energy and vitality from the largely untapped potential of the interior. By so doing, he opened to Brazilian minds a vision of future greatness that has been magnified as this century has unfolded. Of few men in Latin American can this be said.

Voices of Positivism in Chile and Argentina / As positivist ideas reached the lands of southern South America, individual interpretations were filtered through existing social and political conditions. Such was the case in Chile, where its first important exponent was José Victorino Lastarria; the movement, although never as influential politically in Chile as in Brazil or Mexico, proved to be durable, with its last significant exponent, Valentín Letelier, living well into the twentieth century. During the earlier period in Chile, positivism remained close to traditional liberalism, although the ideas of Comte were enthusiastically disseminated. This was not surprising in view of Chilean intellectual development in the years following independence. By mid-century the country had passed through three decades of conservative domination, with nationalistic pride justly based on economic progress, a strong educational system, a relatively homogeneous population, and a small but competent navy to defend its interests.

José Victorino Lastarria (1817–88) attended the University in Santiago, where he studied under Andrés Bello, receiving a degree in law. For several years he was professor of literature and law at the National Institute of Santiago and later taught at the university. The founder of the School of Law and Political Science, he served for years as its dean. On several occasions he was elected to congress and also occupied high diplomatic posts. In addition he found time to acquire considerable public reputation; always interested in national affairs, he strongly believed that, as an educator and scholar, it was his duty to put his ideas into practice. He was an important figure in the Chilean intellectual transition from romantic liberalism to positivism, and by the 1860s his writings were among the most influential in the country. Although an articulate advocate of Comtean views, Lastarria did not accept all of these teachings, preferring a selective adoption of those doctrines that he felt most applicable to Chilean reality.[23]

Lastarria's first important work was published while he was still a young man. In *Elementos de derecho público constitucional* (1846) he showed his early affinity for Comte, largely in his interpretation of history and his belief in progress. Lastarria differentiated between man's sentiments and his intelligence. Sentiment or feeling was described as a conservative drive strengthening the attachment of the individual to things familiar and useful, while intelligence was based on reason, impelling man toward a change of his environment in order to bring about progress. The early societies, he wrote, were dominated by feelings, but in a modern society intelligence should predominate. Feelings were based on customs, intelligence on law; progress, therefore, was dependent upon the predominance of law over custom and tradition.

The young Chilean also differentiated between society and the state. The latter represented an association of men for the enforcement of the law, coexisting with other human associations which had other aims, such as religion, science, or industry. The state dealt only with the political aspects of society. To confuse the aim of the state—the enforcement of the law—with the rest of society was to create political despotism. Law, in Lastarria's view, dealt only with the external aspects of human behavior and therefore should not interfere with its inner life, which he reserved for religion, ethics, and philosophy. The state had the right to use its authority only to enforce the law but was not to become involved in economics, morality, culture, or religion. At this early point in his intellectual formation, Lastarria was merely introducing the early

23. José Victorino Lastarria, *Obras completas* (Santiago: Imp. Barcelona, 1906–14).

glimmerings of positivism, while remaining close to the traditional liberals in Chile. Comtean ideas did not become pronounced until later years, especially with the publication in 1874 of his *Lecciones de política positiva*.

Essentially, Lastarria saw as the important contribution of Comte his emphasis on the scientific bases of social organization, while rejecting the Frenchman's religious and political views. Lastarria regarded the Religion of Humanity as spiritually and philosophically absurd and believed that the application of positivism to politics threatened a despotism of the new order. A libertarian in the tradition of Chilean liberalism, he disagreed with Comte's public praise of the 1851 coup of Louis Napoleon in France and also differed with his praise of the Russian czar as an enlightened statesman. The state was responsible for service to the purposes and needs of individual freedom and, Lastarria believed, should go no further than protecting national independence while assuring domestic peace and order. The state was not to disregard liberty and freedom but should preserve a situation within which individual rights might be enjoyed.

In this same context, Lastarria objected to certain positivist elements in the writings of John Stuart Mill.[24] Despite the impassioned defense of individual freedom by the Englishman, Lastarria believed that Mill erred in maintaining that the state should enjoy the authority to intervene, if necessary, to prevent one person from harming another. This implied a reduction of individual freedoms before state power, with only the state having the capacity to judge its own application of justice. Lastarria's reading of Mill led him to believe that it was fallacious to undertake a reconciliation of progress with order. He regarded the two as being in direct conflict with one another. The social and political aims of the state should not emphasize both order and progress, for this merely encouraged the ever present dangers of absolutism. *Lecciones de política positiva* further underlined Lastarria's belief that politics was but a branch of the science of law, which in turn was a part of sociology. Politics should be based on accurate and scientifically verified knowledge of the society to which it applied. A correct knowledge of all existing social institutions of a country was indispensable to the formulation of a proper theory of its political organization. In this Lastarria clearly mirrored the sociological aspects of Comte's thought, but this was always tempered by his basic belief in individual freedom as inalienable.

The philosophy of Lastarria, then, was in many ways positivist but at the same time embraced only certain elements of Comtean thought. However, for years before the death of Lastarria, a younger generation

24. For a fuller discussion, consult Zea, *Latin-American Mind,* pp. 140–44.

of Chilean *pensadores* was expanding and extending the intellectual applications of positivism to national reality. In the years following 1860, the intelligentsia increasingly adopted positivism as the foundation for the creation of a new and different state. Several different schools of analysis existed, and the convolutions of their running debate cannot be traced in detail. Broadly speaking, however, it is possible to view the division as lying between orthodox and unorthodox positivists. Among the former group, the Lagarrigue brothers, Jorge, Luis, and Juan Enrique, were prominent in upholding a full and unqualified acceptance of Comte's political and sociological teachings. Jorge Lagarrigue in particular was an exponent of original positivism, and after years of debate, he also convinced Juan Enrique of the applicability of the entire fabric of Comtean writing. As it developed, Juan Enrique Lagarrigue became the leading, and one of the very few Chileans to accept the Religion of Humanity along with the rest of positivist doctrine.

The orthodox positivists were sharply opposed by those of heterodox views who, in the tradition of Lastarria, accepted some portions of Comtean thought and rejected others. For years the controversy raged in the Academy of Belles Lettres and other cultural and intellectual institutions. The academy itself, established in 1873 largely under the sponsorship of Lastarria, served as a forum for debate that was reminiscent of the literary salons in which the Generation of 1842 had thrashed out philosophical disagreements. The academy was the site of innumerable polemical debates and influenced the young generation of Chilean intellectuals. José Victorino Lastarria remained the leading spokesman of heterodox positivism until his death in 1888, at which time this role passed into the hands of Valentín Letelier.

Valentín Letelier (1852–1919), born of a French family, studied at the national university and graduated from the faculty of law in 1875. He began his public career as a journalist, became a professor shortly thereafter, and combined these activities with political involvement for the rest of his life. Serving in congress for years as a leader of the Radical party, he retained his scholarly interest in history, law, and political science. In 1906 he was appointed rector of the University of Chile, and until his death enjoyed continental repute. Letelier was firmly convinced that he owed a responsibility to seeking the achievement of his ideas through a public career. He served for a time as a diplomat, and a stay in Germany was marked by his close study of its educational system, some of whose aspects he attempted to introduce to Chile. First and foremost, however, he was a scholar and teacher.

Professor Harold E. Davis has written that Letelier's ideas developed along three main streams: popular education, political science, and a sociological concept of history.[25] With the first, he expressed a concern with the masses, especially the emerging urban worker in Chile. He was influential in the formulation of Radical party doctrine with regard to educational and labor programs. His political science was explicitly positivist, maintaining that any political phenomenon might accurately be understood in terms of the law of causation. His views were developed in two studies published in 1919, the *Genesis del estado* and *Genesis del derecho y de las instituciones civiles fundamentales*.[26] A firm believer in the importance of professional training for those who would participate in the administration of the political system, he advocated the formulation of a science of government, while stressing the importance of a party system for a healthy political community. His two-volume *Evolución de la historia* (1900) dealt with the discovery of the causes of events in order to find a possible sequence that would permit the formulation of a law of history.

Across the Andes to the east, Argentine positivism paralleled to a notable degree the Chilean philosophical evolution, with the development of both orthodox and heterodox positivists. While the Chilean intellectuals debated at the Academy of Belles Lettres, in Argentina the polemical locale was the normal school at Paraná, which had been founded by Sarmiento in 1870. Some twenty years after the fall of the despot Juan Manuel Rosas, Argentine thinkers had largely passed through their period of romantic liberalism in the search for a new social order. The most influential strain of positivism in Argentina, in sharp contrast to that of Mexico, was less concerned with an orderly unification of the nation than with a stimulation of the individual so that the highest possible social and cultural development might be attained. The tendency was therefore in the direction of an individualistic positivism. Among the more prominent figures were J. Alfredo Ferreira and Agustín E. Alvarez Suárez. Ferreira (1863–1935) and his followers encouraged originality and creativity, arguing for the necessity of finding individual answers to national problems. Emphasis was placed on freedom of interpretation, and the end goal of education was seen as liberty to pursue progress without being rigidly bound by any given doctrine. Comte was

25. Harold Eugene Davis, *Latin American-Social Thought: The History of Its Development Since Independence, with Selected Readings* (Washington: University Press of Washington, D.C., 1963), p. 328.

26. For his later and better-known works, see in particular Valentín Letelier, *La evolución de la historia* (Santiago: Imp. Cervantes, 1900). Among the best references is Luis Galdames, *Valentín Letelier y su obra* (Santiago: Universitaria, 1937).

viewed sympathetically but was regarded only as providing very broad guidelines to be followed and revised in accord with Argentine realities. The political and social outlook was generally conservative, and there was an affinity for the Spencerian view that society should permit man to achieve the greatest possible individual freedom.

By the turn of the century, Argentine thinkers were attracted by socialism almost as fully as by positivism. One of the first Latin-American countries to develop an identifiable interest in socialism, Argentina found socialist theory useful in attempting to understand the role in society of the emerging urban proletariat. This was typified by the founder of Argentine socialism, Juan B. Justo, who had first been influenced by the positivism of the Paraná school but later turned to socialism in his quest for social justice. He and other socialists wrote about the relationship of Comtean positivism to socialism and held that positivism recognized the true nature of social problems but was inadequate in providing solutions. There was a conviction that socialism and positivism resembled one another in their concern with social justice by evolutionary means. This socialist tendency meant a dilution of the purer forms of positivism, and Argentina therefore never developed the commitment to Comtean principles that existed in some parts of the hemisphere.

The Argentine variant of positivism was well represented by Agustín E. Alvarez Suárez (1857–1914), who combined the positivism of his formative years with Darwinian evolutionism and, later, a kind of practical idealism. Born in Mendoza, he was first educated in that provincial capital before receiving his degree in law at Buenos Aires. Later he became a founder and distinguished faculty member of the University of La Plata. His legal training was buttressed by a deep interest in sociology, ethics, and collective psychology. A prolific writer, his more important works included *La transformación de las razas en América* (1906), *Manuel de patología política* (1899), and *La herencia moral de los pueblos americanos* (1919).[27] In the first of these, he moved away from such figures as Sarmiento and Alberdi, arguing instead that racial qualities had nothing to do with problems of national development. From this he proceeded to formulate a positivist sociology that emphasized psychological explanation.

In disagreement with *pensadores* who exaggerated the importance of abstract concepts, he believed that too often such philosophical speculations disregarded reality. Thus, for example, Latin-American political

27. Agustín E. Alvarez Suárez, *La transformación de las razas en América* (Barcelona: F. Granada, 1906), and *La herencia moral de los pueblos hispano-americanos* (Buenos Aires: Vaccaro, 1919).

constitutions represented the best of the ideal while ignoring practical matters. Highly developed constitutional complexities meant nothing to millions of people living in an oppressive and semibarbarous condition. Alvarez maintained that Latin America should learn that mere words did not create social conditions and turn instead to an investigation of the realities to which the words should be applied. He felt that backwardness was the result of the collective behavior of a people influenced by outdated customs and institutions. Because of their fanaticism for the abstract, Latin Americans had searched historically for an ideal and utopian formula that would resolve all difficulties. The tendency to move from one philosophical solution to another meant an arbitrary classification of social and political issues into the extremes of black and white; for Alvarez Suárez, moderation within the legal order and the use of reason before the adoption of policies was fundamental. In this, he was in basic agreement with the positivist concept of ordered progress.

Cuban Positivism and National Independence / In Cuba, the influence of Comtean thought was strongly colored by colonial status and the desire for emancipation from Spanish rule. The most representative figure on that island was Enrique José Varona (1849–1933), who found in positivism the doctrine that would simultaneously produce intellectual independence while stimulating the spirit of freedom. Varona received his early education in Camagüey and drew extensively from his parents' large private library. At the conclusion of the Ten Years' War (1868–78) he and a group of intellectuals formed the Liberal Autonomist party. He was elected as representative to the Spanish Cortes in 1884 but soon resigned his position in disappointment over the uncompromising Spanish attitude toward Cuba. He returned to academic life, earned his doctorate of philosophy from the University of Havana in 1894, and inaugurated the publication of the *Revista Cubana*. When Martí founded the Cuban Revolutionary party he joined its ranks in the struggle for independence, becoming the director of *Patria*, the organ of the revolutionaries.

Following the winning of independence from Spain in 1898, Varona served as secretary of education, and he formulated a program of reforms that reflected many aspects of positivism. In 1902 he returned to the University of Havana as professor of philosophy, but the call of politics soon renewed itself. In 1907 he founded the Conservative party, and from 1913 to 1917 served as vice-president of Cuba. Devoting the final years of his life to philosophy and writing, he maintained his active interest in political conditions and emerged from public retirement to support the student movement in protest against the oppression of the dictatorship of Gerardo Machado. His long life was therefore dedicated to political and intellectual freedom, and in this he was an ardent champion whether opposing the shackles of Spanish rule or the authoritarianism of the Cuban government. He was convinced that it was the duty of all educated patriotic Cubans to put their principles into action and maintained a steady stream of writings.

Varona's earlier philosophical writings appeared in the *Revista Cubana* and his *Estudios literarios y filosóficos* (1883). The latter included a series of lectures delivered at the Academy of Sciences between 1880 and 1882. Subsequently, most of Varona's work was concerned with literary analysis and practical politics. His positivism was limited to the use of Comte's scientific thought. Varona was unsystematic, somewhat eclectic, and a realist who sometimes approached outright skepticism. He accepted neither the Comtean theory of the three-stage development of civilization nor the classification of sciences running from astronomy to sociology; he completely ignored Comte's Religion of Humanity. What did influence him was Comte's scientific approach to learning and the establishment of an anti-metaphysical position.[28] Spencerian evolutionism also influenced Varona, for the Cuban's sociological position preserved the concept that social life is man's adaptation to his environment. However, Varona did not agree that force was a leading dynamic ingredient in man's evolution. Opposed to all forms of absolutism, even as a basis for science, he denied Spencer's idea of the evolution of the military state toward the industrial.

As a political philosopher, Varona represented a continuation of Saco's realism.[29] He never lost sight of the special conditions of Cuba, both in domestic and world affairs. Analyses of political events were based on accurate observation, and he kept in mind the interests of Cuban society in general. His realism was noticeable in a study entitled *¿Abriremos los ojos?* (1906). Recognizing that the landed gentry had held economic power in colonial Cuba while the Spanish retained political control, he cited these conditions as largely responsible for the conspiracies, invasions, and rebellious uprisings that early culminated in the first wars of liberation in 1868. In this Varona showed a trace of economic determinism, although he never accepted Marxism, which he described as "the exaggeration of a true fact."[30] Varona's political realism

28. See Medardo Vitier, *Las ideas en Cuba* (La Habana: Edit. El Trópico, 1938), Chapter XI.
29. See Chapter 3.
30. Vitier, *Ideas en Cuba*, p. 188.

was combined with strong feelings of nationalism. Realizing that Cuba had not won full sovereignty after 1898 because of the Platt Amendment, he campaigned at length, though unsuccessfully, for the abrogation of the Cuban constitutional appendix that contained the clause limiting Cuba's right to self-determination. He was, with Manuel Sanguily, among the first to warn the Cubans of the controlling influence of foreign investors, and he portrayed a vividly prophetic vision in *Imperialismo a la luz de la sociología* (1906).[31]

As we have seen, positivism was not universally accepted in Latin America as a rigid and uncompromising system of thought. National variations were great, ranging from the authoritarian applications of the Mexican *científicos* to the semiliberalism of the Chileans. In several countries there were competing positivist schools, as in Argentina and Chile. Yet another characteristic of Latin-American positivism was the fact that many who were trained under positivist educators changed later in life to more idealistic and even to metaphysical positions. Positivism, even at its zenith, was not alone in contributing to a more systematic and critical consideration of overriding social and political problems. In time, disillusionment was engendered. Particularly in the Mexican case, oligarchical monopoly of public affairs and a continuing inequitable distribution of wealth pointed up the difficulties of positivism. Mexico also showed that political tyranny might result, while the increased role of foreign investors encouraged a resurrection of colonialism, notably in the economic realm.

The influence of positivism was observable in countries and authors not discussed here. Eugenio María de Hostos, Puerto Rico's great patriot and educator, was a positivist, as were the Honduran statesman Ramón Rosa, the Paraguayan sociologist Cecilio Báez, and the Salvadoran Victorino Ayala. The popularity of positivism in Latin America stemmed in large part from its self-declared scientific approach to social, economic, and political problems precisely at the moment when the republics were reaching a point of deep frustration in the effort to organize and to order their national lives. There was a need to break with the past, and a wave of dedicated intellectuals was searching for new principles and methods. There was a desire to find what could be described in Comtean terms as the theological and metaphysical stages of history. Political instability, civil wars, and revolution were, for many Latin

31. Enrique José Varona y Pera, *Imperialismo a la luz de la sociología* (La Habana: 1906). For a useful one-volume compendium of representative works, see Enrique José Varona y Pera, *Varona: Prólogo y selección de José Antonio Fernández de Castro* (México: Secretaría de Educación Pública, 1943).

Americans, diseases of the social organism which could only be cured through the creation of a new social structure. Seen in this light, positivism and its emphasis on the scientific explanation of the causes of such disease held out great expectations for the *pensadores,* and their resultant embrace was consequently all the stronger.

SELECTED BIBLIOGRAPHY

Alvarez Suárez, Agustín E. *La herencia moral de los pueblos hispano-americanos.* Buenos Aires: Vaccaro, 1919.
———. *La transformación de las razas en America.* Barcelona: F. Granada, 1906.
Azevedo, Fernando de. *Brazilian Culture: An Introduction to the Study of Culture in Brazil.* Translated by William Rex Crawford. New York: Macmillan Co., 1950.
Barreda, Gabino. *Opúsculos, discusiones y discursos.* México: n.p., 1877.
Da Cunha, Euclydes. *Rebellion in the Backlands.* Translated by Samuel Putnam. Chicago: University of Chicago Press, 1943.
Galdames, Luis. *Valentín Letelier y su obra.* Santiago: Universitaria, 1937.
Lastarria, José Victorino. *Obras completas.* Santiago: Imp. Barcelona, 1906–14.
Letelier, Valentín. *La evolución de la historia.* Santiago: Imp. Cervantes, 1900.
Ramírez, Ignacio. *Obras de Ignacio Ramírez,* 2 Vols. México, Editora Nacional, 1952.
Schulman, Sam. "A Study of the Political Aspects of Positivism in Mexico." Master's thesis, University of New Mexico, 1949.
Sierra. Justo. *Evolución política del pueblo mexicano.* México: La Casa de España en México, 1940.
———. *The Political Evolution of the Mexican People.* Translated by Charles Ramsdell with an introduction by Edmundo O'Gorman. Austin: University of Texas Press, 1969.
Varona y Pera, Enrique José. *De la colonia a la república.* La Habana: Sociedad Editorial Cuba Contemporánea, 1919.
———. *Varona: Prólogo y selección de José Antonio Fernández de Castro.* México: Secretaría de Educación Pública, 1943.
Zea, Leopoldo. *Apogeo y decadencia del positivismo en México.* México: El Colegio de México, 1944.
———. *The Latin-American Mind.* Translated by James H. Abbott and Lowell Dunham. Norman: University of Oklahoma Press, 1963.

5

Idealism

After Rousseau the unlimited faith in reason had slowly declined in Europe, and the conservative writers of the Restoration period launched a frontal attack on reason. In Germany, Hegel, Schelling, and Fichte had brought reason and empiricism before the tribunal of philosophy, thereby initiating a new idealism. The first two men associated reason with the development of the human spirit, conceived as a part of the historical process.[1] Fichte, by contrast, placed man's ideas within the knower and developed his own theory of subjective idealism. Such trends reached Latin America either directly or through a variety of French, Italian, and Spanish interpreters.[2] Among the most important channels through which the German interpretation of idealism reached Latin America was Spanish Krausism.

1. The philosophical historicism of Hegel and Schelling also inspired the German historical school of jurisprudence which exercised considerable influence in the Latin American schools of law. Such jurists of the historical school as Hugo, Savigny, and Puchta were well known and had many followers among lawyers and professors. Their influence tended in some small part to check the rationalism and empiricism of the positivists during the years when this philosophy was so influential in parts of Latin America.

2. Among the now-forgotten or obscure names that held at least fleeting interest for the Latin-American intellectuals, Victor Cousin and Maine de Biran were known; so were the Italians Antonio Rosmini and Vicenzo Gioberti. From Spain came the writings of José Rey Herrera and José Perojo—both Kantians—while Hegelianism was represented by, among others, José Cantero, Antonio Benítez, and Francisco Escudero.

Karl Christian Friedrich Krause (1781–1832), while familiar with the writings of Hegel, was essentially a disciple of Fichte and Schelling. Combining elements of these two masters, Krause developed an idealism that was basically pantheistic. According to Krause, society was a spiritual and not a biological organism; it represented the conscience of its individual components and permitted man to attain personal liberty. Ultimately, man and society progressed toward the image of God. The state was the only part of society with responsibility for its political and legal functions. Krausist philosophical idealism argued for an imprecisely stated synthesis of man and society, whose universal expression was a semireligious humanism heavily interlaced with social consciousness.

The obscure metaphysics of Krause never attracted wide attention in Germany but swiftly became influential in Spain where the development of Krausism was among the most important intellectual events of the nineteenth century. In 1844 the Spanish government sent Julián Sanz del Río (1814–69) to study in Germany, and at Heidelberg he was exposed to lectures by disciples of Krause. Upon his return to Spain, Sanz del Río assumed the chair of history of philosophy at the University of Madrid. In later years he published *Lecciones sobre el sistema de la filosofía analítica de K.C.F. Krause* and *El ideal de la humanidad para la vida*. Although Sanz del Río gave credit for the latter to Krause, it contained his own interpretation of Krausist philosophy. He argued that philosophy was not a systematic discipline but rather an ideal doctrine of man's ethical life. The need for the individual to find freedom in society necessarily presupposed his critical attitude toward existing social values. Although Sanz del Río was denied his chair by the government in 1867 as the result of his defense of ethical liberalism, his ideas were further spread by a small group of devoted followers.

The most distinguished student of Sanz del Río was Francisco Giner de los Ríos (1839–1915), who offered his own interpretations of Krausist idealism.[3] Giner was a professor who taught the philosophy of law at the University of Madrid. Early in his career he became a storm center when his refusal to sign a political oath of allegiance to the government caused his dismissal. A number of his colleagues resigned in protest, and several were imprisoned. As a result, Giner and his associates founded the Institución Libre de Enseñanza, where he taught until his eventual reinstatement at the University of Madrid in 1881. The *institución* was a center of Krausism for many years, attracting outstanding young intellectuals who, in their turn, followed Giner's teaching. While

3. For a recent treatment, see Martín Navarro, *Vida y obra de don Francisco Giner de los Ríos* (México: Ediciones Orión, 1945).

much of Giner's thought was contained in lectures and never reached the printed page, his more important writings were *Resumen de filosofía del derecho* (1898) and *Filosofía y sociología* (1904). His collected works, *Obras completas,* included extensive essays and articles; published posthumously from 1916 to 1929, they comprised a twenty-volume set.

Giner believed that one cannot separate thought from action. To him, ideas were states of consciousness that were always incorporated into history, while history presupposed man's actions. He rejected the static conception of rationalism and the dogma of abstract reason. Following Krause, he conceived of *derecho,* or law, as the total order of life but insisted that law was only a means to an end, the end being the attainment of man's liberty. It is not necessary to insist on other aspects of Giner's thought to appreciate its impact on the Spain in which he lived. If the state and the legal order of society should necessarily aim at the achievement of man's liberty, the first question to be asked was whether the Spanish state was doing its duty. If the answer were negative, the logical conclusion was that the Spaniards had to assure that the state would fulfill its duty. For Francisco Giner de los Ríos, as for the other proponents of Krausism in Spain, this philosophy represented a synthesis of German idealism with liberalism while incorporating a philosophy of action. It was not a perfect reproduction of Krause's thought but a vigorous, autonomous movement of broader and deeper scope.[4]

Critical Idealism

Several of the more eminent intellects of the late nineteenth century could be termed critical idealists. Among these were Juan Montalvo, José Enrique Rodó, and to a degree, José Martí. Somewhat more concerned with contemporary political issues than with philosophical reasoning, they reacted against positivism by seeking new paths toward liberty and the freedom of individual expression. Combining an idealized vision of society with a sharply critical attitude toward existing conditions, they called for a sharp break with the past. None was more outspoken than Ecuador's greatest intellectual figure, the embattled Montalvo (1832–89).

4. Because of the predominance of legal studies in Latin-American universities, Spanish Krausism influenced professors and students there as it did in Spain. Many Spanish jurists, men like Emilio Reus, Leopoldo Alas, and Gumersindo de Azcárate, followed Krausism and were read and discussed through Latin America.

For further discussion see Juan López-Morillas, *El Krausismo español: Perfil de una aventura intelectual* (México: Fondo de Cultura Económica, 1956).

Born in Ambato where he studied in private school, Montalvo attended the National University in Quito but left for Europe before receiving his degree. There he traveled extensively, became an acquaintance of French romantic Alphonse Lamartine, and developed a literary style that was to earn him a reputation as an effective pamphleteer. Away from Ecuador for years, he gained note as a bitter and unrelenting opponent of the remarkable tyrant who controlled Ecuador, Gabriel García Moreno. The latter, scion of an aristocratic family, had studied in Europe and reacted with extreme distaste to the 1848 revolutions. He gained power in 1860 and proceeded to establish the most thorough-going theocracy in nineteenth-century Latin America. A highly intelligent man, García Moreno was a strict disciplinarian who dominated his country completely. As an extreme conservative, he stifled freedom of speech and press, extended ecclesiastical privileges beyond what the Church had ever enjoyed before, and ruthlessly crushed all signs of opposition. In office and out, he ruled Ecuador until his assassination by the steps of the presidential palace in Quito in 1875.

First from Europe and then from Colombia and elsewhere, Montalvo devoted the bulk of his writings to an unending campaign against García Moreno, his political authoritarianism and religious fanaticism. In 1866 Montalvo's journal, El Cosmopólita, was suppressed by the dictator, and he was soon exiled from his country. A succession of attacks upon García Moreno continued, however, including such pamphlets as El antropófago (1872), Judas (1873), and La dictadura perpetua (1874). After the death of García Moreno, Montalvo exultantly claimed that his pen had killed the tyrant. Returning to Ecuador, he edited the newspaper El Regenerador but soon angered conservative Ignacio Veintimilla and was again driven into exile. In Panama, he published the journal Catilinarias for a time and later moved to France. In 1882 Montalvo published Siete tratados,[5] his major work. It is from this that his more significant views emerged.

Like Cuban Martí, Montalvo was confronted with the political reality of his country's oppression. Eternally a man in rebellion, he advocated the customary liberal policies with regard to the Catholic church, criticized its monopoly of education, and suggested economic and political reforms that were later implemented in Ecuador by the liberal movement of Eloy Alfaro in 1895 and after. His insistence on the liberation of

5. For a collection of Montalvo's works, see his Obras escogidas (Quito: Casa de la Cultura Ecuatoriana, 1948). Among the more recent editions of Siete tratados is that prepared by Antonio Acevedo Escobedo, published in Mexico by the Secretaría de Educación Pública in 1942.

man from clerical influence was the heart of the platform advocated from that time forward by the liberals in Ecuador. His political views included the defense of democracy, which he believed would assure justice for the masses. Rebellious but not necessarily a revolutionary, Juan Montalvo called for social changes that should follow the removal of García Moreno and his conservative supporters. He was more concerned with the moral than the economic bases of liberalism, and was among the first Ecuadorans to recognize the condition of the Indian. While unwilling to accept the romanticized concept of the noble savage living in an untouched state of nature, he argued persuasively that the historic oppression of the Indian was among the sources of national backwardness in Ecuador.

In general philosophy Montalvo was essentially an iconoclast in his expression of critical idealism. Widely read, he demonstrated his familiarity with the works of ancient and modern authors as well as with political conitions of the Europe of his day. His personal idealism was alternately utopian and skeptical. Certain of his essays had the flavor of Tom Paine and other critics of the society of the Enlightenment. His faith in progress was unlimited, and a spirit of optimism ran through much of his writing. At the same time, his criticism would occasionally touch on a questioning attitude that suggested an affinity with Montaigne. As an idealist, he was not attracted by the cold scientific analysis of the positivists; neither did he accept what he regarded as the exaggerated emphasis on economic measures suggested by early socialists.

It is difficult to find logically rational or systematic thought in the writings of Montalvo. This is particularly noticeable in his *Siete tratados,* much of which was written in the small village of Ipiales, Colombia, just across the border from Ecuador. He complained that he was forced to write "without books, gentlemen, without books,"[6] As the Uruguayan, Rodó, remarked in his study of Montalvo, the Ecuadoran spent much of his life without "those instruments of measurement and rectification"[7] so necessary to all writers. Even had the environment for writing been different, however, it is likely that his thought would have remained diffuse. Characteristically, *Siete tratados* was a collection of essays covering a variety of topics. It was almost as if the topics themselves were secondary; the important thing was to let his mind flow in the analysis of whatever struck his imagination as worthy of consideration. Rodó put it well when he called Montalvo not a thinker but rather a fencer

6. José Enrique Rodó, "Montalvo," in *Obras completas* (Buenos Aires: A. Zamora, n.d.), p. 531.

7. *Ibid.*

with ideas (*esgrimidor de ideas*). An illustrative passage comes from his description of the death of Bolívar. While it says nothing of his political ideas, it expresses the indomitable spirit with which all his writings are infused.

> By the shores of the Atlantic in a solitary villa is found a man stretched out on a rather humble cot: few people, little noise. The sea crashes against the rocks or groans like a lost spirit when its waves die out on the shore. A few shadowy trees near the house resemble mourners—mourners, for the man is dying. Who is he? Simón Bolívar, liberator of Colombia and Peru. And does the liberator of so much suffer the last agony in neglect? Where are the ambassadors, where the commissioners who surround the bed of this great man? . . .
> If Bolívar had been ambitious by nature, his correct judgment, his admirable tact, his incorruptible magnanimity would have turned his thoughts to things of more importance than a worthless crown which, by being unworthy, would have broken his head. A king is any child of fortune; a conqueror is any strong being; liberators are the envoys of Providence. So great is the value of a superior and noble man that not to know him is a disgrace, to know him and oppose him is unpardonable evil. The enemies of Bolívar disappeared from one day to the next, leaving no heirs to their hatreds. Within a thousand years his figure will be greater and more resplendent than that of Julius Caesar, an almost fabulous hero, magnified with fame and hallowed by the centuries.[8]

Another rebellious example of Latin-American critical idealism, although in many ways defying classification, was the great Cuban *libertador* José Martí (1853–95). Born in Havana where he studied first in a private school and then in public institutions, Martí in his early youth joined the patriots struggling for freedom from Spanish colonialism. He was imprisoned and deported to Spain and received his law degree from the University of Zaragoza in 1873. The following year he received authorization to leave Spain and traveled to Mexico and Central America, where he earned his living teaching and writing. A brief return to Cuba in 1877 again ended in forcible exile, and he went to New York to begin the organization of Cuban patriots for a war of liberation. As he undertook that task, the obstacles were substantial. The majority of Cubans was divided: the autonomists, who wanted political changes and self-government under Spain; the so-called "independentists," who were struggling for full freedom; and the "annexationists." The unification of these groups was not an easy task, but Martí

8. From *Siete tratados* (México: Secretaría de Educación Pública, 1942), p. 3.

was successful in bringing most of them together as members of the Partido Revolucionario Cubano in 1892. Martí believed that Spain had a dual conception of liberty, one for the mother country and another for the colonies. Concluding that the only way to free Cuba was by force of arms, Martí gave the order for insurrection in January, 1895, and patriots on the island took up arms on February 24. In April, Martí landed in Cuba, and he was killed in action on May 19.

A prolific man of letters and a sensitive poet, his *Obras completas* are contained in a number of multi-volume collections.[9] These include drama and poetry, along with innumerable essays and articles. His *Versos libres* and *Versos sencillos* made him one of the forerunners of the *modernista* movement in Latin-American letters. Our concern, however, is with his general thought and political ideas, which in the opinion of some students of Martí, placed particular stress on mysticism and romanticism. In more recent studies, especially those based on new material from his archives, there are strong indications that he had little of the intuitionism of the mystics or the exaggeration of the romantics. He always insisted that a free man must rely on reason and evidence for his knowledge.[10] Philosophyical romanticism is, in a way, similar to mysticism. The romantics believed that logic and reason were inadequate to reach a full understanding of reality. Martí accepted intuitionism as a means of reaching truth, but he also relied on reason and especially on observation, believing in science and the scientific method.

Of the classical philosophies, those which most influenced Martí were stoicism and Platonic idealism. His stoicism was closer to Seneca than to Zeno or, rather, to Seneca as interpreted by Spanish authors of the Golden Age. In all of Martí's writings there is evidence of his interest in man's conduct and a quest for a superior norm governing his behavior. Stoicism influenced his ethics but not his general philosophy, for he did not identify man's soul with nature. He placed man above nature, saying, "Nature is everything that exists in all sorts of forms . . . nature is everything with the exception of heaven and man's soul."[11] From Plato, Martí accepted the identification of God with the good and the conception of ideas as a superior intellectual synthesis of reality. His admiration for nature, which he received from the Stoics, had led some

9. One collection of his writings and letters fills more than seventy volumes. Among the more useful of the various compilations is the misleadingly titled *Obras completas,* 2 Vols. (La Habana: Edición Lex, 1946).

10. This view is expounded at length in Miguel Jorrín, *Martí y la filosofía* (La Habana: Cuadernos de Divulgación Cultural # 11, 1954).

11. Miguel Jorrín, "Ideas Filosóficas de Martí," *Revista Bimestre Cubana* [La Habana] (1941), XLVII, 45.

of his critics to speak of Martí's pantheism. This was not basically a philosophical position, however, but rather a form of expression that was then much in vogue.

The possible influence of positivism and materialism deserves consideration, because some writers have claimed the existence of Marxist thought in the Cuban writer.[12] Positivism was still very strong in Martí's day, but he rejected this philosophy, especially the evolutionism of Darwin and Spencer. He said of Darwin that he had reached only a part of the truth but was never able to understand the whole, and of Spencer that he was too engrossed in excessive detail to achieve full understanding of historical reality. For Martí, the value of positivism was only that of a scientific method; he dismissed the social and political aspects of the philosophy. As to Marxism, Martí left a revealing comment in an article for *La Nación* of Buenos Aires describing the ceremonies held in New York by the socialists and anarchists at the time of Marx's death. In it, he wrote: "Karl Marx is dead. Because he was on the side of the weak, he deserves to be honored. But he who points out the harm done and who burns in generous anxiety to repair the harm is not doing the right thing. Instead he should show a lenient way to right the wrongs. The idea of throwing men against men is frightening."[13] He respected Marx for his lifelong devotion to the defense of the working class, but he did not indicate agreement with his philosophy. Moreover, at no time did the Cuban indicate a philosophical affinity for Hegel or for historical materalism.

The German idealism of Fichte, Schelling, and others exercised a definite influence on Martí, and he was well versed in the writings and formulations of Spanish Krausists. It was during the predominance of Krausism that Martí studied in Spain, and this was apparent in his first important publication, *El presidio político en Cuba*. Martí concurred with the Krausist organic conception of life and society, as well as its spiritual attitude toward reality and the life of man, although he did not accept the whole metaphysical system. At his death he left a notebook for a work to be entitled *El concepto de la vida*, which included a passage wherein he rejected all philosophical systems and suggested that the only way for a philosopher was to find truth for himself. In his political ideas Martí was a liberal; he was more than a political realist concerned solely with the problems of independence in Cuba. His mind led him to examine material conditions as a whole, ever seeking a clearer

12. For example, see Antonio Martínez Bello, *Ideas sociales y económicas de José Martí* (La Habana: La Verónica, 1940).
13. Martí, *Obras completas*, II, 1517.

perspective of man and his society. Like the early forerunners of independence elsewhere in Latin America, he dealt first with the struggle against Spain, organized a political party, and launched the insurrection. However, he did not forget for a moment that his task would not end with the defeat of Spain but that a nation would have to be created out of Cuban colonial society. So it was that he frequently referred to the need for genuine revolution after liberation.

The expression of Martí's liberal faith is apparent from his first political tract, *La república española ante la revolución cubana* (1873), to his final political testament, *Manifiesto de Montecristi* (1895). He desired a representative democracy for Cuba, believing in the co-operative effort of all social groups rather than in a Marxist class struggle. Well aware of the realities of the international position of both Cuba and Puerto Rico, he wanted to keep the two free from British and North American influence. He was convinced that the independence of the last two Spanish colonies in America would be a guarantee of freedom in the rest of the hemisphere. He would have been unhappy with the Platt Amendment and the four years of military occupation that followed the defeat of Spain in 1898. For Cuba he wanted full sovereignty, in practice as well as theory. Moreover, as Felipe Pazos has shown, Martí held liberal economic views, believing in private property and honest profit.[14] At the same time, however, he advocated a "limited" capitalism that would not exploit the poor. Pazos indicates that, before the development of what is elsewhere termed Yankeephobia, Martí warned Cuba and the rest of Latin America of the dangers of imperialism. Distressed over the existence of monoculture and its evils, he suggested the need for diversification and agrarian reform.

During the time he spent in the United States, Martí became well acquainted with its literary, philosophical, and artistic currents; he wrote extensively on North American life and society. Typical was the essay written on Ralph Waldo Emerson when the great transcendentalist died. Martí expressed a clear affinity with the ideas of the New Englander, agreeing with him that the universe was not fully susceptible to scientific explanation and that the important thing for philosophy is man's conduct in life. In this and many other short pieces, Martí showed a knowledge and understanding of the United States which few of his Latin American contemporaries could claim. His political views on the relationship between the United States and its southern neighbors, as well as extensive

14. Felipe Pazos, "Las Ideas Económicas de Martí," in *Vida y pensamiento de Martí*, II, ed. Emilio Roig de Leuchsenring, (La Habana: Municipio de La Habana, 1942), pp. 177–209.

observations on North American political leaders, were frequently critical but never irrational.[15]

Of concrete issues, it can be said that Martí was fully interested in the widest range of Cuban and Latin-American problems. Many of these were domestic rather than international. He was fearful of the dangers of militarism, even during the days of the struggle for independence. He once reminded General Máximo Gómez, for whom he had great respect, that a nation could not be ruled as might be an army. He was aware of the ramifications of Cuba's racial composition, and spoke out strongly in opposition to discrimination, saying, "No hay odios de raza porque no hay razas," or "there are no racial hatreds because there are no races." Like most of the earlier Latin-American liberators Martí was anticlerical, criticizing the role of the Church in supporting the government of Spain as well as its materialistic paternalism toward the Cuban people. Thus he advocated for a free Cuba a lay republic with a clear separation of Church and State. In religious questions he was essentially a free thinker. The development of public education, another issue he had studied at length, was to be free of ecclesiastical influence; he maintained that one of the foremost duties of the state was to provide for the instruction of the people.

Martí also resembled the early nineteenth-century liberators of Latin America in his attention to world affairs. He had served as a delegate from Uruguay to the Monetary Conference held in Washington in 1891 and described the meetings in his role as reporter for Buenos Aires' *La Nación*. He commented at the time on the symbolic implications of a figure of the United States eagle in the conference hall, holding the flags of all the Latin-American republics in its claws. As Enrique Gay-Calbó has noted, Martí was well aware of the inevitability of antagonisms that, despite diplomatic courtesies, existed at the time between the two distinctive cultures of North and Latin America.[16] He was to remark upon this on a number of occasions and, while offering few substantive suggestions, lamented the divisions that existed and could only grow in the future.

Taken as a whole, Martí's thought is scarcely more representative of an identifiable philosophical school than was that of Juan Montalvo. His restless intellectual nature led him to concentrate more on the practical workings of politics than on its doctrinal elements. A revolutionary who advocated first a political liberation and than a socioeconomic trans-

15. These are set forth in the discussion of Yankeephobia in Chapter 11.
16. See the discussion by Enrique Gay-Calbó, "Americanismo de Martí," in Leuchsenring, *Martí*.

formation of his homeland, he emphasized the concept of patriotism and called upon an amorphous kind of individual submission to the nation in the interests of the whole. While writing in a neoromantic tone of liberty and democracy, he concentrated repeatedly on the duties of the citizen toward his government. If any single strand ran through all his writings, it was that of humanitarianism. It was this elevated tone of his writing which combined with ardent patriotism to encourage the cult of Martí which has grown ever since his battlefield death at an early age. The apotheosis of Martí actually began as early as 1889, when his supporter Gonzalo de Quesada y Aróstegui referred to him as the "Apostle."[17] As a heroic national political symbol, Martí has been held up as the larger-than-life idealized Cuban. Gary has written that Martí is perhaps the most important person in the history of Cuba; as the national hero, "he has burst the bonds of mortality to achieve an afterlife in the thought, expressions, and public manifestations of a great number of Cubans."[18]

Among the critical idealists is José Enrique Rodó (1871–1917), the eminent Uruguayan who belonged to a later generation. Much less the nationalist than either Montalvo or Martí, Rodó was more fully universal in his writings, drawing intellectual inspiration from Christian and Hellenic rather than American sources. He inherited a valuable library from his father and became a scholar by dint of his own reading and thought. Eventually he was appointed professor of literature at the University of Montevideo without having received any advanced degree. He founded the journal *Revista Nacional de Literatura y Ciencias Sociales* in 1895 and for many years contributed to the newspapers *El Orden* and *El Diario de La Plata*. He never traveled outside Uruguay until World War I, when he went to Europe as a correspondent for the Argentine review *Caras y Caretas* and died of illness in Palermo, Sicily, at the age of forty-six.

Rodó's first important work of a philosophical nature was *Ariel*, published in 1900,[19] in which he used the name of Shakespeare's ethereal

17. For a discussion of the process of apotheosis, see Richard Butler Gray, *José Martí, Cuban Patriot* (Gainesville: University of Florida Press, 1962), pp. 253–56. Those who do not read Spanish may also consult Jorge Mañach, *Martí: Apostle of Freedom,* tr. Coley Taylor (New York: Devin-Adair, 1950). Also useful is Félix Lizaso, *Martí: Martyr of Cuban Independence,* tr. Esther Elise Shuler (Albuquerque: University of New Mexico Press, 1953). For a selection of his writings, see *The America of José Martí: Selected Writings,* tr. Juan de Onís (New York: Noonday Press, 1953).

18. Gray, *Martí*, p. xiii.

19. For an English translation, see José Enrique Rodó, tr. F. J. Stimson *Ariel* (Boston: Houghton Mifflin Company, 1922).

sprite to represent the part of the human being which is not the slave of the body. His *Liberalismo y jacobinismo* (1906) showed his tolerance in religious and political matters. *Motivos de Proteo* (1909)[20] emphasized the need for a continuous change of the human spirit, and *El mirador de Próspero* (1913) was a brilliant collection of essays covering many topics and world figures.[21] It was the first of these which brought Rodó lasting fame, and *Ariel* was for many years after publication among the most widely read and admired politico-philosophical works in Latin America. Widely studied particularly by Latin-American youth, it helped to prepare the way for the increasingly strong intellectual rebellion against positivism which spread throughout the continent. It also added to the prevailing image of the United States which was later exaggerated, largely for political purposes, and which even today is a serious obstacle to a cultural and intellectual understanding between the Latin and the North Americans.[22]

The central theme of *Ariel* was Rodó's preference for the classical and humanistic values over those of materialism and utilitarianism. Essentially an extended essay, *Ariel* began with the venerable master Prospero taking leave of his students and counseling them as to their course in life. His advice called for a development of the individual personality as far as possible, and this was to be accompanied by an understanding of reality as a whole, without petty misconceptions suggested by the partial and superficial appearance of events. The master condemned the specialization that, he insisted, always leads to mediocrity. Stressing the idealism of life, Rodó, through Prospero, pointed out the limitations of utilitarian positivism. He urged the cultivation of the spirit of selection and the basic superiority of man as a being, which he opposed to the exaggerations of social egalitarianism. Warning his youthful Latin-American followers of the dangers of what he understood as Anglo-Saxon materialism and its expansionist tendencies, he emphasized the spiritual superiority of the Latin cultures. What he feared was a loss of their traditional values because of the attraction of materialistic achievement in the United States. He found the progressive dynamism of the Anglo-Saxons deserving of admiration but felt that it was unsufficient for the enjoyment of a full life. Economic satisfaction was but one aspect of life and could not by itself serve the complete development of the personality of man.

20. This has been translated by Angel Flores as *Motives of Proteus* (New York: Brentano's, 1928).
21. This is contained in Rodó's *Obras completas* (Montevideo: Casa A. Barreiro y Ramos, 1945), a useful collection of his writings.
22. For Rodó's attitudes toward the United States, see Chapter 11.

He warned of North American utilitarianism and its Circean appeal to Latin America:

> The utilitarian conception as the idea of human destiny, and equality at the mediocre level as the norm of social proportion, make up the formula which in Europe they call the spirit of Americanism. It is impossible to think of either of these as inspirations for human conduct or society . . . without at once conjuring up by association a vision of that formidable and fruitful democracy there in the North, with its manifestations of prosperity and power, as a dazzling example in favor of the efficacy of democratic institutions and the correct aim of its ideas. . . .
> The vision of a voluntarily delatinized America, without compulsion or conquest, and regenerate in the manner of its Northern archetype, floats already through the dreams of many who are sincerely interested in our future, satisfies them with suggestive parallels they find at every step, and appears in constant movement for reform or innovation. We have our *mania for the North*. It is necessary to oppose to it those bounds which both sentiment and reason indicate.

Rodó considered the classical Mediterranean culture as superior to the German and Anglo-Saxon because of its respect for the values of the spirit and its reverence for man as a human being. His position was not unlike that of Albert Camus in *The Rebel*, with the crisis of Europe described as the history of the struggle of the German mind against Mediterranean ideology, between German thought and Mediterranean tradition. Beyond this kind of cultural preference, Rodó reflected such sources as Taine, De Tocqueville, Sarmiento, Montalvo, and, most importantly, Renan. Like the latter, he was brought up in the Catholic faith but left the Church early in life. Nevertheless—also like Renan—he retained great respect for the personality of Christ and the values of Christian ethics. One of his most important political studies, *Liberalismo y jacobinismo,* was provoked when a government minister ordered the symbol of the cross to be removed from publicly supported hospitals. Protesting against this directive to eliminate the symbol of Christian charity from places where this value was supposedly being practiced, he condemned the excesses of the false democracy of Jacobinism.

The Uruguayan was an advocate of liberty, but his work reveals the sensitivities of the educated intellectual toward the vulgarity of the masses. Pure democracy he regarded as encouraging a tendency toward leveling mediocrity; unlike Renan, however, he did not go so far as to condemn democratic equality. Instead, Rodó felt that it should be balanced by controls appropriately exercised by a cultured elite. His vision of equality was seen more as a possible utopian ideal than as an absolute reality. Spurred by this theoretical egalitarian possibility, man strives to become the craftsman of his own destiny. This was one of the major themes of both *Motivos v de Próteo* and *El mirador de Próspero,* in which he stressed the individual spirit under his well known slogan "renovarse es vivir"—"to renew oneself is to live." He was opposed to Rousseau's theory of natural education, maintaining that the child should never become isolated from its own cultural environment.

A firm believer in the power of the will, which he considered as important as reason, Rodó nevertheless did not accept the romantic conception of the primacy of will over reason. In *El camino de paros* (1918), a posthumously published collection of chronicles and essays, he restated his main philosophy through the use of diverse social and political topics in which he enlarged and developed his themes. Although concerned with the role of Latin America in its relations with the rest of the world, he was not interested in the inter-American system as a political organization and preferred a sort of spiritual and cultural front of the Latin-American republics. In his customarily cool and detached fashion, Rodó outlined in optimistic terms a continental vision in which the strengths of democracy might outlast the weaknesses, providing an idealistic, even an artistic, creed through which humanity might successfully meet the problems created by the rising tempo of social and economic change. Of all his thought, the most impressive was his clarion call to youth in *Ariel,* urging resistance to materialistic desires and an idealistic renewal of dedicated hopes and spiritual ideals.

For a Brazilian representative of critical idealism we might cite the jurist and statesman, Rui Barbosa (1849–1923). He studied law as São Paulo and from his younger days was interested in political reform, beginning with the abolition of slavery, for which he campaigned intensively. He came of age in the latter years of the empire of Dom Pedro II and became the advocate of numerous reforms, including the extension of public education, legal equality for all citizens, the supremacy of the law, religious freedom, and the integrity of public officials. First joining a group of young abolitionists while studying in São Paulo, Barbosa soon became a leading figure in the movement of protest against the emperor. As the champion of liberty and reform through a constitutional federal government, he opposed the centralization of the imperial government and was a dominant liberal figure when republicanism was introduced into Brazil in 1889.

A major draftsman of the 1891 republican constitution, he served as minister of justice in the provisional government that ensued and was the driving force behind the enactment of important legal reforms. The new charter separated Church and State, enshrined freedom of religion, and removed public education from ecclesiastical hands. Barbosa was a staunch advocate of federalism, arguing that geographical realities and Brazilian history counterbalanced the effects of a less-decentralized arrangement. Ever the advocate of the individual and his liberty, he continued to fight for these ideals through many years' service as jurist, statesman, diplomat, and author. Barbosa epitomized what the Brazilian commentator, Fernando de Azevedo, has described as the type of mentality and culture that predominated within the Brazilian leadership from the late years of the empire until the time of World War I.[23] Predominantly literary and bookish, this culture tended toward excessive reliance upon legalistic formulae. Alongside this mentality, based on the rhetoric and law of the governing class, was that briefly influential strain of positivism that Barbosa himself generally criticized.

In opposing positivism, Barbosa denied occasional allegations that his constitutional work in 1891 revealed Comtean ideals. He said that the document was "derived from the constitution of Hamilton and not from the catechism of Comte,"[24] and he frequently expressed his enthusiasm for the North American constitution. He found positivism incompatible with the religious sentiments of Brazilians and insisted that Comte's religion of humanity could not possibly replace the traditional Catholicism that had endured more than three centuries in Brazil. Moreover, as a liberal he was unwilling to accept the positivist idea of rule by an elite, which he viewed as a form of dictatorship closely akin to theocracy. Regarded by his contemporaries as an atheist, a charge he rejected, Barbosa retained his belief in the Christian values of love of God, emphasizing the importance of man's individual relationship to the deity.

The philosophy of Rui Barbosa is contained in his numerous legal writings and speeches, and in many respects it runs parallel to the critical idealism of Kant. His *Oração aos moços*,[25] a paper presented to the law school of the University of São Paulo, pointed out the importance of the just administration of law. He expressed greater concern for legal application by honest judges than for legal norms themselves. In this he was close not only to Kant but to the neo-Kantianism of Rudolf Stammler. As he told members of one graduating class of the law school,

23. Fernando de Azevedo, *Brazilian Culture: An Introduction to the Study of Culture is Brazil*, tr. William Rex Crawford (New York: Macmillan Co., 1950), p. 413.

24. *Ibid.*, p. 414.

25. Rui Barbosa, *Oração aos moços* (Rio de Janeiro: Casa Rui Barbosa, 1949).

"Legality and liberty are the Tables of the lawyer's calling. On them is inscribed the synthesis of all the commandments. Neither desert justice nor woo it. Neither be lacking in fidelity toward it nor withhold counsel from it . . . . Do not proceed with your consultations except with the true impartiality of the judge in his sentences . . . . Do not be lowly with the great or arrogant with the lowly. Serve the opulent with pride and the indigent with charity. Love your country, and your neighbor, keep faith in God, in truth, and in good."[26]

In his political thought Barbosa, though a progressive for his times, was by no means a pure and unqualified egalitarian. Indeed, he shared the same misgivings over the wisdom of the masses which Rodó expressed in Uruguay. Moreover, he believed in the basic inequality of man, given the fact that no two things in the universe are equal. Socialism he rejected on the grounds that its doctrines were based on material human needs rather than upon the spiritual merit of each individual. For Barbosa, equality consisted in the honest recognition of the existence in society of natural inequality. The principle of social equality he considered "a blasphemy against reason and faith, against civilization and humanity, the philosophy of Misery, proclaimed in the name of the rights of labor." He added that "society cannot make equal those whom nature has created unequal."[27]

Expressions of Philosophical Idealism

The early European idealism of Kant, Hegel, and their followers represented for many Latin intellectuals a reaction against that exclusive dependence on science which marked many Comteans. In later years the idealist statements were extended, leading to a final burst in Latin America which lasted until the 1920s. Certainly the German revival of Kant drew renewed interest from a number of Latin Americans.[28]

26. *Ibid.*, p. 85.
27. *Ibid.*, pp. 33–34.
28. In 1865 Otto Liebmann had published *Kant and the Epigones,* which helped to initiate a return to Kant; the next year Albert Langes' *History of Materialism* marked further movement of purely philosophical speculation in the direction of critical idealism. Additional impetus came as well from the universities at Baden and Madburg. In the former there were the critical teachings of Windelband and Rickert, and in the latter the neo-Kantianism of such figures as Cohen and Natorp. A similar trend occurred in France when Charles Renouvier's *Essais de critique générale* stressed the need to continue and to extend Kant. Frenchmen such as Ravaisson and Lachelier led a concomitant aggressive campaign against positivism.
The German attack on positivism was multi-pronged: from psychology, the intentionalism of Franz Brentano criticized natural science epistemology, paving

Among these were a small group of thinkers who, despite the experience of intellectual formation under the inspiration of positivist teachers, ultimately adopted a highly critical attitude toward positivism. Among the more representative figures in this philosophically oriented idealism were Argentines José Ingenieros and Alejandro Korn, Mexican Antonio Caso, Peruvian Alejandro Deústua, and Uruguayan Carlos Vaz Ferreira.

Each of them, in individual ways, criticized the exclusively scientific concept of reality and the narrowness of Comte which they observed. While all defended the autonomy of man's culture and human freedom against materialistic determinism, they drew inspiration from Italian and French neoidealism.[29] These somewhat isolated efforts toward a renewal of philosophical idealism started in Latin America around the turn of the century, reaching its pinnacle in the years between 1920 and 1950. It was at least mildly ironic that the battle against positivism by this time was over. In studying such men, it is important to keep in mind that these initiators of the final revival of idealism dedicated themselves almost entirely to philosophy. They thereby created a viewpoint and a group of disciples producing a continuity and revival of philosophical speculation. Because of their break with positivism, they were obliged to find their way by independent reading. Their search for new philosophical directions encouraged a critical and independent attitude that was continued by their students, accounting in large part for the recrudescence of philosophical inquiry by Latin-American intellectuals.

Among the major examples of this revival were Argentines José Ingenieros, Alejandro Korn, and Francisco Romero. The first of these (1877–1925), trained in Buenos Aires first in law and then in medicine, was among the intellectual leaders of Latin-American youth during the early years of the century. An outstanding student, he gained early scholarly repute with his 1903 doctorate, *Simulación de la lucha por la vida*. Named professor of psychology a year later, he subsequently lived for several years in Germany and Switzerland following his failure to win a more prestigious faculty appointment in Buenos Aires. It was during

---

the way for the phenomenology of Husserl. In jurisprudence the great exponent of a neo-Kantian philosophy of law was Rudolf Stammler, who conceived an original concept of the state and its normative legal order. And in Italy, Georgio del Vecchio assumed a polemical attitude toward positivistic trends in jurisprudence.

For further discussion, see Luis Recasens Siches, *Los temas de la filosofía del derecho* (Barcelona: n.p., 1935).

29. Especially influential were such figures as Boutroux, Bergson, Croce, and Gentile. Later, the still-evolving German idealistic writings reached Latin America through the influence of the Spaniard Ortega y Gasset and his *Revista de Occidente*.

this time that some of his most significant work was produced. Later returning to Argentina, he founded and for years edited the *Revista de Filosofía,* the first philosophical review in Latin America. Interested in politics in his youth as the result of his father's socialist beliefs, Ingenieros was among the founders of the socialist movement in Argentina, and although eventually withdrawing from public affairs, he never dropped his philosophical inclination toward socialism.

Ingenieros' early philosophical training was in positivism, and in his youth he demonstrated a decided leaning toward Spencer's social evolutionism. Experimental psychology, especially of the school of Tarde, was also a determining element in his intellectual growth. Indeed, much of his work clearly testified to his psychological training. His philosophy was also infused with a strong moral sense; this was especially evident in his most widely read work, *El hombre mediocre.*[30] Published in 1913, it contained idealistic overtones not unlike those of Rodó in *Ariel.* He maintained that spiritual mediocrity was reflected in political and social life, and he proposed the creation of an aristocracy of merit that had positivistic as well as idealistic overtones. Mediocre man, as defined in terms of his relation to the society in which he lived, required a system in which individual merit would receive its just recognition. "Natural selection would be possible and the merits of each one would benefit society as a whole. The gratitude of the less skilled would stimulate those favored by nature. The shadows would respect true men. Privilege would be measured by the effectiveness of abilities and would be thereby removed. The political creed suggested by idealism based on experience is thus clear."[31] This work was widely and enthusiastically received throughout the continent, and even today it is considered among the classics of social and philosophical criticism.

In *Hacia una moral sin dogmas* (1917), Ingenieros offered the thesis that morality was human, natural, and a consequence of inner experience but that it had no connection with any transcendental divinity. For him, the task of the educator was to build the moral conscience of the individual without recourse to the idea of dogmatic authority. He also wrote *La evolución de las ideas argentinas* and *Proposiciones relativas al porvenir de la filosofía,* both published in 1918. The second of these presented his mature thought on philosophical questions. Beginning by restoring the term "metaphysics" to what is unexperiential (*inexperimentable*), he explained that the unexperiential did not correspond

30. José Ingenieros, *El hombre mediocre* (Santiago: Editorial Ercilla, 1937).
31. José Ingenieros, *Obras completas,* 3d ed. (Buenos Aires: L. J. Rosso, 1917), X, 218.

to the supernatural of vulgar beliefs, to the absolute of the pantheists, nor to the unintelligibility of the relativists. For Ingenieros, "the unexperiential is . . . relative to the human possibility of cognition; the objects of experience being infinitely variable in time and space, the perfectibility of human experience never reaches the point of excluding the perpetuity of an inexperiential residuum."[32] But as human knowledge was founded solely on experience, Ingenieros maintained that metaphysics was only a system of provisional hypothesis, subject to verification or correction by experience. Without discarding his scientific and empirical creed, he opened the door to the use of man's imagination in the discovery and verification of truth. It was his faith in the role of science in human progress that made this part of his philosophy especially attractive to the youth of Latin America.[33]

Ingenieros was undoubtedly one of the more original thinkers of his time. Perhaps less imaginative, but also of substantial influence, was his countryman Alejandro Korn (1860–1936), who received his degree in medicine from the University of Buenos Aires. He went into private practice but after some years abandoned that career to become a teacher of philosophy. He had been a positivist but soon turned toward critical idealism, with Kant his philosophical mentor. For him as for Kant, sense experience contributed to man's knowledge but at the same time was limited by one's own consciousness. What distinguished the outside world from man, he maintained, was what separated necessity from freedom. Man sought first to liberate himself from material need by achieving economic freedom. This latter was as important as ethical freedom but should not be confused with it. Economic freedom to Korn was essentially objective, while the ethical sphere was subjective. The error of utilitarianism was that of emphasizing the useful, or economic, without paying adequate attention to the ethical concept of freedom.

Man might only enjoy the full expression of both material and ethical liberty after having first freed himself from the impulses of passion, thereby arriving at a state of moral freedom. This meant that man shared the dualistic economic and ethical ends to human life. In the quest for these two attempts at liberation, the individual through history had created his culture. Freedom therefore became, for Korn, a creative freedom.[34] The Argentine saw as the prerequisite of human freedom

32. Aníbal Sánchez Reulet, *Contemporary Latin-American Philosophy: A Selection* (Albuquerque: University of New Mexico Press, 1954), p. 156.
33. Ingenieros' complete works were published in twenty-three volumes by L. J. Rosso from 1904 to 1940. A more recent collection was published in that city by Ed. Elmer in 1956.
34. Alejandro Korn, *Filósofos y sistemas* (Buenos Aires: Ed. Claridad, n.d.).

the discarding of all subjection to economic limitations, but this was not the only prerequisite, given the close relationship of freedom and ethics. "The heart of the immoral act is that it deprives of freedom, degrades the human condition which is, or ought to be, one of liberty. The good act, on the other hand, has its reward in itself, in the very consciousness that in acting freedom has been achieved. The word consciousness is vital here, for it furnishes as much definition as Korn will ever deign to give."[35]

Korn's greatest influence was personal; his disciples regarded him as a Socratic figure whose teaching could best be learned through lectures and discussions. The general lines of his thought may also be found in his *La libertad creadora* (1930) and *Apuntes filosóficos* (1935). His complete works were published in three volumes by the University of La Plata.[36] Retiring a few years before his death, Korn was succeeded in 1931 in his chair of philosophy by one of his most thoughtful followers, Francisco Romero (1891–1962). Born in Spain but raised and educated in Argentina, Romero chose a military career but later left it for teaching and writing. He followed and developed Korn's philosophical idealism and enriched it with the contributions of the new German philosophical directions, especially the axiology of Scheler and Hartman.

Widely influential throughout Latin America, Romero made a name for himself among philosophical thinkers of Europe and the United States as well as in Latin America. For him the value of philosophy consisted in the sense of the problem *per se* and not in a constructive end. An individual, a group, or a nation should always be aware of the problem of his own existence. Man's conduct as a whole is always directed toward a valuable end. Man, as a spiritual being, transcends his individual interests and appetites.[37] Korn's dualistic conception of freedom, the economic and the spiritual, through the addition of Romero's emphasis on the value of philosophy as a problem, helped to prepare the way for a critical attitude in social and political thought throughout Latin America. This required a re-examination of the role of the state in relation to the individual. The stress was therefore placed upon the realization of higher ends. There appeared an urgency to innovate, to change, and to incorporate man into the whole of his culture. Many writers in more recent years have raised the fundamental question

35. W. Rex Crawford, "The Concept of Freedom in Latin America," in *Freedom and Reform in Latin America,* ed. Frederick B. Pike (South Bend: University of Notre Dame Press, 1959), p. 25.
36. Alejandro Korn, *Obras* (Buenos Aires: Universidad de La Plata, 1938–40).
37. Francisco Romero, *Theory of Man,* tr. William F. Cooper with an introduction by William J. Kilgore (Berkeley: University of California Press, 1964).

as to the values that inspire the behavior of political rulers as well as the ends and purposes of governmental institutions.

Carlos Vaz Ferreira (1873–1958) also represented the antipositivist reaction that characterized Latin-American philosophical idealism. He received a law degree at the University in Montevideo and devoted himself primarily to philosophy. For several years he taught at the university and in 1913 won the unique distinction of being appointed special lecturer (*maestro de conferencias*) for life. His lectures gained him an extraordinary reputation among all Uruguayan social classes. Later he also served for many years as rector of the National University. His first orientation was positivistic, following John Stuart Mill in many ways, but before long he affirmed his own position. Always opposed to rigid systems of thought, this opened him to charges of being a skeptic, although such allegations were less than just. His main ambition was to foster original and independent thinking by his students rather than to propose his own philosophical solutions.

The Uruguayan was consistent in his conviction that it was man's duty to himself to think from reality and never from preconceived ideas. His own thought was highly critical and analytical on a range of topics, and he tended at times to concern himself with minutiae. Always aware of the political and social problems of his day, he gave considerable attention to the examination of both institutional and philosophical trends. In his *Sobre los problemas sociales* (1922) he condemned inflexible thinking as well as the dogmatism of political parties which assumed themselves to be the vessels of eternal truth in the quest for solutions to social problems. Vaz Ferreira not only contributed to the new intellectual climate of his country but engaged himself actively as a concerned citizen when circumstances dictated. The sum total of his teachings was to stress the need for a complete re-examination of social and political conditions in Latin America as a whole.

The revival of philosophical idealism was especially strong in Peru. While its best-known advocate was Alejandro Deústua, there were others who carried similar messages. Among these were Javier Prado in philosophy and Mariano H. Cornejo in sociology. The life of Deústua (1849–1945) covered nearly two-thirds of the independent history of Peru. Born in the mountain town of Huancayo, he studied at Lima's University of San Marcos, became a professor of aesthetics, and retained that post for most of his life; he also served as director of the National Library and rector of San Marcos. A student during the positivist vogue, he began teaching when it was still a strong philosophical current in Peru. His intellectual rejection of positivism and accompanying doctrinal evolution in a sense reflected that of Peruvian intellectual life generally for a comparable span of years. By the turn of the century Deústua and Javier Prado had become the most prestigious professors on the faculty.

His study and writings soon became strongly antipositivist, and his was an early voice in Peru to speak out while positivism was still the dominant philosophical force. For Deústua, positivism was a doctrine alien to the moral and social problems of Peru in particular and of Latin America in general. He held that the need of his country was to create a class to provide national leadership and further argued that this was the mission of the university. There young Peruvians should be taught to sacrifice personal interests for the common good. Moral men should be molded before practical men, and therefore the university was the crucial level of education.[38] Sharply differing with the noted positivist, Manuel Vicente Villarán, and his followers, Alejandro Deústua believed in a conception of liberty that rejected mechanistic explanations. In his view, society was composed of two ingredients, order and freedom. The quest for order had predominated in the fields of politics, economics, and religion, but freedom had never fully influenced any sphere of culture except art. The artist created his own order, while in the other areas of life, freedom had been subordinated to a rigid order and devitalized by it.

Deústua developed this thematic concern in several of his works, especially his *Estética general* (1923).[39] He also wrote about ethical values, opposing the pseudo values of materialism that he saw as threatening man with degradation. Dedicated professionally to instruction in ethics and aesthetics, he elaborated over the years a general aesthetic concept founded on the intuition of liberty. Under the inspiration of the ideas of Bergson, he also formulated a general theory of the life of the spirit in which ethical factors ranged in importance alongside those of order and liberty. This intellectual inquiry over a period of many years frequently touched on the problems of the country, and there were recurrent themes of social concern. Although an excessive intellectual probity caused him to put forward original ideas with great reluctance, the strands of his thought often emerged from his analyses of contemporary

---

38. For a fuller discussion of his educational ideas, see Leopoldo Zea, *The Latin-American Mind,* tr. James H. Abbott and Lowell Dunham (Norman: University of Oklahoma Press, 1963), pp. 191–93.

39. Among his many writings, see Alejandro Deústua's *Las ideas de orden y libertad en la historia del pensamiento humano,* 2 Vols. (Lima: n.p., 1919–22), *La cultura nacional* (Lima: n.p., 1937), and *Los sistemas de moral (apuntes),* 2 Vols. (Lima: Empresa editora de "El Callao," 1938–40).

thinkers. His quest for a better balance of freedom with order came to constitute the ideological premise for a young generation of Peruvians, and the response was a critical analysis of the country, its life, and customs.[40]

Javier Prado (1871–1921), member of a leading family of the *limeno* aristocracy,[41] has been the subject of differing interpretations by Peruvian scholars. Augusto Salazar Bondy has described him as having inaugurated the positivist movement in the university with his thesis in 1888.[42] This seems borne out by his *El método positivo en el derecho penal* (1890) and *La evolución de la idea filosófica en la historia* (1891).[43] By contrast, however, another Peruvian has described him as a major contributor to the revival of the University of San Marcos, introducing for serious attention the study of Peru and the need for a profound social and political revolution.[44] In actuality, Prado expressed a somewhat diffuse set of ideas that lay closer to positivism than the more critical position of Deústua. He did, however, diverge from more traditional positivism in various of his expositions of national problems.

Without being himself an original thinker during a relatively short lifetime, Prado became a spokesman for what emerged as the study of sociology in Peru. Broadly committed to an evolutionary viewpoint that bore some resemblance to Spencerian thought, he portrayed with unusual vigor the realities of Peruvian life. He relied frequently on historical analysis and warned of the dangers of "theoretical and abstract studies" while counseling his students to observe life as they saw it about them. He was critical of economic autarky, racial fragmentation, and the domination of the individual by society and he demanded a true democracy within which social and economic reforms might be enacted. The state, he argued, must liquidate the institutions of its farcical liberal republicanism, adopting new forms where economic and material development could eliminate traditional forms of exploitation. What Peru required was the creation of a national consciousness based upon an equality of rights and of opportunity for all. In this, he went beyond

40. For a detailed discussion of Deústua's philosophy, consult Augusto Salazar Bondy, *Historia de las ideas en el Perú contemporáneo*, I (Lima: Francisco Moncloa, 1965), pp. 149–89.
41. Prado was a brother of the two-term President Manuel Prado (1939–45, 1956–62).
42. Salazar Bondy, *Ideas en el Perú*, p. 40.
43. Following his appointment in 1896 to the faculty in aesthetics, and a year later as the lecturer on the history of modern philosophy, Prado continued to write at a steady rate.
44. Jorge Guillermo Llosa, *En busca del Perú* (Lima: Ediciones del Sol, 1962), pp. 14–16.

the usual boundaries of positivism in Peru and stands in retrospect as far less representative of orthodox positivism than such figures as Jorge Polar and Manuel Vicente Villarán. Had he lived longer, it is not unlikely that his philosophical orientation would have moved increasingly closer to that of Deústua.

In Mexico the reaction against positivism was as strong as the influence previously exercised by the *científicos* in education and politics.[45] It was symbolized in 1908 by the formation of the Ateneo de la Juventud by a group of young intellectuals. Opposed to the official interpretation of positivism and highly critical of the Díaz regime, they launched a movement for ideological, educational, and political reform. Among their membership were many who later became eminent in the Mexican revolutionary movement, such as José Vasconcelos and Alfonso Reyes.[46] In philosophical terms, the most important was Antonio Caso, and it was in his writing that critical idealism recieved its major philosophical exposition in that country. Caso (1883–1946) was born in Mexico City and educated at the National School of Jurisprudence. After practicing law and serving in various diplomatic posts, he devoted the major part of his adult life to teaching and writing. As an instructor in law at the School of Jurisprudence and later as professor of philosophy at the National University, his lectures showed his reasons for changing from positivism to idealism and his admiration for Boutroux and Bergson.

Although he played a significant role in the wave of intellectual defection from Porfirio Díaz and Mexico's positivist era, Caso was more the scholar than the man of action. His lasting impact derived from the hundreds of students who passed through the university, were exposed to his ideas, and then attempted to apply them in practice. Except for brief difficulties in the 1930s when his firm opposition to Lázaro Cárdenas' socialistic education laws forced him out of the classroom for a time, he spent the remainder of his years in that environment. Beginning with the publication of two major works in 1915, his life was largely dedicated to an erudite and humane questioning of life, society, and philosophy. Caso was among the very first to explain and to transmit the philosophy of Bergson to Mexico, as well as German neoidealism and even the briefly fashionable exponent of an individualistic philosophy of history, Berdyaev.

Antonio Caso generally maintained his own independent philosophical position, despite an intellectual debt to others. In such early works as

45. See Chapter 4 for a discussion of Mexican positivism.
46. See Chapter 7 for a discussion of Vasconcelos in relation to the Mexican Revolution.

Problemas filosóficos and *Filósofos y doctrinas morales,* he presented his definitive rejection of positivism. He regarded it as an artificial body of thought that concentrated unduly on isolated and largely materialistic concepts of life and society, and he urged eloquently that modern philosophy should undertake a complete and total synthesis, embracing idealistic and moral considerations on the one hand and material ones on the other. He contended that philosophy could only come to grips with true reality by encompassing a respect for the individual within a universal and environmental setting.

Throughout his writings one finds continual reference to his personal conception of history. In rejecting historical materialism, he believed that the Marxian adaptation of Hegel was only a partial, and therefore an inadequate, formulation in which insufficient attention was given the individual. Thus he wrote that ". . . the materialistic concept of history, in its social philosophy, discards the individual factor. This is as absurd as to insist on eliminating chance in history. In this way economic determinism becomes a lazy fatalism. . . . How is it possible, in the development of a social, moral, or religious doctrine, for the person who principally and eminently engenders it to have been a mere accident? This absurd refusal to recognize the individual in the historical development of humanity will always invalidate the 'collectivist' explanations of Marxism."[47] To Caso, history was a cultural study, revolving about individuals and about personal values, rather than mere events and dates. Values were of overriding relevance to philosophy, and so the latter should be founded upon history if it aspired to significance. Society in all of its manifestations, complex though they were, should be embraced in any approach to an overarching philosophy.

Caso also carried a message to the Mexican people. Perhaps the most striking example appeared in his *Discursos a la nación mexicana* in 1922, where he called for a recognition and awareness of social ideals. Latin America had never experienced genuine constitutionality but had been ruled by personalism and *caudillismo.* In Mexico, this could only be overcome by working for social justice, economic prosperity, and an equitable observance of law. The educational function was vitally significant, for the paucity of properly trained teachers in adequate numbers threatened to stifle the development of free and individual thought. The development of the student's personality lay at the heart of the educational process. For Caso, there could be no doubt that the mission of education in Mexico was a basic factor in the development of the

47. Antonio Caso, *La filosofía de la cultura y el materialismo histórico* (México: Ed. Alba, 1938), pp. 25–26.

nation both spiritually and otherwise. Turning attention in later years to problems of governmental authority and to the international rise of totalitarianism,[48] the Mexican saw the deification of the state as dangerous and abhorrent. While criticizing practical democracy in such places as the United States and Great Britain for confusing means with ends—the ends should be truth, beauty, and justice—he argued that the spirit of man should reach its highest possible fulfillment, something that was wholly impossible under a totalitarian system. Man's freedom in the highest sense should be cultural and spiritual, a product of the rich historical potential of America and the continent.

Caso deeply believed that thinking should never be separated from action, and he therefore condemned all forms of pure intellectualism. In the words of Sánchez Reulet, "A fundamental conviction underlines Caso's work: that together with egotistic, utilitarian and economic activity, there exists in man a disinterested impulse which is manifested in aesthetic creation and in moral action."[49] This position was similar in attitude to that of Deústua, but for the Mexican the reality of values was social, with the community ever struggling to impose its values upon the individual. Against this action of the community, man necessarily reacted in defense of his own personal values. The solution to this struggle was neither individualism nor communism but a society that, conscious of its own values, would respect the free human personality.

SELECTED BIBLIOGRAPHY

Caso, Antonio. *La filosofía de la cultura y el materialismo histórico*. México: Ed. Alba, 1938.
———. *La persona humana y el estado totalitario*. México: Universidad Nacional Autónoma, 1941.
Deústua, Alejandro. *Las ideas de orden y libertad en la historia del pensamiento humano*. 2 Vols. Lima: n.p., 1919–22.
Gray, Richard Butler. *José Martí, Cuban Patriot*. Gainesville: University of Florida Press, 1962.
Ingenieros, José. *El hombre mediocre*. Santiago: Editorial Ercilla, 1937.
Jorrín, Miguel. *Martí y la filosofía*. La Habana: Cuadernos de Divulgación Cultural # 11, 1954.
Lizaso, Félix. *Martí: Martyr of Cuban Independence*. Translated by Esther Elise Shuler. Albuquerque: University of New Mexico Press, 1953.
Llosa, Jorge Guillermo. *En busca del Perú*. Lima: Ediciones del Sol, 1962.

48. Antonio Caso, *La persona humana y el estado totalitario* (México: Universidad Nacional Autónoma, 1941).
49. Sánchez Reulet, *Latin-American Philosophy*, p. 212.

Mañach, Jorge. *Martí: Apostle of Freedom.* Translated by Coley Taylor. New York: Devin-Adair, 1950.

Martí, José. *The America of José Martí: Selected Writings.* Translated by Juan de Onís. New York: Noonday Press, 1953.

Navarro, Martín. *Vida y obra de don Francisco Giner de los Ríos.* México: Ediciones Orión, 1945.

Rodó, José Enrique. *Ariel.* Translated by F. J. Stimson. Boston: Houghton Mifflin Company, 1922.

———. *Motives of Proteus.* Translated by Angel Flores. New York: Brentano's, 1928. Salazar Bondy, Augusto. *Historia de las ideas en el Perú contemporáneo.* 2 Vols. Lima: Francisco Moncloa, 1965.

1928.

Salazar Bondy, Augusto. *Historia de las ideas en el Perú contemporáneo.* 2 Vols. Lima: Francisco Moncloa, 1965.

6

Anarchism

Social and political radicalism appeared in Latin America in close connection with the labor movement. Scholars, intellectuals, artists, and others who early became concerned with labor relations and the welfare of the worker also joined this fairly universal phenomenon. Trade-unionism itself came late to Latin America and was forced to develop under unfavorable circumstances. Agricultural economies, the ignorance of the masses, and ruthless suppression of early labor movements by dictators and assorted strong men also contributed to the retardation. For many years after the coming of independence from Spain and Portugal, freedom of association for the workers was prohibited by law. In this, Latin America and Spain followed the example of France. The original French revolutionaries had dissolved the medieval guilds in the name of the freedom to work, prohibiting all associations created for the purpose of changing artificially the prices of any commodity. Labor itself was viewed as a commodity, subject to the law of supply and demand in a free market. Any association of workers endeavoring to secure an increase in wages, let alone side benefits of any sort, was therefore prohibited by law. This principle was enshrined in the French Chapelier law of 1791 and was soon to be imitated in many European and Latin-American countries.

In the former colonies, much of the nineteenth century passed before the workers attempted collectively to protect their interests through the organization of mutualist associations that provided material aid in cases of prolonged illness or death. Early *sociedades de resistencia,* which often were illegal and operated clandestinely, were not trade unions in the strict sense. In some cases strikes, although prohibited, were employed. Even in Spain, trade unionism as such was not legalized until 1881; it was only after the Mexican Revolution that it recognized the right of labor to organize, and in some Latin-American countries this was a privilege that was witheld until the 1930s. Among the reasons for the belated appearance of a strong and disciplined labor movement was the early influence of anarchism and its anarchosyndicalist and anarcho-communist interpretations. These labor ideologies were not replaced by socialism or democratic trade-unionism until some years after the meaningful initiation of the organized labor movement. To evaluate the role of anarchism in Latin America, it is necessary to have in mind its origin and development in southwestern Europe, especially in Spain.

The European Anarchist Heritage

The Russian anarchist Michael Bakunin (1814–76) was an initiator of peasant movements in western Europe and was the first to contribute   significantly to the organization of the rural workers in Spain. It was only in Spain that his ideas developed into the creation of something resembling a mass movement. In the years between 1868 and 1872, Bakunin had struggled with Marx for control of the First International. Perhaps the major point of difference was whether this organization was to be fundamentally authoritarian or libertarian. Bakunin inclined toward the latter and when, in September of 1868, a revolution broke out in Spain which removed Isabella II from the throne, he sent Giuseppi Fanelli to organize the Spanish workers. At the time, socialism and anarchism were both almost unknown in Spain, although there were a few middle-class intellectuals familiar with French utopian socialism and with Proudhon's formulation of anarchism.

Fanelli's efforts were favorably received by the impoverished rural masses of Andalusia and Levante, as well as by the industrial workers of Catalonia. At a congress held in Barcelona, the anarchists formed the Spanish Regional Federation of the International and adhered to the ideas and leadership of Bakunin. Thus, when Marx forced the expulsion of Bakunin and his followers from the International in 1872, a rival meeting in Switzerland attended by Spanish, Swiss, and Italian anarchists broke away to support the dissident Russian leader. In the years that followed, the attitudes and characteristics of Spanish anarchism emerged with greater clarity; these are particularly relevant because of the parallel they later offered to the early Latin-American movements. All decisions regarding strikes or any form of revolutionary action had to come from, and be approved by, the rank and file. No anarchist group was ever justified in taking action for which it was not both morally and materially prepared. This decentralization was a consistent and marked trait, one that frequently prevented efficient collective action by the workers. Another characteristic that held overtones for Latin America was the concern with agrarian reform, a consideration that was pronounced in southern Spain, where large land holdings were worked by impoverished and landless peasants.

Francisco Pi y Margall (1824–1901), the leader of the Spanish Republic of 1873, was both a federalist and a follower of Proudhon's anarchism. The only thing that divided him from Bakunin was his faith in reform without revolutionary action. As early as 1854, he had written a book entitled *La reacción y la revolución* which provided a rationale in defense of anarchism. The platform of the Spanish First Republic, for which he was significantly responsible, presented an agrarian reform program that included as goals the expropriation of uncultivated land and the creation of peasant communities. During the life of the republic there were several peasant uprisings which, without waiting for government action, took over privately held farms and initiated what was known as the Cantonalist movement until it was suppressed by the government. Spanish rural anarchism included among its beliefs a naïve millenarianism. As Gerald Brenan wrote, "Every movement or strike was thought to herald the immediate coming of a new age of plenty, when all—even the civil guard and the landowners—would be free and happy. How this would happen, no one could say. Beyond the seizure of the land (not even that in some places) and the burning of the parish church, there were no positive proposals."[1] Even today there is great similarity between this and the belief of the Latin-American masses in the notion of the "cure-all revolution."

In its early years, Spanish anarchism was divided into two identifiable tendencies. The workers of Catalonia were reformists who maintained that trade union struggles should be kept within legal bounds. The Andalusian workers, by contrast, favored short strikes accompanied by a maximum of violence and sabotage. The latter group also advocated what was then called "collectivism in the new society," which was to come after the revolution. All property would be held in common, and

---

1. Gerald Brenan, *The Spanish Labyrinth: An Account of the Social and Political Background of the Civil War* (Cambridge: The University Press, 1960), p. 157.

each man had the right to what he could earn by his work. This system presupposed a primitive agrarian way of life that did not exist in industrial Catalonia. Consequently, the Catalan anarchists preferred an approach that was then called anarchocommunism and coincided with the ideas of Peter Kropotkin. Following the revolution, all the people would be entitled to all necessary food and goods according to their needs, and all wealth would be held in common by the people.[2]

It is significant that the first important radical labor movement in Spain appeared in the rural areas, and it was Andalusia that kept alight the fires of anarchist ideology for many years. Later in Latin America, the first important unions to be established after the initial mutualist period were organized and controlled by anarchists. Most of the leaders followed the Andalusian pattern, and although this doctrine fitted the peculiar conditions of rural Spain, in Latin America it was frequently applied in the urban centers rather than the countryside. The decentralized organizational character of anarchism proved not to work well among groups of urban workers, which above all required co-ordination and unity. And in Spain, while anarchist ideas had some appeal to the middle sectors, factory workers never found these to be particularly attractive. For Latin America, there can be little doubt that the early anarchist influence delayed the development of strong urban trade-unionism, a goal that even today has not been fully achieved in some countries.

Another important element of anarchism, especially as practiced in Spain, embraced the activities that were known as anarchist terrorism. The trend developed slowly, emerging fully in the 1890s when middle-class prosperity was growing and Europe in general was enjoying a renewal of economic well-being. The lower classes, unable to share in the increased wealth, sought to shake the complacency of what was regarded as an inert and stagnant society. The subsequent reliance on violence as a meaningful instrument was shared for a time by a number of artists and writers, as well as a few members of the existing elite. The literature of the period fully reveals this frame of mind in the works of such figures as Flaubert, Huysmans, and Wilde. Anarchism became a fashionable literary and pseudopolitical vogue, enjoying its own salons, cafés, and small private intellectual circles. In Spain, anarchist *tertulias* were popular, and in Barcelona, one of the centers was ironically named the Café Tranquilidad.[3] A number of prominent Span-

2. Peter Kropotkin, *The Conquest of Bread* (London: 1906).
3. Brenan, *Spanish Labyrinth*, p. 163.

ish writers participated in anarchist gatherings and flirted with its ideas; at various times, these included Pío Baroja, Azorín, Maeztu, Fernández Flores, and Blasco Ibáñez. The fashion was relatively short-lived, for the fanaticism of the anarchist leaders in time drove away the intellectuals.

The social radicalism of such writers was nevertheless received with interest by widely read Latin Americans. There was also a response to anarchist political ideas, although some objected to the explicit rejection of an organized political party to participate in elections. The anarchists in southwestern Europe advocated direct action of what they called "propaganda by deed," which included sabotage and boycott in order to overthrow the existing social order. They refused to play the so-called "bourgeois game of politics," believing that if they did so, it would only strengthen the established order without bringing about positive results. The corruption of the electoral process, in Spain as in Latin America, meant domination by personal *caciques* and authoritarian figures who, it was argued, could only be brought to action by violent measures. In Spain, it was not until the early twentieth century that anarchist and even socialist groups seriously considered the possible value of electoral participation.

Another anarchist variant that left its mark on the Latin-American labor movement was that of revolutionary syndicalism, or anarchosyndicalism. Appearing in France during the 1890s, it provided a combination of anarchism and Marxism, taking its name from the French word *syndicat,* for trade union. The syndicalists maintained that the workers alone must control the conditions under which they lived and produced. Their purposes could only be achieved by direct action of their own workers' associations. They were opposed to reformist pleas of conciliation with the ruling groups of society, insisting that each class had its own standard of ethics and its own special means of defense and social control. Syndicalism resembled Marxism, but the Marxists wanted to have ultimate control in the hands of the state, while the syndicalists thought it should be exercised by the workers' trade unions themselves.

The French anarchist, Ferdinand Pelloutier, is generally regarded as the initiator of the syndicalist movement, but the most important theorist was Georges Sorel (1847–1922), whose *Réflexions sur la violence* (1908) was highly influential. Sorel developed the theory of the myth of the general strike, contending that a well-organized labor movement had the potential to paralyze the entire economic life of a nation. Even if this proved an impossible myth rather than reality, a mystical faith in the myth itself would give a feeling of power to the workers, helping them by means of revolutionary action to overthrow the social order. Sorel distinguished between force and violence, claiming that the government possessed the power of force or organized coercion while the workers could only respond by violence and revolutionary action. The concept of the general strike and the mystique of violence agreed with the character and mood of both Spanish and then of Latin-American revolutionary leaders. Implicit was the old anarchist notion that everything would be perfect if only the government and dominant social forces could be overthrown.

As already indicated, anarchism found fertile ground among the rural masses of Spain. In Latin America, despite the conditions of *latifundia* which resembled southern Spain, early anarchist interpretations stressed the urban rather than rural areas. Syndicalism was widely employed by the urban workers in their first attempts to create significant labor organization. Spanish immigrant workers from Barcelona and Galicia played an active part in organizing early Latin-American unions, and important syndicalist groups began to appear, first in Argentina, Uruguay, and Brazil. As Brenan has commented, "The Spanish classes were really far more pan-Iberian in their outlook than either the socialists or the bourgeoisie."[4] The movement remained urban and had to compete with less radical associations, especially with the mutualists, as well as facing the severe repression of hostile rulers.

Among other things, the early anarchist influence on Latin America is relevant for an understanding of the revolutionary ferment that exists today in the hemisphere. Even the Cuban Revolution, despite its Marxist orientation, in its early stages reflected the mystique of the "cure-all revolution" that was so typical of the anarchists.[5] The anarchists always rejected the strict discipline demanded by the communists, as well as the frequent tendency of the latter to subordinate moral principles to expedience. Latin-American revolutionary groups frequently have relied more on instinct than on systematic organization and planning. Radical political action in Latin America, even when conducted in the name of communism or another ideology, frequently resembles the "organized indiscipline" of the Spanish anarchists. This is as pertinent to an understanding of today's so-called "revolutionary left" as it was of the early anarchists to whom we now turn our attention. Undoubtedly the best-known anarchist movement was that of the Flores Magón brothers in the years immediately preceding the outbreak of the Mexican Revolution.

4. *Ibid.*, p. 200.
5. See Chapter 9.

The influence of anarchism elsewhere was also important, however, if somewhat more diffuse.

The Influence of Anarchism

As Woodcock has written, "Anarchism has thriven best in the lands of the sun, where it is easy to dream of golden ages and of ease and simplicity, yet where the clear light also heightens the shadows of existing misery."[6] This seems surely so in Italy, Spain, Portugal, southern France, and in parts of Latin America. We have already noted that the influence of anarchism retarded the organization of labor in Latin America and contributed to a scorn for orderly political processes among the working classes in Latin America. Another important contribution to anarchism was the attitude of writers, artists, and intellectuals in general who, although not themselves active anarchists, employed its doctrine as an emotional vehicle of protest against the existing social order. This phenomenon was present in Latin America as well as in Europe. And a third kind of impact was registered through the attachment of political leaders and also the masses to the idea of a revolution bringing about, axiomatically, a true and meaningful transformation of social relationships and economic welfare. This belief in a "cure-all revolution" has survived as exemplified in the Cuban Revolutionary mystique; the emphasis upon extreme individualism was a further component of anarchist doctrine.

Anarchist groups began to emerge as early as the 1870s in Argentina, Mexico, Cuba, and Uruguay. Each of these countries was represented at the Congress of the Anarchist International in 1877. Argentina provides an excellent example of the early anarchism of trade union movements. In Buenos Aires, an Italian immigrant named Ettore Mattei founded the Circolo Comunista-Anarchico in 1884, and a fellow Italian anarchist leader, Eurico Malatesta, published a bilingual Spanish-Italian journal titled *La Questione Sociale*. In 1901, Argentine anarchist workers formed the Federación Obrera Regional Argentina (FORA) under the direction of Pietro Gori. From 1902 to 1909, the FORA was Argentina's most important labor opposition, waging a long campaign of strikes against employers and the government. On May Day of 1909, a large demonstration of anarchists was violently broken up by the police, resulting in many casualties. In retaliation, the anarchists assassinated the chief of police, whereupon the national legislature

6. George Woodcock, *Anarchism: A History of Libertarian Ideas and Movements* (Cleveland: Meridian Books, 1962), p. 425.

passed a rigorous antianarchist law. The FORA continued to operate in defiance of the authorities and exerted considerable influence on the labor movement until the late 1920s, when it abandoned its anarchosyndicalist philosophy to merge with the Socialists.

In Brazil, syndicalism reached its peak in the 1920s, centered on the Confederação Operâría Brasileira and its organ *A Plebe*. Somewhat paradoxically, the Brazilian anarchists later contributed to the development of communism when many of the anarchist unions joined the International.[7] In Chile, despite the early rivalry of that country's burgeoning socialist movement, the anarchists played a major role within labor. One of their syndicalist organizations even affiliated with the Industrial Workers of the World (IWW). In Uruguay, the Federación Obrera Regional Uruguaya (FORU) was under anarchist inspiration early in the twentieth century. And elsewhere, to a somewhat lesser extent, the ideas of anarchism also attracted the workers. Until the hemispheric labor movement developed beyond its early formative period, the violently uncompromising tenets of anarchism, basically simplistic and easily understood, derived substantial support from the preceding migratory wave of European workers, especially in the Plate River region. The leadership also found itself entranced by the promises of rapid and definitive eradication of traditional grievances. It was only with the passing of time that the realization of weaknesses and flaws in anarchist doctrine led to its gradual demise.

Undoubtedly the single most important intellectual figure to respond to anarchist philosophy was the renowned Peruvian, Manuel González Prada (1848–1918).[8] Although philosophically unsystematic and eclectic in his writings, the overwhelming thrust of his thought was a negativism, a bitterly iconoclastic denunciation stemming from Peru's disastrous defeat in the War of the Pacific (1879–83) at the hands of Chile. Born in Lima of a wealthy conservative family, he was educated in the Colegio de San Carlos and the University of San Marcos, where an early exposure to the glimmerings of Peruvian positivism was relatively slight. One of the truly great figures of Peruvian literature, González Prada, in a ferociously poetic style was a rebel, a social combatant whose frustrations grew out of the military debacle and its seemingly unrepentant aftermath in Peruvian national affairs. To González Prada, the War of the Pacific

7. Robert J. Alexander, *Communism in Latin America* (New Brunswick: Rutgers University Press, 1957), pp. 93–95.

8. While defying easy classification, he was clearly much more than a pure anarchist. As this discussion hopefully suggests, however, the anarchist strain was a significant component of his thought and reflected an "antianything" attitude not uncommon to many Latin-American and Spanish intellectuals.

and its outcome gave anguished testimony to the masquerade of allegedly republican life in his country, with its *caudillismo,* its personalistic revolutions, its imported constitutions, and the inequities of social life. Lacking in national unity and a social conscience, Peru, he reiterated, could not even speak of military heroism or sacrifice in the face of Chilean strength. The country had been humiliatingly defeated and its territory mutilated; nothing could more dramatically underline the weakness of society.

With the formation of the Círculo Literario, González Prada initiated a career dedicated to the social problems of Peru and of the world about him. He censured the existing exploitation of the Indians and peasants, he denounced with equal fervor the abuses of the Church in Peru; his target was injustice and inequality wherever he found it. "He was anti-Spanish, anti-Peruvian, anti-Catholic, anti-ruling-class; yet the best that was Spanish or Peruvian or Catholic or aristocratic in his nation and in his people was united in him with a nobility which gainsaid all pessimism and gave buoyance to every hope."[9] Among his extensive writings, some of them collections of articles and essays that were published after his death, included: *Páginas libres* (1894), *Horas de lucha* (1908), *Anarquía* (1936), and *Propaganda y ataque* (1938).[10] His most recurrent theme was a devastating critique of Peru and its institutions, insisting that only a full understanding of historical shortcomings might serve as the proper prelude for renewed growth and progress.

Spain and the past meant the survival of forces that inhibited the fruitful evolution of man. If Peru were to march alongside the leading countries of the world, it would have to dislodge itself from the remnants of eighteenth-century mentality. The Hispanic tradition included regressive customs and a psychological outlook that continued to plague Peru throughout its republican existence. This was not only true in political but in social and philosophical spheres as well. If there was any single key to Peruvian progress, it lay in the eradication of ignorance, and González Prada's early recommendations for educational reform, especially in *Páginas libres,* had a perceptible positivist tinge. Yet this had to be coupled with a complete and total transformation of political life, the press, organized parties, and parliament, as well as the attitudes

9. E. Herman Hespelt, ed., *An Anthology of Spanish American Literature,* II (New York: Appleton-Century-Crofts, 1946), 571.

10. Manuel González Prada, *Anarquía,* 3d. ed. (Santiago: Ediciones Ercilla, 1940), *Horas de lucha* (Lima: Ediciones El Progreso, 1908), and *Propaganda y ataque* (Buenos Aires: Imán, 1939).

of the dominant class. Presenting a revolutionary ideal that was never expanded ideologically, he called upon the pressure of the workers as a means of changing the established order. In no area was his concern more pronounced than with the subject of the Peruvian Indian.

González Prada saw the indigenous mass as holding the destiny of Peruvian society in its hands. He rejected racist explanations of the inferiority of the Indian, which were not uncommon in Peru of that period, and followed the thesis of Le Bon in arguing that Indian degradation and primitiveness was a product of historical ignorance and of the European prejudices that had manufactured the existing artificial social system. He saw as the path to redemption an educational program which, starting with lessons in reading and writing, would in a quarter of a century restore human dignity to the indigenous masses. With the years González Prada became more analytical in his discussions of the Indian. The 1904 essay "Nuestros Indios" and subsequent articles on "La Cuestión Indígena," "Autoridad Humana," and "El Problema Indígena" further outlined his conception of the Indian as basic to a reformulation of national life and the inevitable readjustment of social attitudes.

To González Prada, the solution of the indigenous problem was a part of the larger whole, which demanded salvation for the working classes and a frontal attack on social inequity. In the process of expostulating on these subjects, he unleashed a relentless attack on virtually all aspects and personalities of contemporary life. Those subjected to his wrath included the morally austere political *caudillo*, Nicolás de Piérola, the esteemed man of letters, Ricardo Palma, and many others. In all of this he suggested a pessimistic bleakness of spirit that saw opportunism, servility, and intellectual anemia at all junctures. And yet, this was strongly allied with both the desire and expectation that, in the end, Peruvian qualities would succeed in overcoming the antinational selfishness of the past.

An implicit anarchist inclination emerged from his call for immediate and direct action, his emphasis on the role of the oppressed workers, and his conviction that, given the proper revolutionary guidance, a new and equitable society would rapidly emerge. Between 1904 and 1909, however, he wrote a series of articles for the Lima newspaper *Los Parias* which presented a more articulate defense of the philosophy of anarchism. These were among the pieces later incorporated into a volume under the title of *Anarquía*. Here his familiarity with the theories of such writers as Proudhon, Bakunin, and Kropotkin was apparent. Aware of the prevailing currents of the world anarchist movement, González

Prada clearly expressed his libertarian creed against the authority of the state. In an article entitled "El Estado," he wrote that the "frightened bourgeoisie is beginning to see in anarchy something else besides the bombs of Vaillant and Ravachol. Future generations will judge the present enemies of the state as we today judge the old opponents of the Church; they will see the anarchists and rebels as we today see the impious and the heretics of other epochs."[11] In a piece headed "Anti-políticos," he expressed the typical anarchist hatred of the existing political process. "Among the noises made by the selfish and self-interested, there is a new cry, a redeeming voice resounding among the working classes: *war to politics.*"[12]

Also of note was González Prada's condemnation of the laissez-faire democracy that he saw in Peru, as well as the ideas of democratic socialists. Virtually all the European socialist leaders of his day were condemned, including Bebel, Millerand, Clemenceau, and Jaurès. He wrote in "Fiesta Universal," "Far from oppressive socialism that, in any form whatsoever, is a type of slavery or an imitation of monastic life; far from egotistical individualism that preaches the laissez faire, laissez passer and everybody for himself, everybody in his house, we foresee a distant summit in which only one word is read: *anarchy.*"[13]

Manuel González Prada had many followers among students, workers, and intellectuals; his ideas were greatly influential in the formation of contemporary attitudes and ideas. Certain of his notions were adopted by the Marxist Mariátegui, and his teachings were also important in the later creation of the Alianza Popular Revolucionaria Americana (APRA) under the leadership of Víctor Raúl Haya de la Torre. Many of his disciples, however, followed broadly the ideas of socialism as the preferred course toward social emancipation. They believed, probably correctly, that his anarchism was an intellectual attitude that characterized his outlook, rather than an attainable program for practical political action. His views on the Peruvian Indians also provided inspiration for many of the *indigenistas* who followed.

Anarchism in the Mexican Revolution

Among the intellectual and political precursors of the great Mexican Revolution, few were as striking as Ricardo Flores Magón and, to a lesser extent, his brothers Jesús and Enrique. They gained a distinc-

11. González Prada, *Anarquía,* p. 29.
12. *Ibid.,* p. 79.
13. *Ibid.,* p. 17.

tive niche in their country's history as illustrative of revolutionary anarchism at the turn of the century and immediately thereafter. Although outside the main currents of Mexican intellectual thought, the brothers were nonetheless among the most vigorously active critics of the *científicos,* playing their own individualistic role in helping to overthrow the durable regime of Porfirio Díaz. Ricardo Flores Magón (1873–1922), the best known of the three, was born in Oaxaca of a humble family; his father was an Indian, his mother a *mestiza.*[14] The family moved to Mexico City, where Ricardo attended a preparatory school. After three years' study of law at the School of Jurisprudence, he left before receiving his degree to take up journalism as a career. While a student he had participated in several demonstrations against the dictatorship, especially in May, 1892, to protest Díaz' third consecutive bid for re-election.

Joined by his older brother Jesús and by Enrique, five years his junior, Ricardo founded his own newspaper in 1900, *Regeneración,* and it soon became a leading organ of antiregime propaganda, providing an outlet for all shades of opposition. One year later, anti-Díaz groups met in San Luis Potosí to found the Partido Liberal Mexicano. The Flores Magón brothers attended and joined the movement. Because of their participation in that conference and their virulent editorials in *Regeneración,* the brothers were jailed in 1902 and the paper was suppressed. Ricardo continued his attacks on the government through other liberal newspapers after his release, and eventually went to the United States to continue his campaign from exile. In 1904 *Regeneración* began its second phase, being published in San Antonio, Texas, and smuggled across the border into Mexico. The Díaz government obtained a court order from North American authorities and Flores Magón was arrested. The press and machinery were sold, and he was forced to move, settling in St. Louis where he subsequently revived his newspaper once more.

At this point, Ricardo Flores Magón seemed basically similar to other anti-Díaz Mexicans in his political views. *Regeneración* in its first two periods of publication, although violently nationalistic and moderately critical of the United States, represented the essentially moderate liberal views of those who were calling for the retirement of President Díaz and his close advisers. After the closing of his newspaper by US authorities in San Antonio, however, Flores Magón's ideas began to evolve in the direction of anarchism. In September, 1905, he was instrumental in founding the Organizing Center of the Mexican Liberal party in St.

14. Diego Abad y Santillán, *Ricardo Flores Magón: El apóstol de la revolución social mexicana* (México: Grupo Cultural "Ricardo Flores Magón," 1925).

Louis. Despite fear of Díaz' agents and the ever-present threat of extradition to Mexico, he and his colleagues prepared and issued the *Manifiesto y programa* of the Liberal party in 1906. The document was important in showing that Flores Magón was still basically a liberal in the tradition of Benito Juárez and the nineteenth-century Mexican leaders of the *reforma*. The *Manifiesto* was a sober analysis of Mexico's political and economic problems, and it embodied moderate demands for labor legislation, land reform, and the regimentation of foreign investment. Although Flores Magón himself was already delving into the teachings of revolutionary anarchism, he was not yet prepared to adopt such ideas and tactics.

In the same year of the *Manifiesto,* the liberals planned an armed insurrection in Mexico but, despite sporadic fighting around Veracruz, it amounted to little. Several of the participants were arrested in Texas and Arizona at the request of the Mexican government, but Ricardo Flores Magón escaped to California, where he remained in hiding for months. It was during this period of concealment that he became disillusioned with liberalism and turned to anarchism.[15] He read carefully Kropotkin's *Anarchist Philosophy,* as well as the more familiar works of Karl Marx. The result was to be Flores Magón's transformation from political reformer to anarchist revolutionary conspirator. By 1907 he was once more publishing a newspaper, this time working in Los Angeles with a journal called *Revolución.* And once more a request from Mexico City to Washington led to his arrest and sentencing to federal prison for violation of the U.S. neutrality law. Eventually he participated in another unsuccessful revolt—this one based at El Paso—and was placed in a Mexican prison until the outbreak of the Revolution in 1910.

By this time the years of exile and continual harassment had taken their toll, and Flores Magón had become an anarchist with extreme and undiluted views. Although most of his followers and co-workers had by this time left him, Flores Magón continued his struggle. He was opposed to Francisco Madero's presidency; and he demanded land reform through expropriation and state control of production under the slogan "Tierra y Libertad," which was disseminated and popularized by Emiliano Zapata, the revolutionary warrior from southern Mexico. In and out of prison as a result of continued conspiracy, he next turned his venomous hostility upon the government of Victoriano Huerta, who had assassinated Madero and claimed the presidency for himself. In

15. Myra E. Jenkins, "Ricardo Flores Magón and the Mexican Liberal Party" (Ph.D. dissertation, University of New Mexico, 1953).

due course the anarchist was also opposed to the so-called constitutionalist forces of President Venustiano Carranza. Zapata was the only revolutionary leader for whom he held any sympathy, regarding him as a true revolutionary because of Zapata's seizure of land and burning of property titles on behalf of his landless followers.

Flores Magón was especially vitriolic toward Carranza after the latter accepted the support of the United States. Eventually his interests drifted to world affairs; he welcomed the Bolshevik revolution of 1917, predicted the start of an international proletarian uprising, and in 1918 the final version of *Regeneración* printed a manifesto calling upon all the workers of the world to join in revolution. Along with hundreds of other anarchists, he was again arrested and tried by North American authorities, this time under the terms of the espionage act. Sentenced to prison for twenty years, he soon died in the penitentiary at Leavenworth. Thus ended a remarkably volatile career of a dedicated if increasingly warped individual, one whose anarchistic inclinations were among the most vivid to be found in the annals of Latin-American history.

It had been the failure of the liberal uprising of 1906 which was largely responsible for Flores Magón's disillusionment with political democracy. The 1906 *Manifiesto* was in effect his final gesture toward liberal reform, after which he turned wholeheartedly toward anarchism, presenting his first of many subsequent defenses of its principles in a 1907 article in *Revolución* reflecting the ideas of Kropotkin.[16] The first of his anarchist conspiratorial efforts were reflected within the Mexican labor movement, especially in the Cananea Copper Mine strikes of 1906 and the Río Blanco textile work stoppage of 1907. In advocating syndical unionism, he found receptive ears among the leadership of the labor group at Río Blanco.[17] Increasingly well-versed in revolutionary theories, he also established contacts during his stay in California with the radical Industrial Workers of the World. At the same time he had contacts with the Western Federation of Miners, a group that favored syndical anarchism and approved of direct action. Although little influenced by Marx, Flores Magón read with approval the works of not only Bakunin and Kropotkin but also the Italian-born Argentine anarchist Malatesta.

In September, 1911, his anarchist thought was reflected in the release of a new proclamation by the dying Mexican Liberal party, which officially repudiated the proposals of the 1906 *Manifiesto* and defended

16. *Ibid.*, p. 231.
17. For a fuller treatment see Marjorie E. Clark, *Organized Labor in Mexico* (Chapel Hill: University of North Carolina Press, 1934).

anarchocommunism in explicit terms. The new document, which all three brothers signed, called for the overthrow of all existing institutions by means of force, that the workers and peasants might own the factories and lands in common while sharing equally in the product of their labor. Following Kropotkin, the manifesto of 1911 was based on the principle of the "right to live" as the only inherent right shared by all men. The document claimed credit for the land expropriations of Zapata and invited the urban workers to follow the example in the mines and factories. The manifesto attacked the program of President Madero and asked the proletariat to continue the revolution until all government officials, capitalists, and priests were removed and the ideal of communal society had become a reality. After the victory of the anarchocommunist revolution, "all men were then to be free to choose the kind of work which they wish to do, whether on the land or in industries. Land and factories were to be owned communally and agreements concerning production to be made by common consent. Food and raw materials were to be exchanged for the products manufactured in the factories."[18]

Although Flores Magón's efforts to establish anarchist government in Mexico were unsuccessful, there were others who shared his views. Francisco Moncaleano, for one, established in Mexico City an anarchist group called Luz, as well as the syndicalist club Casa del Obrero Mundial. Later, the Socialists took over the club and expelled the anarchist members. Other anarchist labor groups were organized in the north, but Madero suppressed them in both Tampico and Veracruz. Despite the anarchist influence on several labor organizations, the establishment of the Confederación Regional Obrera Mexicana (CROM) in 1918 followed socialist rather than anarchist lines. This was a severe blow to the few remaining anarchists, and from that time they went into rapid decline. Perhaps the two great influences of Flores Magón on the revolution were his persevering campaign against Díaz and his support of Zapata's agrarian revolution.

It was an irony of history that the liberal *Manifiesto* of 1906 served as a base for the political and economic reforms of the famed Constitution of 1917, the latter coming as it did when the dedicated anarchist had long since lost his faith in constitutional government and bitterly opposed Carranza and the existing regime. In terms of hemispheric importance, Flores Magón was a marginal figure. For these purposes, however, his significance lies in the typification of the anarchist movement in Latin America rather than the originality of his political ideas. Anar-

18. Jenkins, *Magón and the Liberal Party*, p. 251.

chism in Latin America was relatively short-lived, providing an interesting if minor interlude at a time when the rise of the urban proletariat and a disillusionment with positivism in many countries presaged the coming of a new philosophical and political spirit. Nonetheless, anarchism did reflect certain deep-seated sentiments, especially in its impatient demand for immediate transformation and an unrealistic belief that rapid and swift direct action would permit, automatically, the unfolding of a new and better life. It was this latter conviction that was to be resurrected first by Fidel Castro and then by a generation of radical leftists unwilling any longer to bear the continuing inequities and injustices of Latin American life.

SELECTED BIBLIOGRAPHY

Abad y Santillán, Diego. *Ricardo Flores Magón: El Apóstol de la revolución social mexicana.* México: Grupo Cultural "Ricardo Flores Magón," 1925.
Brenan, Gerald. *The Spanish Labyrinth: An Account of the Social and Political Background of the Civil War.* Cambridge: The University Press, 1960.
Clark, Marjorie E. *Organized Labor in Mexico.* Chapel Hill: University of North Carolina Press, 1934.
González Prada, Manuel. *Anarquía.* 3d ed. Santiago: Ediciones Ercilla, 1940.
———. *Horas de lucha.* Lima: Ediciones El Progreso, 1908.
———. *Propaganda y ataque.* Buenos Aires: Imán, 1939.
Jenkins, Myra E. "Ricardo Flores Magón and the Mexican Liberal Party." (Ph.D. dissertation, University of New Mexico, 1953.
Woodcock, George. *Anarchism: A History of Libertarian Ideas and Movements.* Cleveland: Meridian Books, 1962.

PART TWO

*The Conflict between State
and Society*

1900–1970

Introduction

Latin-American political thought of the 1800s has been described in terms of the clash between individual liberty and authority. With the present century, however, the struggle centered on the competing collectivities of state and society. The masses began to show deep dissatisfaction with their political structures. The expected progress dreamed of by the traditional liberals, scientific-minded positivists, and utopian socialists had not come to pass. Many national economies were dominated by foreign interests, while the *latifundia,* peonage, and absentee capitalism plagued the majority. A large and politically influential middle class, viewed as the bulwark of the liberal state, had been slow to develop, and political power remained in oligarchical or military hands. Political thought turned away from the evolutionary concept of society, attempting a more critical analysis of problems. Thinkers grew more independent and nationalistically inclined in studying the characteristic environmental circumstances of individual countries.

The masses insistently demanded a share of the benefits that the state had traditionally offered to but a few. The general attitude with regard to the role of the state also began to change. According to the new concept, the state should be actively engaged in serving the whole of the body politic. Thinkers and writers of both the ideological left and right became attracted by a new version of statism. Although disagreeing about goals and values, they were united in advocating state initiative as the instrumentality whereby society might be transformed. Critical writers on politics at the same time turned against the evolutionary concept of social science, attempting a more realistic and nationalistic investigation of their problems.

In the early years of this century, two events joined with an emerging philosophical revolution to transform the nature of political thought. First, the Cuban war of independence and the defeat of Spain in the 1898 war brought about a major reassessment on the island. This loss of her remaining colonies also stimulated in Spain an intellectual revival known as the Generation of 1898, whose exponents soon were influencing Latin-American thought. Second, the Mexican Revolution of 1910 and the institutional formulation of its principles in the Constitution of 1917 was nearly as significant in its internal repercussions as had been the French Revolution during an earlier period. In its political aspects, the Mexican Revolution represented the demands of the urban lower and lower-middle classes, combined with the aspiration for land reform on the part of rural masses. The nascent Mexican middle class allied itself with the proletariat, represented by the urban workers, integrating a movement without precedent in Latin-American history.

The philosophical revolution was characterized by the arrival of Latin America of a new set of ideas. The reaction against positivism which had previously grown in Europe as neo-Kantianism and neo-Hegelianism had already been felt in Latin America before 1900. However, a renewed emphasis was articulated by the Spanish Generation of 1898, popularizing new directions of German philosophy such as those of Dilthey and Husserl, as well as the existentialism of Kierkegaard and Heidegger. The philosophical revival in Latin America was carried forward eloquently by such men as Antonio Caso, Alejandro Korn, Alejandro Deústua, and Carlos Vaz Ferreira, and then by the generation that followed. This neoidealism contributed to the attitudinal framework for nationalistic populism. New directions such as *indigenismo* also began to appear and in many cases were incorporated into party programs. A sociopolitical creed was elaborated, based on the idea that the cultural history of Latin America was continuous with the pre-Columbian experience. The roles of the *mestizo* and the Negro were widely stressed for the first time.

Latin-American political thoughts since the century's turn has defied neat characterization. The rising economic and industrial technology encouraged greater diversity in thought. As a consequence, the present century has been marked by a rich variety of political ideas and approaches, ranging from communism and socialism to fascism at the other polar extreme. One can find philosophical speculation on a highly abstract plane, as well as pragmatic political programs that are strong on policy proposals but imprecise in ideological orientation. Thus it is possible to identify two rather basic but distinctive kinds of thought, the first largely philosophical, the second more relevant to national political affairs in a temporal sense. In the former case, the philosophical revolution includes existentialism, humanism, and neo-Thomism, with inspiration derived from such diverse figures as Bergson, Unamuno, Nietzsche, and Maritain.

Without denigrating such writings, it must be said that they have generally been of limited relevance for politics. The more avowedly political writings, by contrast, have reflected an intellectual diversity that is equalled by the manifestations of direct political applicability. Not surprisingly, Marxism and its many variants have been among the most pervasive influences. Marxism has of course stressed the role of the state, while the emphasis on a planned approach to economic problems has been somewhat reminiscent of positivism, although adding among other things the component of the theory of class conflict. As will be detailed in Chapter 9, there has been a wide and perceptible division between socialism and communism; each has in turn been subjected to a number of native adaptations. The socialist element has proven more striking intellectually and can be traced back to the appearance of socialist clubs and publication at the beginning of the century in Argentina, Mexico, Colombia, Brazil, and Chile. Labor in its nascent period reflected strong ideological tendencies, and the anarchosyndicalism brought to the continent by Spanish and Italian workers in the late 1800s gave way to more Marxian influences. Labor also was to receive consideration in a long succession of modern constitutions, beginning with the Mexican charter of 1917. These documents, moreover, adopted the pattern of legislating on cultural, economic, and labor problems with strong nationalistic emphases, in place of the earlier tendency to enshrine abstract principles of traditional liberalism.

The emergence of socialism as an active political force, most notably in the republics of the River Plate region, was more democratic and reformist than conspiratorial or revolutionary. An early example of socialist influence was seen in the version of nationalistic populism introduced by the reforms of Uruguayan President José Batlle y Ordóñez early in the century. Despite classic treatments of Marxism penned by such men as Peru's José Carlos Mariátegui and Argentina's Alfredo Palacios, an ever greater historical impact emerged with the rise of social democratic parties. Beginning with Peru's Alianza Popular Revolucionaria

Americana in the 1920s, which blended with Marxist philosophical bases a socially conscious *indigenismo* with nationalistic overtones, the movement of social democracy later spread to a number of other countries. Venezuela's Acción Democrática, some of whose leaders had initially leaned toward communism, and Costa Rica's Liberación Nacional, which had first taken the name of "Social Democratic," were leading examples, and are discussed in Chapter 11.

Communism itself has demonstrated an uneven development through the years, although certain basic doctrinal features have been constant. The affiliation of communist leaders with the international movement, accepting in most cases tactical as well as ideological direction from Moscow, has contributed a flavor of opportunism that has in the long run reduced the efficacy of its appeal. Ideological divisions have become deeper within the past decade, reflecting both the Sino-Soviet split and the impact of *fidelismo* in Cuba. The original goals advocated by Castro were akin to those formulated by nationalistic Cuban reformers as early as 1933 and later enacted into the Constitution of 1940. As will be seen, the strain of Cuban nationalism has been a consistent thread running through the ideological fabric of Cuban revolutionary expositions. The charismatic and doctrinal appeal of *fidelismo* for a new generation of Latin-American radicals added another interpretation of Marxism, as it suggested in Chapter 9. Most of the writing by orthodox Communists themselves has come from political activitists who merely provide party-line polemics; typical are such men as Blas Roca and Juan Marinello of Cuba and the Machado brothers of Venezuela, none of whom has made significant ideological contributions to Latin-American communism.

Political events in the early years of the twentieth century were also important in encouraging the enunciation of new ideas and doctrines as well as contributing to a greater awareness of social problems. Most significantly, university students began to participate more actively in contemporary political struggles. The historical context for this development lay in the fact that Latin-American universities were long modeled upon the Spanish University of Salamanca, which in turn had copied early Italian universities in which student guilds had dealt on an equal basis with the professors' guilds. As early as the seventeenth century, students in Latin-American educational centers had participated in the election of rectors, and such practices have been revived and continued in the present century. Particular impetus has been acquired followed the spread of the university reform movement after its appearance at Argentina's University of Córdoba in 1918. The status of university autonomy has provided the students with license to participate freely in politics, especially in revolutionary and antigovernmental activities. As a rule, students are among the first to protest political oppression, the first to offer open opposition to dictatorships. And it is primarily at the universities, of course, that fledgling politicians receive their philosophical indoctrination.

Following World War I, there was a change in the tone of political thought. Democratic socialism as advocated in Europe had been overwhelmed by the force of nationalism and seemed to have failed in preventing the holocaust. The Russian Revolution of 1917 had assured that the split between Communists and Social Democrats would be enduring. All of this was viewed with interest by educated Latin Americans, and the subsequent failures of parliamentary liberalism and the impotence of the League of Nations contributed to a deepening of the interwar liberal crisis. One of the results was a growth of ideologies on the right, with fascism and corporatism gaining in strength and prestige. These movements were not without their appeal in Latin America, leading to the versions of nationalistic populism adopted for a time in Argentina and Brazil. The *justicialista* philosophy of Juan Perón, based in part upon theories of conflict derived from Hegel and Marx, attempted to assert for itself a third position that would harmoniously balance the four elements of materialism, idealism, collectivism, and individualism. While many have argued that the *peronista* ideology was false and artificial, the fact remains, as discussed in Chapter 8, that *justicialismo* provided a contextual framework for nationalistic populism in Argentina which has survived to the present.

In the wake of European expositions of fascism, comparable views gained some currency in Latin America during the years immediately preceding the outbreak of World War II. The most prominent example was the Brazilian "Estado Novo" of Getulio Vargas, which represented a self-proclaimed "authoritarian democracy" claiming to provide a balance between liberty and authority. Vargas' minister of justice and chief ideologue, Francisco Campos, published a work in 1940 which credited the regime with a Fascist outlook while paying homage to the example of corporativism established by the Salazar regime in Portugal. While Brazilians themselves failed to take seriously the officially inflated importance of the regime's ideological statements, what existed until the early 1940s was a Luso-Brazilian variant of Fascist corporativism that at the same time heightened the rising populism that had been latent in Brazil. The inspiration of Generalissimo Francisco Franco's political system in Spain was also echoed by exponents of *hispanidad,* and for a time this gained some prominence in Columbia. There it was sponsored by the conservative *caudillo* Laureano Gómez, who in the early 1950s was in the process of adopting a corporativist constitution for his country when he was toppled from power by a military *golpe de estado* headed by Lieuteuant General Gustavo Rojas Pinilla.

There are other intellectual bodies of thought that have also marked the recent and contemporary period. The Yankeephobia engendered by North American policies in the Caribbean early in the century gave rise to a largely irrational and polemical body of writings that nonetheless was widely read. The attacks of Eduardo Prado, Manuel Ugarte, Rufino Blanco Fombona, and Isidro Fabela were overflowing in vitriol and indignation, although purely philosophical merits were generally minimal. And in more recent years, broadly similar criticisms of allegedly imperialistic North American policies have been put forward by such men as former Guatemalan President Juan José Arévalo. A wholly different philosophy is that of Christian Democracy, which attained prominence only toward the close of the 1950s. Deriving from the attacks on secularism by Jacques Maritain during and after the Spanish Civil War of 1936–39, neo-Thomist thought was strengthened through a series of social-minded papal encyclicals. The intellectual and philosophical expositions of such Latin Americans as Brazilian Alceu Amoroso Lima gave added impetus to the movement, and Chilean Eduardo Frei headed the formation of a Christian Democratic movement in his country which eventually carried him to dramatic victory in 1964 presidential elections.

Twentieth-century intellectual contributions to political thought in the region, striking in their diversity and relative lack of cohesion, have ranged over a broad spectrum. Underlying much of the thought, however, has been the continuing effort to find a rationale upon which progress and development might be systematically and effectively based. At least implicitly, writers have reiterated what they have felt to be a need for a distinctive, original, and uniquely indigenous set of ideas that would prove timeless in validity and hemispheric in constructive applicability. It has been this spirit that has perhaps been strongest in the continuing intellectual inquiry of the present century. The emergent forms of contemporary political thought have also been marked by the prominence given to statism. Latin-American political thinkers, aware that their area has lagged in the march of civilization, are determined to catch up with it.

Whatever their location on the political spectrum, twentieth-century thinkers have argued that the activity of the state is vitally essential, necessitating intervention in economic and social matters in order to build a more advanced and enlightened citizenry. For the Communists, a proletarian dictatorship has been the avowedly indispensable step toward the utopian paradise of their classless society. Nationalists have stressed the necessity of removing the traditional influence and domination of foreign capitalism. Social Democrats have focused their statism on a major commitment to intervention that attempts to maintain and to strengthen democratic political processes. The Christian Democrats have advocated sweeping social and economic changes supported by a moral renewal based on Christian ethics. Even parties and factions that were traditionally conservative have, in many cases, come to advocate important social and economic reforms. Among the younger generation there is a revolutionary and nationalistic feeling that demands the eradication of conditions that have encouraged past political dictatorship and socioeconomic injustice. Whatever the specific ideological or philosophical formulations of recent and contemporary political thinkers, the instrumental magic in enunciated formulae for change and reform has rested upon the initiative and leadership of the state. Traditional nineteenth-century liberalism is regarded as outmoded, incapable of coping with the problems of the times. Its values have been rejected, but new ones have agreed on little besides the dominant role of the state.

Latin-American political thought has not succeeded in creating a new or original theory of the state. The basic political culture in intellectual terms is western, and the *pensadores* have generally followed the ideas of this tradition and civilization. On the other hand, they have evolved theories that seem native to the area. Among the most important is the concept that a successful political revolution is a source of law, all revolutionary acts being legal and obligatory for the population. It is true that this notion is based on the teachings of European jurists like Stammler and Duguit and on the principles of public international law, but in Latin America it has been developed and implemented. The Latin-American concept of private ownership is also important, for it holds that property, as defined in nearly all of the twentieth-century constitutions, is a social function and no longer the absolute right asserted by the older liberal philosophies. Property is understood to be a privilege granted to the individual as long as it is useful to society. Furthermore, contemporary political thought in Latin America has fully accepted the idea that the state is not only the guarantor of the constitution and the laws but has an incontrovertible social and economic mission. Representative government and civil liberties are not the only goals to be attained, for the state must also contribute to economic improvement and social justice.

The present concept of the state is not exclusively a Latin-American phenomenon, to be sure, for it exists in the majority of the world's developing areas. It is nonetheless critical to an understanding of political thinking in Latin America, where the determination to progress rapidly accepts the necessity of sacrificing the traditional established order and the temporary well-being of a generation. It is the natural opposition of vested interests and the traditional socioeconomic elite which has underlain the more serious and severe stresses that plague contemporary politics and society. As noted previously, Latin-American thought has turned against the traditional evolutionary concept of the state, undertaking in its stead a realistic, dynamic, and nationalistic approach to the resolution of problems. Intellectuals are determined to direct the destinies of the Americas by their own methods rather than shaping political, social, and economic life about the patterns of the nineteenth century.

7

Nationalistic Populism in Mexico and Uruguay

The growth and dissemination of explicitly political and ideological thought in twentieth-century Latin America has represented in considerable degree an opposition to the *status quo* position. From this have flowed several identifiable streams, of which three are especially important: populism, Marxism, and democratic socialism. Common to all three has been the element of nationalism, although variously interpreted and articulated. Nationalistic populism stands as the least ideological and doctrinal of the three, although having significantly influenced the course of politics and the rise of participation in a number of countries. As it evolved over the years, nationalistic populism came to reflect a vague but genuine concern over the needs of the masses, especially the underprivileged peasants and workers. A sociologist at the University of Buenos Aires has recently defined populism "as a political movement which enjoys the support of the mass of the urban working class and/or peasantry but which does not result from the autonomous organizational power of either of these two sectors." Moreover, it is "also supported by non-working class sectors upholding an anti-status quo ideology."[1]

1. Torcuato S. Di Tella, "Populism and Reform in Latin America," in *Obstacles to Change in Latin America,* ed. Claudio Veliz (London and New York: Oxford University Press, 1965), p. 46.

The same author further identifies three major sources of populist strength: an opposition to the *status quo* at the middle or upper-middle levels of society, a mobilized mass emerging from the revolution of expectations, and an ideology or emotional state that encourages communication between leaders and followers while stimulating collective enthusiasm.[2] Defined in these terms, there are several examples; the most illustrative of these are discussed in this and the following chapter. Strictly doctrinal or ideological tenets of populism can and do vary widely, as seen in such diverse movements as *peronismo* in Argentina and the Mexican Revolution. But it is important to note that ideological positions represent but one of the characteristics of populist movements, while the nature of class-oriented support is also of major relevance. It is possible to regard the Social Democratic movements as a version of populism; this is Di Tella's opinion. However, the Marxist underpinnings of social democratic theory are sufficiently distinctive to justify a separation of populistic and social democratic movements. Moreover, the "autonomous organizational power" of urban workers in the latter movements has provided a further basis for a classificatory distinction.

Early in the twentieth century, the tumultuous Mexican Revolution and the gradualistic but far-reaching reformism of Uruguayan *batllismo* stood out as leading examples of nationalistic populism. In the former case, a protest initially directed against the political *status quo* soon spread in disorganized fashion into the realm of social and economic concerns, involving diverse groups, classes, and subclasses in a destructive undertaking that in time reoriented itself toward a positive set of goals representing a major national transformation. Also prominent was a heterogenous but powerful emotional commitment that, although defying easy characterization, epitomized the demands of the urban proletariat and the peasantry. For Uruguay, the quiet but revolutionary transformation initiated and implemented by José Batlle y Ordóñez and his successors was led by middle and upper-middle class leaders who succeeded in mobilizing popular support for their programs. Some might argue that the pacific Uruguayan experience achieved a more striking set of basic changes than did the violence-ridden Mexican Revolution. Be that as it may, nationalistic populism in both countries underlay the dramatic alterations that emerged over time. The contrast with Argentina under Perón and Brazil under Vargas, expressed in more ideological terms, will become more apparent through the discussion in Chapter 8. But within the specified framework, these historical experiences were all illus-

2. *Ibid.*, p. 53.

:rative of the populism that emanated from indigenous national
movements.

The Mexican Revolution

The Mexican Revolution stands out as one of the earliest genuine
revolutions of the twentieth century. Today, more than fifty years later,
many in Mexico regard it as the most basic factor in the country's
life and politics. For the student of political ideology, however, the revolution is striking by its lack of an explicit, unifying body of thought.
The accumulation of analyses, interpretations, and polemics over more
than fifty years has led to a further dispersion of intellectual writings
in Mexico.[3] Unlike the tumultuous Cuban Revolution, the Mexican was
marked by neither a single dominant political figure nor an ideological
leader. And as the revolution was consolidated, there continued to be
many and varied spokesmen. It would be neither feasible nor appropriate
to present a full study of the revolution and all its schools of thought
here.[4] Instead, the more significant Mexican political writers of this
period will be discussed individually; as for an "ideology of the Revolution," only an indication of broad politico-philosophical trends can be
undertaken.

Precursors of the Revolution / While an authentic historical explosion, the Mexican Revolution lacked a universal and easily identifiable
ideology, for the political movement that led to the outbreak of fighting
in late 1910 had no set program. Moreover, the overthrow of Porfirio
Díaz came so swiftly and easily that there was little time for a definite
ideology to develop. Only by understanding the outlines of the movement
can one place in proper perspective the names and writings of a small
band of intellectual precursors. Perhaps the earliest set of factors revolved
about the spread of social unrest, based largely upon economic conditions.
Years under the *porfiriato*—the long rule of Porfirio Díaz dating from
1876—had cumulatively extended the discontent. The small aristocracy,
which by 1910 owned 70 percent of the Mexican land surface, controlled
an agriculture in which the peasantry lived under virtual slavery on

3. For a useful compendium of views on the revolution, expressed largely
by Mexicans, see Stanley R. Ross, ed., *Is the Mexican Revolution Dead?* (New
York: Alfred A. Knopf, 1966.). Also note Ross's perceptive "Introduction," pp.
3–34.
4. One of the basic sources for the serious student of the Mexican Revolution
is the monumental work of Daniel Cosío Villegas, *Historia moderna de México*,
5 Vols. (México and Buenos Aires: n.p., 1955–63).

the *haciendas*. Furthermore, the nascent working class had grown restless. The passage of progressive legislation had not prevented the regime from violently suppressing all organizational efforts, including several strikes. Moreover, the rise of a new generation increased the depth of feeling that demanded a change. Many saw the Díaz regime not only as a government of the privileged but one of elderly men who refused stubbornly to relinquish authority.

Voices of protest were raised increasingly. As early as 1893 Félix Requelme was attacking the labor system of the *hacienda* as a form of slavery. In 1904 Juan Pedro Didapp demanded political change in his *Explotadores políticos de México*. Others who symbolized the intellectual opposition to Díaz included Juan Sarabia, Antonio Villareal, and Filomeno Mata.[5] The influence of Ricardo Flores Magón and his brothers has already been traced. Of all these men, it is probably true that none had "formulated Mexico's situation as a problem to be solved and . . .[none] offered a new historical project."[6] No precursor was more genuinely representative of anti-Díaz intellectual currents than Andrés Molina Enríquez. His *Los grandes problemas nacionales*,[7] published in 1909, was perhaps the major contribution of this late prerevolutionary period. Basically a discussion of the agrarian problem, the work provided a penetrating study of Mexican reality. The first part traced the land question from the *conquistadores* to Díaz; the second focused on contemporary problems and their solution. The result was a forceful indictment of the Díaz regime.

In the view of Molina, the North American and European foreigner stood at the apex of the social pyramid. The small Mexican aristocracy, the so-called *criollo* group, collaborated as sycophants with the outsiders. The *mestizos* were praised as the most constructive social class, although Molina noted that neither they nor any other Mexicans could be said to constitute a middle class. At the bottom of society stood the peasantry and the Indians. Molina's lengthy discussion of contemporary problems represented a virtual demand for the overthrow of Díaz, although it was not so worded. Leadership of a revolution would necessarily be *mestizo*, for the *criollo* interests were tied to existing conditions, while the peasant, despite admirable qualities, was lacking in a sufficiently broad

5. Jesús Silva Herzog, *Meditaciones sobre México* (México: n.p., 1946). For his analysis of later ideological currents, see his *Trayectoria ideológica de la revolución mexicana, 1910–1917* (México: Cuadernos Americanos, 1963).

6. Octavio Paz, *The Labyrinth of Solitude: Life and Thought in Mexico*, tr. Lysander Kemp (New York: Grove Press, 1961), p. 136.

7. Andrés Molina Enríquez, *Los grandes problemas nacionales* (México: A. Carranza e hijos, 1909).

national view. The future was therefore dependent upon the mounting of a *mestizo*-directed revolutionary movement.

While Molina was not violently anti-*yanqui,* he did fear the effects of "americanization." Indeed, all foreigners were regarded as constituting a threat to Mexican nationality. For Molina, then, the revolution should be both nationalist and antiforeign. He advocated the creation of a Mexican nationality, defining the concept of *patria* or the fatherland as encompassing both a patriotic ideal and the institution of the family. True Mexican nationality was dependent upon a pair of factors: the unity of the family and unity in pursuing the ideal of the *patria.* The former awaited the meaningful division of the land while the second required a continual process of assimilation. For Molina, basically, the fundamental necessity was the creation of a Mexican nation. Despite an emphasis on social problems, he foresaw an essentially nationalistic movement evolving. Thus he could write in the book's final paragraph, "The time has come for us to form a nation, properly speaking, the Mexican nation, and we must make that nation absolutely sovereign over her destinies, mistress and queen of her future."[8]

While demanding basic reforms, Molina was staying within the broad framework of an evolutionary positivism that was not totally foreign to the earlier approach of Sierra. As he was writing, however, the concepts of positivism as advocated by members of the regime were being sharply and directly attacked by the Ateneo de la Juventud, or Youth Atheneum. This group of young intellectuals gathered about Antonio Caso in criticizing positivistic teachings in the National University. By so doing, they also filled the role of critics of official dogma in social, economic, and philosophical terms. The intellectual antecedents of the Ateneo membership were diverse, ranging from the economic theories of socialism to the abstractions of such philosophers as Bergson, Kierkegaard, and Unamuno. Given the political situation in Mexico, the common strand of idealism, blended with scornful attacks on the official interpretation and application of positivism, strongly implied the need for direct action against Porfirio Díaz. Perhaps the most important figures in what Paz has termed a "vast intellectual renovation" were Antonio Caso and José Vasconcelos.

The full impact of these two men is examined below within a broader context. As young leaders of the Ateneo, however, our interest lies in their critiques of positivism. Caso himself delivered a series of lectures in which he systematically dissected first Comte, then Mill, Spencer,

8. *Ibid.,* p. 361.

and Taine. Rejecting what he regarded as a nonphilosophical pragmatism inherent in the official application of positivism, Caso eloquently pleaded for the purity of philosophical speculation. Calling himself an idealist, he hailed the metaphysical values of Plato, Hegel, and others. Vasconcelos, by contrast, was largely intuitive in his criticisms. Wedded to the belief that emotion rather than intellect held the key to an understanding of reality, he was far more negative than was Caso. Despite the importance of these and others of the Ateneo as intellectual forerunners of the revolution, the role was essentially destructive. For Caso and Vasconcelos personally, greater and more meaningful contributions lay ahead in their more mature years. For the group in general, little was offered in positive terms; there was but minimal relationship between their theorizing and the specific demands of the people.

While young intellectuals were attacking positivism and Molina was formulating his analysis of Mexican reality, prerevolutionary literature also incorporated a number of more issue-oriented political tracts. In 1908 a lawyer, Querido Moheno, in *Hacia donde vamos?* urged popular participation while calling the attention of the people to their civic responsibilities under the dictatorship. That same year Francisco de P. Senties wrote a polemic entitled *La organización política de México* which advocated the formation of new political parties as a step leading to the overthrow of the regime. It was left for a modest volume by Francisco Madero to kindle the passions of the discontented. His *La sucesión presidencial de 1910,*[9] published in 1908, provided a narrative of Mexican history which concluded that civil strife and militarism in government had been highly deleterious to national development. Although critical of Díaz, Madero accepted the assumption of yet another re-election for the aging president in 1910. Calling for a set of reforms within the existing system, Madero argued for a closer and more scrupulous application of existing laws. This, he felt, would be preferable to a drastic alteration of constitutional prescriptions.

In his desire for wider participation in preparation for the eventual passing of the *porfiriato,* Madero was consistent with the traditions of Mexico's nineteenth-century political liberalism, and this contributed to the popularity of his book. A mystical quality to his writing also added to his stature as the symbol of the anti-Díaz movement. He was not wholly unaware of social and economic problems; nonetheless, Madero believed that political reform should be antecedent to social revolution. Having come under the philosophical influence of Krausism during Euro-

9. Francisco I. Madero, *La sucesión presidencial de 1910* (México: 1910).

pean travels, he had returned to Mexico with an idealistic humanitarianism in which pacifism and spiritual values were important. This intellectual proclivity underlay in part his judgment that socioeconomic reforms might be realized within the existing power structure. Madero rapidly came to epitomize mass protest. With a slogan of "effective suffrage and no re-election," he became the apostle of the revolutionary movement. Assuming the presidency in 1911 upon the overthrow of Díal which followed the outbreak of fighting, he served but two years before being swept away by overpowering forces. Despite his violent removal at the hands of assassins, however, he had opened the way for change. With the unfolding of the revolution, the land would never again be the same.

Constitutionalism and the Quest for Nationality / Beginning with the deadly conspiracy against Madero in 1913, Mexico's *tormenta* spread with a vengeance. This reign of terror was typified by the unbridled passions of competing revolutionaries whose differing ideas supported personal ambitions. To the south, Emiliano Zapata in his Plan of Ayala called for *tierra y libertad,* today revered as a cornerstone of the revolutionary heritage. Articles 6 and 7 of the plan called for expropriation of the great *haciendas* and a redistribution of the land to Indian communities. As the first major revolutionary leader to champion a solution of agrarian problems, Zapata and his counselors envisaged a return to past traditions. In the advocacy of communal farms, the goal was in effect a restoration of preconquest agricultural and land patterns. As such, Zapata was proposing the elimination of the semifeudalistic past on behalf of the landless. In the north, Francisco "Pancho" Villa, although an unscrupulous revolutionary without a program, crudely epitomized *machismo* as a leader of popular discontent. In Padgett's words, he "was a warrior, not a statesman, but as a warrior figure he contributes essential zest and color to the nationalist revolutionary tradition."[10]

During the early years of *la tormenta,* various figures claimed alternatively that the revolutionary goals were constitutional, political, social, agrarian, anticlerical, anti-imperialist, and so forth. With the country paralyzed by virtual civil war, the Mexican intelligentsia remained unable to formulate a systematic ideological whole out of the diverse popular aspirations. When Venustiano Carranza gained control, he assumed the role of victorious military Caesar. An unreserved nationalist whose political notions were vaguely set in the tradition of Mexican political

10. L. Vincent Padgett, *The Mexican Political System* (Boston: Houghton Mifflin Company, 1966), p. 25.

liberalism, Carranza nonetheless was influenced by his advisers and confidants. It was the work of this small group that led to the formulation of the Mexican Constitution of 1917, the single most important document of the period. The result was a concerted effort to deal with central issues of national history. Among these were the land problem, the role of the Church, the place of the Indian, foreign economic interests, and centralization versus decentralization. Among the most influential of Carranza's advisers at this point was Luis Cabrera.

A leading intellectual of the revolutionary period, Cabrera had been prominent during the Madero period and later took a large part in the administration of the Carranza government. On the eve of the constitutional convention he wrote that the revolution had been a popular insurrection against the Díaz regime and the system that supported it. The uprising had been the only means at hand to destroy that system and to undertake the construction of a new and better one. By 1917, he wrote, the destructive revolutionary period had completed the dismantling of existing socioeconomic and political forms. The responsibility of the Carranza government became that of proceeding with the effort at reconstruction. Once this had been completed, it would be "possible to return to a legal regime no longer based upon the old legislation and the obsolete system, but upon new principles that become the new legal system, that is to say, the new regime."[11] For Cabrera, such was the situation facing the drafters of the new document.

The Constitution of 1917 enshrined the role of the state, in contrast to the traditional *laissez faire* concepts represented in the earlier 1857 charter. Accompanying the establishment of a strong presidential system was a major commitment in the social and economic realm. The description of a federal system barely cloaked what in practice proved a highly centralized government. The two most important constitutional articles regarding the revolution were 27 and 123. The former claimed national jurisdiction over "all minerals, or substances in veins, masses, or layers . . . such as minerals from which are extracted the metals and metaloids used in industry, precious stones, salt deposits from seawater, mineral or organic materials to be used as fertilizers, solid mineral fuels, petroleum; and all solid, liquid, or gaseous hydrogen carbide." The article thereby staked out Mexico's ownership and control over all subsoil deposits. This upheld Mexican nationalism, the central economic role of the state, and a repudiation of foreign domination of the country's

---

11. Luis Cabrera, "The Mexican Revolution—Its Causes, Purposes, and Results," *The Annals of the American Academy of Political and Social Sciences,* Supplement to XIX (January 1917), p. 15.

own resources. Article 123 was a virtual labor code which was a pioneering effort for the hemisphere. Working hours, minimum wages, social benefits, and organizational opportunities were guaranteed to both industrial and agricultural workers.

Many Mexicans came to regard Article 27 as the single most important base for the emerging revolutionary mystique, and it was fully used in this sense during the long controversy of the 1920s and 1930s with the United States over the development and exploitation of subsoil petroleum deposits. In a less concrete sense, the gradual stabilization of government and politics in the years after the adoption of the constitution provided a setting within which the quest for nationality took place. This intellectual and popular search did not always follow doctrinal or philosophical lines, but it was essential to the gradual creation of the revolutionary ideology. There was a basic cleavage as to whether the Spanish conquest constituted a part of national history. Debate was endless over the multifaceted problem of redeeming the Indian. As efforts at truly national integration were taken, the clash between the heritage of the past and contemporary problems of erecting a modern state was unending.

The decade of the twenties saw the beginning of a resurrection of Aztec civilization as an integral part of Mexican evolution. Archaeological activities received tremendous impetus, while a host of writers delved into anthropological and racial analyses. Scholars dug amidst the ruins of Yucatán and Teotihuacán, and Mexican artists provided even greater contributions in reviving the ancient past. Such men as Rivera, Siqueiros, Orozco, Tamayo, and others created a theme and style of Mexican painting which gained them international repute. The glorification of the Indian at the expense of his exploiters—from Spaniards of the conquest to the invading soldiers of the French and the North Americans—provided a virtual sanctification of the humble virtues. In the process, the Indian was placed at the vortex of the revolution and everything for which it stood. As one observer has written, "The Mexican art of this decade fulfilled two functions. It interpreted Mexican history to the Mexican people, thus creating a visual memory which aided in establishing a new national identity, overcoming the alienation which had disturbed Mexico since the days of Cortés. In addition, Mexican art made the world aware of Mexico's struggle and in the process obtained universal reach, becoming an integral part of contemporary art."[12] Literature provided a similar orientation; from the revolution

12. Gerhard Masur, *Nationalism in Latin America: Diversity and Unity* (New York: Macmillan Co., 1966), p. 81.

came the epic struggles that inspired the leading novels of the period. Mariano Azuela, Jaime Torres Bodet, and a host of others were to elaborate artful variations on the same revolutionary theme.

With the conclusion of the military phase of the Revolution, young intellectuals became involved in the construction of a new nation and its creed. Many played their parts in government, while others were either publicly or privately influential on political leadership. Perhaps none was more representative than José Vasconcelos (1882–1959), one of the towering intellectual *pensadores* of twentieth-century Mexico. As a young man prominent in the Ateneo de Juventud, he wrote voluminously during a long life, seeking a Mexican identity with sound philosophical bases. An imaginative thinker whose writings derived from various sources while attempting to transcend them all, he gave extensive thought to the problem of race. Titling some of his works by such labels as *Indología* and *La raza cósmica*,[13] Vasconcelos undertook an effort at synthesis in which each race was given its due. Drawing the kind of contrasts between Latin and North Americans typical of so many colleagues, he argued that the breakdown of isolation was leading to the development of an Ibero-American reality. For Mexico, there were many rich traditions from which a superior and unique being was emerging.

In the two works cited above, Vasconcelos argued that the potential for the future was limitless. He saw in the reconciliation of Indian, African, and European traits the ingredients for his "cosmic race." The *mestizo* was not the inferior being that many had portrayed, but a fortuitous mixture that had been handicapped by the environmental and historical circumstances surrounding him. Mexicans were descended from both European and Indian aristocracies, and this meant a process of assimilation in which the infusion of African characteristics would also be beneficial. The ultimate result would be nothing less than a new cultural being, containing the highest and purest qualities. The inhumanity of positivism, the grossness of Anglo-Saxon pragmatism and materialism would all be subordinated to a higher order. For Mexico and indeed for all of Latin America, the most important cause was that of effective integration. With a cultural and racial fusion, the supreme achievement in civilization would be realized. The material stage of civilization would evolve into the intellectual and then, ultimately,

13. José Vasconcelos, *Indología: Una interpretación de la cultura iberoamericana* (Barcelona: Agencia Mundial de Librerías, 1927), and *La raza cósmica: Misión de la raza iberoamericana* (Paris: Agencia Mundial de Librerías, 1925).

into the aesthetic. At that juncture, "The principal task of society will not then be to defend itself against each man doing that which is right in his own eyes, as in the second period; nor against social injustice, as in the third; nor will it be the task of insuring production adequate to meet the needs of all. . . . It will be to prepare the soul for its endless rising and transcending of the material."[14]

The underlying philosophical bases of Vasconcelos' thought lies in his massive trilogy on metaphysics, ethics, and aesthetics.[15] In his all-embracing conceptualization, the Mexican attempted a universal synthesis of philosophical writings. In the volume entitled *Etica,* he argued that man could be free only by the liberation of his own thought, with philosophical guidance giving true meaning to practical action. Naturalism and emotion rather than the logic of social science should provide the impetus; for Vasconcelos this would ideally be couched in mystical intuition rather than rational intellectualism. In *Estética,* which he conceived first but published third, he declared that such considerations were paramount. True knowledge and a comprehension of society and of civilization could emanate only from intuition. Of all the various forms of knowledge, only the emotional and the aesthetic coud be ultimately satisfactory. It was the aesthetic method rather than the scientific or the intellectual which might bring to one the comprehension of the nature of things. Moreover, the highest ethical values were those inherent in the aesthetic.

If the mystical quality of Vasconcelos' thought was most obscure and disorganized in his philosophical writings, some clarification was provided by his actions as a public servant. Rising to the position of minister of education at a critical time, he was greatly responsible for the building of cultural nationalism. In large part the founder of modern education in Mexico, he carried out the earlier work of Justo Sierra by improving the quality of instruction while moving well beyond the elementary and introductory plane. Viewing education as a process demanding active involvement, he encouraged intellectual contact with the masses. Schools were built in rural areas, textbooks prepared and distributed, literary classics translated and made available in cheap editions, special teaching institutes founded, and traveling groups of teachers dispatched through the countryside. The popular arts were revived, while artists were given both moral and material support. Education was placed squarely in

14. Vasconcelos, *Indología,* p. 217.
15. José Vasconcelos, *Tratado de metafísica* (México: Botas, 1929), *Estética* (México: Botas, 1939), and *Etica,* 2d ed. (México: Botas, 1936).

the midst of revolutionary currents, and past traditions were stressed in the effort to eliminate class-oriented traditionalism. The past, in effect, was invoked on behalf of a dynamic and vigorous future.

Throughout a stormy public life Vasconcelos was often inconsistent, for he was in many ways a unique figure. Never forgetting entirely a strong Catholic upbringing, he was nonetheless a dissenter who stressed secularism in Mexican education. Although in many ways sympathetic toward the United States, he nonetheless wrote bitter diatribes[16] that were often petty, as when he mocked the investigations of the Smithsonian Institution of Washington. Regarding himself as fully knowledgeable in philosophical and artistic matters, he coveted a chair in philosophy although never having taken a course in the subject. At a time when Debussy and Ravel had gained universal recognition as original and innovating musical giants, he bragged of his inability to understand or appreciate their music. An ardent nationalist with almost fanatical pride in the Mexican Revolution, he tended to idealize the Spanish influence although castigating its impact upon Mexican history. A man of great ambition, he withdrew permanently from politics following his unsuccessful race for the presidency in 1930, rapidly squandering his substantial power and authority through a long succession of attacks on his former colleagues.[17] Yet if he was a contradictory figure, Vasconcelos was a true son of the Mexican Revolution. Just as he can be understood only within the context of that great event, so can the revolution itself be appreciated more fully through an awareness of Vasconcelos, his works and his writings.

Another Mexican who typified certain of the intellectual responses to the events of the revolution and its aftermath was Samuel Ramos (1897–1959), whose writing was as rigorously coherent as that of Vasconcelos was diffuse.[18] The most pertinent of his works for this discussion is *El perfil del hombre y de la cultura en México*.[19] Appearing in 1934,

16. José Vasconcelos, *Bolivarismo y monroismo*, 2d ed. (Santiago: Ercilla, 1935).

17. For a remarkable account of his life and times, see Vasconcelos' four-volume autobiography, published by Botas from 1935 to 1939: *Ulises criollo, La tormenta, El desastre*, and *Proconsulado*. An abridged translation of the first of the series is available as *A Mexican Ulysses*, tr. William Rex Crawford (Bloomington: Indiana University Press, 1963).

18. For a pertinent discussion, see Fernando Salmerón, "Mexican Philosophers of the Twentieth Century," in Mario de la Cueva et al., *Major Trends in Mexican Philosophy* (Notre Dame and London: University of Notre Dame Press, 1966), pp. 246–87.

19. Samuel Ramos, *El perfil del hombre y de la cultura en México* (México: Imprenta Mundial, 1934). For a translation by Peter G. Earle, see *Profile of Man and Culture in Mexico* (Austin: University of Texas Press, 1962).

the volume was an effort to probe in orderly psychological fashion into the mind and heart of Mexico. Arguing that to do this would lead to an understanding of national culture and society, Ramos began with a consideration of the *pelado,* a kind of urban vagabond. Noting the *pelado's* concern with strength and masculine virility as a means of compensating for a strong feeling of inferiority, Ramos continued by arguing that an innate mistrust was also characteristic of the middle-class Mexican. The long heritage of colonialism, which for Ramos extended until the outbreak of the revolution, had bred a form of cultural subordination that was deeply engrained in the great majority of Mexicans.

To overcome this, in Ramos' view, was one of the pressing necessities of his day. Pursuing a middle course, he believed that there were inherent evils in either an overemphasis on European traditions or an inward isolation from all foreign influences. While Mexico should resist the encroachments of the mechanistic view of its northern neighbor, this should not mean a concomitant rejection of European civilization as a whole. Mexican cultural development in the twentieth century owed much to adaptations of European achievements, a factor which could not be ignored. Ramos argued cogently that Mexicans should be continually questioning themselves in the quest for self-understanding.

Ramos' efforts to dissect the Mexican personality had their bases in deep philosophical convictions that were best expressed in *Hacia un nuevo humanismo.*[20] Ramos had an intuitive distrust of pure intellect—not an uncommon characteristic among other Mexican thinkers—which was at times reflected in concern over individual dehumanization before the power of the machine. Echoing the voices of Unamuno and Ortega y Gasset, he identified the crisis of mankind as the abdication of the philosopher before the expedients of materialism. This had led to a dangerous loss in the higher values, and the critical task should therefore be a careful personal re-examination of man and his place in society. As Ramos argued, philosophy could define for man his spiritual values, his intuitive beliefs that could lead to the "new humanism." This would permit a renunciation of the lower morality for the sake of the higher, with the individual free to recognize and to develop the values of his personality and of the culture in which he might live.[21]

Vasconcelos and Ramos were, of course, but two of many who contributed to an elaboration, extension, and critical understanding of Mexico, its culture, and its revolutionary creed. The importance of many

20. Samuel Ramos, *Hacia un nuevo humanismo* (México: La Casa de España, 1940).
21. *Ibid.,* pp. 134–35.

others cannot be gainsaid. There was the individualistic Jesús Silva Herzog, a leading economist who founded and edited the esteemed *Cuadernos Americanos*. There was Jorge Cuesta, a perceptive critic who differed with Ramos on the role of European ideas and attacked the influence of French rationalism while arguing that revolutionary Mexico was without a past. The quest for self-understanding was followed by historian and economist Daniel Cosío Villegas; founder of the prestigious and influential publishing house Fondo de Cultura Económica, he has recently become better known in the United States with the English publication of some of his writings.[22] The literary brilliance of man of letters Alfonso Reyes gave a lyric touch to an understanding of the revolution. Leopoldo Zea in his studies of philosophy and especially of positivism has also provided enlightenment, and some of his work has happily become available in English. While these writings covered a considerable time span, most were written in the spirit of the quest which was inaugurated even before 1917. It remained for political events to spell out in specific terms the concrete policies and goals of the revolution.

Revolutionary Politics / The institutional bases of the revolution had gradually taken root during the 1920s, and by the start of the next decade, the setting was ready for the introduction of policies implementing the ideals of the 1917 constitution. The initiator of such measures was Lázaro Cárdenas (1895———), whose six-year presidential term began in 1934. Only fifteen years old when the fighting had begun, Cárdenas was a product of the revolution rather than one of its initiators. Rising to importance through first the military and then the government, he came to the presidency as leader of the left wing of the revolutionary movement. While by no means a pure ideologue, he had developed a closely reasoned, if personal, view of the revolution. In contrast with the conservatism of his immediate predecessors, he regarded the revolutionary responsibility to the peasants and workers as unfulfilled. Important reforms remained to be introduced, and for Cárdenas this meant extensive state intervention. His administration proved to be the most active in developing the kind of fundamental change implied by the revolution in its early years. Himself a revolutionary in the full sense of the word, Cárdenas headed a government that dedicated itself in

22. Daniel Cosío Villegas, *American Extremes,* tr. Américo Paredes (Austin: University of Texas Press, 1964). Also see Cosío Villegas, *Change in Latin America: The Mexican and Cuban Revolutions* (Lincoln: University of Nebraska Press, 1961).

practical terms to the extension and solidification of Mexican nationality. Certainly it represented the most active period of nationalistic populism in Mexico, one measure of which has been Cárdenas' prestige and popularity for more than a quarter-century following his presidency.

Cárdenas' first challenge in office was largely political. He had to assert his own primacy over a predecessor as well as suppressing the last vestiges of private armies that had remained after the years of violence. He first began to shift military commanders and to court the favor of younger officers; this soon gave him a preponderance of his own supporters within the armed forces. Similar manipulation led to the elimination by 1938 of the last of the self-made revolutionary generals, who for years had regarded themselves as largely independent of national authority. An extensive and unending effort to solidify his personal popularity with the peasantry, begun during the 1934 presidential campaign, brought Cárdenas a greater degree of popular identification with the revolution than any others had enjoyed. This contributed further toward the pillars of strength from which he could build toward more distant revolutionary goals.

Among Cárdenas' most significant contributions to Mexico was the nonideological but indispensable organization of the revolution. He undertook to make the existing government party more effectively representative. The Partido Revolucionario Mexicano[23] was reorganized into four separate sectors: the peasantry, labor, "popular" organizations including government employees and businessmen, and the military. All but the last remain in today's official party. Organizational reforms also extended to the the the establishment of a national peasant confederation, the Confederación Nacional Campesina (CNC), as a parent body for the country's agrarian leagues. In the labor field the Confederación de Trabajadores de México (CTM) was formed. The encouragement of a woman's organization and of a federation of government employees also served in the effort to provide an effective and rational basis for the structuring of a popular movement exercising meaningful contact and communication with the masses.

While these were all necessary and important steps for Cárdenas, they

---

23. This was a forerunner of today's Partido Revoluciosario Institucional (PRI). Among a number of treatments in English, see L. Vincent Padgett, "Mexico's One-Party System: A Re-evaluation," *American Political Science Review*, LI, No. 4 (December 1957), pp. 995–1007; Martin C. Needler, "The Political Development of Mexico," *American Political Science Review*, LV, No. 2 (June 1961), pp. 308–12; and Philip B. Taylor Jr., "The Mexican Elections of 1958: Affirmation of Authoritarianism?" *Western Political Quarterly*, XIII, No. 3 (September 1960), pp. 722–44.

merely provided the political strength required for the initiation of social and economic reforms. In the agricultural realm he revived the process of land distribution and succeeded in granting twice as much land to new owners as all his predecessors had since 1915. He also doubled the number of beneficiaries. By the end of his presidency roughly one-third of the population had received land under the auspices of the revolution. Cárdenas also altered the over-all shape of the agricultural program. Landless villages that previously had been ineligible to receive a government grant were now included. Moreover, Cárdenas strongly advocated the development of the local community in socioeconomic affairs. Unenthusiastic over extensive grants of land to individuals, the president therefore distributed land to the communal *ejidos*. Expropriation of large *hacienda* lands was also pushed further than before, and the result was a perceptible shift in the organizational structure of Mexican agriculture. By 1940, nearly half the rural peasantry had been drawn into the agrarian program and, by implication, into involvement with the revolution itself.

In the urban areas Cárdenas moved in the direction of more highly centralized labor organization and a greater degree of government paternalism. The creation of the CTM under Vicente Lombardo Toledano was followed by strong and often direct official intervention on its behalf. Typical was the hosting and financing in 1938 of a hemispheric meeting of trade union leaders which brought into being the Confederación de Trabajadores de América Latina (CTAL) under the presidency of Vicente Lombardo Toledano. Frequent government pressure on management in its relations with labor also furthered the growth of the latter, while the CTM brought an end to much of the divisive strife that had previously characterized the labor picture. By the close of Cárdenas' administration, Mexican labor had become an effective supporter and collaborator of the regime and the party, while helping to provide a broader base for popular identification with the government.

The controversy over oil and the role of foreign capital provided a major test of Cárdenas' revolutionary convictions, and his response assured him of a hallowed niche in the pantheon of revolutionary heroes. The creation of an effective petroleum workers' union had led to a series of demands that foreign management had rejected. By May, 1937, a general strike was called, and the workers requested government assistance, charging that the conflict was a matter of national interest. Following the report of a federal arbitral agency that largely supported the workers' demands, a series of additional irritations further inflamed sentiment. Cárdenas, who had at first worked on behalf of labor without confiscating the companies, ultimately found it necessary in March, 1938, to decree expropriation of the enterprises. This move, while creating serious diplomatic problems with the United States and Great Britain, served as an enormously propelling force in the mobilization of popular support. National sovereignty and independence had been defended, while Cárdenas emerged as a larger-than-life defender of the revolution.

The sum of Cárdenas' administration included the political stabilization of the revolution, the incorporation of new groups into the official party, the dissemination of the revolutionary myth through educational reforms, the insistence upon a new and reduced role for foreign investment, the furtherance of agrarian egalitarianism through the communal emphasis of the *ejidos,* the elevation of organized labor from its formerly subordinate position, and a co-ordination of government and private industry on behalf of economic development. As a leader of nationalistic populism in Mexico, Cárdenas knew no peer. Under his guidance, ". . . surgery was performed upon economic and social institutions of long standing. Social realignments and change in stratification arrangements took place, and national sentiment and unity triumphed in these changes. . . . Cárdenas is a folk figure whose renown in his own lifetime makes mention of his name in some planned way a matter of only secondary importance. He is a part of the nationalist, revolutionary tradition, the national myth."[24]

One of the leading activists during Cárdenas' administration was labor leader Vicente Lombardo Toledano (1894-1968). A leading figure in Mexico for much of his life, Lombardo Toledano was a Marxist whose prominence has come more from public affairs than from theoretical formulations. However, his influence on the revolution, both direct and indirect, justifies a short discussion here. As a university student he came under the influence of many who had belonged to the Ateneo de la Juventud. In particular he was attracted by the teachings of Caso, especially the humanistic ideal of the full and happy realization of human potential. Caso's nationalism also was reflected in Lombardo Toledano, although this was scarcely atypical of Mexican intellectuals. Probably the greatest lasting impact of Caso was Lombardo Toledano's lifelong concern with the practical fulfillment of human capacity. This was accompanied by an anti-Marxism that survived until the 1920's. It was at this time that his social consciousness, added to working experience in the leading labor organization of the decade,[25] gradually pointed him in the direction of socialism.

24. Padgett, *Mexican Political System,* pp. 39-40.
25. Then known as the Confederación Regional Obrera Mexicana (CROM).

His first major work, *La libertad sindical en México,* appeared in 1926. A strong nationalism was blended with partially formulated ideas about the desirability of the socialization of wealth. In the next few years, both extensive reading in Marxist literature and a growing disillusionment with the growing conservatism and complacency in the pre-Cárdenas period contributed to his further intellectual development. In 1932 he resigned from the CROM and, at the same time, declared himself to be a "radical Marxist" dedicated to changing bourgeois society in Mexico. From that time forward, Lombardo Toledano's thought was basically Marxist, whatever the occasional variations brought about by the contingencies of immediate political pressures. Accepting customary ideas about the internal contradictions of capitalism and imperialism, he also adopted the concept of dialectical materialism. The superiority of the latter to antirational philosophy, he argued, would improve future prospects for all humanity.

Lombardo Toledano's position regarding Mexican nationalism was a continuing element in his thought. Certainly it was present in his youthful as well as his more mature writings, although in the latter period a note of anticapitalism was usually present. He often gloried in Mexico's cultural heritage, recognizing both the Spanish and the Indian elements. One of the major means of combatting North American imperialism, he argued, is through a strengthening of Mexico's awareness of its own native culture and a feeling of indebtedness to such great "creators" as Las Casas, Inés de la Cruz, Juárez, Zapata, and many others. The revolution has accomplished a great deal in destroying the *hacienda* system, developing industrial production, and pursuing state ownership of utilities and numerous other activities. Yet it is far from complete, for many of the original goals, to Lombardo's thinking, have not yet been achieved. The economy remains a hostage of North American capitalism, agrarian reform is incomplete, and the inequitable distribution of wealth has worsened. It is through a total socialization of the Mexican economy, for Lombardo, that the revolution may realize its greatest fulfillment.

His blueprints for this process have been spelled out frequently in the publications of the Partido Popular Socialista (PPS), a Marxist political party that he founded under a different name in 1948. The party, but one of several leftist organizations in contemporary Mexico, has consistently stressed the theme of anti-imperialism. Through the PPS Lombardo Toledano advocated the creation of a so-called "popular democracy" in Mexico, a government based on representation of various groups and sectors under working class leadership. Development of national productive forces would in time permit the coming of socialism, at which point the means of production and distribution will have become public property, thus presumably ending the exploitation of the class system. The further nationalization of foreign-operated enterprise, the extension of state controls and additional responsibilities in social welfare, a further division of large landholdings among the peasantry, and improved representative procedures—all of these were prescribed as steps necessary for the transition to socialism.

In his long career as a political activist, Lombardo Toledano expressed his views at great length, on many subjects, and through a variety of different media. An embattled nationalist whose struggle to establish pure socialism in Mexico had failed, Lombardo Toledano often provoked criticism for a slavish and uncritical acceptance of the polities and doctrines of Soviet communism. Long denying any Communist affiliation, he often clashed with orthodox Mexican Communists. Whatever the validity of these allegations, they do not alter the fact that as a Marxist in the post-1917 period, Lombardo Toledano was for years a significant political and ideological figure. Yet his standing within the world of Mexican intellectuals suffered from his lack of independence in, for example, accepting the Soviet brutality in the Hungarian fighting of 1956. If this lack of independence stands in contrast to that of a man such as Mariátegui, it left the Mexican as a highly intelligent figure who, in seeking the practical achievement of socialism in Mexico, contributed little truly original in terms of philosophy or ideology.[26]

Nationalism and the Revolutionary Ideology / It has been a commonplace observation that the Mexican Revolution has lacked any single theoretical or systematic ideological formulation. The movement was too spontaneous for the emergence of either a single dominant political personality or the elaboration of a logical and well-articulated doctrine. As Scott has written, the problem of the revolution was that it had too many ideologies, not that it had none.[27] Thus the intellectual explanations have ranged across the political and philosophical spectrum. It has been persuasively argued that, in essence, the revolution developed an ideology of pragmatic experience. "Through trial and error over the years . . . [the revolution] has come to mean integration of the

26. A useful if unduly sympathetic study is that of Robert Paul Millon, *Mexican Marxist—Vicente Lombardo Toledano* (Chapel Hill: University of North Carolisa Press, 1966). The reader should be wary of accepting unreservedly some of the author's conclusions, given his evident agreement with many of his subject's ideas.

27. Robert E. Scott, *Mexican Government in Transition* (Urbana: University of Illinois Press, 1959), p. 99.

Indian into the national life, improved social and economic conditions for farmer, laborer, bureaucrat, or any other Mexican and, gradually, a greater participation in the political life of the country for all of them."[28]

If there has been no single voice of the revolution, however, it is perhaps true that one intellectual has, more than any other, symbolized by his inquiry and his enlightened thinking the best in the spirit of the revolution. That man, whose writings have sometimes appeared with those of Vasconcelos and Ramos, is Antonio Caso. An advocate of philosophical idealism, Caso was as a youth a leading figure in the Ateneo de la Juventud before later becoming one of the most influential teachers and thinkers of twentieth-century Mexico. While he had much to say on a variety of subjects, including political economy and a deep concern for national development, Caso was perhaps most deeply interested in philosophy, which he regarded as the highest of all subjects for intellectual investigation. It was from him that Mexicans gained their greatest exposure to major philosophical trends of the times, and it was his voice that, for more than a quarter-century, was raised again and again in his pleas for humanity, justice, and civilized understanding.

In his broad humanism and an eminently sane advocacy of the higher values of the spirit, Caso called for the environmental conditions that would be morally as well as materially conducive to a realization of the revolution. The history of that phenomenon itself, beyond the government-published versions disseminated widely for many years, is one of a revolutionary nationalist myth upon which the legitimacy of the entire national system has been based. The history of this great movement has served as a unifying factor for Mexican society at the same time that it has been supportive of the existing regime. This again lends itself to an emphasis on ideological pragmatism. One experienced observer has argued that the revolution possesses a "motivating ideological image" consisting of a set of fundamental objectives. The resultant "Revolutionary Creed" contains a number of components, all of which combine in forming an ideological picture of the revolution.

To summarize the specifics, he has written: "An overall synthesis would reveal the Revolutionary Creed's insistence that reason govern tradition, that secular authority supersede divine right, that nationalism transcend particularism, and that the state perform welfare functions that historically depended on religious charity. The basic objectives further hold that state intervention is indispensable to economic growth; that social, political and economic integrations on a national scale are

28. *Ibid.*, p. 100.

intrinsically good; and that international stature is gained and held by the adherence to recognized principles of diplomatic conduct."[29] The populistic strain of nationalism remains the indispensable ingredient of revolutionary thought and sentiment, no matter how much Mexicans themselves may debate over the meaning and accomplishments of the movement. It is this vital intangible that the contemporary Mexican poet and essayist, Octavio Paz, has expressed:

> Villa still gallops through the north, in songs and ballads; Zapata dies at every popular fair; Madero appears on the balconies, waving the flag; Carranza and Obregón still travel back and forth across the country in those trains of the revolutionary period. . . . It is the Revolution, the magical word, the word that is going to change everything, that is going to bring us immense delight and a quick death. By means of the Revolution the Mexican people found itself, located itself in its own past and substance. Hence the Revolution's fertility, compared with our nineteenth century movements. Its cultural and artistic fertility resulted from the profound manner in which its heroes, bandits and myths stamped themselves forever on the sensibility and imagination of every Mexican.[30]

Uruguay and Batllismo

Uruguay shares with Mexico the distinction of having initiated a movement of nationalist populism early in the twentieth century. Although lacking the dramatically tumultuous and violent stage through which Mexico passed, Uruguay nonetheless experienced social and political reforms of great and lasting significance. Furthermore, the Uruguayan movement contrasted with the Mexican in having a single dominant personality at its head. José Batlle y Ordóñez (1856–1929) was of such central importance to his country that one observer has even suggested, "Probably in no other country in the world in the past two centuries has any one man so deeply left his imprint upon the life and character of a country as has José Batlle y Ordóñez upon Uruguay."[31] If perhaps an exaggeration, this statement nonetheless gives some measure of the man and his national role. Before examining Batlle and his movement, however, a brief discussion of the Uruguayan background is in order.

A neglected backwater of the Spanish colonial empire, Uruguay came

29. Frank R. Brandenburg, *The Making of Modern Mexico* (Englewood Cliffs: Prentice-Hall, 1964), pp. 7–8.
30. Paz, *Labyrinth of Solitude*, p. 148.
31. Russell H. Fitzgibbon, "Uruguay: A Model for Freedom and Reform in Latin America?" in *Freedom and Reform in Latin America*, ed. Fredrick B. Pike (Notre Dame: University of Notre Dame Press, 1959), p. 233.

into being as an independent republic in 1828, serving as a buffer state between Brazil and Argentina. Riven by political strife and by repeated intervention from its two large neighbors, Uruguay did not begin to achieve prosperity and stability until the institution of military rule in 1875. From 1890 on, civilian politicians took control of national affairs, and in 1903 Batlle began the first of two nonconsecutive presidential terms. In the meantime, the philosophical trends of Uruguayan thought were gradually moving away from a strong if relatively brief advocacy of positivism. The most important philosophical and political expositions, at least for a few years, emanated from the members of the Ateneo del Uruguay after 1880. Concerned over the country's unenlightened and unproductive past, these intellectuals also opposed the role played by the military. Critical of the form of order being imposed by the armed forces, these men believed that eventual liberation from the evils of Uruguay's political traditions could come only from the people themselves. The primary task, therefore, was educational; the prophet of this view was José Pedro Varela (1845–79).

This great exponent of educational reform had become deeply impressed by a year's travel through Europe and the United States in 1867. He was also influenced by brief contact with Sarmiento in Washington. Upon returning home, he reported his experience in Montevideo newspapers and began to work toward his goals. A lengthy exposition appeared in his two-volume *La educación del pueblo*[32] in 1874, and a shorter work two years later outlined drastically a proposed revision of educational legislation. He began to implement his views during the regime of the progressive Colonel Lorenzo Latorre, although widely criticized by fellow intellectuals for this collaboration with the existing dictatorship. With Latorre enacting many of Varela's proposals by executive fiat, Uruguay began to develop educational professionalism. Centralized national control brought about a standardization of the schools, the reduction of political favoritism in the appointment of teachers, and the strengthening of the principle of free and universal public education. Denying bitter charges from former colleagues that he was a tool of the Latorre dictatorship, Varela retorted that the "surest way of combatting dictatorship is by changing the moral and intellectual character of the people, and this character cannot be changed except through education.[33]

32. José Pedro Varela, *La educación del pueblo* (Montevideo, n.p., 1874).
33. From *Proceso intelectual del Uruguay*, quoted in Leopoldo Zea, *The Latin-American Mind*, tr. James H. Abbott and Lowell Dunhom (Norman: University of Oklahoma Press, 1963), p. 241.

In outlining his educational proposals, Varela carefully kept in mind the particular conditions that characterized his country. Noting the small-ness of the population, he believed that Uruguay was undergoing a political, economic, and financial crisis. An unrealistically large budget, economic overdependence on sheep and cattle, and the overpowering position of Montevideo were all serious problems that, he contended, were becoming progressively worse. Moreover, the social history of the country was an uninterrupted story of urban domination by the Monte-video elite and rural *caudillismo* that blocked progress in the countryside. The ongoing political system was not encouraging the proper policies, thus social inequities flourished. "Governments are not the cause but the effects of social conditions. . . . [It is not true] that a change of government or, better said, of personnel in government, changes the essential conditions of the life of a people. . . . Bad governments, then, are not what bring permanent disgrace to nations, [but instead] the social conditions of these same nations. . . ."[34]

Varela was consistently outspoken in attacking various elements of the *status quo*. In addition to the views already noted, he was vocal in his opposition to the Church, both as an educational and as a social force. Advocating secular schools, he criticized the alleged religious rather than social function of Catholic education. For Varela, the state was nationally responsible for schools, with tax support being paid by all citizens, including a large number of Protestant immigrants. The encour-agement of Church education implied both clerical regulation of educa-tion and an absence of objectivity in the classroom. Varela was equally forthright in his observations concerning the National University. Its graduates, especially those of the law school, regularly allied themselves with the existence of Uruguay's social and political elite, thereby con-tributing to the survival of historical weaknesses and defects. The answer to all of this was the major theme of all Varela's writings: only a well-designed educational system could bring to Uruguayans a comprehension of national problems which might lead to the necessary reforms.

The pragmatism of North American education blended in Varela with a strong strain of positivism. Indeed, he was charged at one point with having merely paraphrased Spencerian writings on education. Varela responded that Spencer's work had not antedated his own initial work on the subject. At the same time, however, Varela abetted the brief enshrinement of positivist thought in Uruguay, which continued after his premature death in 1879. Positivism, in its criticism of Uruguayan

34. José Pedro Varela, *De la educación escolar* (Montevideo: n.p., 1876), pp. 24–25, 27.

reality, opposed the political influence of militarism with a strong moralistic approach. Denying the attacks of a small group of idealists who alleged that positivism was actually amoral, the defenders of the latter school of thought insisted that they were simply supporting the scientific in opposing the irrational impulses of politics and society. True positivism was held to be a humane approach to a solution of the problems of mankind. As the philosophy of democracy, it was essential to all nations in working toward the collective good. Therefore, positivism encouraged a kind of humane, practical realism whereby significant reforms might properly be oriented. It was with this line of argument that positivism, with Spencer rather than Comte its official spokesman, became a dominant philosophical force in Uruguay.

Although less influential in national politics than in some neighboring countries, positivism provided Uruguay with the base of a growing social consciousness and a realistic pragmatism that was harmoniously attuned to the ideas of José Batlle y Ordóñez. It was under the leadership of Batlle that, in some fifteen years after 1903, Uruguay experienced its sweeping socioeconomic change. The resultant reorganization of life and society actually antedated the Mexican Revolution by a few years, and in a nonviolent sense was more extensive. With the large immigration of Italians and Spaniards to Uruguay toward the close of the nineteenth century, a *mestizo* population had been greatly altered, while the prosperity engendered by the increased production of meat, wool, and wheat was in the process of transforming the country's economic base. It became the task of Batlle and his Colorado party to move the country in the direction of a largely urbanized society based on popular democracy and organized within the framework of moderate socialism.

Although standing out in historical retrospect as more of a pragmatic innovator than a political theoretician or ideologue, Batlle spent his formative years in a serious philosophical consideration of political problems. The son of a Colorado party leader and Uruguayan former president, Batlle attended the National University during the time of brief, but heated, debate between the positivists and the idealists. Attracted for a time to the arguments of Prudencio Vázquez y Vega, the leading idealist spokesman in Uruguay, he was at least indirectly influenced by the writings of Krause. Batlle wrote in later years about his youthful affinity for a book by Belgian Krausist E. Ahrens entitled *Course on Natural Law*.[35] Ahrens' exaltation of the individual personality was com-

---

35. For a short discussion of Batlle's early philosophical interests, see Milton I. Vanger, *José Batlle y Ordóñez of Uruguay: The Creator of His Times, 1902–1907* (Cambridge: Harvard University Press, 1963), pp. 16–24.

bined with a desire for social reforms that might enhance the dignity of man, and in later years this concern was evident in many of the policies of *batllismo*. In 1878 he helped establish a short-lived journal, *El Espíritu Nuevo,* which advocated "the total emancipation of the American spirit from the tutelage of the Old World." Significantly, it published philosophical rather than political items before its closing. After several years of political activism and a period of study in Europe, Batlle in 1886 established a new daily, *El Día;* selling for the equivalent of two cents a copy, it was the first Uruguayan paper intended for mass readership.

From that date until winning the presidency in 1903, Batlle was involved predominantly in political affairs and especially with the task of reorganizing and popularizing the Colorado party. While using the pages of *El Día* regularly to increase public awareness of national conditions and problems, he progressed through a rising level of political posts, achieving the presidency of the Senate in 1899. From within the leadership of the Colorados, he called for true civic participation in Uruguayan affairs; political rather than socioeconomic issues received the bulk of his attention. Moreover, he viewed the rejuvenated Colorado party as necessarily and properly being centered on the worker and his problems. As one Uruguayan student of *batllismo* wrote in later years, the movement became constituted largely of workers and employees. "It includes in its ranks the working class from the city and the country, which is guided by an intuitive perception of its utility. It incorporates both the employee in private activity and the official of the public administration, who see in *batllismo* an organization adequate to the expression of their concerns and for the achievement of their aspirations. The interests of each social sector demand, therefore, a political organization which can coordinate, instruct, and organize them."[36] The beliefs of *batllismo* gradually evolved during this period, although not receiving a full or systematic statement until a party declaration in 1921, well after the conclusion of Batlle's second presidential term. "During Batlle's life this program remained the avowed goal of the country's major party. . . . If it can be said that Uruguay possesses a national ideology today, it is clear that it is based as much on this program as on any other public statement."[37]

In 1903 José Batlle y Ordóñez reached the presidency after negotiating

36. Roberto M. Giudice, *Los fundamentos del batllismo* (Montevideo: n.p., 1946), p. 17.

37. Philip B. Taylor, Jr., *Government and Politics of Uruguay,* Tulane University Studies in Political Science, Volume VII (New Orleans, 1960), p. 112.

a series of political deals in accordance with past Uruguayan custom. Facing down an armed rebellion by the Blanco opposition in 1904, he followed this with a massive victory in 1905 congressional elections and, when he left office in 1907, personally selected his Colorado successor. During his first term, Batlle gave various indications of his concern with social questions. Primary education was broadened, with substantial emphasis placed on its expansion outside the urban center. Labor received sympathetic treatment, although the brief but strong influence of an-archosyndicalist leadership mitigated against the adoption of meaningful reforms. Batlle's time, however, was largely devoted to purely political matters. With the tradition of armed politics giving way to representative electoral procedures, Batlle was able to solidify the situation while establishing himself firmly as both the party and the national leader. Representing a determined if moderate nationalism committed to a centralization of political authority, Batlle began to move Uruguay in new directions, "toward concern for working-class well-being; the moralizing of personal life; an expanded government role in the economy; and the popularization of political action."[38]

After leaving office in 1907, Batlle departed the country for an extended trip through Europe, during which time he devoted study and thought to the perennial Latin-American phenomenon of undue executive authority. His observation of the Swiss collective executive later bore fruit in Uruguayan constitutional reforms. Upon his return to the presidency in 1911, however, he launched the program of social and economic policies for which he became famous. First and foremost a nationalist, Batlle undertook a massive program of nationalization which, among other things, was intended to substitute state control for foreign. This led to the creation of three major state banks and the nationalization of such services as telephones, railroads, light and power, insurance, and Montevideo port facilities. Meat-packing and processing was nationalized while government agencies assumed monopolistic responsibility for tobacco, cement, chemicals, and the refining of petroleum. A set of overlapping planning organs was set up, and the number has continued to grow in more recent years.

Batlle was an economic nationalist, and a variety of measures were at least mildly antagonistic to foreign investors, especially the British. Native manufacturing was encouraged through the extension of protective tariffs, and preferential treatment was provided for the importation of raw materials required by national industries. All of these steps were fully acceptable to the Uruguayan socialists, but Batlle's inspiration

38. Vanger, *José Batlle*, p. 272.

was one of nonideological nationalism. He regarded the state as the most appropriate instrument for economic development. National control of public services and utilities was necessary, as was the avoidance or prevention of foreign-dominated enterprise. As Batlle wrote in *El Día* years after his second term in office, "The tendency for the industrial enterprises of the State to increase is characteristic of the present epoch. It obeys, fundamentally, three causes. First a fiscal cause, which is the need for new resources to cover the constantly increasing costs of national progress. Second, a social cause, that of limiting the profits of capitalism, the dividends of which come from the money of the people. Finally, a political cause, which consists of the unquestionable need in democratic society to tie as closely as possible the social activity of the State to the masses of the nation of which the State is the juridical expression."[39]

This "social activity of the state" was also far-reaching. A lengthy succession of social and labor laws issued forth from the second *batllista* administration. A broad-based social security system gave extensive coverage plus a host of fringe benefits. In the labor field Uruguay pioneered along paths followed only later by Mexico, Chile, and then the other hemispheric nations. Legislation included workmen's compensation, an obligatory weekly day of rest, and leave with pay for women for one month before and another after pregnancy. Proposals for an eight-hour working day were adopted shortly after Batlle left office. A variety of laws established the legal basis for effective trade union organization, and the Batlle government was friendly to labor while refusing to meddle in its internal affairs. Educational policy continued to emphasize rural schools, as well as an innovating development and suport of vocational training. The advance of agriculture received impetus from the creation of experimental stations, the removal of tariffs on the importation of farm machinery, a liberalization of credit, and reforestation. Although Batlle did little to deal with the problem of the *latifundia*, owing in part to a tacit understanding with the rural-dominated Blanco opposition, he hoped to defend the economic importance of grazing while at the same time developing manufacturing and light industry.

In the political field Batlle also worked toward a recasting of institutions, procedures, and attitudes. Convinced that overwhelming executive authority and the Hispanic cultural proclivity toward *caudillismo* remained an omnipresent threat to political stability, he became the champion of collegiate government. He had returned from Europe in early 1913 to advocate the substitution of a nine-man governmental council;

---

39. *El Día* (Montevideo), November 10, 1923, quoted in Jorge Batlle, ed., *Batlle: Su vida y su obra* (Montevideo: Editorial "Acción," 1956), p. 183.

by including representatives of the minority, moreover, it would hopefully contribute constructive bipartisanship to national politics.[40] The idea of the so-called *colegiado* lacked popular support, and it led to a schism among the Colorados which despite periodic changes and permutations has persisted to the present. Only with difficulty did Batlle win partial acceptance at the 1917 constitutional convention for his program. The unsatisfactory compromise that emerged created a nine-man National Council of Government, dividing executive authority with the president. Batlle regarded this as the capstone of his career.

The 1933 *golpe de estado* destroyed the arrangement, but popular interest in a plural executive revived during the late 1940s. A family feud between the sons of Batlle and his nephew, President (1947–51) Luis Batlle Berres, attracted even greater public attention, and the eventual adoption of a new constitution in 1952 introduced a *colegiado* fully in accord with the ideas of the first Batlle. A nine-man executive board was established; the majority party would receive six of the seats, and the minority the remaining three. Chairmanship of the *colegiado* rotated annually among the members of the majority. This experiment, unique in Latin America, was undertaken at a time during which Uruguay was confronted with a series of taxing economic problems, and the demands for effective action were not met by the plural executive. Instead of the responsibly bipartisan collaborative direction that Batlle had anticipated, executive disorder and inefficiency resulted. The division of authority among the membership of the *colegiado,* heightened by factionalism within both the Blancos and the Colorados, paralyzed the nation's leadership and encouraged executive policy-making sterility. Public disillusionment was registered in the 1958 election of the Blancos after more than sixty years in the minority. When this failed to alter the situation fundamentally, popular discontent increased; in 1966, a nationwide plebiscite returned the country to a more traditional one-man presidential system.

Batlle's political contributions transcended his idea of a plural executive, inventive and imaginative though it was. Political order and regularized governmental succession became a part of the Uruguayan tradition, notwithstanding the interregnum of a military dictatorship in the 1930s. Party policies and the interplay of countervailing forces was also popularly accepted, even while the Blancos long remained unable to win elections. The democratic heritage was also strengthened by various mechanical improvements to the electoral process, including the secret bal-

40. Batlle's proposal appeared in *El Día* on March 4, 1913, under the title "Apuntes sobre el poder ejecutivo colegiado y su posible organización."

lot, proportional representation, and a general reorganization of voting procedures. The freedom of dissent, an unfettered press, increased local autonomy, the encouragement of civic participation, and a renewed emphasis on the sovereignty of law and the courts all gave added substance to the national tradition of popular government. Having said all the above, it remains to note the negative products of *batllismo,* for these too have survived as a part of Batlle's remarkable influence in the decades since his death.

The long succession of Colorado governments that followed Batlle y Ordóñez continued and extended many of his policies. One of the major results was the establishment of the hemisphere's most highly developed welfare state. In fact, Uruguay joined New Zealand and certain of the Scandinavian countries as the world's most advanced welfare systems. This gradually created financial demands beyond the power and limited capacity of the nation's economy. In many enterprises it became possible for a worker to retire while still in his forties; many workers received pensions although still actively employed; as an extreme illustration, even foreign indigents over the age of sixty were entitled to a pension. Moreover, the multiplication of government agencies to operate the welfare program and to administer the many state-owned enterprises led to an excessively large bureaucracy. Fully one-third of all working Uruguayans are on the government payroll, and it is not uncommon for the employee to hold two jobs, neither of which is done efficiently, while drawing two salaries.

As this situation has become aggravated, a working atmosphere embracing all the evils of an overindulgent and unproductive bureaucracy has added to the nation's economic burdens. In the late 1940s under Luis Batlle Berres, Uruguay continued to extend the direct responsibilities of the state even further. At the same time, a policy designed to protect and to stimulate the growing of wheat was adopted, although Uruguay had long remained essentially a grazing country. Production costs remained higher than those in competing Argentina, however, and overpricing made it impossible to sell all the wheat at home. Argentine and North American competition on the international wheat market could not be met, and the government was forced into the expensive and uneconomic position of subsidizing wheat. At the same time, high tariffs had been raised even further during World War II to stimulate native industry. In the postwar period, however, this well-intentioned effort to diversify the economy left Uruguay in the position of maintaining uncompetitive industry at a high cost. The resultant financial crisis has worsened ever since. Spiraling inflationary pressures by the

1960s brought the country to the brink of bankruptcy, and it was a belated recognition of this fact which increased popular discontent and contributed in part to the repudiation of the plural executive in 1966.

While it is unjust to blame Batlle for events that took place long after his death in 1929, there is no denying that Uruguay has fairly consistently followed *batllista* guidelines. Critics and supporters alike are in agreement as to his inordinately crucial role in national development. It was through his leadership that Uruguay was transformed from one of the more unstable and backward countries of the hemisphere to one of the most advanced. Batlle pioneered as a social reformer and economic nationalist and was among the very first of the Latin-American political leaders to recognize and make use of centralized governmental authority to stimulate economic growth directly. His views and approach became a part of Uruguayan political thought, accepted and supported by the public and the majority of intellectuals. *Batllismo* accepted many socialist criticisms of pure and unalloyed capitalism while instituting a *criollo* socialism that attacked national problems without undue attention to doctrinal or philosophical issues. Thus, in practical terms *batllismo* long outlived its creator. By 1929, as Taylor has remarked, the principle of extended government intervention in the economy and concern for social welfare had been established solidly. "In a number of important respects, it can be argued that the thinking of the country has not progressed substantially since the death of Batlle."[41]

It must be remembered, finally, that socioeconomic reforms, no matter how important and innovative, were but a part of *batllismo*. A fervent democrat, Batlle combined a highly developed social conscience with an equally deep commitment to liberty and popular participation. Himself a civil *caudillo* in many respects, Batlle was a highly successful politician who desired political awareness for the urban lower and middle classes as well as improved social and economic status. Whatever history's judgment of his ideas about executive authority, the latter will not supercede the single dominant theme of nationalistic populism. As two students of Latin-American nationalism have written, "Under their great leader the Colorados established for Uruguay a modern identity that harmonized in most respects with the social and economic trends of the times. An orientation toward urban areas, a firm commitment to social welfare programs, a strong assertion of economic nationalism, and an inventive if controversial solution to the problem of the too powerful chief executive were all elements in this Uruguayan national identity."[42]

41. Taylor, *Politics of Uruguay*, p. 12.
42. Arthur P. Whitaker and David C. Jordan, *Nationalism in Contemporary Latin America* (New York: Free Press, 1966), p. 127.

It is the building of this national identity that stands today as the lasting contribution of *batllismo* to Uruguay.

SELECTED BIBLIOGRAPHY

THE MEXICAN REVOLUTION

Alba, Víctor. *The Mexicans: The Making of a Nation.* New York: Frederick A. Praeger, 1967.

——. *Las ideas sociales contemporáneas en México.* México: Fondo de Cultura Económica, 1960.

Brandenburg, Frank R. *The Making of Modern Mexico.* Englewood Cliffs: Prentice-Hall, 1964.

Caso, Antonio. *Discursos a la nación mexicana.* México: Porrúa Hermanos, 1922.

——. *La filosofía de la cultura y el materialismo histórico.* México: Ed. Alba, 1936.

——. *La persona humana y el estado totalitario.* México: Universidid Nacional Autónoma, 1941.

Cline, Howard F. *Mexico: Revolution to Evolution, 1940–1960.* New York: Oxford University Press, 1963.

——. *The United States and Mexico.* Cambridge: Harvard University Press, 1953.

Cockcroft, James D. *Intellectual Precursors of the Mexican Revolution, 1900–1913.* Austin: University of Texas Press, 1968.

Cosío Villegas, Daniel. *American Extremes.* Translated by Américo Paredes. Austin: University of Texas Press, 1964.

——. *Change in Latin America: The Mexican and Cuban Revolutions.* Lincoln: University of Nebraska Press, 1961.

——. *Historia moderna de México.* 5 Vols. México and Buenos Aires: n.p., 1955–63.

De la Cueva, Mario, et al. *Major Trends in Mexican Philosophy.* Notre Dame and London: University of Notre Dame Press, 1966.

Haddox, John H. *Vasconcelos of Mexico: Philosopher and Prophet.* Austin: University of Texas Press, 1967.

James, Daniel. *Mexico and the Americans.* New York: Frederick A. Praeger, 1963.

Millon, Robert Paul. *Mexican Marxist—Vincente Lombardo Toledano.* Chapel Hill: University of North Carolina Press, 1966.

Padgett, L. Vincent. *The Mexican Political System.* Boston: Houghton Mifflin Company, 1966.

Paz, Octavio. *The Labyrinth of Solitude: Life and Thought in Mexico.* Translated by Lysander Kemp. New York: Grove Press, 1961.

Ramos, Samuel. *El perfil del hombre y de la cultura en México.* México: Imprenta Mundial, 1934.

——. *Hacia un nuevo humanismo.* México: La Casa de España, 1940.

——. *Profile of Man and Culture in Mexico.* Translated by Peter G. Earle. Austin: University of Texas Press, 1962.

Romanell, Patrick. *The Making of the Mexican Mind.* Lincoln: University of Nebraska Press, 1953.

Ross, Stanley R., ed. *Is the Mexican Revolution Dead?* New York: Alfred A. Knopf, 1966.

Schmitt, Karl E. *Communism in Mexico.* Austin: University of Texas Press, 1965.

Scott, Robert E. *Mexican Government in Transition.* Urbana: University of Illinois Press, 1959.

Simpson, Eyler N. *Many Mexicos.* Berkeley: University of California Press, 1941.

———. *The Ejido: Mexico's Way Out.* Chapel Hill: University of North Carolina Press, 1937.

Tannenbaum, Frank. *Peace by Revolution.* New York: Columbia University Press, 1933.

———. *The Struggle for Peace and Bread.* New York: Alfred A. Knopf, 1951.

Vasconcelos, José. *Bolivarismo y monroismo,* 2d ed. Santiago: Ercilla, 1935.

———. *Estética.* México: Botas, 1939.

———. *Etica.* 2d ed. Mexico: Botas, 1936.

———. *Indología: Una interpretación de la cultura iberoamericana.* Barcelona: Agencia Mundial de Librerías, 1927.

———. *Mexican Ulysses.* Translated by William Rex Crawford. Bloomington: Indiana University Press, 1963.

———. *La raza cósmica: Misión de la raza iberoamericana.* Paris: Agencia Mundial de Librerías, 1925.

———. *Tratado de metafísica.* México: Botas, 1929.

Whetten, Nathan L. *Rural Mexico.* Chicago: University of Chicago Press, 1948.

URUGUAY AND BATLLISMO

Batlle, Jorge, ed. *Batlle: Su obra y su vida.* Montevideo: Editorial "Acción," 1956.

Fitzgibbon, Russell H. *Uruguay: Portrait of a Democracy.* New Brunswick: Rutgers University Press, 1954.

Hanson, Simon G. *Utopia in Uruguay: Chapters in the Economic History of Uruguay.* New York: Oxford University Press, 1938.

Rama, Carlos M. *Ensayo de sociología uruguaya.* Montevideo: Editorial Medina, 1957.

Taylor, Philip B., Jr. *Government and Politics of Uruguay.* Tulane University Studies in Political Science, Volume VII. New Orleans: Tulane University Press, 1960.

Vanger, Milton I. *José Battle y Ordóñez of Uruguay: The Creator of His Times,* 1902–1907. Cambridge: Harvard University Press, 1963.

Varela, José Pedro. *La educación del pueblo.* Montevideo: n.p., 1874.

Zea, Leopoldo. *The Latin-American Mind.* Translated by James H. Abbott and Lowell Dunham. Norman: University of Oklahoma Press, 1963.

Zum Felde, Alberto. *Proceso intelectual del Uruguay.* Buenos Aires: Editorial Claridad, 1941.

8

Nationalistic Populism
in Brazil and Argentina

The democratic form of populism represented by *batllismo* in Uruguay stands in contrast with the authoritarianism of Getúlio Vargas in Brazil and Juan Perón in Argentina. These latter political movements have frequently been described as "fascist" in the semipopular literature; yet this rubric provides little insight into regimes that are also illustrative of nationalistic populism. Only by a closer examination can the unquestionably antidemocratic governments of Vargas and Perón be placed within a proper setting.

Brazil And Vargas

While its nineteenth-century historical evolution was atypical of its Hispanic neighbors, Brazil gradually moved toward the threshold of substantive political and socioeconomic change. Following the economic disturbances resulting from World War I, Brazilian conditions became rife for nationalistic populism. With the intellectuals dissatisfied over an unsettled and unresponsive *status quo,* the national climate gradually changed, culminating in the populist movement of 1930. The heightened awareness that made possible the events of that year stemmed from a variety of influences, but perhaps the single most influential contribution intellectually was Euclydes da Cunha's *Os sertões,* published in 1902.[1] Called by João Cruz Costa the first true example of political thought in Brazil, [2] this masterful account of life in the interior departed from the usual propensity of intellectuals to look toward Europe. Rather, attention was concentrated upon the country's kaleidoscopically varied regional cultures, leading in time to a new national consciousness. This intellectual ferment, added to an imposing array of social grievances and dramatized by the growing impact of the international depression, emerged in a movement guided and directed by Getúlio Dorneles Vargas (1883–1954).

Vargas' Early Years: Socioeconomic Reforms / The dominant political figure in Brazil from 1930 until his suicide in 1954, Getúlio Vargas helped to formulate and to capitalize upon the populist wave. Whatever his shortcomings as a paternalistic authoritarian, Vargas played a paramount role; the magic of his name has survived more than a decade after his death. It was under his leadership that Brazil moved from semicolonial status toward genuine nationhood. Not only were natural resources significantly developed for the first time but, perhaps more importantly, "the Brazilian people acquired an appreciation for their own abilities . . . which made them shed once and for all their traditional tendency to pattern their political, economic, and cultural institutions on those of other countries."[3] Serving as chief of state from 1930 to 1945 and then again from 1950 until his death, Vargas represented both the symbolic and pragmatic elements of nationalistic populism. Ample evidence, both administrative and ideological, was to be provided during his quarter-century of leadership.

Getúlio Vargas was born in the town of São Borja, in Brazil's southernmost state of Rio Grande do Sul. Raised amid the frontier spirit of the Brazilian Gauchos, he was surrounded by politics from an early age, eventually gaining prominence regionally before advancing to the national scene. A shrewdly intelligent youth who received both military and legal training, he was also influenced by positivist thought. Vargas' father was a strong advocate of this philosophy, as was the founder of the Republican party in Rio Grande do Sul, Júlio de Castilhos. The positivistic emphasis on strong government and executive control over

1. For the English translation by Samuel Putnam, see *Rebellion in the Backlands* (Chicago: University of Chicago Press, 1943).
2. See his mimeographed "Nationalism and the Evolution of Brazilian Thought in the Twentieth Century," in *International Congress for the History of Ideas* (Mexico City: November 1962).
3. Robert J. Alexander, *Prophets of the Revolution: Profiles of Latin American Leaders* (New York: Macmillan Co., 1962), p. 219.

the legislature had been deeply implanted in the region, and the young Vargas could scarcely be immune. The firm rule he later established from the presidency in Rio de Janeiro was consistent with regional experiences during Vargas' formative years. And while the subsequent ideological justification of his lengthy rule was not positivistic, its emphasis on orderly government was not dissimilar.

The political circumstances of the 1930 crisis revolved about the traditional rotation of the presidency between citizens of either Minas Gerais or São Paulo. When the outgoing president attempted to impose as his successor a fellow resident of São Paulo, Julio Prestes, a discontented Minas Gerais threw its support behind the southerner Vargas at the head of the Liberal Alliance. When the government-supported Prestes predictably won the election, Vargas temporarily withdrew to Rio Grande do Sul but soon decided to contest the results. In October he mounted an armed uprising, supported by a group of restless young *tenentes,* or lieutenants. Socially minded nationalists who opposed the establishment as represented by the rule of the landed oligarchy, the *tenentes* had already staged unsuccessful revolts in 1922, 1924, and 1926. Demanding justice for the rural citizenry while protesting Brazilian economic subservience to foreign interests, they willingly collaborated with Vargas, who had campaigned in defense of the masses. The existing government was deposed in a characteristically relaxed Brazilian fashion, and Vargas was proclaimed provisional president. Effectively outmaneuvering the *tenentes* and preventing their organization into a meaningful political group, Vargas soon freed himself of all commitments. He also succeeded in neutralizing Plínio Salgado and his integralist movement (Ação Integralista Brasilera), a green-shirted Fascist movement that employed extremist methods of the right in an effort to capitalize on middle-class resentments. The pragmatist par excellence was thus ready to guide the energies of populism.[4]

Vargas was to remain in office without interruption until 1945, and efforts to ascribe an official ideology to his regime began only after the drafting of the Constitution of 1937. Long before then, however, the populistic movement was taking shape. Indeed, the years from 1930 to 1934 were productive ones, during which time he legislated by decree while making the preparations necessary for future national development.

4. For a discussion of the 1930 revolution and its impact, see Jordan M. Young, *The Brazilian Revolution of 1930 and the Aftermath* (New Brunswick: Rutgers University Press, 1967). A detailed account is also found in John W. F. Dulles, *Vargas of Brazil: A Political Biography* (Austin: University of Texas Press, 1967).

The cornerstone of these early years was the newly created Ministry of Labor, Industry and Commerce, popularly termed the "ministry of the revolution." Headed by Lindolfo Collor, one of Vargas' major supporters in Minas Gerais, the ministry provided the bureaucratic framework through which social problems were attacked. The result was an attempt to grapple with the burgeoning industrialization that had begun in the first decade of the century. Such a commitment of administrative concern, appropriate to the accumulating pressures for action, contrasted with the traditional attitude that, as an earlier administration had remarked, regarded "The social problem as a police problem."

Vargas and Collor proceeded to adopt what amounted to extensive social legislation, principally in the realm of labor. Eight-hour days and six-day work weeks were decreed, while minimal salary guarantees and a variety of fringe benefits were also approved. The Retirement and the Pensions Institutes were created for public employees, and benefits were later provided to other federal workers. Brazilian labor was encouraged through the registration of all trade unions, and old-time labor leaders were replaced by government-supported organizers. Internal direction of the labor movement fell into the hands of government backers, and from that time on the workers became a bulwark of support for Vargas. With regional labor offices enforcing national decrees and government officials directing the course of nascent collective bargaining, Vargas paternalistically if meaningfully benefited the lot of the expanding urban proletariat while re-enforcing the popular base of his authoritarian rule. Vargas also committed himself to the support and expansion of a social security system, and while the program was frequently administered with political patronage as an objective, it also became widely accepted as basic to nationalistic reformism.

Vargas' early years included a variety of additional state-controlled activities, especially in the wake of economic crisis. A National Coffee Council was granted sweeping powers to deal with the problems of the country's major export crop, while other areas of agriculture were encouraged, notably sugar and rubber. Industrialization was also promoted, with a high tariff wall protecting new enterprises. The rationing of foreign currency was imposed, and native industry was favored through a complex of preferential legislation. Beyond the alteration of economic policies, Vargas was directing the overhauling of the nation's educational system while initiating a literacy campaign and attacking major endemic diseases, especially malaria. Vargas was all the while improving and strengthening bureaucratic mechanisms, at the same time deriving all possible political advantage through patronage and favoritism. Although himself a man of scrupulous financial honesty, Vargas had few qualms about the value of favoritism, whether political or financial.

While concentrating in his early years on socioeconomic reforms, Vargas was also active in assuring his own primacy. Legislating by decree in the absence of congress, he directed state affairs through the appointment of trusted friends or allies as "interventors." At all levels, political participation was minimal; opponents of the regime had little fear of serious physical reprisal but found themselves frozen out of all political authority. An early indication of dissent came with a brief uprising from São Paulo in 1932, although it was easily quelled. Partly in response to this, Vargas permitted elections for a constituent assembly, which in due course passed the Constitution of 1934. After three years of rule as a nominally constitutional president, however, Getúlio Vargas chose to alter further the nature of presidential succession.

Consolidation of Dictatorship and the Estado Nôvo / The constitution had provided for presidential elections in January, 1938, and political activity increased in late 1937 with the entry of two major presidential candidates. Vargas carefully laid the groundwork for a *golpe de estado,* which occurred on November 10. On that date he broadcast to the country that national unity was threatened by inflamed partisanship. Congress was described as irresponsible, and the alleged alternative was therefore a strong government that would work "in order to adjust the potlitical organism to the economic necessities of the country." The Constitution of 1937 was adopted by presidential decree, with the preamble justifying the seizure of power:

> Whereas, the legitimate aspirations of the Brazilian people for political and social peace, seriously disturbed by manifest factors of disorder, created by growing party dissensions, which a malicious demagogic propaganda attempted to transform into class warfare, and which, through the extreme force attained by the ideological conflicts, tended, in its natural process of development, to solve itself by violence, thus subjecting the nation to the imminent threat of a disastrous civil war;
>
> Whereas, the state of apprehension caused throughout the country by the infiltration of communism, which was growing daily more widespread and deeper, calls for a remedy, both radical and permanent in character . . .
>
> Now, therefore, it is resolved to insure to the nation its unity, its honor, and its independence; and to the people of Brazil, under a regime of political and social peace, the necesary conditions for their security, their welfare, and their prosperity;

The President of the Republic of the United States of Brazil decrees the following constitution. . . .[5]

The 1937 coup, in Skidmore's words, "was possible because the middle class, that small but important social group . . . was confused and divided." Getúlio Vargas thereupon set forth into the second half of his fifteen-year tenure. "The goals of social welfare and economic nationalism, much debated earlier in the decade, were now to be pursued under authoritarian tutelage. The result was a deepening of the dichotomy between a narrow constitutionalism which had neglected social and economic questions and a nationalistic social welfarism which had become unequivocally anti-democratic."[6] The dictator was not to organize an official government party, despite later ideological overtones to his movement. Rather, the so-called Estado Nôvo that emerged was a personalized hybrid under which Vargas undertook the guidance of national social change and economic development.

Among the major sources for Vargas' Estado Nôvo was the Constitution of 1937, "the extraordinary brain child of Francisco Campos,"[7] the minister of justice. While the document combined features of what at that time was the authoritarian Polish constitution with the explicit corporativism of Portugal, its political essence lay in Article 180, "Until the National Parliament meets, the President of the Republic shall be empowered to issue decrees on all matters of legislation for the Union." As Loewenstein observed, these words represented the core of the Estado Nôvo, while "all the rest of one hundred and eighty-six articles are legal camouflage."[8] As events were to prove, President Vargas ruled in the absence of legislative meetings until falling from power in 1945. Constitutional tenets included the outlawing of all political parties, extensive press censorship, the control of domestic travel, and the jailing or forced exile of troublesome critics. A state of national emergency was also declared, thereby placing political conflict outside the jurisdiction of the courts. A promised plebiscite to ratify the constitution was never held, and for Vargas the national emergency was to remain throughout his period in power.

5. Preamble to the Constitution of 1937, as quoted in Austin F. Macdonald, *Latin-American Politics and Government,* 1st ed. (New York: Thomas Y. Crowell Company, 1949), p. 140.
6. Thomas E. Skidmore, *Politics in Brazil, 1930–1964: An Experiment in Democracy* (New York and London: Oxford University Press, 1967), pp. 30–31.
7. Dulles, *Vargas,* p. 172.
8. Karl Loewenstein, *Brazil under Vargas* (New York: Macmillan Co., 1942), p. 48.

As represented both inside the constitution and out, the Estado Nôvo was strongly nationalistic, a fact that was underlined by Vargas' periodic exaltations of patriotism and loyalty. Articles 145 to 153 of the constitution were highly nationalistic and clearly reminiscent of the spirit of Mexico's Constitution of 1917. Attention was given to subsoil mineral deposits, all of which were to be reserved to Brazilians. Banks and insurance companies were also to be operated only if the majority of stockholders were citizens. The evident intention, aside from the political value of nationalistic sloganeering, was to prevent foreign ownership or domination of steel, oil, and comparable industries. Additional constitutional prescriptions stressed the same nationalistic orientation through controls over bureaucratic administrators, leadership of labor unions, and the registration of sea-going ships. Vargas added similar decrees to constitutional requirements in the following years. Having capitalized upon nationalistic sentiment for reasons of political opportunism, the dictator predictably revived popular passions at appropriate times. But if concrete requirements were sometimes unrealistic or unnecessary, it was equally true that popular support for Vargas and his government included a genuine and deep-felt pride that, before Vargas, had remained beneath the surface. Political considerations aside, the Estado Nôvo legitimately contained a strong nationalistic element. In short, "the idea of nationalism was the rallying point for the Estado Nôvo."[9]

Given the rise of fascism in Europe, many professed to see similar trappings to Vargas' regime. The Constitution of 1937 suggested a corporate state, although few of the key provisions were ever implemented. Numerous councils, committees, and executive agencies were created as outgrowths of the executive power. Nominally under the direction of the president instead of a given cabinet minister, there was a concomitant suggestion that they might function as agencies of a state-controlled collectivism. In practice, however, few ever enjoyed more than nominal authority; most were advisory, and a number were never formally established and made operative. A corporate approach never became effective under Vargas, and most state activities continued to follow more traditional lines. So while the Estado Nôvo called on paper for a reorganization of the nation's policy-making organs, few of the recommended revisions were ever enacted.

It was in the field of labor that the corporativist inclination came closest to fruition. Workers and employers alike were to be members of *sindicatos*, classified by economic activity. Above the municipal level,

9. Gerhard Masur, *Nationalism in Latin America: Diversity and Unity* (New York: Macmillan Co., 1966), p. 134.

these were to be combined into a series of confederations. Nationally, these latter were to encompass all areas of economic activity. At least in theory, they would also have provided political support for the regime. Vargas never pursued the possibilities, however, and even on the economic side organizing activities were but minimal. The *sindicatos* proved useful as channels for social welfare affairs, but all remaining freedom in collective bargaining was erased. An extensive complex of labor courts began with local Boards of Conciliation and reached through regional organs to the Superior Labor Tribunal in Rio de Janeiro. These remain in effect today, although functioning differently than they once did under Vargas.

As the Estado Nôvo went into effect, Vargas encouraged efforts to create an official ideology. Aside from scattered analogies to European fascism, the rationale came from the writings of Francisco Campos, author of the 1937 Constitution. Although the Portuguese colonial heritage led some to describe Vargas' system as a copy of the existing despotism in Portugal, Campos himself referred to a variety of other foreign influences. Both the constitution itself and Campos' *O estado nôvo*[10] were ideologically eclectic. While the book was hailed at first as the authoritative exposition of Vargas' allegedly unique regime, few in Brazil took its intellectual pretensions seriously. Loewenstein aptly concluded that *O estado nôvo* itself was largely an apology for the constitution rather than an original ideological blueprint. In short, "the solutions are less Fascist than authoritarian; it does not extol violence nor does it indulge in state mysticism. Moreover, it is so legalistic in its entire approach that one easily understands why the volume completely failed to serve the purposes of a persuasive and dynamic ideology."[11]

Until Getúlio Vargas muted his pro-Axis stance and moved smoothly to the side of the democracies after Pearl Harbor, characterizations of his government as Fascist were common.[12] Entirely aside from the claims of official spokesmen, many were inclined to equate the Estado Nôvo with existing Italian and Portuguese political systems. Yet the parallels were strained at best. The fact that Vargas' government was authoritarian and antidemocratic was apparent; moreover, it reached an accommodation with national mores by leaving private life largely unaffected. If the constitution called for the establishment of a fundamentally cor-

10. Francisco Campos, *O estado nôvo: Sua estructura, seu conteudo ideologico* (Rio de Janeiro, José Olympio, 1940).
11. Loewenstein, *Brazil under Vargas*, p. 126.
12. For the multi-volume collection of Vargas' speeches and public statements, see his *A nôva política do Brasil* (Rio de Janeiro: 1930–45).

porativist system, the restricted application of the document, other than in the labor field, diluted the operative nature of the system. The peculiarly Brazilian brand of authoritarianism, infused wherever possible with open permissiveness and reliant upon the considerable personal talents of Getúlio Vargas, gathered the energies of a latent national revolution and directed them along a gradualist path.

More important than the ideological trappings of the regime were changes in administrative and political institutions. Under Vargas there was a transformation of the relationship between federal and state authority, resulting in a highly centralized and more truly national government. Many traditionally state and regional duties were transferred to the capital, making possible a truly national effort for socioeconomic change and development. There were concomitant political repercussions; increased centralization under Vargas meant, among other things, "a reaction to the decentralization imposed by the Republican constitution-writers of 1889–91, who had wished to undo what they regarded as the harmful overcentralization of the Empire (1822–89)."[13] Moreover, Vargas was in a sense preparing for his later career as a democratic leader in which he relied substantially upon a new popular movement in addition to traditional support from industrialists and rural landowners. The political implications of his policies of economic nationalism were great, creating widespread approval for heightened state intervention, especially in the realm of industrialization. Mechanistically speaking, the significant element was the handing down of pertinent policies from above, as would be the case with Perón in Argentina.

From the Estado Nôvo to the Return of the "Democrat" / If many a populistic aspiration went unfulfilled under the Estado Nôvo, that was at least in part a function of Vargas' opportunistic pragmatism. An eclectic realism permeated his rule, with the role of ideology peripheral. The social reforms of the regime, uneven though they were, registered a lasting impact on Brazil. Although the Vargas era from 1930–1945 was far from revolutionary, it offered a climate and attitude within which political institutions were reshaped and revitalized. Within the authoritarianism of the Estado Nôvo, populistic energies and demands were recognized; unless political demands proved contradictory, responsive policies were adopted. All the while, the threatened disintegration of national identity in 1930 was avoided, and the historically strong centripetal forces of regionalism were quelled and subordinated by Vargas' strong hand on the central government. It was his early success

13. Skidmore, *Politics in Brazil*, p. 35.

in restoring the recognized legitimacy of the national government which permitted the dictator to undertake the reforms that followed.

The Brazilian tradition of oligarchical domination was altered, if not erased. Again citing Loewenstein, Brazil under Vargas was run by a "numerically small, thoroughly bourgeois, and highly qualified governing class. . . . [However,] the monopoly of the governing is traditional rather than deliberately planned and . . . is mitigated by the common sentiment of social equality. Moreover, the oligarchy shares with the mass of the people the belief in the democratic values of social life."[14] In addition, the emergence of a middle sector in Brazil created the bridge between the oligarchy and the discontented masses.[15] Major political groups, including both the urban middle class and the military, accepted with enthusiasm the nationalism of Vargas' economic policies, and the antiforeign excesses of prewar days served a positive function in Vargas' drive toward broadly generalized reforms. From 1930 the voices of the people became important for national affairs; in this sense Vargas' contribution was a lasting one.

Nationalistic populism in Brazil called first for social reforms and not meaningful political participation. The ideals of freedom and reform were separate, and the masses failed to see the interrelationship of the two. As one Brazilian commentator remarked, "What the people wanted was security, better wages, low costs of living, various protective laws, strong unions, in short, tangible values, not votes. Therefore . . . instead of liberty first, the slogan became reform first—reform in the sense of new social legislation and a new status for workers."[16] Central to the era inaugurated by Vargas were the factors of social legislation, industrialization, economic nationalism, the political role of labor, and a crucially important, if intangible, national awareness. Whatever the corporativist overtones of the 1937 Constitution, whatever the ideological expressions of Campos' writings, and notwithstanding superficial similarities to European fascism, the Vargas era symbolized for Brazil the rise of nationalistic populism.

When Vargas was finally ousted by the military in 1945, it was suggested that he was no longer accepted as a populist prophet. However, in a matter of months he had been elected to the national legislature, and his presence hung over the government that succeeded him. In

14. Loewenstein, *Brazil under Vargas,* p. 372.
15. For a discussion of the rise of the Brazilian middle sectors, see the country chapter in John J. Johnson, *Political Change in Latin America: The Emergence of the Middle Sectors* (Stanford: Stanford University Press, 1958), pp. 153–80.
16. Alceu Amoroso Lima, "Voices of Liberty and Reform in Brazil," in *Freedom and Reform in Latin America,* ed. Fredrick B. Pike (Notre Dame: University of Notre Dame Press, 1959), p. 299.

1950 the Partido Trabalhista Brasileiro (PTB) nominated him for the presidency, and Vargas returned to office with a clear majority. Inaugurated as democratic ruler in January, 1951, the political veteran found himself confronted by changing conditions, and he was soon floundering amid economic disorder and a climate of official corruption. In August, 1954, a chain of incidents culminated in a military demand that he resign. Realizing that the end had been reached, the septuagenarian Vargas chose suicide.

His turbulent career closed with a farewell letter; melodramatic though it was, the message effectively assured the continuation of Vargas' populistic appeal from the grave. Brazilian nationalism and a love for the common man were emphasized amid more specific charges against political enemies. Excerpts included the following:

> After years of domination and looting by international economic and financial groups, I made myself chief of an unconquerable revolution. I began the work of liberation and I instituted a regime of social liberty. I had to resign. I returned to govern on the arms of the people. . . .
> I wished to create national liberty by developing our riches through Petrobras, and a wave of sedition clouded its beginnings. Electrobras was hindered almost to despair. They do not wish the workers to be free. They do not wish the people to be independent. . . .
> I fought against the looting of Brazil, I fought against the looting of the people. I have fought bare-breasted. The hatred, infamy and calumny did not beat down my spirit. I gave you my life. Now I offer my death. Nothing remains. Serenely I take the first step on the road to eternity and I leave life to enter history.[17]

Argentina and Peronismo

Contrasting starkly in many ways with the Brazilian movement of nationalistic populism is that of Argentina. The twentieth-century evolution of political ideas in Argentina has emphasized the unique aspects of what is perhaps the most paradoxical and enigmatic country of South America. The study of recent and contemporary thought in Argentina requires particular attention to the government of Juan Domingo Perón and to his official ideology of *justicialismo*. But while Perón in various ways headed a populistic movement accompanied by powerful nationalistic sentiment, his regime needs to be understood within the framework of Argentina's twentieth-century development.

17. Among a variety of sources, see the text in Alexander, *Prophets of the Revolution*, pp. 240–41.

Both Perón the political leader and *justicialista* thought were in consonance with deep-felt national attitudes and values. Thus the origins of *peronismo* itself follow upon the heritage that preceded Perón's rise to supreme power in the mid-1940s.

Argentinidad / The country emerged into a new historical era in the 1890s, one that for forty years was to be marked by growing nationalism and a desire to become assertively independent in hemispheric affairs. Economic development and early industrialization began to arouse the nascent urban masses. As the traditional oligarchy encountered growing pressure from popular forces, the Radical Civic Union and the Socialist party mounted an attack on the socioeconomic *status quo*. Electoral reforms adopted in February, 1912, brought about the effective enfranchisement of the middle sector, and the Radicals swept to power in 1916 behind their great and controversial leader, Hipólito Irigoyen.[18] For fourteen years the radicals controlled the country. Popular expectations were consistently disappointed, and social-minded radicals grew disillusioned. Irigoyen refused to attack the power and status of the landowning oligarchy; instead, exponents of reformism found themselves isolated and ineffectual. Military seizure of power in 1930 merely aggravated the situation and introduced a thirteen-year era of conservative domination known as the *concordancia*. Despite the fragmentation of populistic forces, however, the writings of Argentine intellectuals continued to express the thoughts and aspirations that Juan Perón was later to enunciate as official dogma.

Among the most influential was Ricardo Rojas (1882–1957), a versatile and gifted writer whose talents were prodigious. His *La restauración nacionalista*[19] in 1909 produced a clarion call for national progress and reform; it was perhaps the most influential of the patriotic evocations and euphoric perorations that grew common in the years to follow. Dedicated to the description and definition of *argentinidad,* Rojas stressed the spiritual and cultural bases of Argentine history. Harking

18. Peter Snow, *Argentine Radicalism: The History and Doctrine of the Radical Civic Union* (Iowa City: University of Iowa Press, 1965).

An extended consideration of the *peronista* era is enhanced by an understanding of both the 1890–1916 period and the post-Irigoyen years of 1930–43. Insightful accounts in English include a pair of recent works: Peter H. Smith, *Politics and Beef in Argentina: Patterns of Conflict and Change* (New York: Columbia University Press, 1969), and Robert A. Potash, *The Army and Politics in Argentina, 1928–1945: Irigoyen to Perón* (Stanford: Stanford University Press, 1969).

19. Ricardo Rojas, *La restauración nacionalista: Crítica de la educación argentina y bases para una reforma en el estudio de las humanidades modernas*, IV (Buenos Aires: J. Roldán, 1909).

back to the nobility of purpose and strength which he found in nine-teenth-century national history, Rojas envisioned in *argentinidad* a mys-tique that suggested a virtual patriotic religion. As the high priest of the "nationalistic restoration," Rojas' nationalism was principally cultural in thrust. Yet it also embraced a strong antiforeign sentiment. This was even more evident in *Eurindia*.[20]

Published in 1924, its very title was intended as suggestive of both the European and Indian sources of Argentine culture. For Rojas, the vitality of the country's heritage came not from the colonial but from more recent tradition. Critical of evidences of foreign influences on his fellow citizens, Rojas argued for the originality of national literature. Indeed, eight volumes from his prolific pen concentrated upon a critically positive overview of Argentine literary currents. Where Sarmiento had drawn contrasts between civilization and barbarism, Rojas—believing himself an heir of the former—devoted his analysis to the conflicting values and beliefs of cosmopolitan materialism versus agricultural ideal-ism. In *Eurindia* Rojas set forth, much as did Vasconcelos in Mexico, a personal faith in that special Americanism that drew upon the richest sources of both the European and native cultures. Indianist influences, he argued,

> should not be a militant xenophobia, but a peaceful creation of American culture, a nativist rejustification by means of intelligence, the spiritual conquest of our cities by the American genius. Toward this synthesis we march, and it will be achieved in a philosophical and artistic renaissance whose proximity is already to be noted. . . . We now await the absorption of the exotic civilization by the Indian tradition, so that its synthetic expression may appear in philosophy and art. . . .
>
> *Exotismo* is needed for our political growth, as is *indianismo* for our aesthetic culture. We wish neither gaucho barbarism nor cosmopolitan barbarism. We wish a national culture as the source of a national civilization; an art which may be the expression of both phenomena.
>
> *Eurindia* is the name of this ambition.[21]

The direction and force of Rojas' works were not dissimilar from that of many other writers, for he was enunciating widely popular views. The most notable of his colleagues was Manuel Gálvez (1882———). Author of some forty volumes of poetry, prose, novels, and essays, this literary critic combined a fervent nationalism with a belief in authority, discipline, and hierarchy. This latter strain, which is missing in the work

20. Rojas, *Eurindia*, V (Buenos Aires: J. Roldán, 1922).
21. *Ibid.*, p. 133.

of Rojas, was to be echoed in the philosophy and practice of *peronismo*. In his earlier phase, however, the stress was on Hispanic spiritual values and the role of Christianity. The enemy was urbanism and materialism, against which all citizens should struggle. In *El solar de la raza*, Gálvez produced a paean of Hispanism reminiscent of Spain's own Generation of 1898. A typical passage reads, "Let us build Argentine idealism, drawing it out of the depths of our race, that is to say, from the Spanish and the American qualities that we carry within us. And perhaps in some not distant day the efforts of this generation will fructify in a typical and modern form of Argentine idealism."[22] And later in the same work he declares, "Let us love Spain. She is perhaps the most noble nation which has existed upon the earth. . . . We possess hidden energy. But ours will not be a barbarous and automatic energy, like that which boils incessantly in the United States of North America. Ours is and will be a harmonious energy, a force tempered by Latin elegance, an intelligent impulse, the spiritual arm of a being in whom action has not destroyed the ability to dream."[23]

Gálvez moved in later works toward a position that provided more than a little inspiration for subsequent *peronista* ideologues. Although his *El espíritu de aristocracia* in 1924 called for the conciliation of democratic and illiberal ideals, this soon gave way to a reactionary, antimaterialistic authoritarianism that permitted highly sympathetic biographies of such *caudillos* as Juan Manuel Rosas and Gabriel García Moreno. By the decade of the 1930s Gálvez was expressing views that proved usefully convenient for subsequent exponents of *justicialismo*. *Este pueblo necesita*[24] described ten "needs" of the nation, each of which received an individual chapter for discussion. Typical were such items as patriotism, moral reform, order and discipline, social hierarchy, and political authority. Democracy was subjected to particular disdain, with Gálvez attacking politics in general while describing the trappings of representative government as inimical to the unity that only a highly centralized authority might provide.

Neither Gálvez' fervent nationalist nor the pro-Fascist coloration of his later writings were peculiar commodities in Argentina. Another common ingredient was a generalized antiforeign bias that in some writers centered primarily upon the United States. But one of many examples

22. Manuel Gálvez, *El solar de la raza* (Madrid: Ed. Saturnino Calleja, 1920), p. 27.
23. *Ibid.*, p. 60.
24. Manuel Gálvez, *Este pueblo necesita* (Buenos Aires: A. García Santos, 1934).

was Manuel Ugarte (1878–1951), whose role as an exponent of Yankee-phobia is described elsewhere.[25] Venom was directed toward the United States, its society, and its culture. Concerned over the encroachments of North American economic activity and scornful of Anglo-Saxon civilization in general, he feared that Latin America's European heritage might be lost. A later expansion of Ugarte's views received the benefit of a widely disseminated English translation. Thus *El destino de un continente*[26] in 1925 extended his criticism of North American economic self-interest while attacking both the Monroe Doctrine and Pan-Americanism as he understood them. Pleading for a South American hemispheric arrangement to counter the United States, Ugarte envisioned Argentina as the natural leader of such a bloc.

While Argentine intellectuals continued to vent their nationalistic sentiments, sympathy for European fascism grew in the latter years of the 1930s. With the period of the *concordancia* characterized politically as a conservative return to the oligarchical tradition, it was not surprising that Axis propaganda received wide circulation. The class designs of the rulers found ready support in Fascist sloganeering. In Masur's words, "The nation had two choices: It could follow the example of Great Britain, France, or the United States, accepting a moderated socialism or a New Deal policy; or it could follow the path of fascism, German-or Italian-style. Fascism won the day."[27] Argentine reactionaries, especially in the light of Hitler's early victories, vocally praised such events while the Germans established the *Deutscher Volksbund für Argentina* in 1937 and later expanded their pro-Nazi activities.

Not all the intellectual currents followed precisely these channels, however; others were also to influence the *peronista* movement. Traditional radicalism long survived Hipólito Irigoyen, and underlying its contemporary policy demands was a strong attraction to caudillistic leadership and personal charisma. Of relevance for the ideology of Juan Perón was the doctrine of a group of pro-Radical intellectuals known as the Fuerza de Orientación Radical de la Joven Argentina, or FORJA. The *forjista* program included a demand for neutrality during World War II, immediate industrialization, a severing of economic ties with Great Britain, and an expansion of state responsibilities.[28] All of these principles were to be embraced by Perón. Although many elements of *peronismo*

25. See Chapter 12.
26. Manuel Ugarte, *El destino de un continente* (Madrid: Editorial Mundo Latino, 1923).
27. Masur, *Nationalism in Latin America* p. 162.
28. See the exposition by the *forjista* Arturo Juaretche, *F.O.R.J.A. y la década infame* (Buenos Aires: Coycacán, 1962).

were in conflict with the *forjistas,* the similarities contribute to a more complete understanding of the precursors of *peronismo.* Neither is it purely coincidental that following the dissolution of FORJA in 1945, many of its members followed pamphleteer Arturo Juaretche into the *peronista* movement.

The Nationalism of Peronismo / The emergence of Juan Domingo Perón as a public figure came with an army coup in 1943. This interruption of formally constitutional government was carried out by the Grupo de Oficiales Unidos (GOU), which since 1930 had come to include nearly half of the officers on active duty. Highly nationalistic, anti-United States and avowedly pro-Fascist, this group espoused a brand of authoritarianism that was presumably to cleanse Argentina of corruption, bringing about sound and orderly administration of national affairs. "Our government will be an inflexible dictatorship, although at the beginning we will make the necessary concessions needed to put it on a solid basis."[29] Prominent within the GOU leadership was Colonel Perón.

Born in 1895 of a middle-class family, Perón entered a military academy at sixteen and followed a career in the army. Observing the Mussolini regime at first hand while serving in Rome as a military attaché in the 1930s, he found political processes in that country to his liking. The currents of nationalism and fascism which he encountered upon his return to Argentina proved congenial, and with the 1943 *coup d'état,* he began his drive for national rule. Appointed both secretary to the war ministry and president of the labor department, he rapidly built his strength through the beginnings of a long and fateful courtship of the Argentine worker. The labor department was soon elevated to ministerial status. Perón was later to say that when "we created the secretariat of labor and welfare . . . [was] for me the first day of our movement."[30]

After seizing power the GOU leadership first made overtures to the country's industrialists. When the latter indicated their preference for new elections and a return of the Radical party, however, the regime turned to the leading labor organizations. As secretary of labor and social welfare, Perón was in a position to encourage greater trade unionism. Previously inactive workers such as those from the sugar plantations and packing-houses were stimulated, while Perón's frequent intervention

29. Quoted in José Luis Romero, *A History of Argentine Political Thought,* tr. Thomas F. McGann (Stanford: Stanford University Press, 1963), p. 245.

30. George I. Blanksten, *Perón's Argentina* (Chicago: University of Chicago Press, 1953), p. 55.

in bargaining processes forced prolabor settlements upon the business community. Extensive social security coverage was provided; the Institute of Social Security, established in 1945, gave far greater benefits than labor had known before. As Perón built a political machine based on the trade unions, he also gained substantial control over the national Confederación General de Trabajo (CGT). Wage increases, low-cost housing, and a growing panoply of fringe benefits further cemented his hold on the loyalties of the workers. Most important of all, he gave them "a feeling of self-esteem and importance which they had never felt before. . . . He made them feel a part of the civic life of the nation in a way which they had never felt before."[31]

When the military prepared a return to elected government, Perón became a presidential candidate. Supported by the Partido Laborista (Labor party), which was founded in November of 1945, he mounted a campaign that drew the bulk of its popularity from Buenos Aires' urban proletariat. The platform espoused extreme economic nationalism, pledging the nationalization of foreign-owned utilities and an attack on non-Argentine interests. Echoes of *argentinidad* were strong, and the Partido Laborista championed "national scientific and cultural development." Demagogic promises of social welfare measures were reiterated, frequently couched in terms of antiforeign xenophobia. Aided by government favoritism and lackadaisical opposition from an anti-Perón coalition of disparate forces, he heightened his chances by requiring employers to pay their workers a Christmas bonus equalling 25 percent of their annual wage. And finally, when the U. S. Department of State issued a Blue Book on Argentina which documented wartime Axis affiliations and likened Perón to Hitler, the culminating issue was provided. Attacking former Ambassador Spruille Braden, who had inspired the publication, Perón told the electorate that the choice was "Braden or Perón," Yankee interference or Argentine independence. Twelve days later he won office by a substantial margin.

Taking office in June, 1946, Juan Perón immediately launched his program of economic nationalism and social justice. The former, he declared, required that major economic components be in the hands of the state. With Argentina enjoying status as a creditor nation and a war-swollen foreign exchange surplus of $1.5 million, Perón began to "repatriate" non-Argentine interests. Following a rapid nationalization of the Central Bank, he negotiated the purchase of the British-owned railroads. The telephone system, long a subsidiary of International Tele-

31. Robert J. Alexander, *Prophets of the Revolution: Profiles of Latin American Leaders* (New York: The Macmillan Company, 1962), p. 250.

phone and Telegraph Company, was expropriated. Cash was paid for the recovery of a wide assortment of British, French, and North American enterprises. Nationalistic pride was served with highly visible but uneconomical steps such as the growth of a national merchant marine; by 1951 the tonnage had grown from 45 ships to 386. Gold reserves were also used to pay off the foreign debt. Within three years' time, Perón could claim major achievements in the drive for economic independence. At Tucumán in July, 1949, he issued a Declaration of Economic Independence, marking the success of "the peoples and governments of the Argentine provinces and territories . . . [in breaking] the dominating chains which have bound them to foreign capitalism. . . ." Perón announced, "Following the course of conduct and the example of San Martín, we have come to Tucumán, we have entered the historical house, we have endeavored to create a similar atmosphere, we have taken the same oath, and we are also ready to die, should it be necessary, to obtain our economic independence."[32]

Economic nationalism also called for a transformation of Argentina from a pastoral to an industrial basis. Perón had said that the nation's economy "rested almost exclusively on the products of the earth, which were processed in a most inferior manner; later . . . we acquired them again as manufactured goods. . . . All that money left the country without benefitting our economy, our industries, or the working class whom it could have fed."[33] And so, seemingly striking at the traditional power of the landowning oligarchy, he centralized the control of the country's agricultural export products through the creation in March, 1946, of the Instituto Argentino de Producción e Intercambio (IAPI). As the co-ordinating agency responsible for the Five-Year Plan of economic development, the IAPI bought meat and grain from the producers at low prices, sold them abroad at the highest price available, and kept the profit for official use. Much of the profit was channeled into the purchase of capital goods, and all possible encouragement was given to native industry. The urban industrialist was the beneficiary of such policies, while the agricultural landowner suffered.

For several years the economic resources built up during the wartime boom was sufficient to underwrite such policies. At the same time Perón also was enacting a broad range of welfare measures. It was not coincidental that they contributed to the genuine popular support the regime enjoyed. Social security coverage continued to be extended; increased housing was provided; higher education was made free, although univer-

32. Blanksten, *Peron's Argentina,* p. 238.
33. Quoted in Romero, *Argentine Political Thought,* pp. 250, 252.

sity autonomy was dealt a series of devastating blows; and new labor legislation was passed. Above all, the extended honeymoon with the workers showed no sign of waning. Rural laborers were organized into the Federación Argentina de Secciones Agrarias, and for the first time in history the farm workers bargained with their employers. The government progressively brought the CGT under its control, and the dominant figure was Perón's one indispensable colleague, his wife Evita.

Eva Duarte, born out of wedlock in 1919 and raised in the provinces, had undertaken a career in radio when she met Juan Perón. At first his mistress and after 1945 his second wife, she had been instrumental in arousing the public demonstrators who forced the GOU to end his one-day imprisonment after a brief setback in 1945. Following his election she built up her own political organization, based upon control of the labor movement and her own María Eva Duarte de Perón Foundation. The latter, supported budgetarily by the government but financed primarily by forced donations from private individuals and businesses, became the instrument by which she dispensed huge funds in assorted social programs. Ambitious, energetic, and completely devoted to her husband and his cause, she combined a genuine sympathy for the lower classes with a bitter resentment toward the socially privileged, who never accepted her. With an unerring personal touch that led to a popularity rivaling her husband's, she actively engendered the class hostilities and social antagonisms that increasingly marked the *peronista* regime. The opulence with which she surrounded herself merely endeared her further to the masses, while the aid given out personally through the Eva Perón Foundation, unencumbered as it was by any public accounting for its funds, served to strengthen her position even further.

Having championed with her husband the rights of women, she symbolized amid her glamorous surroundings an awakened feminine mystique in Argentina. Her autobiography[34] testified to Evita's love of the oppressed and of children in particular, while emphasizing the completeness of her dedication to *peronismo*. Always referring to her husband simply as "Perón," she epitomized her attitude in writing that Perón "was great and I small; he was the master and I pupil, he was the figure and I the shadow." Her own ambitions reached their apogee when, in 1951, she prepared to run for vice-president on the official ticket. At that juncture the armed forces, already disturbed by her power and appalled at the thought of a woman on the threshold of the presidency, brought pressure to bear on Perón. Well understanding the sentiments of the military, he acceded to their demands, and Evita withdrew at a mass

34. Eva Perón, *My Mission in Life* (New York: Vantage Press, 1953).

rally as an emotional act of renunciation. Her health broken by extreme exhaustion and the onslaught of cancer, she was too ill to attend Perón's second inauguration, and in July, 1952, she died at the age of thirty-three. Although her virtual canonization provided a renewed source of popularity for her husband—who took the official title of First Widower—Evita's absence deprived him of his most trusted and effective collaborator.

In the international field, nationalistic populism included *peronista* ambitions of hemispheric leadership; this too was nothing new in the context of Argentine political thought. Seeking economic union with its neighbors, Argentina signed a series of treaties with Paraguay, Bolivia, and Chile, while the Vargas government in Brazil considered for a time the possibility of a formal agreement. Perón undertook to build a hemispheric labor organization, the Agrupación de Trabajadores Latino Americanos Sindicalizados (ATLAS). It sought to capitalize on the rivalry of the communists' CTAL and the democratic Organización Regional Interamericana de Trabajadores (ORIT), and Argentine money poured in for several years before the effort was abandoned. In the meantime, labor attachés were sent to many Argentine embassies, even going so far as to finance a newspaper in Rio de Janeiro. Public declarations repeatedly called for a "Third Position" designed to provide an independent stance between the great antagonists of the cold war, while less public diplomacy attempted to create an informal South American bloc. It was only with the onset of domestic fiscal problems and the necessity of seeking economic aid from the United States that Perón reluctantly retreated from such undertakings and modified his outspoken anti-Yankee stance. But his basic course was again one that was consistent with national sentiment and by so doing helped to buttress his mass appeal, at least temporarily.

Perón's policies of economic nationalism, social justice, and hemispheric diplomacy all struck powerfully responsive chords in Argentina. In the meantime his drive for personal power led to the gradual creation of a virtual dictatorship. Notwithstanding his broad popularity, he erected an authoritarian structure within which dissent was forbidden. And it was this which led many foreign observers to classify *peronismo,* often on superficial bases, as a Latin variant of fascism. Organized party opposition was curbed over a period of time. Following a substantial victory in 1948 congressional by-elections, Perón introduced a campaign of harassment against the radicals and others. Arrests and extended detentions became common, and a law of *desacato* or disrespect legalized the jailing of any who criticized either the Peróns or the government.

Large *peronista* majorities in congress impeached the entire Supreme Court, and the hallowed sanctity of judicial independence was crushed. Press censorship grew in severity, while *peronista*-financed dailies, weeklies, and radio stations spread the gospel of *peronista* glory. Perón himself frequently wrote editorials under the pseudonym of Descartes. Both *La Nación* and, in 1951, the famed *La Prensa* were forced to discontinue publication. The voices of dissent were first muted and then totally silenced.

The Elaboration of Justicialismo / By the time of Perón's re-election in 1951, the trappings of hero-worship and the cult of the leader were growing in magnitude. The old Partido Laborista had long since been converted into the Partido Peronista, notwithstanding Perón's inclination to permit a number of minor parties, as long as they all contributed to the advancement of *peronista* interests. Special anthems and songs were written, adopted, and chanted by the well-organized masses that would gather to hear Perón from the balcony of the Casa Rosada, Argentina's presidential palace. Informers and secret agents were employed to ferret out opposition, while cities, provinces, schools, ships, airports, and other entities were named for either Juan or Evita. Perón, unlike the unassuming Getúlio Vargas, was a magnetic figure and commanding orator, and he relished extreme adulation while playing his role to the hilt. Applying his personal flair to the fullest, he proved highly sensitive to the nuances of opinion-molding.

His goal of permanent rule suggested the value of an official ideology, and the intelligent if nonintellectual Perón recognized both the pragmatic and the self-satisfying potentialities of a "unique" and original state doctrine. So it was that at a Congress of Philosophy meeting at Mendoza in April, 1949, he first sketched in broad philosophical terms what Argentina came to know as *justicialismo*. Derivative, eclectic, and opportunistic as it was to be, it nonetheless stands as one of the few carefully articulated political expositions of twentieth-century Latin America. Described by the regime as an alternative to both capitalism and communism, *justicialismo* was presented as worthy for adoption throughout the world. Although the initial discussion of *justicialismo* was brief and rather general, later presentations were to spell out the vaunted "Third Position" in detail. By 1951 the first of several books on the subject had appeared,[35] and Perón himself was proudly referring to the virtues of his new doctrine. As he told congress on one occasion,

35. The leading official statement was that of Perón's minister of technical affairs, Raúl A. Mende, *El justicialismo* (Buenos Aires: Imprenta Nacional, 1950).

"When I think that we have been the first to announce this solution to men, and when I demonstrate that we have been the first to realize it . . . [my] soul is filled with emotion when I think that the day cannot be far off when all of humanity, seeking some star in the night, will fix its eyes on the flag of the Argentines."[36]

Basing its philosophical precepts upon the writings of Hegel and Marx, *justicialismo* regarded society as an entity characterized by the clash of conflicting forces. It was toward the resolution of such competitive rivalry that *justicialismo* was directed. Four basic elements were identified as playing a necessary social role: idealism, materialism, individualism, and collectivism. The *justicialista* task was to bring about the harmonious resolution of these forces; only by the proper exercise of all four could society develop in a constructive fashion. Should any of these forces gain ascendency over the others, tyranny would result. Moreover, if any two forces combined in opposition to the other two, a further variety of tyrannies and social injustice would follow.

The triumph of idealism, it was argued, would lead to a clerical dictatorship or theocracy in which materialism, individualism, and collectivism would be destroyed. On the other hand, a victory for materialism would lead to a machine-dominated technocracy to which the individual would be subordinated. Should extreme individualism gain the upper hand, anarchy would reign. For in the words of Perón, individualism unfettered "leads to a society of inhuman egoists who think only of getting rich, although to do so it may be necessary to reduce millions of their less fortunate brothers to a state of starvation, poverty, and desperation."[37] In the event of extreme collectivism, finally, the spirit of man would be stifled by a communal tyranny in which the state would be deified. Given the victory of any single force, in short, society would be subjected to unacceptable consequences. But it was the combination of two of the four basic elements which was regarded as a more likely source of social conflict.

Justicialista thought regarded an alliance of idealism and collectivism as descriptive of fascism and nazism. In the government's postwar renunciation of the Axis, fascism was anathematized almost as much as communism. The combination of materialism and collectivism, which produced communism, implied the annihilation of idealism and individ-

36. By far the best treatment in English is that of Blanksten, *Perón's Argentina,* in his chapter entitled "Southern Dialectic." Excerpts are reproduced in John D. Martz, ed., *The Dynamics of Change in Latin America* (Englewood Cliffs: Prentice-Hall, 1965).

37. From Juan Domingo Perón, *The Voice of Perón* (Buenos Aires: Subsecretaría de Informaciones de la Presidencia de la Nación Argentina, 1950), p. 133, as quoted in Blanksten, *Perón's Argentina,* p. 287.

ualism; with communism, mankind would know its bitterest hour. Domination by materialism and individualism, in overcoming idealism and collectivism, brought about capitalism. As seen through *justicialista* eyes, capitalism resulted in "dehumanized capital." The absence of idealism and collectivism would permit the abuse of property, as was allegedly true of the United States. The anti-Yankee strain of Argentine nationalism was rife at the time of the introduction of *justicialismo,* thus the criticism of capitalism was especially vigorous. This was a form of tyranny to be avoided at all costs. Said Perón: "Capitalism, glorious perhaps in the eighteenth century in its constructive stage, is arriving at its final stage. New forms—as has been the custom of humanity throughout the ages—struggle and contend in the world to replace capitalism in its final stage."[38]

Seven different tyrannies, then, were theoretically possible in society; four could emanate from the triumph of one given force, while the final three were produced by an alliance of a pair of the four societal elements. The avoidance of all such results was the task of *justicialismo,* thus its "Third Position" would provide a new system conducive to the collaborative interrelationship of idealism, materialism, individualism, and collectivism. Conflict would be neutralized, with each force contributing in a constructive fashion to social harmony. Blanksten's synthesis says it well: "*Justicialismo* or the 'Third Position' is the 'new Argentina's' version of Aristotle's 'Golden Mean,' insofar as that concept sought the avoidance of extremes. The *Peronista* who knows his doctrine defines it thus: *Justicialismo* is 'that doctrine whose objective is the happiness of man in human society achieved through the harmony of materialistic, idealistic, individualistic, and collectivist forces, each valued in a Christian way.' . . . *Justicialismo,* then, envisages a temperate social order compounded of 'just the right amounts' of idealism, materialism, individualism, and collectivism."[39]

The persuasiveness of *justicialismo* was perhaps weaker in its constructive than in its negative aspects. The identification of major social elements and the critique of the seven resultant forms of tyranny set forth clearly a philosophical dialectic of conflict. The subsequent analysis of *justicialismo* as a conciliating and yet positive alternative tended more to the superficial. Described as a theory of equilibrium, it was stylistically clear but offered little in the way of explicit content. The result was a rampant imprecision that was not susceptible to specific formulations. A balance was sought among idealism, materialism, individualism, and

38. From Leonard T. Richmond, *Argentina's Third Position and Other Systems Compared* (Buenos Aires: Acme Agency, 1949), p. 10.

39. *Ibid.,* pp. 290–91.

collectivism. Each of the forces had its own value, yet the four were not weighted equally. Idealism and individualism bore greater intrinsic worth than materialism and collectivism. Consequently, the point of equilibrium would lie closer to the first two forces than to the latter pair. The "Third Position" of *justicialismo,* located somewhere between the four elements, was fluid. And being changeable rather than static, it would move about, depending upon the given issue in question. Perón was lucid in treating this point. "We are not sectarians, *Peronismo* is not sectarian. Some say, in grave error, that it is a centrist party. A centrist party, like a rightist or leftist party, is sectarian, and we are totally antisectarian. . . . Our 'Third Position' is not a centrist position. It is an ideology which is in the center, on the right, or on the left *according to specific circumstances.*"[40]

In practice, *justicialismo* therefore became a theoretical justification for whatever specific policy Perón chose to adopt. With the "Third Position" moving and dynamic, it provided a rationale for *peronismo* in both domestic and foreign policy. The identification of the magical point of equilibrium depended on Perón's personal decision, after which the propaganda organs of the state would hail the policy as exemplary of official doctrine. Domestic policy in general held that *justicialismo* required a position between rich and poor, with the economically underprivileged masses receiving the greatest possible support and encouragement. Internationally, of course, the "Third Position" supported nationalistic independence of both East and West, justifying anti-Yankee and anti-Communist policies at one and the same time.

The ideology and program of *justicialismo* provided ample opportunity for sloganeering and propagandizing. Only a small number of politicians and intellectuals were familiar with the extended philosophical treatments of *justicialismo,* and even a lesser number took it all seriously. But the short catch phrases and symbols were widely disseminated and became for a time a part of the national vocabulary. "The Third Position," "national dignification of labor," "political independence and economic sovereignty," "humanization of capital," and "solidarity among Argentines" were among the more familiar. The "Twenty Truths of *Justicialismo*" as expounded by Perón in 1950 were also common knowledge to many. The flavor was suggested by the following excerpts:

> 2. *Peronismo* is an eminently popular movement. Every political clique is opposed to the popular interests and, therefore, it cannot be a *Peronista* organization. . . .

40. My emphasis.

5. In the New Argentina, work is a right because it dignifies man, and a duty because it is only fair that each one should produce at least what he consumes. . . .

9. Politics do not constitute for us a definite objective, but only a means of achieving the homeland's welfare as represented by the happiness of the people and the greatness of the nation. . . .

20. The best of this land is the people. . . .[41]

A brief synopsis of the meaning of *justicialismo* to the ordinary Argentine worker was best revealed in these "truths":

14. *Justicialismo* is a new philosophical school of life. It is simple, practical, popular, and endowed with deeply Christian and humanitarian sentiments.

15. As a political doctrine, *justicialismo* establishes a fair balance between law and society.

16. As an economic doctrine, *justicialismo* achieves a true form of social economy by placing capital at the service of the economy and the economy at the service of society.

17. As a social doctrine, *justicialismo* assures an adequate distribution of social justice, giving to each person the rights to which he is entitled. . . .[42]

Despite its weaknesses and occasional self-contradictions, this ideology was an important element of *peronismo;* certainly it was pertinent for an understanding of Perón's particular formulation of nationalistic populism. Aside from its political value in the mobilization of mass support, it gave him a further means of incorporating Argentine twentieth-century ideas and sentiments into the totality of his movement. Only in the final days of *peronismo,* as conditions mounted over which the regime had little control, did the ideology of Juan Perón recede from public view. With the coming of the 1950s, the seeds of economic and political turmoil which had been planted in the preceding decade germinated to bring forth the thorny fruits of earlier mistakes. It was largely the deterioration of economic conditions for which Perón was responsible that hastened his collapse. As will be seen, his departure from office and from Argentina did not, however, mean an end to either the popular sentiments or the social and political alterations that had been encouraged and implemented.

41. Quoted in Macdonald, *Latin-American Politics,* 2d ed. (1954), pp. 92–93.
42. *Ibid.*

An Assessment of Peronismo / Despite short-run nationalistic achievements in the economic field, the ultimate costs proved to be expensive. The race toward industrialization and independence of foreign influence rapidly drained the treasury, and accumulated wartime reserves were soon depleted. The nationalized railway system lost staggering sums, while the large-scale importation of capital and luxury items contributed to a foreign debt of alarming proportions. The drive for industrialization suffered from official interference and mismanagement, and in the meantime agricultural production fell. IAPI maintained its low price levels, and producers were discouraged from broadening their activities. By the end of Perón's rule in 1955, the amount of cultivated land was actually less than in 1940. The industry-based economic nationalism of *peronismo,* while a necessity for Argentina, demanded a gradualistic program that required years for fulfillment. Perón, however, insisted upon a rate of transformation that was impractical and unrealistic. The chimera of total self-sufficiency in a short period of time was beyond the realities of the situation.

In the years following Evita's death, the repercussions of *peronista* economic policies multiplied with growing urgency. The mismanagement and corruption of state-operated agencies grew, while inflation made it difficult to meet the demands of labor. Wage increases were rapidly eaten up by spiraling prices. Perón was forced to seek economic assistance from the United States; when he signed an exploration contract with a North American oil company, his vaunted anti-Yankee position disintegrated, and the labor confederation defined Perón by rejecting the agreement. Church support was also forfeited when Perón, desperate for public scapegoats, expelled high-ranking Church officials. Deserted by close associates and for the first time unsure of himself, he ordered the legalization of prostitution, a further insult that helped lead to his excommunication in June, 1955. When a military *golpe de estado* in the same month failed to unseat Perón, he adopted yet more extreme measures. Opposition continued to grow while his laboriously erected pillars of support crumbled. Finally, in September, 1955, another military uprising spread from Córdoba to Buenos Aires and, after brief hesitation, the dictator fled the country.

In the years since his departure, Perón has continued indirectly to influence the course of national affairs. More than a dozen years' turmoil has seen a succession of governments, both military and civilian, grapple with the legacy of *peronista* economic policies. Although Perón has remained in Spanish exile, rival groups of *peronista* leaders have retained control over much of the labor movement, and no one has yet succeeded in capturing *peronista* loyalties. Efforts by the military and by two radical factions have failed to incorporate these elements into a constructive political force. The tough-minded military regime that seized control in the mid-1960s adopted harsh anti-*peronista* measures, but the demands and pressures of nationalistic populism were not met. Domestic wounds are unhealed and the body politic remains badly fragmented. The movement of *peronismo,* like its *justicialista* doctrine, was divisive, based on conflict. Encouraging class hostilities, it fragmented rather than united Argentina. In short, Perón's bequest to Argentina was "a feeling of insecurity, a lack of confidence in its identity, a confusion and equivocation within its basic political institutions."[43]

For students of political thought, *peronismo* was a vigorous and highly articulated movement that, in addition to its strongly pragmatic flavor, was consistent with contemporary currents of Argentine sentiment. The inculcation of nationalism, the aggressive independence in international affairs, and the objective of social justice under highly centralized direction were appropriate components of public policy during the decade of Perón. Whatever the ultimate results, *peronismo* spoke of using state power to bring about a moral regeneration, to create the kind of harmonious social equilibrium of which *justicialismo* preached. Traditional values of hispanic culture—*hispanidad*—were asserted with little qualification. Perón made this clear on many occasions, of which a 1947 speech was indicative: "The spiritual richness endowed upon us by Spain with the cross and the sword . . . withered until it became unrecognizable. . . . [But today,] Spain, Our Mother, eternal daughter of immortal Rome, heiress of gentle Athens and strong Sparta, we are your Sons of the clear name; we are Argentines of the land with silver tinklings, and we possess your golden heart!"[44]

Although *peronismo* performed less than far-reaching revolutionary functions in Argentina, there were certain areas in which it achieved major changes. The status that was given to both urban and rural workers was something that can never again be effectively and lastingly denied. Notwithstanding the unrelenting opposition of large landholders, Perón altered the century-long tradition of national domination by the rural oligarchy. Coming to power despite the opposition of *status quo*

43. Masur, *Nationalism in Latin America,* p. 197.
44. Quoted by Alberto Ciria in his "Peronism—Mythology or Ideology?" mimeographed paper later published by the Latin-American Research Program, University of California at Riverside, 1967.

groups, he was largely successful in transferring a significant degree of political and economic power to the lower and lower-middle classes, especially in the cities.[45] The popular strength of both the industrial worker and the agricultural laborer forced upon post-*peronista* leaders the necessity of vying for their support. Although the land tenure system itself remained intact, the social and political levers of power were altered.

A final consideration concerns the controversy over use of the term "fascism" in characterizing Perón's movement. While the application of broad labels always invokes the dangers of oversimplification, a brief discussion is in order. To judge *peronismo* as a South American variant of European fascism is to yield to imprecise generalization. Moreover, although there was "great resemblance between the policies and techniques of the Peronista group and those of European fascism . . . it was in the methods and techniques rather than in the ideology that the resemblance lay."[46] And the persecution of opposition, muzzling of press opinion and a broad disregard for individual rights was but one element in the broader phenomenon of *peronismo*. A highly significant distinction between *peronismo* and classic European fascism lay in Perón's mass lower-class support. Unlike the traditional fascist reliance on a *declassé* middle class, *peronismo* encouraged and capitalized upon the *descamisados*, the "shirtless ones." Although some middle-class elements did indeed provide support, their role was essentially secondary. The sectors of the population which Perón converted and incorporated into Argentine political and social life were primarily those of the lower strata of society. These, then, were the Argentines who derived genuine social and economic advantage from *peronismo*.

One analyst has referred to *peronismo* as a "fascism of the left," resting as it did on the working class.[47] To him, labor-oriented *peronismo* was an anticapitalist populist nationalism appealing to the lower strata. This led to his conclusion, "If Peronism is considered a variant of fascism, then it is a fascism of the left because it is based on the social strata who would otherwise turn to socialism or Communism as an outlet for their frustrations." Critics of this characterization respond that true fascism does not attack the interests of the dominant oligarchy, as did Perón. Moreover, fascism does not customarily attempt to meet the

45. For a discussion of the Argentina middle sectors under Perón, see Johnson, *Political Change in Latin America*, pp. 112–23.

46. William W. Pierson and Federico G. Gil, *Governments of Latin America* (New York: McGraw-Hill Book Company, 1957), p. 327.

47. Seymour Martin Lipset, *Political Man: The Social Bases of Politics* (Garden City: Doubleday & Co., 1960), pp. 172–73.

workers' demands for equality.[48] And lastly, fascism brings about a total state supremacy that Perón never achieved.[49] Whether Argentina experienced a true "fascism of the left" thus remains a subject of debate, but the parallels to European fascism were largely selective, not inclusive.

Setting aside the controvery over labels, the fact remains that, under Juan Perón, Argentina experienced a manifestation of nationalistic populism which looms large in its contemporary evolution. If the regime was less than fully revolutionary, it nonetheless instituted societal alterations more extensive and durable than did Vargas and his Estado Nôvo in Brazil. While Perón built his regime on a variety of power bases—including labor, the military, the Church, a limited number of "bourgeois industrialists," and his own personal charisma—he also gave vent to historical currents of Argentine thought that included *argentinidad, hispanidad,* and antiforeign nationalism. A fitting conclusion is provided by the words of a leading Argentine student of *peronismo:* "Granting due weight to ideological and personal factors (such as the devotion of many Argentine common people towards Perón and Eva), Peronism can also be seen as a mass movement with a bourgeois ideology. . . . Its most valid achievements were made in the social sphere; but in no instance [did] Peronism push authentic revolution into the economic and political fields. . . ."[50]

SELECTED BIBLIOGRAPHY

BRAZIL AND VARGAS

Alexander, Robert J. "Getúlio Vargas, 'The Father of the Poor,'" in his *Prophets of the Revolution: Profiles of Latin American Leaders.* New York: Macmillan Co., 1962.

Amoroso Lima, Alceu. "Voices of Liberty and Reform in Brazil," in *Freedom and Reform in Latin America.* Edited by Fredrick B. Pike. Notre Dame: University of Notre Dame Press, 1959.

Araujo Lima, Claúdio. *Mito e realidade de Vargas.* Rio de Janeiro: Editora Civilização Brasileira, 1955.

Azevedo, Fernando de. *Brazilian Culture.* Translated by William Rex Crawford. New York: Macmillan Co., 1950.

48. John H. Kautsky, "An Essay in the Politics of Development," in John H. Kautsky, ed., *Political Change in Underdeveloped Countries: Nationalism and Communism* (New York: John Wiley & Sons, Inc., 1962), p. 110.

49. For a lucid and insightful analysis of Argentine "anti-nationalism," as well as a demurrer to Lipset's views, see Kalman H. Silvert, "The Costs of Anti-Nationalism: Argentina," in *Expectant Peoples: Nationalism and Development,* ed. Kalman H. Silvert (New York: Random House, 1963), especially pp. 365–69.

50. Ciria, "Peronism," p. 18.

Burns, E. Bradford, ed. *A Documentary History of Brazil.* New York: Alfred A. Knopf, 1966.
———, ed. *Perspectives on Brazilian History.* New York: University of Columbia Press, 1967.
Campos, Francisco. *Educacão e cultura.* Rio de Janeiro: n.p., 1940.
———. *O estado nôvo: Sua estructura, seu contendo ideologico.* Rio de Janeiro: José Olympio, 1940.
Cruz Costa, Joâo. *History of Ideas in Brazil: The Development of Philosophy in Brazil and the Evolution of National History.* Translated by Suzette Macedo. Berkeley: University of California Press, 1964.
———. "Nationalism and the Evolution of Brazilian Thought in the Twentieth Century," in *International Congress for the History of Ideas.* Mexico City: November 1962.
Dulles, John W. F. *Vargas of Brazil: A Political Biography.* Austin: University of Texas Press, 1967.
Jaguaribe, Hélio. *O nacionalismo na atualidade brasileira.* Rio de Janeiro: n.p., 1958.
———. *Economic and Political Development: A Theoretical Approach and a Brazilian Case Study.* Cambridge: Harvard University Press, 1968.
Horowitz, Irving Louis. *Revolution in Brazil: Politics and Society in a Developing Nation.* New York: E. P. Dutton, 1964.
Loewenstein, Karl. *Brazil under Vargas.* New York: Macmillan Co., 1942.
Masur, Gerhard. *Nationalism in Latin America: Diversity and Unity.* New York: Macmillan Co., 1966.
Mendes de Almeida, Cándido Antônio. *Nacionalismo e desenvolvimento.* Rio de Janeiro: n.p., 1963.
Poppino, Rollie. *Brazil: The Land and People.* New York: Oxford University Press, 1968.
Rodrígues, José Honório. *The Brazilians: Their Character and Aspirations.* Translated by Ralph Edward Dimmick, with foreward and notes by E. Bradford Burns. Austin: University of Texas Press, 1967.
Skidmore, Thomas E. *Politics in Brazil, 1930–1964; An Experiment in Democracy.* New York and London: Oxford University Press, 1967.
Smith, T. Lynn, ed. *Brazil, People and Institutions.* Baton Rouge: Louisiana State University Press, 1963.
Vargai, Getúlio Dorneles. *A nôva política do Brasil.* 12 Vols. Rio de Janeiro: n.p., 1930–45.
Walker, Harvey. "The Vargas Regime," in *Brazil.* Edited by Lawrence Hill. Berkeley: University of California Press, 1947.
Young, Jordan M. *The Brazilian Revolution of 1930 and the Aftermath.* New Brunswick: Rutgers University Press, 1967.

ARGENTINA AND PERONISMO

Alexander, Robert J. "Juan Domingo Perón and 'the New Argentina,'" in his *Prophets of the Revolution: Profiles of Latin American Leaders.* New York: Macmillan Co., 1962.
———. *The Perón Era.* New York: Columbia University Press, 1951.
Barager, Joseph R., ed. *Why Perón Came to Power.* New York: Alfred A. Knopf, 1968.

Belloni, Alberto. *Peronismo y socialismo nacional.* Buenos Aires: Coyoacán, 1962.

Blanksten, George I. *Perón's Argentina.* Chicago: University of Chicago Press, 1953.

Fillol, Tómas Roberto. *Social Factors in Economic Development: The Argentine Case.* Cambridge: M.I.T. Press, 1961.

Gálvez, Manuel. *Este pueblo necesita.* Buenos Aires: A. García Santos, 1934.

Germani, Gino. *Política y sociedad en una época de transición.* Buenos Aires: Editorial Paidós, 1965.

Johnson, John J. *Political Change in Latin America: The Emergence of the Middle Sectors.* Stanford: Stanford University Press, 1958.

Kennedy, John J. *Catholicism, Nationalism, and Democracy in Argentina.* Notre Dame: University of Notre Dame Press, 1958.

Mende, Raúl A. *El justicialismo.* Buenos Aires: Imprenta Nacional, 1950.

Pastor, Reynaldo. *Frente al totalitarismo peronista.* Buenos Aires: Bases, 1959.

Perón, Eva. *My Mission in Life.* New York: Vantage Press, 1953.

Perón, Juan Domingo. *The Voice of Perón.* Buenos Aires: Subsecretaría de Informaciones de la Presidencia de la Nación Argentina, 1950.

Peralta, Jerónimo M. *Perón y la revolución justicialista.* Buenos Aires: n.p., 1951.

Rojas, Ricardo. *Eurindia,* Vol. V of *Obras de Ricardo Rojas.* Buenos Aires: Juan Roldán y Cía., 1924.

———. *La restauración nacionalista: Crítica de la educación argentina y bases para una reforma en el estudio de las humanidades modernas.* Buenos Aires: J. Roldán, 1909.

Romero, José Luis. *A History of Argentine Political Thought.* Translated by Thomas F. McGann. Stanford: Stanford University Press, 1963.

Scobie, James R. *Argentina: A City and a Nation.* New York: Oxford University Press, 1964.

Silvert, Kalman H. "The Costs of Anti-Nationalism: Argentina," in *Expectant Peoples: Nationalism and Development.* Edited by Kalman H. Silvert. New York: Random House, 1963.

Snow, Peter. *Argentine Radicalism: The History and Doctrine of the Radical Civic Union.* Iowa City: University of Iowa Press, 1965.

Whitaker, Arthur P. *Argentine Upheaval: Perón's Fall and the New Argentina.* New York: Frederick A. Praeger, 1956.

———. *The United States and Argentina.* Cambridge: Harvard University Press, 1954.

9

Marxism in Theory and Practice

Of all genuine political thought and ideology in twentieth-century Latin America, none has been as intellectually popular or politically influential as Marxism. While vaguely socialistic ideas reached the Americas in the late 1800s through the importation of European utopian socialism, Marxist ideas first acquired significance with the wave of European immigrants reaching the Plate River region at the turn of the century. Orthodox socialism acquired an immediacy with the convulsion in Russia in 1917, and within a few years Soviet agents and propagandists from the Communist International were carrying their ideological and organizational message throughout the Western Hemisphere. With native Communist parties customarily responsive to the dictates of Soviet international policy, the popular appeal of the movement temporarily waned. At the same time there began to appear a group of intellectuals who, although highly critical of "antinational" Communist groups, advocated Marxian solutions to pressing social and economic problems. Later, the alleged failure of the United States after World War II to provide anticipated technical aid and economic assistance on a large scale, combined with North American policies that many saw as a more insidious and subtle form of imperialism, contributed to a climate in which more radical and virulent strains of Marxism began to emerge. The rise of Fidel Castro in Cuba then presented a major charismatic figure about whom emotional passions rapidly formed.

By the decade of the 1960s, several generations of young university students, increasingly sensitive to the social injustice and economic deprivation surrounding them, had found in Marxism a seemingly complete philosophy that, especially in its material emphasis, appeared to promise a new and genuinely better world. Although the ranks of disillusioned former Communists have been numerous, many Latin Americans have retained a Marxist orientation while bitterly criticizing what they regard as the antipatriotic stance of orthodox communists who slavishly follow the dictates of foreign masters. The variants of Marxism have presented differing interpretations and applications to individual visions of Latin American society and politics. Among these have been the practical exponents of Social Democracy, whose movement is described later. Probably there has been no time during the past half-century when exponents of Marxism have not been significant in at least a few of the twenty American republics. And while the area has provided relatively little originality in its adaptations of Marxism, this has not substantially reduced the ideological attraction of the broad philosophical and political movement. Following an overarching historical review of socialism and communism, attention must be directed to the tumultuous outpourings of *fidelismo* in Cuba, as well as the resurgence of the new radical left with its anarchistic impulse toward violence and terrorism.

Socialism and Communism

The antecedents of Marxism in Latin America first appeared in the second half of the nineteenth century with the importation of European utopian socialism. The ideas of such philosophers as Saint-Simon were current in literary circles, and interest by a tiny minority in the revolutionary wave that swept Europe in 1848 also provoked a degree of attention to such social-minded dogma. However, until the end of the century this was largely in the nature of a fashionable curiosity, and little real impact was registered in the area. The situation changed as a result of the social and economic developments that accompanied a wave of European immigrants (notably to Argentina, Uruguay, Chile, and southern Brazil) and a major infusion of foreign capital. A vocal urban proletariat began to form, and in barely a generation, ideologically sensitive labor unions and political organizations began to spring up. As one authority has written, "radical socio-political concepts moved from the salons of the literati to political rallies in the streets of Latin America."[1]

1. Rollie Poppino, *International Communism in Latin America: A History of the Movement, 1917–1963* (New York: Free Press of Glencoe, 1964), p. 217.

Contingents of immigrants, many from southern Europe, had already been exposed to ideologically oriented trade-unionism before crossing the Atlantic, and their familiarity extended to the doctrines and tactics of not only Marxian socialism but of anarchism and syndicalism as well. Indeed, the latter were very influential upon leaders of the incipient trade union movement in much of Latin America. It was also true that countries previously untouched by European immigration soon responded to similar ideas. Thus the Mexicans and Cubans, for example, both adopted an assortment of Marxist and anarchosyndicalist concepts at the turn of the century. The latter, derived largely from Spain, France, and Italy, were based upon the conviction that private property and capitalism were responsible for all social misery. It was argued that the inherent conflict between worker and employer could be resolved only by the total defeat of the latter; as already seen, all means of direct action were recommended. With capitalist interests controlling the organs of the state, ordinary political action became meaningless; parties, elections, and constitutional government were thus regarded as instruments of oppression in the hands of the rulers.

The anarchosyndicalists therefore sought a total destruction of the state as they knew it. Later, this would lead to a condition of communal ownership of industry through organized syndicates. The early history of the labor movement in Latin America was characterized for a time by anarchosyndicalist doctrine, in addition to the first glimmerings of socialism.[2] With supporters of the latter accepting the anarchosyndicalist goal of destroying capitalism and establishing regulation of the means of production, the collaboration of these two groups was unsurprising. Certainly the anarchosyndicalists and socialists constituted the dominant elements in the labor movement until after the Russian Revolution. Among the earliest examples were Chile, Argentina, Brazil, and Mexico.[3] In each of these, Marxist thought was concerned almost totally with the achievement of social benefits for the workers. Certainly the ideological origins of Marxism in Latin America were founded upon a rigidly class-oriented interpretation of society.

2. For a general survey that examines on a country-by-country basis the evolution of labor from its mutualist and anarchosyndicalist origins to the present, see Robert J. Alexander, *Organized Labor in Latin America* (New York: Free Press of Glencoe, 1965).

3. Brief but informative accounts of this early stage in the Latin American labor movement are found in Moisés Poblete Troncoso and Ben G. Burnett, *The Rise of the Latin-American Labor Movement* (New York: Bookman Associates, 1960). For a more detailed treatment, consult Víctor Alba, *Politics and Labor Movements in Latin America* (Stanford: Stanford University Press, 1968).

In Argentina the socialists were instrumental in founding the Federación Obrera de la República Argentina in 1890, and within five years the regular Partido Socialista had been established. In 1901 the anarchosyndicalists gained the upper hand, rechristening the labor organization as the Federación Obrera Regional Argentina (FORA). The socialists soon established the Unión General de Trabajadores (UGT). Unity of the movement could not immediately be achieved, but in 1909 a wave of anarchist-inspired violence led to official repression, and after 1910, the socialists came to dominate the labor movement. In Chile a series of trade unions developed in the Valparaiso area at the century's turn and were strongly dominated by socialists. The country's first federation of unions, the Federación Obrera de Chile (FOCH), was organized in 1909 under Marxist control. In Brazil the introduction of anarchism by Italian immigrants was especially strong, with a dozen unions coming together as early as 1892. In 1906 they united as the Federação Operária Regional Brasileira (FORB); not until unsuccessful general strikes in 1917 and 1918 did they lose their primacy. As for Mexico, the anarchist leadership of the brothers Flores, Magon was strong both before and after the fall of Porfirio Díaz. Only with the founding of the Confederación Regional Obrera Mexicana (CROM) in 1918 did the anarchosyndicalists go into decline.

While gradually eclipsing the anarchosyndicalists within the labor movement, the socialists also hastened to create formal political parties. The first was the Argentine, which began in 1895. Although never winning power, it came to exert great influence in Buenos Aires, and was strong with the working class until the advent of Perón. The founder and for years the head of the Socialist party was Juan Bautista Justo (1865–1928), a graduate in medicine from the University of Buenos Aires who later became famous as a surgeon. Influenced in part by his exposure to European socialism during a period of studies there, he became an ardent and socially conscious Marxist who, among other things, translated into Spanish the first volume of *Das Kapital*. Obliged by his personal commitment to social action to enter public life, he edited the socialist daily *La Vanguardia* while directing the party's organizational affairs. Less a true Marxist than an admirer of the German socialist Edward Bernstein, he became a noted political thinker in Argentina, and his publications included, among others, *La teoría científica de la historia y la política argentina* (1898) and *El socialismo argentino* (1910).[4]

---

4. The works of Justo's later years were largely repetitive of his earlier writings.

He was succeeded by Alfredo Lorenzo Palacios (1880–1966), who for several decades stood as Argentina's leading socialist intellectual and political figure. At various times either a senator or deputy, head of the Faculty of Juridical and Social Sciences at the University of La Plata and a professor in law and social sciences at the University of Buenos Aires, he voiced for years an eloquent nationalistic reformism along Marxian lines. Speaking on behalf of the urban workers while himself an intellectual par excellence, Palacios was prolific both as a writer and speaker. Among his many works, notable contributions included *La defensa del valor humano* (1939), *La justicia social* (1954), and *Soberanía y socialización: Industrias, monopolios, latifundios, y privilegios del capital extranjero* (1946).[5]

In neighboring Uruguay the Socialists organized politically before World War I,[6] and in 1917 responded sympathetically to the news of the Russian Revolution. At a 1920 conference the party accepted Russian overtures by affiliating with the Communist International. The following year the organization renamed itself "Communist," and a dissident group withdrew and re-established an official Socialist party. The Brazilian case reflected the prominence of anarchism in the labor movement, and a weakly organized socialist group turned to communism and joined the Communist International in 1921. In the 1930s formal Socialist parties began appearing in such countries as Colombia, Peru, Ecuador, Cuba, Bolivia, and Panama.

In all of their organizations, the socialist parties adopted an orthodox Marxian approach to national problems. While economic nationalism and government intervention were prescribed for the achievement of true social justice, in truth it was only the welfare of labor that received close attention. A degree of political freedom, extensive economic planning, and of course the social ownership of the means of production and distribution were advocated. Between the Russian Revolution in 1917 and the death of Lenin in 1924, the existing Socialist parties divided. In most cases the majority chose to affiliate with the Soviet Union, leaving a minority to break away and rechristen itself "Socialist." Although the situation varied from one country to another, in most cases the avowed Socialists were forced to play a role secondary to the Communists. Furthermore, due in large part to their penchant for copying

5. Also representative are his *Libertad de prensa* (Buenos Aires: Editorial Claridad, 1935), and *Nuestro América y el imperialismo* (Buenos Aires: Editorial Palestra, 1961).

6. Emilio Frugoni organized a Centro Carlos Marx in 1904 and six years later led in the formation of the Socialist party. Frugoni remained for many years the dominant figure of Uruguayan socialism.

European models, they found themselves supplanted by those who emerged in the 1930s and after as Social Democratic parties. Within a few years of the conclusion of World War I, in short, the majority of self-titled Socialist trade unions and party organizations had been relegated to a peripheral role. For political purposes, the furtherance of Marxism rested in the hands of the emergent Communist parties.

In Latin America these latter regularly altered and adapted their tactics in accordance with the dictates of Moscow.[7] Through the years they have been consistent in adhering to the requirements of existing international events. With but few exceptions of any real importance, the Latin-American Communists have placed the interests of their own countries second to those perceived by their Soviet comrades. An important result has been the fact that while independent Latin-American Marxists have applied its doctrines in the light of native conditions, the formally organized, card-carrying party members and their organized movement have been essentially alien. Poppino has commented perceptively along these lines: "From its inception each [Latin-American Communist party] . . . has looked exclusively to Marxism, as interpreted by the head of the Soviet state. . . . No Communist party has sought to draw upon Latin America's heritage of indigenous 'communistic' societies or seriously to identify itself with the surviving communal practices of the descendents of Aztecs, Mayas, or Incas. . . . From the beginning the first loyalty of every Communist party has been to the Soviet Union, not to the republic in which it operates."[8]

As loyal members of the world-wide Communist movement, the Latin Americans have been responsive to the series of stages through which the international movement has passed. At least seven such historical periods can be identified: (1) the early period from the 1917 Revolution to the 1924 death of Lenin; (2) the 1924–29 years that preceded collectivization and industrialization in the Soviet Union; (3) the years to 1935 during which Stalinism emerged unchallenged; (4) the era of the Popular Front and Communist collaboration with non-Marxist parties of the left; (5) at the signing of the Nazi-Soviet Pact, the brief reversal of the Popular Front; (6) a return to co-operation with representative governments and organizations during World War II; (7) postwar rigidity accompanying the introduction of the Cold War; and

---

7. In addition to Poppino, a standard reference is Robert J. Alexander, *Communism in Latin America*, 2nd pr. (New Brunswick: Rutgers University Press, 1960). Also see the excellent "Introduction" by Luis E. Aguilar in his anthology, *Marxism in Latin America* (New York: Alfred A. Knopf, 1968), pp. 3–59.

8. Poppino, *Communism in Latin America*, p. 55.

(8) the more fluid and uncertain period marked by Nikita Khrushchev's speech to the Twentieth Congress of the Soviet Communist party in 1956 and dramatized by the rise of Fidel Castro and the international schism between Peking and Moscow.[9]

The details of the half-century of Communist activity in the hemisphere provide a history of international relations and of short-run tactical considerations rather than basic ideological issues; as such, they need not be outlined here.[10] It is sufficient to append a pair of observations relevant to the evolution of Communist dogma. The first is a restatement of the Latin-American fidelity in reflecting the international Communist movement. Even the rise of Castro in Cuba, as will be seen, has changed this relatively little. At the same time, nonetheless, the Latin-American parties have enjoyed a greater maneuverability than their European counterparts. This has stemmed from the Soviet expectation that the United States would not permit the seizure of power by Communists in its own sphere of influence. Secondly, it must be remembered that communism in Latin America has sought mass support from the urban industrial proletariat. Although agrarian reform has been given lip service, practical political calculations have concentrated on urban laborers and young intellectuals. Only with recent *fidelista* writings about peasant-based rural violence have such basic assumptions been challenged.[11]

As a philosophical construct, Marxism has made substantial inroads upon the thinking and attitudes of Latin Americans. Taken in terms of a nonrevolutionary emphasis upon planning and economic progress, it has been faithful to the deep-rooted cultural bias favoring collectivism and centralized control by the state. In this sense, Marxist ideas have spread through the urban middle classes as well as the intelligentsia. Insofar as Marxism advocates economic centralization and industrial development, its acceptance is widespread. Certainly this has had much to do with the popular successes of the Social Democratic movements studied in later chapters. Although the doctrinal insistence on the classical postulates of class strife have not been abandoned, in some quarters they are not taken seriously. Until Castro, theoretical formulations tended to emphasize a gradualistic rather than rapid approach to the seizure of political and economic power. This apparently struck relatively few Latin Americans as a source of discomfort.

9. Alexander, *Communism in Latin America,* pp. 18–19.
10. Poppino, Alba, Alexander, and Aguilar are all useful in this context.
11. For an elaboration of these points, see Federico G. Gil, "Latin America," in *The New Communisms,* ed., Dan N. Jacobs (New York: Harper and Row, Publishers, 1969).

The most successful adaptations of Marxist thought in political terms have been, again, those of the Social Democratic movements, but our concern for the moment is related to purer expositions of Marxism. What can be regarded as Communist thought has been largely the plodding, uninspired, party-line writings of Moscow-oriented political hacks. The enthusiasm of such eminent artistic figures as Diego Rivera and Pablo Neruda emerges more in aesthetic than in doctrinal terms; for such sympathizers, the attraction is largely that of revolutionary social protest as expressed artistically. Philosophically valid and doctrinally sound expositions of Marxism in Latin America have been relatively few. Given the adherence of the party faithful to dictates from the Soviet Union, it is natural that the more perceptive expositions of Marxism have come from independent-minded intellectuals. One in particular has earned high marks, being highly influential in his own country and beyond for many years. This is the remarkable Peruvian, José Carlos Mariátegui (1895–1930).

Mariátegui stands as an intriguing figure who is quite likely the most important Marxist theoretician of Latin America. Emerging from an impoverished childhood to become a journalist at an early age, an omnivorous reader who was largely self-educated, Mariátegui founded the daily *Nuestra Epoca* in 1918. Returning to Peru in 1923 after four enriching years of European travel, he then founded the journal *Amauta,* in which much of his subsequent writing appeared. Founder of the Peruvian wing of the Communist Third International, he combined a full life of literary and journalistic activity with dedicated political involvement. His *La escena contemporánea*[12] appeared in 1925, and the essays that constituted *Defensa de marxismo*[13] were published following his death by Julio Portocarrero, an early leader of the Peruvian Communist party. His major work, however—one of the most important in twentieth century Latin America—was the collection of *Amauta* writings entitled *Siete ensayos de interpretación de la realidad peruana.*[14]

In these "Seven Essays," Mariátegui undertook a consideration of the critical areas of Peruvian society: economic evolution, the problem of the Indian, the problem of the land, regionalism and centralism, the process of public instruction, the religious factor, and the process of literature. Much of his attention was primarily economic, and the author devoted attention to the pre-conquest development that he be-

12. José Carlos Mariátegui, *La escena contemporánea* (Lima: Ed. Minerva, 1925).
13. José Carlos Mariátegui, *Defensa de marxismo: La emoción de nuestro tiempo y otros temas* (Santiago: Ediciones Nacionales y Extranjeras, 1934).
14. José Carlos Mariátegui, *Siete ensayos de interpretación de la realidad peruana: Escritos de Mundial y Amauta* (Lima: Ediciones Amauta, 1928).

lieved had been grievously retarded by Spanish colonialism. The latter had interrupted an orderly evolutionary pattern, and more current difficulties should be met by a renewal of the four-hundred-year-old tradition. Thus, after praising the social utility and efficient collectivism organized by the Incas, he continued: "The Spanish conquerors destroyed . . . this formidable machinery of production. Indigenous society, the Inca economy, fell to pieces and died under the blow of the Conquest. The links of unity broken, the nation dissolved into scattered communities. Indigenous labor ceased to function in an organic manner."[15]

The Spanish actions led to the formation of a feudal economy, and this characterized the system in Peru for generations. The second stage of the economic emerged from military and political factors born of national independence. At this point, "The ideas of the French Revolution and the North American constitution were favorably diffused in South America because its bourgeoisie, although in embryonic form, had needs and interests which enabled it and caused it to be infected with the revolutionary spirit of the European bourgeoisie."[16] Latin America in general and Peru in particular then turned toward capitalist England for the support of industrialists and bankers that Spain could no longer provide. Continuing his vivid portrayal of Peruvian reality—which even today is enlightening for an understanding of the country—Mariátegui identified elements of three distinct economies as coexisting in Peru: a residue of the communal Indian economy in isolated mountain regions, a feudal economy based upon the Spanish conquest, and a coastal bourgeois economy that came to enjoy social and political preeminence.

Mariátegui saw Peru as essentially an agricultural country in which the tilling of land occupied most of the people. The Indian was largely a farmer. Even granting the sketchy and incomplete nature of statistics in the early 1900s, it was clear that agriculture was of great importance to the Peruvian economy. At the same time, the extractive activities of mining had earned large sums of income despite the fact that only a small number of workers were required. Mining as well as commerce had fallen into the hands of foreign capital, while Peruvian landowners supported the *status quo*. The latter had developed into a powerful capitalist bourgeoisie while retaining a feudalistic organization in agriculture. For Mariátegui, the combination of these and lesser factors had brought about the creation of a capitalistic system that, while pressing

15. *Ibid.*, in the 1955 edition published in Santiago by Ed. Universitaria, pp. 5–6.
16. *Ibid.*, p. 10.

upon the unhappy masses, mantained for the agricultural workers a state of servitude. An instructive excerpt from *Siete ensayos* read:

> His Spanish heritage and education weigh down the *criollo* proprietor, preventing him from perceiving and understanding clearly all that distinguishes capitalism from feudalism. The moral, political, and psychological elements of capitalism do not seem to have found their climate here. The capitalist, or rather the *criollo* proprietor, has the concept of income rather than of production. . . .
>
> Capitalistic concentration has been preceded by a state of free concurrence. . . . the rise of the great modern property required the fragmentation or dissolution of the large feudal estate. Capitalism is an urban phenomenon. It has the spirit of the industrial, manufacturing, mercantile town. . . .
>
> In Peru, contrary to the spirit of the republican emancipation, the creation of a capitalist economy has been entrusted to the spirit of the feudal fief—the antithesis and negation of the spirit of the city.[17]

In much of his writing, Mariátegui was preoccupied with the Indian, whom he regarded as having the right to the land that was once his. Land redistribution had long been blocked by political caudillism and traditional liberal-conservative conflicts. Added to this was the damaging influence of militarism, which supported a flourishing landed aristocracy. It became impossible in Peru for a true bourgeois class to grow, for the aristocracy assumed this function without losing colonial and elitist prejudices. With the subordinate position of the Indian reflecting disinterest and, indeed, hostility on the part of many Peruvians, he insisted that only a reshaping of the basic class structure and an alteration of aristocratic economic interests would permit a ray of progressive hope for the Indian as a group. Peru's basic indigenous question arose from the nature of the economy and its roots in the system of land ownership. He argued that the problem was a complex of interrelated socioeconomic factors and was not susceptible to solution by bureaucratic reforms, police action, or educational programs. Administrative action was not capable of protecting and encouraging the Indian, while legislation had consistently favored the absorption of indigenous property by the *latifundias*. Ethnic and moral elements were also relevant, and an entirely new and total rather than piecemeal approach was required.

The existence of *latifundista* conditions had imposed virtual slavery

17. *Ibid.,* pp. 20–21.

on the Peruvian farmer, with the landowners at the same time standing indebted before the power of foreign capitalists. To remedy this condition would require the application of Marxism in accordance with Peruvian reality. Arguing that the industrial proletariat would be too weak for revolutionary activity for many years, the Peruvian writer suggested that the role of the peasant had a great and immediate potential. In his anguished calls for an end to injustice and exploitation, José Carlos Mariátegui tended to obscure the traditional Marxist doctrine of class struggle in his preoccupation with the peasant and the Indian. One of the several sources for the ambiguous and changing position of the Communists toward him was the mystical nationalism with which his Marxist solutions were embued. While Peruvian Communists and socialists since his death have claimed him as their source of inspiration, they conveniently forget that the official Communist party had denounced him as a Trotskyite just months before his death. The Alianza Popular Revolucionaria Americana (APRA) under his old colleague and competitor, Víctor Haya Raúl de la Torre, has also been vaguely uneasy in discussing its relationship to Mariátegui. These, however, are political questions that, in our context, are tertiary. Mariátegui's writings were imaginative, insightful, and informed. If the application of Marxist ideas was not always consistent with party-line positions, this was a credit to the independence of a dedicated and honest intellect.

Cuba and Fidelismo

The Cuban Revolution, it has been said, shook the Western Hemisphere as the French Revolution once rocked Europe. Domestic politics have been affected in every country since 1959, while inter-American relations and the intrusion of the politics of the Cold War have altered basic foreign policy considerations. The Communist movement was also directly influenced, bringing about a reshaping of the problems confronted by individual organizations. With the rise of Fidel Castro in the "Pearl of the Antilles," ideological factors also came to receive more intense analysis than ever before. The debate over the true nature of the Castro movement has raged bitterly since the late 1950s. Before examining the tenets of *fidelismo,* changeable though they have proven, the historical and philosophical setting from which the Cuban Revolution emerged must be considered. It cannot be understood merely as an aberrational outgrowth of international communism. Above all else, it has developed as a manifestation of Cuban nationalistic sentiment—first moderate, then increasingly radical.

The Reformist Background and Castro's Rise / The colonial history of Cuba differed from that of its Latin-American neighbors. The struggle for independence was longer and more bitter. A series of uprisings and a violent conflict from 1868 to 1878 proved unsuccessful, and it was only through the involvement of the United States in 1898 that the Spanish were expelled from the island. Following a four-year occupation by the United States, the Cuban republic was inaugurated in 1902. The immediate result was the gaining of power by conservative elements of the business elite. In the years to follow, the country never enjoyed true democratic rule. A lack of civic experience, economic problems, and public apathy plagued Cuba; as Federico Gil has written, the corrupt and the inept rose to political power. Moreover, "Two great evils have consistently plagued Cuba's political history: electoral fraud and administrative corruption. Since the founding of the republic in 1902, the country never had a single government free of graft and immorality."[18]

With the coming to power of Gerardo Machado in 1925, an unhappy political situation grew increasingly worse. Machado instituted a dictatorship that became especially savage after students and workers initiated a lengthy struggle against him in 1930. Revolution was staved off until 1933 when, after a turbulent twenty-day strike involving thousands of students, laborers, businessmen, and white collar workers, the military forced Machado's resignation. As intellectuals renewed the cry of "regeneración" that had been raised in the 1920s, the Generation of 1930 entered politics with the avowed goal of genuine political socioeconomic revolution. Comprised of essentially middle-class students and professional men, this movement clashed with old-line politicians and influential veterans of the earlier fight for independence. The new reformers wanted to right existing injustices and blamed these latter groups for the republic's ills. There was a desire for a greater Cuban role in controlling its own economic life and in regulating foreign business interests. Such slogans as *Cubanidad* and *Cuba libre* became current; in the immediate months after Machado's overthrow, there was a strong nationalistic emphasis on Cuban destiny and the national potential for progress and development.

The pre-eminent figure of the revolutionary undertaking was Dr. Ramón Grau San Martín. Governing briefly in late 1933 before being pushed aside for a time, he merged several groups into a new Partido Revolucionario Cubano (*auténtico*). Thus a formal structure was pro-

18. Federico G. Gil, "Antecedents of the Cuban Revolution," *The Centennial Review*, VI, No. 3 (Summer 1962), 373–74.

vided for those who sought a genuine revolutionary transformation in Cuba. At the same time a sergent named Fulgencio Batista had risen to become the power behind the presidential chair, and in 1940 he assumed that position himself. Four years later, under the auspices of the Constitution of 1940, the PRC and Grau San Martín won national elections. Eight years of *auténtico* rule were thereby initiated, for the party candidate in 1948, Dr. Carlos Prío Socarrás, also won election. These years of PRC rule provided a fully democratic setting within which economic progress took place, notwithstanding administrative shortcomings and rampant public immorality. Again quoting Gil, the genuine achievement of "a remarkable record of accomplishments in economic development and social justice . . . was later to be discredited by administrative ineptitude and tolerance of personal dishonesty."[19] The libertarian climate was dissipated in March, 1952, when presidential candidate Batista, sensing imminent electoral defeat, seized power with a classically executed *golpe de estado*. The resultant dictatorship was to continue until its collapse in 1959 under the attack of Fidel Castro.

Through much of the republican period preceding the rise of Castro, Cuban intellectuals had espoused various reformist programs in the hopes of bringing into being a modern, progressive democracy. Initially, it was the veterans of the independence struggle who failed in the implementation of their program and ideals. Their sense of responsibility was reassumed by the Generation of 1930; a prime example was the economic plan of the major anti-Machado organization, the ABC. Among the tenets of the ABC were: elimination of the *latifundios;* nationalization of public services; reduction of North American economic influence; producers' co-operatives; and an extensive program of social legislation. Fundamental political rights included liberty, social justice, and the reconquest of the land.[20] With the incorporation of the ABC into the *auténtico* party, these proposals were largely retained through their inclusion in the PRC program. Thus when the newly organized party first met in February, 1934, it adopted a program stressing the broad themes of nationalism, economic development, and social reform.

As the new repository for constructive nationalistic ideals, the PRC was fully committed to basic reforms, promising fervently that Cubans should and would share more fully in the country's economic resources. Although lacking a strong ideological orientation, the *auténticos* detailed an extensive array of policies: government control and regulation of

19. *Ibid.,* p. 376.
20. Ramón Grau San Martín, *La revolución cubana ante américa* (México: Ediciones del Partido Revolucionario Cubano, 1936), pp. 104–5.

the sugar industry, the stimulation of organized labor, educational reforms, an effective social security system, improved budgetary procedures, an improvement of the tax system, and firm independence in Cuban-North American relations. In short, *regeneración* or *renovación* was pledged in all realms of Cuban life.

The PRC also played a major role in the preparation of the Constitution of 1940, a document that itself symbolized both the problems and the hopes of the country.[21] Dr. José Manuel Cortina, a prominent jurist, was the guiding force behind the drive for constitutional reform. As early as 1930 he had demanded a new document, and his crusade reached fruition ten years later. Dedicated to mechanical reforms that might better regulate executive-legislative relations, Cortina advocated a semiparliamentary system in the hopes of regularizing procedures, identifying political responsibility, improving the observance of civic participation, and, perhaps most importantly of all, restoring public confidence in the government. What Cortina termed a "regulated parliamentary system" included an effective cabinet, legislative right of interpellation, and the authority to censure ministers; also notable was an extensive listing of socioeconomic rights reminiscent in broad outline of the Mexican Constitution of 1917. *Auténtico* labors on behalf of the new document were Herculean, and the underlying principles of the constitution became embodied in the program of the party.

Led by the popular Grau San Martín and, after 1948, by Prío Socarrás, the PRC enacted numerous reforms consonant with programmatic pledges. While economic diversification was initiated, the production and pricing of sugar was stabilized and the distribution of wealth improved. The educational system was significantly strengthened, and both a National Bank and a Tribunal of Accounts were instituted in an effort to rationalize administrative procedures. The *auténticos,* as already noted, were scrupulous in their observance of civil liberties, and this respect for political democracy added a new and vital dimension to the sphere of Cuban public affairs. Among the failures were an unwillingness or inability to inaugurate agrarian reform and, to repeat, a flowering of graft and corruption unprecedented in the country's history. Instead of a promised purification of public life, dishonesty became the order of the day, and cynicism toward the PRC was rampant.

Just as nationalistic ideals had passed from the veterans of indepen-

21. For an analysis, see William S. Stokes, "The Cuban Parliamentary System in Action, 1940–1947," *Journal of Politics,* XI, No. 2 (May 1949), 335–64. Much the same material appears in Chapter 18 of Stokes's *Latin-American Politics* (New York: Thomas Y. Crowell Company, 1959), pp. 437–56.

dence to the Generation of 1930, they were in turn transferred in time from the PRC to a new organization, the Partido del Pueblo Cubano (PPC). An offshoot of the PRC, it developed from its 1946 formation into a solid popular force. Its guiding spirit, Eduardo Chibás, enunciated a five-point program that promised to rescue avowed *auténtico* principles through a new party of revolution. Popularly known as the *ortodoxos,* the PPC issued a call for economic independence, political liberty, and social justice. Rapidly incorporating into its ranks the new generation of students and professional men—including Fidel Castro, then a law student—the *ortodoxos* gained popular acceptance as heirs to Cuban national reformism. Chibás campaigned tirelessly for public rectitude and morality; even after his suicide in 1951, the *ortodoxos* were expected to win the 1952 elections when Batista overthrew the constitutional order. Given the benefit of hindsight, it is apparent that from that time on, the republic was once again in search of a leader and a movement that would fulfill the historically unanswered cries for a genuine political reformation. Given the circumstances, it was ultimately ironic that what might have been a genuine movement of nationalistic populism under Fidel Castro ultimately became a personalistic variant of communist revolution. For among the major elements in the rise of *fidelismo* in Cuba was a deeply engrained nationalistic sentiment that, at least in 1959, was consistent with historical trends in Cuba.

The first public awareness of Fidel Castro came with the suicidal attack upon Santiago's Moncada Barracks on July 26, 1953. While it failed abysmally and Castro himself was sentenced to a fifteen-year prison term, his impassioned speech at the military trial provided a measure of his political beliefs at that time. In his "History Will Absolve Me" speech, as it became known, he outlined for those who wished to hear a broad program fully consonant with the principles of Cuban nationalism reformism. In large part his statement might well have been that of Chibás, of Grau San Martín in his early years, or of the exponents of *regeneración* some thirty years previous. Giving utterance to popular criticisms of Batista and insistent upon the inevitability of revolution, he sketched five "revolutionary laws" that would be proclaimed.[22]

First, the people would regain sovereignty through the re-establishment of the Constitution of 1940. As soon as possible, elections would be held. As for agriculture, plots of land would be granted to the peasantry, while productive enterprises would be established for the common use of equipment, seed, fertilizer, and the like. The third "revolutionary

22. Fidel Castro, *Pensamiento político, económico y social de Fidel Castro* (La Habana: Editorial Lex, 1959), pp. 29–31.

law" promised the workers 30 percent of the profits from industrial, mercantile, and mining enterprises, while agricultural businesses would be exempted. Fourth, agricultural workers would be given the right to 50 percent of the income from the harvesting and sale of sugar. Lastly, property and "ill-gotten gains of those who had committed frauds during previous regimes" would be confiscated. Elaborating only briefly on these points while devoting greater attention to a cataloguing of Batista oppression,[23] Castro also cited the major problems that would confront the promised revolutionary government: "The problem of the land, the problem of industrialization, the problem of housing, the problem of unemployment, the problem of education, and the problem of the people's health; these are the six points to which our efforts would have been resolutely turned, together with the conquest of the public liberties and political democracy."[24]

In the political realm, Castro's views were set forth in a variety of additional sources. In a signed article in *Coronet*,[25] he strongly suggested that all necessary changes in Cuba might be achieved within the framework of the 1940 Constitution. Castro promised that representative government would be established by "truly honest" elections within twelve months, while "full and untrammelled" freedom would be observed. In his later "Manifesto of the Sierra Maestra,"[26] dated July 12, 1957, he insisted again on the importance of "truly free, democratic, impartial elections." And in a December, 1957, letter to Cuban exiles and again in a May, 1958, interview with Jules Dubois,[27] he repeated his position. The July, 1958, Pact of Caracas, a joint statement by various anti-Batista forces, committed them to guide Cuba "after the fall of the tyrant, to normality, by instituting a brief provisional government that will lead the country to full constitutional and democratic procedures."[28] Castro signed the document as head of the Twenty-Sixth of July Movement.

His economic and social proposals at this early time were suggested already by several "revolutionary laws" in his 1953 trial defense. Support for grants of land to small farmers and the rights of workers to a form of profit-sharing were repeated in references to land reform in the *Coro-*

---

23. Brief excerpts from several important Castro speeches are included in Paul E. Sigmund, ed., *The Ideologies of the Developing Nations* (New York: Frederick A. Praeger, 1967), pp. 306–38.

24. *Ibid.*, p. 31.

25. Fidel Castro, "Why We Fight," *Coronet* (February 1958), pp. 80–86.

26. Contained in Gregorio Selser, ed., *La revolución cubana: Escritos y discursos* (Buenos Aires: Editorial Palestra, 1960), pp. 393–422.

27. For the details of the interview plus a close early look at Castro, see Jules Dubois, *Fidel Castro* (Indianapolis: Bobb-Merrill, 1959).

28. For the full text see *ibid.*, pp. 280–83.

net article. The "Manifesto of the Sierra Maestra" also spoke of a distribution of land through agrarian reform, while a program of industrialization was also mentioned. The brief 1953 reference to some unspecified
form of co-operatives was not repeated at this time. Castro's early mention of nationalization with regard to public utilities was withdrawn
in the *Coronet* statement, and he later denied the efficacy of extensive
nationalization in an interview with Dubois. Thus, "Never has the 26th
of July Movement talked about socializing or nationalizing the industries. . . . We have proclaimed from the first day that we fight for
the full enforcement of the Constitution of 1940, whose norms establish
guarantees, rights, and obligations for all the elements that have a part
in production."[29]

The politics and ideology of Fidel Castro during his fight for power,
to summarize, were unexceptional in content. Goals and objectives varied
little from those of earlier Cuban reformers. Idealistic, almost utopian
statements about the customary liberties of democratic government over-
shadowed the inattention to socioeconomic specifics, and there was no
plan or set of priorities to be pursued following the anticipated defeat
of Batista. In fact, for nearly three years after the attack on Moncada
Barracks, Castro remained officially an *ortodoxo,* apparently regarding
himself as faithful to the principles of Eduardo Chibás. Thus he wrote
an *ortodoxo* gathering in 1955 that the Twenty-Sixth of July Movement was the "revolutionary apparatus of *Chibasismo.*"[30] Not until
March, 1956, did Castro formally break away from the *ortodoxos,* and
even then he claimed to be continuing the work of Chibás. Only later did
Castro and his movement strike out as an explicitly independent force,
and the consistency of his statements throughout the 1953–59 period
was notable dispite his formal withdrawal from the organized PPC.

Such being the context and tenor of his statements, it was natural
for Castro to win the support of the masses. His personal demonstration
of bravery and the nationalistic myth of revolution also added to his
stature. This is relevant, especially in light of subsequent *fidelista* claims
to have won a military victory by means of maoist-inspired guerrilla
warfare.[31] In truth, the campaign in the Sierra Maestra triumphed
through the withering of Batista's own support, the disheartened disintegration of the armed forces, who simply quit fighting, and the desertion

29. Dubois, *Castro,* p. 263.
30. Quoted by Thodore Draper in his *Castroism: Theory and Practice* (New
York: Frederick A. Praeger, 1965), p. 10. For excerpts see Luis Conte Agüero,
Los dos rostros de Fidel Castro (México: Editorial Jus, 1960), pp. 104–7.
31. See the later discussion of Ernesto "Che" Guevara's writings on revolutionary theory and related military strategy and tactics.

of the dictator's closest aides and colleagues. When the fabric of Batista's regime began unraveling in the final months of 1958, the aura and charisma of Castro was greatly magnified. When he took power in January, 1959, Castro did so with the heartily enthusiastic best wishes of the great mass of the Cuban citizenry. "It was precisely the kind of promises Castro made that enabled him to win the support of the overwhelming majority of the Cuban middle and other classes; a 'peasant revolution' would hardly have been expressed in quite the same way."[32]

During the early stages of the Cuban Revolution, there was frequent reference to the allegedly peasant nature of the revolution—one of the several myths that, although initially accepted by many, has been largely dispelled by cold analysis. A related myth that fails to withstand impartial examination of the facts has claimed that pre-1959 domestic conditions on the island had made inevitable both the Castro revolution itself and the radicalism that soon set in. When Communist ideologues in time prepared retroactive official explanations of what had happened before January, 1959, it was suggested that, in accordance with Marxism-Leninism, conditions of mass discontent and economic grievances had characterized Cuba. It was further stated that Cuba had had a weak and ineffective middle class, severe economic dislocations as a result of primitive native industry, unacceptable and unworkable social structures, a predominance of agricultural workers, and a widespread sentiment repudiating the principles of representative democracy. Such was not the case; Cuba was neither an exceedingly underdeveloped country nor was it a peasant society.

The facts speak for themselves: 57 percent of the population was urban; in 1950 only 44 percent of the national labor force was agricultural; less than half the people were dependent upon agriculture; the agricultural system itself was more advanced and less feudal than in most Latin-American countries; and the standard of living was fourth highest in the region (behind Venezuela, Argentina, and Chile). The middle sectors were numerous and growing rapidly, while political democracy received deep and unqualified support. Even the landowning oligarchy and bourgeois capitalists were allied with rather than hostile towards one another. The workers were comparatively satisfied with their status and remained passive through most of the climactic confrontation leading to Batista's defeat. A leading Cuban Communist himself conceded in 1961, "Cuba was not one of the countries with the lowest standards of living of the masses in America but, on the contrary, one

32. Theodore Draper, *Castro's Revolution: Myths and Realities* (New York: Frederick A. Praeger, 1962), p. 20.

of those with the highest standard of living."[33] Certainly Cuba was among Latin America's most middle-class countries.

Economic development was also progressing well by hemispheric standards, granted the uneven distribution of wealth seen in the fact that an estimated 8 percent of the total population held three-fourths of the economic resources. Some 40 percent of the sugar industry was controlled by North American interests. Sugar was the major source of Cuban foreign exchange, which in turn had traditionally been used to import food and consumer goods. Whenever the price of sugar was low, there would be talk of diversification and the development of local industries, but with the eventual rise in prices, Cuba would bend its efforts instead toward the planting of greater acreage. The United States did little to strengthen the occasional efforts toward diversification and, notwithstanding the exaggerations of *fidelista* attacks on that country, it was true that the North Americans shared with Cuba the guilt in permitting the continuation and extension of monocultural exports.

The Cuban Revolution, then, did not take place in a country wherein domestic conditions met the classical Marxist-Leninist prerevolutionary pattern. Moreover, the Twenty-Sixth of July Movement was not essentially one of peasants. Its leadership was almost totally middle class; although there was some peasant support in the Sierra Maestra, there was a great deal from the urban middle class, especially its younger generation. There was a noticeable difference between the old and the young middle class, with the former comprising the bulk of the industrially and commercially oriented, while the youth gravitated largely toward political-legal professionalism. It was not uncommon for middle-class parents to be drawn into the anti-Batista camp by their children. In other cases, the generational difference caused a sort of middle-class schizophrenia in which families were estranged, the young from the old.

While Castro and his lieutenants themselves were of middle-class origins, this did not imply that the leadership of the Cuban middle class itself was strongly behind the revolutionary movement. The Cuban Revolution was not sufficiently class-conscious in its composition and attitudes to be called, strictly speaking, a middle-class revolution. Boris Goldenberg upheld this view in writing that the movement did not represent any single social class. Yet it did have a sociological base—a heterogeneous conglomeration of Cubans without roots in society. It was these "rootless ones," lacking in any common national consciousness, who provided the

33. Aníbal Escalante, writing in *Verde Olivo* of July 30, 1961, as quoted in *ibid.*, p. 22.

basis for the revolution in its early period. Moreover, the revolution was characterized by three major features: initiation by a charismatic leader; an early "humanist" phase from which the rootless and under-privileged gained immediate benefits; and the later transition from demo-cratic to authoritarian, even totalitarian, procedures.[34]

The Cuban phenomenon, even before its swing toward radicalism, was genuinely revolutionary rather than merely representative of tradi-tional Latin-American revolt. The distinction, as Spanish José Ortega y Gasset has written, lies in the fact that while a revolt is directed against the abuses of power, a revolution demands a change of the conditions that made possible the abuses. The overthrow of Batista was the Cuban revolt, while events under Castro's rule constituted true revo-lution. In January, 1959, the mood in Cuba was clearly revolutionary. The younger generation in particular was tired of the old order, its leaders, and its policies. There was a revolutionary mystique and popular emotionalism that supported ill-defined but strong aspirations for basic change. Such sentiment permeated all social classes, compounding the near-utopian expectations facing Castro when he took power.

Radicalism and the Fusion with Communism / The preceding brings into focus the background, antecedents, and evolution of the Cuban Revolution in the pre-1959 period. Political and ideological phases were to evolve following Castro's accession to power. In view of the crucial role to be played by Cuban communism, a summary of that movement in the pre-1959 era is also pertinent. The initial impact of the Russian Revolution four decades earlier was inconsequential until the administration of Alfredo Zayas (1921–25). The boom of the "Dance of the Millions" in the 1920s was followed by a deep decline that stimu-lated labor unrest and intellectual protest. At the University of Havana, Julio Antonio Mella initiated a reform program against negligent profes-sors; it developed into a student strike that closed the university for three months. A band of intellectuals known as the Grupo Minorista joined with the students and provided intellectual guidance.

In 1925 several of these intellectuals joined with Mella to form the Partido Comunista Cubano (PCC); later adherents to the movement included the poet Rubén Martínez Villena and the writer Juan Mari-nello. The inauguration of Gerardo Machado to the presidency soon brought swift suppression of the student movement, however. Mella him-self was jailed, exiled, and mysteriously murdered in Mexico in 1929.

34. Boris Goldenberg, "The Cuban Revolution: An Analysis," *Problems of Communism*, XII, No. 5 (Sept.–Oct. 1963), 5–7.

During the rest of the decade the PCC made little progress, only returning to public attention as a part of the anti-Machado movement. The
party role in the decisive general strike of 1933 was equivocal, and
after Machado's fall the Communists opposed the nationalistic reformers
who followed. Through much of the 1930s the Communists remained
in opposition, but a reversal of Fulgencio Batista's attitudes led to the
beginning of opportunistic collaboration.

In 1937 Batista permitted the formation of a front party headed by
Juan Marinello, and the following year he legalized the Communist
party. In 1940 the PCC supported Batista's presidential candidacy, and
during the next four years exerted substantial influence on the Department of Labor. The party also won ten representatives to the Chamber
of Deputies in 1940 and over one hundred members of municipal councils. While backing the Allied wartime effort, the party changed its name
to the Partido Socialista Popular (PSP); under this label the Communists backed the chosen Batista candidate in 1944. Although winning
three Senate and nine Chamber seats that year, the party went into
decline during the eight years of *auténtico* administration. Efforts were
concentrated upon the labor movement, with Communist Lázaro Peña
a dominant figure in the national Confederación de Trabajadores de
Cuba (CTC). It was only upon the return of Batista in 1952 that
the Communists began to rebuild their status significantly, although the
Soviet break of relations with Cuba in late 1953 complicated things.

The early response of the Communists to Fidel Castro was scornful.
The attack on Moncada Barracks was termed a "petit bourgeois putsch,"
and when Castro's invasion in December, 1957, initiated guerrilla warfare, he was derided as an amateur. Party leaders rejected the idea
of collaboration and as late as April, 1958, played an important part
in nullifying Castro's call for a general strike. Ideologically committed
to a massive popular uprising led by a workers' movement in the cities,
the PSP saw no way for the Twenty-Sixth of July Movement to bring
about revolution. Before long, however, party leaders concluded that
Castro could not prudently be ignored, and in June, Carlos Rafael
Rodríguez was sent to the Sierra Maestra to confer with the rebel leader.
By the end of the year Communists were in the mountains fighting
alongside Fidel, although their number was small.

To summarize the course of the Cuban Revolution after 1959 is to
identity at least four distinctive phases: democratic humanism, the transition to radicalism, fusion with the Communists, and administrative stabilization of the revolution. Of these, the first was the briefest, constituting
no more than the first nine months of 1959. A Cuban "humanist" move-

ment had been organized in 1950 by the intellectual Rubén Darío Rumbaut and represented unfulfilled hopes of creating a Christian Democratic movement on the island. This had been largely forgotten when Castro suddenly characterized his regime as one of "humanism." As an alleged alternative to both capitalism and communism, humanism was temporarily employed in both public and private explanations of his movement's political thought. During an April, 1959, visit to the United States Castro said, "We believe that there should not be bread without liberty, but neither should there be liberty without bread. We call that humanism. We want Cuba to be an example of representative democracy with true social justice."[35] For the next month or so Castro repeated his definition of humanism as "liberty with bread without terror" but by mid-1959 dropped the phrase from his vocabulary. None of Castro's supporters attempted to develop the train of thought, and orthodox Communists regarded it, in the words of party theoretician Aníbal Escalante, as "ideological confusion."

If the humanist stage was ideologically inconsequential, in political terms it was the utopian phase of the Cuban Revolution. Moderates of the Twenty-Sixth of July Movement played significant roles, and there were few indications that the pre-1959 promises would not be honored. Of those who accompanied Fidel at this time, many remembered the disappointments in 1902 and again in 1933; they were determined not to repeat earlier failures. The ill-defined Generation of 1950 saw itself in terms of parallels to the 1930 group, with the former attacking the integrity of the latter while promising meaningful alterations. Recognizing the broad public repugnance toward politics, most of the young *fidelistas* revealed an ethical, almost puritanical strain, which had already been evidenced by such as the strict discipline and unswerving morality reported in rebel camps during the fighting. One observer commented on "their apparently great popular appeal . . . their salutory effect in shaking the rather widespread cynicism among Cubans towards their leaders, and . . . their kindling the embers of a political crusade in which each citizen saw himself as an active participant in the task of reorganizing the country."[36]

At the outset, in short, many of the moderates stressed the importance of developing a stronger sense of civic consciousness. The first step in this direction had to be a restoration of public confidence in official morality and competence. This was also a factor in the public trials of suspected Batista collaborators, notwithstanding procedural aspects

35. Quoted in Draper, *Castroism,* p. 39.
36. Gil, "Antecedents of the Cuban Revolution," p. 387.

that were distasteful to many outsiders. A related trait was the importance of the role promised to the provinces. Havana had historically been the vortex of national affairs, although the Constitution of 1940 had granted extensive powers to the municipalities, which in practice had been rarely exercised. With Castro's movement having fought its way to power from the eastern province of Oriente, there was reason to expect a degree of effective local autonomy. This, too, was verbally praised during the humanist period and further illustrated the broad path toward effective civic participation that many of the revolutionary leaders espoused.

The provisional government during this brief time span was headed by Manuel Urrutia, a career lawyer and judge, although Castro was, as always, the heart and soul of the movement. An early cabinet crisis occurred in February, leading to the departure of Premier José Miró Cárdona, a well-known politician of pre-Batista years. By July a further disagreement led to the resignation of Urrutia from the presidency and his replacement by former Communist Osvaldo Dorticós. The decisive step in Castro's movement away from the humanist phase came with his arrest of revolutionary hero Hubert Matos in October. Matos, who had privately protested the gradual replacement by Communists of Twenty-Sixth of July members in a variety of positions, was charged with treason for having endangered the regime. Before Matos' eventual sentencing to twenty years' imprisonment, concerned moderates had lodged a protest that led to their resignation. Before the close of 1959, with Castro openly intervening on the side of Communists in their rivalry with the Twenty-Sixth of July Movement, the moderation of the humanist phase had passed. At that point the revolution began its transition to radicalism.

This shift gathered impetus rapidly in the wake of Matos' removal and the resignation, both voluntary and forced, of prominant moderates. By the close of 1959 the glories of the rebel army had been largely forgotten as a regularized militia took its place, with traditional Communists holding positions of influence. Radicalism became noticeable as well in the labor movement, where Castro forced the leadership of the reorganized CTC from the hands of the Twenty-Sixth of July Movement. David Salvador, Castro's leading labor organizer and one of his most ardent and effective supporters, was removed from authority and, within a year, had been imprisoned. By early 1960 anti-communism was openly equated with treason to the revolution, and public diatribes against critics and opponents of communism grew in frequency.

This second phase, which ran through the end of 1960, was also characterized by a sharp realignment in the international field. Relations steadily deteriorated with the United States. In June of that year three British- and North American—owned oil refineries refused to process Soviet crude oil and were swiftly seized by the government. The following month the Eisenhower administration suspended the Cuban sugar quota, and Castro retaliated with the expropriation of United States businesses. When Washington levied an export embargo in October the Cubans responded by heightening the speed of expropriation, and economic war between the two grew more serious. Cuba, which had signed an economic pact with the Soviet Union during the visit of Anastas Mikoyan in February, announced that henceforth all sugar would be sold to the Communist bloc, while purchases of military equipment also became common. At the close of the year Castro demanded a substantial reduction of the United States Embassy staff, and Eisenhower responded by breaking relations.

Perhaps the major indicator of Castro's growing radicalism came with the massive nationalization decreed by Revolutionary Law No. 890 on October 13, 1960. By this stroke 376 all-Cuban enterprises were taken over, thus virtually destroying the bourgeoisie. Over two million acres of Cuban-owned land were expropriated, in addition to more than three million owned by United States interests. Such a move was in direct contradiction to Castro's many earlier denials of the efficacy or desirability of nationalization. The magnitude of the measure dramatized not only his transitional shift to the far left but, at the same time, was to symbolize the initiation of the critical third phase—fusion with communism. Both the Cuban Communists and later Fidel Castro himself were to identify the date of this action, October 13, 1960, as marking the initiation of what was officially termed the "socialist" stage of the revolution.

The first public recognition of the fact of fusion came on April 16, 1961, when Castro briefly mentioned that the Cuban Revolution was "socialist." Speaking but a day before the Bay of Pigs invasion, he proclaimed that "we have effected a socialist revolution under the very nose of the United States." He was to be more explicit in his forthcoming May Day speech. Declaring "the birth of a patriotic democratic and socialist revolution," he henceforth referred to the Cuban Revolution as socialist. The meaning of this latter term was suggested by his praise for the Soviets and the Chinese as international leaders of socialism. So it was that in 1961 Cuba avowedly embarked along the path toward an ultimate dictatorship of the proletariat. It remained for Castro to set in perspective the evolution of the "socialist revolution." This he did on December 1, 1961, in a speech that marked one of the milestones in the ideological evolution of the Cuban Revolution.[37]

Castro was faced with the necessity of explaining his shift to "socialism" without defacing his revolutionary image. Moreover, there were the contradictory statements and promises of earlier years to be dealt with. Thus he spoke on the one hand of his past primitive ideological uncertainty while explaining the importance of Marxism-Leninism to the revolution. Calling himself ignorant and a "political illiterate" at the time of his entrance into the university, he claimed to have moved, almost unconsciously, toward Marxism-Leninism during that period. Part of his dilemma was suggested in the following: "Do I believe absolutely in Marxism? I believe absolutely in Marxism. Did I believe in it on the first of January? I believed in it on the first of January. Did I believe on the 26th of July? I believed on the 26th of July. Did I understand it as I understand it today, after almost ten years of struggle? No, I did not understand it as I understand it today. . . . Could I call myself a full-fledged revolutionary on the 26th of July? No. I could not call myself a full-fledged revolutionary. Could I call myself a full-fledged revolutionary on the first of January? I could not then call myself a full-fledged revolutionary." Adversely influenced as a student by malicious propaganda against Cuban communism, he had not been sympathetic toward the party for some time. Now, however, he admitted to seeing things more clearly. In short, "I am a Marxist-Leninist, and I will be one until the last day of my life."

Also significant was Castro's announcement in this address of the creation of a Socialist party; how else could a true socialist revolution be brought into being? Denying the permanence of his personal leadership and calling for a party that might guarantee revolutionary continuity, he pledged himself to rule by a party that would exercise leadership in accordance with Marxist-Leninist principles. The new party was to draw its membership from workers, students, intellectuals, peasants, and the small bourgeoisie, but qualifications for full participation would be rigidly demanding. Actually, the organizational fusion had begun a year earlier when Castro, in December, 1960, had overseen the establishment of so-called Escuelas de Instrucción Revolucionaria to provide a preparation for a subsequent united party. The youth wings of the crumbling Twenty-Sixth of July Movement and of the PSP were also initiating

37. The full text appeared in the December 2, 1961, issues of *El Mundo, Revolución,* and *Noticias de Hoy.*

a merger. By the time of his famous December, 1961, speech, therefore, Castro was already moving toward the practical realization of fusion with the Communists.

Formation of the monolithic party was designed in two stages: first, the preparatory Organizaciones Revolucionarias Integradas (ORI) and then, when appropriate, the Partido Unido de la Revolución Socialista (PURS). The ORI was a merger of the Twenty-Sixth of July Movement, the Partido Socialista Popular, and the Directorio Revolucionario, a disintegrating student group that had opposed Batista before 1959. The result was a Communist-dominated ORI, in which Castro, brother Raúl, and Ernesto "Che" Guevara, at that time the economic czar, were joined by prominent old-line Communists like Blas Roca and Lázaro Peña. As for this projected PURS, "since . . . we are conscious of the great enthusiasm of the masses, and of their revolutionary spirit, a party that is developing and becoming articulate . . . has all favorable conditions to select the best elements and the most positive and valuable people from the masses, and, to make them members of this organization."[38] Furthermore, "every citizen can be a member of the United Party of the Socialist Revolution apart from whether he is a worker or not. That is, the gates are open for every true revolutionary who builds the revolution and is disposed to carry out his assignments and accept the program of the United Party of the Socialist Revolution fully and with complete conviction. . . ."[39]

Tensions between orthodox Communists and *fidelistas* were not easily relaxed, however, as became plain when on March 26, 1962, Castro launched a bitterly critical speech purging Communist theoretician Aníbal Escalante from the ORI. While Escalante was the only leading Communist to be named, Castro was clearly attacking alleged assumptions of unchallenged authority by members of the PSP. This was a milestone indicative of the problems inherent to fusion. But never before had there been public acknowledgment of inner struggle between young revolutionary leaders and the traditional communists. The role of the Communists, Castro insisted, was one of orienting rather than managing the state. Reviving the glories of the Sierra Maestra campaign, he recalled that the Communists were not the ones who made the revolution and had no call to act as if it were theirs. Communist militants, he charged, had been guilty of "idiocies" and of "criminal errors" in seeking to impose traditional party-style control over the newly created ORI.

38. For the non-Spanish reader, excerpts of this speech appear in Sigmund, *Ideologies,* pp. 322–30. This quotation is found on page 329.
39. *Ibid.*

Castro's reassertion of his personal role underlined his determination to remain the master of the revolutionary movement. In all of this, however, he was attacking individuals and tactics; there was no denial of his belief in communism. For he reminded his audience that his speech was not a discussion of ideological definitions. Rather, "the Revolution is absolutely defined as Marxist-Leninist, and we are making this self-criticism of our errors within the context of Marxism-Leninism. Let no one dream of anything else or entertain any illusion about this!"[40]

A more recent statement by Castro, addressed to the first meeting of the Central Committee of the renamed Partido Comunista de Cuba (PCC), expressed the depth of commitment that ultimately emerged. During a gathering held between September 30 and October 3, 1965, the "Maximum Leader" referred to the party as being representative of the laboring masses, while the organizational core of the PCC was composed of the hundreds of cell members dispersed throughout the island. The result, he argued, was a more truly revolutionary and representative organization than had ever existed in Cuba before. Recalling the evolution through the stages of the ORI and later the PURS, he declared that the official Communist Party of Cuba was now fighting for a higher type of society. This would be "a thousand times more just and perfect than that rotten bourgeois imperialist society which discriminates against men and sacrifices them, which condemns women to prostitution and children to misery, which shows no mercy and has no ideal but the worship of riches and money." Consequently, he concluded, Cuba was "fighting for a new higher type of society which no nation today has achieved, and I think we can compete in this effort to try to be among the first to achieve these more advanced forms of human society. . . . And therefore to adopt a name which implies both the absolute unity of all the people and at the same time expresses the final goals of our Revolution, we have suggested the name of the Communist Party of Cuba. . . ."[41]

Economic policies during the period of fusion provided great difficulty. Through 1959 and much of 1960 the regime had formulated economic policy in accord with political factors. Funds were spent on housing, public works, educational reform, and other important but economically nonproductive programs. Removal of the United States sugar quota was officially welcomed as freeing the island from imperialistic controls while liberating Cuba economically and permitting meaningful diversification.

40. Theodore Draper, "L'Affaire Escalante," *The New Leader* (April 16, 1962). This was later reproduced in Draper, *Castro's Revolution,* pp. 201–11.
41. Sigmund, *Ideologies,* pp. 337–38.

This too made effective politics but disastrous economics. The growing reliance upon the Communist bloc for trade was but another matter in which political advantage was offset by economic miscalculation. The October, 1960, nationalization soon brought nearly 90 percent of Cuban industry under state control, creating a situation beyond the existing administrative capacity of the state. The flight of many Cuban middle-class technocrats by the end of 1960 robbed the government of precisely that trained expertise that it critically needed.

Although Guevara had previously insisted that economic development could be achieved without a period of Stalinist-type sacrifice and deprivation, shortages in time forced a variety of stop-gap measures, including the rationing of food. By 1962 the unco-operative stance of the peasants, who insisted upon selling their own products independently, had generated a serious agricultural crisis. This led to the appointment in February, 1962, of prominent Communist Carlos Rafael Rodríguez as president of the Instituto Nacional de Reforma Agraria (INRA), a key organ of the revolution. Under Rodríguez, stringent measures were introduced to improve both production and distribution, but the result was a virtual war against the farmer. What was styled by the regime as "the year of education" (1961) gave way to "the year of planning" (1962). This in turn was followed by the years of "organization" (1963), of "industrialization" (1964), "agriculture" (1965), and "solidarity" (1966). Among the major efforts that followed, each was intended as a means of fully socializing the economy of the revolution. It was the shifting of ideological orientation and pragmatic daily administration which marked the fourth revolutionary phase—one which basically characterizes the Castro regime at this writing.

Agricultural problems stemmed not only from the peasant desire of selling for a profit but also from the inefficiency of the state farms, the *granjas del pueblo*. The co-operatives first established in early 1960 had been intended as the cornerstone of Cuba's Agrarian Reform law of 1959. In 1962 the co-operatives had been incorporated into the state farms, leaving the peasants without any voice whatever. Not even *pro forma* meetings were held, and members merely served their allotted hours and received a fixed wage from the INRA. Administration of the *granjas* was inefficient, and the entire agrarian reform program suffered as a consequence. In the meantime, the decision to de-emphasize sugar production had brought about a drastic decline in export income. This in turn crippled the vaunted drive for accelerated industrialization. Minister of Industries Guevara recognized that the expense of raw materials was great and that declining national income made purchases economically unwise. A resultant balance of payments crisis was averted only through major assistance from the Soviet Union in 1960 and 1961. By 1962 this flow became less generous as Russian technical experts began to demand an accounting from Cuba before extending additional support.

In 1963 "Che" Guevara admitted to a pair of fundamental miscalculations—one the "declaration of war on sugar cane," the other the commitment to industrialization without considering the acquisition of raw materials. By the end of 1963 this "year of organization" saw a number of confessional declarations of errors by Castro, Guevara, Rodríguez, and others. The result was a basic reversal of Cuban economic policy. The pace of industrialization was gradually reined in, sugar production was encouraged once more, and an effort to pursue the systematic administration of the economy was undertaken. In October, 1963, Castro also proclaimed the Second Agrarian Reform law. By changing the former balance of 60-40 in favor of the private sector to 30-70 in the hands of the state, another wave of expropriation was introduced. At the same time the increased state ownership was to be controlled through a more decentralized machinery, in the hope of improving productivity as well as the effectiveness of local administrators. All this provided a setting for the years ahead in which the regime attended more diligently to the intended fruition of the economic goals of the revolution while muting somewhat the ideological and doctrinal issues.

For Castro himself, personal ascendancy was guaranteed by his action during the March, 1962, Escalante scandal. His charisma has remained a fundamental element of the revolution, with his ultimate authority unchallenged. Nearly as indispensable, it appeared, was his Argentine-born confidant Guevara. So it was that a wave of speculation surrounded the disappearance of the latter in 1966. After months of rumor and mystery, "Che" re-emerged in Bolivia, where his failure at mobilizing an effective revolutionary force concluded with his death in late 1967.

Spokesmen of the Revolution / Of the several champions or ideological defenders of the Cuban Revolution, easily the most widely read were Guevara himself and a young Frenchman, Régis Debray. The writings of the former have been particularly noteworthy, and the views of Castro's former deputy and confidant have been disseminated widely across the hemisphere. The single most famed work was *La guerra de guerrillas*,[42] in which Guevara provided an instructional guide on the

42. Ernesto Guevara, *La guerra de guerillas* (La Habana: Ediciones Minfar, 1960). Also see the English translation by J. P. Morray, *Guerrilla Warfare*

tactics, strategy, and technical aspects of guerrilla warfare. Most relevant to the present context is his conception of revolutionary theory; for "Che" three features stood out. Thus, he argued that (1) popular forces can defeat a regular military force; (2) insurrection may precede the existence of all revolutionary conditions; and (3) the countryside should be the locale for revolution in Latin America. Guevara expanded at length upon each of these points. Regarding the first, he scoffed at those who would concede the field to professional military forces; for Guevara, Cuba thoroughly disproved the decisive capacity of regular armed forces. On the second contention, he held that popular forces themselves can force the kind of conditions in a given country whereby these revolutionaries may triumph. Thirdly, Guevara strongly criticized urban-based revolution; by so doing he implied that ordinary Communist movements in Latin America are destined to failure. Since armed rebellion, a vital ingredient, can more effectively be sustained in the countryside, he concluded that the rural setting was indispensable.

For Guevara, only a very small band of guerillas was required. Again mindful of the Cuban example, he believed that a minimal number could, over time, improve their situation and create the conditions requisite to the country in question. The guerrillas at the same time must advocate meaningful agrarian revolution, since this is the best way to assure the peasant support that he described as indispensable. Thus what is occasionally called a "peasant revolution" would take place, although actually being a revolutionary movement aided and abetted by peasant support in its early phase, nothing more. Later, with industrialization replacing agrarian reform as the major policy goal for the regime, presumably the peasant element itself would be supplanted as a revolutionary force by the urban. Notwithstanding Guevara's insistence upon the "peasant" nature of the Castro movement, both his own writings and subsequent policy actions taken in Cuba tended to weaken the purity of his argument.

A further vital aspect of Guevara's thought was his application of the Cuban revolutionary experience to the other Latin-American republics. On many occasions he maintained that the Cuban road to revolution was appropriate elsewhere. Conceding that every revolution would have certain peculiarly distinctive characteristics, he saw these in Cuba as having been the person of Castro, the unwisdom of United States policy,

---

(New York: Monthly Review Press, 1961). In the wake of Guevara's death, an important reflection of his thoughts and attitudes was presented under the title *Reminiscences of the Cuban Revolutionary War* (New York: Monthly Review Press, 1968).

and the "proletarianized" peasantry. But in broad terms, the Cuban conditions for revolution were found throughout the hemisphere, and thus he concluded that similar tactics would assure victory. Power was to be seized by means of armed conflict; an urban environment was inappropriate for this, hence guerrilla warfare would be pursued, ideally in the revolutionary program. More pragmatic than ideological or doctrinal in its logic, this reasoning was to be reiterated ceaselessly in the attempted exportation of the Cuban Revolution to the rest of the hemisphere. The response of Latin-American Communists elsewhere is described later in the chapter.

Shortly before the Bolivian capture and execution of Guevara, the same authorities had captured Régis Debray (1941——), a young Marxist philosopher who had first visited Havana in 1961. His *Revolution in the Revolution?* first published in French in 1966, appeared in a huge 200,000-copy edition in Spanish in January, 1967.[43] Expounding upon his interpretation of *fidelista* revolutionary theory, he largely agreed with Guevara in his criticism of Communist orthodoxy, at least within the Latin-American setting. The historical failure of the traditional Communist parties to bring about the establishment of socialist governments was cited as proof of their ideological inadequacy. Thus, the Cuban lesson was regarded as appropriate for the region. His explicit reference to Cuba was somewhat misleading, however. Among other factors, he overlooked the demoralization of the Batista regime, the full impact of Castro's personality (although it was mentioned in passing), and especially the duping of the Cuban middle class. Castro himself had observed in his December, 1961, speech that had he been frank about his intentions before 1959, he could not have gained power. Yet Debray insistently contended that revolutionary forces should be public and explicit in stating their objectives from the very outset. Thus, "In order to convince the masses, it is necessary to address them, that is, to address speeches, proclamations, explanations to them—in brief, to carry on political work, 'mass work.' Hence the first nucleus of fighters will be divided into small propaganda patrols which will cover the mountain areas, going into villages, holding meetings, speaking here and there, in order to explain the social goals of the Revolution, to denounce the enemies of the peasantry, to promise agrarian reform and punishment for traitors, etc."[44] This meant, in short, that armed propaganda and military action

43. For an English translation, see Régis Debray, *Revolution in the Revolution? Armed Struggle and Political Struggle in Latin America,* tr. Bobbye Ortiz (New York: Grove Press, 1967).
44. *Ibid.,* p. 47.

were to be conducted simultaneously. "Armed propaganda has more to do with the internal than with the external guerrilla front. The main point is that under present conditions the most important form of propaganda is successful military action."[45] Also implicit throughout Debray's work, much of which focused on military tactics for the revolutionary guerrilla force, was the conviction that all of Latin America was sufficiently homogeneous for the same tactics to be effective everywhere. Little attention to the importance of individual indigenous conditions emerged.

The writings of Guevara and Debray, along with the speeches and proclamations of Fidel Castro, all combine to present a composite picture of that variant of communism which has emerged in Cuba as *fidelismo*. To draw firm conclusions about a dynamic and animated phenomenon such as the Cuban Revolution is presumptuous at the present time. It seems improbable, however, that the Castroite version of communism will change greatly. Further developments will likely depend upon practical politico-economic forces within Cuba itself. The record in the policy area does show certain achievements to date: nationalization has removed foreign private interests; the eradication of illiteracy has been realized in substantial part; public health and housing have been measurably advanced; and social and racial inequities have been lessened. Balanced against these are the erection of an authoritarian regime; the suppression of ordinary freedoms and liberties; the destruction of an independent peasantry and displacement of a competent middle class; the serious if temporary damage to the sugar industry; the whole series of economic imbalances brought about by unrealistic policies; and the replacement of North American by Soviet influence.

The Cuban Revolution has evolved over time into a movement and government that is unquestionably Communist. At the same time it has retained a powerful nationalistic undercurrent; Fidel Castro has never forgotten this fact, although the Cuban Communists have occasionally done so. Above all, the Cuban Revolution must be understood as having been in part one man's personalistic revolutionary movement. A commanding personality but unoriginal thinker who chose to bring about a drastic restructuring of society, Castro in time sought the support of the Communists in instituting his plans. And if his pre-1959 promises were forgotten, the Communists also bent or broke their orthodoxy in the interests of capitalizing upon the mercurial presence of a unique national leader. Among the few certainties of the flambuoyant Castro personality is its stubborn, even defiant, independence. He said as much in celebrating the sixth anniversary of Batista's defeat in 1965. "We

45. *Ibid.*, p. 56.

are a people with the right to speak with our own thought and voice . . . what every Marxist party should do in each concrete situation cannot be told by anyone from anywhere. . . . It is clear that each country has concrete conditions under which each revolution developed. . . . If some persons have doubts about whose head we are using, we must clearly answer that we do not need to ask anyone to lend us his brains."[46]

Castro and the Radical Left

Following the advent of the Cuban Revolution, a wave of political and ideological repercussions washed across the hemisphere. While the achievements of Castro brought new prestige to the Latin-American Communists, they also led to serious rifts between pro-*fidelista* elements and old-guard Communists. For those who accepted the Cuban revolutionary variant, the very radicalism of Castro himself became a basic component. Members of this radical, revolutionary left, almost always ideological Marxists, in many cases preferred to stand independent of the international Communist movement. Committed to bringing about the "national liberation" of their respective countries, they generally followed the guidelines of the Castro experience in seeking basic political and socioeconomic change. While many traditional Communist parties rejected the Cuban interpretations, groups of the radical left found the *fidelista* inspiration most congenial. As already suggested, the sources of ideological friction were apparent in the ideas of Castro and of Guevara.

To begin with, Castro was committed to a personal vision—however eccentric—of absolute justice. This was inconsistent with the historical dialectic of Marxism that presents communism as the inevitable pinnacle of socioeconomic development. Guevara's contention that the path to social revolution must be that of armed violence and guerrilla warfare also ran counter to the usual Marxist belief in the urban proletariat as the crucial revolutionary element. Yet a third source of ideological division was the Cuban insistence that violence could and would triumph even in the absence of traditional Marxist "revolutionary conditions." The acceptance of this argument strongly implied a basic rejection of the long-standing insistence by Latin-American Communists that conditions for revolution were not yet ripe.

Such basic ideological issues contributed substantially to the rivalry

46. Quoted in Gerhard Masur, *Nationalism in Latin America: Diversity and Unity* (New York: Macmillan Co., 1966), p. 224.

in Cuba between the *fidelistas* and the orthodox communists. Much the same conflict took place elsewhere. By and large, the regular Communist parties have stood apart from *fidelismo*. Faithful to their belief in a peaceful transition to socialism, they have continued to pursue moderate policies of accommodation. Brazil's near-legendary Communist leader Luis Carlos Prestes, for one, wrote that conditions in his homeland were not conducive to an armed rebellion. Revolution and violence were not necessarily synonymous, he argued, thus in much of Latin America events would have to wait upon the ripening of the proper situation. In Chile, Luis Corvalán was only slightly less categorical. Although conceding that the path of violence might in unusual instances be appropriate, the peaceful transition was in most cases preferable. The Argentine Communists also rejected for themselves the violent path, although praising the Cuban Revolution. At their Twelfth Party Congress in 1963, the Argentines outlined plans for a national front that would seek power within the prevailing rules of the game in that country.

While national variations were inevitable, the orthodox Communists generally remained loyal to their theoretical traditions. Striking witness was provided by articles appearing in the *World Marxist Review* in 1964.[47] Panamanian Orso Alba flatly declared that the revolutionary process in his country would succeed without civil war. From Guatemala, Alfredo Guerra Borges complimented the Cuban influence but noted that local circumstances in his country were not yet appropriate for armed insurrection. The Peruvian rejection of the Cuban path was clear, as Jorge del Prado emphasized. Peruvian communism lacked the mass support necessary for revolution; what was more pertinent, he said, was a concerted effort to gain popularity and strength over a period of time. Argentina's Victorio Codovilla was somewhat ambiguous but in essence concluded that the Cuban Revolution itself was little more than a mildly different variant of Communist revolution and that ideological conflict was therefore minimal.

With the major exception of Venezuela, the *fidelista* ideological position has been questioned or meaningfully diluted by the Communist

---

47. Much of this discussion is derived from the following articles, all of which appeared in 1964 issues of *World Marxist Review:* Orso Alba, "Panama in the Fight for National Sovereignty," April, pp. 15–21; Alfredo Guerra Borges, "The Experience of Guatemala: Some Problems of the Revolutionary Struggle Today," June, pp. 12–18; Jorge del Prado, "Mass Struggle—The Key to Victory," May, pp. 11–18; and Victorio Codovilla, "The Ideas of Marxism-Leninism in Latin America," August, pp. 40–49.

A fine synthesis of relevant ideological clashes appears in Aguilar, *Marxism in Latin America*, pp. 42–59.

parties of Latin America. That is not to say that the Cuban Revolution has lacked for converts; indeed, only the Venezuelan Communist party has officially and publicly defied Castro's doctrine. Throughout Latin America there are groups that ardently support *fidelista* ideology. Its exportability has therefore in one sense been proven, although the recipients have in most cases been not the traditional Communists but rather the movements of the radical left. They are irrefutably Marxist-Leninist in sympathy and revolutionary in action, but it is the Cuban brand of communism that is most admired. Several identifiable characteristics may be noted: (1) these groups anticipate the creation of broad-based national movements rather than parties, arguing that the latter are static and presuppose a division of opinion within the country; (2) they are willing to take great political and personal risk, although thereby being denounced by regular Communists upon occasions as adventurers and political extremists; (3) their intellectual as well as personal radicalism frequently includes a commitment to the old Trotskyite concept of "permanent revolution"; (4) among the membership are students, intellectuals, and professionals, but there are few from organized labor; (5) while rejecting preachings of peaceful coexistence and substituting the advocacy of guerrilla tactics, they maintain independence in international affairs—Soviet or Chinese influences are more opportunistic than ideological; (6) a great unifying factor is admiration for the person of Fidel Castro and the achievements of his movement in Cuba—this is in addition to the moral and material support that has been provided from Havana through clandestine channels.

There have been several such organizations of the radical left, with their durability highly variable. A partial list taken from the decade of the 1960s would include the Fuerzas Armadas de Liberación Nacional (FALN) and the Movimiento de la Izquierda Revolucionaria (MIR) of Venezuela; the Frente de Liberación Nacional (FLN) of Peru; the Movimiento 14 de Junio of the Dominican Republic; the Movimiento de Liberación Nacional (MLN) of Paraguay; the Movimiento Revolucionario 13 de Noviembre (MR-13) and the Fuerzas Armadas Rebeldes (FAR) of Guatemala; and the Frente Unido de Acción Revolucionaria (FUAR) and the Movimiento Revolucionario Liberal Izquierdista (MRLI) of Colombia. Of these, the most important to date have been the Venezuelan FALN and the FUAR of Colombia. Their roles in national affairs have upon occasion been substantial, certainly far more so than any of their counterparts elsewhere. Of more direct relevance have been the writings of their leadership.

In the Venezuelan case, let us examine the ideas of Domingo Alberto

Rangel, especially as expressed in his *Venezuela país ocupado* (1960).[48] A brilliantly polemical economist who by 1958 had become one of the leading figures in Venezuela's Acción Democrática (AD), Rangel became a critic of the gradualist policies of the party. This led in time to his expulsion from the party and the creation of the Movimiento de la Izquierda Revolucionaria (MIR). An aggregation comprised largely of the former left wing of the AD, the *miristas* were ideological Marxists impatient for "true revolution" in Venezuela. In time the group joined in the violent FALN effort to overthrow the government of Rómulo Betancourt. While much attention centered on tactical questions, the fundamental socioeconomic goals resembled those espoused by Cuba. Rangel, whose writings were ideologically more facile than they were profound, espoused an economic nationalism based upon radical agrarian reform. The Betancourt agricultural program, among the most effective in Latin America, was nonetheless too moderate and piecemeal for his liking. The role of North American investment, especially in Venezuelan petroleum, was sharply criticized. Rangel's general view toward Castro's revolutionary path was favorable, although he at least implicitly opposed the neglect or violation of individual rights.

Rangel's writings were less extreme than his support of violence. He and other radicals of the left gave witness to the kind of revolutionary dilemma that emerged in the wake of Fidel Castro.[49] There was the usual argument between the old-line Communists and the FALN and MIR, with the former preferring open participation within the constitutional prescriptions of the day rather than armed rebellion. Going one step further, however, there was a tactical controversy within the radical groups over the proper *means* of violence. At first it was generally accepted that the Cuba-style revolutionary movement was ideal; thus the FALN began a campaign in the interior, especially the Andean region. An effort was made to gather aid and support from the local peasantry, after which the guerrilla warfare against regular military forces might be expanded. When the government's popularity with the peasantry caused a thwarting of revolutionary hopes, it was decided to resituate the violence in the urban centers.

Bombings, running gun battles with authorities, attacks on public buildings, and indiscriminate terrorism became the order of the day.

48. Domingo Alberto Rangel, *Venezuela país ocupado* (Caracas: Pensamiento Vivo, 1960).

49. For a sympathetic analysis of the FALN and MIR position during this period, see Timothy F. Harding and Saul Landau, "Terrorism, Guerrilla Warfare and the Democratic Left in Venezuela," *Studies on the Left*, IV, No. 4, (Fall 1964), 118–28.

The radicals believed that a wave of lawlessness and violence would cause the spread of public dismay and fear. The armed forces would eventually seize power from civilian authorities in order to restore public order. Then, the inevitable military dictatorship would provide the proper conditions for a popular revolution in which the radicals might assume the dominant role. When this campaign failed to prevent national elections in December, 1963, some of the FALN began to return to the countryside; they argued that the Cuban pattern was correct after all but that it would take many years of effort. Others maintained that constant pressure from urban violence would ultimately be fruitful.[50] And all the while, Venezuela's regular Communists inclined toward a truce with the government in order to re-enter public politics legally.[51]

In Colombia, the FUAR has been but one of several small groups of the radical left. It is of particular interest because of its leader, Luis Emiro Valencia, an economist and intellectual married to the daughter of the controversial martyred liberal leader of the 1940s, Jorge Eliecer Gaitán. Valencia as well as his wife was strongly sympathetic to the Castro revolution. In 1961 he wrote *Realidad y perspectiva de la revolución cubana*,[52] in which Castro was described as the model for future revolutionary leadership in Latin America. Hoping to capitalize on the still-vivid Colombian recollections of the popular Gaitán, Valencia expressed the hope of reviving *gaitanismo* in combination with revolutionary activity. This was more sensible in terms of practical politics than it was in ideological terms, in view of the fact that Gaitán had not been an advocate of violence. Valencia in the FUAR platform incorporated the rhetoric of Marxism, calling for a centralized state under the control of workers and peasants. Extensive nationalization and a fully planned economy were proposed, along with fervent pleas for international peace and for freedom from omnipresent colonialist evils.

The most prominent figure of the Colombian radical left, however, was a Catholic priest and sociologist whose briefly meteoric career has already become legendary to Latin-American youth. Camilo Torres

50. A Communist viewpoint reflecting in part the dilemmas of the mid-1960's is that of Héctor Mujica, "La táctica comunista en Venezuela," *Rinascita*, 16 (April 1966), 14–15.

51. Terrorist tactics and the official response are treated, along with the 1963 elections, in the latter sections of John D. Martz, *Acción Democrática: Evolution of a Modern Political Party in Venezuela* (Princeton: Princeton University Press, 1966).

52. Luis Emiro Valencia, *Realidad y perspectivas de la revolución cubana* (Cuba: Casa de las Américas, 1961). Another excellent Marxist treatment of Colombia is Diego Montaña Cuellar, *Colombia pais formal y país real* (Buenos Aires: Editorial Platina, 1963).

(1929–66) combined elements of antisystemic radicalism, socialism, and ecumenical Catholicism, but in the final analysis his political thought was distinctive and unique. A member of the post-1925 generation in Colombia which was to a large degree nurtured and grew to maturity in an atmosphere of extreme partisan conflict and the societal agonies of *la violencia*,[53] Father Torres was a scholarly and deeply religious man. Trained as a sociologist, his political thought was formulated from an amalgam of his academic training, professional analysis of Colombian social reality, and the most progressive elements of contemporary Catholicism.

Camilo Torres was strongly influenced by exposure to the ecumenical environment of western Europe and by advanced study at the University of Louvain, an institution that represented the vanguard of creative Catholic thought. Only gradually and somewhat reluctantly did he come to the conclusion that only a true revolutionary challenge to existing power groups in Colombia could bring about a meaningful transformation of society. The intellectual application of economic and social sciences to Colombian life and politics brought him into increasing disagreement with the church hierarchy in Bogotá. On June 24, 1965, he requested release from his clerical duties, "for reduction to the lay state and for exoneration from obligations inherent in the clerical state."[54] In an accompanying statement he declared in part:

> I chose Christianity because I thought it contained the purest way to serve my neighbor. I was chosen by Christ to be a priest forever, motivated by the desire to commit myself totally to the love of my fellow man. As a sociologist, I had wished that that love might become effective through technology and science. In analyzing Colombian society I have realized that a revolution is necessary in order to give food to the hungry and drink to the thirsty, to clothe the naked and to obtain the welfare of the majority of our people. I think the revolutionary fight is a Christian and priestly fight. Only through it, in the concrete circumstances of our country, can we accomplish the love which men must have for their neighbors.[55]

53. During the years from 1947 to 1958 Colombia experienced an unparalleled blood-letting in the rural areas, during which time it is conservatively estimated that some 200,000 Colombians lost their lives. In more recent years the remnants of *la violencia* have largely taken the form of apolitical banditry and lawlessness. For a controversial but in many ways extraordinary study of this phenomenon, see Germán Guzmán, Orlando Fals Borda, and Eduardo Umaña Luna, *La violencia en Colombia* (Bogotá: Ediciones Tercer Mundo, 1962).

54. For a translation of the full text, see Germán Guzmán, *Camilo Torres*, tr. John D. Ring (New York: Sheed and Ward, 1969), p. 131.

55. *Inquietudes* (Bogotá), No. 5, p. 27.

The Archbishop of Bogotá granted the petition, culminating a lengthy controversy during which Torres had become unwillingly but increasingly criticized and ostracized by the conservatively inclined Church heirarchy.

Earlier in 1965 Father Torres had proclaimed in a "Platform for a Movement of Popular Unity" the necessity of structuring a pluralist political apparatus capable of seizing political power. Directing the message to trade unions, co-operatives, popular associations, and peasant leagues, he demanded that national decisions be taken away from those wielding power. "Those who actually possess real power constitute an economic minority which makes all the fundamental decisions of national politics. This minority will never make necessary decisions which might affect their own interests or the foreign interests to which they are tied. . . . These circumstances make indispensable a change of the structure of political power so that the majorities might produce the decisions."[56] In the following months he undertook the creation of a "United Front of the People," but after a series of organizational setbacks deriving from the disunity and rivalry of progressive sectors, he disappeared from public view late in the year. After some weeks of rumors it was learned that he had gone to the mountains to join existing groups in armed rebellion against the government. On February 15, 1966, he was shot and killed by government troops during a guerrilla attack on a small rural village. The intervening years have added to his legend, and today he stands alongside "Che" Guevara as a martyred apostle of the hemispheric struggle against oppression, injustice, and the historic inequities of Latin-American society.

The subtleties of Camilo Torres' personal ideology require more extended attention than is possible here; they were based on deep religious conviction, teachings of Catholic progressives, and a somewhat idiosyncratic and personalized vision of sociological reality. Advocating what Fals Borda has termed "utopian pluralism," Torres sought to change the existing rules as a means of transforming the social order; the final goal was "socio-economic revolutionary development conceived as the creation, resolution, and advancement of a neo-socialist subversion."[57] What he envisaged was a society of co-operative understanding, constructed upon the mutual collaboration of diverse progressive movements. Dreaming of "a system oriented by brotherly love,"[58] he advocated what

56. From *Frente Unido,* as quoted in Guzmán, *Camilo Torres,* pp. 96–99.
57. Orlando Fals Borda, *Subversion and Social Change in Colombia,* tr. Jacqueline Skiles (New York: Columbia University Press, 1969), p. 162.
58. Camilo Torres, *Biografía, plataforma, mensajes* (Medellín: Ediciones Carpel-Antorcha, 1966), p. 35.

one sympathetic Colombian has termed "the vision of a completely open society in which differences of opinion, belief, or attitude are respected for the higher purpose of achieving as commonwealth progress within a just structure."[59]

Although many of his specific proposals were still evolving and changing at the time of his death, his recommendations in the March, 1965, declaration are revealing. Among the more important objectives were agrarian reform, state planning, nationalization, free and obligatory public education, and a reshaping of international relations.[60] Land would belong to those directly working it, while the government would be responsible for supporting and developing co-operative and community systems, and for providing credit and technical assistance in accord with a national agrarian plan. Industrialization and development demanded extensive state intervention, including mechanisms to articulate a plan for import substitution, increase of exports, and the more equitable distribution of national goods and products. Nationalization was to be extensive, incorporating banks, hospitals, clinics, public transportation, the communications media, and insurance companies. Subsoil deposits were to be the property of the state, and he incorporated specific guidelines for the regulation of foreign investment, especially in the exploitation of petroleum. His pluralistic system also demanded an antiimperialist orientation, for he regarded the Colombian elite as having surrendered the national patrimony to United States economic interests.

Underlying many of Father Torres' recommendations was a commitment to the ideal of communalism. Both agrarian and urban reforms were based on various forms of collective action, and communal activities were to include worker participation in decision-making and profit-sharing plans. This was further intended as yet another means of strengthening the dignity of the individual, a concern that was always at the forefront of Torres' thought. He also dedicated attention to the place of violence and counterviolence within society. Although thereby subjecting himself to strong and critical attack, he insisted upon the moral justification of rebellion and violence. Moreover, this was seen as contributing to the rebirth of the worth of the individual, which he felt had suffered increasing depradation through the continuation of traditional patterns of power in Colombia. Condemning the oligarchy for having itself employed both covert and overt forms of violence and

59. Fals Borda, *Social Change in Colombia*, p. 167.
60. The text, which Torres regarded as a "working document" demanding study, discussion, and further refinement, is reproduced in Guzmán, *Camilo Torres*, pp. 96–99.

social pressure, he argued that counterviolence by the masses was an appropriate and indeed one of the few means whereby the latter might struggle to protect and to develop their own needs and interests. In order to achieve the well-being of the masses, it was necessary to take power away from the privileged minorities. "The revolution may be peaceful if the minorities do not resist violently."[61] It was the apparent inability of the masses to assert and to defend their own interests which ultimately led Torres to the belief in the necessity for armed struggle. It was, of course, this same conviction that led the embattled and dedicated priest to the mountains and, tragically, to his death.

In Peru, there have been several exponents of the radical left. Perhaps the most respectable intellectually are the academically inclined writings of members of the small Movimiento Social Progresista (MSP), including a number of outstanding scholars who became advisers to the military regime that seized power late in 1968. While by no means convinced of the utility of violent revolution, there are far-reaching proposals for truly meaningful socioeconomic reform. The most prominent radical activist has been Hugo Blanco, a young man who inspired Indian uprisings in the south of Peru in the early 1960s. Denounced by orthodox Communists as a Trotskyite, he has been more concerned with actual amelioration of living conditions in that region than with ideologically fastidious theorizing. Among the most notable works is Carlos Malpica's *Los dueños del Perú*.[62] The author, a Cajamarca-born agricultural engineer, served for a time as secretary general of the MIR. Writing about the socioeconomic transformation of Peru, he concentrated upon agricultural problems and the over-all land-man relationship in the country. His book is a highly damning treatment of the Sociedad Nacional Agraria (SNA), a leading organization of large landowners; considerable attention is also devoted to the Asociación de Criadores de Lanares del Perú, which is representative of similar views and interests. Examining official tax and property records, he documents an extraordinary record of large landholdings which dramatizes the extent to which a few families dominate the ownership and control of lands and productive activities in Peru. As one of several findings, he notes that thirty large coastal *hacendados* controlled 191,276 hectares of land, or 28.7 percent of the area of cultivation.[63] He concludes with an examination of the composition of the Peruvian congress, maintaining that the possibility of a *true*

61. Torres, *Biografía*, p. 34.
62. Carlos Malpica S., *Los dueños del Perú* (Lima: Fondo de Cultura Popular, 1965).
63. *Ibid.*, pp. 6–7.

agrarian reform, in the light of the interests represented there, is virtually nonexistent. This work created a considerable stir upon publication, and since that time Malpica has continued his criticisms.

These movements of the revolutionary left, whatever their particularistic traits, have shared in most of their tactics and methods. Among these are: (1) a rejection of normal political action as a solution for national problems; (2) advocacy of the general strike as an effective means of challenging authority; (3) a belief in the imminent nature of a total and fundamental revolution; (4) the advocacy and practice of direct action (including robbery, kidnappings, burning of selected targets, and the like); (5) the use of insurrectionary tactics and a preference for guerrilla activities; (6) and the building of peasant support and, if geography and politics permit, the seizure of land and establishment of individual peasant communities (such as Sumapaz and Marquetalia in Colombia). It is striking to note the similarities between these revolutionaries of the left and the old anarchist thought of days past.[64] This is true in organization as well as tactics, since the movements of the revolutionary left operate in small semiautonomous groups with little or no central authority.

The survival of this anarchistic temper is relevant to an understanding of contemporary revolutionary ferment in Latin America. Even the Cuban Revolution, despite its eventual embrace of communism, in its early stages gave signs of the mystique of the total revolution, of insurrectionary tactics and the alleged importance of peasant support. The traditional anarchist has rejected the form of strict discipline demanded by Communists, as well as the practice of subordinating moral principles to party expedience. Revolutionaries of the left in Latin America tend to rely more on instinct and intuitive judgment rather than on organization and careful planning. Thus the political action of these groups, whether conducted in the name of communism, Marxism-Leninism, or some other doctrinal position, resembles the historical "organized indiscipline" of the anarchists.

While the impact of Castro and the Cuban Revolution provided both an idealized inspirational hero and suggestive doctrinal and revolutionary ideas to the revolutionaries of the left, there were other external forces. The impact of the Sino-Soviet dispute was felt across the hemisphere, both within the Communist parties and among independent Marxists. The ideological as well as practical political division of international communism was not without its implications for the hemisphere. Granted the stresses already created by the Cuban Revolution, the cumulative

64. See the discussion of anarchism in Chapter 6.

result was a more fragmented and self-destructive Communist movement than ever before in Latin America. The conflict has raged largely among various factions of the Communist parties and groups, and significant or original doctrinal writings have not emerged. However, the dispute continues to be fought out on ideological grounds. Basically, it has centered upon the methods appropriate to effect social revolution and erect a Communist state.

Communist China argues, as does Cuba, that violence is the most immediate and effective path to revolution. Peaceful coexistence is derided as being opportunistic. vacillating, and a betrayal of the purity of Communist ideals. The struggle against imperialism must be constant and unremitting and should be founded on a united front of the workers and the peasants. The initial importance of the peasantry in particular is stressed, and the Cuban Revolution provided a natural boon to the Chinese in furthering their argument. They also stressed the anti-imperialist nature of the Cuban struggle, praising the breaking of colonial chains that had long been held by the United States. Deriding Soviet accommodation with the United States, the Chinese cried betrayal while holding up the Cubans as exemplary of the possibilities for those with proper doctrinal insights. For the Chinese, in short, the Latin Americans should join in repudiation of Soviet moderation in Cold War politics. Violent revolutionary struggle should be universally applied in the promotion of communism, and as an underdeveloped region, Latin America should replace reliance upon circumstantial similarities to Cuba.

As already suggested, the Latin-American Communist parties have generally followed the Moscow line rather than that of Peking. As for Cuba, praise of the revolution and its accomplishment has come primarily from the radical left. These movements have found the Cuban and Chinese ideas an attractive interpretation of Marxism-Leninism. Thus, although traditional Latin-American Communists have at a series of international gatherings reaffirmed their pro-Soviet allegiance, the impact of the Cubans and Chinese is not to be overlooked. Certainly the cry for immediate revolution, the heroic self-sacrifice that is demanded, and the over-all zeal and militancy of the non-Soviet position have held considerable psychological as well as doctrinal appeal. The continuing activity of Castro's agents throughout the hemisphere, along with the cumulative intensification of Chinese operations in Latin America, have added fuel to the fires of conflict within the left.

The similarity of Chinese and Cuban appeals in the reliance on revolutionary violence has been especially appealing to youth groups and to intellectuals. For the Chinese, eventual capture of the Communist movement in the hemisphere stands as the ultimate goal; for Cuba and Castro, the creation of a more sympathetic climate is perhaps as important as the assertion of personal and national leadership in Latin America. Certainly the regular Communists have generally represented the evolutionary sector of the left. Given the revolutionary needs of much of Latin America, it seems inevitable that, whatever the course of events in Cuba or elsewhere, radical movements will continue to be active, vocal, and deeply committed to a violent overturn of existing society.[65]

SELECTED BIBLIOGRAPHY

SOCIALISM AND COMMUNISM

Aguilar, Luis E. *Marxism in Latin America*. New York: Alfred A. Knopf, 1968.

Alba, Víctor. *Historia del comunismo en América Latina*. México: Ediciones Occidentales, 1954.

Alexander, Robert J. *Communism in Latin America*. 2d. pr. New Brunswick: Rutgers University Press, 1960.

————. *Organized Labor in Latin America*. New York: Free Press of Glencoe, 1965.

Allen, Robert Loring. *Soviet Influence in Latin America: The Role of Economic Relations*. Washington: Public Affairs Press, 1959.

Bazán, Armando. *José Carlos Mariátegui*. Santiago: Zig-Zag, 1939.

Dillon, Dorothy. *International Communism and Latin America: Perspectives and Prospects*. Latin American Monograph No. 19. Gainesville: University of Florida Press, 1962.

Halperin, Ernst. *Nationalism and Communism in Chile*. Cambridge: M.I.T. Press, 1965.

Mariátegui, José Carlos. *Defensa de marxismo: La emoción de nuestro tiempo y otros temas*. Santiago: Ediciones Nacionales y Extranjeras, 1934.

————. *La escena contemporánea*. Lima: Ed. Minerva, 1925.

————. *Siete ensayos de interpretación de la realidad peruana: Escritos de Mundial y Amauta*. Santiago: Ed. Universitaria, 1955.

Poblete Troncoso, Moisés, and Ben G. Burnett. *The Rise of the Latin-American Labor Movement*. New York: Bookman Associates, 1960.

Poppino, Rollie. *International Communism in Latin America: A History of the Movement, 1917–1963*. New York: Free Press of Glencoe, 1964.

Ravines, Eudocio. *The Yenan Way*. New York: Charles Scribner's Sons, 1951.

Schmitt, Karl M. *Communism in Mexico: A Study in Political Frustration*. Austin: University of Texas Press, 1965.

Schneider, Ronald M. *Communism in Guatemala: 1944–1954*. New York: Frederick A. Praeger, 1959.

65. For a more detailed discussion of this material, see John D. Martz, "Doctrine and Dilemmas of the Latin-American 'New Left,'" *World Politics*, XXII, No. 2 (January 1970).

CUBA AND FIDELISMO

Castro, Fidel. *Pensamiento político, económico y social de Fidel Castro*. La Habana: Editorial Lex, 1959.

Casuso, Teresa. *Cuba and Castro*. New York: Random House, 1961.

Conte Agüero, Luis. *Los dos rostros de Fidel Castro*. México: Editorial Jus, 1960.

Debray, Régis. *Revolution in the Revolution? Armed Struggle and Political Struggle in Latin America*. Translated by Bobbye Ortiz. New York: Grove Press, 1967.

Draper, Theodore. *Castroism: Theory and Practice*. New York: Frederick A. Praeger, 1965.

————. *Castro's Revolution: Myths and Realities*. New York: Frederick A. Praeger, 1962.

Dubois, Jules. *Fidel Castro*. Indianapolis: Bobbs-Merrill, 1959.

Dumont, René. *Cuba: Socialisme de développement*. Paris: Editions du Seuil, 1964.

Goldenberg, Boris. *The Cuban Revolution and Latin America*. New York: Frederick A. Praeger, 1965.

Guevara, Ernesto. *La guerra de guerrillas*. La Habana: Ediciones Minfar, 1960.

————. *Pasajes de la guerra revolucionaria*. La Habana: Ediciones Unión Narraciones, 1963.

————. *Reminiscences of the Cuban Revolutionary War*. Translated by Victoria Ortiz. New York: Monthly Review Press, 1968.

————. *The Diary of Che Guevara: Bolivia, November 7, 1966–October 7, 1967*. New York: Bantam Books, 1968.

Huberman, Leo, and Paul M. Sweezy. *Cuba: Anatomy of a Revolution*. New York: Monthly Review Press, 1960.

Jackson, D. Bruce. *Castro, the Kremlin, and Communism in Latin America*. Baltimore: Johns Hopkins Press, 1969.

Julien, Claude. *La revolución cubana*. Translated by Mario Trajtenberg. Montevideo: Ediciones Marcha, 1961.

Mallin, Jay, ed., *"Che" Guevara on Revolution*. Coral Gables: University of Miami Press, 1969.

Matthews, Herbert L. *The Cuban Story*. New York: George Braziller, 1961.

McGaffey, Wyatt, and Clifford R. Barnett. *Twentieth Century Cuba: The Background of the Cuban Revolution*. New York: Doubleday & Co., 1965.

Meyer, Karl E., and Tad Szulc. *The Cuban Invasion*. New York: Ballantine Books, 1962.

Mills, C. Wright. *Listen, Yankee!* New York: Ballantine Books, 1960.

Roca, Blas. *The Cuban Revolution*. New York: New Century Publishers, 1961.

Ruiz, Ramón Eduardo. *Cuba: The Making of a Revolution*. Amherst: University of Massachusetts Press, 1968.

Suárez, Andrés. *Cuba: Castroism and Communism, 1959–1965*. Cambridge, MIT Press, 1967.

Seers, Dudley, ed. *Cuba: The Economic and Social Revolution*. Chapel Hill: University of North Carolina Press, 1964.

Selser, Gregorio, ed. *La revolución cubana: Escritos y discursos*. Buenos Aires: Editorial Palestra, 1960.

Suchlicki, Jaime. *University Students and Revolution in Cuba, 1920–1968.* Coral Gables: University of Miami Press, 1969.

Urrutia, Manuel. *Fidel Castro & Company, Inc.* New York: Frederick A. Praeger, 1964.

Wilkerson, Loree. *Fidel Castro's Political Programs from Reformism to "Marxism-Leninism."* Latin American Monograph, Second Series, No. 1. Gainesville: University of Florida Press, 1965.

Zeitlin, Maurice. *Revolutionary Politics and the Cuban Working Class.* Princeton: Princeton University Press, 1967.

CASTRO AND THE RADICAL LEFT

Gerassi, John. *The Great Fear in Latin America.* New York: Macmillan Co., 1965.

———, ed. *Venceremos: The Speeches and Writings of Che Guevara.* New York: Macmillan Co., 1968.

Guzmán, Germán. *Camilo Torres.* Translated by John D. Ring. New York: Sheed and Ward, 1969.

Malpica S., Carlos. *Los dueños del Perú.* Lima: Fondo de Cultura Popular, 1965.

Montaña Cuellar, Diego. *Colombia país formal y país real.* Buenos Aires: Editorial Platina, 1963.

Pareja, Carlos Henrique. *El padre Camilo: El cura guerrillero; 4 ensayos sobre la lucha entre el pueblo y la oligarquía en la historia de Colombia.* México: Editorial Nuestra América, 1968.

Rangel, Domingo Alberto. *Venezuela país ocupado.* Caracas: Pensamiento Vivo, 1960.

Taber, Robert. *The War of the Flea.* New York: Lyle Stuart, 1965.

Torres, Camilo. *Biografía, plataforma, mensajes.* Medellín: Ediciones Carpel-Antorcha, 1966.

Valencia, Luis Emiro. *Realidad y perspectivas de la revolución cubana.* Cuba: Casa de las Américas, 1961.

IO

Social Democracy
in the Andean States

The early advent of socialist thought, heightened by the impact
of the Russian Revolution and subsequently affected by Moscow-based
Communist directives, reflected in part a widening social consciousness.
There were, obviously, a number of Marxist thinkers whose inclinations
were toward intellectual theorizing rather than political activism. But
among those who chose to participate in public affairs, many worked
within the orthodox Socialist parties, especially in the Plate River countries and in Chile. In addition, there was another group of individuals
who, after frequently unhappy experience with Communist organizations,
pursued their political goals through parties and movements that may
be termed "Social Democratic."[1] While accepting many basic postulates
of traditional Marxism, these groups were tactically and doctrinally pragmatic; they consciously adjusted to the political and socioeconomic realities of their individual countries.

The characteristics of these partisan political activists have been at
least three. First, they have sought sweeping social and economic change,
with attention centered on land reform and the integration of the lower
classes into the political process. While the ultimate Marxist utopian

1. Despite the dangers of assuming parallels to similar groups in western Europe, such a denomination of these parties seems more accurate descriptively
than any of the alternatives.

state has not always been repudiated, the achievement of practical and realizable goals has been emphasized. Secondly, the overriding approach has been democratic rather than authoritarian. Party declarations are heavily larded with pledges to popular participation, untrammeled electoral competition, and responsive representative government. Militarism and violence have been condemned, and there has been in most cases a rejection of force as a legitimate political weapon. Thirdly, they have represented a movement that is strictly native to the area; international connections have been largely continental. In the words of one of the first North American scholars to use the term "Social Democratic," "This extremely ideological group believes in the establishment of full service states, with the government as an active orienter of economic policy. They are generally distrustful of private business organizations of the size and power of oil companies and banks, but are willing to make a peace with them so long as they are not pushed substantially to the right and in order to avoid being forced into the Castro camp by extremists within their own countries."[2]

A number of Latin-American political parties can be termed "Social Democratic," although other terms have also been used, including "modern,"[3] "indigenous nationalistic,"[4] and most frequently, *"aprista."* Indeed, this final term has proved an enduring one in speaking of the Social Democratic parties, and although somewhat misleading, is among other things a tribute to the early arrival, hemispheric reputation, and political durability of the Peruvian Aprista party, from which the name derives. Thus a major section of this chapter must discuss the voluminous and strongly ideological literature of the *apristas.* Among other things, the Peruvians may be distinguished from many other Social Democrats by dint of their concern with the indigenous masses in their country. The major Social Democratic party in the Andes, the APRA's party doctrine has been infused with a large dosage of *indigenismo.* While all the Social Democrats have been deeply concerned with the plight of the masses, most of them have been located in countries such as Costa Rica where the Indians are either negligible or nonexistent.

It is also natural that, in such countries as Peru, Ecuador, Bolivia, and Columbia, a sympathetic and deeply felt preoccupation with the

2. Kalman H. Silvert, *The Conflict Society: Reaction and Revolution in Latin America* (New Orleans: The Hauser Press, 1961), p. 256.
3. William Whatley Pierson and Federico Guillermo Gil, *Governments of Latin America* (New York: McGraw-Hill Book Company, 1957), pp. 318–20.
4. Asher N. Christensen, "The General Nature of Political Parties in Latin America," in *The Evolution of Latin American Government,* ed. Asher N. Christensen (New York: Henry Holt, 1951), p. 508.

plight of the Indian has extended beyond the ranks of political activists. Especially as recent anthropological and sociological studies have brought out the truly abysmal circumstances in which the Indians live, an increasing number of scholars and intellectuals have raised their voices on behalf of the indigenous masses. Entirely aside from *aprista* contributions, then, an aroused social consciousness has devoted itself to the welfare of the Indians, for the vast preponderance of whom national life has been alien. The advent of Indian-oriented social thought, commonly known as *indigenismo*, has resulted in a flourishing and influential body of literature. In this, the first of two chapters on Social Democratic thought, attention must be devoted to evolving *indigenista* analyses as well as the ideology of the Peruvian *apristas*, whose concern has been combined with a philosophically flavored elaboration and restatement of Marxist thought.

The Social Conscience and Indigenismo

A quarter of the countries of Latin America have been predominatly Indian in ethnic composition—Peru, Bolivia, Ecuador, Mexico, and Guatemala. In several others a substantial proportion of the population remains Indian, while elsewhere the dominant *mestizo* strain reflects the indigenous presence. The traditional pattern was one of a class- or race-oriented differentiation of social and political functions, with the Indians on the bottom. Effectively excluded from active political participation, they lived in rural, often isolated mountainous regions. Social customs and attitudes have remained basically unchanging through the passing of generations. For all practical purposes the Indians have stood apart from "national" life, only rarely affected by urban change, economic growth, and the Western cultural heritage. Thus in Guatemala, as a typical example, the Indian traditionally has spoken only his own language, accepted the values of his own heritage, and has been regarded by the dominant, Spanish-speaking *ladino* elite as an inferior, even subhuman being deserving of treatment no different than an ordinary beast of burden. Such attitudes on the part of whites and *mestizos* have survived to the present, but the champions of the Indian have grown legion since the turn of the century.

Through the intervening years, there has developed an awakening appreciation that the Indian population comprises a vital and potentially productive element. This has also led more recently to an understanding of the importance of preserving indigenous customs and cultures while developing a unifying sentiment of national pride. In its earliest stages, what evolved into *indigenismo* stemmed from the intellectual search for an American doctrine reflecting the total experience of the hemisphere. This was supported by an accumulation of anthropological and archaeological studies which has continued to the present. Perhaps more noteworthy in the present context has been the effort to construct theories of cultural pluralism. Latin Americans have examined "Indianism" or "native Americanism," at the same time striving to identify a composite ideology containing elements of the presumably unique native genius of the culturally and racially mixed population. The results have often been couched in idealistic rather than purely anthropological or scientific terms. Among the many examples, one thinks of the Argentine Rojas' vision of "Eurindia," or that of the Mexican Vasconcelos' "cosmic race."

Many of the *indigenista* writers, by centering their studies on spiritual and cultural values, turned their backs on the bitterly contested debate between Americanists and Europeanists which had raged through much of the nineteenth century. Among the important byproducts of the movement was a broadened intellectual interest in social justice. This received positive political treatment from such movements as the Movimiento Nacionalista Revolucionario (MNR) of Bolivia, the Peruvian APRA, and the short-lived Guatemalan revolutionary movement of Juan José Arévalo. In Mexico the influence of *indigenismo* emerged as a dominant interest for students of national history, and Mexican intellectuals still continue to wrestle with the problems of assimilating the Indians into national life. The concomitant concept of the continuity of Indian history, through the generations of European domination, in Davis' words, "has resulted in a distinctly new perspective in American history and, accordingly, has produced a number of efforts to establish the significant epochs or decisive historical movements from this standpoint."[5]

Unsurprisingly, the general interest in the Indian heritage encouraged the appearance of indigenous novels, especially in the Andean region. Ecuadorean Jorge Icaza wrote in his famed *Huasipungo* and *Cholos* about the social conditions of Indian life on the *sierra*,[6] while Bolivian Alcides Argüedas painted a bleak picture in *Raza de bronce*[7]—*Race of Bronze*—and Peru's Ciro Alegría penned *El mundo es ancho y*

5. Harold Eugene Davis, "Trends in Social Thought in Twentieth-Century Latin America," *Journal of Inter-American Studies,* I, No. 1 (January 1959), 65.
6. Jorge Icaza, *Huasipungo: The Villagers, a Novel,* tr. Bernard M. Dulsey (Carbondale: Southern Illinois University Press, 1964); Jorge Icaza, *Cholos, novela* (Quito: Litografía e imprenta Romero, 1938).
7. Alcides Arguedas, *Raza de bronce* (La Paz: González, 1919).

ajeno[8]—*Broad and Alien Is the World.* Historical works glorified the qualities of the pure Indian, as with Mexican accounts of Benito Juárez or the Ecuadorean Benjamín Carrión's vivid if larger-than-life biography of the Inca, Atahualpa.[9] There was a generous portion of romanticism in some of these works which was reminiscent of Rousseau's "noble savage." Yet the social conscience of many writers found expression in starkly brutal portrayals of Indian life, as in the case of the gifted Icaza. It was not coincidental that the bulk of these works emanated from the Andes. An estimated 40 percent of the twenty-five million Latin-American Indians live in this region.

Indigenismo in Bolivia and Ecuador / Boliva is a vertical country geographically, ranging from the extremes of a tropical jungle area on the east to the *altiplano*, that imposing highland plateau of twelve thousand to fifteen thousand feet on which most Bolivians live. Although until recently the vast majority of its people have in practical terms lived outside the currents of national life, the ancient heritage of Kollasuyu, a territorial subdivision of the Incan empire Tawantinsuyu, has provided a mystical sense of communality among the Quechua-speaking Indians. Although independence from Spain was soon followed by a brief and unsuccessful attempt to create a single Peruvian-Bolivian Confederation, the Indianist tradition survived, at least in narrow intellectual circles. The humiliating defeat at the hands of Chile in the War of the Pacific (1879–83) brought disastrous territorial losses that cost Bolivia its outlet to the Pacific. In the wake of that defeat, essentially positivist thinkers began to reconsider the role of the Indian, and this led to the flourishing of a virtual cult of *indigenismo*.

After years of numbing shock in the war's aftermath, Bolivia began to regain a modicum of balance with the victory of the liberal faction in 1889 and after. As this group stabilized its rule in the next few years, the influence of positivism was felt in various fields, most notably education. Traditional Church authority was reduced, with education becoming strongly secular rather than ecclesiastical. At the same time, explanations of historical weaknesses, and especially the defeat by Chile, were expressed in relentlessly damning fashion. Spencerian positivism was widely accepted by the Bolivian intelligentsia; it was used as a means of outlining the evolution toward progress and change which might lead

8. Ciro Alegría, *Broad and Alien is the World,* tr. Harriet de Onís (New York: Farrar & Rinehart, 1941).
9. Benjamín Carrión, *Atahualpa,* 3d. ed. (Quito: Editorial Casa de la Cultura Ecuatoriana, 1956).

to a fundamental transformation of the nation. Among the more prominent neo-Spencerians were Daniel Sánchez Bustamante and Luis Arce
Lacaze. The former, a professor in La Paz, set forth his ideas in *Principios
de derecho* and *Principios de sociología*.[10] Implicit was the suggestion
that the Indian was a source of national weakness but might in time
come to play a more constructive role if accepted by existing white
society. Arce Lacaze, also a professor, generally shared the views of
Sánchez Bustamante.[11] A few years later, the writings of Ignacio Prudencio
Bustillo proved even more influential on a generation of Bolivian
students.[12]

A teacher of legal philosophy at the University of Sucre, Bustillo
(1895–1928) discussed the problems of improving Bolivian society in
his *Ensayo de filosofía jurídica*,[13] which appeared in 1923. Giving extended consideration to educational problems, the Bolivian advocated
what he called the realistically practical North American approach. The
educational process in Bolivia, he argued, had been excessively rhetorical.
Bolivia needed fewer literary and professional men, while the shortage
of trained technicians required an emphasis on the study of the land
and its problems. Among other things, he urged the establishment of
"model farms" on which Indians might learn modern agricultural
methods. Bustillo's major concern was philosophical, and his interest
in the improvement of the Indian, although genuine, was relegated to
a secondary position. Nonetheless, he gave witness to the breakdown
of earlier intellectual reluctance to concede any social value or worth
to the Indian. It was, indeed, precisely this kind of concession that
indirectly encouraged the appearance of more explicitly *indigenista*
thought in Bolivia.

Among the most significant exponents of the latter was Franz Tamayo,
whose *La creación de la pedagogía nacional*[14] first appeared in 1910
and gained wide popularity with the intelligentsia in the 1930s and
1940s. As Francovich remarked, Tamayo envisioned a humanitarian kind
of nationalism by which the higher social values might be regenerated.[15]
A critic of foreign ideologies, Tamayo called for a Bolivian cultural

10. Daniel Sánchez Bustamante, *Principios de derecho* (La Paz: n.p., 1905),
and *Principios de sociología* (La Paz: n.p., 1903).
11. Luis Arce Lacaze, *Filosofía del derecho* (La Paz: n.p., 1892).
12. For a discussion of these Bolivians, see Guillermo Francovich, *El pensamiento boliviano en el siglo XX* (México: Fondo de Cultura Económica, 1956).
13. Ignacio Prudencio Bustillo, *Ensayo de filosofía jurídica* (Sucre: Imp. Bolívar, 1923).
14. Franz Tamayo, *La creación de la pedagogía nacional: Editoriales de "El
Diario"* (La Paz: Ministerio de Educación de Bolivia, 1944).
15. Francovich, *Pensamiento boliviano*, p. 55.

nationalism which was not unlike that of Ricardo Rojas in Argentina. The Indian was central to the development of a sense of nationality. To Tamayo the Indian was a man of action who had successfully preserved his heritage in the face of Spanish colonialism and constituted a fundamental source of energy for Bolivia. The dignity of the Indian and his past achievements, in short, constituted a vital and undeniable component of Bolivian nationality. Much the same general attitude was expressed with burning conviction by Gustavo A. Navarro, who created a stir in the 1920s with his advocacy of social revolution and a recognition of the rights of the Indian.

Writing under the pseudonym of Tristán Marof, he called for violent revolution as the best way of introducing meaningful reforms. One of the earlier *indigenistas* to extol the glories of the Incan empire in flaming prose, Navarro demanded a social revolution that would represent a return to what he understood as the Incan social and political tradition. Describing Incan collectivism in almost utopian terms, he demanded "land to the Indians, mines to the state." The latter meant outright nationalization of the mines and all productive foreign-controlled enterprise. Sympathetic to socialist ideals, Navarro later founded the Partido Socialista Obrero de Bolivia, the country's earliest Socialist party. He was primarily an *indigenista* and only secondarily a Marxist, at least in his writings. With Navarro as with many contemporaries, *indigenismo* contained a mystical sentiment of attachment to the land. The reality of life on the *altiplano* and the exceptional environmental demands that confronted the Indian were poetically transformed into a semireligious phenomenon. The cultural and social adjustments adopted by the Indian were praised as symbolizing man's ability to conquer the worst that nature could offer. In the final analysis, this tendency ascribed to the Andean physical setting "the source of a spirit which is communicated in some mystic way to the subconscious in man, thus giving form to American culture and American thought."[16]

Alcides Argüedas (1878–1946), among the most noted of Bolivian writers, vividly portrayed the life and status of the Indian in novels, essays, and historical interpretations. While his *Raza de bronce* described the degrading life of the Indian on the *altiplano,* he elaborated on the subject in many other works. His *Un pueblo enfermo*[17] undertook an examination of geographic and cultural factors, of which the former

16. Gustavo A. Navarro (Tristán Marof), *Ensayos y crítica: Revoluciones bolivianos, guerras internacionales y escritores* (La Paz: Librería y Editorial "Juventud," 1961); also see *La tragedia del altiplano* (Buenos Aires: Editorial Claridad, 1955).

17. Alcides Argüedas, *Un pueblo enfermo: Contribución a la psicología de los pueblos hispano-americanos* (Barcelona: n.p., 1910).

received greater emphasis. Racial components, he argued, were for all practical purposes a function of the geographic and topographic environment. The ungrateful soil of the *altiplano* and the numbing cold contributed to a state of depression from which the Indian could not rise. Added to this was what he viewed as the tragic history of Bolivia, which served to aggravate the state of moral and socioeconomic depradations that existed. Argüedas stressed the conditions of *altiplano* life rather than presenting an articulate program for reform; there are few *indigenistas* who have depicted the life of the highland Indian in equally stark and realistic fashion.

A logical political outgrowth of Bolivian *indigenismo* was the Movimiento Nacionalista Revolucionario (MNR), which was organized officially in 1941, struggled for power until the revolution of 1952, and remained in control until its overthrow a dozen years later.[18] The party ideology was a rather peculiar admixture of national socialism, pluralistic collectivism, and concern for the Indian; in practice, this was combined with a frequent disregard for democratic processes. The *indigenista* strain was prominent in MNR doctrinal writings. The first official Program and Principles of Action, adopted in 1942, gave early recognition of the fact. It said in part, "We demand the identification of all Bolivians with the aspirations and necessities of the peasant, and we proclaim that social justice is inseparable from the redemption of the Indian for the economic liberation and sovereignty of the Bolivian people. . . . We demand the study of a scientific basis of the Indian agrarian problem so as to incorporate into the national life the millions of peasants now outside of it, and to obtain an adequate organization of the agricultural economy so as to obtain the maximum output."[19] Its early commitment to an improvement of life for the Indian was also noted by the early writings of such people as Víctor Paz Estenssoro, the dominant figure in the MNR.[20] The party republication of the writing of Tamayo in 1944 was further evidence of its *indigenista* proclivities.

18. For a sympathetic discussion of the MNR up to 1958, see Robert J. Alexander, *The Bolivian National Revolution* (New Brunswick: Rutgers University Press, 1958). The fall of the MNR in 1964 is detailed in William H. Brill, *Military Intervention in Bolivia: The Overthrow of Paz Estenssoro and the MNR* (Washington: Institute for the Comparative Study of Political Systems, 1967).

Among the most incisive and thoughtful analyses is James Malloy, "Revolution and Development in Bolivia," in *Constructive Change in Latin America,* ed., Cole Blasier (Pittsburgh: University of Pittsburgh Press, 1968), pp. 177–233.

19. Quoted in Alexander, *Bolivian National Revolution,* p. 59.

20. For a useful treatment of Paz Estenssoro and the MNR rise to power, see José Fellman Velarde, *Víctor Paz Estenssoro: El hombre y la revolución* (La Paz: Editorial "Don Bosco," 1954).

The story of the MNR reform program, its successes and failures, cannot be recounted here. It should be recalled, however, that the vague pro-Indianism of the MNR in early years led to a series of specific commitments after it came to power. There were four major reforms that the MNR attempted to institute, each of which implied the elevation of the Indian through a conversion of his status into that of independent and productive peasant with a role to play in national life. These were nationalization of the large tin mines, agrarian reform, educational reform, and electoral reorganization. Among the virtues of these policies, it was believed, would be a fulfillment of the obligation to liberate and educate the Indian, molding him into a responsible participant in Bolivian life and society. Perhaps the most lasting revolutionary change was that undertaken through agrarian reform. Significantly, pressure from Indian organizations forced upon the MNR a more rapid and far-reaching program than had been anticipated in 1952. The resultant Agrarian Reform Law of August, 1953, like its counterparts in several other countries, led at least for a time to a decline in productivity. Moreover, an elaborately designed system of Indian communes met with little success. Nonetheless, the MNR moved further along the road to the assimilation of the Indian than had any of its predecessors in power and introduced an irreversible change that survived the 1964 eclipse of the party.

The advent of *indigenismo* in Ecuador came chronologically later than in Bolivia. It first emerged perceptibly in the 1920s and 1930s through several philosophical and anthropological studies. The seriousness of the Ecuadoran commitment was illustrated by the creation of the Institute Indigenista del Ecuador in September of 1943. Its first director and for many years its driving force was the pioneer of Ecuadoran *indigenistas*, Pío Jaramillo Alvarado (1889–1968). Historian, essayist, and man of letters, he was both versatile and prolific.[21] His classic study *El indio ecuatoriano* first appeared in 1922 and since that time has gone through four editions. The last two of these have also included his *Del agro ecuatoriano*,[22] which had appeared separately in 1936. Jaramillo Alvarado gave a detailed description of the various racial mixtures in Ecuador, as well as reciting his findings on the customs, tradi-

21. Among his numerous works, see Pío Jaramillo Alvarado, *El indio ecuatoriano*, 4th ed. (Quito: Casa de la Cultura Ecuatoriana, 1954); *El régimen totalitario en América* (Guayaquil: Editora Noticia, 1940); *Estudios históricos* (Quito: Casa de la Cultura Ecuatoriana, 1960); *Historia de Loja y su provincia* (Quito: Casa de la Cultura Ecuatoriana, 1955); and *La nación quiteña: Biografía de una cultura* (Quito: Imp. Fernández, 1947).

22. Pío Jaramillo Alvarado, *Del agro ecuatoriano* (Quito: Imprenta de la Universidad Central, 1936).

tions, and characteristics of the various Indian regions and communities in the country. His observations on agricultural reality have presented a depressing if carefully drawn view of the daily lives of the Indians, especially in the intermontane Andean basins.

In the original edition of El indio ecuatoriano, Jaramillo Alvarado outlined the poverty and virtual servitude within which the ordinary Indian was born, lived, and died. In later editions his views were increasingly supplemented by precise data, especially that provided by Italo Paviolo, an Italian agronomist who undertook extensive studies for the Ecuadoran government. After documenting the shape of latifundismo and its attendant ills, he noted that the dispersed rural population of over one million Indians constituted perhaps Ecuador's major national problem. Related to this was the nullity of the Indian as a creative producer of wealth. Jaramillo Alvarado called for a radical change in the cultural condition of the Indian. While quoting Vasconcelos to the effect that, for the Indian, the door to the future must be that of modern culture, he added that the situation in Ecuador was much different from that in Mexico. As late as the 1950s, Jaramillo Alvarado saw no reason to alter his conviction of 1922 that Ecuador's indigenista movement had been more intellectual than practical.

In the most recent edition of this work, moreover, the Ecuadoran lamented that the Instituto Indigenista del Ecuador had realized only modest results, given its limited budget and inadequate government financing. He also remarked that the Constitution of 1945, drafted under the auspices of a liberal-socialist government, represented "a marvelous constitutional conquest for Indian protection" but was then ignored rather than implemented.[23] While the Ecuadoran did not agree wholeheartedly with those of his countrymen who saw the Indian as the salvation of the country, he did feel that only through the redemption of the indigenous sector would meaningful social justice and economic development be feasible. "For Ecuador, there has arrived the decisive epoch for the planning and execution of new forms of economic life, which means a profound transformation of the aged systems of working the land and the labor of the Indian population. May the servitude of Indian concertaje disappear, for it has enslaved them and has kept them in the misery of routine to their patrons; may the land be a just extension of all that works; and may Ecuador—even today an essentially agricultural country—reach prosperity by peaceful Agrarian Reform or by the right of insurrection."[24]

23. Jaramillo Alvarado, El indio ecuatoriano, p. 509.
24. Ibid., p. 526.

One of the most significant *indigenistas* in Ecuador, José de la Cuadra (1903–41), centered his attention on racial problems of those living away from the Andes. In *El montuvio ecuatoriano*,[25] he examined the life and society of those who lived in the country's western zone, especially along the banks of the littoral rivers. The *montuvio* is basically a *mestizo* whose ancestors, according to De la Cuadra, included the ethnic and cultural attributes inherited from a tribe of Indians who antedated the Incas. Estimating that one-tenth of the Ecuadorean population was *montuvio*, De la Cuadra wrote that the majority of the group worked in transitory fashion on large *haciendas*. Although not tied to the land and *patrón* as was the highland Indian, the *montuvio* materially was scarcely better off. More independent and less passive than his mountain cousins, the *montuvio* was eager to move away from past traditions in an effort to improve himself. Yet he could not do this unassisted. De la Cuadra remarked that the local Communist and Socialist parties were the only ones to undertake the politicization of the *montuvio* but, because of internal rivalries, had been largely ineffective. Likening the *montuvio's* attitude toward the land to that of the Russian kulak, De la Cuadra said that slowly but inevitably, his lot would gradually change for the better. In the meantime, "social revolution will never attract him if it does not guarantee the exclusive dominion over a plot of land that he works and cultivates, and over the fruits that he makes it produce."[26]

Among the most interesting of the Ecuadoran *indigenistas* has been Segundo B. Maiguashca, himself a full-blooded Indian, who became a lawyer and writer devoted to the status of his Ecuadoran brothers In 1949 his *El indio, cerebro y corazón de América*[27] provided a knowledgeable discussion in which he proposed a variety of means to solve the retarded development of the Indian. To incorporate him into national culture, wrote Maiguashca, attention should be devoted to measures attacking psychological, economic, juridical, and educational shortcomings. As to the first, he urged that the Indian should learn to trust the white, while the latter in turn should discard his instinctive repudiation of the Indian. Economically, the Indian should receive the lands that had once been his, while receiving credits and various forms of agricultural assistance. In the juridical sphere, protective agencies and special legislation should be enacted. Educationally, the Indian should

25. José de la Cuadra, *El montuvio ecuatoriano* (Buenos Aires: Ediciones Imán, 1937).
26. *Ibid.*, p. 92.
27. Segundo B. Maiguascha, *El indio, cerebro y corazón de América: Incorporación del indio a la cultura nacional* (Quito: Edit. "Frey Jodoco Ricke," 1949).

be provided opportunities in special schools, including vocational training and also artistic opportunities for self-expression.

At the same time Maiguashca rejected several of the approaches that white *indigenistas* have proposed. He was unimpressed with the argument that compulsory military service, for example, would train and prepare the Indian for assimilated adult life. Furthermore, he opposed the sending of Indian children to schools with whites, arguing that in practice the Indians would be left out. He also believed that the Indian would not be transformed through mere contact with whites and thus was opposed to the extensive employment of Indians in domestic service. Ultimately, Maiguashca urged the Indian not to be ashamed of his heritage or race but to work to improve himself in society. He was told to initiate a campaign that would vindicate his personality and race, although it should be neither vengeful nor violent. As his fundamental thesis, he wrote: "My purpose is to put within the reach of the Indian all the elements that are necessary to bring about a species of social osmosis, letting the vernacular form of attitudes toward us disappear in the minds of the other social classes, a thing which would mean our true injection . . . into the Ecuadoran nation. My fundamental thesis is: ALL OR NOTHING."[28]

Space prohibits an exhaustive analysis of many other *indigenista* works. A number have been more scientific than rhetorical, however, and the study of the Indian in Ecuador has brought much wider knowledge and understanding, along with a series of specific proposals for the betterment of their situation. Luis Monsalve Pozo, for instance, has classified the geographic zones of Indians in Ecuador, buttressing his analysis with data on the number and location of different groups.[29] Víctor Gabriel Garcés has outlined a series of positive actions that should be taken by the national government,[30] and Angel Modesto Paredes has included in his writing an economic and sociological picture of the Indian and his world.[31] Gonzalo Rubio Orbe has contributed a series of works,[32]

28. *Ibid.*, p. 83.
29. Luis Monsalve Pozo, *El indio: Cuestiones de su vida y su pasión* (Cuenca: Editorial Austral, 1943).
30. Víctor Gabriel Garcés, *Indigenismo* (Quito: Casa de la Cultura Ecuatoriana, 1957).
31. Angel Modesto Parades, *Problemas etnológicos indoamericanos* (Quito: Casa de la Cultura Ecuatoriana, 1947).
32. Gonzalo Rubio Orbe, *Aspectos indígenas* (Quito: Casa de la Cultura Ecuatoriana, 1965); *Promociones indígenas en América* (Quito: Casa de la Cultural Ecuatoriana, 1957); and *Punyaro: Estudio de antropología social y cultural de una comunidad indígena y mestiza* (Quito: Casa de la Cultura Ecuatoriana, 1956).

including anthropological studies that have provided enlightenment as to the values, attitudes, and patterns of life in selected small communities. All of these contributions shared in assessing the moral and philosophical status of the Indian. There was agreement that the future development of Ecuador required a recognition and elevation of the Indian. While proposals for reform varied, all of them basically attempted to uphold the inherent ability of the Indian, the worth of his individual personality, and the necessity of preserving his cultural heritage while working for his incorporation into national life.

Indigenismo in Peru / If the output of *indigenista* writing in Ecuador has exceeded that of Bolivia, the quantity in Peru is even greater. In a broad sense, there are few Peruvian thinkers who have not dedicated themselves in one fashion or another to the problem of the Indian. Such major figures as González Prada, Deústua, and Haya de la Torre, although not primarily *indigenistas*, have nonetheless given considerable thought to the Indian and his role in national life. More narrowly defined, however, Peruvian Indianists are those whose major focus is directed toward this sector of the population. Among the first indications of concerned Indianism came early in the century with an intellectual group sometimes termed the *arielistas* (Arielists), after the work of the Uruguayan Rodó. Composed of those who gave precedence to spiritual over economic values, they believed that only a spiritual revival could bring about national progress. Economic development in itself was insufficient. It was the Rodó-like emphasis on the cultural legacy of Latin America which provided the basis for *arielista* thought.[33]

Reacting to the anarchistic pessimism of González Prada, who had derided the study of the past as fruitless, the *arielistas* undertook to seek and to identify in Peruvian history the lessons from which the future might benefit. As a result, "For the first time in Peruvian intellectual circles it became fashionable to seek a deep and integrated understanding of the national reality."[34] Concerned with the need to reincorporate the Indian masses into Peruvian life, the *arielistas* were outspoken in their belief that the latter embodied innate values of dignity and spiritual worth. This meant that it was an ethical as well as utilitarian responsibility of the ruling elite to encourage the assimilation of indige-

33. For a useful if brief discussion of the *arielistas,* see Frederick B. Pike, "The Old and the New APRA in Peru: Myth and Reality," *Inter-American Economic Affairs,* XVIII, No. 2 (Autumn 1964), 6–11. This also offers an interpretation of *aprismo* which differs sharply with the uncritical treatment by Harry Kantor.

34. *Ibid.,* p. 7.

nous Peruvians. The spiritual qualities of the Indians were an irreplaceable national asset, and material progress stood as a necessity if these people were to become Peruvian citizens in the fullest sense. The *arielistas* saw the task as more of a moral than a pragmatic duty. There was a resultant contrast to *indigenista* writers elsewhere, who often advocated the elevation of the Indian as a means of strengthening their country economically.

Given this ethical and spiritual concern, it is unsurprising that some, although not all of the *arielistas* were at the same time spokesmen of Catholicism. Outstanding examples were José de la Riva Agüero and Víctor Andrés Belaúnde,[35] although others such as Francisco García Calderón remained agnostics until their deaths. José de la Riva Agüero (1885–1944) was an historian of Peru's Generation of 1905 who, as a recognized advocate of Catholic thought, expounded a concerned paternalism toward the Indian. An erudite scholar whose whole life and being centered about his native Lima, Riva Agüero sought with encyclopaedic thoroughness to study Peru as an historical creation and a collective spiritual being. Critical of the *criollismo* that the Spanish race had established, he called for a national renaissance in which the Indian would have a share.[36] He imagined Cuzco, the former center of Incan glories, to be "the heart and symbol of Peru" and contrasted the achievements of the preconquest era with the contemporary state of misery in which the Indians lived. The ancient indigenous virtues had endured, he argued, and represented a potential source of national benefit. Unlike most of the *arielistas,* Riva Agüero held that the Indian problem was fundamentally economic. The solution, in his view, lay in economic progress for the mountainous regions; only thereby might true redemption be brought to the native population.[37]

The genuine if paternalistic social consciousness of the *arielista* writers anticipated the introduction of reforms from above. There was no intention of overturning the existing class system but rather an implicit narrowing of the gigantic gulf separating the Indians from *mestizos* or white Peruvians. Certainly none of these men followed González Prada

35. For Belaúnde's Catholicism, see the discussion of Christian Democracy in Chapter 12.

36. In his *Elogio* Riva Agüero painted a picture of the Inca Garcilaso de la Vega which extolled the indigenous characteristics of that great historical figure. See his *Obras completas,* 5 Vols. (Lima: Pontificia Universidad Católica del Perú, 1962).

37. Important individual works were *Por la verdad: La tradición y la patria* (*opúsculos*) (Lima: 1937), and *Civilización peruana: Época prehispánica* (Lima: Talleres gráficos de la Editorial "Lumen," 1937).

in advocating the salvation of the Indian through the destruction of the traditional ruling elite. What the *arielistas* desired was the encouragement of *mestizaje*, the blending of ethnic groups to construct a new kind of Peruvian. One of the most eminent men to present this view of Jorge Basadre, among the very greatest and most influential historians of twentieth-century Peru. Beginning as a young man in the decade of the 1920s, Basadre (1903————) demonstrated his philosophical views clearly in such works as *Perú: Problema y posibilidad* (1931) and *Meditaciones sobre el destino histórico del Perú* (1947).[38] Especially in the former, he examined national history through a study of evolving social classes and traditions, insisting upon the value of the past as a road toward the comprehension of future needs and difficulties.

For Basadre, history was not a mere recitation of dates and events but an account of the creation, development, and growth of Peru as an entity. Different historical epochs testified to the continuity of the territory and its people. The Spanish Conquest actually marked the birth of the Peruvian collectivity, since it has never before existed as such. The Indian, however, had been chained by the shackles of both colonial and republican forces. These, he argued, were responsible for the retarding effect on national life which the Indian unwittingly and unwillingly exercised. In what was at the time an unorthodox position, Basadre explained that the written history of the state was not that of the Peruvian nation. The latter demanded an understanding of all human factors, among which the Indians were important. Basadre criticized the elite for lacking the social conscience that should have been a part of its legacy. Among its errors had been the failure to recognize the part that the native races might play. Basadre's lasting fame in Peruvian intellectual annals will stem from contributions far more extensive than his *indigenismo*, but he remains an important figure in the evolution of national concern over the Indian.

In a very real sense, it was the accumulated influence of the *arielistas* and the declining neo-Spencerians which led to the rapid growth of Indianist literature. Among its many more recent exponents, a representative sampling would include José Uriel García, Hildebrando Castro Pozo, and Luis E. Valcárcel. García (1884–1965), who taught at the University of Cuzco, best expressed his views in *El nuevo indio: Ensayos indianistas sobre la sierra superuana*,[39] published in 1930. This noted

---

38. Jorge Basadre, *Perú: Problema y posibilidad* (Lima: Librería Francesa Científica y Casa Editorial E. Rosay, 1931); and *Meditaciones sobre el destino histórico del Perú* (Lima: Ediciones Huascarán, 1947).

39. José Uriel García, *El nuevo indio: Ensayos indianistas sobre la sierra superuana*, 2d ed. (Cuzco: H. G. Rozas Sucesores, Librería e Imprenta, 1937).

writer presented a new interpretation of the Indian while arguing the necessity of creating a cultural synthesis capable of eliminating race as a traditional limiting factor to national progress. García postulated that his biological creation of a "new Indian" would be a productive vindication of Peru's native races. Although praising the qualities of the Indian as he presently existed, García insisted that the future depended upon a new racial mixture that would assimilate the best qualities of both the European and the Indian heritages.

> The traditional Indian, the same as the *"mestizo"* and the *"criollo"*—those racial fruits which appeared from the discovery of our America—are merely superimposed humanities. . . . Without doubt the world of the "Indian," of the *"mestizo,"* and of the *"criollo"* lived on, as did the creative impulse and spiritual force stemming from their corresponding blood, but all that was produced is simply the traditional, and the man who overcomes these individual [organic] simplicities will be the creator of the future; he will be the synthesis. . . .
> While "race" lives on as "blood," tradition endures. In America blood is only tradition. But when it grows in a spiritual sense . . . culture will advance. Blood limits and separates; the spirit unifies . . . .[40]

Hildebrando Castro Pozo (1890–1945), a native of Piura and lawyer by profession, was a Marxist who for many years served as a leader of the Peruvian Socialists. His major works were *Nuestra comunidad indígena* (1924) and *Del ayllu al cooperativismo socialista* (1936).[41] In the former he described the indigenous community as socially *sui generis,* representing a form that had not varied basically since the precolonial era. Carefully detailing the communal institutions of the Indians, he wrote of their social customs, agricultural methods, system of irrigation, and of their form of land ownership and property. Despite the degradation of servitude under the *patrones* of the large *haciendas,* the Indian in his own community had retained his cultural heritage and traditional social values. Thus he still bore the ancient traditions of his collective organization of labor, his sociopolitical practices, his arts, songs, and superstitious folklore. All such values should be retained, and in later years Castro Pozo formulated specific proposals along these lines.

In *Del ayllu al cooperativismo socialista* he outlined his conviction that the solution lay in the proper handling of the land problem. After

40. *Ibid.,* pp. 6–7.
41. Hildebrando Castro Pozo, *Nuestra comunidad indígena* (Lima: n.p., 1924); and *Del ayllu al cooperativismo socialista* (Lima: P. Barrantes Castro, 1936).

a devastating critique of colonial and capitalist systems, he postulated a form of modern co-operativism, thereby giving "a new ideological content to the conscience of our social masses." By so doing, "the future of the social masses . . . is intimately tied to the country's agrarian collectivism, the normal biological unfolding of which was brutally disrupted by the Spanish conquest."[42] This judgment was, for Castro Pozo, ideologically consistent with historical materialism. Marxist philosophy provided a useful framework for his proposals, and he believed that the result was an appropriate application of Marxism to Peruvian reality. This meant to him the proper adaptation of old sociocultural forms "with which, across the centuries, the spirit of 'señor don Carlos Marx' will rejuvenate that of the ayllus."[43]

In Luis E. Valcárcel (1891———), an exponent of cultural anthropological analysis, *indigenismo* found one of its most learned and articulate spokesmen. The author of numerous ethnic studies of ancient Peru,[44] he was an ardent defender of the Indian, penning strongly polemical defenses of indigenous virtues in *Tempestad en los Andes* (1927) and the two-volume *Mirador indio: Apuntes para una filosofía de lacultura incaica* (1937 and 1941).[45] Beginning with a radical negation of traditional paternalistic approaches, his thesis held that Peru was fundamentally an ancient land. Its highest values, therefore, were those of its original inhabitants and their direct descendants. Such events as the conquest and colonial rule were but passing episodes in a lengthy history. The great unity of Peru lay in its native peoples, and future greatness depended upon an extension and continuation of fundamental and overriding social and spiritual values originating with the Indians. The only acceptable action was therefore a total vindication and restoration of the native. "Peru is Indian. So many centuries are needed for the realization of this primordial fact. A profound evolution in thought has been necessary in order that one might proclaim this fact."[46]

The *sierra* on which the Indian lived was the most important region of the country. As long as it was ruled from the coast, necessary social

42. Castro Pozo, *Del ayllu al cooperativismo socialista,* p. 210.
43. *Ibid.,* p. 212.
44. Luis E. Valcárcel, *Del ayllu al imperio: La evolución político social en el antiguo Perú y otros estudios* (Lima: Editorial Garcilaso, 1925); *Historia de la cultura antigua del Perú,* 2 Vols. (Lima: Imprenta del Museo Nacional, 1943 and 1949); and *Etnohistoria del Perú antiguo,* 2d ed. (Lima: Universidad Nacional Mayor de San Marcos, Departamento de Publicaciones, 1964).
45. Luis E. Valcárcel, *Tempestad en los Andes* (Lima: Biblioteca Amauta, 1927); and *Mirador indio: Apuntes para una filosofía de la cultura incaica,* 2 Vols. (Lima: Imprenta del Museo nacional, 1937 and 1941).
46. Valcárcel, *Tempestad en los Andes,* pp. 116–17.

and political changes would be impossible. It was the survival of the ethical values of the Incan society which constituted the moral fibre of the contemporary indigenous masses. Therefore, in a frankly racist formulation, Valcárcel opposed the process of *mestizaje* which some thinkers advocated. "The collectivities with a strong *mestizo* element— Indians, negroes, yellow, and black all mixed in—are the most retarded in cultural development, in constant political disequilibrium and with a distinct inferiority on moral indices. Those places, like the United States, in which the races live without intermingling, but with an equailty of rights and without prejudices, demonstrate their effective capacity for a democratic organization and an elevated level of culture and morality."[47] Arguing elsewhere in defense of his beliefs, Valcárcel declared, "Defending the purity of Indian collectivities from any abusive *mestizo* or white intromission, it is possible to maintain that the human who would [thereby] be saved would not be destroyed by oppression, vices, or the infirmities introduced from the discovery and conquest of this hemisphere."[48]

In a later work,[49] a matured Valcárcel was less extreme in his views, Nonetheless, he continued to insist that the soul and spirit of Peru was Indian. The latter should therefore be protected against the incursions of foreign, e.g. non-Indian cultural influences. He conceded a willingness to adopt useful technical and scientific achievements from other peoples but never the religious, political, philosophical, or juridical forms. Any acceptance of the superficial benefits of the Western way of life would introduce harmful effects into the ancient Peruvian legacy. To promote the proper revival and restoration of the indigenous masses and their values, a massive educational program was required, one that might assimilate useful elements of modern life while preserving true Peruvian culture. Linked to this was "a radical agrarian reform" that would redistribute lands, but on a collective or group rather than an individual basis. Ultimately, this would enhance the movement toward that revitalized Peruvian nationality that might then take its proud place alongside its fellow republics.

Peruvian *indigenismo* reached beyond the orthodox boundaries of cultural anthropology and philosophical speculation. Typical of this breadth was the artistic influence of José Sabrogal and the archaeological pioneering of Julio C. Tello. Sabrogal created his own authentic artistic school

47. *Ibid.*, p. 120.
48. Valcárcel, *Mirador indio*, pp. 51–52.
49. Valcárcel, *Ruta cultural del Perú* (México: Fondo de Cultura Económica, 1945).

with disciples and an aesthetic creed of its own. While Sabrogal has achieved personal fame from his painting, his influence has extended to other spheres. A discerning observer who traveled extensively through the Andes, he created a form of popular art that had won wide acceptance in Peru. His artistry was complemented by literary essays, and in recent years his impact has also been felt in the plastic arts, where his telluric and *indigenista* orientation looms large. Julio C. Tello's contributions have come from his lifelong uncovering of the remainders of past civilizations. Such findings as the Chavin relics and the excavation of the necropolis of Paracas were followed by major discoveries of *huacas* and other artefacts near Pachacamac, Lima, and Cajamarca. The author of systematic studies of the ancient coastal cultures, he has been justly regarded as the father of Peruvian archaeology. Tello has helped to promote a major revival of archaeological investigations by both Peruvians and foreigners. In theoretical terms he has suggested a cyclical view of the civilizations of antiquity, described within a framework of national unity and the contrasting territorial regions. He has viewed the early forms of culture as proceeding from the jungle area to the mountain regions and finally descending to the coastal plain. For Tello, it was the inhabitant of the last who achieved the greatest spiritual development.

Through the years Peruvian *indigenismo* has emerged as a movement of social conscience which exalts the value of the native peoples as the purest and most genuine expression of *peruanidad*, of true nationality. While the approach has varied, running the gamut of extremes from an elitist paternalism to a demand for violent warfare against white oppression, there has been a consensus on the importance of the Indian to Peru. Moreover, there has been a common linking of his future development to the progress of the country; the former is regarded as a necessary precondition for the latter. For some Indianists, this can be realized through civil and penal reforms or more enlightened legislation. Others stress agricultural development and economic modernization, while some are more attracted to educational measures as promising a moral and spiritual awakening of the Indian. In any event, all of these attitudes have influenced the thinking of urban intellectuals and the landowning aristocracy. The search for a systematic political doctrine embodying necessary governmental policies and actions has endured since the 1920s and is best exemplified by the teachings of *aprismo* and, more recently, of Acción Popular. It is to an elaboration of these ideas and proposals that we must now turn.

Peru and Aprismo

Few political movements have been as embattled and controversial as Peru's Alianza Popular Revolucionaria Americana (APRA), known in more recent years as the Partido Aprista Peruano (PAP). Today, after more than forty years' existence and the pronouncement of countless obituaries by its opponents and critics, the APRA remains one of the fundamental components in any equation of Peruvian politics. All of this is in defiance of the fact that never has the party won full control of national politics. Perhaps the most self-consciously doctrinal political group in the hemisphere—with the exception of the Radical Left—it is precisely on ideological grounds that *aprismo* has been subjected to the most intensive and heated analysis. Moreover, the movement politically is no less controversial than its almost legendary founder and leader, Víctor Raúl Haya de la Torre. An extraordinarily prolific writer of great intellectual curiosity, the task of analyzing comprehensively his philosophical contributions is staggering. Only the barest outlines of *aprista* ideology can be presented in this space, and many pertinent areas of controversy can only be suggested in passing.

The Formative Years and Original Programs of APRISMO / Víctor Raúl Haya de la Torre (1895———) was born of a prominent family in the northern coastal city of Trujillo. As a university student at Lima's San Marcos, he became a leader of the restless discontent provoked by the hemispheric movement of university reform and aggravated social conditions following World War I. The student federation, of which Haya became president in 1920, undertook the reorganization of student-university relations and the encouragement of the nascent labor movement in Lima. It also established a series of adult education centers known as the Universidades Populares González Prada, providing training for rank-and-file labor members. Inevitably, the students adopted a position of defiance toward the dictatorial government of President Augusto B. Leguía, and open rebellion was sparked by the effort of the latter to negotiate a concordat with the Vatican and to dedicate the republic "to the Sacred Heart of Jesus." Haya was arrested for his leadership of a national protest movement and, shortly thereafter, was deported from Peru in the company of other student leaders. After traveling to both Europe and the United States, he proceeded to Mexico on the invitation of José Vasconcelos. There, in May, 1924, he proclaimed the doctrine of the Alianza Popular Revolucionaria Americana.

As announced at that time, the program of the APRA had five points. These were first published by Haya in a 1926 English journal under the title "What is the APRA?" and later were developed in a series of essays, first written in 1928, which appeared eight years later in a volume called El antimperialismo y el Apra.[50] The five points were the following: (1) action against Yankee imperialism; (2) for the political unity of Latin America; (3) for the nationalization of land and industry; (4) for the internationalization of the Panama Canal; (5) for solidarity with all oppressed peoples and classes of the world. The first point represented to aprismo Latin America's most pressing problem. Imperialistic penetration of the region, especially by the United States, was bringing about foreign domination of the area's industry and agriculture. Given the nature of international capitalism, Latin America found itself a weak economic dependency, unable to benefit from the fruits of its labors. The improper introduction of foreign capital served only the interests of industrial capitalism, not the masses themselves. As Haya wrote elsewhere, "What aprismo considers ruinous for Peru is that in the name of our need for foreign capital, the country is converted into a slave of this capital, and . . . becomes its servant. . . . A country without its own economy and subject only to dependence on foreign capital is nothing more than a colony. With a nation subordinated to the yoke of foreign capital, which exploits the workers, the merchant, the small proprietor, the taxpayer and the consumer, the State lacks all support to defend its sovereignty and becomes an instrument of foreign capital which directs the economy of the country."[51]

Having established the dangers of imperialism, Haya and the apristas suggested by their second point a means of opposing it. Concluding that significant outside help was improbable, the APRA therefore advocated Latin-American unification. Viewing the region as a natural entity, the party argued that existing political boundaries were merely arbitrary lines, serving no practical purpose. Despite individual national differences, they held that the overriding problems of the hemisphere were parallel and that the peoples were united by common bonds of history and tradition. Unification would promote rapid industrial development, thereby raising the standard of living. Collectively rich in natural resources and sufficiently populated to provide a mass market, Latin America could also develop subregional specialization through a carefully planned program of economic priorities. In practical terms, the APRA

50. Víctor Raúl Haya de la Torre, El antimperialismo y el Apra (Santiago: Ediciones Ercilla, 1936).
51. Ibid., pp. 147–48.

believed the first step should be the creation of customs union, from which the movement to total unity would evolve. Over forty years after first presenting their concept of unification, the *apristas* in 1967 would hail the results of a hemispheric conference of presidents at Punta del Este as committing all the countries to this *aprista* plank.

The demand for the nationalization of land and industry was justified both as an anti-imperialist device and as a proper means of organizing the state. Although the detailed form of nationalization was not made clear at this early point, the commitment was unqualified and provided an illustration of Marxist influences—about which more later. Nationalization was seen as embracing a system of extensive state ownership over economically significant enterprise. Foreign property would not revert to domestic private hands but rather to the state, thus mitigating the weaknesses of existing capitalism. This would lead to the situation Haya later outlined in *El antimperialismo y el Apra*. The new organization of the state was compared to the "state capitalism" developed in Germany during World War I. "In the Anti-Imperialist State, a state of defensive economic war, it is also indispensable to limit private initiative and control the production and circulation of wealth. The Anti-Imperialist State, which must *direct* the national economy, will have to deny individual or collective rights in the economic field when the use of these rights implies an imperialist danger."[52]

The two final points of the early "maximum program" of *aprismo* underlined its explicit intention of presenting proposals with hemispheric applicability. Opposition to North American control of the Panama Canal, consistent with the demands of many who criticized the United States presence there, argued that the internationalization of the canal would contribute to Latin-American unification and the struggle against Yankee imperialism. This led in turn to the final point, an emotional statement suggesting a sentiment of kinship with the colonial peoples of the world. The *apristas* did not offer specific policies for implementation. The implications of this initial APRA program were described by Haya de la Torre in the following terms:

> Our historic experience in Latin America, and especially the very important contemporary Marxian experience, shows us that the immense power of Yankee imperialism cannot be confronted without the unity of the Latin American peoples. But since this unity is conspired against jointly by our governing classes and imperialism, and since the former aid the latter, the State, an instrument of oppression of one class by another, becomes an

52. *Ibid.*, pp. 138–39.

arm of our national ruling classes and imperialism to exploit our producing classes and to keep our peoples divided. Consequently, the fight against our governing classes is indispensable; political power must be captured by the producers; production must be socialized, and Latin America must constitute a Federation of States. This is the only road to victory over imperialism, [applying] the political objectives of APRA as the International Revolutionary Anti-Imperialist Party.[53]

While the *apristas* have retained the five-point "maximum program" through the years, Haya has introduced two alterations. One of these was a substitution, in 1941, of the term "interamericanization" for "internationalization" in discussing the Panama Canal. Although the original term seemingly implied a form of collective world control, this point was never clarified. The tacit *aprista* preference was for a hemispheric arrangement; the 1941 rewording simply recognized formally the intention of diminishing the United States role while improving the defense of continental interests through practical Latin-American control. The other change in the original program was more significant, calling for the deletion of "Yankee" form the anti-imperialism of the first point. As the prominent *aprista*, Luis Alberto Sánchez, explained, there had never been a thought of combatting *only* North American imperialism while ignoring that of other foreign nations. But since the overriding imperialism of the 1920s had appeared to be Yankee, it was natural to apply the term. A decade later this circumstance had been changed, and the party decided to omit the "Yankee" reference.[54] Parenthetically, it should be noted that this alteration also reflected the shift in attitudes toward the United States which the APRA experienced with the approach of World War I and its political implications for Latin America.

Haya de la Torre continued to travel through the final years of the 1920s, expounding his views in hemispheric terms. He made few explicit proposals regarding Peru in particular until returning home to organize his 1931 presidential campaign. At the first National Aprista Congress that followed Haya's arrival in Lima, the party adopted for the campaign its immediate or "minimum program." With minor exceptions, this has remained the basic formulation of the party's domestic policy ever since. Ratified at both clandestine and legal congresses through the years, it outlined a program that it hails as being a true reflection of Peruvian conditions. Basic to such policy recommendations was the view of na-

53. *Ibid.*, p. 37.
54. Luis Alberto Sánchez, *Haya de la Torre y el APRA: Crónica de un hombre y un partido* (Santiago: Editorial del Pacífico, 1955), pp. 152–53.

tional reality that Haya held. During a major campaign speech on August 31, 1931, he described the picture before him. Peru, he declared, reflected the fact that independence from Spain was achieved by a *latifundista* class lacking in ideological direction. As a consequence, the defeat of the Spanish meant the consolidation rather than liquidation of feudalism. Republican government in Peru had proven unable to grasp the meaning of economic reality, remaining instead the instrument of a small and selfish oligarchy. The state had merely paid lip service to the formalities of democracy while preserving the inequities of the traditional system.

Peru's dominant group was the only one to have a clearly defined concept of its own interests, and these were naturally reflected through the governments. Haya demanded the creation of a legitimately representative national state that would recognize and deal with the needs of the three oppressed sectors—the *campesinos*, the proletariat, and the growing urban middle class. Promising to be the instrument of a popular alliance symbolizing the interests of these groups, Haya became the first national political leader to pledge the establishment of a regime founded on social classes and interests. Thus, he affirmed that *aprismo* was not a sectarian movement but rather an organic entity representing the strength of popular forces. *Aprismo* meant a national phenomenon that symbolized a new and revitalized Peru. In these terms, Haya suggested in part the vision from which he and the party had arrived at the specific pledges that constituted its "minimum program." Only a few of the highlights can be mentioned here.

Proposing a transformation of the country, the APRA called for a democratic, anti-imperialist state based upon the three oppressed classes mentioned above. The *aprista* government would first undertake a careful and systematic collection of statistical information, after which the convening of a special economic congress would devise a rational national plan of production, distribution, and consumption. Peru would be divided into appropriate geographical regions through which political and economic rule would be decentralized. Each would enjoy administrative autonomy in formulating its individual economic programs, while the national government would provide technical advice and assistance. Calling themselves "anticentralists," the *apristas* promised thereby to repudiate the overwhelming domination of Lima and *limeño* interests in national policy making. Once the system of regionalism was established, a reorganized unicameral legislature would be created on the basis of economic rather than territorial constituencies. Within this distinctly Peruvian arrangement, the *apristas* would move in the direction of modified socialism. Both Haya de la Torre and his close associate Manuel

Seoane referred to the ultimate goal of "state capitalism," visualizing the role of the state as one of planning and stimulating economic development. This meant state ownership of key economic sectors and the establishment of a variety of co-operative enterprises. The result would appear to be a variant of socialism permitting the operation of free enterprise in selected spheres of activity. Nationalization with compensation was regarded as instrumental for the formation of the *aprista* state. Foreign investment would be permitted, but only after careful scrutiny and continuing state supervision.

Agricultural development was basic to economic progress, and therefore was regarded as an area of special interest. The 1931 "Plan de acción"[55] enumerated a five-point program that focused on such matters as production, colonization, agricultural education, and agrarian public administration. Closely related to this was a commitment to assimilate the Indian into national life. Reflecting a form of *indigenismo* that praised the qualities of the Indian while recognizing the degradation of his subsistence-level existence, the "Plan de acción" offered six specific proposals. These included the creation of a national Bureau of Indian Affairs, the evaluation and census of community property, the surveying of boundaries and titles to property, and the expropriation of *haciendas* bordering on communal Indian lands. The redemption of the Indian was seen as necessary for the eradication of economic injustices. Living as if alien to Peru, the Indian was to be uplifted from his traditional condition of exploitation so that he might be incorporated into the life of the republic. This problem, for the APRA, was largely economic rather than racial or even social.

Education was viewed as an important means of redeeming the indigenous masses. The APRA advocated the creation of a system of special "rural schools" in which the Indian child might learn practical techniques preparing him for entry into modern life. Instruction would include not only reading and writing but also improved agricultural methods, notions of conservation, and such basics as personal hygiene and ethical behavior. Indian teachers would be employed, and the curricula would be drawn up with a mind to regional traits and customs. Small industries and native art would be encouraged by the state, and a system of Indian co-operatives would be introduced. To those who called them Indian nationalists, the *apristas* retorted that they were committed to social justice for all Peruvians, which obviously included

55. Bearing the full title "Plan de acción inmediata o programa mínimo," this is found in Víctor Raúl Haya de la Torre, *Política aprista* (Lima: Editorial Cooperativa Aprista Atahualpa, 1933), pp. 9–29.

the Indians, constituting as they did the largest single sector of the population.

> Our Party cannot seek a retrogression of history nor an elimination of all that is not Indian in Peru. We aspire to the material and spiritual reincorporation of the Indian into national life, and to the reappearance of the eternal virtues of the Peruvian race. . . . We do not renounce European culture nor the contribution which the whites have brought to our soil. But we repudiate the colonial mentality which until now has adopted the anti-Peruvian attitude of scorning the Indians or whatever is Indian. We believe that a Peru should rise which assimilates within its new national features what is ethnically and culturally modern, uniting it with what is permanent in the imperial traditions.[56]

Related to *aprista* policies for the rejuvenation of the Indian was Haya's own personal image of Latin America and its peoples. As expressed in *A dónde Va Indoamérica?*[57] a collection of writings from the years 1927–31, there was substantial importance to the substitution of "Indoamerica" for more common terminology. This new term was regarded as the most descriptive way of stressing the indigenous component along with the extracontinental element. To say either "Hispanic America" or "Ibero-America" was to imply colonial connotations, while he called "Latin America" a French term and considered "Pan America" an imperialistic label. "Indoamerica," wrote Haya, permits a clearer understanding of the region, as well as being useful for the outside world. Haya has emphasized throughout the bulk of his writings the uniqueness of Indoamerica while criticizing those who would look primarily to Europe for guidance and inspiration. It was important to bring about a mental emancipation from traditional stereotypes, just as *aprismo* was intended as a distinctively regional effort to formulate a program for the entire continent. Political unification was therefore intended to create a United States of Indoamerica which might collaborate in the resolution of mutual difficulties while dealing with North America on a basis of equality.

The Marxist Bases of Aprista Leadership / During his wanderings of the 1920s, Haya de la Torre attended a number of Communist

---

56. El Buro de Redactores de "Cuaderno Aprista," *40 preguntas y 40 repuestas*, p. 28, as quoted in Harry Kantor, *The Ideology and Program of the Peruvian Aprista Movement* (Berkeley and Los Angeles: University of California Press, 1953), pp. 86–87.

57. Víctor Raúl Haya de la Torre, *A dónde va Indoamérica?* (Santiago: Ediciones Ercilla, 1935).

gatherings, including the Fifth Congress of the Communist International. As a Marxist-oriented revolutionary leader, he engaged for a time in a flirtation with Russian-style communism. The many accounts of these years by both friends and critics have never satisfactorily clarified his involvement. Undoubtedly Haya's own ambitions, as well as his personal independence and an ambivalent relationship to José Carlos Mariátegui, contributed to his ideological development of a distinctive, doctrinally unorthodox, Marxism. Before returning home to campaign for the presidency in 1931, he had made clear his choice of a native Peruvian variant of socialism. Whatever the nature of *aprista* revisionism in more recent years, the bulk of Haya's earlier writings were clearly Marxist-oriented. The result was an effort to adapt certain elements of Marxist dogma for the development of a socialist system appropriate to Indoamerican conditions.

As early as 1928, Haya de la Torre declared, "The doctrine of APRA means within Marxism a new and methodical confrontation of Indo-american reality with the theses that Marx postulated for Europe and that emanated from the European reality in which he lived and studied." Furthermore, "We accept in Marxist terms the division of society into classes and the struggle of those classes as an expression of the process of History."[58] In 1933, he also stated categorically that "our party is Marxist. And therefore I am in a position to declare that, being Marxist, its present doctrinaire position corresponds perfectly to the conditions of our social and economic reality."[59] For Haya, in short, the commitment to a Marxian intellectual framework was given; his task was its adaptation for Peru and Indoamerica. He gave particular emphasis to the ideological importance of the concept of imperialism. Of crucial importance to *aprismo*, it was expressed thus: "In Europe imperialism is 'the last stage of capitalism'—meaning the culmination of a succession of capitalist stages—which is characterized by the emigration or exportation of capital and the conquest of markets and of productive zones of primary products toward countries with incipient economies. But in Indoamerica what in Europe is 'the last stage of capitalism' becomes the first. For our peoples, immigrating and imported capital establishes the initial stage of its modern capitalist age. The economic and social history of Europe is not repeated in Indoamerica."[60] While imperialism was the final stage of capitalism in the developed countries, then, just the reverse was true in such underdeveloped areas as Indoamerica. Consequently,

58. Haya de la Torre, *El antimperialismo*, pp. 117, 119.
59. Haya de la Torre, *Política aprista*, p. 172.
60. Haya de la Torre, *El antimperialismo*, p. 51.

the weak nations should actually encourage the advent of imperialism in order to foster the conditions from which a new proletariat might prepare the way for socialist revolution. The people would only be ripe for the latter after having experienced capitalist imperialism and a subsequent growth of political consciousness.

This has long stood as one of the more intriguing of Haya's formulations. Certainly there was relevance to the contention that the existence of an organized and politicized, if downtrodden, urban proletariat in Europe stood in contrast with the situation in much of Latin America. In a country such as Peru, Haya argued that a strict interpretation of Marxism would imply that, because of the weak and diffuse nature of a backward proletariat, true socialism would be impossible. Hence, his reformulation of the stages and preconditions for revolution had a basis in Peruvian reality. At the same time, this left him in a contradictory position as an avowed champion of anti-imperialism. As Pike has appropriately remarked, "Just how Haya de la Torre proposed to cooperate with United States imperialism, which in effect he had identified with Yankee investments, as a means of developing capitalism in Peru and thus hastening the socialist revolution, while at the same time urging the immediate end of imperialism, which he so often did, is not quite clear."[61] If imperialism was the necessary first stage of capitalism, it is hard to reconcile with this his oft-expressed concern over the increasing pace of North American investments. It was perhaps more than coincidental that, through the decade of the 1930s, Haya and the *apristas* were more articulate in their reiterated demands for anti-imperialist revolution than they were in discussing the "last stage-first stage" theory.

Throughout his long and durable career, Haya has paid tribute to his philosophical debt to Hegel. As early as 1927 he proclaimed his affinity for Hegelianism, advocating the value of the dialectical approach. It was through the Hegelian concept of the competing interplay of social forces that the ultimate classless society might evolve. Among other things, this implied a willingness to accept violent measures; for over three decades, one of the sharpest criticisms of many anti-*apristas* has been the contention that the party willingly accepts violence as an instrument to achieve its goals. There seemed little ambiguity in Haya's 1927 statement that within all societies, "the classes and systems evolve, deny-

61. Pike, "The Old and the New APRA in Peru," p. 20. For a current and incisive reassessment of *aprismo* by a graduate student at The University of North Carolina at Chapel Hill, see Richard L. Clinton, "APRA: A Party of Sorrow and Acquainted with Grief," to appear in the *Journal of Inter-American Studies and World Affairs* in 1970.

ing each other mutually [through the dialectical process of thesis and antithesis]. Out of the conflict emerges the new society [synthesis], the fruit of violence. Contrary forces can only be overcome by revolution."[62] It must be noted that for years the *aprista* leadership has heatedly and consistently denied its acceptance of violent measures. At the same time, the party *has* been involved in violent activity on more than one occasion, especially during the domestic turmoil of late 1948. The tenor of many *aprista* writings in the early years suggests that violence might indeed be permissible under extraordinary conditions.

Ideologically, the importance of Marxist thought clearly overshadows that of any other doctrine, although there is occasional evidence of other influences, particularly from Manuel González Prada. One of the best expositions of the affinity for Marxism is that of the Peruvian party's most dedicated North American student, Harry Kantor.

> As the Apristas understood Marx's philosophy it included four parts: dialectical materialism, the materialistic conception of history, Marxian economics, and the idea that there was a certain evolutionary development in history which proceeds almost despite men's wishes. Of these four the Apristas never made much use of Marxian economics, but the other three were of great importance in the development of their ideas. Dialectical materialism gave them the idea that everything in the world is in a state of flux. The materialistic conception of history impressed upon them the importance of economic factors in the development of society. From their understanding of Marxism also came their view of man. They saw man as the product of his environment who would be superior or inferior, good or bad, better or worse, depending upon how the forces within society affected him.[63]

Aprista Revisionism and "Historical Space-Time" / Notwithstanding the occasional inconsistencies or internal contradictions of Haya's thinking during his earlier years, it contributed to the formulation of a party program that, for many observers, represented a fairly original and imaginative message for the Peruvian people. However, the decade of the 1930s brought a gradual shift in *aprista* ideology, and this was reflected in Haya's writings from that time forward. Changing hemispheric conditions had some influence, for the implementation of Franklin D. Roosevelt's Good Neighbor Policy brought both material and intangible alterations to the role played by the United States. Not only was "Yankee" dropped as an adjectival modifier of imperialism in the first point of the "maximum program," but the development of a new

62. Quoted in Pike, "The Old and the New APRA," p. 24.
63. Kantor, *Peruvian Aprista Movement,* p. 24.

industrial philosophy by foreign investors and internal economic growth in Latin America seemed to draw the sting from old charges of imperialist penetration. The rise of fascism in Europe was also a factor, and *aprista* attacks on the United States were muted. Haya wrote in a 1940 letter that

> . . . the *apristas* have not changed their attitude but—fortunately—the government of the United States has. The imperialist policy of the "Big Stick" of the Republicans changed radically with the arrival of President Roosevelt. And we have the right to believe that this change in attitude was much influenced by all of the anti-imperialists of our great Indoamerican nation. . . .
> We *apristas* have seen with profound sympathy this modification of North American government policy. . . . And even though the phenomenon of imperialism in its roots and its economic phase still exists, it has been profoundly modified by the "good neighbor" policy. . . .[64]

The revision of *aprista* attitudes toward the United States proceeded further with the coming of World War II, and this led to the publication in 1941 of the so-called Plan for the Affirmation of Democracy in America. Declaring that Indo-American unity was even more necessary in the face of Nazi aggression, the plan set forth several specific actions as a means of improving relations with the United States. The *apristas* called for creation of an American Committee for the Defense of Democracy with delegates of democratic political parties as well as government officials in attendance. Each country was also to convene its own special economic congress, representative of all relevant sectors, which would formulate national plans that might be co-ordinated at the hemispheric level. An Inter-American Economic Congress would hold supervisory powers whereby such measures as a unified system of currency and a series of export-import banks might be created. Additional proposals included the creation of an Inter-American Tariff Union and the equalization of transit fees in the Panama Canal. Significantly, a fruitful and vigorous collaboration between Indo-America and the United States was anticipated.[65] This revision of hemispheric policy, especially with regard to the North American presence, was more tactical than doctrinal; furthermore, it was a not illogical consequence of the *aprista* interpretation of the changing nature of imperialism. However, Haya de la Torre was also moving toward a recasting of his basic ideology, and this took form in his exposition of the theory of "Historical Space-Time."

Haya was gradually moving away from the Hegelian dialectic and unalloyed determinism. With anti-imperialism no longer the *apristas'* clarion call for action, it became necessary to go beyond Marxist theory. The Peruvian therefore began to develop a theory of relativity that, borrowing from concepts of the physical sciences, could serve to justify changes of party policy. Haya's intellectual curiosity about such notions was not new; as far back as 1928 he had written about the relativity inherent in basic historical and geographical factors. And even before that, he had attacked "the false concept of untouchable truths and of eternal principles in this hour of profound scientific revolution and of the uncompromising relativist current, the precursor of new and different fundamental affirmations of all kinds."[66] His subsequent interest and readings of such men as Spengler and Toynbee led to an increasingly strong proclivity for the concept of relativism. This reached its fullest exposition with the publication of a series of essays in 1948 under the title *Espacio-tiempo histórico.*[67]

Transposing philosophical terms derived from Einstein's treatment of natural phenomena, Haya de la Torre ambitiously undertook the statement of a new and distinctive interpretation of social forces. His central thesis postulated that there are varying factors of historical space-time which correspond to the differences of world cultures. As an alleged outgrowth of the Marxist interpretation of history, the theory of historical space-time is relativity as applied to history. The process of world development had progressed beyond that observed by Marx in nineteenth-century Europe, and the contemporary scientific revolution was affecting the very foundations of human knowledge, for it was bringing "the negation of the great scientific truths, held unimpeachable until now, upon which we have erected our conception of the world, of nature, of the cosmos, of time, and of space."[68] This revolution had also extended to the social sciences, according to Haya, and the ideas developed by Einstein and others should appropriately be included in a philosophy of history. In the theory of historical space-time, he argued, history becomes a universal co-ordination of processes, each of these inseparable from its own space, time, and motion.

The ingredients of his concept were termed historical space and his-

66. Víctor Raúl Haya de la Torre, *Espacio-tiempo histórico* (Lima: Ediciones La Tribuna, 1948), p. xvi.
67. *Ibid.*
68. *Ibid.*, p. 87.

torical time. The former was the relation of space with the given population as it develops group consciousness, comprising the sum of geography,
of man, his ethnic composition, and his interrelationship with social
awareness. Historical time is the stage of a people's socioeconomic, political, and cultural development that flows from its relations with historical
space. Historical space and historical time are inextricably linked with
one another to include everything that affects the life of a social group.
In each historical space-time, there is an innate rhythm determined by
the collective consciousness of its own development. The world is divided
into "continental peoples," including Indo-America, the United States,
western Europe, Russia, China, and the Arab states. One cannot speak
of a single universal scheme—as did Marx—because history is a series
of processes, varying greatly from one "continental people" to another.
Indo-America therefore stands apart and, as the *apristas* had always
maintained, could not expect the same historical economic development
through which Europe passed. Once again, *aprismo* concluded that new
political formulae were requisite for the solution of uniquely Indo-American problems.[69]

The *apristas* interpreted the relativism of historical space-time as justifying their own unique comprehension of Indo-American problems. Presumably, only Haya's philosophical insights permitted a clear and pure
vision of social reality. Others failed to appreciate the latter, as for
example the orthodox Marxists who still insisted, from their European
orientation, that the fundamental approach must be based upon the
fact of imperialism constituting the final stage of capitalism. Reiterating
the lengthy exposition of his views, Haya concluded in the following
terms: "Each historical space-time forms a system of cultural coordination, a geographical stage, and an historical event which determine the
relationship of thought and 'becoming' inseparable from the spatial concept and from the chronological stage. . . . And if a people reaches
cultural adulthood only when it achieves consciousness of its own process
of economic and social development, that consciousness is only complete
when it discovers, with the passing of its history, the non-transferable
and indivisible nature of its own space-time. And this is the background
of the philosophy of *aprismo* in attempting an interpretation of the
'People-Continent of Indoamerica'."[70]

The next major work by Haya appeared in 1957 under the title
Toynbee frente a los panoramas de la historia: Espacio-tiempo histórico

69. Consult *ibid.*, pp. 21–100.
70. Víctor Raúl Haya de la Torre, *Y después de la guerra ¿qué?* (Lima:
Ed. Talleres PTCM, 1946), p. 182.

Americano.[71] Again putting together the theses of earlier articles and essays, he attempted to demonstrate the compatibility of historical space-time with the major positions of the British historian and philosopher. Accepting Toynbee's "challenge and response" theory on the origin of civilizations, Haya observed that they came into being as the result of man's clash with his environment. This was the way in which the hemisphere had emerged as a civilization. In North America the backward and nomadic natives had been unable to confront the geographical challenge successfully, and the area therefore evolved as an extension of western Europe. In Indo-America, however, the conquest presented major hardships for the arriving Spanish and Portuguese; the challenge was both human and geographic, emanating as it did from the established indigenous cultures as well as the problems of size, altitude, and terrain. The application of the Toynbeean "challenge and response" once more led to Haya's conclusion that a new and distinctive civilization had been created on that territory that he chose to call Indo-America.

Additional Voices of Aprismo / Although Haya de la Torre has always stood out as the unchallenged spokesman and ideologue of *aprismo,* there have been others to discuss the movement and its ideas cogently. Second only to Haya himself is Luis Alberto Sánchez (1900———), one of the leading *apristas* and an intellectual of hemispheric repute.[72] One of Peru's leading literary critics and intellectual historians, his massive bibliography includes a number of political works. Prominent among these are *Carta a una indoamericana* (1932), *Aprismo y religión* (1933), *Los Fundamentos de la Historia de América* (1943), and *El Perú: Retrato de un país adolescente* (1958).[73] An early sympathy for Marxism appeared in the first of these, as well as in the notable introduction to his translation of excerpts from the writings of Marx.[74] Sánchez prefaced the latter translation by stating that the German philos-

---

71. Víctor Raúl Haya de la Torre, *Toynbee frente a los panoramas de la historia: Espacio-tiempo histórico americano* (Buenos Aires: Compañía Editora y Distribuidora del Plata, 1957).

72. Sánchez emerged in the mid-1960's as the single most powerful *aprista* in public office, combining the position of president of the Peruvian Senate with the rectorship of the University of San Marcos during the presidency of Fernando Belaúnde Terry.

73. Luis Alberto Sánchez, *Aprismo y religión* (Lima: Editorial Cooperativa Aprista Atahualpa, 1933); *Carta a una indoamericana, cuestiones elementales del aprismo* (Quito: n.p., 1932); *Los fundamentos de la historia de América* (Buenos Aires: Editorial Americalee, 1943); *El Perú: Retrato de un país adolescente* (Buenos Aires: Ediciones Continente, 1958).

74. Carlos Marx, *Principios filosóficos* (Buenos Aires: Ed. Inter-americana, 1945).

opher was the greatest single thinker of the contemporary world. For Latin America, Marx had taught that the governing classes favored imperialism while attempting to keep the people ignorant of basic economic conditions. They maintained their own dominant position by delivering the resources of the continent to foreign interests so that the subjugation of the masses might be continued. Economically, Sánchez further noted the utility of the concept of class struggle for socially motivated Latin-American revolutionaries, although saying little about Haya's "first stage-last stage" theorizing about imperialism. He made clear his commitment to the supervisory responsibility of the state in guiding underdeveloped nations toward prosperity and a liberation from the shackles of economic colonialism.

Sánchez was virtually the only *aprista* to give a detailed treatment to the party's attitude toward religion, a vexing issue about which Haya was uncharacteristically uncommunicative. The APRA has often been charged with anticlericalism, although the party, while opposed to undue Church involvement in politics, has consistently denied hostility toward religious observance. In Sánchez' 1933 work on the subject, he wrote that the APRA was neither religious nor antireligious. Arguing with little substantiation that Marxism itself was not antireligious, he stated that *aprismo* believed the fields of politics and religion to be separate and distinct. The party did not engage in "a struggle against religion, but against a religiosity that is tied to the system of existing exploitation."[75] For Sánchez, both Marxism and *aprismo* were theories calling for the radical transformation of man on materialistic bases, indifferent to the question of religion. Religion stands as a science of the absolute, politics the science of the possible. Thus, "*Aprismo* leaves to the conscience of each one of its members the resolution of the religious problem. Through experience it knows that mixing religion and politics kindles terrible fires."[76] As for the religious establishment in Peru, Sánchez drew a distinction between partisan and neutral members of the Church. "In Peru, as in the other countries of Latin America, both a high and a low clergy exist. The high clergy is composed of descendants of rich families which have donated their riches to the Church and received ecclesiastical positions for their members. This high clergy, oligarchical and allied to the '*civilista*' politicians, to whose class they belong, scorns and lower national clergy. The separation is absolute. The lower national clergy, *criollo* or Indian, feels itself displaced. . . . It sees . . . an alliance between the high clergy and the foreign clergy against the low

75. Sánchez, *Aprismo y religión*, p. 14.
76. *Ibid.*, pp. 36–37.

national clergy (*criollo* or Indian)."[77] *Apristas,* says Sánchez, were born in the Catholic faith and respect it but also embrace a humanistic tolerance to spiritual ideas and attitudes.

A subject that has held Sánchez' interest for many years is that of his interpretation of history. His explicitly Marxian view has attempted to prove the importance of ancient cultures of America, which for Sánchez revealed that so-called New World was actually the old. He argued that the recognition of American antiquity and its constructive qualities had repercussions on social thought, which in turn encouraged an anti-European, anti-imperialist, and essentially Socialist outlook. What he regarded as the flourishing of Marxism, especially through the philosophical updating of Haya's historical space-time, gave evidence to the spiritual depth and intrinsic social significance of life in the rechristened "old" world formed in Indo-America. Pride in the long lineal heritage had brought about in the contemporary period an intellectual ferment reflecting concern with endemic native conditions. There was a concomitant awareness of the dual character of Latin-American history, combining the indigenous and the Europeanized elements. In less abstract terms, this had contributed to a reassessment of the Indian and a renewed interest in the scientific and systematic study of economics. In the rising effort to study and to understand Latin America with a new maturity, Sánchez saw *aprismo* in the vanguard of the new historical consciousness.[78]

A man of great erudition and a strong telluric sense of unfolding Peruvian history, Sánchez often responded in an intuitive fashion to the study of his country's problems. He has been characterized by fellow Peruvians as the epitome of the *criollo* mentality, portraying a heterogeneous, even fragmented culture from which a new tradition and spirit might emerge.[79] Standing in contrast is the more philosophically inclined Antenor Orrego (1892—). His early books, especially *Notas marginales* (1922),[80] were heavily metaphysical in nature, reflecting exposure to the writings of Bergson. Knowledge was postulated as the endeavor most worthy of man's dignity. Life reflected the confrontation of reason and intuition, of science and one's inner core of experience. An appreciation of truly cosmic life could be achieved by either of two paths, "The

77. *Ibid.,* pp. 38–39.
78. An exposition of his views for North Americans appeared in Sánchez' "A New Interpretation of the History of America," *Hispanic American Historical Review,* XXIII, No. 3 (August 1943), 441–56.
79. For example, see Jorge Guillermo Llosa, *En busca del Perú* (Lima: Ediciones del Sol, 1962), pp. 104–6.
80. Antenor Orrego, *Notas marginales* (Trujillo: Tipografía Olaya, 1922).

road of pure science, that of experimental rigor that tests and analyzes fact, and the road of intuition, that of revelation, whose only instrument is the very spirit of man. . . ."[81] For Orrego, the choice was clearly in favor of the latter, thereby permitting the fullest aesthetic experience while implying a philosophical comprehension superior to earth-bound rationalism. The tenor of his speculation was mystical, with the power of logical reasoning and modern technology condemned as failing to encompass the true spirit of man.

In 1939 Orrego wrote *Pueblo-continente*,[82] the most political of his works. In it he presented a conceptual framework for theories of Indo-American unity. Writing as an *aprista*, Orrego argued the validity of the movement's ideology in its portrayal of continental nationalism. Approaching his subject as would a revolutionary, he set forth an almost Messianic historical exaltation of the emerging racial character that Vasconcelos had called "cosmic." A new culture was in its formative process, one inherently superior to those which in the Orient and Occident had entered into a period of crisis. "The density of America is to resolve, by superior human unity, the anguished grief, the tragic crossroads out of which the contemporary world has flowed, and to be itself the continuity of the world."[83] Each *pueblo-continente* will have individual beliefs and intuitions by which its own unique circumstances may be confronted. For Indo-America, this was translated into a necessary social and political revolution. In view of the historical conditions of American society, there could be no path other than the revolutionary, if genuine spiritual and material well-being were to be achieved.

Also deserving of mention is Manuel Seoane (1900–1963), long Haya's right-hand man until his withdrawal from politics a year before his death. A brilliant party organizer and leader with training as an economist, Seoane both founded and edited a variety of journals and periodicals, including the *aprista* daily *La Tribuna*. Most of his writing appeared in short articles and newspaper commentaries, of which the most representative collection was *Páginas polémicas*,[84] containing speeches and editorials from the 1931 election campaign. In a short pamphlet that same year,[85] Seoane presented a synthesis of the party's domestic program, demanding the liberation of the Peruvian worker as a precious

81. *Ibid.*, p. vii.
82. Antenor Orrego, *Pueblo-continente*, 2d ed. (Buenos Aires: Ediciones Continente, 1957).
83. *Ibid.*, p. 68.
84. Manuel Seoane, *Páginas polémicas* (Lima: Editorial La Tribuna, 1931).
85. Manuel Seoane, *Nuestros fines*, 2d ed. (Lima: Partido Aprista Peruano, 1931).

national commodity. "Our true capital is not only the Peruvian citizen but the riches of our soil, which are also enslaved. The principal Peruvian products . . . are monopolized by imperialist enterprises or by *criollo* minorities who exploit and tax the country without giving any benefit. . . . Constructive work must be completed by breaking the selfish centralism of Lima with a system of scientific administrative decentralization by the young and honorable forces of the country."[86] Seoane was forthright in his defense of democracy; this contrasted in degree with Haya de la Torre, frequently charged with being a personally ambitious, elitist-oriented political *caudillo*. The party's number two leader firmly disagreed with the thesis that Latin America was not yet ready for democracy. While its peoples lacked the political maturity to be observed in Anglo-Saxons, this was the result of mere historical accident. The Latin Americans had an affinity toward representative government which lacked only experience, and a democratic framework was a basic necessity for progress and modernization.

In his later *Nuestra América y la guerra*,[87] Seoane reflected the *aprista* change in outlook toward the United States which developed by the time of World War II.[88] Arguing that the conflict was attributable to economic rivalries between the great powers, he maintained that the peace terms in the Treaty of Versailles had been instrumental in exacerbating national sentiment in the competing countries. In neo-Marxian terms, he discussed ideological as well as economic factors in the long drift toward conflict. However, the war was different from its predecessors in that the contest was between democratic and dictatorial imperialists. For Latin America, co-operation with the United States and western Europe was necessary. In such a universal struggle between democracy and fascism, he explained, the choice had to be clear. A victory by Fascist imperialism was by far the greater of the two evils. Moreover, Latin America would itself be a kind of battleground, being rich in raw materials while weak militarily. Participation rather than neutrality was therefore the proper course of action. The victory of democratic imperialism would leave the door open to the possibility of economic progress and independent development, while that of the Axis would not.

86. *Ibid.*, p. 31.
87. Manuel Seoane, *Nuestra América y la guerra* (Santiago: Ediciones Ercilla, 1940).
88. In the introduction to *ibid.*, Seoane wrote that the contents represented the consensus of *aprista* leadership.

Contemporary Aprismo. The political history of the *apristas* has been one of hardship, persecution, and disappointment, with only brief moments of apparent triumph. The 1931 elections have always been regarded as stolen from Haya through official fraud, although the evidence is mixed and the controversy unresolved. Following years of exile, the party was permitted to participate in the 1945 elections, although this did not include a presidential nominee. The party won a major victory, capturing a legislative majority while providing the popular base for President José Luis Bustamante y Rivero. For three years the party experienced the handy wine of political dominance. Runing roughshod over the opposition, its attitude was at least superficially similar to that of Venezuela's Acción Democrática during the same three-year period. However, only scattered and unsystematic reforms were introduced. Furthermore, the relationship between Bustamante and Haya de la Torre grew strained, eventually leading to a complete break. Shortly after an abortive uprising that included *aprista* elements, the military intervened, ousting Bustamante and initiating an eight-year regime under General Manuel Odría which was marked by dictatorial controls and economic growth. It was during this time that the 1949–1954 presence of Haya de la Torre in Colombia's Lima Embassy—the result of Odría's denial of a safe-conduct pass out of the country—became a hemispheric *cause célèbre.*

Despite Odría's unrelenting harassment of the APRA, which was driven to clandestine operations, quiet overtures were inaugurated toward the regime by the *apristas.* Eventually the party regained legal status at the time of 1956 elections, although again prohibited from running its own presidential candidate. After extensive negotiations the party threw its support behind Manuel Prado, who was easily elected to his second, nonsuccessive presidency.[89] During his six-year term the APRA, under the tactical command of party secretary general Ramiro Prialé in the extended absence of Haya, co-operated with the conservative Prado government in a so-called *concordancia.* While this permitted a rebuilding of the party organization and in 1962 the presidential candidacy of Haya, it also caused the defection of young intellectual supporters and provoked charges that the APRA had opportunistically sold its revolutionary soul as the price for respectability and acceptance by the Peruvian establishment. Without opening a Pandora's box to detailed consideration of such charges, there could be no doubt that the APRA

89. During his earlier term from 1939–45, Prado had relaxed somewhat the earlier persecution of the APRA although still denying it legal status.

had moved a considerable distance to the right of its traditional position in the political spectrum. Haya apparently won a narrow but disputed victory in 1962; amid widespread charges of electoral fraud, the bitterly anti-*aprista* military stepped in and annulled the results. One year later the same three major presidential contenders repeated their contest, and Haya ran second to a younger and newer exponent of socioeconomic transformation, former *aprista* Fernando Belaúnde Terry and his Acción Popular (AP). Since that time the APRA has renewed an informal agreement with its once-hated oppressor, Manuel Odría. The result has been a rather conservative alliance opposing its legislative majority to Belaúnde's mild reformist proposals. With the October, 1968, seizure of power by the military, the APRA had found itself once again relegated to a secondary position.

For the APRA, which has changed its official name to the Partido Aprista Peruano (PAP), the years since 1956 have marked a pragmatic political reorientation. Notwithstanding frequent denials, the party has become closely aligned with a slowly-modernizing national elite, having largely abandoned its original revolutionary posture. One can offer tangible political reasons for this shift; in ideological terms, however, the sheer fact of such a major alteration is more significant that the causes. The movement in general, always dominated by middle- and upper-middle-class leadership, has become essentially bourgeois, and its appeals to the urban proletariat today carry limited popular attraction. Collaboration with such former antagonists as Odría, Prado, and conservative newspaper publisher Pedro Beltrán has alienated many intellectuals. Much of the party's youth wing broke away in the early 1960s as the Apra Rebelde, later rechristened the Movimiento de Izquierda Revolucionaria (MIR). Marxist-oriented intellectuals have also turned their backs on today's PAP; characteristic was the Movimiento Social Progresista (MSP), a modern and technically oriented group that was concerned with economic underdevelopment and a scientific attack on traditional problems. Moderate reformers flocked to the banner of Fernando Belaúnde, seeing in him a leader who promised to achieve more important and effective reforms than Haya de la Torre.

The party is by no means dead,[90] retaining a hard core of supporters

90. Among the first works to argue that the party had entered into serious decline was that of an embittered former *aprista*, Víctor Villanueva, *La tragedia de un pueblo y de un partido (páginas para la historia del Apra)* (Santiago: Ediciones Renovación, 1954). A sharp attack was also mounted by Carlos Miró Quesada in *Autopsia de los partidos políticos* (Lima: Ediciones "Páginas Peruanas," 1961). It should be noted that the Miró Quesada family, which publishes

comprising from one-fourth to one-third of the electorate. The gradual revision of both its practical and its doctrinal position has nonetheless been perceptible. In ideological terms, this process stemmed in part from the *aprista* realization that its original radicalism held little appeal for the essentially conservative middle sectors. The virulence of economic nationalism and attacks upon imperialism—especially with the label "Yankee"—receded and by the close of World War II had virtually disappeared. While maintaining its demand for the unification of Indo-America, the party's basic motives changed. Instead of advocating an independent counterweight to North American economic interests, the APRA adopted a policy of uncritical co-operation. As Pike observed, this has been translated into a greater emphasis on the generation of wealth rather than upon its distribution.[91] The early *aprista* antagonism toward the Peruvian socioeconomic elite has been changed, through a series of rather subtle permutations, into a collaboration with the upper-class establishment. Related to this has been a frenetic and vociferous anticommunism which, although once grounded on ideological bases, came to resemble a McCarthyite crusade, especially in the hands of the shrewd Luis Alberto Sánchez.

To some, the drama and tragedy of the APRA has been its inability during more than four decades to win and exercise full national power, despite Haya's apparent victory in 1962 and a possible triumph in 1931, as well as the genuinely substantial popular appeal which has existed during much of this time. Others lament that Haya himself, until Castro the most renowned political figure of twentieth-century Latin-American politics, has never been able to apply his unquestionably gifted and imaginative intellect to the full administration of Peruvian government. And for many embittered former *apristas,* there is both anger and anguish in the belief that Haya and his movement sold out their principles in the interests of material comfort and an accommodation with retrogressive domestic and international capitalist interests. In the present context, however, stress must be placed on ideological adjustments. Haya's contention that imperialism was actually the first stage of capitalist evolution in underdeveloped societies was ingenious, but it also created doctrinal problems from which he never fully extricated himself. Haya has not satisfactorily formulated a statement of the additional stages that in

the Lima daily *El Comercio,* is among the traditional foes of the APRA. Several works have appeared in the 1960's with the contention that the party is dead or dying. A characteristic example is that of Hernando Aguirre Gamio, *Liquidación histórica del APRA y del colonialismo neoliberal* (Lima: Ediciones Debate, 1962).

91. Pike, "The Old and the New APRA," p. 37.

underdeveloped areas would follow that of imperialism. This has left him uncomfortable with the evolution of events from the mid-1930s on; while he has softened the tone and tempo of anti-imperialist writings, he has provided little that might explain changing circumstances. As the party has tried to move with the times, it has therefore done so on short-range opportunistic, rather than doctrinally rational, bases. This, combined with the taste of power from 1945 to 1948, has widened—perhaps definitively—the chasm between *aprista* theory and practice.

Haya's ideological response to such matters was the enunciation of historical space-time. The reader of his expositions on the subject is struck by Haya's breadth of intellect but also with a verbal pomposity that suggests his familiarity with the topic is superficial. The only lasting impact comes from the discussion of relativity, and this tends to suggest that, in a fluid and volatile world of rapid change, *aprismo* might be applied to justify a wide range of diverse, even contradictory policies. Otherwise, an attempt to seek guidance for the unending choice of political alternatives is fruitless. More recent efforts to correlate historical space-time with Toynbeean theories of civilization and culture are even further removed from political issues. The only lasting impression is that of a fertile and restless intellect attempting to crown its own somewhat disjointed philosophizing with the ideas of one of the world's great minds. *Apristas* may hail this theorizing as proving the universality of Haya's thought, but it contributes little to party thinking or to the solution of Peruvian problems.

The future of today's Partido Aprista Peruano remains a hotly debated issue in Peru. The party organization is relatively effective, and large numbers of *aprista* followers—especially in its traditional northern stronghold—remain highly politicized and blindly loyal. Question has been expressed over the quality of second-generation leaders, for the dominant figures remain Haya, Sánchez, Prialé, Cox, Heysen, and a few other storied veterans of the near-legendary struggles of the 1920s and 1930s.[92] In view of the clearly authoritarian structure of the party, this question

92. At this writing, the septagenarian Haya de la Torre remains vigorous and active. The junior author, during an extended research stay in Peru in 1967, observed the *aprista* leader's zest for politics. Haya was present almost nightly in his office at the party headquarters, the Casa del Pueblo, where he received a stream of visitors from all walks of life. Opponents who anticipated his forthcoming retirement from politics found themselves confronted with the possibility that in the national elections of 1969, at the age of 74, Haya might launch one final effort to crown his career by capturing the long-elusive presidency. The military *coup d'etat* in 1968 seemingly foreclosed this final possibility, however.

assumes even greater relevance. Whatever vagaries a capricious future may hold for the PAP, its ideological and philosophical contributions lie in the past. History may ultimately record that these were the imaginative and significant years of *aprismo,* when the movement provided inspiration for socially conscious revolutionaries the hemisphere over. As for Víctor Raúl Haya de la Torre, whatever the inconsistencies of his thought, the weaknesses of his ego, and the quirks of a remarkable if complex personality, it was his voice that, at an historically critical period in Latin America, rose above all others as an eloquent and impassioned prophet of the revolution.

SELECTED BIBLIOGRAPHY

THE SOCIAL CONSCIENCE AND INDIGENISMO

Basadre, Jorge. *Meditaciones sobre el destino histórico del Perú.* Lima: Ediciones Huascarán, 1947.
———. *Perú: Problema y posibilidad.* Lima: Librería Francesa Científica y Casa Editorial E. Rosay, 1931.
Bustillo, Ignacio Prudencio. *Ensayo de filosofía jurídica.* Sucre: Imp. Bolívar, 1923.
Castro Pozo, Hildebraond. *Del ayllu al cooperativismo socialista.* Lima: P. Barrantes Castro, 1936.
De la Cuadra, José. *El montuvio ecuatoriano.* Buenos Aires: Ediciones Imán, 1937.
Francovich, Guillermo. *El pensamiento boliviano en el siglo XX.* México: Fondo de Cultura Económica, 1956.
García, José Uriel. *El nuevo indio: Ensayos indianistas sobre la sierra superuana.* 2d ed. Cuzco: H. G. Rozas Sucesores, Librería e Imprenta, 1937.
Jaramillo Alvarado, Pío. *El indio ecuatoriano.* 4th ed. Quito: Casa de la Cultura Ecuatoriana, 1954.
———. *La Nación quiteña: Biografía de una cultura.* Quito: Imp. Fernández, 1947.
Llosa, Jorge Guillermo. *En busca del Perú.* Lima: Ediciones del Sol, 1962.
Maiguashca, Segundo B. *El indio, cerebro y corazón de América: Incorporación del indio a la cultura nacional.* Quito: Edit. "Fray Jodoco Ricke," 1949.
Rubio Orbe, Gonzalo. *Aspectos indígenos.* Quito: Casa de la Cultura Ecuatoriana, 1965.
———. *Punyaro: Estudio de antropología social y cultural de una comunidad indígena y mestiza.* Quito: Casa de la Cultura Ecuatoriana, 1956.
Salazar Bondy, Augusto. *Historia de las ideas en el Perú contemporáneo.* 2 vols. Lima: Francisco Moncloa, Editores, 1965.
Tamayo, Franz. *La creación de la pedagogía nacional: Editoriales de "El Diario."* La Paz: Ministerio de Educación de Bolivia, 1944).
Valcárcel, Luis E. *Ruta cultural del Perú.* México: Fondo de Cultura Económica, 1945.

PERU AND APRISMO

Aguirre Gamio, Hernando. *Liquidación histórica del APRA y del colonialismo neo-liberal.* Lima: Ediciones Debate, 1962.

Chang-Rodríguez, Eugenio. *La literatura política de González Prada, Mariátegui y Haya de la Torre.* México: Ediciones de Andrea, 1957.

Cossio del Pomar, Felipe. *Haya de la Torre: El indoamericano.* Lima: Editorial Nuevo Día, 1946.

Cox, Carlos Manuel. *Dinámica económica del aprismo.* Lima: Ediciones La Tribuna, 1948.

Haya de la Torre, Víctor Raúl. *A dónde va Indoamérica?* Santiago: Ediciones Ercilla, 1935.

———. *El antimperialismo y el Apra.* Santiago: Ediciones Ercilla, 1936.

———. *Espacio-tiempo histórico.* Lima: Ediciones La Tribuna, 1948.

———. *Política aprista.* Lima: Editorial Cooperativa Aprista Atahualpa, 1933.

———. *Toynbee frente a los panoramas de la historia: Espacio-tiempo histórico americano.* Buenos Aires: Compañía Editora y Distribuidora del Plata, 1957.

———. *Y después de la guerra ¿qué?* Lima: Ed. Talleres PTCM, 1946.

Kantor, Harry. *The Ideology and Program of the Peruvian Aprista Movement.* Berkeley and Los Angeles: University of California Press, 1953.

Llosa, Jorge Guillermo. *En busca del Perú.* Lima: Ediciones del Sol, 1962.

McNicoll, Robert E. "Intellectual Origins of Aprismo," *Hispanic American Historical Review,* XXIII, No. 3 (August 1943).

Miró Quesada Laos, Carlos. *Autopsia de los partidos políticos.* Lima: Ediciones "Páginas Peruanas," 1961.

Orrego, Antenor. *Pueblo-continente.* 2d ed. Buenos Aires: Ediciones Continente, 1957.

Pike, Fredrick B. "The Old and the New APRA in Peru: Myth and Reality," *Inter-American Economic Affairs,* XVIII, No. 2 (Autumn 1964).

———. *The Modern History of Peru.* New York: Frederick A. Praeger, Publishers, 1967.

Saco, Alfredo. *Programa agrario del aprismo.* Lima: Ediciones Populares, 1946.

Salazar Bondy, Augusto. *Historia de las ideas en el Perú contemporáneo,* 2 vols. Lima: Francisco Moncloa, Editores, 1965.

Sánchez, Luis Alberto. *Aprismo y religión.* Lima: Editorial Cooperativa Aprista Atahualpa, 1933.

———. *Carta a una indoamericana: Cuestiones elementales del aprismo.* Quito, n.p., 1932.

———. *Haya de la Torre y el APRA: Crónica de un hombre y un partido.* Santiago, Editorial del Pacífico, 1955.

———. *Los fundamentos de la historia de América.* Buenos Aires: Editorial Americalee, 1943.

———. *El Perú: Retrato de un país adolescente.* Buenos Aires: Ediciones Continente, 1958.

Seoane, Manuel. *Nuestra América y la guerra.* Santiago: Ediciones Ercilla, 1940.

———. *Nuestros fines.* 2d ed. Lima: Partido Aprista Peruano, 1931.

———. *Páginas polémicas.* Lima: Editorial La Tribuna, 1931.

II.

Social Democracy
in Venezuela and Costa Rica

Although the *apristas* were the first important group to emerge within the pattern of Social Democracy, they are neither the only nor, indeed, the most successful. Among the political parties that have sometimes been similarly classified are Venezuela's Acción Democrática, Liberación Nacional of Costa Rica, the Partido Revolucionario Dominicano in the Dominican Republic, the *febreristas* of Paraguay, and the Partido Popular Democrático in Puerto Rico. Of these, the most prominent have been the Venezuelan and Costa Rican groups. Each has provided the major political and doctrinal orientation in its nation's politics for an extended period of time; each has won national elections on more than one occasion and has long stood as the leading party organization of the country. Ideologically, each has espoused a statist position in which governmental authority in the economic and social realm is extensive, while the commitment to democratic processes is fundamental.

The Marxist origins of Venezuela's Acción Democrática are striking, and include the youthful membership in the Communist movement of its greatest leader, Rómulo Betancourt. As described below, he and his colleagues as young men became imbued with Marxist ideas and, although soon breaking with the orthodox Communists, retained a Socialist cast in their thinking. Passing from an early revolutionary radicalism to a more gradualistic reformism in recent years, the party has retained its basic goals while accepting the need for greater patience and moderation in their achievement. In Costa Rica, the Social Democratic movement was first organized under that name—the Partido Social Demócrata—and the subsequent change to Liberación Nacional merely lessened the opprobrium that the term "socialist" carries for many Costa Ricans. This has not altered the fact that basic organizational and doctrinal objectives assume the importance of state intervention in socioeconomic affairs. Democratic processes are emphasized, along with explicit encouragement of civic participation in political life.

Venezuela and Acción Democrática

Among the Social Democratic parties of Latin America, Venezuela's Acción Democrática (AD) ranks with the APRA as the most widely known. Its electoral record is exceptional; until 1968 the party was undefeated in a succession of contests dating back to 1946. The far-reaching evolutionary changes introduced into Venezuelan life and society during roughly a quarter-century have been primarily the responsibility of *adeco* leadership in attempting to meet the demands of the citizenry. Only in the past few years have the Christian Democrats and political independents begun to share significantly in the formulation and implementation of the patient and gradualistic alteration of the country. Perhaps the most significant historical role played by Acción Democrática, whatever its future, has been the broad popular consensus that has formed about major policy issues first raised and articulated by the AD. Throughout its history the party has been an extremely politicized entity; its leadership has been dedicated wholly and without reservation to the political game and all it means. At the same time, it has expressed a Social Democratic doctrine that has become a part of national values and attitudes. Among its ideologues, none has been as influential as Rómulo Betancourt, for years the inspirational leader of the movement. An examination of his intellectual development tells us a great deal about the AD doctrinal position.[1]

The Marxist Background and Venezuelan Social Democracy /
Born in Guatire in February, 1908, Rómulo Betancourt was schooled

1. The Betancourt bibliography is too extensive for a complete listing here. Among the more important works are: *Dos meses en las cárceles de Gómez* (Barranquilla: n.p., 1928); *Interpretación de su doctrina popular y democrática* (Caracas: Editorial Suma, 1958); *Posición y doctrina* (Caracas: Editorial Cordillera, 1958); *Tres años de gobierno democrático, 1959–1962*, 3 Vols. (Caracas: Imprenta Nacional, 1962); and *Venezuela: Política y petróleo* (México: Fondo de Cultura Económica, 1956).

in Caracas and entered the Universidad Central with the intention of studying law. He rapidly became prominent within the student organization, which continually agitated against the aging tyrant Juan Vicente Gómez, from 1908 the unquestioned authority of the country. Politics were discussed by these youths in what were euphemistically termed "cultural meetings," and in February, 1928, dissension erupted into student demonstrations that later served to identify its participants as members of the Generation of '28.[2] Reprisals by *gomecista* officials drove them into exile, but for the participants the experience had been profound. As Betancourt later told a Colombian newsman, "I had the first concrete revelation that the popular mass was beginning to intervene in Venezuelan history as a new factor. . . . We students considered ourselves . . . as chosen to transform the country. Then our people suddenly made known their presence; and without leaders, without labor and political organizations, without action committes or strike funds, the people organized a massive demonstration in Caracas. . . ."[3]

It was during this first period of exile that Betancourt and his colleagues began the quest for an all-embracing ideology. They were first inclined toward a revolutionary overthrow of the Gómez dictatorship, although having but a partial understanding of national problems. A small informal discussion group—the Agrupación Revolucionaria de la Izquierda (ARDI)—was marked by a brief flirtation with Marxism. One of the top *adecos* for many years, Gonzalo Barrios, later noted that the revolutionaries had seen Marxism as a convenient framework within which to analyze national conditions and formulate possible solutions.[4] This was echoed in Betancourt's own recollection of the period. Writing in his *Venezuela: Política y petróleo,* he elaborated upon the intellectual climate. "We [of the Generation of '28] shared a phenomenon common to the majority of students exiled in the thirties. . . . We began to dream of a bolshevik revolution, with the 'czar of Maracay'[5] shot at dawn. Nevertheless, none of those who later would found Acción Democrática became members during this first exile of political groups subordinated to the Third International. . . . The small group of our countrymen, already embryonically organized at that time, which later

2. For a detailed treatment see John D. Martz, "Venezuela's 'Generation of '28': The Genesis of Political Democracy," *Journal of Inter-American Studies,* VI, No. 1 (January 1964), 17–33.

3. Luis Enrique Osorio, *Democracia en Venezuela* (Bogotá: Editorial Litografía Colombia, 1943).

4. Interview with Gonzalo Barrios by Martz, November 27, 1962.

5. This was in reference to Juan Vicente Gómez, who spent much of his time at a ranch near Maracay.

would become the Communist Party of Venezuela, proceeded to deepen the abyss between their group and ours, unleashing an abusive campaign against us in which they still persist. . . ."[6]

For Betancourt, this was a period of intellectual and political groping toward a satisfactory doctrinal framework. Settling in Costa Rica, he played a significant part in that country's Communist party. His emphasis on purely national issues soon caused a clash with those whose primary loyalty was to the Communist International rather than to Costa Rica. Disillusioned, Betancourt resigned in 1935 from the party. This experience provided him with a harsh lesson in the pragmatic realities of communism and its ties with Moscow. Commenting in later years, he wrote: "I joined a small Communist group in Costa Rica in 1930. I came with high hopes of an armed invasion against the tyranny of Gómez. Desperation over our inability to overthrow the hated tyrant, as well as ignorance of the socio-economic realities of the American people . . . all provided fertile terrain for the messianic hope of a revolution 'a la rusa'. . . . During this transitory stage within the Communist Party, I was never one of the drawing-room bolsheviks who discoursed on social revolution while hoping that there might be a *golpe*. . . . I was seeking a truly American doctrine or ideology or set of answers."[7] Betancourt's experience was not unlike that of many revolutionary young Latin Americans of the 1920s and 1930s. Initially ignorant about national conditions and largely unaware of economic subtleties, they undertook a search for a set of answers which led to Marxism as an intellectual tool for study and knowledge. Betancourt and others of today's AD "old guard" went through this period together, although not always becoming card-carrying party members. Out of the eventual rejection of communism, however, came an affinity for broadly Marxist or socialist ideas which remained in later years.

During clandestine activity under the López Contreras regime, 1937–39, the Partido Democrático Nacional (PDN), the illegal forerunner of Acción Democrática, underwent mounting stress from the division between Communist and non-Communist elements, and the schism of 1938 created the circumstances for an extended struggle between the two, in which Betancourt and his colleagues eventually won ascendency. Writing in 1949, he discussed at length the split within the PDN. "The Venezuelan Left was divided into two well-defined groups. One of these based its strategy and tactics not so much on Marxist doctrine as on the successive changes ordered by the Comintern and later by the

6. Betancourt, *Política y petróleo*, pp. 69–70.
7. *El País* (Caracas), February 15, 1944, p. 11.

Cominform . . . The other, ours, which in the underground was the PDN and later became Acción Democrática, formed by those who, professing a revolutionary concept of the social struggle, thought as Americans and thought of themselves as Americans, did not believe that a transplanted formula or an imported line varying with the international strategy of a certain great power should be the guide to popular action to be carried out with realism and effectiveness."[8] In addition to the question of a national versus international outlook, Betancourt and the non-Communist left rejected the idea of a class-oriented party, as the Communists advocated. "The thesis advanced by the communists was hardly realistic . . . [for] urban middle classes, the students and professionals, the varied body of small farmers . . . would not join in workers' parties, but rather would join those of full and comprehensive national revolutionary plans."[9] Instead, there were efforts to organize what was termed a *policlasista* or multi-class organization. ". . . we advocated and organized a much more amply based party than one based only on the proletariat, since it had within its ranks men and women coming from all of the non-parasitic classes of the population, forming a movement which fought for democracy and sought to adapt it to our time, with emphasis on social justice and economic redemption. It was a movement, finally, which was not guilty of insularity, but on the contrary, aspired to establish relations with similar groups elsewhere in America, while always refusing to subordinate national interests to the very special objectives of Russian political strategy."[10] The earliest lengthy exposition of what may be termed Social Democracy in Venezuela emerged from the first national conference of the PDN in September, 1939. The *pedenista* declarations were subsequently broadened, elaborated, and rationalized in the doctrine of Acción Demoncrática. They provide much illumination, however, into the early ideological formulations of Rómulo Betancourt and his associates.[11] The introductory "political thesis" described the PDN as enjoying a solid doctrinal base, "having been organized after extended analyses of Venezuelan reality. Its program and tactics have not been born of capricious will . . . but from a dedicated study of the fundamental problems of the Nation. . . ." The subsequent declaration was divided into four sections: the commitment to participa-

8. Betancourt, *Rómulo Betancourt: Pensamiento y acción* (Mexico: n.p., 1951), p. 141.
9. Betancourt, *Política y petróleo*, p. 787.
10. Betancourt, *Pensamiento y acción*, pp. 141–42.
11. Major excerpts from the PDN declaration are reproduced in Luis Troconis Guerrero, *La cuestión agraria en la historia nacional* (Caracas: Editorial Arte, 1962), pp. 42–51.

tory democracy, Venezuelan economic reconstruction, labor legislation, and the reform of education and health. The democratic commitment was stated in terms of full constitutional guarantees and individual liberties, with the municipality the "true basic cell" for national political life. This was discussed at less lengthy than was the economic analysis and related proposals, however.

Venezuela was termed "a semicolonial, semifeudal country, a country tied to economic, fiscal and political imperialism, with an economy predominantly rural, chained by *latifundismo* and incapable in its present form of assuring for itself economic independence and progress." Consequently, the PDN called for "scientific study of the economic potentialities of the country," which would be guided by a state-sponsored Council for National Economic Development. Their commitment to centralized state action was strong, appearing in promises of activity through technical and credit programs for agriculture, public corporations for the exploitation of subsoil riches, and a controlled parceling of lands and estates still belonging to the heirs of the Gómez era. In the area of labor, the state would guarantee an extension of benefits to workers in all sectors as well as legislating an obligatory social security law. Government assistance was pledged to labor in building a national labor movement. The state also would undertake to guide the modernization of secondary education, the encouragement of normal and vocational schools, and the introduction of an anti-illiteracy campaign.

In somewhat disjointed fashion, Betancourt and the Partido Democrático Nacional were enunciating a Social Democratic commitment to a statist system within a democratic setting. As is seen, the commitment to centralized governmental direction was clear. "Analysis leads to the conclusion that the State is, in fact, more capable in Venezuela than in other Latin American countries to exercise . . . a determining influence on the life of the Nation."[12] Ultimately, a general democratization of the national economic system was intended. "We conceive of democracy as nothing less than a government that at the same time permits the free play of social forces and . . . by means of abolishing the *latifundio,* as well as feudal relations, intervenes in the cities through industrial production and the development of commerce, especially and admittedly protecting . . . in particular the sectors benefitting the least in the present distribution of riches, namely the manual workers and the intellectuals."[13] During the next few years, especially with the legali-

12. Shorter PDN excerpts are also found in Acción Democrática, *Acción Democrática: Doctrina y programa* (Caracas: Editorial "Antonio Pinto Salinas," 1962).
13. *Ibid.,* pp. 20–21.

zation of the party in 1941, stress was placed on organizational development and the politicization of the electorate. Not until the late 1950s did Acción Democrática present a systematic and modernized collection of party theses detailing its programmatic position. In the meantime, however, it participated in a revolution that brought it to national power for three years beginning in October, 1945. A brief examination of the policies of this so-called *trienio* shed further light on the party's stance.

The provisional government headed by Rómulo Betancourt during most of this period first undertook political reforms, stressing electoral democratization and a new constitution embodying the principles of participatory government that the country had not known before. At the same time the AD government was committed to the importance of providing better living conditions. One of the leading *adeco* theoreticians of that period, Luis Lander, explained that the AD felt the masses would be prepared for economic advances only after experiencing the unfettered play of political democracy. By participating in elections, Venezuelans might thereby "see in practice how the causes of their misery can be eradicated, and how to solve their problems by democratic means. They see the denial of liberty, systems of dictatorial government, and the effect of economic methods of exploitation as being . . . cultivated by the spread and growth of communist ideology."[14]

The commitment to central economic planning led to the creation of a major state agency in May, 1946, the Corporación Venezolana de Fomento (CVF). Rómulo Betancourt described it thus:

> The Development Corporation, charged with fulfilling the industrialization program of the democratic regime, conceived of this process as taking place in four stages. . . . The first stage was to stimulate basic industries: electricity, without which development of industry is impossible; and those related to human welfare, such as foodstuffs, clothing, fuel and housing. . . . In the second stage were included industries complementary to those already named; in the third stage, medium heavy industries were to be pushed, and in the fourth step, the production of machines, heavy industry. But there was no rigid formula, only a working guide, to be carried out with flexibility.[15]

In addition to the CVF, a variety of semiautonomous agencies with economic responsibilities were established in other areas, including a workers' bank and the Banco Agrícola y Pecuario, an agrarian credit

---

14. Luis Lander, "La Doctrina Venezolana de Acción Democrática," *Cuadernos Americanos,* IX (julio-agosto 1950), 23.
15. Betancourt, *Política y petróleo,* p. 384.

institution. By 1948 the government had also elaborated an agrarian reform law, but a military overthrow of the recently elected AD-dominated administration of famed novelist Rómulo Gallegos prevented its implementation at that time.[16] Social welfare and education were brought under the aegis of state direction, with perhaps the single most important achievement the virtual eradication of malaria. In his *Venezuela: Política y petróleo*, Betancourt summed up the commitment to the role of the state in economic affairs by writing the following:

> All of this has relative importance in the face of a fundamental fact: we had demonstrated with deeds, in agriculture as well as in industry, that it *was* possible to stimulate specifically Venezuelan production. We showed that it was mere speculation of those who were afraid to act and were prophets of defeatism to insist that the country must continue to depend only on petroleum. If the State undertook a creative role of encouraging, orienting and stimulating specifically Venezuelan production, the industrious spirit and the will to work of the people of our land would do the rest. The results obtained in three years in the various fields of economic activity provide an impressive list of achievements to sustain this optimistic thesis.[17]

The reforms undertaken during the *trienio* cannot all be cited here. A word is appropriate on one of that government's most widely heralded policies, that dealing with Venezuela's black gold, petroleum. The party collectively and Betancourt individually had long argued that the country needed to share more fully in the exploitation of this, its greatest national resource. The leading AD spokesman on petroleum policy, Juan P. Pérez Alfonzo, devised a nationalistic policy that avoided what were seen as the evils of expropriation.[18] The result was the "50–50" formula that soon became an objective elsewhere. Pérez Alfonzo argued that while the earnings of petroleum should be used to encourage balanced economic development, Venezuela was not presently capable of administering the enterprise itself. The result was a series of renegotiated contracts whereby the government received half the profits of the industry, either through ordinary royalty payments or by a revised tax structure. Betancourt explained that the party "had always rejected the possibility of applying, in the beginning of an administration with a revolutionary

16. For Rómulo Gallegos' account of these events, see his *Una posición en la vida* (México: Ediciones Humanismo, 1954).

17. Betancourt, *Política y petróleo*, pp. 406–7.

18. His exposition of views appears in Juan Pablo Pérez Alfonzo, *Petróleo: Jugo de la tierra* (Caracas: Editorial Arte, 1961).

367 / Social Democracy in Venezuela and Costa Rica

orientation, a measure similar to that which is the greatest claim to fame of the Mexican regime of Lázaro Cárdenas."[19] Thus, Acción Democrática refused to nationalize the industry, at the same time seeking the greatest possible contribution to Venezuelan growth and development.

The Elaboration of Party Doctrine / During the ten-year period of exile that followed the 1948 overthrow of the Gallegos government, party leaders scattered to different corners of the hemisphere and beyond. Following the ouster of the dictatorship of Colonel Marcos Pérez Jiménez in January, 1958, however, a reorganized and revitalized party published a lengthy reconsideration of Venezuelan problems and party doctrine. After intensive work by a series of study groups and commissions, the AD issued a set of six "theses" describing party ideology more fully than ever before.[20] Eight areas of interest were outlined: political, economic and fiscal, administrative, social, health, agricultural, educational, and international. One of the present authors has previously identified three strands running through the text of the theses, all of them consistent with the thinking of Betancourt and other party leaders.[21] Moreover, these have their parallels in Social Democratic movements elsewhere in the hemisphere. They can be labeled under the broad rubrics of political freedom and democratic government, advocacy of state planning, and state responsibility for the betterment of all sectors of Venezuelan society.

The party initially declared its support for democratic government "as the true expression of the will of the national majority," stating that sovereignty resided in the people, "who exercise it by means of the organs of public power." Civil liberties and individual freedoms were guaranteed, with the party pledging "absolute respect for all religious beliefs, reaffirming the principle that religion is a matter reserved to the individual conscience." Civilian government was defended and, although the military drew brief praise for its high moral and material state of development, the party added that the armed forces did not

---

19. Betancourt, *Política y petróleo*, p. 235.
20. Issued in 1958 by the Caracas Editorial "Antonio Pinto Salinas," these six publications of Acción Democrática were *Tesis agraria, Tesis educativa, Tesis organizativa y estatutos, Tesis petrolera, Tesis política,* and *Tesis sindical.* In 1962 they were republished in one volume under the title *Acción Democrática: Doctrina y programa.*
21. For a more lengthy discussion than is possible here, see John D. Martz, *Acción Democrática: Evolution of a Modern Political Party in Venezuela* (Princeton: Princeton University Press, 1966), pp. 228 ff.

constitute a deliberative body and must submit to "the authority of the freely elected organs of the State and to the norms that are determined by the Constitution and the Laws of the Republic." In the international field the party ratified "conciliation, arbitration, and discussions in the International Organs that must be the means for the resolution of conflicts among States." Sovereign equality for all peoples was defended, with the AD proclaiming its frank solidarity with regions struggling to free themselves from a colonial past.

The party commitment to centralized planning was strong and unreserved. National resources were to be subject to state regulation as the means of developing industries that might bring about an economic transformation. This meant the creation and extension of state-operated enterprises for the fuller exploitation of natural resources, with industrialization intensified through the drafting of technical programs encouraging over-all economic diversification. Article 10 of the *Bases programáticas* called for the use and management of the national budget in favor of planned economic development, thereby "maintaining the measure of public investment at a high level, orienting public expenditures toward a geographic distribution that favors all regions of the country in accord with the needs of progress." The party promised governmental participation in the creation of "a national organ within the governmental structure whose task will be the coordination of the planning process on a national, state and municipal scale."

Chapter IV of the *Bases programáticas* spoke of those social principles applicable in particular to labor conditions and to social security. There was an explicit reiteration of state responsibility for the elevation of the citizenry, and this led to lengthy discussion of the rights of labor and the encouragement to be provided by the government. This fairly general treatment of labor concluded that Acción Democrática supported "the right of workers to group in their specific organizations and, as a consequence, considers that the State must guarantee free association and the perfect exercise of labor liberties. Labor freedom must be effective and must be fully guaranteed." Chapter V followed by outlining questions of health and social assistance; all Venezuelans were guaranteed state facilities for the protection of their health. Beyond this, the elevation of living conditions required particular attention to the peasantry, with the government dedicated to effective collaboration in a series of rural centers of social assistance.

The *Bases programáticas* provided an overview of *adeco* ideology as published and disseminated in 1958. Changes since that time have been largely ones of detail, with the commitment to basic goals remaining unchanged.[22] The following succession of party theses spelled out in greater detail the means envisioned for the achievement of broad goals. Space prohibits lengthy repetition, but a few of the highlights serve to add flavor to party doctrine.[23] Perhaps the most revealing single thesis is that of labor, which provides a useful if partisan history of Venezuelan labor before setting down specific recommendations. Labor is not to be considered a mere offshoot of the party, for its independence must be maintained.[24] Its own commitments and interests relative to business and commerce cannot at all times be identical with those of the party. However, labor is called "an important ally of Acción Democrática in its struggle for a free Venezuela, a Venezuela for Venezuelans, since this is the struggle of the people themselves." The party repeats its conviction that the peaceful Venezuelan revolution is essentially a gradual march toward a form of socialism. The full force of labor can only be achieved through a strong and united organization. To put it bluntly "workers possess nothing more than their strength and force of labor, and they live by selling it to the capitalists who possess the instruments of production. Between these two classes [labor and conservative property holders and managers] a continual war is waged, an unceasing war that is . . . ended only when those owners of a progressive mentality agree to make concessions to the workers." Through concerted efforts, the labor movements can contribute to the welfare of the working man, and thus it must struggle relentlessly against all concentration of capital and all monopoly.

Turning to agriculture, Acción Democrática again argued that the two polarized sectors in the struggle between democracy and dictatorship were the people and the forces of reaction. The former, lacking the privileges of power and wealth, included the middle sectors, the working class, and the peasantry. In the countryside, *latifundismo* is the major obstacle. The demand for agrarian reform was therefore fundamental. Referring back to the short-lived Agrarian Reform Law of 1948, the party declared that a national consensus existed on the need for measured, nonviolent reform, one that should pay just prices for expropriated lands while leaving untouched those large holdings where efficient and modern means of production were employed. There was criticism of

22. The party planned on an updated set of "theses" for the 1968 elections, but the internal schism delayed the effort indefinitely.

23. All of the theses listed in note 20, with the exception of the *Tesis organizativa y estatutos*, were used for these passages.

24. For a fuller discussion, see John D. Martz, "The Growth and Democratization of the Venezuelan Labor Movement," *Inter-American Economic Affairs*, XVII, No. 2 (Autumn 1963), 3–18.

both capitalistic and socialistic approaches. The first was seen as leaving intact the structure of land ownership, while traditional nationalization of land and socialization of agricultural production contradicted the structure of a country founded largely upon private property and free enterprise. "We must not be animated by any preconceived prejudice. Each country must realize the agrarian reform that is appropriate to its needs. . . . The political, social, demographic and economic reality of the country . . . [is] what must stamp its course and the positive forms of change."

Petroleum policy has been expounded frequently and at length, with important statements in the writings of Betancourt as well as Pérez Alfonzo's *Petróleo: Jugo de la tierra*. The party has repeated its basic thesis that petroleum can, through proper planning, hasten a more balanced national development. Recalling the "50–50" formula of the *trienio*, the party has again rejected a policy of nationalization. A ten-point set of propositions outlined such steps as creation of a national petroleum company, increased stated participation in the exploitation of petroleum, and a denial of further exploratory concessions to foreign private enterprise. Efforts to bring rationality to the setting and maintenance of international prices meant the establishment of an international agreement—such as was worked out with Middle Eastern oil producers in the Organization of Petroleum Exporting Countries (OPEC). A useful summary of the importance of petroleum was that of Pérez Alfonzo written from exile in June of 1954. "Venezuela has a great resource in its petroleum, but it is also faced with great responsibility. It must not impede a use of this resource to satisfy the needs of other people, but in protecting its own national interest, it must never let the industry become dilapidated.

"Petroleum is the principal of all indispensable fuels in modern life. . . . The future of the product is absolutely certain; its prices will continue to rise. Venezuela needs to maintain and even to increase the income it receives from petroleum. With a policy of just participation, the exploitation of present concessions is enough for the country."[25]

In the area of education, party doctrine sets forth three major goals: the promotion and defense of democracy, the interpretation and transmission of the nation's historical and social patrimony, and the effort "to form the personality of the Venezuelan within a concept of human solidarity, making him able to understand and to exercise the principles of democracy." The state must lend assistance to those who traditionally could not avail themselves of education, and the entire system should

25. Pérez Alfonzo, Petróleo, pp. 83–84.

be operated as a co-ordinated entity. Unified control of educational policy and its effective administration is the duty of the Ministry of Education. Such supervision is felt to be an appropriate state responsibility, one that must not be delegated either implicitly or otherwise. Above all else, perhaps, the *Tesis educativa* stressed that education had to be planned.[26] In short, the educational policy was succinctly summarized in the prefatory passages of the 1948 Organic Law of National Education. "Education is an essential function of the State . . . [having] as its object the achieving of the harmonious development of the personality, forming citizens preparing for the exercise of democracy, fortifying the sentiments of nationality, nourishing the spirit of human solidarity and promoting national culture . . . oriented preferentially toward the value of work as a fundamental civic duty . . . and the development of the productive capacity of the Nation."[27]

Assessing the Movement / While it is neither appropriate nor feasible to undertake a survey of AD policies in office,[28] it is useful to observe the gradual evolution of the party in doctrinal terms. At the outset, Betancourt and the others faced a country in need of revolutionary change in many areas of national life. Both the political heritage and existing socioeconomic conditions were primitive, and the emergence of a rebellious, social-minded group of revolutionaries was natural. The Generation of '28 began with the intention of overturning the existing tyranny, and as they came to study and to understand national problems, it was realized that national power had little intrinsic value of its own but was mandatory if societal and other changes were to be introduced. Communism was rejected as an embracing ideology, but there were tenets of Marxism which became a part of AD thought. In the 1940s, Bentacourt himself was known to refer to the party as Socialist, although this was later dropped from usage. The massive effort to remake the

26. Fuller discussions by Dr. Luis Beltrán Prieto Figueroa, long an *adeco* leader and a professional educator, are found in his *De una educación de castas o una educación de masas* (La Habana: Editorial Lex, 1951); *El concepto del líder: El maestro como líder* (Caracas: Editorial Arte, 1960); and *El humanismo democrático y la educación* (Caracas: Editorial Novedades, 1959). For a brief statement in English, see Prieto's "Education for Latin America," in *Latin America: Evolution or Explosion?*, ed., Mildred Adams (New York: Dodd, Mead & Company, 1963), pp. 169–78.

27. Chapter I, Articles 1 and 2 of the *Ley orgánica de la educación nacional* (Caracas: Imprenta Nacional, 1948).

28. For a detailed and sympathetic account of the policies of Betancourt's administration, 1958–63, see Robert J. Alexander, *The Venezuelan Democratic Revolution* (New Brunswick: Rutgers University Press, 1964).

country from 1945 to 1948 was a turbulent undertaking in which the overriding spirit was that of impatience and radicalism. Procedural purity was not always observed, and if the AD represented democratic socialism during that era, it might be said that the emphasis was less democratic than it was socialistic.

The *trienio* experience saw the party pugnaciously override or ignore the sensitivity of many groups, engendering a discontent that encouraged the military *golpe de estado*. The resultant decade of exile led to a diminution of previous intransigence toward opposition, effectively muting the youthful radicalism of the party's first period in power. By 1958, the revolutionary phase of the party was past history for the leadership, which came to recognize that the party was neither monolithic nor all-knowing. The years since 1958 have seen an institutionalization and bureaucratization of the party; in organizational terms, this has meant that earlier reliance on ideological or personal appeals gave way to a reliance on the party *aparato* as the major source of strength. Betancourt and his more experienced colleagues accepted the pragmatic necessity of a more gradualistic approach. It was believed that with the days of virtual domination forever gone, the AD needed to make adjustments in a spirit of conciliation rather than to continue the unrestrained militancy of the past.

While certain goals were modified, the major shift was tactical rather than ideological. The deliberate slowing of reforms soon caused the less-experienced party radicals to break away, carrying with them most young student activists. The dispute that has since continued centers largely on methods. Marxists and leftist radicals argue in doctrinaire terms that the measured pace of reforms indicates that the party has surrendered to imperialist and capitalist influences. There is little basis for this contention, but the issue is not meaningless, even if pragmatic more than genuinely ideological. The approach of national elections in 1968 saw the growth of internal division between the *betancouristas,* who supported continued moderation and collaboration with other democratic parties, and those who felt that the time had come to press forward again, with little regard to the opposition of assorted social and political forces. The pre-electoral division of the party into factions supporting the respective presidential candidacies of Gonzalo Barrios and Luis B. Prieto cast serious doubt about the long-range future of Acción Democrática in addition to assuring the victory of a Christian Democratic leader.

Whether or not the party would survive this basic dispute to continue its remarkable record of electoral success, it has long since made its indelible mark on the twentieth-century transformation of Venezuela. The basic outlines of its policies, both practical and doctrinaire, have become a part of national values and attitudes. It is true that Rómulo Betancourt was first a brilliant practicing politician and only second an ideologue; both he and Acción Democrática have learned from experience, and the strain of pragmatism is readily evident. Setting that aside, however, both the man and the party have stood in the forefront of Social Democracy in Latin America. Emanating from a revolutionary nationalism that had a vision of political and socioeconomic change, they were influenced by Marxist ideas, tempered by a commitment to democratic processes and a rejection of domination by international communism.

As with all of those Latin American movements labeled Social Democratic, it was a common practice to apply the term *aprista*. *Adeco* leaders themselves have long rejected this description. Regarding their party as uniquely Venezuelan, AD leaders understandably have had little taste for being tagged by a name created for another party in a different country. To the AD, the APRA is distinctly Peruvian in outlook, program, and composition. To regard it as a prototype is wholly unacceptable. AD leaders, rightly or wrongly, believe Peruvian *aprismo* to be a vivid reflection of Marxist thought that has been too doctrinaire in applying foreign ideas to national problems.[29] The once-common use of "socialism" as a descriptive term has long since been dropped. Raúl Leoni, Betancourt's successor to the presidency, once suggested to the junior author that the party was essentially "national revolutionary," and this term has received considerable currency in recent years. Without belaboring the point further, there is little question that the party fits well into Silvert's usage of Social Democracy.[30]

Costa Rica and Liberación Nacional

Among similar movements, one of the best-known is found in the small but progressive Central American republic of Costa Rica. There the Partido Liberación Nacional (PLN) and its leading spokesman, José Figueres (1906——), have become established as the country's most important force for political continuity over the past twenty years. The

29. Based on Martz's interviews with various party leaders, including Raúl Leoni, October 29,1962; Gonzalo Barrios, November 27, 1962; and Mercedes Fermín, November 19, 1962.
30. Kalman H. Silvert, *The Conflict Society: Reaction and Revolution in Latin America* (New Orleans: Hauser Press, 1961), pp. 256–57.

party itself has been in and out of power, and national elections to a considerable degree revolve about popular attitudes toward the PLN.[31] Figueres has long been the party's major source of guidance, and at the same time he has built a broad hemispheric reputation as one of the most articulate of Social Democratic reformers. In the decade since leaving the presidency he has lectured widely on a variety of Latin-American questions, particularly the ever-thorny relationship of Latin America with the United States. While the major exponent of PLN doctrine, Figueres has, like Betancourt in Venezuela, shared political leadership with a number of colleagues. Our concern, as always, is primarily one of doctrine, and only secondarily the political history of the movement.

José Figueres and the Rise of Liberación Nacional / Born in San Ramón to recent immigrants from Catalonia, José Figueres was educated in Costa Rica, irregularly attended classes in the United States for a time, and began a career as owner and operator of a coffee *finca* in the rugged mountains south of San José, which he named "Lucha Sin Fin," or "The Unending Struggle." For some fifteen years Figueres worked to build up the property, adopting the kinds of approaches that were later applied to Costa Rica as a whole. A loose form of mixed socialism was employed, wherein some five hundred sharecroppers harvested their fields and had a choice of selling to Figueres at market prices or elsewhere if a better offer were available. Modern agricultural methods were introduced, water resources developed, and housing provided along with a small dispensary giving medical services. A communal vegetable farm was begun, as was a dairy that produced free milk for the children of the farm workers.

Figueres first came to national attention in 1942 when a radio broadcast criticizing the government was interrupted by authorities who arrested and exiled him briefly. Upon his return, Figueres renewed his attack on the administration; in 1943 his first work was published under the title *Palabras gastadas*,[32] or "wasted words" (referring to liberty, democracy, and socialism). In this early statement he voiced an ardent defense of individual liberty. Figueres insisted that if man lacked "an altar where there burns the sacred flame of dignity, and an unquenchable

---

31. For an electoral study that notes the importance of emotional responses to the party, see John D. Martz, "The Costa Rican Elections, 1953–1966," *The Western Political Quarterly*, XX, No. 4 (December 1967), 888–910.

32. José Figueres, *Palabras gastadas: Democracia, socialismo, libertad*, 2d ed. (San Jose: n.p., 1955). For an excellent survey of the development of philosophy in Costa Rica, see Constantino Lascaris, *Desarrollo de las ideas filosóficas en Costa Rica* (San José: "Las Américas, Ltda.," 1964). Figueres is discussed on pp. 312–23. Also see the treatment of an affiliated exponent of Social Democracy, Rodrigo Facio, on pp. 323–29.

thirst for liberty, he may be reduced to a more miserable existence than that of his savage forebears in the untrammeled forest."[33] Democracy rather than dictatorship provided the only path to the ennoblement of the human spirit. Thus, "democracy is optimistic, because it needs the conscious action of each citizen, and it believes in the gradual advance of culture. The one degrades, the other dignifies. Dictatorship looks backwards, and is stagnant, Death. Democracy looks forward, and is evolution, splendor, Life."[34]

Figueres' economic ideas were beginning to take shape as well. While refusing to make a sharp doctrinal commitment, he stressed the point that production was an essentially social rather than private activity. All too often, the gap between the producers and those who directed their labors was growing in magnitude. For Figueres, major concern should be directed toward a fruitful and co-operative relationship between employer and employee. "Social revolution? So be it. Let it be the revolution against inefficient methods of work, which are not good enough to bake bread enough for all, and against retrogressive methods which are useful to no one. But let the struggle of ideas, the struggle of classes and the social revolution be contests among rational beings, in a democratic battlefield, where each brain is a cannon, where each enemy is a friend. And above all let it never be a fratricidal struggle among the elements necessary for production. . . ."[35]

By the mid-40s Figueres became the center of a group of young intellectuals who sought to introduce socioeconomic reforms to Costa Rica. They organized as the Partido Social Demócrata (PSD) but made few inroads into the existing system of traditional Costa Rican parties and factions. In 1948 they joined with the conservative Partido Unión Nacional (PUN) in supporting newspaper publisher Otilio Ulate against the official government candidate. When the legislature attempted to annul Ulate's electoral victory, civil war broke out in normally nonviolent Costa Rica; Figueres led the revolutionaries from the mountainous region in which "Lucha Sin Fin" was located. The fighting lasted nearly two months, and during this time the Communists assumed a major role on behalf of official forces. It was this that led Figueres to make subsequent claims that his movement had actually been the first in Latin America to take up arms against the encroachments of communism.[36]

33. Figueres, *Palabras gastadas,* p. 34.
34. *Ibid.,* p. 18.
35. *Ibid.,* p. 27.
36. Two useful narrations of the events leading up to and including the 1948 civil war, both of them sympathetic to the PLN, are Alberto F. Cañas, *Los 8 años* (San José: Editorial Liberación Nacional, 1955), and Hugo Navarro Bolandi, *La generación de '48* (México: Imprenta Olimpo, 1951).

The rebels were ultimately victorious, and in due course Otilio Ulate assumed the presidency. First, however, came an eighteen-month period during which Figueres headed the self-styled Junta Fundadora de la Segunda República. Several important and revealing reforms were introduced during this period.[37]

The *junta* issued a decree that nationalized Costa Rica's banking system. Arguing that private banks had been concerned only with the financing of export-import trade, thereby making it a virtual impossibility for small farmers to receive necessary credits, the *junta* believed that only nationalization could democratize the system sufficiently to benefit the ordinary agricultural worker. The nationalized banks were then used by the *junta* to initiate a program of planned economic development. The government provided additional capital, and extensive loans were negotiated with large numbers of both businessmen and small farmers. An autonomous Instituto Constarricense de Electricidad (ICE) was created as a means of developing a truly national system of electricity that could provide the power necessary for agricultural development and the growth of light industry. These and similar steps were financed in part by a 10 percent capital levy that the *junta* decreed soon after taking power. Among the results was a wave of opposition from conservative interests, and the Partido Social Demócrata received limited support in the 1949 elections for a constituent assembly. Consequently it was unable to introduce into the new constitution the far-reaching reforms that had been envisaged.

During the Ulate administration that followed, Figueres dissolved the PSD and created the Partido Liberación Nacional, with its objective, as one observer wrote, "an ideological party which would be capable of conducting Costa Rica along the path of modern economic and social development while at the same time conserving and expanding the country's political democracy."[38] Its electoral mottoes were "Social Justice with Liberty" and "Progress with Democracy." The party became a fully developed organization with which Figueres swept to the presidency in 1953, and since that time anti-PLN elements have mounted a variety of alliances in opposing it. Figueres' close friend and chosen successor, Francisco Orlich, won the presidency for Liberación Nacional in 1962 after a temporary party rift had cost him victory in 1958.[39] The party

37. An informative biography that stresses Figueres' career before his 1953 election is Arturo Castro Esquivel, *José Figueres Ferrer: El hombre y su obra* (San José: Imprenta Tormo, 1955).

38. Robert J. Alexander, *Prophets of the Revolution: Profiles of Latin-American Leaders* (New York: Macmillan Co., 1962), p. 157.

39. A brief but ill-timed division resulted in two PLN members running for

narrowly lost the presidency to a coalition opponent in 1966, although retaining a slender legislative majority. However, the party returned to power when Figueres won another term in the 1970 elections. But already both the record of his own 1953–58 administration and Figueres' extensive writings and public declarations through the years gave a detailed picture of his formulation of Social Democratic thought.

The Ideology and Program of Costa Rican Social Democracy / Figueres, in a 1950 speech, reviewed the history of the hemisphere and noted the obstacles that had retarded the growth of genuine participatory democracy.[40] Three deficiencies struck him as particularly serious: the imperfections in performance of the political system, with the rights of man too often respected only by paper constitutions; the economic contrast between a well-to-do minority and a deprived majority; and a similar cultural duality in which the educated elite stood in contrast to a large illiterate mass. These, argued Figueres, gave meaning to what he saw as a contemporary cultural and economic crisis. The solution lay in the social control of economic activities, which he described as increasing throughout Latin America. He praised the beneficial role of state-owned enterprises combining the operating advantages of private corporations with governmental protection of general interests. It was important for Liberación Nacional, therefore, to create an over-all plan for economic institutions. The party pledged itself to entrust autonomous agencies "with the rendering of certain general services such as credit, electric power, the principal means of transportation, scientific stabilization of prices, regulation of a balanced production; and [to] encourage a large number of private enterprises to function freely within defined limits."[41]

If democracy were to adapt itself to a changing world and support

the presidency in 1958 against opposition candidate Mario Echandi Jiménez. Their vote total was larger than Echandi's, but the split permitted his election as a minority president. For an account of this schism, see James L. Busey, *Notes on Costa Rican Democracy* (Boulder: University of Colorado Press, 1962), p. 23 ff. For a searching self-critical analysis of internal party weaknesses and the "unnecessary" loss of the presidency in 1958, see Joaquín Zalazar Solórzano, *De una derrota a la victoria del P.L.N.* (San José: Imprenta Vargas, 1962).

40. José Figueres, "Unity and Culture," address delivered to the Inter-American Conference for Democracy and Freedom, Havana, May 12, 1950, translated by Figueres and reproduced in Harold Eugene Davis (ed.), *Latin-American Social Thought: The History of Its Development Since Independence, with Selected Readings* (Washington: University Press of Washington, D.C., 1963), pp. 463–81.

41. *Ibid.*, p. 470.

the drive toward social revolution with the least possible dislocation, in short, a whole panoply of centralized agencies would be necessary. The co-operation of such autonomous organs with private businesses would introduce efficiency into the economy, stimulate high productivity at low cost, and spread administrative responsibility while insuring an equitable distribution of wealth among the several social classes and groups. It would be folly to permit the operation of a "so-called 'free' economy," for this had already demonstrated its inability to bring about an orderly, efficient prosperity. For Costa Rica, as for the entire hemisphere, the over-all picture was that of rising wages, increased production, and improving standards of living. The application of technology, research, and improved education would assure the progress that was fundamental to socioeconomic development.

Through the years Figueres has continued to stress the need for national development, with science and technology regarded as basic components of a philosophically eclectic welfare state. He has envisioned a mixed economy, seeking "a combination in which the organisms of the state give the general direction, with the public welfare in mind, while private enterprises attend to the business of production and distribution."[42] Central planning is viewed as a fundamental necessity. Given the state of economic development in Costa Rica, Figueres is fully committed to the providing of services through centralized governmental agencies. The stimulation of growth and development must be undertaken in accordance with a scientifically planned set of long-range priorities. Economic forces are too irrational to be permitted a decisive influence in the ordering of national affairs. Rather, there should be a combination of state agencies and private producers as a means of maximizing economic efficiency. The state is responsible for using its agencies to provide a positive social orientation to development.

In a speech delivered in Miami in 1952, Figueres reiterated that state intervention was the soundest means of providing expanded benefits to the mass of the people. Private business itself was unequal to the task.

> The notion that all business is "private" is an illusion. In practice we accept every kind of social regulation, from the moment at which a company is founded and organized, passing then to control of quality and characteristics of their products, until the moment at which the benefits are distributed. Then comes the direct tax to ring the final bell of social responsibility to free enterprise.
> If we could educate ourselves and accept the principle of the

42. Charles W. Anderson, "Political and Development Policy in Central America," *Midwest Journal of Political Science*, X, No. 4 (November 1961), 335.

social functions of productive property and of economic activity, the majority of our problems would become simplified. . . . The beneficial collaboration of the state, that we not tolerate unwillingly as "government interference in business," and that we condemn to a partial failure by our lack of vision, must be accepted more complacently. . . . All life in society implies the renunciation of certain liberties in exchange for certain guarantees.[43]

Taking his writings as a whole, it can be said that Figueres has devoted the greatest attention to three topics: democracy in Latin America, economic development, and economic relations with foreign nations, especially the United States. In the first of these, his views have never wavered from those first enunciated in *Palabras gastadas.* In 1950 he noted that the strengthening and preservation of democratic ideals required a continual sacrifice, one that the United States and all of Latin America shared. He reminded his audience that, during World War II, the hemisphere had played its part. "To prevent the consolidation of tyranny elsewhere, we have made a truce in our own struggle for the rights of man. Probably at such price we have forestalled a possible attack on the hemisphere. If so, we have confirmed once more that before one can philosophize one must survive."[44] International obligations are incumbent upon those who would nurture democracy for themselves. "The democratic nations of America, led by the United States, have had to sacrifice in this hemisphere the very principles for which they fought abroad . . . This is an attitude which the oppressed peoples cannot understand, although it is understandable in the light of the overall situation. But even though it is explainable it is deplorable. It is a sacrifice imposed by international actions. The interdependence of nations is a force which sustains established regimes, whatever be their political ideology or their moral worth."[45]

The same theme was elaborated in a 1955 article that appeared in the *Journal of International Affairs.*[46] Figueres presented five points in his discussion as fundamental to an understanding of democracy and its implications in Latin America. In the first place, he argued, the

43. José Figueres, "Crusade of Moral Rearmament: The Just Man," address delivered to the Assembly of the Americas, Miami, January 1952, as quoted in John D. Martz, *Central America: The Crisis and the Challenge* (Chapel Hill: University of North Carolina Press, 1959), pp. 242–43.
44. Figueres, "Unity and Culture," in Davis, *Latin-American Social Thought,* p. 476.
45. *Ibid.*
46. José Figueres, "Problems of Democracy in Latin America," *Journal of International Affairs,* IX, No. 1 (January 1955), 1–15.

masses of the hemisphere were ripe for democracy. Although many of the people had little direct experience, nonetheless all shared in the political aspiration for the dignity of man, individual freedom, and a broad democratic creed. Secondly, the struggle for democracy in Latin America was inextricably linked to the social and economic struggle; only by dealing with the latter problems could democracy be advanced. From this, he continued by observing that over-all development could either take place independent of the United States or in conjunction with truly inter-American co-operation. He expressed the opinion that the effort would have to be truly and fully hemispheric. Consequently, his next contention held that Latin America demanded North American leadership, which would be along Western lines of conduct. Finally, the two main contributions of the United States should be those that reflected its characteristic national virtues—namely, its native political genius for living in a spirit of mutual self-respect, and its economic capacity of producing goods and services at an unprecedented pace.

In his discussions of economic relationships, Figueres particularly stressed the problems of foreign investment, traditionally one of the most inflammatory and controversial points in Latin-American relations with the outside world. He accepted the importance of foreign private investment for Latin-American economic development. This required that basic guarantees be given, such as those of nondiscrimination and the remittance of profits. At the same time, however, the entire question was rife with complexity. For one thing, Figueres was not interested in private investment in public utilities. He believed that no Latin-American nation should have its power facilities, port capacities, and other public services subjected to foreign-based commercial control. Furthermore, foreign investment should not be permitted if based on the employment of cheap labor. Rather, the incentives for foreign business should be "the desirability of industrializing our raw materials locally, the economy of supplying certain markets from here, [and] the payment of moderate taxes during a reasonable period."[47]

The Costa Rican appreciated the fact that foreign investors were anxious to maintain low wage scales so that goods might be sold inexpensively. For Latin America, however, this also meant the maintenance of a low standard of living, and therefore he saw no reason to encourage new investments. Rejecting the sometimes demagogic and antagonistic view that unreservedly condemned those North American enterprises operating in Latin America, he willingly accepted their need for satisfac-

47. Figueres, "Unity and Culture," in Davis, *Latin-American Social Thought*, p. 474.

tory earnings. What he opposed was the all too prevalent practice of refusing to pay the workers fair wages and a reluctance to contribute toward government expenditures or to the welfare of the employees. "It is short-sighted to believe that this attitude benefits one community, the consuming country, at the expense of the other community, the producing country. In the long run, poverty in any section of the hemisphere retards the development of the whole."[48]

In one article[49] Figueres wrote that foreign ownership of a large segment of a country's economy constituted a form of economic occupation. "Large ownership is . . . a means of limiting local authority, especially when it operates under 'contract laws' or discriminatory 'concessions' such as the colonial companies have exacted from the weak nations."[50] What the underdeveloped Latin-American countries required was higher income, so that more could be saved and therefore invested. In most such countries, income depended on the prices of exports, of raw materials. Thus foreign investment was, in the long run, less important than stabilization of the world markets. "The so-called law of supply and demand is the law of the strong. Economics should be an ethical science. Prices can be stabilized, and they should be in a civilized world."[51] During a public lecture at Grinnell College in Iowa, he reiterated the idea that the soundest way of strengthening Latin-American economies was the payment of just prices.

> It may not be untimely to repeat that during World War II the coffee market was fixed by the Office of Price Administration at a level that turned out to be one-half of the market price when controls were released. This meant that coffee-producing countries contributed to the war effort, during three or four years, fifty percent of the gross value of their main crop. We do not complain . . . but we think the North American people should know about these things, especially since they are so frequently told of the inequities imposed upon them by the expense of their foreign aid programs. . . . The healthiest source of income for any nation, as for any man, is the fair compensation for its own efforts.[52]

In summing up this argument, Figueres outlined the following formula: "Pay [the underdeveloped nations] for their products; tell them how

48. *Ibid.*
49. José Figueres, "We Don't Want Foreign Investments," *New Leader,* August 31, 1953, pp. 2–4.
50. *Ibid.,* pp. 3–4.
51. *Ibid.,* p. 4.
52. José Figueres, "A Latin American Looks at Point Four," address delivered at Grinnell College, Iowa (San José: n.p., 1953), pp. 4–7.

to produce more; tell them how to save, and to grow from earnings; if absolutely essential, grant loans to proper agencies or make temporary investments; but do not try to own them!"[53]

The policies of Figueres' government reflected the concrete aspects of many of his writings and speeches. For one thing, they testified to his faith in the centrality of state responsibility. The Instituto Nacional de Vivienda Urbana (INVU) was created to cope with housing, and during his administration built houses for some twelve thousand people in sixty-four different municipalities. The social security program was revitalized, with coverage extended far beyond its previous boundaries. Through the Institute Costarricense de Electricidad, the national power capacity was more than doubled. A major effort was also undertaken in the field of agriculture, which provided the foundation of the Costa Rican economy. Production was stimulated through the co-operative fiscal encouragement of the nationalized bank system, a price stabilization board, and the Technical Assistance Organization of the Ministry of Education. Contractual renegotiation with the United Fruit Company of Boston raised Costa Rica's share of the profit from 15 to roughly 42 percent, while the Standard Fruit Company was encouraged to renew and expand activities on the abandoned east coast banana plantations. In his *Cartas a un ciudadano,* Figueres summarized the agricultural achievements of his administration. "Agricultural methods are being improved by technical means and by economic means. In the cultivation of grains, seeds are being used which are selected by the Ministry of Agriculture, the purchase of machinery and fertilizers and the control of plagues are being financed by loans from the State Banks. The propagation of agricultural information has been well accepted by our peasants. The system of price stabilization is being perfected. . . ."[54]

If the writings of Figueres represent Social Democratic political thought, it should be obvious that much of his concern was and continues to be pragmatic in cast.[55] Especially in the economic realm, the Costa

53. Figueres, "We Don't Want Foreign Investments," p. 4.
54. José Figueres, *Cartas a un ciudadano* (San José: Imprenta Nacional, 1956), p. 92.
55. The Secretaría de Capacitación y Cultura of the PLN issued a series of pamphlets in late 1961 and early 1962 outlining the specifics of party doctrine for forthcoming national elections. Representing detailed proposals consistent with Figueres' broader formulation, these party documents were: *La nacionalización bancaria; Política campesina y ley de reforma agraria; Programa de educación;* and *Programa económico.* All were published in San José by Editorial Eloy Morua Carrillo. The party also included in the series Figueres' comments on the Cuban Revolution, entitled *Dos revoluciones: La alianza para el progreso, la revolución cubana.*

Rican has been concrete rather than abstract, practical instead of philosophical. There is also a secular morality that runs as a constant thread through the fabric of *figuerista* writings. Davis has remarked upon this idealistic touch, which he sees as adding an ethical note to Figueres' advocacy of social progress and a mixed economic system.[56] An apt illustration is the final section of a speech delivered to the Inter-American Conference for Democracy and Freedom in 1950. Entitled "Unity and Culture," it concluded with the following words:

> . . . we have found no magic formula for the problems of democracy in America. We do think that political problems cannot be examined by themselves, apart from the social, economic, and cultural efforts. . . .
>
> The success of the Movement of National Liberation is due to Culture and Unity. To Culture, because for half a century we have had almost no illiteracy in Costa Rica. To Unity, because some democratic forces of Latin America lent us their support. Unity and Culture like some old medicines, tried and true!
>
> So when we are asked to bring before this Conference our ideas on the problems of democracy in America, we come with nothing new; just the same recommendations of the leaders of the past: Unity and Culture.
>
> If we could send a herald with a silver trumpet, who, poised upon the peaks of the Andes and the Rockies, would announce to the American Republics a sacred watchword, surely the echoes in the valleys of the New World, from the Great Lakes to the Pampas, would ring with the slogan: Unity and Culture.[57]

SELECTED BIBLIOGRAPHY

VENEZUELA AND ACCIÓN DEMOCRATICA

Acción Democrática. *Acción Democrática: Doctrina y programa*. Caracas: Editorial "Antonio Pinto Salinas," 1962.

Alexander, Robert J. *The Venezuelan Democratic Revolution*. New Brunswick: Rutgers University Press, 1964.

Barrios, Gonzalo. *Los días y la política*. Caracas: Editorial "El Nacional," 1963.

Briceño-Iragorri, Mario. *Ideario político*. Caracas: Editorial "Las Novedades," 1958.

Betancourt, Rómulo. *Dos meses en las cárceles de Gómez*. Barranquilla: n.p., 1928.

———. *Hacia américa latina democrática e integrada*. Caracas: Editorial Senderos, 1967.

———. *Interpretación de su doctrina popular y democrática*. Caracas: Editorial Suma, 1958.

56. Davis, *Latin-American Social Thought*, p. 463.
57. Figueres, "Unity and Culture," in *ibid.*, pp. 479–81.

———. *La revolución democrática en Venezuela, 1959–1964.* 4 Vols. Caracas: Imprenta Nacional, 1968.
———. *Posición y doctrina.* Caracas: Editorial Cordillera, 1958.
———. *Rómulo Betancourt: Pensamiento y acción.* México: n.p., 1951.
———. *Trayectoria democrática de una revolución.* Caracas: Imprenta Nacional, 1948.
———. *Tres años de gobierno democrática, 1959–1962.* 3 Vols. Caracas: Imprenta Nacional, 1962.
———. *Venezuela: Política y petróleo.* México: Fondo de Cultura Económica, 1956.
Gallegos, Rómulo. *Una posición en la vida.* México: Ediciones Humanismo, 1954.
Gilmore, Robert L. *Caudillism and Militarism in Venezuela.* Athens: Ohio University Press, 1964.
Lieuwen, Edwin. *Venezuela.* London: Oxford University Press, 1961.
Machín, José María. *Caudillismo y democracia en América Latina.* México: Ediciones Humanismo, 1955.
Magallanes, Manuel Vincente. *Partidos políticos venezolanos.* Caracas: Tip. Vargas, 1960.
Martz, John D. *Acción Democrática: Evolution of a Modern Political Party in Venezuela.* Princeton: Princeton University Press, 1966.
Pérez Alfonzo, Juan Pablo. *Petróleo: Jugo de la tierra.* Caracas: Editorial Arte, 1961.
Prieto Figueroa, Luis Beltrán. *De una educación de castas o una educación de masas.* La Habana: Editorial Lex, 1951.
———. *El concepto del líder: El maestro como líder.* Caracas: Editorial Art 1960.
———. *El humanismo democrático y la educación.* Caracas: Editorial Novedades, 1959.
Rangel, Domingo Alberto. *Una teoría para la revolución democrática.* Caracas: Editorial Arte, 1958.
Serxner, Stanley J. *Acción Democrática of Venezuela: Its Origins and Development.* Latin American Monograph Series. Gainesville: University of Florida Press, 1959.
Troconis Guerrero, Luis. *La cuestión agraria en la historia nacional.* Caracas: Editorial Arte, 1962.
Uslar Pietri, Arturo. *Venezuela: Un país en transformación.* Caracas: Tip. Italiana.

COSTA RICA AND LIBERACIÓN NACIONAL

Bosch, Juan. *Apuntes para una interpretación de la historia costarricense.* San José: Editorial Eloy Morua Carrillo, 1963.
Busey, James L. *Notes on Costa Rican Democracy.* Boulder: University of Colorado Press, 1962.
Cañas, Alberto F. *Los 8 años.* San José: Editorial Liberación Nacional, 1955.
Castro Esquivel, Arturo. *José Figueres Ferrer: El hombre y su obra.* San José: Imprenta Tormo, 1955.
Figueres Ferrer, José. "A Latin American Looks at Point Four," address delivered at Grinnell College, Iowa. San José: n.p., 1953.

————. *Cartas a un ciudadano.* San José: Imprenta Nacional, 1956.

————. *Dos revoluciones: La alianza para el progreso, la revolución cubana.* San José: Editorial Eloy Morua Carrillo, 1962.

————. "Commerce between Rich and Poor Countries as a Source of Tensions," in *Latin America: Evolution or Explosion?* ed., Mildred Adams, New York, Dodd, Mead & Co., 1963.

————. "Crusade of Moral Rearmament: The Just Man," address delivered to the Assembly of the Americas, Miami, January 1952.

————. *Palabras gastadas: Democracia, socialismo, libertad.* 2d ed. San Jose: n.p., 1955.

————. "Problems of Democracy in Latin America," *Journal of International Affairs,* IX, No. 1 (January 1955).

————. "Unity and Culture," address delivered to the Inter-American Conference for Democracy and Freedom, Havana, May 12, 1950. (See excerpts in Harold Eugene Davis, ed., *Latin American Social Thought: The History of Its Development since Independence with Selected Readings* [Washington, The University Press of Washington, D.C., 1963] pp. 463–81.)

————. "We Don't Want Foreign Investments," *New Leader,* August 31, 1953.

Lascaris, Constantino. *Desarrollo de las ideas filosóficas en Costa Rica.* San José: "Las Américas, Ltda.," 1964.

Navarro Bolandi, Hugo. *La generación de '48.* México: Imprenta Olimpo, 1951.

Ortuño Sobrado, Fernando. *El monopolio estatal del Banco de Costa Rica.* San José: Trejos Hermanos, 1963.

Partido Liberación Nacional. *Carta fundamental del movimiento Liberación Nacional.* San José: Imprenta Vargas, 1953.

Zalazar Solórzano, Joaquín. *De una derrota a la victoria del P.L.N.* San José: Imprenta Vargas, 1962.

12

International Perspectives

Given the nature of internal dislocations, political turbulence, and socioeconomic inequities, the Latin-American concentration on domestic problems is natural. While those who have adapted foreign teachings as a basis for their own thinking have often recognized their intellectual indebtedness, this has not altered the preoccupation with things internal. A kind of inbred insularity has been perceptible through the years, and the enduring belief in the uniqueness of Latin-American culture and civilization has further underlined the tendency to minimize international affairs. Only with the advent of mass communications media in recent years—notably the impact of television in urban areas and the horizon-opening dissemination of transistor radios in the countryside—has an awareness of the outside world led to a fuller awareness of other societies, their accomplishments and failures. Politically, this has frequently revolved about the competition of the Cold War, with ideological overtones emanating from views of North American capitalism and the international activities of communism.

Having said the preceding, it must also be recognized that, among narrow intellectual, diplomatic, and governmental circles, the unfolding narrative of twentieth-century history has been a subject of no little interest. Especially as a result of the pre-eminence of relations with the United States and the omnipresence of its economic and commercial interests in Latin America, international perspectives have been vividly colored by the image of the Colossus of the North. Consequently, a body of political literature has emerged which reflects this historical circumstance. A portion of this, referred to by the inelegant but expressive term "Yankeephobia," has been sufficiently voluminous to merit separate treatment. The same is true of the more truly international attitudes that have become current in the years since World War II. If neither body of writings can be regarded as truly philosophical, doctrinal, or ideological, both are interwoven through the fabric of Latin-American intellectual thought; in many countries, they have also been significant in the formulation of popular attitudes on which national policy has been based.

Yankeephobia

For a small but influential group of Latin Americans, political thinking has been shaped in part by the direct impact of political events. The result has often been explicit reference to such developments. Given the predominant role of the United States in Latin-American affairs by the turn of the century, it was predictable that more than a generation of writers would concern themselves with the impact and significance of the United States. This led to the emergency of the literature of Yankeephobia.[1] The abstract diffuseness of much nineteenth-century speculative writing is largely absent in its characteristic works. But if such writings frequently do not qualify as legitimate political thought, they are nonetheless an important component of certain Latin-American opinions and attitudes.

The history of United States diplomatic policy in the hemisphere is itself a major subject for study. Events in the early years of the 1900s included the military occupation of several Caribbean countries, the establishment of official economic and financial controls, and the onslaught of the imperialism that characterized the United States at that juncture. While "Yankee Imperialism," "Dollar Diplomacy," and "Wall Street Imperialism" were popular cries of opprobrium for years—and indeed, remain xenophobic slogans even today in Latin America—this critical literature included outspoken and often highly popular expressions of such sentiment. Given the heightened awareness of the omnipresent Colossus of the North throughout the hemisphere, Yankeephobia was to become a major ingredient of Latin America's international awareness

---

1. The junior author benefited in the preparation of this section from the bibliographic survey of Robert Carter Burns, "Some Recent and Modern Latin-American Criticism of the United States," unpublished paper, Institute of Latin American Studies, The University of North Carolina at Chapel Hill, 1955.

until its dilution began with the coming of the Good Neighbor Policy in the 1930s. While a number of the "Yankeephobes" were essentially pamphleteers with a set of propagandistic slogans to peddle, others were among the leading political writers of the time. This was the case with such men as José Martí, José Enrique Rodó, and Rubén Darío, the first two of whom were discussed at greater length in connection with critical idealism.

Martí was among the earlier critics of the United States to gain a wide audience, although his significance was of course much greater as leader of the Cuban independence movement. Moreover, Martí was among those who, regarding themselves as friendly toward the United States, had little difficulty in finding things to admire. Through essays and letters he formulated a view that was exemplified by his remarks upon the death of Ulysses S. Grant. The United States, he wrote, displayed a consciousness of power and appetite for wealth which could well endanger the independence of neighboring countries and perhaps of the human spirit itself. Yet it was nonetheless a great country, wherein man realized his self-fulfillment without hindrance other than the natural limitations imposed by coexistence with his fellow beings.[2] The materialistic strain that he regarded as generally characteristic of North Americans provided further cause for concern. Motivations of money and extravagance were strong, he believed, while there was relatively little true culture or any desire for love and glory.

Foreseeing the rise of imperialism as a basic tenet of United States foreign policy, he was sharply critical of Grant's effort to annex Santo Domingo and of later maneuvering to obtain a naval base from Haiti. Secretary of State James G. Blaine, often hailed in the United States as the father of Pan-Americanism, stood out for Martí as a personification of evil. "Blaine, versatile and unbridled, perspicacious and dreaded, never great . . . Blaine, purchasable, who true to his character, buys and sells in the markets of men . . . it seems that the mass of people see their own image and absolve themselves of all guilt, and that they find in this triumphant political sinner the sanction for their own unbridled desire for success."[3] Consistently fearful as well that the precious commodity of North American support for Cuban independence might lead instead to the annexation of the island, Martí held views that were generally colored by his involvement in the struggle for independence from Spain. Writing shortly before his battlefield death, he concluded,

2. José Martí, *The America of José Martí*, tr. Juan de Onís (New York: The Noonday Press, 1953), p. 46.
3. *Ibid.*, pp. 57–58.

"I know the monster because I have lived in its lair, and my sling is that of David."[4]

Famed Uruguayan José Enrique Rodó was far less interested and indeed less informed on matters of direct political relevance. For him, as for a generation of intellectual disciples, the great weakness of the United States lay in its cultural materialism. Unlike Martí, Rodó had no first-hand knowledge of the country, and while he claimed to be understandingly sympathetic of the United States, his writings were heavily critical. The publication of *Ariel* in 1900 set forth in detail his opinions.[5] While summoning the youth of the Americas to a life consistent with the spiritual values of the ancient Greco-Roman-Hebraic tradition, he epitomized the United States as a land of crass materialism, wherein the work ethic and technological genius left little room for the philosophical and the aesthetic.

Rodó saw the fundamental weakness of the United States as a tendency to emphasize total equality at the expense of personal excellence. The result was a leveling mediocrity that offset the achievement of quality. The utilitarian emphasis of life contributed to the nation's cultural paucity; no matter how prodigal the North American might be in terms of material accomplishments, he never acquired good taste. North American manifestations of power and prosperity, he warned, should not be permitted to dazzle the onlooker to concomitant flaws. The admiration of many Latin Americans for their northern neighbors he regarded as a potentially disastrous evil. Expressing his misgivings, Rodó remarked, ". . . the vision of a voluntarily delatinized America, without compulsion or conquest, and already through the dreams of many who are sincerely interested in our future, satisfies them with suggestive parallels they find at every step, and appears in constant movements for reform or innovation. We have our *mania for the North*. It is necessary to oppose to it those bounds which both sentiment and reason indicate."[6]

Perhaps the only other Latin American writer of this *genre* to enjoy similarly wide reputation was Nicaraguan Rubén Darío (1867–1916). One of the great poets of his time and a man who won international acclaim during his brief life-time, Darío traveled widely throughout a tortured and unhappy career, lecturing and reading his poetry in Europe, the United States, and Latin America. Having immigrated to Chile

---

4. Quoted in Manuel Pedro González, *José Martí* (Chapel Hill: University of North Carolina Press, 1953), p. 21.
5. For a general assessment of Rodó, see Chapter 5.
6. José Enrique Rodó, *Ariel,* tr. F. J. Stimson (Boston: Houghton Mifflin Company, 1922), p. 89.

in 1886 after traveling through Central America, he became editor of *La Epoca*, immersed himself in world literature, especially French, and in 1888 published a collection of poems entitled *Azul*. After a period of collaboration with Buenos Aires' *La Nación*, for which he spent time writing reports from Spain, he gained acclaim with his *Prosas profanas*, a seminal contribution to the emerging literature of *modernismo*. Later works included *Cantos de vida y esperanza, Canto epico a las glorias de Chile, Peregrinaciones, España contemporánea*, and others. Named Nicaragua's minister to Spain in 1908, he remained largely in Europe until his early death from a lifetime of dissipation.

While the political significance of his poetry is slight, in a few selections it nonetheless expresses a Yankeephobic position that deserves mention because of his literary reputation. With much of his poetry infused with a spirit of rebellion and a magnetic buoyancy, Darío turned his fire in particular on the *bête noir* of Latin American intellectuals—Theodore Roosevelt. In his *To Roosevelt*,[7] the Nicaraguan was, if poetically uninspired, slashingly brutal in depicting the accepted Latin view of the North American President. As he concluded,

> Long live Spanish America!
> A thousand cubs of the Spanish lion are roaming free.
> Roosevelt, you must become, by God's own will,
> the deadly Rifleman and the dreadful Hunter
> before you can clutch us in your iron claws.
> And though you have everything, you are lacking one thing: God!

Most of the exponents of Yankeephobia were both unreserved in their criticism and undistinguished in stylistic talent, yet their writings were widely disseminated for many years. Moreover, they accurately voiced the views of most concerned and informed Latin Americans of the time. It is therefore unjustified to dismiss them on the grounds of pedestrian writing or unoriginal political ideas. One of the earliest and most widely read was the Brazilian Eduardo Prado (1860–1901), author in 1893 of *A ilusão americana*, or *The American Illusion*.[8] In expressing the views of what might be termed the school of unadulterated hate, he identified domestic corruption and international treachery as characteristically North American. Describing the internal social and economic system as a materialistic plutocracy, Prado alleged that the United States intended by means of a far-reaching network of international economic

7. Rubén Darío, "To Roosevelt," in *Selected Poems of Rubén Darío*, tr. Lysander Kemp (Austin: University of Texas Press, 1965), pp. 69–70.
8. Eduardo Paulo da Silva Prado, *A ilusão americana* (Rio de Janeiro: Civilização Brasileira, 1933).

treaties to become the dominant power in a global monopoly of natural resources. Violence was basic to the North American who, for Prado, took greater joy in riots and lynchings than in sport or more orthodox entertainment. Certainly the United States had nothing of intellectual or cultural value to contribute. In its relations with Latin America the United States had given ample evidence of its unfettered and brutish economic drive. Pretended ties of friendship with Brazil were a mere fiction behind which the United States was formulating nefarious plans for economic dominion. For Prado, the demolition of all things Yankee was a driving passion, and the result was some of the most virulent savagery to be found in all the literature of Yankeephobia.

A comparable Mexican writer was Carlos Pereyra, a legal expert and long-time professor of sociology at the University of Mexico. The author of two bitter diatribes against the nation to the north,[9] Pereyra (1871–1942) undertook an interpretive history of the United States as the setting for his criticism. From the very outset, the United States represented a conspiracy of the rich against the interests of the common man. The composition of its Constitutional Convention was that of rich men only, with the very adoption of the constitution the result of violence, corruption, and bribery. Thus reified from the beginning of national independence, plutocratic interests in the country extended their influence to all areas of life and society. Following the westward expansion to the Pacific, the greed of the ruling class cast covetous eyes abroad. The result, as detailed in *El mito de Monroe*, ridiculed any altruistic sentiment while stressing the economic benefits of United States diplomatic policy. The North American failure to apply the tenets of the Monroe Doctrine, in such episodes as the Pastry War of 1838, the British occupation of the Falkland islands, and the acquisition by conquest of large portions of Mexican territory, only served to emphasize the selfishness of national policy. A long succession of secretaries of state—Fish, Bayard, Blaine, Olney, and others—were described as apostles of hypocrisy and aggrandizement. Theodore Roosevelt symbolized the culmination of North American greed for power and territory.

Among the exponents of Yankeephobia, one of the most influential was the Argentine Manuel Ugarte (1878–1951), especially through his *El destino de un continente* (1923).[10] Calling the United States—

9. Carlos Pereyra, *La constitución de los Estados Unidos* (Madrid: Editorial-América, 1917); and *El mito de Monroe* (Madrid: Editorial-América, 1914).

10. Manuel Ugarte, *El destino de un continente* (Madrid: Editorial mundo latino, 1923). The English version, translated by Catherine A. Phillips and with an introduction by J. Fred Rippy, was published in 1925 by Alfred A. Knopf as *The Destiny of a Continent*.

Mexican border the dividing line between Anglo-Saxon and Latin civilizations, he viewed the two as separate and distinct entities in which the boorish motives of the former threatened to inundate the latter with a cultural and philosophical atavism. The exclusively European heritage of Latin America set the area apart from the United States, and the very survival of Latin society had become seriously endangered. Economic rather than blatant militaristic aggression provided the source of North American ambitions. Ugarte proposed a "United States of the South" to offset the immensity of the Colossus, its leadership naturally falling upon the shoulders of the Argentines. What he sometimes called "Latin-Americanism" was to provide the bulwark against North American economic imperialism, with the latter embodied by the unilaterality of the Monroe Doctrine and of Pan-Americanism.

Two Venezuelans also shared in the general assault. Rufino Blanco Fombona (1874–1944) and, to a lesser extent, his brother Horacio were relentless in their criticism. The former remarked in his *Los grandes escritores de América* that

> South America detests the United States because of its fraudulent elections, its commercial deceit, its ridiculous Colonel Roosevelt, its shirt-sleeve diplomacy, its university professors who write about Spanish America with extreme ignorance, its sinking of the *Maine,* the secession of Panama, its seizure of the finances of Honduras, its usurpations of the customs of Santo Domingo; the blood that it shed and the independence that it frustrated in Nicaragua; . . . its conversion of its cables and newspapers into instruments of discredit for each of the Spanish American republics; its aggressive imperialism; its conduct toward Spanish America during the past half-century.[11]

Horacio was writing his own hateful paean in *Crímenes del imperialismo norteamericano.*[12] Giving a detailed account of Wall Street involvement in the 1912 intervention in Nicaragua, he charged that the imperialism of the United States was a serious and enduring threat to the "permanent interests of our race." Among his specific targets were the United States role in the Panamanian rebellion against Colombia, the interference with Haitian affairs, the enactment of the Platt Amendment for Cuba, and especially the actions of military forces in Santo Domingo. Added fillips came from tales of atrocities and crimes against Dominican civilians.

11. Rufino Blanco Fombona, quoted in A. Curtis Wilgus, *The Development of Hispanic America* (New York: Farrar & Rinehart, Inc., 1941), p. 695.
12. Horacio Blanco Fombona, *Crímenes del imperialismo norteamericano* (México: Ediciones "Churubusco," 1927).

Similar themes were echoed by Rafael Nogales (1879–1944), a Venezuelan adventurer whose observation of Nicaraguan events led to the publication in English of *The Looting of Nicaragua*.[13] On the very first page he wrote: "While Mr. Secretary Kellogg was modestly taking the world's most honoured prize for peace, he was waging war. His marines, his machine guns, his destroyers and gunboats were "protecting" the American Banana Trust and other vested interests in the foreign land of Nicaragua. And Mr. Kellogg's ironclad, holster-hipped diplomats were 'assuring a fair election' for a handful of traitorous Nicaraguan sycophants who would do blindly the will of Wall Street and the State Department of Washington, D.C. . . ."[14] The Nicaraguan guerrilla leader Sandino was widely praised as a defender of national independence against the Yankee Marines and was held up as typifying the spirit necessary if Latin America was to stand up against encroachments from the north. Citing the adventurer of the 1850s, William Walker, as the first in a long line of North Americans dedicated to bringing Nicaragua under the control of Washington, Nogales concluded that only force and violence might throw back the Yankee tide.

Another manifestation of this literature—and the preceding examples could be added to at considerable length—was the Spaniard Luis Araquistaín (1886———), whose *El peligro yanqui*[15] was published in 1921 following a visit to the United States. His personal observations led to the conclusion that the machine had established a tyranny over man, with wealth concentrated in the hands of the few while the vaunted democracy of the system operated to the exclusion of individual liberty. Among his targets were William Randolph Hearst, the press in general, and a rising tide of feminism that weakened matrimonial bonds. All spiritual values had receded before the onrush of commercialism. Although less extreme than some, Araquistaín left no doubt about his disdain toward the inferiority of North American society.

He also devoted considerable attention to international politics, a subject that was pusued more fully in *La agonía antillana*.[16] Written at the close of the 1920s, this book critically related the activities whereby the Caribbean was being transformed into a "North American Mediterranean." The United States, having first prevented European encroachment through the Monroe Doctrine, had then undertaken an attack

13. Rafael de Nogales y Méndez, *The Looting of Nicaragua* (London: Wright & Brown, n.d.).
14. *Ibid.*, p. 1.
15. Luis Araquistaín, *El peligro yanqui* (Madrid: Publicaciones España, 1921).
16. Luis Araquistaín, *La agonía antillana: El imperialismo yanqui en el mar Caribe* (Madrid: Editorial España, 1930).

upon the sovereignty of the hemisphere. Deploring North American involvement in Cuba, Haiti, and Santo Domingo, the Spaniard also devoted a lengthy discussion to the status of Puerto Rico. Araquistaín commented ironically that North American protestations of a basic commitment to liberty and freedom were meaningless in the face of the refusal to grant independence to Puerto Rico. The Spaniard saw the United States as engaged in the process of "North Americanization" in Puerto Rico, hoping thereby to weaken all nationalistic sentiment on the island.

While the brunt of the Yankeephobic attacks came in the earlier years of the century, more contemporary works carry on the tradition. While many are propagandistic polemics that merely mimic the views of international communism, others follow a less ideological course. Alberto Wagner de Reyna of Peru has criticized the specialization and mechanization that he sees in both communism and capitalism, defending in *arielista* fashion the values of Hispanic culture.[17] Vicente Sáenz has pursued a familiar path in concentrating his fire on foreign (e.g., North American) enterprise in Latin America, damning the imperalism of United States plutocracy and charging allegedly sycophantic governments in the region with the crime of *entreguismo* (giveaways to Yankee capitalism).[18] The embittered attacks of former Guatemalan president Juan José Arévalo have also been translated into English,[19] and there have been similar works by other Guatemalans regarding the North American role there in the early 1950s.[20]

From the more thoughtful criticisms of Martí to the unqualified diatribes of Nogales and the brothers Blanco Fombona, common strands were woven through the literature of Yankeephobia. Fundamental emphasis was placed on two issues: the cultural inferiority of materialistic North American civilization, and the aggressive imperialism of hemispheric policy. The classic exposition of the former was, of course, Rodó's description of the crass Caliban in *Ariel*, contrasting the mechanistic technological development of Anglo-Saxon life with the aesthetically refined character of Latin culture. North American involvement in con-

17. Alberto Wagner de Reyna, *Destino y vocación de iberoamérica* (Madrid: Ediciones Cultura Hispánica, 1954).

18. Vicente Sáenz, *Hispano américa contra el coloniaje* (México: Unión Democrática Centroamericana, 1949).

19. Juan José Arévalo Bermejo, *The Shark and the Sardines,* tr. June Cobb and Raúl Osegueda (New York: Lyle Stuart, 1961); also *Anti-Kommunism in Latin America: An X-Ray of the Process Leading to New Colonialism,* tr. Carleton Beals (New York: Lyle Stuart, 1963).

20. For an illustration, see former foreign minister Guillermo Toriello's *La batalla de Guatemala* (Santiago: Editorial Universitaria, 1955).

tinental matters, especially in view of the expansionistic proclivities of the United States early in the century, gave all too adequate and frequent grounds for the criticisms that were expressed in predictably vehement terms. With the masses verging on popular breakthroughs in the more advanced countries of Latin America, a heightened national consciousness made the tone of Yankeephobic literature far from surprising.

Pan-Americanism and Internationalism

Yankeephobic literature declined in volume in the 1930s when a drastic reversal in United States policy brought about a change in the circumstances that had largely inspired Latin-American critics. Although anti-Yankee writing has not disappeared, the more venomous expositions have narrowed to a small group composed primarily of Marxists. The adoption of the Good Neighbor Policy introduced a substantially different contextual framework, and as a consequence political writings tended to broaden their perspectives, encompassing a world that reached beyond continental shores. A growing awareness of the outside world came to have cultural and intellectual as well as politico-economic overtones. Thus, the policy of the Good Neighbor led to a recasting of the literature, and vilification of the United States became less frequent. Even before this, however, a small minority had attempted to recognize the merits of the United States as well as the shortcomings. A trio of Cubans exemplified this school of Pro-Americanism in the early years of the century.

Roque E. Garrigó (1876–1936), a Cuban congressman during that country's early independence years, wrote *América para los Americanos* in 1910.[21] He took the unusual and unpopular position that Latin America should repudiate the Spanish heritage in favor of an effective relationship with the United States. Like many Cubans for whom the long struggle against Spanish control held vivid memories, Garrigó reflected an antagonism toward Spain which, given the historical context, other Latin Americans did not share. Emphasis was placed on Cuba's indebtedness to the United States for the island's liberation, and for Garrigó the hearts of all Cubans were filled with love and admiration for the *"pueblo yanqui."* Rejecting the thesis of North American imperialism, he praised the constructive civilizing effect of the United States. An enthusiastic admirer of education in the United States and a realist

21. Roque E. Garrigó, *América para los Americanos* (New York: The Garrick Press, 1910).

in his views of commercial and economic development in the hemisphere, he believed that the United States could not abdicate its position of leadership even if it so desired. Garrigó prophesied a future in which hemispheric relations would be governed by an international organization, with disputes to be resolved by an arbitral tribunal. The seeds of Pan-Americanism were clearly evident in his writing.

A countryman, Francisco Caraballo Sotolongo, shared in the effort to dispel Yankeephobic sentiment. In his *El imperialismo norteamericano*,[22] which appeared in 1914, Caraballo flatly declared that "imperialism does not exist in the foreign policy of the United States."[23] The pressures of public opinion would not consent to imperialistic ambitions, for libertarian traditions were too fundamental to permit the acceptance of the imposition of rule upon foreigners. Caraballo conceded the expansionism of Theodore Roosevelt, but at the same time praised the reversal of attitudes that he read into the 1912 election of Woodrow Wilson to the presidency. Indeed, he even went to the extreme of denying Theodore Roosevelt's complicity in the Panamanian independence movement against Colombia, notwithstanding overwhelming evidence to the contrary. The Monroe Doctrine, a major target of criticism for generations, was praised as having countered all possibility of European colonization. Furthermore, he cited objections to the French intervention in Mexico and insistence upon British-Venezuelan arbitration in 1895 as testimony to United States sincerity in upholding the Doctrine. Ultimately, Caraballo contradicted his earlier insistence upon the total absence of imperalism but explained that North American intervention was a function of a national civilizing mystique. Echoing the thrust of arguments typified by exponents of a "white man's burden" position, the Cuban ended on the note that hemispheric coexistence required United States involvement.

Perhaps the most scholarly treatise sympathetic to the United States came from the pen of a third Cuban, Raúl de Cárdenas. As a study in inter-American relations, his 1921 *La política de los Estados Unidos en el continente americano*[24] stood for years as a careful if friendly treatment. The territorial expansion of the United States was studied within the context of Manifest Destiny and the abandonment of isolationism. Noting the role played in the Pacific as well as the Caribbean,

22. Francisco Caraballo Sotolongo, *El imperialismo norte-americano* (La Habana: Imprenta "El Siglo XX," 1914).
23. *Ibid.*, p. 78.
24. Raúl de Cárdenas, *La política de los Estados Unidos en el continente americano* (La Habana: Sociedad Editorial Cuba Contemporánea, 1921).

Cárdenas conceded the aggressive quality of United States policy, while emphasizing both economic and civilizing functions. An extended look at the Monroe Doctrine concluded with his declaration that historically, both its observance and its violation had been dependent upon United States national interest. Noting as had the Yankeephobes the failure to apply the Doctrine in such conflicts as the Pastry War and the Falkland Islands, he explained that more pressing national problems forced Washington to the conclusion that its commitment was not called for. Cárdenas also differed with the Yankeephobes in characterizing North American intervention in the Caribbean as fundamentally political, not economic. This led to his contention that the United States was not interested in territorial gains, and that annexation was not a serious threat to Latin America. Finally, he lavished grateful praise upon the United States for its part in the expulsion of Spain from Cuba.

With the United States retreat from interventionism during the Hoover administration and the enunciation of the Good Neighbor Policy by Franklin D. Roosevelt, the ground rules for inter-Americanism were almost completely changed. The spread of Pan-Americanism brought the erection of what became the world's leading regional entity, the Organization of American States. Accompanying the champions of Pan-Americanism—who are discussed below—came a renewed emphasis on international law and its implications for the western hemisphere. The most influential Latin-American scholar in this legal realm was the famed Chilean jurist, Alejandro Alvarez. It was Alvarez who advanced the thesis that the hemisphere should be guided by "American international law" as a unique and distinctive body of rules and usage. While many have subsequently disagreed with him, this contention remains a part of the juridical writing and thought from which today's inter-American system is derived.

Alvarez was one in a long line of Latin-American students of international law. Among the earlier ones had been Andrés Bello with his *Principios de derecho internacional*[25] in 1832, and a half-century later Argentine Carlos Calvo made a major contribution with his multi-volume *Le droit international théorique et practique*.[26] Alvarez' writings appeared in the twentieth century, his best-known contributions being *Le droit international américain*[27] in 1910 and *Le nouveau droit interna-*

25. Andrés Bello, *Principios de derecho internacional,* in *Obras completas de Andrés Bello* (Caracas: Ministerio ed Educación, n.d.).

26. Carlos Calvo, *Le droit international théorique et practique,* 6 Vols. (Paris: A. Durand, 1896).

27. Alejandro Alvarez, *Le droit international américain* (Paris: A. Pedone, 1910).

tional public et sa codification en Amérique[28] fourteen years later. The specific juridical issues need not be detailed, but the philosophical bases deserve consideration. Among Alvarez' overriding concerns was the delimitation of inter-American relations by means of a consideration of hemispheric juridical traditions. Noting the historical failure of hispanic efforts toward confederation, he maintained that the resultant relations between a host of sovereign and independent countries should be governed by standards that reflected endemic cultural and historical similarities. American international law was therefore viewed as peculiarly appropriate to the Western hemisphere. In this he was presenting a view which had been shared by various Latin-American governments through the years. "For Alvarez, the definition of American internationl law meant the aggregate of institutions, principles, rules, doctrines, conventions, customs and practices which are characteristic of the American republics in the domain of international relations. The existence of this law is due to the geographic, economic, and political conditions of the American continent, to the way in which the new republics were formed and entered into the international community, as well as to the solidarity which exists among them."[29] Five characteristics identified this law: pacifism, idealism, and optimism; respect for law and international morality, condemning all violations of their precepts; an American moral conscience; an American juridical conscience; and a sentiment or spirit of continental solidarity. Critics of Alvarez have noted that, by and large, the first four elements are requisite to traditional international law and that civilized international behavior shares in these idealized goals. As to the fifth, many have felt that its abstract nature renders it inoperable as a practical matter. Alvarez nonetheless declared by implication that his principles were not universal in their acceptance or application and therefore could not be assumed for all nations everywhere.

While articulate in his conviction regarding the uniqueness of his philosophico-juridical propositions, Alvarez also enumerated rules for inter-American relations which were less than fully international, at least in his opinion. Among these were the Drago Doctrine, recognition of the legal status of revolutionaries, their right of asylum, and acceptance of such principles as *uti possidetis* and *ius soli*. Controversy over these and other juridical issues, especially between the United States and Latin

28. Alejandro Alvarez, *Le nouveau droit international public et sa codification en Amérique* (Paris: A. Rousseau, 1924).

29. Alejandro Alvarez, *Después de la guerra,* as quoted in Ann Van Wynen Thomas and A. J. Thomas, Jr., *The Organization of American States* (Dallas: Southern Methodist University Press, 1963), p. 190.

America, has come down to the present. But if these are beyond the scope of our discussion, there is no gainsaying the lasting impact of Alvarez' ideas on legal aspects of hemispheric relations. Despite various critical assessments by some Latin Americans, one still encounters frequently the belief in the concept of American international law as a singular Latin American contribution.

As technological development, improved communications, and events in Europe all combined to increase the momentum behind Pan-Americanism, Latin Americans became policy-oriented in their thinking along international lines. Overshadowing all else was the inevitable tension and abrasiveness of dealings with the northern colossus. Sentiment warmed with the coming of the Good Neighbor Policy, remaining cordial for the most part through the wartime period. As the burgeoning inter-American system developed formal machinery, optimism ran high. Both national and international personalities expressed their confidence in a partnership with the United States. Among many, three may be cited as particularly representative: Luis Quintanilla, Carlos Dávila, and Ezequiel Padilla.

Luis Quintanilla (1900——), a Mexican diplomat long active in the Organization of American States, expressed high regard for the United States during World War II in *A Latin American Speaks.*[30] Believing Pan-Americanism to be "the first successful experiment in the friendly orgaization of an entire hemisphere," Quintanilla argued that the Bolivarian advocacy of equal rights and equal responsibilities had been reincarnated in inter-American relations. While the Monroe Doctrine itself was attacked—largely on grounds of inefficacy—the enunciation and promotion of the Good Neighbor Policy was the true measure of the contemporary North American attitude toward Latin America. The multilateralization of hemispheric duties and responsibilities, he argued, testified to existing bonds of friendship. With Latin America yet to attain economic emancipation, and with intracontinental trade almost nonexistent, the role of United States capital was necessarily large. While primarily concerned with hemispheric matters, Quintanilla made a point of rejecting Rodó's allegation of cultural mediocrity. In a passage atypical of the customary Latin-American view, he wrote: "The plain truth is that the people of the United States are essentially artistic. . . . I believe that nothing has been more detrimental to mutual understanding in the Americas than the continental prejudice according to which all spir-

30. Luis Quintanilla, *A Latin American Speaks* (New York: Macmillan Co., 1943).

itual culture belongs to Latin America and all material civilization to the United States."[31]

Much the same tenor was expressed in *We of the Americas*[32] by Carlos Dávila. An eminent Chilean newspaperman and diplomat who had once served briefly as his nation's president, Dávila (1884–1955) had risen to the post of secretary general of the Organization of American States before his death. Long convinced that the future of humanity rested upon the vitality and energy of the New World, he had earlier written that Pan-Americanism was the magical panacea. "Juridically, it is a monumental conception. Never has a continent set up such a near-perfect rule of conduct to maintain peace and settle disputes among a group of nations. . . . Economically, Pan Americanism has been not one, but a rosary of errors and neglects."[33] While the free enterprise system was fundamental to North American economic development, it embraced a sense of social responsibility which mitigated the evils of "unbridled capitalism." The view of United States materalism was unacceptable, for if less artistic than Latin Americans, their neighbors had a more tolerant nature. To Dávila, Rodó's characterization of North American materalism was "one of the clichés of Latin American literature."[34] Neither was unqualified denunciation of the Monroe Doctrine appropriate, although the doctrine had been used improperly for many years as a justification for intervention. Lamenting the failure of an abortive attempt to establish a League of American Nations after World War I, he concluded that the Organization of American States, with strong backing from the United States, provided the best hope for fruitful and harmonious hemispheric development.

Similar views were expressed by Ezequiel Padilla (1890——) in his *Free Men of America*.[35] The Mexican foreign minister during World War II, he was to preside over the Inter-American Conference on Problems of War and Peace in Mexico City in 1945. A major architect of the Western hemisphere regional system and an ardent admirer of the United States, Padilla saw multilateral relations between North and South as the key to postwar progress and prosperity. So pro–United States that it was to affect his presidential ambitions adversely, Padilla

31. *Ibid.*, p. 43.
32. Carlos Dávila, *We of the Americas* (Chicago: Ziff-Davis Publishing Company, 1949).
33. *Ibid.*, pp. 23–24.
34. *Ibid.*, p. 135.
35. Ezequiel Padilla, *Free Men of America* (Chicago: Ziff-Davis Publishing Company, 1943).

reiterated at length the critical role of that country for meaningful and co-operative Pan-Americanism. Sharing the contemporary fear that the great powers would dictate to the small nations of the world through the machinery of the United Nations, he advocated the establishment of several regional entities as the best protection for the small powers. As he told delegates to the Mexico City meeting, "The small nations do not pretend to equal participation in a world of unequal responsibility. What they do desire is that, in the hour in which injustice may strike at the doors of the small nations, their voice may be heard; that they may appeal to the Universal Conscience, and that their complaints and protests against injustice shall not be shrouded in the silence and blind solidarity of the great powers."[36] As passionate an exponent of political democracy as he was of Pan-Americanism, Padilla felt that the classical concept of Western libertarianism was best typified in the United States and that a genuine understanding of the practical political implications would redound to the benefit of all Latin America.

As leading apostles of Pan-Americanism, Quintanilla, Dávila, and Padilla gave vivid testimony to an influential body of option. Yet there were less familiar positions that advocated a variety of different international relationships. For some, the nineteenth-century concept of Pan-Hispanism was attractive. Based on political, ethnic, linguistic, and cultural ties with Spain, Pan-Hispanism had flourished in the latter part of the nineteenth century, when the antagonisms against three hundred years of colonialism gave way to growing apprehension over North American intentions. Its champions based their thesis on the affinity of Spanish America for the mother country. A brief flurry of interest in the twentieth century diminished with the triumph of Francisco Franco in the Spanish Civil War, however, and prodemocratic liberals consequently rejected the thought of closer ties to Spain. Even less widespread was the idea of Pan-Latinism, which proposed a closer relationship with France. Almost forgotten for decades, this was revived to a degree in the 1960s following the triumphant tour of Charles de Gaulle through several Latin-American countries.

Greater attention was occasionally directed toward Pan-Hispanic Americanism, which argued that the United States should be excluded from special regional arrangements. Pan-Hispanic Americanism had first

36. Ezequiel Padilla, quoted in *Inter-American Conference on Problems of War and Peace, Mexico City, February 21–March 2, 1945: Report Submitted to the Governing Board of the Pan-American Union by the Director General* (Washington: 1945), p. 10.

appeared during the mid-nineteenth century when a series of meetings were held by various of the West Coast countries of South America. Convened largely in response to the threat of renewed Spanish incursions, these gatherings represented a feeling that Latin America should unite for the achievement of its goals, exclusive of Spanish, French, North American, and any other foreign involvement. In the twentieth century the idea was promoted in general by critics of the United States and in particular by the Argentines. The latter, historically defensive on behalf of their own hemispheric role and jealous of North American influence, spoke out with particular vigor in the 1930s. As United States prestige mounted during the Roosevelt administration, Argentina actively vied for diplomatic pre-eminence, guided by foreign minister Carlos Saavedra Lamas, winner of the Nobel Peace Prize for his part in settling the Chaco dispute between Paraguay and Bolivia. There was an implied commitment to the ideals of Pan-Hispanic Americanism by Perón, although stated in different language. The currency of the concept has declined more recently, at least partially because of Argentine preoccupations with domestic problems.

The most recent thinking of Latin Americans on international affairs—setting aside policy oriented issues of the moment—has reflected more than ever before the nature of United States foreign policy. While opinion is in many cases directly related to the ideological views of the writer, there are intellectuals whose thinking is relatively free of limiting preconceptions. Attention has naturally dealt at length with the Alliance for Progress, initiated in 1961 under the leadership of John F. Kennedy. While final assessments of its accomplishments and failures are presently premature, a variety of responses have already been stimulated. While both Marxists and rightists have, for different reasons, opposed the program and its objectives, those between the two extremes on the political spectrum have differed substantially. For those with a strong pragmatic orientation, the 1963 *Report on the Alliance for Progress to the OAS* was revealing. A pair of hemispherically noted former presidents, Juscelino Kubitschek of Brazil and Alberto Lleras Camargo of Colombia, presented a critique in which a variety of flaws were described. Kubitschek was particularly sharp in his criticisms, while Lleras spoke in more moderate language.

The Brazilian called for "Latinization" of the alliance as a remedy to United States mismanagement. "Between the words and intentions of President Kennedy and the timid and cumbersome course followed by the measures of the Alliance there is a discrepancy. . . . In lieu of a vital dialogue of the Americas, a sort of discouraging monologue has been going on."[37] In contrast, Lleras stressed the Latin as well as North American errors. In his view, "Certainly, as of today, the manner in which the Alliance has been administered by the United States is open to criticism, but it must be admitted that the countries of Latin America, despite the progress made recently, have made a very poor showing of their ability to organize administratively the coordination of the gigantic efforts to which they have committed themselves. . . ."[38] Among the sharpest and most acute critics has been Víctor Alba, a Spaniard by birth who has lived and traveled in Latin America for years. In an impassioned attack[39] that divides blame between North American bureaucratization and the selfish blindness of Latin oligarchs, his "a plague on both houses" approach is at once brutal and uncomfortably accurate. A small but increasingly influential body of moderate reformists has recently been voicing similar sentiments.

The international perspectives of Latin-American political thought, whether philosophically abstract or issue-oriented, have consistently emanated from existing political occurrences. From the Yankeephobic vehemence through idealistic Pan-Americanism to the social and economic interests in the second half of the twentieth century, writers have been primarily concerned with the United States—its culture, its social life, its hemispheric policy, and its omnipresence for all Latin America. Among the newest currents of thought with international connotations has been the so-called ideology of economic development. This provides the subject of the final chapter.

SELECTED BIBLIOGRAPHY

Alba, Víctor. *Alliance without Allies: The Mythology of Progress in Latin America.* New York: Frederick A. Praeger, 1965.

Alvarez, Alejandro. *Le droit international américain.* Paris: A. Pedone, 1910.

———. *Le nouveau droit international public et sa codification en Amérique.* Paris: A. Rousseau, 1924.

Araquistaín, Luis. *La agonía antillana: El imperialismo yanqui en el mar Caribe.* Madrid: Editorial España, 1930.

———. *El peligro yanqui.* Madrid: Publicaciones España, 1921.

Arévalo Bermejo, Juan José. *Anti-Kommunism in Latin America: An X-Ray of the Process Leading to New Colonialism.* Translated by Carleton Beals. New York: Lyle Stuart, 1963.

37. Juscelino Kubitschek, *Report on the Alliance for Progress Presented to the OAS* (Washington, June 15, 1963), p. vi.

38. Alberto Lleras Camargo, *Report on the Alliance for Progress Presented to the OAS* (Washington, June 15, 1963), p. 25.

39. Víctor Alba, *Alliance without Allies: The Mythology of Progress in Latin America* (New York: Frederick A. Praeger, 1965).

————. *The Shark and the Sardines.* Translated by June Cobb and Raúl Osegueda. New York: Lyle Stuart, 1961.

Blanco Fombona, Horacio. *Crímenes del imperialismo norteamericano.* México: Ediciones "Churubusco," 1927.

Burns, Robert Carter. *"Some Recent and Modern Latin-American Criticism of the United States."* Unpublished paper, Institute of Latin American Studies, The University of North Carolina at Chapel Hill, 1955.

Caraballo Sotolongo, Francisco. *El imperialismo norte-americano.* La Habana: Imprenta "El Siglo XX," 1914.

Cárdenas, Raúl de. *La política de los Estados Unidos en el continente americano.* La Habana: Sociedad Editorial Cuba Contemporánea, 1921.

Darío, Rubén. *Selected Poems of Rubén Darío.* Translated by Lysander Kemp. Austin: University of Texas Press, 1965.

Dávila, Carlos. *We of the Americas.* Chicago: Ziff-Davis Publishing Company, 1949.

Dozer, Donald M. *Are We Good Neighbors? Three Decades of Inter-American Relations, 1930–1960.* Gainesville: University of Florida Press, 1959.

Garrigó, Roque E. *América para los americanos.* New York: The Garrick Press, 1910.

Martí, José. *The America of José Martí.* Translated by Juan de Onís. New York: The Noonday Press, 1953.

Nogales y Méndez, Rafael de. *The Looting of Nicaragua.* London: Wright & Brown, n.d.

Padilla, Ezequiel. *Free Men of the Americas.* Chicago: Ziff-Davis Publishing Company, 1943.

Pereyra, Carlos. *El mito de Monroe.* Madrid: Editorial-América, 1914.

————. *La constitución de los Estados Unidos.* Madrid: Editorial-América, 1917.

Prado, Eduardo Paulo da Silva. *A ilusão americana.* Rio de Janeiro: Civilização Brasileira, 1933.

Quintanilla, Luis. *A Latin American Speaks.* New York: Macmillan Co., 1943.

Rodó, José Enrique. *Ariel.* Translated by F. J. Stimson. Boston: Houghton Mifflin Company, 1922.

Saénz, Vicente. *Hispano américa contra el coloniaje.* México: Unión Democrática Centroamericana, 1949.

Wagner de Reyna, Alberto. *Destino y vocación de iberoamérica.* Madrid: Ediciones Cultura Hispánica, 1954.

13

Christian Democracy

The array of diverse doctrinal and ideological formulations that have paraded across the pages of twentieth-century life in Latin America emanated largely from earlier years. While it can be argued that some versions of nationalistic populism—especially those of Vargas and Perón—were relatively recent, this general orientation in political and socio-economic thought had its origins in events and developments of earlier years. Communism and orthodox Marxism are far from new, and even the radicalism adopted by, and disseminated from, Castro's Cuba has philosophical bases that include the anarchism of the late 1800s as well as the advent of international communism in the first quarter of the twentieth century. The leading exponents of Social Democracy also date from the 1920s and 1930s, although these parties did not achieve political ascendency in most cases until the conclusion of World War II and after. Among the more recent intellectual currents, however, that of Christian Democracy stands out in particular.

Even this is by no means philosophically new. To be sure, the Christian Democratic parties have only come to hemispheric prominence within the past decade. The Chileans rose from minor status in the 1950s to impressive electoral victory in 1964, while in Venezuela the "Social Christian" Comité de Organización Política Electoral Independiente (COPEI), organized in 1946, did not come into its own until the close of the 1950s. Yet the doctrinal roots extended back to social-minded papal encyclicals and the writings and actions of such Europeans as

Jacques Maritain and Luigi Sturzo, prominent more than a generation ago. Neo-Thomist philosophical currents have been present in Latin America for some years. It is only the recent and rapid emergence of Christian Democratic parties politically which has given the impression of newness to the movement.

As many have noted, questions "concerning the role of the Church in society and its relation to the state have persistently formed one of the central issues in the politics of Latin America."[1] With the emergence of the Christian Democrats, the whole panoply of Church-related problems, issues, philosophies, and doctrines have risen anew. The widely publicized 1964 presidential election of Chilean Eduardo Frei Montalva has highlighted the surge of such parties, the most successful of which have been built in the last ten to fifteen years. While the Christian Democrats themselves have been overly sanguine in predicting their ultimate triumph across the entire hemisphere, foreign observers as well have hailed their movement as likely to replace the Social Democratic pre-eminence of recent years among representative democratic political forces. North Americans viewed Frei's "revolution with liberty" as a new and viable alternative to *fidelismo,* and policy-makers in Washington eagerly extended almost embarrassingly effusive praise and aid to the new Chilean government. Whatever the exaggerations of Christian Democratic claims to future successes—and there have been many—the fact remains that the ideological force of the movement has assumed major proportions. Moreover, it has been belatedly recognized that the neo-Thomist tradition itself dates back a number of years and that Christian Democracy has a variety of strong philosophical bases that are by no means new. To understand the doctrinal evolution over the years, one must also appreciate the traditional role of the Catholic church in Latin-American history.

Historical Church Influence and the Rise of Social Consciousness

The universality of Latin-American Catholicism originated with the coming of the Spaniards and the Portuguese. During the colonial era, the partnership with royal authority led to economic privilege, educational and spiritual predominance, and a sharing of meaningful political

---

1. John J. Kennedy, "Dichotomies in the Church," *The Annals,* CCCXXXIV (March 1961), 55.

For a highly perceptive treatment of the contemporary Church in Latin America, see Ivan Vallier, "Religious Elites: Differentiations and Developments in Roman Catholicism," in *Elites in Latin America,* eds. Seymour Martin Lipset and Aldo Solari (New York: Oxford University Press, 1967), pp. 190–233.

power with the agents of the crown. Despite geographic variation and the pressures of changing times, the basic similarity of individual religious experience was strong. As a social institution with a hierarchical structure, the Church in the early independence period generally followed a preference for like-minded political leaders, and among the results was a strong element of intellectual anticlericalism that did not abate significantly until the present century. Social policy of the Church was founded on the principle of charity, and where deemed necessary, this was applied with political ends in mind. This did little to soften the force of the conflict over Church-State relationships, and much of the storied nineteenth-century political struggle between liberals and conservatives was couched in terms of clericalism, with the conservatives closely allied to the Church. Clergymen were often appointed to political office, while others provided informal counsel at the highest governmental levels. Thus, for one example, the extreme dictatorial theocracy of Gabriel García Moreno consecrated Ecuador to "the sacred heart of Jesus" in the 1870s. The overlapping of political and ecclesiastical authority was, in short, a common phenomenon.

A basic act of faith was the conviction that God was immanent in human society, and natural occurrences were often explained in theological terms that stressed the element of the supernatural. The faithful official of the Church therefore believed himself the vessel for broad truths that were politically as well as socially and religiously valid. The impact of anticlericalism during the early independence period merely sharpened the bases of disagreement. The vehemence of anticlerical political leaders served to drive the Church further to the right than might otherwise have been the case. While divisions within the Church itself slowly mounted, the predominant belief continued to hold that political issues should be viewed and dealt with in terms of official Catholic dogma. Anticlericals reacted by adopting a wide range of European-based philosophies; thus we have seen that anticlericalism was an element in Latin-American adaptations of positivism. While this did little to alter the basic position of the Church, the rise of the new middle sectors at the close of the 1800s forced upon many clergymen a reluctant self-evaluation.

Long aligned with elitist elements dedicated to a preservation of the *status quo,* the Church first reacted with suspicion to the emerging middle groups. As Pike, a noted authority on the subject has written, "Traditionally . . . the Church in Latin America had prospered best when allied with the owners of the huge landed estates. Its ability to retain temporal control, or to reacquire it in those countries where it had been diminished or totally suppressed, seemed to depend upon the continuing strength of the landed aristocracy. . . . The rise to power of a new urban group, over which the Church had virtually no control, threatened the supremacy of an established order in which the Church was strongly entrenched."[2] Although hostility between the clergy and middle-sector leaders was gradually muted with the passage of time, little was achieved toward the incorporation of the lower groups into political life. Direct contact by the Church has been complicated by a grave shortage of priests, even in the urban areas, and only in very recent times has the Church, often spurred by Christian Democratic intellectuals, begun to reassess its position and to undertake genuine programs of social assistance. While Church conservatives still view the answer as being one of paternalism and an expansion of charitable works, progressive elements have called for a social pluralism in which the rights of all groups and classes enjoy the opportunity for advance and self-betterment. Here too, the writings of many Christian Democrats have been influential.

Today the Church is responding increasingly to the revival of Thomist thought that followed the proclamation of 1891 of Leo XIII's papal encyclical *Rerum novarum*. Both in Europe and in Latin America, the implications of this statement were sweeping, although tardy in development and exposition. A truly revolutionary document, it can be said to have inspired the entire Christian Democratic movement, albeit somewhat indirectly. *Rerum novarum* stated that the labor movement was theoretically similar to the family, in that both are natural communities. Therefore, the right of labor to organize and to conduct genuine trade-union activities was inherent and should not be denied by either temporal or spiritual authorities. The social concern of the papacy was later reiterated by Pius XI's *Quadragesimo anno* in 1931 and, with increased urgency, by the more recent *Mater et magistra* and *Pacem in terris* of John XXIII. The pontificate of the latter proved highly inspirational to the Christian Democrats, both emotionally and intellectually.

In addition to the series of papal encyclicals, the roots of Neo-Thomism and of the Christian Democratic movement in Latin America significantly included the French school of "New Catholicism," of which Jacques Maritain was the major exponent. Other prominent spokesmen were Etienne Gilson and Yves Simon. The influence of Maritain in particular has been strong ever since the 1930s, and following the Spanish

2. Peter G. Snow (ed.), *Government and Politics in Latin America: A Reader* (New York: Holt, Rinehart and Winston, 1967), p. 331.

For an optimistic view of progressive, modernizing forces within the Church and related groups, see Edward J. Williams, "Latin-American Catholicism and Political Integration," *Comparative Political Studies*, II, No. 3 (October 1969), 327–49.

Civil War—a traumatic experience for many Latin-American intellectuals—even greater attention was given to his ideas. Eduardo Frei himself later wrote, "Jacques Maritain occupies a central position. Renovator of scholasticism, he has made operable and intelligible its fundamental philosophy."[3] With the revival of philosophico-religious speculation by progressive minds, there was renewed inquiry into the thought of Aquinas. As Davis has written, "Whether these Neo-Thomists and neo-Aristotelians really restore God and theology to the heart of philosophy as they claim, or whether they merely create an illusion to that effect, their influence upon social thought has been great, if for no other reason than the emphasis they give to social voluntarism and their consistent opposition to Marxism."[4]

The Neo-Thomist intellectual trend preceded the establishment of full and effective Christian Democratic political organizations. Nowhere was this as evident as in the case of Brazil. It was seen earlier that the powerful positivist current in that country eventually gave way to a return to idealism, whose leading exponent was Raimundo de Farías Brito. Although not a Catholic, he helped to pave the way for Neo-Thomist thought in Brazil, the most influential exponents being Jackson de Figueiredo and Alceu Amoroso Lima. Jackson de Figueiredo (1891–1928), born in Arajacú and first educated in a Protestant missionary school, continued as a student of law at the University of Bahia. Later he became a prominent lawyer in Rio de Janeiro while pursuing an active political life. After some years as a materialistic skeptic, he returned to Catholicism and became devoted to philosophical inquiry. Strongly attracted by the speculations of Farías Brito, he defended the idealism of the latter but criticized his individualistic mysticism in *Algumas reflexões sôbre a philosofia de Farías Brito*[5] in 1916. Advocating a subordination of philosophical rationality to meaningful religious faith, he approached pure Neo-Thomism in *A questão na philosofia de Farías Brito*.[6]

For many years the best known Brazilian voice has been that of Alceu Amoroso Lima (1893——). Educated both in Brazil and in France, he has been active in law, literary journalism, and politics, and from

3. Eduardo Frei Montalva, *Pensamiento y acción* (Santiago: Editorial del Pacífico, 1956), p. 52.

4. Harold E. Davis, *Latin-American Social Thought: The History of Its Development Since Independence, with Selected Readings* (Washington: University Press of Washington, D.C., 1963), p. 373.

5. Jackson de Figueiredo, *Algumas reflexões sôbre a philosofia de Farías Brito: Profissão da fé espiritualista* (Rio de Janeiro: Rev. dos Tribunais, 1916).

6. Jackson de Figueiredo, *A questão na philosofia de Farías Brito* (Rio de Janeiro: n.p. 1922).

1941 held a chair in philosophy at the Pontifical Catholic University in Rio de Janeiro. He served as director of the Department of Cultural Affairs of the Pan American Union from 1951 to 1953 and for over a quarter-century wrote literary criticism in *O Jornal* under the name of Tristâo de Ataide. A founder of his country's Catholic student movement, he was active for a time in the Christian Socialist party, and for many years participated in the Social Action movement devoted to achieving the social objectives set forth in *Rerum novarum*. A prolific writer, he has shown an intellectual debt to Jackson de Figueiredo as well as to Maritain. Much of this was evidenced in his study of the social aspects of labor problems, *O problema do trabalho*.[7] First appearing in 1917, this work gave a clear indication of Neo-Thomist influences, with a sprinkling of Aristotelian thought.

Labor he defined as habitual human effort directed toward an end, with work and industry the characteristic element. Labor could take one of three different forms—mechanical, instinctive, and rational. It was the last of these that held meaning for man, as true labor had to be a freely chosen effort. Imposed labor was a violation of freedom, he wrote, and therefore labor should include both liberty and rationality. It was man's consciousness of work activity and its products that was authentic, and the true conception of labor for Amoroso Lima joined together conscience and intelligence with liberty. "Labor, therefore, is indissolubly linked to the human personality."[8] It was with this conviction that the Brazilian dealt with social and religious matters. He argued that non-Catholic forces were too often indifferent to labor as a whole, emphasizing material considerations at the expense of the social, the moral. Although the destiny of modern societies revolved about labor, much was lost in the general "morass of indifference." One might easily explain but never excuse the lack of social dynamism, the uncommitted boredom, and the ignorance that thrives in all classes and groups. The great task was that of educating and catechising so that labor might truly develop a moral and social consciousness.

In the past, Amoroso contended, it had appeared that the Church was closely tied to a conservative social order. Many Catholics themselves believed in the identity of their faith with the spirit of conservatism. In fact, some even held the belief that to be a Catholic and a conservative was synonymous. The political result was often an alliance with reactionary regimes that mistreated the workers while failing to appreciate the

7. Alceu Amoroso Lima, *O problema do trabalho* (Rio de Janeiro: AGIR, 1947).
8. *Ibid.*, p. 49.

ultimate social values of labor. So it was in colonial Brazil, where "the chaplains of the feudal lords of the times counseled the slaves, as today they do the workers, to be docile under social injustice."[9] The task of the modern Church, by contrast, should be a pure Christianizing support- ive of the social and economic aspirations of the people. In political terms this would imply a resolution of the conflict between conservatives and radicals, between reactionaries and revolutionaries. Instead of de- fending an unjust and static social order, and rather than permitting either partial or unqualified Marxist totalitarianism, Brazilians should follow the dictates of common sense and natural law. Such would be possible "only through the sanctification of labor and through its eleva- tion to the position which it deserves in a just balance of social forces."[10]

In his firm advocacy of basically Christian Democratic ideals, Amoroso insistently supported its international movement, which was formally established at Montevideo in 1947. Having once written that "history will likely record the passage from nationalism to continentalism as one of the most characteristic signs of our times,"[11] he argued that this would, among other things, provide a counterbalance to international communism. The latter, if successful in gaining significant organizational influence throughout the hemisphere, could only mean tyranny, proletar- ian dictatorship, foreign ideological imperialism, and indefinite obstruc- tion along the path to rational social justice. The continent stood in need of a Christian revolution, from which Latin-American civilization itself might progress. Historical periods of "Official Christianity" and "Official Agnosticism" would be transcended by a "Free Christianity," guided by a nonconfessional leadership in accord with the principles of Christian humanism. For mankind, this would mean an end to irre- sponsible freedom of the individual and the encouragement of responsible freedom of the human person. Only thus might Brazil and its neighbors move toward the true common good, avoiding the atomizing fragmenta- tion of individualistic freedom on the one hand and authoritarian, de- humanizing collectivism on the other.

The Political Founders of Christian Democracy

Easily the best-known of the hemispheric Christian Democrats is Chile's Eduardo Frei Montalva (1911———), whose election as presi-

9. *Ibid.*, p. 25.
10. *Ibid.*, p. 26.
11. Alceu Amoroso Lima, "An Interpretation of Brazilian Politics," *Social Science*, XXVI (October 1951), 202.

dent in 1964 dramatized the political growth of the movement. It should not be forgotten, however, that he has also been one of its leading intellectual spokesmen. Born in Santiago, Frei took his law degree at the Catholic University, where he was active as president of the Catholic student association. His first work was published in 1933,[12] and he gained wider attention with the appearance four years later of *Chile desconocido*.[13] Among his later writings, many of them published as collections of philosophically oriented newspaper articles and speeches, a representative sampling includes *La política y el espíritu* (1940), *Sentido y forma de una política* (1951), *La verdad tiene su hora* (1955), and *Pensamiento y acción* (1956).[14] While a teacher of labor law at the Catholic University, he joined in the formation of the Social Christian National Falange in 1936 and thirteen years later became its first national senator. The *falange* became the Partido Demócrata-Cristiano (PDC) in 1957, and he ran third in the 1958 presidential race before winning an historic victory in 1964.

Frei described the thought of Christian Democracy as implying "an organic and coherent concept, inspired in the values and principles of Christian philosophy. It is . . . an interpretation of man and his fate, and, as a reflection of it, a concept of the human personality that cannot be based on money, class, or race."[15] The central tenet is the belief that an exhausted world is giving way to a rebirth of civilization with man as its primary concern, and "its inspiration will be based on human values and concepts of Christianity."[16] Christian Democracy has affirmed its commitment to democracy and stands prepared to do whatever might be necessary in defense of liberty and freedom, for only through the enjoyment of freedom of speech and of conscience can man live with true dignity. He characterized Christian Democracy as a moral force; those who would provide political leadership cannot serve their own political interests but must work in accord with the sustaining force

12. Eduardo Frei Montalva, *El régimen del salariado y su posible abolición* (Santiago: Editorial del Pacífico, 1933).

13. Eduardo Frei Montalva, *Chile desconocido* (Santiago: Ediciones Ercilla, 1937).

14. Eduardo Frei Montalva, *La política y el espíritu* (Santiago: Ediciones Ercilla, 1940); *Sentido y forma de una política* (Santiago: Editorial del Pacífico, 1951), and *La verdad tiene su hora* (Santiago: Editorial del Pacífico, 1955); *Pensamiento y acción* (Santiago: Editorial del Pacífico, 1956).

15. Eduardo Frei Montalva, "Paternalism, Pluralism, and Christian Democratic Reform Movements in Latin America," in *Religion, Revolution, and Reform: New Forces for Change in Latin America*, eds., William V. D'Antonio and Frederick B. Pike (New York: Frederick A. Praeger, 1964), p. 37.

16. *Ibid.*

of a clear philosophical ideal. This Christian Democratic ideal is an interpretation of human life, dedicated to the sanctity of individual rights. "The right to life, to independence, to worship of God, to self-expression . . . depends upon something which God gave us and of which only God can deprive us; thus we are free."[17] And so Christian Democratic philosophy will provide the inspiration for new forms of human creativity, by which society can achieve new ideals as yet unrealized in history.

Old and inefficient social organizations in Latin America, says Frei, have led to a paralysis of the economic system and a stagnation within society. A true revolution is necessary, and it is this that becomes the overriding political consideration of Christian Democracy. Marxist solutions are unacceptable, thus better means must be devised. Although Christian Democracy is deeply opposed to Marxism, it is far more than a mere destructive, negative anticommunism. Thus it must do more than follow the barren path of fearful anticommunism that seeks to preserve order through military seizures of power and the unrelenting application of force. Christian Democracy, rather, must point the way to genuine freedom and democracy. Philosophically, it does this through a faith in its own ability to interpret man and his society as a prelude to greater self-fulfillment in freedom. Therefore it aspires to a politico-socioeconomic system which enshrines human and social rights.

Christian Democracy, according to Frei, stands unflinchingly at the side of the poor. Instead of separating itself from the lower classes, the movement accepts the obligation to work unremittingly toward social justice. That position is buttressed by a dedicated effort to achieve meaningful economic development, by means of which society can be elevated. Institutional, administrative, and substantive reforms are all necessary to achieve the basic structural transformation, and they must rely upon the civic participation of all the people. The "mainspring for reform" is symbolized by Lincoln's dictum of "government of the people, by the people, and for the people." This has been missing in Latin America, but it must be restored. To establish a democracy respectful of human values, the movement must help in the birth of a state which emanates "from innermost reaches through a human process in which the people will feel that they are generating power and creating wealth, and sharing in their creation and distribution."[18] The Christian Democrats work

17. Eduardo Frei Montalva, *Una tercera posición* (Lima: Ed. Universitaria, 1960), p. 105.
18. Frei Montalva, "Christian Democratic Reform Movements, in D'Antonio and Pike, *Religion, Revolution, and Reform,* p. 39.

alongside the people, the poor, in their struggle for justice and self-fulfillment.

Society is conceived of as a social organization which, according to *Sentido y forma de una política*, "has its origin in man and has as its end the creation of the conditions in which man realizes his ends."[19] The common good in society comes from the integration of individual human rights and duties. Basic for the harmonizing of justice with liberty is the concept of social pluralism, an idea shared by all Christian Democratic thinkers. The several intermediate societies within the pluralistic whole must collaborate for the fullest realization of man's potential. It is the task of these intermediate communities to prevent anarchical atomization of the individual and to combat the potential dehumanization of man under collectivism. In other words, social pluralism implies the legitimacy of many distinct groupings which, together, form the basis for a Christian Democrat society. Of these, the most important unit is the family, without which there can be no society. In this, Frei is expressing one of the most universally accepted beliefs of Christian Democracy in Latin America.

The state itself is regarded as "the expression of an ideology, and follows it in the organization of society."[20] Impinging upon man in many ways, it must serve as an instrument for the use of its members, and it has no meaning or existence apart from man. The state provides leadership and guidance, for upon it rests the responsibility for social transformation. Rapid evolution is necessary; especially in Latin America, the contemporary crisis gives special urgency to a planned governmental alteration of the *status quo*. The state must therefore be charged with a missionary task of undertaking fundamental social and human changes; political as well as socioeconomic reforms must be wrought. Latin America has reached the point at which the organized mobilization of all national resources is mandatory, and the scope of such an effort demands centralized direction. As Frei told a hemispheric congress of Christian Democrats at Lima in 1959, "Christian Democracy is ready to take its stand on an economic position, planning and giving its ideas to the end of organizing the economic development of Latin America, to increase the rate of capital investment, to change the agrarian and economic structures, to change the structures of our international commerce which are now stifling all our peoples."[21]

19. Frei Montalva, *Sentido y forma*, p. 83. For a fuller ideological and philosophical treatment of the Christian Democratic view of the "communitarian" state, see Jacques Francois Chonchol and Julio Silva Solar, *Qué es el social-cristianismo? Ensayo de interpretación* (Santiago: Casa Hogar San Francisco, 1948).
20. Frei Montalva, *La política y el espíritu*, p. 33.
21. Frei Montalva, in *Una tercera posición*, p. 102.

Over a period of years Frei and his Chilean confreres have spelled out the specific policies that would lead to a "revolution with liberty" in contrast to a "revolution with dictatorship." These emerged clearly at the time of the 1964 campaign and after. While repeating the advocacy of a so-called "Communitarian Society," to be typified by social pluralism and political democracy, Frei set forth his government program in the following terms: agrarian reform for the landless peasant; public housing to eliminate urban slums; reorganization of national administrative structures; higher progressive income taxes; nationalization of public utilities; closer control over foreign investment; higher import duties to support domestic industries; and "Chileanization" of the country's mineral wealth.[22] This last focused primarily on the problem of United States—dominated copper industries—which the socialists and communists proposed to solve by outright nationalization—and envisioned a process whereby the government would buy stock in the North American firms up to 51 percent of the total.

The record of the Frei administration at this writing is incomplete. A major victory in 1965 congressional elections gave the PDC a larger representation than any other party had enjoyed in many years. The impossibility of meeting high popular expectations, however, was reflected in a setback in 1967 municipal elections. Frei's avowed effort to play a role of hemispheric leadership was also diminished that same year when an opportunistic coalition of opposition senators denied him permission to pay an official state visit to Washington. Prospects of a second Christian Democratic president in 1970 dimmed with the fragmentation of the party a year earlier, when the left wing broke away to create the Movimiento de Acción Popular Unitaria (MAPU). Whatever the 1970 outcome, however, Frei had earlier put together an imposing political organization of unquestioned popular strength which based its program on a well-defined doctrine and in the process has infused the entire hemispheric movement with a vigorous, dynamic, and optimistic activism. Of the other organized parties, the most successful in electoral terms has been the Venezuelan COPEI, headed by the second most prominent Christian Democrat in the hemisphere, Rafael Caldera.

Like Eduardo Frei, Caldera (1916——) has long been the guiding spirit of his country's Christian Democratic movement. While a student

22. For an exposition directed at North American readers, see Eduardo Frei Montalva, "The Aims of Christian Democracy," *Commonweal*, LXXXI (October 9, 1964), 63–66.
An insightful assessment of internal party divisions is found in Federico G. Gil, "Ideology and Pragmatism: The Crisis in Chilean Christian Democracy," in *Artists and Writers in the Evolution of Latin America*, ed., Edward D. Terry (University: University of Alabama Press, 1969), pp. 155–67.

he attended the Congreso Internacional de la Juventud Católica in Rome in 1934, where other young Latin American delegates included Frei, Mario Polar of Peru, and Venancio Flores of Uruguay. In 1936, following a declaration by the Federación Estudiantil Venezolana (FEV) calling for the expulsion of Jesuit clergymen from the country, Caldera and other angered Catholic students formed the Unión Nacional Estudiantil (UNE). Later the same young men organized the Acción Electoral, and he was one of two members who subsequently won election to the Chamber of Deputies. The dominant intellectual strain was conservative, and this remained a characteristic for some years. In January, 1946, shortly after the revolution headed by Acción Democrática, Caldera proclaimed the formation of the Comité de Organización Política Electoral Independiente (COPEI).[23] Thus was initiated the group that has grown to become the second fully national, "modern" party of Venezuelan politics.[24]

As COPEI has evolved through the intervening years, Caldera has become increasingly well known in the hemisphere, and among Christian Democrats his stature is second only to that of Eduardo Frei. Although an intelligent and thoughtful spokesman, Caldera is more the political activist and less the ideologue and theoretician. To be sure, his speeches and assorted articles have been published through the years. Among the more important are El bloque latinoamericano (1961) and La idea de justicia social internacional y el bloqne latinoamericano (1962).[25] These, however, give a less clear picture of his general position than the many official publications of COPEI itself. And while Caldera has made contributions to Christian Democratic thought which must be noted, it is more appropriate to trace the development of copeyano sentiment and the party program. It is interesting to note that the party has been gradually moving to the left since 1946 and that it nonetheless is a more centrist entity today than the PDC in Chile.

COPEI was ideologically imprecise during its early years, and there were affiliations with landholding interests in the Andean states of

23. The official name today is the Partido Social-Cristiano COPEI.
24. For a definition and further discussion, see John D. Martz, Acción Democrática: Evolution of a Modern Political Party in Venezuela (Princeton: Princeton University Press, 1966), pp. 9–10. The evolution of COPEI from a narrow regional and traditional into a modern party is sketched on pp. 381–82.
25. Rafael Caldera, El bloque latinoamericano (Santiago: Editorial del Pacífico, 1961), and La idea de justicia social internacional y el bloque latinoamericano (Caracas: Editorial Sucre, 1962). Also see Caldera's Democracia cristiana y desarrollo (Caracas: "Colección Desarrollo y Libertad," No. 2, 1964); Idea de una sociología venezolana (Caracas: Empresa "El Cojo," 1953); and Moldes para la fragua (Buenos Aires: Librería "El Ateneo" Editorial, 1962).

Táchira, Mérida, and Trujillo, where the party has always been strongest. During its first electoral campaign in 1946, the party issued a general declaration in favor of democracy, and verbal praise was directed to "social Christian" thought. In September of that year a manifesto set forth the party commitment to progress and reform. COPEI promised to fight for social justice for all, and particular attention was given to the improvement of labor conditions, although this was not to exclude other sectors. "COPEI proclaims that social justice demands, on the one hand, the recognition of the rights of the workers and, on the other, the respect of rights of the other classes. . . ."[26] The family was recognized as bearing fundamental importance to national life, and Caldera himself publicized his advocacy of social welfare measures. At that time, however, the party still included significant elements representing the earlier dictatorship of López Contreras, and it frequently seemed to mirror the position of less enlightened clerical circles.

COPEI survived the subsequent ten-year dictatorship of Marcos Pérez Jiménez and was reinvigorated in the years following the re-establishment of representative government in 1958. The party entered into a government coalition, with the Acción Democrática of President Rómulo Betancourt the senior partner. The five-year collaboration brought a number of prominent *copeyanos* into the government, several at the ministerial level. Indeed, the role of COPEI's Víctor Giménez Landínez as minister of agriculture was important in the initiation of what became one of the few meaningful agrarian reform programs in Latin America.[27] Caldera himself served for a time as presiding officer in the upper chamber, and by the time of national elections in 1963, COPEI had become a reformist party whose platform was similar to that of the AD. During the campaign, COPEI argued basically that it would maintain and extend the reforms already initiated by the AD but would implement them more effectively.

Existing social security projects were deemed inadequate, and COPEI promised a "unification and simplification of administrative structure and a progressive extension of . . . services." The AD pledge of 375,000 new homes in the next five years was called inadequate, and COPEI upped the ante by pledging 100,000 per year, or a total of 500,000. A peculiarly Christian Democratic plank called for a Law of Family

26. As quoted in Manuel Vicente Magallanes, *Partidos políticos venezolanos* (Caracas: Tip. Vargas, 1960), p. 153.

27. By the close of the Betancourt administration at the beginning of 1964, roughly 57,000 families had been settled on 1.5 million hectares by the Instituto Agrario Nacional (IAN).

Loans; based on the spirit of the papal encyclicals, it outlined a program of family subsidies that would be provided nationally. While COPEI ran second nationally, with presidential candidate Caldera drawing 20.2 percent of the vote, it was the only major party in the country which increased its popular strength, and the party expressed optimism over the vision of a national victory in 1968. In the meantime the party withdrew from the government coalition and adopted a position of responsible independence under the slogan "AA," for "autonomy of action." Caldera himself had succeeded in establishing a progressive and social-minded orientation within the party, with old-line conservatives pushed aside. In fact, although his leadership remained unchallenged, a younger group advocated more extensive reforms, and the vigorous youth wing of the party, the Juventud Revolucionaria Copeyana (JRC), shared this less moderate position while assuming the leadership of non-Marxist student forces in the universities. In 1968 Caldera capitalized on an AD division to win the presidency by a slender margin. As a minority president, he soon found himself gravely handicapped by an opposition-dominated legislature and a series of economic problems. By 1970, after a year in office, Caldera was clearly unable to introduce many of his proposed programs.

While Caldera cannot be regarded as an original thinker, he has devoted increasing attention in recent years to the continental movement, and this has led to a number of doctrinal statements that deserve note. Perhaps the most important has been his concept of international social justice. On the domestic or national front, Christian Democrats agreed that the individual should go beyond the fulfillment of minimal obligations as a means of contributing to the common good. Caldera extended this to the international realm, arguing that a nation itself should also do more than the minimum in striving for international progress. Expanding his views in *El bloque latinoamericano,* he recalled that "There is a social justice which obligates the stronger with regard to the weaker; it demands from the richer an obligation with regard to the poorer; it demands duties which can neither be figured by machines nor the mathematics of communitive justice. There is a social justice which establishes inequality of duties to reestablish fundamental equality among men; that social justice, which exists in the name of human solidarity, imposes whatever is necessary for the common good."[28] Internationally, he continued, a prosperous country could fulfill its corporate duty toward social justice in a variety of specific ways.

For example, economically developed countries should not apply the

28. Caldera, *El bloque latinoamericano,* pp. 25–26.

principle of supply and demand in their trade with producers of raw materials. The latter should not be compelled to open unprotected domestic markets for the return of manufactured goods. Moreover—and this had obvious relevance for Latin-American trade with the United States—raw materials producers should be assisted in their struggle against uncontrollable price changes. A country earning its foreign exchange from one major export product, therefore, should not be forced to face the wildly fluctuating vagueries of international prices without receiving substantive aid from the producer of finished goods. A logical extension of this argument brought Caldera to an advocacy of regional common markets.[29] While this in itself was consonant with Christian Democratic doctrine on questions of international agreements, Caldera attempted to provide further ideological justification. The obligations of international social justice bound the economically developed countries to encouragement of multilateral agreements on regional bases. In all of this, wrote Caldera, the more fortunate countries could give meaning to their growing awareness of a national responsibility to combat international injustice. Caldera's international concept, it must be added, was adopted as a basic principle by the Christian Democrats at their hemispheric congress in 1959.

Among the Christian Democrats, Caldera's voice was also prominent in arguing the necessity of political cooperation with rival political groups. Obviously influenced by the highly beneficial and fruitful collaboration of COPEI with the AD, he showed none of the reluctance with which many Christian Democrats faced the prospects of political alliances. Caldera specified two conditions for collaboration: "One, a clear and concise definition with regard to Communist forces which offer social change, but deny to man the use of representative democracy and the inviolable guarantee of human rights; the other, respect for the spiritual values which inform our movement even when they do not share them as the base of their philosophical position."[30] This too was subsequently adopted at an international convocation of Christian Democrats. The Third World Conference in 1961 resolved that member parties be willing to consider "the convenience of collaboration or understanding with those advanced social currents which, even without being founded on a Christian inspiration, are disposed to struggle, respecting

29. Following his 1969 inauguration, however, Caldera moved slowly in the face of strong opposition—including much *copeyano* opinion—to proposed Venezuelan participation in the sub-regional "Andean Pact."

30. Rafael Caldera, as quoted in Edward J. Williams, *Latin-American Christian Democratic Parties* (Knoxville: The University of Tennessee Press, 1967), p. 191.

the spiritual values which inspire us, for the achievement of social justice within the defense of democracy and of liberty."[31]

These issues aside, the basic writings of Rafael Caldera have been little different than those of Christian Democrats elsewhere. He has consistently advocated the necessity of profound change, which is to be realized by nonviolent social revolution. "Revolution," he wrote in 1963, "must be understood as the acceleration of history . . . [and] the rupture with that part of the past which retards the accomplishments of social aims, and the adoption of those measures and systems which can bring about the realization of the Christian concept of man."[32] And as he said on another occasion, "We will either have a peaceful, constructive and Christian revolution, or the people will be swept toward a violent, materialistic, and destructive revolution."[33]

The intellectual vigor of Christian Democracy in Peru has given it nearly as much influence as the Venezuelan movement, notwithstanding its lesser importance in terms of national politics. Its leading contemporary ideologue has been the acerbic and combative Héctor Cornejo Chávez, although the intellectual roots of Catholic thought in Peru antedate his rise to prominence. Traditional yet socially concerned views were expressed from the 1930s in many of the writings of Víctor Andrés Belaúnde (1883-1966), one of the great figures in twentieth-century Peruvian letters. Of particular significance was his *La realidad nacional*,[34] in which he undertood a refutation of Mariátegui's *Siete ensayos*. Criticizing the latter's Marxist position on philosophical grounds, he called for a harmonious synthesis of social forces which would draw inspiration from the social doctrine of the Church. The worth of the individual was to orient society so that, while the values of work and of the human spirit might be enhanced, there would be none of the atomization that threatened modern society. Convinced that religious unity through Catholicism provided the fundamental base for the building of national Peruvian attitudes, he argued that *peruanidad* required a continued extension of social-minded Catholic endeavor.[35]

31. *Ibid.*

32. Rafael Caldera, "Crucial Test for Christian Civilization," in *The Alliance for Progress: A Critical Appraisal,* ed., William Manger (Washington: Public Affairs Press, 1963), p. 23.

33. Rafael Caldera, "El Crecimiento de la Democracia Cristiana y su influencia sobre la Realidad Social de América Latina," lecture given in Chicago, January 1965, as quoted in Gerhard Masur, *Nationalism in Latin America: Diversity and Unity* (New York: Macmillan Co., 1966), p. 236.

34. Víctor Andrés Belaúnde, *La realidad nacional* (Paris: Editorial "Le Livre libre," 1931).

35. For his full analysis, see Víctor Andrés Belaúnde, *Peruanidad*, 3d ed. (Lima: Ediciones Librería Studium, 1965).

More explicit Christian Democratic ideals were expressed by José Luis Bustamante y Rivero (1893———), once the nation's president and an eminent jurist who was elected presiding officer of the International Court of Justice in 1967. Not himself a party member,[36] Bustamante concerned himself with Catholic formulations of Peruvian socioeconomic problems. In 1955 his *Mensaje al Perú*[37] expressed his belief that they had not been adequately dealt with in the past; furthermore, Bustamante recognized the explicit need for genuine change. Critical of both traditional liberalism and the statism of Marx, he raised a Catholic cry for social justice, firmly reproaching the Church in Peru for its affinity to traditional conservatism and for inadequate personal contact with the working class. The official activities of the Church were inadequate to contemporary needs; moreover, "Peruvian Catholics lack a basic understanding of the dogma of their religion and have not known how to assume their responsibilities as men and as believers in the face of the social phenomena that characterizes the existence of the classes."[38] Bustamante's questioning analysis has been reflected in other writings by contemporary Peruvian Catholics, many of whom have shared a commitment to the renovation of the Church in their country.[39]

The organizational bases of political activism were initiated in 1947 with the formation of the Agrupación Demócrata Cristiana (ADC). This was followed a year later by the merger of the ADC with several other small groups into the Movimiento Democrático, and in 1955 the Partido Demócrata Cristiano (PDC) came into being. Among its founders, the most vocal in doctrinal matters was a young lawyer from Arequipa, Héctor Cornejo Chávez. Until the mid-1960s, it was his voice that spoke for Christian Democracy in Peru. Once the secretary to President Bustamante, he mounted a slashing attack upon what he regarded as a continuing national crisis. Among his major targets was the Peruvian oligarchy, "which has controlled political power from behind the throne by means of financial power. It has managed and continues to manage the country as if it were a *hacienda* and tries to manage Peruvians as if they were peons of that *hacienda*."[40] Moreover, "The oligarchy means a government of the few, holding in its hands tremendous power

36. Bustamante was elected to the presidency in 1945 at the head of a multi-party coalition in which the major electoral force was the APRA.

37. José Luis Bustamante y Rivera, *Mensaje al Perú* (Lima: n.p., 1955).

38. José Luis Bustamante y Rivera, *Perú, estructura social* (Lima: Editorial Universitaria, 1960), p. 168.

39. For example, see Antonio San Cristóbal, *El ordén económico socialcristiano: Documentos de Pío XII* (Lima: 1959).

40. Héctor Cornejo Chávez, *¿Qué se propone la democracia cristiana?* (Lima: Ediciones del Sol, 1962), p. 110.

whereby it decides things arbitrarily; this is what the Dictionary says, and this is what the bitter experience of the country says."[41]

Cornejo Chávez joined in the general contention that Christian Democracy was and had to be revolutionary. "Revolution" did not imply violent methods but rather an ultimate goal of total socioeconomic transformation. During his 1962 presidential campaign he promised "an authentically revolutionary program." He furthered explained as follows: "We do not understand the word 'Revolution' to mean the act of overturning automobiles or of throwing stones at the windows of commercial establishments; neither do we understand it as an act of finding a Colonel with the pretext of saving the *Patria,* for he will only save his own patrimony. We call revolution a substantial, a profound and deep-rooted structural change. And this is what we intend to do by means of six basic reforms: agrarian reform, the reform of business, tax reform. the reform of credit, educational reform, and the reform of the State."[42] Basic to this "revolution," in Cornejo Chávez' eyes, was a policy of economic development guided by central planning. "We need to establish an order of priorities to know what needs our government must first meet; it will be necessary to establish objectives and periods of time for the fulfillment of these objectives . . . it will be necessary, within this task of planning, for the promotion and coordination of the sectors of production in order to avoid a misarticulated or unbalanced growth of those different sectors."[43]

Social justice and a removal of class inequities can only be achieved by extensive state activity. Among the many economic obligations of the state are the creation of basic industries such as steel works, the manufacture of machinery, petrochemical plants, and the production of fertilizer. Economic direction must also deal with rural problems, where the most important necessity is true agrarian reform. While Cornejo believes that the suffocation of private initiative will reduce man to being a mere cog in a society of mechanistic omnipotence, he also opposes laissez-faire policies as being responsible for capitalistic injustice. Christian Democracy is obligated to accept the importance of economic phenomena as well as the existence of class conflict, and should "combat the unjust distribution of wealth and struggle for a more just distribution of goods among all."[44] Social justice means equal treatment

41. *Ibid.,* p. 111.
42. *Ibid,* p. 118.
43. *Ibid.,* p. 40.
44. Héctor Cornejo Chávez, *Nuevos principios para un nuevo Perú* (Lima: Publicaciones de la Juventud Demócrata Cristiana, 1960), p. 206.

for all; Christian Democratic doctrine means a radical attack on the sources of class inequities, and the vast distances and high barriers separating Peruvian social sectors have to be removed.

A strong and characteristic element of Cornejo's thought has been his effort to place specific problems within the framework of a philosophical morality. Christian Democracy stands as a defender of the human person, enshrining the spirit and freedom of the individual. This is basic to the anticipated rivalry with communism and with local variants of Marxism. The conflict is fundamental to spiritual values and ideological expression.

> The incompatibility between Christian Democracy and communism is notorious. . . . Christian Democracy believes, to begin with, that man is made of spirit and matter, and it therefore rejects the Marxist conception according to which the spirit and manifestations of thought are simple reflections of the unique reality, which would be material. Christian Democracy maintains the eminent dignity of the human person and thereby rejects the Marxist thesis according to which man is converted into a defenseless instrument at the service of the State or a plaything of economic phenomenon. . . . Christian Democracy believes in the essential principle of equality and fraternity among men and therefore rejects the Marxist posture of class struggle as the inexorable motor of history. Christian Democracy maintains that wealth must be distributed among those who produce and rejects, thereby, the Marxist thesis that capital is always accumulated labor. . . .[45]

An ardent champion of Christian Democracy whose opponents have often charged him with narrow-mindedness and undue concentration on doctrinal questions, Héctor Cornejo Chávez has effusively extolled the movement as ushering in a great historical era no less significant than the fall of the Roman Empire or the French Revolution. To him, the movement was born and organized by the free determination of Peru's popular sectors, with its Christian basis flowing from the proclamation of the eminent dignity of the human person with rights and duties anterior and superior to the state. In synthesizing his beliefs, the Peruvian has outlined the fundamental rights of man in terms typical of the continental movement: the right of defending and developing one's own moral and intellectual life; the right to worship God; the right to matrimony, family and domestic society; the right to work and the free choice of a way of life, with unqualified equality of opportunity; and the right to private property, be it individual or communitarian. The basic and

45. *Ibid.,* pp. 88–89.

overarching doctrine draws inspiration from a spiritual point of view in which an active respect for the individual and the promotion of the common good are universal and unalterable.[46]

The political role of the Peruvian PDC has shown the stresses engendered by the often radical, semicaudillistic leadership of Cornejo Chávez and the pragmatic stance of more moderate elements. Following the unsuccessful 1962 campaign in which the party gained but 5 percent of the vote, the Christian Democrats took advantage of the military annullment of elections by entering into an agreement with Fernando Belaúnde Terry and his Acción Popular (AP). The result in 1963 was the victory of Belaúnde at the head of an avowedly reformist AP-DC government coalition of Acción Popular and the Christian Democrats. The latter received more than their share of important positions, but after two years of fairly effective co-operation, the alliance was weakened when Cornejo Chávez returned to the party presidency in 1965 and adopted critical belligerence toward the reluctance or inability of Belaúnde to initiate substantive reforms. In December, 1966, the party split, with the more flexible moderates forming the Partido Popular Cristiano (PPC) around the movement's strongest vote-getter and presidential aspirant, Mayor Luis Bedoya Reyes of Lima. Cornejo Chávez retained personal control of the radical wing, including the support of most younger Christian Democrats; the PPC, however, soon established a more effective and extensive organization through the countryside. Cornejo's intransigence in the face of the hard fact of Peruvian social and political conservatism and traditionalism seemed unrealistic. The collapse of constitutionality in 1968 left the future muddled and uncertain. Whatever the final outcome, it remained certain that Cornejo personally would maintain the vigorous and revolutionary position that he had long since established in his interpretation of Latin-American Christian Democracy.[47]

Christian Democracy Today

In practical terms, the greatest electoral successes of the Christian Democratic parties have been, respectively, those of Chile, Venezuela,

46. Héctor Cornejo Chávez, *¿Qué es la democracia cristiana?* (Lima: Imp. "El Escritorio," 1960), pp. 4–5.
47. For additional sources of Peruvian Christian Democracy, see the party's *Ideario del partido demócrata-christiano* (Limo: n.p., 1956); *Programa de gobierno* (Lima: n.p., 1962); and Héctor Cornejo Chávez, "Una tercera fuerza para un nundo mejor," in *La democracia christiana y América Latina: Testimonios de una posición revolucionaria,* ed. Rodríguez-Arias Bustamante (Lima: Editorial Universitaria, 1961), pp. 137–47.

and Peru. And in the third of these, the articulate doctrinal statement of Cornejo Chávez have failed to accompany an effort toward truly national political organization. There have been glimmerings of strength in El Salvador, where the CD elected fourteen members of the Legislative Assembly in 1964 and for a time held the mayoralty in the capital city. Two years later the party slipped back, but by the close of the decade again was on the ascendence. It is important to bear in mind that in the vast majority of the Latin American countries, the Christian Democratic parties are new and weak. This is not to say that some may not mobilize popular support with the passing of time, but neither may this be automatically assumed. While the Christian Democratic parties as a whole clearly represent a significant new force, it is premature to take seriously their claims for eventual domination across the hemisphere.

The major ideological tenets have been reflected in the preceding syntheses of their leading figures. It is not irrelevant to note that, increasingly, the doctrinal statements are collective declarations of party platforms. Moreover, the emphasis has generally been placed on specific recommendations for the solution of particular national problems, and broader theoretical formulations have been somewhat slighted. While Catholic thinkers will continue to discuss the principles of the movement, its major positions have long since been staked out. Theoretical statements concerning peaceful revolution, social justice, the role of the state, communitarian pluralism, and the nature of man and society have been extensive, and it is unlikely that much will be added. Many of these positions have been sufficiently broad to permit a degree of latitude in the formulation of specific policies. Thus, it is neither surprising nor especially inconsistent to find that different Christian Democratic parties stand at varying positions on the political spectrum.

On the philosophical plane, there are inconsistencies that have not been reconciled. One of these revolves about the concepts of the state and social pluralism, while the other deals with corporatism and communitarianism. In the first instance, it would appear that a strong state actively engaged in centralized economic planning contradicts the emphasis on social pluralism. As Williams has observed, "It is difficult to see exactly how strong, independent groups can achieve full maturity in a society with a penchant for dynamic, active central government, which has been so characteristic of Latin America. Achieving a workable harmony between the two will be a great challenge to Christian Democracy."[48] The Christian Democrats respond that individual groups will

48. Williams, *Christian Democratic Parties*, p. 233.

naturally gravitate toward their proper and harmonious sphere in society. This reply begs the question, however, especially in terms of practical application. The second doctrinal conflict appears both more serious and more complex. Christian Democrats are not accustomed to accepting the characterization of their movement as Catholic corporatism; yet their belief that separate economic endeavors should have the authority to deal with their own problems is strongly reminiscent of European corporative theory. They have not really grappled with the problem, and perhaps they will not. Moreover, their parties have not attempted to introduce a corporative system into political institutions, and there seems no such likelihood. The question is sufficiently imprecise, in any event, so that practicing politicians can evade the theoretical implications.[49]

To summarize an ideology or political movement that has only fairly recently begun to attract attention and study is somewhat arbitrary. However, it is fair to expect little in the way of further ideological additions; in the area of political activism, the future is uncertain. A concluding point should emphasize the very brief experience with governmental administration which the Christian Democrats have had. Until 1964 they had never enjoyed the challenge of putting into practice their doctrinal ideas. Their expectations have been unrealistically high. The effect of the inevitable confrontation with political reality and existing socioeconomic forces can only be sobering, and for some, disillusioning. The Frei government has faced this situation, although enjoying the advantages of an almost unprecedented popular mandate in Chile. By the mid-point of that administration there were powerful conflicts between those who posited the necessity of compromise with opposing elements and others who rejected any such accommodation. The challenges of governing are inevitably great; as Christian Democracy continues to mature, its responses will have great intrinsic value in helping to chart the future course of the movement, its doctrine, and its electoral potential.

SELECTED BIBLIOGRAPHY

Amoroso Lima, Alceu. *O problema do trabalho.* Rio de Janeiro: AGIR, 1947.
Belaúnde, Víctor Andrés. *La realidad nacional.* Paris: Editorial "Le Livre libre," 1931.
————. *Peruanidad.* 3d ed. Lima: Ediciones Librería Studium, 1965.
Bustamante y Rivera, José Luis. *Perú, estructura social.* Lima: Editorial Universitaria, 1960.

49. For a full discussion of this pair of dilemmas, see *ibid.,* pp. 232–37.

Caldera, Rafael. *Democracia cristiana y desarrollo.* Caracas: "Colección Desarrollo y Libertad," No. 2, 1964.
———. *El bloque latinoamericano.* Santiago: Editorial del Pacífico, 1961.
———. *Idea de una sociología venezolana.* Caracas: Empresa "El Cojo," 1953.
———. *La idea de justicia social internacional y el bloque latinoamericano.* Caracas: Editorial Sucre, 1962.
———. *Moldes para la fragua.* Buenos Aires: Librería "El Ateneo" Editorial, 1962.
Considine, John J., ed. *The Religious Dimension in the New Latin America.* Notre Dame: Fides Publishers, 1966.
Cornejo Chávez, Héctor. *Nuevos principios para un nuevo Perú.* Lima: Publicaciones de la Juventud Demócrata Cristiana, 1960.
———. *¿Qué es la democracia cristiana?* Lima: Imp: "El Escritorio," 1960.
———. *¿Qué se propone la democracia cristiana?* Lima: Ediciones del Sol, 1962.
D'Antonio, William V., and Fredrick B. Pike, eds. *Religion, Revolution, and Reform: New Forces for Change in Latin America.* New York: Frederick A. Praeger, 1964.
Figueiredo, Jackson de. *Algumas reflexões sôbre a philosofia de Farías Brito: Profissão de fé espiritualista.* Rio de Janeiro: Rev. dos Tribunais, 1916.
Frei Montalva, Eduardo. *Chile desconocido.* Santiago: Ediciones Ercilla, 1937.
———. *El régimen del salarido y su posible abolición.* Santiago: Editorial del Pacífico, 1933.
———. *La política y el espíritu.* Santiago: Ediciones Ercilla, 1940.
———. *La verdad tiene su hora.* Santiago: Editorial del Pacífico, 1955.
———. *Pensamiento y acción.* Santiago: Editorial del Pacífico, 1956.
———. *Sentido y forma de una política.* Santiago: Editorial del Pacífico, 1951.
Gil, Federico G. *The Political System of Chile.* Boston: Houghton Mifflin Company, 1966.
Halperin, Ernst. *Nationalism and Communism in Chile.* Cambridge: M.I.T. Press, 1965.
Mecham, J. Lloyd. *Church and State in Latin America.* rev. ed. Chapel Hill: University of North Carolina Press, 1966.
Pike, Frederick B., ed. *The Conflict between Church and State in Latin America.* New York: Alfred A. Knopf, 1964.
Silvert, Kalman H., ed. *Churches and States: The Religious Institution and Modernization.* New York: American Universities Field Staff, 1967.
Vallier, Ivan. "Religious Elites: Differentiation and Developments in Roman Catholicism," in *Elites in Latin America.* Edited by Seymour Martin Lipset and Aldo Solari. New York: Oxford University Press, 1967.
Williams, Edward J. *Latin-American Christian Democratic Parties.* Knoxville: University of Tennessee Press, 1967.
Zañartu, Mario. "Religious Values in Latin America: An Appraisal," in *The Religious Dimension in the New Latin America.* Edited by John J. Considine. Notre Dame: Fides Publishers, 1966.

14

Ideologies of Development

Although customarily labeled in the sloganeering jargon of the present era as "underdeveloped," Latin America is both economically and socially dissimilar in many respects from the countries of the Middle East, Africa, and Asia. As a whole the region has progressed much further in the quest for modernization. Moreover, it must be recognized that it is inaccurate to treat the entire hemisphere as uniformly underdeveloped. The scale along which these countries range is extensive, running from the lower extremes of an underdeveloped and stagnating Haiti to the upper reaches of a well-developed Uruguay or Argentina. In much of Latin America, the period since World War II has been characterized by change and growth, even though frequently uneven and disorganized. With technological development, increasing production, and general economic growth, Latin-American intellectuals have often felt themselves surrounded by all-encompassing programs with a strictly practical policy orientation.

The pragmatism of economic planners and a newly emerging technocratic elite, formed largely by problem-directed men of middle-class origins, is a phenomenon the likes of which these countries have not regularly experienced. Increasingly, theoretical arguments are being presented as a means of rationalizing specific economic and social policies. These have contributed toward the expression of what may be termed ideologies of development. In some cases, these bear fairly orthodox philosophical explanations, such as those of the Christian Democrats or the Social

Democrats when confronted with the demands of an increasingly restless and vocal populace. Thus it can be said that the ideologues of such political organizations must present official programs within the context of party history and their respective views of society and the external world. At the same time, however, the new generation of economic planners frequently arrives at policy decisions without the overarching rationale of a given political doctrine. These men are concerned primarily with the amelioration of existing economic inequities and social injustices. While their solutions are embodied within an inclusive set of beliefs, these do not comprise what would traditionally be regarded as political theory.

New technocratic elites are acquiring great importance in several countries; in Venezuela under Acción Democrática and COPEI, in Chile under the Christian Democrats, and in Mexico under its institutionalized revolution, their impact has been consequential. An entire generation has been spawned from the commitment to national development in Brazil, while a similar if less articulate element in Argentina is struggling in the face of that country's divided populace. In any discussion of contemporary intellectual trends in Latin America, the spokesmen of the rising technocracy must be heard; some are technical experts and economists, others are intellectuals concerned with socioeconomic development. It is somewhat difficult to identify clearly defined schools of thought, although some classification is possible. What must be carefully understood, however, are the kinds of formulations that have been offered in recent years. The trends that have emerged, such as those emphasizing state entrepreneurial planning and regional or hemispheric integration, can be broadly regarded as among the ideologies of development current in Latin America today.

Postwar Conditions and Developmental Doctrine

In the final analysis there must be an economic framework within which the ideologues of development can apply their formulae. The survival of historical Latin-American trade patterns after World War II meant the continuing exportation of raw materials to the outside world as the basic support for national economies. Although industrialization was becoming for many a magical panacea promising significant progress and modernization, by and large manufactured goods were still being obtained from foreign sources. The early effort in the direction of national industries did little to meet the growing demands for consumer goods. The majority of Latin Americans continued to labor in the agricultural sector, tightly bound by social and economic structures that dated from the colonial era. Low productivity and agrarian stagnation were the order of the day—even as remains the case in some countries now. International trade patterns also followed traditional paths, with the exchange of raw products for finished goods perpetuating an unfavorable situation. Moreover, Latin America's share of world trade was small and diminishing, while intracontinental trade remained minimal. Observers could only note in dejection that the heritage of three centuries' colonial experience had created a set of practices that were still customary.

The unevenness of development in different countries was of course striking, and many of the republics themselves contained two or more economically distinct and largely independent areas. National structures were internally heterogeneous, and separate regions were often marked by a lack of complementarity. The stereotypical dichotomy between rural and urban societies was frequently disruptive, combining with technological shortcomings to maintain obstacles of staggering magnitude. Fiscal aspects of the economies were complex, while the lack of co-ordination of currency policies encouraged a widespread insufficiency of public savings. The usual sociopolitical instability, aggravated by the inevitable revolution of rising popular expectations, joined with unchecked inflationary pressures to discourage significant investment, both domestic and foreign. Such was the panoramic view that the exponents of economic development beheld in the late 1940s. If the obstacles seemed to some realists virtually insurmountable, there was at the same time a determination to undertake a systematic, rational, and internally consistent attack on historical practices and structures. The first efforts took as their point of departure a set of ideas supported by belief in evolutionary economic theory.

Exponents of economic evolution believed that development would progress through a set of identifiable stages, moving ever onward and upward. At each step of the way, technical and statistical indices would show an increasingly productive, complex, and rationally organized economy in the trend toward modernization. By definition, each new stage represented an achievement superior to its predecessor. For the Latin Americans, there were various expositions that were attractive. Perhaps the best-known was that of Walt W. Rostow.[1] He devised a five-stage evolutionary analysis that began with a traditional phase, followed in

1. Among Rostow's many writings, see *The Process of Economic Growth* (London: Oxford University Press, 1953), and *The Stages of Economic Growth* (New York: Cambridge University Press, 1960).

turn by a period of preconditions, the take-off, sustained growth, and the ultimate leveling off of a developed economy. As Blanksten noted, the first three stages were of particular relevance to Latin America.[2] The traditional stage was to be found in the indigenous communities of such countries as Ecuador, Peru, Bolivia, and Guatemala. The period of preconditions saw the growing influence of Westernizing ideas, while the take-off had been reached in such economies as the Mexican and the Brazilian. Change became more spectacular, economic transformations began to take place, and those in power were more explicitly dedicated to the continuing of policies they believed would encourage economic development and growth. Thus the leading countries of Latin America were experiencing a significant alteration of socioeconomic structures and institutions.

There were critics who denounced the implied inevitability of evolutionary theory, and some argued that it was unduly mechanistic and formal for meaningful application to varying countries. At the same time the commitment to development and modernization remained foremost in the minds of economic thinkers, and emphasis continued to be placed upon the worth of technological innovation. Added impetus came from the implicit rationale behind United States assistance programs, which came to have influential byproducts of their own. Technical co-operation had actually begun in 1939, with innovating techniques being introduced in the fields of education, agriculture, health, and sanitation. The increasing tempo of such programs in the late 1940s included the elaboration of multilateral arrangements in addition to more bilateral pacts. It was the impact of fully international efforts and the concern of the Organization of American States and the United Nations which saw the emergence of a new entity as the most important force for an internally consistent approach to the problems of development. The theory and writings of this organ—the United Nations Economic Commission for Latin America (ECLA)—became central during the decade of the 1950s.

Organized in 1948 as a United Nations regional commission with its seat in Santiago, ECLA set about the elaboration of basic economic doctrine applicable to the entire area.[3] The leading theoretician and

2. George I. Blanksten, "The Aspiration for Economic Development," *The Annals*, CCCXXXIV (March 1961), 13–14.
3. An outstanding discussion of ECLA doctrine and related issues is Albert O. Hirschman, "Ideologies of Economic Development in Latin America," in *Latin-American Issues: Essays and Comments*, ed. Albert O. Hirschman (New York: Twentieth Century Fund, 1961). The junior author is much indebted to this discussion in the present passage.

driving force behind this undertaking was the first director of ECLA, Raúl Prebisch. It was from his efforts that there emerged a body of principles to guide Latin-American developmental policy. The first major exposition of ECLA doctrine appeared in 1950 under the title *The Economic Development of Latin America and its Principal Problems.*[4] At the outset, the highly stratified international system was seen as divided into two identifiable camps: the developed or modern, and the underdeveloped or traditional.[5] Judged in terms of power, prestige, and economic status, Latin America therefore stood with Asia and Africa toward the lower end of the scale. For Prebisch, this was described in terms of the center and the periphery of international trade, with Latin America naturally belonging to the latter. Under existing conditions, "the specific task that fell to Latin America, as part of the periphery of the world economic system, was that of producing food and raw materials for the great industrial countries. There was no place within it for the industrialization of the new countries. . . . [Nevertheless] two world wars in a single generation and a great economic crisis between them have shown the Latin American countries their opportunities, clearly pointing the way to industrial activity."[6]

Giving a sophisticated and persuasive statement of the view that trade may serve an exploitative function harmful to the less developed countries, Prebisch presented empirical data to support his contention that the terms of trade were biassed in favor of the industrialized giants of the international system. The unequal distribution of production gains, he argued, led in point of fact to a deteriorating situation for Latin America. And as a result, there were serious and increasing discrepancies in the use of income, with the percentage expenditure on imports from the periphery declining. This led in turn to balance-of-payments weakness and the absence of adequate capital imports for the periphery. Countries

A perceptive treatment is also found in James H. Street, "The Latin-American 'Structuralists' and the Institutionalists: Convergence in Development Theory," *The Journal of Economic Issues,* I, Nos. 1 and 2 (June 1967), 44–62. For a careful assessment of conflicting economic theories, a fine discussion is that of John P. Powelson, "Toward an Integrated Growth Model: The Case of Latin America," in *Constructive Change in Latin America,* ed., Cole Blasier (Pittsburgh: University of Pittsburgh Press, 1968).

4. United Nations Economic Commission for Latin America, *The Economic Development of Latin America and Its Principal Problems* (United Nations, 1950).

5. For an analysis that accepts the basic premise of a dichotomous international economic system, see Gustavo Lagos, *International Stratification and Underdeveloped Countries* (Chapel Hill: University of North Carolina Press, 1963).

6. United Nations Economic Commission, *Development of Latin America,* p. 1.

in this latter group would be unable to influence through their own imports the purchasing policies of the center. The general train of thought, then, held the regional backwardness in large part stemmed from the system of international trade. Latin America therefore had to move toward policies that might make congenial a change in existing conditions. Industrialization required protective legislation and extensive import controls. Export controls could not provide the necessary encouragements of economic development, and therefore import substitution should be consistently practiced.

ECLA doctrine has been firm in its insistence that the governments of the underdeveloped periphery must actively promote and guide developmental policies. These must focus upon the availability and use of adequate capital, both national and international. The demand for added resources from such sources as the International Monetary Fund (IMF) stemmed naturally from ECLA doctrine, and this sometimes meant sharp criticism of the orthodox approach to fiscal and exchange problems which the IMF frequently applied. Clearly, there was little of a startling or innovative nature in the ECLA position of support for the massive assumption of economic responsibilities by the state. However, Prebisch and his colleagues sought to encourage and assist in the long-range approach to developmental planning. It was with this in mind that, by 1953, ECLA entered upon a second stage, in which it concentrated upon interesting individual governments in systematic programming. The first document to express this goal was *An Introduction to the Technique of Programming*,[7] presented at ECLA's fifth annual conference.

In Hirschman's words, this represented an attempt "to provide guidance in the drawing up of medium- and long-term aggregate and sectoral projections of economic growth on the basis of empirical knowledge and various theories that were then being rapidly accumulated by economists concerned with development problems; the projection of domestic demand in accordance with consumer budget studies; the projection of the capacity to import on the basis of an estimate of foreign markets; estimates of savings and capital-output ratios; and the application of various investment criteria and of input-output analysis."[8] Implicit was a reliance on forthright action by the state; in the next few years, ECLA provided counsel and assistance to Colombia, Argentina, and Peru, among others. Greater impetus derived from the legitimacy provided by tacit Organization of American States (OAS) approval at the 1954

7. United Nations Economic Commission for Latin America, *An Introduction to the Technique of Programming* (Rio de Janeiro: mimeographed report, 1953).
8. Hirschman, *Latin-American Issues*, p. 17.

economic conference in Petrópolis, Brazil. The ECLA report discussed and in part adopted at that time also included a detailed presentation of possible developmental policies and their probable outcomes. Among these, a partial listing included expansion of infrastructure; monetary, fiscal, and tariff policies; encouragement of domestic savings, accompanied by growth incentives; a reorientation of foreign private investment; and improved economic programming machinery.[9]

Again using the words of the highly perceptive Hirschman, the programming activities of ECLA were "a protest, both pathetic and subtle, against a reality where politicians relying on brilliant or disastrous improvisations hold sway, where decisions are taken under multiple pressures rather than in advance of a crisis and emergency situations, and where conflicts are resolved on the basis of personal considerations . . . rather than in acordance with objective principles and scientific criteria."[10] ECLA, rejecting old arguments about the destructive and negative forces of Latin-America society and politics, argued that the weaknesses of the periphery were the product of policies arbitrarily dictated by the center. For ECLA, the response was a developmental ideology based on the premise of a revolutionary change in policy-making. The ultimate hope was for the eradication of those traditional obstacles—structural, attitudinal, and societal—that have long frusrated the achievement of genuine growth and development.

Despite the dominant nature of ECLA and of Prebisch's writings, there have been those who found his theses unacceptable. One argument contended that the basic capacity of the state in Latin America is unequal to the tasks demanded of it by such mean as Raúl Prebisch. Governmental corruption has often been cited as an insurmountable obstacle; even greater emphasis has been placed on commonly exhibited bureaucratic inadequacies. The ECLA insistence upon extensive state activity and the role of centralized semiautonomous public agencies has been held to be totally unrealistic, notwithstanding the postwar advances in the preparation and training of technical experts. In the nineteenth century it was common for Latin-American intellectuals to dwell gloomily on the problem; Alberdi is a case in point. Typical of current opponents the ECLA's general thrust is the Brazilian Eugênio Gudin, who has argued that what governments must do "is simply *not to disturb or prevent* . . . [economic development] by indulging in such evils as political warfare,

9. United Nations Economic Commission for Latin America, *International Cooperation in a Latin-American Development Policy* (United Nations, 1954).
10. Hirschman, *Latin-American Issues,* p. 22.

demagogy, inflation, hostility . . . to foreign capital, unbalanced or excessive protection to industry and/or agriculture, etc."[11]

Ideologies of Brazilian Development

An illustrative case of evolving developmental ideology is that of Brazil. In the quest for an overarching theoretical framework within which to attack problems of development three lines of reasoning emerged: the neoliberal, the developmentalist nationalist, and the radical nationalist.[12] The first has contended that orthodox fiscal and monetary policies, with an effort toward balanced budgets and control over the supply of money, would encourage the national self-discipline requisite for economic progress. Eugênio Gudin was among the best known economists identified with this position, and the influential publishing empire of Assis Chateaubriand gave important support.[13] In recent years broadly neoliberal views have been expressed by Roberto de Oliveira Campos, who emerged as the chief formulator of economic policy while minister of economic planning under the presidency of Humberto Castello Branco. It was from this position of authority that he engineered the policies of balanced development and fiscal austerity.

Although too pragmatic and eclectic to be regarded as a pure neoliberal, Campos became identified with the fairly orthodox policies embodied by the anti-inflationary controls that were introduced after the fall of the Goulart government. As early as 1957 and 1958 Campos had questioned ECLA doctrine, expressing his doubts over the contention that the substitution of state for private enterprise would create new economic resources. While serving with the National Bank for Economic Development, he denied that social progress could precede significant economic gains. The emphasis on industrialization at the expense of the agricultural sector struck him as an unwise ordering of priorities. Campos was a frequent defender of the free enterprise system and, for Brazil, foreign involvement in national economic development. Although critical of past economic imperialism, he was concerned by what he re-

11. Eugênio Gudin, discussion paper presented at Rio de Janeiro round table of the International Association, 1957, as quoted in Hirschman, *Latin American Issues*, p. 25.

12. See the lengthier discussion by Thomas E. Skidmore in his *Politics in Brazil, 1930–1964: An Experiment in Democracy* (New York: Oxford University Press, 1967), pp. 87–93.

13. An articulate presentation of Gudin's views appeared in his *Análise de problemas brasileiros: Coletânea de artigos, 1958–1964* (Rio de Janeiro: n.p., 1965).

garded as monopolistic and phantasmagoric nationalism that employed ideological arguments in defiance of practical considerations.

For Campos, the problem was that of mobilizing the positive content of nationalism without adopting self-defeating xenophobic extremes. He was prepared to capitalize upon United States foreign aid programs, therefore; moreover, he placed greater blame on Latin-American ambivalence than on selfish North American intentions for the shortcomings of assistance programs. Consistent in his strong emphasis on practical questions, he preferred to avoid the "useless and frustrating dispute on planning versus free enterprise."[14] This was precisely the kind of doctrinal controversy that he saw as clouding more pressing daily considerations. Although appreciating the strong social pressures for rapid development. Campos feared the restraining countereffects on private initiative, which deserved encouragement rather than restraint. "It is far from easy to maintain a correct balance between private motivation and planned growth, and it may be expected that tensions will arise between governments and private enterprise, particularly foreign enterprises. The use of the leverage of external assistance to interfere with a government's freedom of choice in allocating tasks between the public and the private sector may generate dangerous frictions which must be avoided if the Alliance for Progress is to succeed."[15]

Distinguishing in his writings between "pragmatic" or functional nationalists and "romantic" nationalists, Campos has charged the latter with a near-fanaticism whereby they lose sight of realistic objectives and ultimately support outright revolution, at least by implication. Opting for pragmatic nationalism, Campos has written that he opposes "the temptation of mobilizing resentment in order to gain the authority to plan development. I would rather strengthen the national entrepreneur than merely antagonize the foreigner. I would want the State not to do what it cannot do, in order to do what it should do."[16] Even by the standards of Brazilian pragmatism, Campos stands out as pre-eminently realistic in his assessment of developmental problems.

The developmentalist-nationalist school in Brazil emerged in the early 1950s, taking much of its intellectual inspiration from ECLA. A number of developmentalist intellectuals participated in the Instituto Superior de Estudos Brasileiros (ISEB) created in 1955. A federally financed

14. Roberto de Oliveira Campos, "Relations between the United States and Latin America," in *Latin America: Evolution or Explosion?* ed., Mildred Adams (New York: Dodd, Mead & Co., 1963), p. 50.

15. *Ibid.*, pp. 53–54.

16. For further expression of his opinions, see Campos' *Reflections on Latin-American Development* (Austin: University of Texas Press, 1967).

entity created by the Ministry of Education as a high-level center for independent study and research, ISEB was urged to adopt and to apply the analytical techniques of modern social science for the elaboration of policies designed to stimulate national development. Despite a torrent of criticism that was generated over alleged political and ideological preconceptions,[17] ISEB issued a series of publications in which a variety of problems were examined. While not producing a truly comprehensive single statement, ISEB withstood political attacts and irregular government support while typifying the hemispheric effort to bring to bear the knowledge of modern techniques and experience upon an analysis of national conditions.[18]

Among those active with ISEB, one of the most prominent was Hélio Jaguaribe. The principal author of one of ISEB's earliest publications, the collaborative *A crise brasileira*,[19] Jaguaribe followed with his own *O nacionalismo na atuadidade brasileira* in 1958 and *Burguesía y proletariado en el nacionalismo brasileño* in 1961. In the 1958 work he began from the position that the advanced nations had imposed economic servitude on the underdeveloped nations. He called for a calculating application of a neutral and independent foreign policy that would serve national interests by playing off East against West. For Jaguaribe, the basic goal of Brazilian nationalism was the modernization resulting from economic development. In the second of these works, he continued by arguing that the existing entrepreneurial group held the key to such development. It would be the efficiency of entrepreneurial activity which would meet popular demands while reducing class privileges and equalizing opportunity.

Advocating a characteristically Brazilian pragmatism that refused to choose between capitalism and socialism, Jaguaribe followed an iconoclastic path in his treatment of foreign investments. Typically, he expressed unorthodox views on the politically explosive issue of Petrobras, the state-owned oil corporation. "What makes the present petroleum policy nationalist is not the fact that Petrobras . . . is directed by native-born Brazilians, etc. In a general way, the nationalist policy could as well be realized through Standard Oil or any other firm, provided that, in the country's actual situation, this proved the most efficient

17. By 1959, an internal schism emerged with the radical nationalists bitterly attacking such moderates as Hélio Jaguaribe, while from the right came charges that even the developmentalist nationalists were tainted with communism.

18. A review of ISEB thinking during its early period was published as *Introducão aos problemas do Brasil* (Rio de Janeiro: ISEB, 1956).

19. Hélio Jaguaribe, "A crise brasileira," *Cadernos de nosso tempo*, 1, (October–December 1955).

way of exploiting Brazil's petroleum and providing the national economy with the full use and control of that raw material." This realistic nationalism was sharply opposed by Cándido Mendes de Almeida (1928——) in a work entitled *Nacionalismo e desenvolvimento*.[20] For Mendes, although himself more a developmentalist than a radical nationalist, the winning of Brazilian independence and the acceptance of economic liberalism permitted a foreign penetration that subjected the country to colonial status at the hands of the developed nations. The international economic system gradually evolved into the now-familiar dichotomy between the center and the periphery, which he termed "the historical proletariat." The emancipation of this downtrodden proletariat would be achieved by a stubbornly nationalistic developmental program. There was no other way to reduce the existing degree of subordination to outside influences.

With a program of nationalistic development the key to Brazilian modernization, he demanded a rejection of all foreign aid, whether emanating from individual governments or international agencies. It was his belief that the International Monetary Fund, to take a leading example, was dominated by the nations of the center, and therefore would inevitably pursue policies inimical to the interests of the periphery. By way of illustration, he studied the IMF assistance to the inflation-plagued Argentine government of Arturo Frondizi in 1958, which he interpreted as a classic case of orthodox fiscal stabilization designed to maintain traditional economic interests in that country. He contrasted to this the "authentic" and independent revolution being interpreted and articulated by Castro in Cuba. As a corollary, Mendes advocated a neutralist foreign policy that he praised as intelligent self-interest designed to increase Brazil's bargaining power with both international power blocs. In this, he was in agreement with Jaguaribe, whom he regarded as expressing a number of heretical antinationalist views. It should be added as a footnote that Mendes' lengthy study was published under the auspices of the Instituto de Estudos Afro-Asiaticos, a newly organized group founded by President Quadros in 1961 which identified Brazil with other underdeveloped areas while suggesting an independence from the United States and western Europe.

Among the most prominent and profound Brazilian economic thinkers has been Celso Furtado (1920——). Once the chief of ECLA's Development Division, his national responsibilities have included service as direc-

20. Cándido Mendes de Almeida, *Nacionalismo e desenvolvimento* (Rio de Janeiro: Instituto de Estudos Afro-Asiaticos, 1963).

tor of the National Bank of Economic Development, executive head of the Agency for the Development of the Brazilian Northeast, and minister of planning. An extensive traveler and lecturer in Europe and the United States, Furtado's voice has been one of the most respected on developmental matters. Moreover, his writings have a strong philosophical basis, unlike those of some of his contemporaries. Recent translations have made several of his works available in English, the most theoretical of which is *Desenvolvimento e subdesenvolvimento*, or *Development and Underdevelopment*.[21] Discussing the change of intellectual approach which developmental theorists and planners have undergone, he notes that it began with an emphasis on the traditional economic concept of general equilibrium, moving through an elaboration of Keynesian thought, and following this with Marxian analyses.

Although the last of these approaches holds the dangers of inflexible philosophical dogmatism, it also has encouraged the understanding of accelerated social change in the underdeveloped world. If these contributions were to be synthesized, it could be said that "Marxism has spurred the critical and nonconformist approach, whereas the classic economies has served to impose methodological discipline without which analysis swerves toward dogmatism, and the Keynesian outburst has favored a better understanding of the role of the state in economic processes, opening up new vistas in the process of social reform."[22] Developmental thinking has, by means of this intellectual process, reached the point at which theoretical inquiry should concentrate on the identification of factors that hold specific relevance for each given economic structure. The result will be the establishment of a heuristically valuable typology of economic structures.

Much of Furtado's writing delves into abstract economic theory, and for the present purposes can be placed to one side. He deals with such matters as the developmental ideas implicit in the English classics of the literature, early efforts toward explaining the process of growth, and the identification of categories of economic analysis with universal validity in explaining development. Furtado has also employed the historical method in considering the Western cultural origins of industrial economy. He has noted that the classic model of industrial development

21. Celso Furtado, *Development and Underdevelopment*, tr. Ricardo W. de Aguiar and Eric Charles Drysdale (Berkeley and Los Angeles: University of California Press, 1964). Also see his *Diagnosis of the Brazilian Crisis*, tr. Suzette Macedo (Berkeley and Los Angeles: University of California Press, 1965).
22. Furtado, *Development and Underdevelopment*, p. vii.

does little more than reveal extraeconomic variables that influence the rate of production growth in a given economy. He views such theory as being based on a unique historical phenomenon, the Industrial Revolution, which therefore has limited applicability to the contemporary study of development. Historically, underdevelopment in Latin America was a part of the dualistic international economic system that grew out of the Industrial Revolution. Penetration of capitalistic enterprise from abroad did not necessarily change the basic archaic structures of the underdeveloped regions; thus underdevelopment stands as a special condition, and those theorists who attempt to draw analogies from the history of the industrialized areas are likely to achieve no more than a partial understanding.

Furtado has devoted great attention to the specific problems of his own country, including an economic history that traces the series of transitions carrying Brazil from its old slave economy in agriculture and mining to the present industrial phase; he has analyzed at length the impact of class conflict, ideological struggle, and political factors on the national economy. Observing that the state is the most powerful organization within society, he sees as natural its dominant role in the developmental process. Given the fact that development implies structural changes in both the systems of production and of income distribution, what he calls the "state-machine" must accept a major responsibility. Domestic capitalism requires protection, agriculture must receive credit support, and the exporting sector needs an underlying structure of basic services. In these and related matters, the rapid expansion of the state-machine is inevitable.

The radical nationalist approach to development in Brazil has been more polemical than economic in nature; this third "school" has demanded a doctrinal acceptance of the exploitive character of the existing system. Strong in aggressive tone but weak on precise policy recommendations, it has tended to reiterate continual demands for total state control of all economic enterprises. While Marxists adopted this position, its appeal was much broader in intellectual circles, and many others found the highly nationalistic implications attractive. Indeed, the nationalistic element was by no means absent in the writings of any of the three interpretations of developmental thought in Brazil. Often the individual expositions have represented a mixture of two of the three positions, and the nationalistic factor has rarely been absent. The reawakening of vocal nationalism in Brazil—popularly termed the *tomada de consciência*—became an underlying characteristic of the ideologues of development. With the rise in influence of popular forces in the decade of the 1950s, the *tomada de consciência* was symbolized by an articulate and self-conscious pride in the presumably unlimited potential for future development.

For Brazil, the twentieth-century evolution of its economy stimulated a growth of structural tensions. Three decades of a movement toward industrial capitalism have brought major alterations, but the process is far from complete. Transitional economic problems have included inflation, a deterioration in the terms of trade since 1955, and, temporarily, a decline in the growth rate. In short, the process of industrial capitalism has encountered structural obstacles that are difficult to overcome within the existing institutional framework, given the attitudes of the ruling classes. Furtado describes as inherently dangerous the "populist game" that the ruling classes have played since the days of Vargas. Interlacing his economic writings with a concern over related political problems, he regards the attainment of an open democracy as a fundamental precondition for genuine socioeconomic progress. The important political objective is to provide a pluralist democratic setting for development, and this means the creation of conditions under which both urban workers and the peasantry may enjoy effective participation. Today, the activities of both the urban and rural masses are of fundamental importance to Brazilian socioeconomic development, and these activities must be incorporated into the political process. He sees Brazil as having entered a period of social revolution, and the broadening of political bases is necessary if social change is to proceed with a minimum of community discontinuity.

At present, he argues, the ruling class represents a small fragment of the politically active participation, and the present exclusion of the Brazilian masses dare not be continued. Otherwise, conditions of revolutionary turmoil will become inflammatory in the extreme. Brazil remains a country in transition. The greatest obstacle to a gradual national change ". . . lies in the fact that the most urgent reform—which would give the system a greater capacity for self-adaptation, and make it easier to introduce further reforms—happens to be the most difficult to introduce. This, of course, is political reform, aimed at increasing the representativeness of the organs that act in the name of the people. Once this higher degree of effective democracy has been achieved, other changes in the institutional framework can be introduced without excessive tensions in the political system."[23]

23. Furtado, *Diagnosis*, p. 94.

Regional and Hemispheric Integration[24]

Toward the end of the 1950s there was a gradual decline of the high optimism that had earlier marked the postwar period; industrialization in particular was recognized as providing less than axiomatic assurance of rapid and genuine socioeconomic transformation. The voices of the experts were heard to shift key, progressing through a series of modulations that resolved themselves in integrationist chords. And suddenly, intellectuals, party leaders, industrialists, and businessmen were all beginning to examine the potential for regional agreements and multilateral arrangements. In this, the broad conception extended, as before, beyond the purely economic sphere to social and political development. The Economic Commission for Latin America was again in the forefront of developments.

The earlier phases of ideological elaboration and the programing of long-range needs gave way in 1958 to a shift of study and interest to various forms of hemispheric and subhemispheric collaboration. This placed particular emphasis on the creation of a Latin-American common market, and by 1960 ECLA staff members were conducting a series of inquiries into the possibilities. At the same time, the inter-American system was marked by a perceptible shift in economic relations. The psychological impact of the European Economic Community (EEC), a customs union contemplating increased economic integration in that area, proved highly suggestive to many Latin Americans, notwithstanding the fundamental differences between western Europe and Latin America. The appeal of free trade among the Latin-American countries as a means of industrial and agricultural development dated back to the prewar period, notably to the 1939 industrial integration pact between Argentina and Brazil and a group of Central American trade agreements. However, it was much later until consequential integrationist structures were created. Of these, three must be cited: the Inter-American Development Bank, the Central American Common Market, and the Latin-American Free Trade Area.

The first was established in December of 1959, with nineteen Latin-American countries and the United States becoming subscribing members. Beginning formal operations in October, 1961, the Inter-American Development Bank (IADB) was committed, among other things, to the

24. Much of the following discussion is adapted from Federico G. Gil and John D. Martz, "The Integration of Latin America," in *Comparative Politics and Political Theory: Essays Written in Honor of Charles Baskervill Robson*, ed., Edward L. Pinney (Chapel Hill: University of North Carolina Press, 1966).

acceleration of economic development, both individual and collective. Concerned at the outset with the financing of individual projects judged on their intrinsic merits, the IADB soon turned to wider planning. After the hemispheric states at the Punta del Este economic meeting committed themselves to the formulation of national development plans, the bank began to evaluate projects in terms of their relationship to over-all national programs. In time the emphasis shifted to frankly integrationist concerns, with proposals appraised largely in terms of their relevance for integration. The financial operations of the bank were seen as supporting the integrationist movement in four ways: the study and financing of regional projects; the financing of national industrial projects with regional ramifications; assistance to work improving economic infrastructure; and the study of frontier integration. Typical programs receiving bank support were the study of an international highway passing through the eastern jungles of Colombia, Ecuador, Peru, and Bolivia, and a series of loans in 1963 and 1964 to assist the Central American Bank for Economic Integration in that area's industrial and infrastructural development.

By the late 1950s, the Central American Common Market had already achieved substantial progress in evolving a true customs union for its five member republics.[25] A Committee for Economic Co-operation had first met in 1952, and during the next five years a wide variety of studies were conducted with the advice of regional and international organizations, as well as a set of bilateral treaties that culminated in the 1958 signing of the Multilateral Treaty of Free Trade and Central American Economic Integration. During the next two years some eight separate trade agreements were also signed, with the purpose of encouraging Central American industry. All of this provided the setting within which, on December 13, 1960, the five Central American republics created their common market in Managua. By June, 1961, the ratification of the first three members rendered the agreement operable, and the two remaining members followed suit by the close of 1962. The terms of the treaty established free trade for all the products of the area, excluding selected terms that were made the subject of special conditions for a specified period of time. The common market was to become fully effective by June, 1966; actually, it was to be considerably later, as events proved.

25. For a fuller discussion, see Carlos M. Castillo, *Growth and Integration in Central America* (New York: Frederick A. Praeger, 1966). Castillo was at that writing executive secretary of the General Treaty on Economic Integration of Central America.

Two notable features of the Central American Common Market were the founding of the Central American Bank for Economic Integration, located in Tegucigalpa, and an emphasis on integrated industries, whereby the promotion of new industry would center upon regional rather than smaller local markets. Outside financial support was to be drawn through the activity of the bank, which was capitalized through equal member contributions at the sum of $20 million. A series of organs and institutions have grown up through the inspiration of the regional common market. Of particular note are the Instituto Centro Americano de Investigación y Technología Industrial (1956), supported by the United Nations Special Fund for the study of industrial services and scientific investigation; the Escuela Superior de Administración Pública para la América Central (1954), to provide training for the necessary corps of administrative technicians; and the Consejo Monetario Centroamericano (1964), which emerged out of periodic meetings conducted by the five national banks.

The multinational drive for regional development also encouraged the formation of a variety of private organs. The rectors of the five national universities moved toward the unification of higher education by establishing the Consejo Superior Universitario Centroamericano. Newspapermen founded the Federación Centroamericana de Periodistas, and businessmen, the Federación de Cámaras y Asociaciones Industriales Centroamericanas. In the political realm, the signing of the Charter of San Salvador in 1951 has led, after some years' inactivity, to the founding of the Organización de Estados Centroamericanos (ODECA).[26] All of these measures were in consonance with the historical interest in restoring the regional federation that had emerged after the fall of Spanish colonialism but shattered amid personalistic and localistic rivalries in 1838.[27] For Central America, the early record has been promising: a significant list of products has been freed from internal tax barriers; incentives for foreign investment have been rationalized; and at this writing, the majority of important agricultural products are covered by the common market. Intraregional trade grew from $3.6 million in 1950 to $32.7 ten years later, and by 1965 it was over $70 million. The outbreak of war between Honduras and El Salvador in 1968 gravely disrupted regional progress, however, leaving the future of the Central American Common Market uncertain.

26. For a useful if dated account, see James L. Busey, "Central American Union: The Latest Attempt," *The Western Political* Quarterly, XIV, No. 1 (March 1961), pp. 49–63.
27. For a detailed historical narrative, see Thomas L. Karnes, *The Failure of Union: Central America, 1824–1960* (Chapel Hill: University of North Carolina Press, 1961).

Given a similarity of national history, the emphasis on agricultural products, and the retarded state of industrial development, the Central American republics faced less imposing obstacles to regional integration than those that confronted the Latin-American Free Trade Association (LAFTA). Preliminary studies were conducted by the Economic Commission for Latin America in 1956, and after a lengthy period of debate and disagreement, LAFTA was inaugurated in 1960 with the signing of the Treaty of Montevideo by seven nations.[28] The specified goal was the origination of a free trade zone by means of a general tariff reduction, special treatment for the least developed members, and assorted arrangements to provide complementary support.[29] Extensive multinational talks led to a complicated procedural structure intended to lower tariffs by a minimum of 8 percent annually for twelve years, culminating in a reduction of at least 96 percent. It was hoped that a complementary pattern would emerge in manufactured goods, while regional industry might be encouraged. As trade barriers are dropped, the participants anticipate that improved transportation and communications will lead to a relative standardization of monetary systems and a workable free trade area.

Among the barriers to the effective establishment of the free trade area, two questions are of critical centrality: "first, whether Latin American economic integration will reduce or increase the evident inequalities in the development levels of the different countries; second, whether it will help or hinder the programming of Latin American economic development."[30] There are vivid disparities in living standards and levels of development among the member states. A wide range of escape clauses permit preferential treatment for such members as Ecuador and Paraguay. With more favorable terms available to the least developed countries, it has been hoped that the latter would not fail to benefit, thus contributing to a general elevation of economic standards within LAFTA. Nothwithstanding these and other special adjustments, the early record of LAFTA has not been impressive. Although intraregional trade grew by 40 percent in the first two years of operation, this represented a mere 8.5 perecnt of the total international trade of LAFTA members. Whether the anticipated free trade area can develop in the specified twelve-year period remains questionable. It is partially in response to

28. By the latter years of the 1960s, LAFTA membership included Argentina, Brazil, Chile, Colombia, Ecuador, Mexico, Paraguay, Peru, Uruguay, and Venezuela.
29. For further details see Gil and Martz, "Integration of Latin America," in Pinney, *Comparative Politics*, pp. 133–34; also see Víctor L. Urquidi, *The Challenge of Development in Latin America*, tr. Marjory M. Urquidi (New York: Frederick A. Praeger, 1964), pp. 132–34.
30. Urquidi, *Development in Latin America*, p. 133.

growing pessimism over LAFTA that six of the South American republics were developing a subregional Andean Pact by the start of the 1970's.

As the preceding suggests, public officials and international experts have contributed in collaborative fashion to the formulation of integrationist doctrine. There is no single dominant figure in the movement. However, recent impetus has come from the expansion of hemispheric training and research organizations. Two of the more promising have been the Instituto para la Integración de América Latina (INTAL) and the Facultad Lationamericana de Ciencias Sociales (FLACSO). The former was established in Buenos Aires in 1965 by the Inter-American Development Bank under the direction of Chilean Gustavo Lagos, and the latter is a UNESCO-sponsored institute in Santiago providing graduate level training in sociology and political science to young Latin Americans. Both are attempting to alleviate the shortage of competent experts by providing thorough grounding in modern techniques and methodologies of social science as well as informed analyses of existing developmental problem areas. INTAL in particular, as its title suggests, is concerned with problems of integration.

Presently, the international position of Christian Democracy is joining in the integrationist movement. In January, 1965, Eduardo Frei addressed a letter to four of the most influential Latin-American economists: Prebish, José Antonio Mayobre, Felipe Herrera, and Carlos Sánz mists: Prebisch, José Antonio Mayobre, Felipe Herrera, and Carlos Sánz ization of economic integration. "In the matter of institutions I would like to make this suggestion: labor as well as managerial forces, either on an individual or cooperative basis, should be given clear participation in the movement for integration. The integration of Latin America, as is the case with the entire process of structural changes, demands essentially a broad popular base. Narrowing integration exclusively to official technical and financial circles regardless of how competent these may be would only lead to failure."[32] In a reply one week later, the four responded in terms that reflected the new and growing emphasis on the importance of political organs and decisions.[33] A variety of specific

31. The Venezuelan Mayobre had followed after Prebisch as director of ECLA; Herrera was the Chilean president of the Inter-American Development Bank; and Sánz de Santamaría was the Colombian heading the Comité Interamericano de la Alianza para el Progreso (CIAP).

32. Eduardo Frei Montalva, *Carta del presidente de Chile Eduardo Frei, a los srs. Raúl Prebisch, José Antonio Mayobre, Felipe Herrera y Carlos Sánz de Santamaría* (Mimeo., January 6, 1965).

33. The text of these proposals is contained in "Perspectivas para la creación del mercado común latinoamericano," an annex to *La integración latinoamericana: Situación y perspectivas* (Buenos Aires: Instituto para la Integración de América Latina, 1965), pp. 189–217.

proposals included the creation of a ministerial-level Council of Ministers, an Executive Board, and advisory committee of specialists, and a Latin-American Parliament. The first to be founded was the parliament, which was chartered in Lima in August, 1965.[34] As a regional forum for discussion of general integrationist problems, it is intended as an additional mechanism to provide a favorable atmosphere for the adoption of decisions, rather than as a supranational legislative assembly.

The approach of Latin-American thinking toward integration has changed somewhat from its original conception of successive evolutionary stages advancing toward broad co-ordination and integration. Economic regional integration is no longer advocated as an alternative to national integration but rather as a means of co-ordinating individual efforts toward social justice and reform in the member republics. Regional integration has become, then, a means of promoting national development. It is also understood that the necessary institutions of implementation must be political as well as socioeconomic.[35] An institutional framework is slowly emerging which will exercise decision-making authority without continuous negotiation among the various member governments. And overriding all substantive questions is the importance of a *mystique*, an identifiable integrationist ideology. Integration is no longer seen as a panacea promising the resolution of all difficulties, but as a promising and potentially fruitful approach. Clearly, the first realistic steps toward integration have been taken—ones that can contribute significantly to economic development. Whatever the future holds, it will require as a solid foundation an unqualified psychological and intellectual commitment.

SELECTED BIBLIOGRAPHY

Anderson, Charles W. *Politics and Economic Change in Latin America: The Governing of Restless Nations.* Princeton: D. Van Nostrand Company, 1967.
Campos, Roberto de Oliveira. *Reflections on Latin-American Development.* Austin: University of Texas Press, 1967.

34. For a brief overview of developments, see Harry Kantor, "The Latin-American Parliament: A New Attempt to Stimulate Economic and Political Unification," *South Eastern Latin Americanist*, IX, No. 3 (December 1965), pp. 1–3.

35. For a pro-integrationist statement that stresses cultural and ethical elements, see Roger E. Vekemans, "Economic Development, Social Change, and Cultural Mutation in Latin America," in *Religion, Revolution, and Reform: New Forces for Change in Latin America*, ed., William D'Antonio and Frederick B. Pike (New York: Frederick A. Praeger, 1964), pp. 129–42.

Castillo, Carlos M. *Growth and Integration in Central America.* New York: Frederick A. Praeger, 1966.

Daland, Robert. *Brazilian Planning: Development Politics and Administration.* Chapel Hill, University of North Carolina Press, 1967.

Dell, Sidney. *A Latin American Common Market?* New York: Oxford University Press, 1966.

Furtado, Celso. *Development and Underdevelopment.* Translated by Ricardo W. de Aguiar and Eric Charles Drysdale. Berkeley and Los Angeles: University of California Press, 1964.

———. *Diagnosis of the Brazilian Crisis.* Translated by Suzette Macedo. Berkeley and Los Angeles: University of California Press, 1965.

Gil, Federico G. and John D. Martz. "The Integration of Latin America, in *Comparative Politics and Political Theory: Essays Written in Honor of Charles Baskervill Robson.* Edited by Edward L. Pinney. Chapel Hill: University of North Carolina Press, 1966.

Jaguaribe, Hélio. "A crise brasileira," *Cadernos de nosso tempo,* 1 (October–December 1953).

———. *Economic and Political Development: A Theoretical Approach and a Brazilian Case Study.* Cambridge: Harvard University Press, 1968.

———. *O nacionalismo na atualidade brasileira.* Rio de Janeiro: n.p., 1958.

Hirschman, Albert O., ed. *Latin American Issues: Essays and Comments.* New York: Twentieth Century Fund, 1961.

Mendes de Almeida, Cándido. *Nacionalismo e desenvolvimento.* Rio de Janeiro: Instituto de Estudo Afro-Asiaticos, 1963.

Skidmore, Thomas E. *Politics in Brazil, 1930–1964: An Experiment in Democracy.* New York: Oxford University Press, 1967.

United Nations Economic Commission for Latin America. *The Economic Development of Latin America and Its Principal Problems.* United Nations, 1950.

Urquidi, Víctor L. *Free Trade and Economic Integration in Latin America.* Berkeley and Los Angeles: University of California Press, 1962.

———. *The Challenge of Development in Latin America.* Translated by Marjory M. Urquidi. New York: Frederick A. Praeger, 1964.

INDEX

Index